Frommer's

Alaska
day BY day

1st Edition

by Charles P. Wohlforth

WILEY

John Wiley and Sons, Inc.

> *A mother harbor seal checks in on her pup.*

Contents

Juneau,
Skagway
Ketchikan
Seward

1 **Chapter 1: The Best of Alaska**
4 My Favorite Alaska Moments
5 My Favorite Small Towns
6 The Best Scenery
8 The Best Encounters with Alaska Native Cultures
9 The Best Wildlife Viewing
10 The Best Backcountry Trips
11 The Best Wilderness Lodges
12 The Best Inns & Bed & Breakfasts
14 The Best Restaurants
15 The Best Adventures on the Water

17 **Chapter 2: Strategies for Seeing Alaska**

27 **Chapter 3: The Best All-Alaska Itineraries**
28 Kenai Fjords and Denali Highlights
32 Southeast Alaska Highlights
36 Kenai Peninsula to the Arctic in 2 Weeks
42 *Spotlight: A Dangerous Time*
44 The Best of Southeast & Southcentral Alaska
48 The Best Undiscovered Towns
52 The Best Outdoor Adventures in 2 Weeks
56 Kenai Fjords & Denali, Car-Free
58 Alaska with Kids in 2 Weeks

63 **Chapter 4: Anchorage**
64 My Favorite Anchorage Moments
68 The Best of Anchorage in 1 Day
72 The Best of Anchorage in 2 Days
74 The Best of Anchorage in 3 Days
76 Anchorage with Kids
80 A Stroll Through Downtown Anchorage
84 A Drive on Turnagain Arm
88 The Best of Anchorage Outdoors
94 *Spotlight: Going to Extremes*
96 Anchorage Shopping Best Bets
97 Anchorage Shopping A to Z
102 Anchorage Restaurant Best Bets
103 Anchorage Restaurant A to Z
110 Anchorage Hotel Best Bets

111 Anchorage Hotels A to Z
116 Anchorage Nightlife & Entertainment Best Bets
117 Anchorage Nightlife & Entertainment A to Z
122 Anchorage Fast Facts

125 **Chapter 5: Denali & Mat-Su**
126 My Favorite Denali & Mat-Su Moments
130 Denali & Talkeetna in 3 Days
136 Denali & Mat-Su in 1 Week
146 The Best of the Denali Park Road
152 A Denali Camping Adventure
158 The Best Denali Adventures
164 Where to Stay Near Denali
170 Where to Dine Near Denali
172 Talkeetna
178 Denali & Mat-Su Fast Facts

181 **Chapter 6: Prince William Sound & the Copper River Country**
182 My Favorite Prince William Sound & Copper River Country Moments
186 *Spotlight: The Secret Lives of Whales*
188 The Best of Prince William Sound & the Copper River Country in 3 Days
192 The Best of Prince William Sound & the Copper River Country in 1 Week
200 Prince William Sound, Car-Free
204 A Prince William Sound and Copper River Country Outdoor Adventure
210 Cordova
214 Kennicott & McCarthy
220 Matanuska Glacier Area
222 Valdez
226 Prince William Sound & the Copper River Country Fast Facts

229 **Chapter 7: Kenai Peninsula**
230 My Favorite Kenai Peninsula Moments
232 The Best of the Kenai Peninsula in 3 Days
236 The Best of the Kenai Peninsula in 1 Week
244 The Best of the Kenai Peninsula with Kids
250 A Kenai Peninsula Outdoor Adventure
254 *Spotlight: Salmon*

256 The Best Kenai Peninsula Fishing in 1 Week
260 Homer
268 Seward
274 Kenai & Soldotna
278 Kenai Peninsula Fast Facts

281 **Chapter 8: Fairbanks & the Interior**
282 My Favorite Fairbanks & the Interior Moments
284 The Best of Fairbanks & the Interior in 3 Days
290 *Spotlight: The Amazing Aurora*
292 The Best of Fairbanks & the Interior in 1 Week
304 Fairbanks & the Interior with Kids
310 Extreme Driving: A Dalton Highway Road Trip
316 Fairbanks
326 Fairbanks & the Interior Fast Facts

329 **Chapter 9: Southeast Alaska**
330 My Favorite Southeast Moments
334 The Best of the Southeast in 3 Days
338 The Best of the Southeast in 8 Days
346 The Southeast with Kids
354 *Spotlight: Towering Totems*
356 The Southeast's History & Culture
362 The Southeast's Best Wildlife & Scenery
368 A Southeast Camping Adventure
374 Juneau
386 Sitka
394 Ketchikan
402 Petersburg
406 Gustavus & Glacier Bay
410 Haines
414 Skagway
418 Southeast Alaska Fast Facts

421 **Chapter 10: The Alaska Bush**
422 My Favorite Alaska Bush Moments
426 Barrow
430 Nome
434 Unalaska & Dutch Harbor
440 *Spotlight: Russian America*
442 Kodiak
448 Alaska Bush Fast Facts

PAGE 278

PAGE 327

ALASKA 43

PAGE 418

PAGE 356

PAGE 424

PAGE 475

451 **Chapter 11: Alaska's Natural History & Culture**
452 A Timeline of Alaskan History
454 *Spotlight: Gold!*
456 A Brief History of Alaska
461 Alaska's Natural History
468 Alaska's Native Peoples
471 Alaska in High & Popular Culture
475 Eating & Drinking

477 **Chapter 12: The Best Special Interest Trips**
478 Escorted General Interest Tours
478 Organized Tours: Finding Your Guide to the Great Outdoors
479 Self-Guided Tours
480 Outdoor Activities A to Z

486 **Chapter 13: Guide to Alaska's Flora & Fauna**
488 Land Mammals
491 Marine Mammals
493 Fish
496 Birds
499 Trees & Plants

503 **Chapter 14: The Savvy Traveler**
504 Before You Go
506 Getting There
507 Getting Around
508 Tips on Accommodations
508 Fast Facts

516 **Index**

PUBLISHED BY

Wiley Publishing, Inc.

111 River St., Hoboken, NJ 07030-5774

ISBN 978-0-470-56233-8; ISBN 978-1-118-02337-2 (EBK); ISBN 978-1-118-02338-9 (EBK); ISBN 978-1-118-02339-6 (EBK)

Frommer's®

Editorial by Frommer's

EDITOR
Linda Barth

PHOTO EDITOR
Cherie Cincilla

CARTOGRAPHER
Guy Ruggiero

CAPTIONS
Kathryn Williams

COVER PHOTO EDITOR
Richard Fox

COVER DESIGN
Paul Dinovo

Produced by Sideshow Media

PUBLISHER
Dan Tucker

MANAGING EDITOR
Megan McFarland

PROJECT EDITOR
Alicia Mills

PHOTO EDITOR
John Martin

DESIGN
Kevin Smith, And Smith LLC

SPOTLIGHT FEATURE DESIGN
Em Dash Design LLC

For information on our other products and services or to obtain technical support, please contact our Customer Care Department within the U.S. at 800-762-2974, outside the U.S. at 317-572-3993 or fax 317-572-4002.

Wiley also publishes its books in a variety of electronic formats. Some content that appears in print may not be available in electronic formats.

MANUFACTURED IN CHINA

5 4 3 2 1

How to Use This Guide

The Day by Day guides present a series of itineraries that take you from place to place. The itineraries are organized by time (The Best of the Kenai Peninsula in 1 Week), by region (A Drive on Turnagain Arm), by town (Homer), and by special interest (A Denali Camping Adventure). You can follow these itineraries to the letter, or customize your own based on the information we provide. Within the tours, we suggest cafes, bars, or restaurants where you can take a break. Each of these stops is marked with a coffee-cup icon ☕. In each chapter, we provide detailed hotel and restaurant reviews so you can select the places that are right for you.

The hotels, restaurants, and attractions listed in this guide have been ranked for quality, value, service, amenities, and special features using a **star-rating system.** Hotels, restaurants, attractions, shopping, and nightlife are rated on a scale of zero stars (recommended) to three stars (exceptional). In addition to the star-rating system, we also use a kids icon **kids** to point out the best bets for families.

The following **abbreviations** are used for credit cards:

AE American Express	**MC** MasterCard
DC Diners Club	**V** Visa
DISC Discover	

A Note on Prices

Frommer's lists exact prices in local currency. Currency conversions fluctuate, so before departing consult a currency exchange website such as **www.oanda.com/currency/converter** to check up-to-the-minute conversion rates.

In the "Take a Break" and "Best Bets" sections of this book, we have used a system of dollar signs to show a range of costs for 1 night in a hotel (the price of a double-occupancy room) or the cost of an entree at a restaurant. Use the following table to decipher the dollar signs:

COST	HOTELS	RESTAURANTS
$	under $100	under $10
$$	$100–$200	$10–$20
$$$	$200–$300	$20–$30
$$$$	$300–$400	$30–$40
$$$$$	over $400	over $40

How to Contact Us

In researching this book, we discovered many wonderful places—hotels, restaurants, shops, and more. We're sure you'll find others. Please tell us about them, so we can share the information with your fellow travelers in upcoming editions. If you were disappointed with a recommendation, we'd love to know that, too. Please email us at frommersfeed back@wiley.com or write to:

Frommer's Alaska Day by Day, 1st Edition
Wiley Publishing, Inc.
111 River Street
Hoboken, NJ 07030-5774

Travel Resources at Frommers.com

Frommer's travel resources don't end with this guide. **Frommers.com** has travel information on more than 4,000 destinations. We update features regularly, giving you access to the most current trip-planning information and the best airfare, lodging, and car-rental bargains. You can also listen to podcasts, connect with other Frommers.com members through our active reader forums, share your travel photos, read blogs from guidebook editors and fellow travelers, and much more.

An Additional Note

Please be advised that travel information is subject to change at any time—and this is especially true of prices. We suggest that you write or call ahead for confirmation when making your travel plans. The authors, editors, and publisher cannot be held responsible for the experiences of readers while traveling. Your safety is important to us, so we encourage you to stay alert and be aware of your surroundings.

About the Author

Charles Wohlforth is a life-long Alaska resident and prize-winning author of numerous books about Alaska. Besides travel, his work includes writing about science and the environment, politics, history and biography. A popular lecturer, he has spoken all over the United States and overseas. His articles have appeared in *Discover, The New Republic, Outside,* and many other magazines. Wohlforth lives with his wife, Barbara, and their four children. They reside in Anchorage during the winter, where they are avid crosscountry skiers, and in summer on a remote Kachemak Bay shore reachable only by boat. Wohlforth's recent book *The Fate of Nature: Rediscovering Our Ability to Rescue the Earth* (St. Martin's Press, $28) uses Alaska as a microcosm to understand the cultural roots of humankinds' will to protect the planet.

Acknowledgments

I've received help from scores of friends and journalists to develop my knowledge of Alaska and its travel industry over more than 15 years of writing on this subject. I've drawn on that store of knowledge throughout this book, and my debt of gratitude owes to more people than it is appropriate to name here. Long-time colleagues whose work is essential to these pages include Eric Troyer, Kris Capps, and Charlotte Glover. The critical help that always comes through when most needed, year after year, depends on Karen Datko. She is the researcher every writer dreams of; she has spoiled me and I know I'll never find another like her.

About the Photographers

Ken Cedeno is a Washington, DC-based photojournalist who has covered politics and breaking news for over 20 years.

David Fulton has been a professional photographer for over 30 years; see his work at www.davidroyfultonphotography.com.

Orin Pierson is a self taught photographer who lives in Petersburg.

Matt Hage and **Agnes Stowe** met at the University of Alaska Fairbanks, and provide photography for editorial and commercial clients.

Ryan Long lives and works as a writer and photographer in Wrangell and owns Ryan M Long Photography.

Daniel Buckscott is an award-winning, Juneau-based photographer; see his work at www.WildernessPeaks.com.

Bailey Kirkland is from Unalaska, where she plans to open a photography studio.

Audrey Kang spent 2 years in Alaska before moving to New York to work at the International Center of Photography.

John Wagner is a staff photographer at the Fairbanks Daily News-Miner.

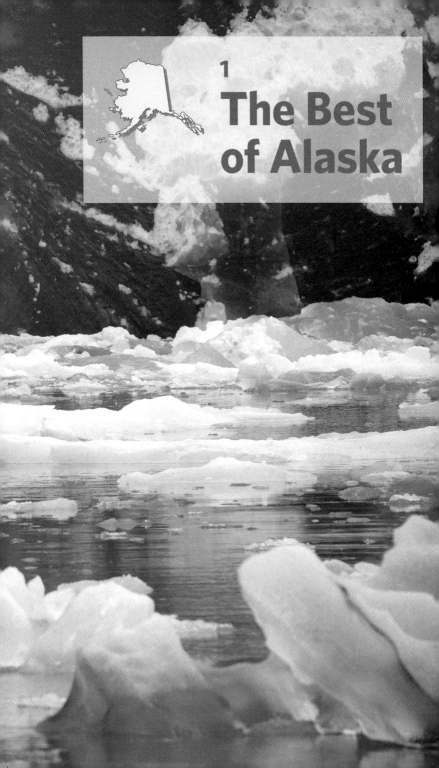

1
The Best
of Alaska

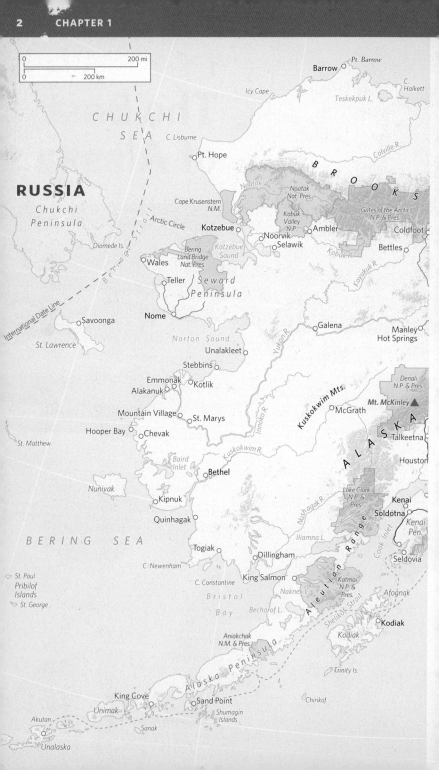

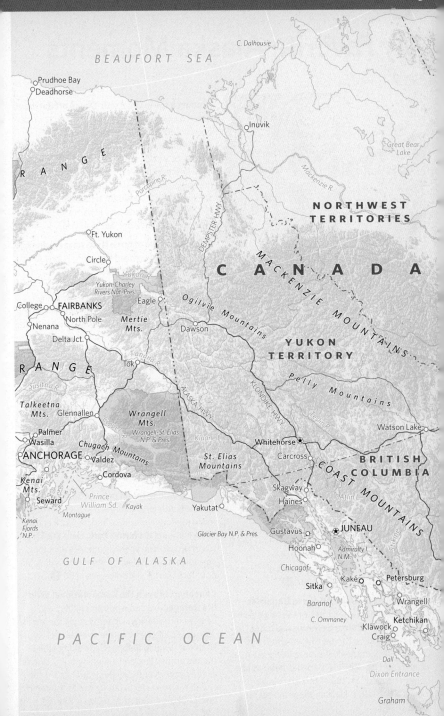

My Favorite Alaska Moments

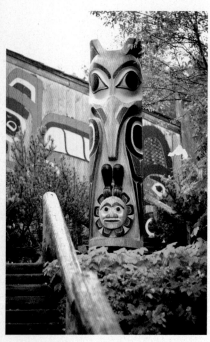

> PAGE 1 Ice floes off Tracy Arm. THIS PAGE Totem poles tell the story of the Tlingit.

Seeing a humpback whale breach. A 45-foot-long giant weighing 45 tons suddenly shoots from the surface of the ocean, hangs briefly, then drops with an enormous splash. It's the first leap that is always unexpected. Missed it? Just wait; once humpbacks start breaching, they'll often keep it up. You'll have an excellent chance of seeing whales in the waters near several communities, but **Icy Strait** off Gustavus may be the best. See p. 367, **13**.

Summiting a mountain ridge in Denali National Park. The small trees of the taiga grow thinner and disappear as the view around you opens over alpine tundra toward countless rocky peaks. Suddenly it's clear how vast this place is and how little a mark has been left by human beings. The top of Mount Healy overlook is a half-day hike from the visitor center. See p. 31, **6**.

Dipping a toe in the Arctic Ocean off Barrow. The gravel beach in front of the Arctic town of Barrow seems like the edge of the Earth. Standing here, you'll feel as though there's nothing but water and ice between you and the North Pole. Discover whale bones and Eskimo hunting equipment stored for use by people who still feed their community in harmony with 1,000-year-old traditions; sometimes you'll even see them at work. See p. 429, **3**.

Skiing over hills of birch trees near Anchorage. Anchorage has some of the nation's best cross-country skiing. Within the boundaries of the state's largest city, you speed silently through the forest, its black tracery of tree branches outlined by white hoarfrost. Low-angle morning light called alpenglow outlines Mount McKinley in orange against the light blue of the sky and the snowy land. See p. 92.

Hooking into a king salmon on the Kenai River. Position yourself on Alaska's most famous salmon stream at the height of a run, and feel the wrenching jerk of a huge, silver-sided giant that can fight long enough to leave your arms rubbery and exhausted. The key is to find the right spot at the right moment, when the fishing is hot, with a guide who knows the river. See p. 256, **2**.

Walking among totem poles in Sitka. Great art and extraordinary history stand together in the misty rainforest of spruce and hemlock at the **Sitka National Historical Park.** Here the Tlingit fought Russian invaders 2 centuries ago; their descendents recorded the story (and still do) in dour faces on carved poles. See p. 32, **1**.

Canoeing through the Kenai National Wildlife Refuge. Anyone who can paddle can venture into Alaskan wilderness via the small, connected lakes and gentle rivers of the Kenai National Wildlife Refuge. Glide along while trailing a trout lure and watching puffy clouds as they soar over the rustling birches. At the end of the trip, a local family can pick up and take back your rented gear. See p. 249, **11**.

My Favorite Small Towns

> The quiet artists' colony of Halibut Cove lies across Kachemak Bay from Homer.

Petersburg. Norwegian fishermen built this waterside community among the channels and mountains of Mitkof Island, and the fishing life still makes the streets hum. Many of the streets are in fact docks, spanning a quiet slough and reaching into the enormous boat harbor. Use the charming town as a starting point for some of Alaska's best outdoor opportunities: hiking, biking, sea kayaking, fishing, or whale-watching. See p. 340, ❺.

McCarthy. Deep within Wrangell–St. Elias National Park, the nation's largest park, McCarthy is a tiny former mining community that would be called a historic ghost town if it weren't still full of interesting frontier folk. At the end of a long dirt road and then a footbridge, McCarthy can't be reached by private car, but helpful locals ferry everyone around. Nearby is Alaska's largest and most memorable historic site, the true ghost town and former copper mine of Kennicott, well preserved by the National Park Service. See p. 217, ❼.

Cordova. In a forgotten corner of the spectacular, forested waterways of Prince William Sound, this friendly little town offers close access to some of the best self-guided wilderness activities in Alaska: bird-watching, glacier viewing, canoeing, and river fishing, as well as sea kayaking and ocean fishing. Yet few visitors ever make the trip, so you'll feel as though you have the place to yourself. See p. 210.

Homer. This town with a 5-mile finger of land reaching into the sea offers Alaska's easiest access to spectacular coastal waters and wildlife. That access has given rise to the state's most active artistic community and some of its best dining and lodgings. The town itself isn't much to look at, but there's nowhere else you can spend a full day of such interesting and diverse activities. See p. 260.

Nome. This classic Alaska gold-rush town hasn't changed that much, even though hardly a building stands from its legendary Wild West days. It's the spirit that remains in this fun, freewheeling community between the tundra and the Bering Sea. And the roads around Nome reach some of Alaska's best bird- and wildlife watching country. Where else can you go for a drive to look at musk oxen? See p. 430.

The Best Scenery

> *More than 100 years ago, Scottish-American naturalist John Muir visited "nobly sculptured" Tracy Arm.*

Tracy Arm, near Juneau. Boats on day trips from Juneau follow the towering fjords of the Tracy Arm–Fords Terror Wilderness, working their way up to the glaciers at the end, where seals are often seen lounging on icebergs. But the terrain itself—waterfalls tumbling thousands of feet down cliffs carved by ice; mountains jutting a mile high, straight from the sea—is what blows minds. See p. 381, **14**.

Turnagain Arm, near Anchorage. Driving the Seward Highway or riding the Alaska Railroad south from Anchorage, you'll see the cliffs of the Chugach Mountains standing on the left, often with Dall sheep balanced on their crags. On the right roil the furious glacial waters of Turnagain Arm, where beluga whales chase salmon. The route is always spectacular, but never more so than when the evening sunshine picks out patches of snow in orange, high on the surrounding peaks. See p. 84.

Mount McKinley, Denali National Park, from above. North America's highest mountain is one of the largest objects on Earth that can be seen in its entirety, because it stands on relatively low ground. When you fly among the mountain's intricate, icy folds, your whole concept of "big" may change as the immensity of nature sinks in. When your plane lands on one of its glaciers, that feeling is further magnified by the realization of how tiny you are within this landscape. No one should miss the experience. See p. 130, **1**.

The snowy landscape, Interior Alaska. Winter makes the land more beautiful by

> *A bush plane takes passengers flightseeing over the spectacularly pristine Denali National Park.*

smoothing and simplifying the terrain, creating soft, sinuous shapes that reflect the warm colors of the sun, which never rises far above the horizon during the colder months. Vistas empty of any sign of activity lie in perfect peace. Visitors who come in the winter have to endure icy roads, cold temperatures, and limited tourism activities, but they see the essence of Alaska. See p. 287.

Chena Hot Springs during the northern lights. The springs, outside Fairbanks, are away from city lights and far enough north that the aurora borealis shows frequently and brightly, right up in the middle of the sky. Since the best viewing occurs in the coldest, darkest months, the hot pools make it a perfect occasion. Swimmers can float in steamy water in below-zero weather while lights whip through the sky above them. See p. 289, **8**.

Childs Glacier, near Cordova. From the viewing area across the vast Copper River, which cuts through its face, the glacier stands as an immense wall of blue ice, filling your field of vision from side to side and hundreds of feet above. You can actually feel the deep groaning of the glacier's movement. If you're lucky, you may witness massive chunks of ice falling

into the river and launching waves that run right toward you, occasionally flooding the picnic area. Truly exceptional waves have been known to toss salmon up into the trees. See p. 212.

Richardson Highway. This little-used rural road crosses the Alaska Range east of Mount McKinley, winding through scenery that sometimes exceeds Denali National Park in its breadth, variety, and grandeur. Breathtaking views crop up at several places along the drive, but my favorite vistas include the alpine lakes north and south of Paxson, which lie like great fields of silver in the treeless tundra bowls between the mountains. See p. 36, **9**.

Wrangell Narrows at dusk. South from the town of Petersburg toward Wrangell, in Southeast Alaska, the Narrows extend like a corridor, 24 miles long between shores—so close, ships can barely fit through. The largest to attempt it are the ferries of the Alaska Marine Highway System, which slalom between glowing navigational lights so close to shore that passengers can sometimes see wildlife among the trees. In a region full of extraordinary views from the decks of ships, this is the most thrilling. See p. 340, **9**.

The Best Encounters with Alaska Native Cultures

> *The Iditarod dog sled race starts from 4th Avenue in Anchorage every March, though the race route alternates each year.*

Ketchikan's totem poles. The art of the Tlingit and Haida is both preserved and created in Ketchikan. It's preserved in two outdoor totem pole parks and a museum that contains historic poles too old to be exposed to the elements. And it's created in a workshop where visitors can stop in and see some of the greatest living masters of totem carving at work on new poles that tell new stories. See p. 396, ⓐ.

Alaska Native Heritage Center, Anchorage. A living museum with enough going on to keep you busy most of the day, this place was built by Alaska Native groups to teach about their cultures. There's a lot to see in the mock village, museum, and theater, where dance and storytelling go on all day, but the highlight for me is meeting Native craftsmen who are eager to talk about their lives, homes, and art. See p. 72, ⓐ.

Iñupiat Heritage Center, Barrow. The residents of this Arctic community build sealskin boats, repair drums, and hear elders' stories at the center, but visitors are welcome, too. In the summer, one can often see an afternoon dance performance. Even when nothing special is happening, the center's exhibits on Iñupiaq culture and history are well worth a visit. See p. 426, ⓐ.

Sled dogs and festivals, Anchorage. Alaska comes alive in late winter when the snow is deep and the skies are bright, and that energy hits its peak in early March, when the 1,500-mile Iditarod Trail Sled Dog Race leaves from Anchorage. Besides the Iditarod, it's a wonderful time across the Southcentral and Interior regions of the state. Many communities hold races (for dogs or human beings), winter festivals, or ice carving competitions, and there's even a winter fishing derby in Homer. See p. 122.

The Best Wildlife Viewing

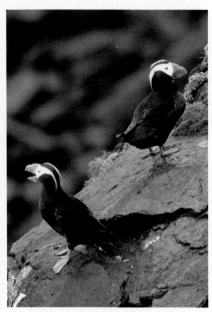

> *Tufted puffins on the Pribilof Islands.*

> *Black bears go hunting for salmon.*

A low-cost safari, Denali National Park. The park's shuttle system sends visitors on one of the world's great wildlife-viewing expeditions many times a day, for less than the cost of dinner in a good restaurant. You never know what you'll see, but it's common to encounter bears, moose, caribou, and even wolves. Bring binoculars. See p. 149.

World-renowned bird-watching, Pribilof Islands. Many places in Alaska offer birders a chance to see species that few others have encountered, sometimes in great numbers, but nowhere are rare sightings more frequent or is the setting more grand than in the Pribilofs. Getting there is expensive, accommodations are rough, and there is simply nothing else to do there, but the wildlife watching is widely regarded as among the world's best. See p. 481.

Black bear viewing, Juneau. An unusual situation of mutual benefit has developed between a group of black bears near the Mendenhall Glacier and the people who watch them: The female bears with cubs are somewhat protected from male bears, which may attack cubs, because they tend to shy away from humans. Meanwhile, we get to watch the bears from just yards away, on boardwalks near a U.S. Forest Service visitor center. See p. 380, ⓫.

The birds and mammals of Kenai Fjords National Park, from Seward. Boats venture into a park that's virtually inaccessible by land but penetrated from the sea by narrow fjords of towering rock. Sentinel islands swarm with puffins, auklets, and other seabirds. Killer and humpback whales commonly show up along the way as well. The park is easily done as a day trip from Seward. See p. 234, ❺.

The Best Backcountry Trips

> *Tributaries of the Copper River rage through Wrangell-St. Elias National Park.*

Floating an Arctic river. Hiking the trackless lands of Alaska's Arctic can be challenging or even impossible. The Alaska Natives of the North Slope travel in winter when the land is frozen or in summer by boat. Hardy visitors can do the same. Riding down the Kongakut or Hulahula rivers in the **Arctic National Wildlife Refuge** with a skilled guide opens up lands that are entirely unaffected by human presence. And thanks to your low-impact mode of travel, you need not leave a trace of your passage, either. See p. 479.

Hiking in Wrangell–St. Elias National Park. The largest of all the nation's parks contains a seeming infinitude of mountains and hardly any people. By joining a guided trek, you can learn to climb some of these peaks, or even summit a mountain that no human ever has before. You could charter a bush plane to set up a base camp and explore, or make your own route over land without trails; either way, the sense of adventure is real and your own outdoor skills are the key to your safety. See p. 55, ⑥.

Tide pooling at China Poot Bay, near Homer. A boat leaves the Homer Boat Harbor behind, bound for the Center for Alaskan Coastal Studies on the roadless south side of Kachemak Bay. There, naturalists take visitors for a day's walk through the coastal forest and among tide pools that teem with odd and wonderful little creatures you can examine. Children love the trip, with its feeling of immersion in the wild, but the safety of town and a comfortable bed for the night are not far off. See p. 248, ⑩.

Fly-in fishing, Bristol Bay region. Imagine a floatplane departing in the distance, leaving your group on a stream bank where only the sounds of gurgling of water and your own voices will be heard until the pilot comes to fetch you at the end of the day—or after a few days in a camp or lodge. You can do this almost anywhere in coastal Alaska, although the Bristol Bay region is the best. The key is timing your visit with the running of the salmon. Hit it right, and your fishing experience could be among the fastest-paced and most exciting available in the world. See p. 259.

Dayhiking in Denali National Park. Getting deep into the Alaska wilderness commonly costs thousand of dollars. At Denali, though, it can cost less than $30, thanks to a transportation system that prohibits private vehicles but carries visitors up to 90 miles into the park on shuttle buses. Get off the bus; the wilderness is at the bottom of the steps. It's open for exploration on even a casual dayhike, until you return to the road and catch a ride back. See p. 134, ⑥.

Sea kayaking in Glacier Bay National Park. Near the park headquarters you can often paddle, guided or alone, among humpback whales. But the most intense experience of the park comes on multiday sea kayaking expeditions into the farthest reaches of the glacial fjords. Far from any habitation, you can explore the ice among marine mammals and sleep in a tent on the shore, amid the pure air and an intense quiet you may never have encountered before. See p. 407, ③.

The Best Wilderness Lodges

> *Kachemak Bay Wilderness Lodge features comfortably rustic accommodations, with eight naturalist guides on staff.*

Kachemak Bay Wilderness Lodge, near Homer. The magic of the lodge emerges both from its location, on an isthmus next to an unimaginably rich tidal estuary, and from the charisma of its warm and adventurous owners, Michael and Diane McBride, who have introduced this paradise to visitors since the 1970s. The lodge buildings, which reflect the McBrides' eco-philosophy, are appropriately rustic for the setting but also comfortable and subtly elegant. See p. 264.

Winterlake Lodge, west of Anchorage. Alongside placid waters in the deep wilderness along the Iditarod Trail, this lodge is like a five-star hotel housed in a remote log cabin. Besides the setting and the activities, which include massage, yoga classes, and helicopter exploration, the food is especially remarkable. It is produced by a gifted chef working with local ingredients and the best of what can be brought in daily by floatplane. Even the wine is extraordinary. See p. 168.

Camp Denali, Denali National Park. Ensconced well within the best part of Denali National Park, this lodge has worked to protect and honor the area by interpreting nature for visitors in an environmentally sensitive way. Guests sleep in primitive log cabins that, alone among all facilities at the park, have stunning views of Mount McKinley. Outings are led by expert guides with special access to the heart of the park. There's no better way to visit Denali. See p. 166.

The Best Inns & Bed & Breakfasts

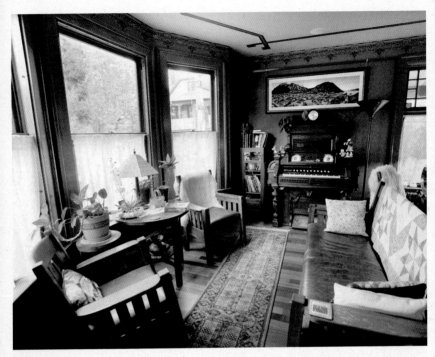

> *Guests often meet over a drink or a cup of tea in the sitting room at Alaska's Capital Inn.*

Copper Whale Inn, Anchorage. The clapboard buildings that make up the Copper Whale overlook Cook Inlet, at the edge of downtown Anchorage's most stylish neighborhood. You can rent a bike on-site for the Tony Knowles Coastal Trail, or walk to the state's best museums and restaurants. The inn is loaded with quirky charm but run attentively for travelers with high expectations. See p. 111.

Lake Hood Inn, Anchorage. This aviation-themed B&B was designed and built by a pilot to showcase his love of flying. The location, on Lake Spenard, is busy with floatplanes, including those tying up at the foot of the lawn. You can even listen to the tower transmissions. The inn is clean, light, comfortable—and handy to the airport. See p. 113.

Bowman's Bear Creek Lodge, Hope. Way off the beaten track, in the forgotten gold-rush town of Hope, south of Anchorage, these little cabins around a pond are simple and share a bathhouse for plumbing. Anything the place lacks in sophistication, however, it more than makes up for in the friendliness and charm of the owners and their sleepy community. See p. 246.

Driftwood Inn, Homer. Some might question the presence of this economical and well-worn inn on a list of Alaska's best, but it deserves inclusion because it serves so many kinds of travelers so well. Those on a budget will enjoy trim little compartments with bunks, while others can choose among beautifully appointed units such as beach houses. All face Kachemak Bay, with the beach only yards away. See p. 266.

Aurora Express B&B, Fairbanks. The hosts, the Wilson family, bought a collection of rail cars and hauled them up a mountain on the south side of Fairbanks, remodeling some into delightful themed rooms and leaving others as nostalgic accommodations true to their past in the romantic days of Pullman sleepers. See p. 322.

A Taste of Alaska Lodge, Fairbanks. Although it's just an easy drive from Fairbanks, this family-operated B&B feels more like a wilderness lodge. The log house sits on its own 280-acre homestead on a sloping lawn that commands a sweeping view of Mount McKinley. You can arrange a dog-sled ride from the grounds. See p. 322.

Pearson's Pond Luxury Inn & Adventure Spa, Juneau. On a residential street near the Mendenhall Glacier, the inn offers rooms that all have the qualities of a bridal suite, with every luxury included and every need anticipated. Many weddings do happen here, on lovely grounds above a small pond, or on the glacier itself, reached by helicopter. See p. 384.

Alaska's Capital Inn, Juneau. A lovingly restored mansion from Juneau's gold-mining days stands half a block from the capitol building, within walking distance of all downtown sites. Rooms are marked by comfort and authenticity. The hosts create a friendly sense of community among guests at evening gatherings in the parlor and over elaborate breakfasts. See p. 383.

Gustavus Inn, Gustavus. A special sense of relaxation envelops this cozy, historic spot in the tiny town of Gustavus, on the edge of Glacier Bay National Park. Breezes caress the meadow outside, where a big vegetable garden provides much of the justly famous food. This superb example of a classic country inn could just as soon be called a wilderness lodge, for the opportunities to get out into nature are boundless. See p. 409.

> *Grab a seat and enjoy the view from Bowman's Bear Creek Lodge.*

Fly-In Fish Inn, Sitka. The air-taxi fishing operation came first; then followed the elegant, friendly waterfront inn to take care of clients. But even if you don't want to fish, you'll enjoy the ambience of this well-made lodging, with its spacious rooms, wonderful views, and beautiful harborside bar. See p. 392.

Black Bear Inn, Ketchikan. Amid waterfront gardens, with a path to a private beach, the inn contains exquisite rooms. A separate unit in an old cannery building was remodeled with floors of slate and porcelain. The owners pay attention to every detail and offer services ranging from satellite TV to lessons in how to smoke salmon. See p. 399.

The Best Restaurants

> *The old-standby steakhouse Channel Club recently got a swanky makeover.*

Jens' Restaurant, Anchorage. Alaska's most adventurous cuisine comes from this remarkable restaurant, incongruously set in a strip mall in the Midtown commercial district. Inside, the look and ritual of the best traditional dining are observed, while the food defies categorization, representing the creativity of a brilliant chef, Jens Hansen. See p. 105.

The Marx Bros. Cafe, Anchorage. The pioneers of elegant food in Alaska still serve some of the state's best meals in a little house downtown. Chef Jack Amon's creations with fresh Alaska seafood have become often-copied classics. See p. 107.

The Homestead Restaurant, Homer. A log roadhouse among the trees and meadows east of town is the setting for local seafood prepared with flair and skill, beautifully finished meat from the grill, and an extensive and reasonably priced wine list. There's no better finish to a day outdoors. See p. 267.

The Saltry Restaurant, Halibut Cove. A meal here is a total experience, beginning with a boat ride across Kachemak Bay from Homer to the picturesque artists' colony of Halibut Cove, where boardwalks and a placid ocean channel take the place of sidewalks and roads. The restaurant, specializing in local seafood (of course), is a jewel box full of lovely touches and a destination well worth the journey. See p. 240, ⑩.

Lavelle's Bistro, Fairbanks. In the middle of muscular Fairbanks, land of greasy-spoon diners and touristy, themed restaurants, here is an eatery decorated in chrome, stone, and glass, serving excellent meals in a wide variety of culinary styles. Started by a couple hoping to educate the town about fine food, the bistro hosts wine classes, too, and keeps a well-stocked cellar. See p. 285, ②.

Zyphyr, Juneau. A short walk from the capitol building, this former old-time grocery store was beautifully remodeled into a romantic dining room with high ceilings and tables set far apart, giving it a sense of velvety privacy. The traditional Mediterranean cuisine has been perfect on each of my visits, and the service charming and professional. See p. 385.

Channel Club, Sitka. A recent redo resurrected one of Alaska's most famous old-fashioned restaurants. This classic steakhouse along the water outside of town went from straight-up masculine to elegant and calming. The salad bar remains truly remarkable and is worth the visit alone. The grilled steaks are done just right as always, and now the club also offers a full range of local seafood. See p. 393.

The Best Adventures on the Water

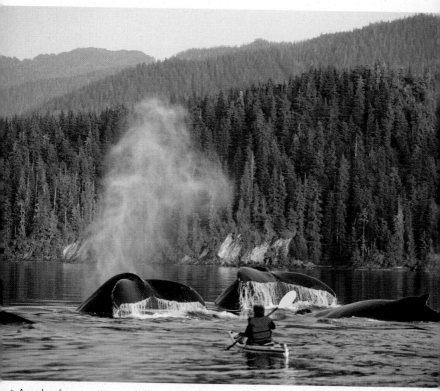

> *A sea kayaker encounters a pod of humpback whales.*

Halibut fishing, Homer. Lurking near the dark sea floor, hundreds of feet below the surface, halibut can grow for 50 years to more than 300 pounds. It's common for anglers on charter boats from Homer (and a number of other coastal towns) to bring in fish that weigh 100 pounds. The advantages of this port are a huge fleet of vessels and a derby for the biggest fish of the summer, carrying a jackpot that often exceeds $40,000. See p. 259, ❹.

Sea kayaking, Petersburg. Every reasonably fit visitor to Alaska should try a sea kayaking day trip. This is your chance to experience the wildness of Alaska at your fingertips, not through glass or along a well-trodden trail. Sea kayaking companies in every coastal community offer outings. Petersburg's advantage is its extensive protected waters for exploration that you can reach right from town. See p. 404.

Prince William Sound glacier cruise, Whittier. You can sail among the wooded islets of this protected inland sea on a day trip from Anchorage, feeling the cold breath of a glacier at midday and dining at a top-rated restaurant back in town that same evening. The scenery is extraordinary, and the trip is easy. See p. 202.

2
Strategies for Seeing Alaska

Strategies for Seeing Alaska

Alaska is synonymous with adventure. It contains some of Earth's remaining great wilderness, free-roaming wildlife, and interesting and exotic people. Faced with the unknown, visitors can be tempted to wrap up in layers of comfort and security—and insulate themselves from the very adventures that could have been their most memorable experiences. You can choose to be pampered, but remember to include the spontaneous and authentic in your planning. This is your chance to try something new, beyond your comfort zone. Here are some tips to make that happen.

> PREVIOUS PAGE *Kenai National Wildlife Refuge's Swan Lake Canoe Route.* THIS PAGE *Lake Hood is the world's largest floatplane base.*

Tip #1: Set realistic goals.

You have reasons for planning a trip to Alaska. Before you decide exactly where you will go or what you will do, think about those reasons and talk them over with your traveling companions. What originally captured your imagination?

Whales? Tundra? Snow? Tour promoters will try to sell you their ideas, so be sure to know your own heart.

Although Alaska is known for its immensity, many visitors still make the mistake of trying to see too much of it in too short a time. You

> *The ice on Johns Hopkins Glacier (named after the American university) moves about 3,000 feet per year.*

wouldn't plan to visit both Florida and Maine on the same vacation, but that's essentially the same as deciding to go to Ketchikan and Nome on a trip to Alaska. This book offers some 3-day tours designed to give you a sense of the area you're visiting, but if you really want to experience a region, plan to spend at least a week there. The exception: 1-day side trips by air (which tend to be expensive). You'll find plenty of itineraries in the book that will let you encounter a microcosm of the state within any one area.

Tip #2: Decide what is essential.

Given how many people talk about wanting to see wildlife and scenery when they come to Alaska, I'm always surprised by how much time visitors seem to spend in museums, gift shops, and made-for-tourists attractions. Setting your own priorities and planning your trip around them will help steer you away from Alaska's plentiful ticky-tacky tourist traps and into the wilderness where, absent the touring crowds, authentic encounters with nature are possible.

About twice as many visitors come to Alaska annually as the number of people who live here. Plenty of businesses look for ways to entertain tourists, usually in large groups. These activities can be fun but are best taken in moderation. The real Alaska is discovered on your own and cannot be prepackaged or repeated at hourly showings.

Tip #3: Use all of your senses.

Remember that visiting Alaska isn't all about "seeing." A glacier certainly is a spectacular sight, but if you get out from behind the glass of a bus or boat window, you'll find it can create other remarkable sensations, too, as its cool breath flows over you and the groan of moving ice rumbles in your gut. Even better, arrange a hike or flight to a glacier and touch it, absorbing a sense of its incredible scale.

Tip #4: Make a plan.

If you go to Paris, you can figure out what to do when you get there. On a trip to Hawaii, the beach always awaits. But the heart of a trip to Alaska is the outdoor excursions you make to see wildlife or scenery, or to try paddling a kayak or riding a raft. Some spots are good for mountain climbing and others for bear viewing. It makes sense to decide first *which* activities appeal to you and then plan *where* you will go accordingly, rather than the other way around.

> *Summer is the best time to see humpback whales, which have come north to feed.*

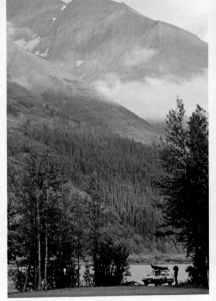

> *Driving is the most cost-efficient way to see the middle of the state.*

Tip #5: Pace yourself.

Here are two good reasons to slow down your itinerary and schedule extra days around each adventurous activity. First, a practical one: Alaska's weather is unpredictable and sometimes severe. Your activity may be cancelled or simply not worth the effort in bad weather. For example, you probably don't want to go whale-watching in a storm and risk getting seasick. Second, a philosophical reason: If you're in a rush to go somewhere else, you may miss the best of the place where you already are.

Tip #6: Reconsider your comfort level.

Traveling in first-class luxury certainly has its appeal, but on an Alaskan trip you could be trading comfort for authenticity. Passengers on escorted tours offered by luxury cruise lines will meet few or no Alaskans and rarely find themselves outside the protective shell of a vehicle or building. Staying in B&Bs means you meet real Alaskans and experience their stories and hospitality. Camping means you fall asleep to the scent of the campfire and wake to the sound of the birds.

Tip #7: Hit the road when you can— otherwise, save time by flying.

A unique aspect of traveling in Alaska is that you can't use every mode of transportation to get everywhere. Most towns in Southeast Alaska have no road access, including the state capital of Juneau. Air is the only way to reach most of the Arctic region or western Alaska. But in the central part of the state, near Anchorage and Fairbanks, driving is the cost-effective and convenient way to get around. You can fly to either city, rent a car for touring, and then return the car before departing. The most popular itineraries in the book are set up for that plan. As an alternative, think about renting an RV and camping along the way.

Except for short stretches of divided highway near the largest cities, Alaska's major highways are all paved, two-lane roads through sparsely populated country. In the summer there is plenty of traffic, but gas stations and restrooms may be broadly spaced. Unpaved routes reaching small rural communities, such as the Dalton, Denali, Taylor, Top of the World, and Steese highways, require preparation for emergencies and special arrangements for your rental vehicle, since most agencies will not allow driving on gravel. (Some that will are listed in chapter 6, p. 194, and chapter 14, p. 509.)

Winter highway driving in Alaska is an adventure all its own. It calls for a properly equipped vehicle and cold-weather gear to keep you warm in case of a breakdown. Most winter visitors should fly between towns instead.

The Alaska Department of Transportation & Public Facilities provides up-to-date road reports and lots of other handy information at http://511.alaska.gov, or call the automated line by dialing ☎ 511 or 866-282-7577.

Distances between Alaskan towns are long. If time is at a premium, you usually can fly instead of driving or taking the ferry, often saving an entire day of vacation time for the cost of a couple hundred dollars. This strategy is especially valuable in Southeast Alaska, where the alternative is taking a boat from place to place. Seeing Alaska from the window of a low-flying plane is an adventure that no visitor should miss. Lots of "flightseeing" opportunities are listed throughout the book, but you can also hop from town to town on propeller-based flight services, enjoying the view and the thrill and saving time on the way. There are typically no security lines to get through, so it's more convenient than flying with an airline.

Tip #8: Ride the rails and the ferries, fly by floatplanes, and ride bikes.

Although it's impossible to take a train *to* Alaska, there are two railroads *within* the state: a short excursion line in Skagway (p. 361, **7**) and the state-owned Alaska Railroad, which runs from Seward through Anchorage and Denali National Park to Fairbanks. Riding the Alaska Railroad is expensive and slow, but well worth it for the entertainment value of the trip.

The Alaska Marine Highway System, a primary transportation link throughout coastal Alaska, is also a fun, inexpensive, and scenic way to travel. Unlike cruise ship passengers, ferry riders can stop off in towns along the way for as long as they like and meet lots of real Alaskans. If you can avoid bringing a car on the ferry, you can be spontaneous, with little need for advance reservations.

Board a floatplane, and soon you'll be landing on a remote lake with little more than a

> *Many of the state's trails are open to mountain bikers.*

fishing rod. Or put down on a mountain glacier, or visit a bear-crowded river. Flight services abound, taking visitors beyond the end of the road to places of unspoiled beauty, where you can get out and experience the setting for yourself—but still get back to town for dinner and a comfortable bed.

Rent a bike instead of a car. If you travel by ferry, you'll find most coastal towns nearly as accessible by bicycle as by car. The miles of Anchorage bike paths can be quite handy, too. Advantages of bike travel include simplicity, flexibility, and proximity to the local people. For those who want more of an escape, most trails

> *Planes can save valuable travel time and get you to Alaska's most remote, and unspoiled, natural spots.*

in Alaska are open to mountain biking, and the national forests offer extensive networks of little-used dirt roads.

Tip #9: Stay put.

Most visitors to Alaska spend only a day or two in each place they visit. Consider whether such a broad, quick survey of the place really matches your interests. After learning about what one family liked to do, I advised them to spend their entire vacation in one tiny Alaska town. There they were able to do all the outdoor activities they wanted, and they got to feel like locals and make real friends. They told me it was one of their best vacations ever.

Tip #10: If you need to budget, plan ahead.

Because Alaska is considered an expensive, once-in-a-lifetime destination, economic downturns hit tourism businesses here very hard. Prices for Web specials and last-minute bookings can reduce costs by half or more. Taking advantage of those deals takes some nerve, however, because if you wait too long, your first choices may book up (see "Making Advance Reservations" on p. 505).

Careful planning saves money. Reserving ahead means you have more choices, which may include the best values. More important, it allows you to focus on the true highlights of your experience. You should pay for the parts of the trip that hold real meaning for you, economizing on the other stuff that doesn't matter as much. That takes some thought.

Driving a rented car and taking the ferry are generally the least expensive ways to travel in Alaska. Flying is next, followed by taking the train. (Cruising can be inexpensive, but that's beyond our scope here.) On the other hand, taking a car on the ferry can be expensive. The bottom line is that if you're on a serious budget, tour an area you can reach by driving from Anchorage or Fairbanks, or visit Southeast Alaska by ferry without a car.

> *The Great Outdoors might be the best accommodations Alaska has to offer.*

Tip #11: Some things are worth spending a little extra money on, while others are not.

You'll need a guide for some of the best experiences available. I wouldn't recommend that a beginner go sea kayaking alone. But you can do many other activities just as Alaskans do: Drive yourself to the trailhead and hike, bait your own line and fish in a stream, or rent a mountain bike and explore. These may be your most memorable and least expensive days in Alaska.

There are good meals to be had, but Alaska is not a dining destination where food represents a major part of the experience. Do visit some of the special restaurants I recommend in the book, and try the local cuisine, but also think about lodgings with simple cooking facilities where you can produce your own meals, even if that's just heating up a packaged meal in a microwave oven. The time and money you save will let you do more.

Skip the big hotels when you can. The least-expensive private lodgings in most towns are bed-and-breakfasts run by families in their homes. It's not unusual to save $50 to $100 over a comparable room in a hotel. As a side benefit, the host may become a new friend, providing the color and advice that make your visit more interesting and authentic.

Tip #12: Give camping a try.

If there is any place to give camping a try, this is it. Traveling in a full-sized RV doesn't save money over staying in hotels, because the rigs are expensive to rent and fuel, but smaller camper vehicles can be cost-effective. Tent camping is very inexpensive and can get you in touch with Alaska's natural world firsthand. Families especially should consider it. You can rent the equipment you need for the bulk of your visit, then stay in a hotel every few days to get cleaned up. For more information, see chapter 12, "The Best Special Interest Trips" (p.476).

Tip #13: Stretch your limits.

A trip to Alaska is the perfect time to try something new. How deeply you delve into the experience may depend on it. You may never encounter a greater variety of outdoor opportunities. Where else can you paddle among whales or walk on a glacier? With the right attitude, you may get much more from the trip than you ever expected.

Try sea kayaking. Paddling with a guide is a safe activity and need not be physically taxing, even for those for whom a trail hike might not be a good idea. Sitting right on the water gives the closest possible view of the marine environment, and it's a relaxing and fun way to see

> *Camping in a tent or RV will let you stay closer to Alaska's natural beauty.*

the scenery and wildlife. You can do it in virtually any coastal town listed in the book.

Hike off the trail. The vast majority of Alaska is public land. That means if you are driving through a tundra-covered mountain valley, there's no reason you can't get out of the car and explore. At Denali National Park, hiking away from the road and trails is the heart of the experience. You'll need proper shoes, your common sense, and a little preparation if you're undertaking a long hike, but this is well within the abilities of most healthy people.

Tip #14: Consider visiting in winter.
Alaska is at its most beautiful when clothed in snow, and community activities take off in the late winter, with sled dog and ski races, ice carving competitions, and wacky community festivals. Ski, watch the aurora, snowshoe, or ride a dog sled. Yes, it's cold, but that's the real essence of Alaska, too.

Tip #15: Book a wilderness trip.
To get away from humanity and into the deep wilderness, consider a guided trip for an extended rafting, sea kayaking, or hiking expedition. Most visitors aren't up to organizing such a trek on their own, but join one of Alaska's experienced outfitters and you can go to spectacular places few other people (including most Alaskans) will ever witness. Your trip doesn't have to be very challenging; consider a "soft" adventure package to get off the beaten track.

Tip #16: Put some thought into your packing.
The key to packing for a trip to Alaska is to bring layers of clothing that can be combined or peeled off, depending on the circumstances. During the warmer months, you may encounter dry days in the 80s within the Interior region— or you could find yourself on a boat in front of a glacier, battling wind and rain in temperatures in the 40s. The more time you plan to spend outdoors in the real Alaska, the more layers you should bring.

Besides your T-shirts, bring heavy, long-sleeved shirts and pants; a wool sweater or fleece equivalent; a jacket; and a waterproof raincoat and rain pants. Gloves and wool hats are a good idea, too, especially for boating trips. If you'll be camping, add synthetic, thermal long underwear and wool socks, and make your jacket a thick synthetic fleece. For wintertime trips, add a parka and insulated boots, plus whatever you'll need for your activities, such as skiing. Lodges and guides often lend or rent the extreme winter equipment required for their activities, so make sure to ask before buying stuff needlessly.

Tip #17: Use common sense when outdoors.
The most important piece of safety equipment for outdoor activities is a properly functioning brain. Only you know your limits and skills. Books can tell you about some unique Alaskan hazards, but the most dangerous ones are obvious: for example, falling into freezing cold water. If you're unsure of yourself, go with a guide. Ask plenty of questions. Next time, you may be ready to go on your own. Everyone was a beginner once.

The other side of common sense is not to be scared off by unreasonable fears. You should avoid attracting bears and learn basic rules about how to behave around wildlife, but don't be deterred from enjoying the outdoors because of the extremely low probability of being hurt by wild animals.

I guess it all depends on where you're from. My kids are used to being around bears, but they can't believe people in the Lower 48 go outdoors in places where they could be bitten by poisonous snakes or spiders, which we don't have here.

Outdoor safety tips are in chapter 14, "The Savvy Traveler" (p. 502).

> *Alaska Railroad offers transportation and tour packages.*

Tip #18: Look into travel insurance.
Most trips to Alaska involve deposits or prepayment for reservations—money that, in most circumstances, is lost if you have to cancel or can't make it because of weather. And it's not unusual for weather to foul up plans here. That means trip cancellation or interruption insurance is a good idea.

For a price tag that's around 5% to 7% of the cost of the trip, you can get coverage for your expenses and a ride home or other emergency help. I don't bother with luggage insurance or added coverage on rental cars, but it's worth sizing up your situation to determine if that coverage is right for you. You can comparison shop for travel insurance at www.insuremytrip.com. Don't buy travel insurance from the same outfit that sells your trip to you, just in case they go bust.

Tip #19: Forget your goals.
Am I contradicting myself? I don't think so. Once you're traveling, its time to give in to the experience of Alaska. Frequently, the best experiences are unexpected and unplanned. Don't spend your trip chasing what you hoped to find. Instead, open yourself up to the wonderful surprises that can fill your days and nights in this unique place.

3
The Best
All-Alaska
Itineraries

Kenai Fjords and Denali Highlights

Many first-time visitors to Alaska consider Denali National Park a can't-miss site—and with good reason. This itinerary connects Denali and another of the state's great national parks, Kenai Fjords. Not surprisingly, it is the most popular route for independent travelers on their first trip to Alaska. You'll board a boat to view glaciers and towering mountains from the ocean, and later ride a bus over alpine tundra to experience the continent's highest peak. Possible wildlife sightings include whales, sea otters, seabirds, brown bears, caribou, and wolves. You can enter the wilderness by sea kayaking, hiking, or flying in a small plane. It's a lot to do in a week, but it makes the most of your time and money. You'll need to rent a car to get around on this week-long trip.

> PREVIOUS PAGE *A park tour bus yields to a grizzly sow and her cubs.* THIS PAGE *Mount Healy's majestic ridgeline.*

START Anchorage. Fly into Ted Stevens Anchorage International Airport. **TRIP LENGTH** 761 miles.

❶ Anchorage. Take a walk or bike ride on the **Tony Knowles Coastal Trail** (p. 70, ❻). This paved pathway leads from the downtown area along the shore of Cook Inlet for 10 miles, ending up in wooded Kincaid Park. A mile south of your start, at Westchester Lagoon, see the waterfowl and the salmon from the viewing boardwalk.

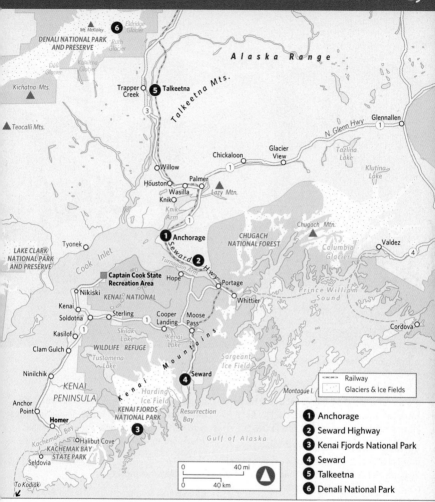

Railway
Glaciers & Ice Fields

1 Anchorage
2 Seward Highway
3 Kenai Fjords National Park
4 Seward
5 Talkeetna
6 Denali National Park

If time allows (or rain requires), stop in at the **Anchorage Museum at Rasmuson Center** (p. 68, **1**). Alaska's largest museum, it contains exhibits of art, history, anthropology, and natural history, as well as a children's science museum, not yet open at this writing.

On the morning of Day 2, pay a visit to the **Alaska Native Heritage Center** (p. 72, **1**). Alaska's Native peoples joined together to create this living museum that showcases their cultures. A trip includes dance and storytelling presentations, exhibits, craft studios where artisans invite discussion with visitors, and outdoor village settings where guides explain traditional lifestyles. ⏱ **Half-day.**

In the afternoon, drive south from Anchorage to Seward, a 127-mile journey.

2 Seward Highway. The first 40 miles of the drive trace the rushing gray waters of Turnagain Arm. Be on the lookout for Dall sheep on the cliffs above—use the right-hand pullouts to view them, the scenery, or (if you're lucky) beluga whales in the Arm. Next, the road rises into the mountains of the Kenai Peninsula, where (if you have time) you can get out for a ramble in the heather. Make a stop at Tern Lake for bird-watching. ⏱ **2½ hr.**

In the late afternoon, you'll arrive in Seward, where you'll spend the next 2 nights. Reserve

> Steller (or northern) sea lions, a threatened species, pile onto a rock.

ahead for a morning tour-boat departure from the Seward harbor to Kenai Fjords National Park, where you'll spend Day 3.

❸ Kenai Fjords National Park. The park's dramatic vertical scenery can be reached only by boat. Pick an all-day tour that goes into the park proper, at least to Aialik Bay, to see Holgate Glacier or Aialik Glacier as well as wildlife that may include whales, otters, and sea lions. You'll also spy an abundance of seabirds,

including puffins. The largest operator is **Kenai Fjords Tours** (p. 234, ❺). They offer trips with park rangers on board to explain what you're seeing—be sure to book one of those. ☺ 1 day.

Spend Day 4 exploring:

❹ Seward. Don't miss the **Alaska SeaLife Center** (p. 268, ❶), a unique research aquarium with dramatic exhibits of marine birds and mammals that give a close-up and educational look at what one can see in Kenai Fjords National Park.

Finish your day by sea kayaking along the shore of Resurrection Bay, south of Seward. You'll likely see otters and maybe spawning salmon, as well as intertidal creatures. **Sunny Cove Sea Kayaking** (p. 252, ❹) offers 3-hour paddles from Lowell Point, including outings that make use of the midnight sun, leaving at 6pm. ☺ 1 day.

Retrace your drive to Anchorage to spend the night so you'll be that much closer to Denali National Park on the morning of Day 5. Get

A Rainy Day Option

If the weather is bad, you may want to delay your boat tour to the next day. It's smart to include an extra day in your planning for this eventuality. A good backup outing is a trip to **Exit Glacier** (p. 235, ❼), at the end of a 9-mile road that branches from the Seward Highway 3⅔ miles north of Seward. You can walk right up to the glacier and even hike along its side to the top. Admission is free.

an early start and take the Glenn and Parks highways 114 miles north to the little town of Talkeetna.

⑤ Talkeetna. Flight services that land climbers on the flanks of Mount McKinley, North America's highest peak, also take visitors to look at the mountain and, for an added fee, to step foot on one of its glaciers. Don't miss this opportunity for some of the most magnificent and memorable hours of your trip to Alaska. By going in the morning you greatly improve your chances of clear, smooth weather, so getting to Talkeetna for an early flight should be a priority. Several good operators offer flights, including **Talkeetna Air Taxi** (p. 130, **①**). ⏱ 3 hr. See p. 172.

Continue the drive from Talkeetna to Denali National Park, a trip of 154 miles. Stop at the Wilderness Access Center to pick up tickets for the buses that allow access into the park proper. You'll spend 2 nights here.

⑥ Denali National Park. After getting settled, check out the **Denali Visitor Center** (p. 133, **④**), a museum of the park with ingenious and informative modern exhibits that explain its science, nature, and culture. Out back is the start of the stunning **Mount Healy Overlook hike** (p. 135, **⑧**)—begin at the Taiga Trail). Without using the bus system, this climb at the park entrance allows you to break above

> *Ethnographic artifacts in the Anchorage Museum at Rasmuson Center.*

the tree line and see the lay of this expansive, unpopulated land. The entire hike is a strenuous 5-mile round trip, but you can climb to good views without going so far.

On Day 6, you'll want to get an early start once again, this time for a one-of-a-kind outing, the **Denali shuttle bus ride** (p. 149). There is no other way into the main part of the park, and for that reason the wildlife and unspoiled scenery at Denali remain truly pristine and accessible. All visitors ride buses beyond the entrance area and can travel up to 90 miles over a gravel road into the heart of the park. Here is your chance for a remarkable wildlife safari to see bears, caribou, and wolves and to take a wilderness dayhike, for a ticket that costs only around $30. Plan well ahead to take the earliest bus you can manage, as wildlife are most active in the morning and a good start gives you more time to explore on your own. You can get off and back onto passing buses at will.

Start your last day at Denali with a raft ride on the glacial Nenana River, which roars through a rock canyon just outside the national park. Lots of silty water comes aboard the rafts during 2-hour canyon runs in class III and IV rapids. Float with **Denali Outdoor Center** (p. 135, **⑥**). ⏱ 2½ days.

Retracing your drive on the Parks and Glenn highways, return 239 miles to Anchorage.

Making Adjustments

All the itineraries in this chapter are fast-paced, showing the most you can expect to do in the allotted time. My aim is to demonstrate ways to fit these locations and activities together. Traveling at such a pace requires a lot of early mornings and good luck with the weather. Going on a sightseeing cruise on a stormy day isn't much fun, and you may want a down day now and then to sleep in, shop, and explore casually. I recommend expanding a 7-day itinerary to 9 days, adding a day around any weather-dependent activity. That way, you can postpone an outing without having to sacrifice something else from your trip. The extra days you don't need are for spontaneous fun or just to relax. They may end up being the best days of your trip.

Southeast Alaska Highlights

This route touches the Southeast's highlights, which include many of Alaska's best offerings. In Sitka, the capital of Russian America, you'll find evidence of the state's most important and interesting history, as well as lots of marine wildlife. In Juneau, discover the current capital city and its amazing topography and culture. Then visit Glacier Bay National Park and its charming gateway community, Gustavus, with big ice, lots of whales, and lovely countryside to explore. This trip will take a week, but if time allows, add days to your plan for weather contingencies.

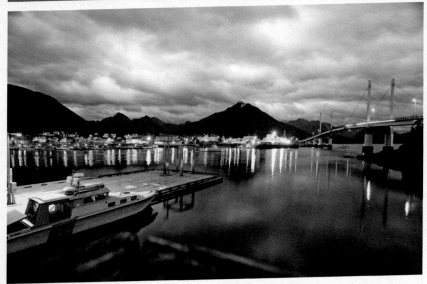

> O'Connell Bridge links Sitka on Baranof Island with the smaller Japonski Island.

START Sitka. Fly into Sitka Rocky Gutierrez Airport. **TRIP LENGTH** 240 miles.

1 Sitka. Castle Hill, with its cannons and flagpole, is a perfect starting point, as it marks the beginning of Alaska's history as part of the United States. Here, the Russian flag came down and the American flag was raised in 1867 when the U.S. bought Alaska for $7 million (see p. 456). The site is entirely casual, as befits Sitka's style.

Next, head to **St. Michael's Cathedral** (p. 389, **5**). Founded in 1848, it was the first Russian Orthodox cathedral in the New World and contains antique furnishings and icons dating to the 17th century. A fire burned the structure in 1966, but townspeople miraculously saved the contents by forming a human

chain. This exact replica was completed 10 years later from the original plans.

The **Russian Bishop's House** (p. 389, ❸) was built for Bishop Innocent Veniaminov, architect of St. Michael's and the great humanizing figure of Russian America, who moved into the extraordinary structure of interlocking logs in 1843. It is the finest of only three authentic buildings from Russian America that still survive from a time when Sitka was the largest city on the American West Coast. Do not miss the National Park Service tours of the second floor.

The **Sitka National Historical Park** (p. 388, ❷) is the moving site of a great battle between invading Russians and the Tlingit in 1804. Copies of historic totem poles stand along the shady rainforest paths, and the originals are in a dramatic gallery in the visitor center. The center combines this extraordinary art with a history exhibit, a film, and workshops where contemporary Tlingit masters make art and interact with visitors.

The **Alaska Raptor Center** (p. 390, ❼) cares for injured birds of prey from around the region that are brought here for medical attention and recuperation. Visitors can learn about the work, see bald eagles up close, and watch them in an extraordinary flight training facility.

Sitka Sound is a lovely setting for a wildlife cruise. The island-dappled waters in front of the town are famous for their humpback whales, sea otters, and abundance of seabirds. The **St. Lazaria Island bird colony** is the best spot for seeing puffins, murres, and other pelagic birds. A variety of half-day cruises are available, including the old favorite **Sitka Wildlife Quest** (p. 389) or, with underwater viewing, **Sea Life Discovery Tours** (p. 389). ◷ 2 days.

Take the ferry 150 miles from Sitka to Juneau. The spectacular ride traverses the amazingly narrow Peril Straits, where you can sometimes see wildlife on shore.

Travel Tip

The Juneau ferry terminal is near the airport but far from the downtown area. If time allows, consider renting a car at the airport—just for the first day of this 2-night visit to the capital city—and touring the portion of Juneau near the ferry dock and airport.

> *A natural history exhibit and a clan house will interest children at the Alaska State Museum.*

Depending on whether you take the fast or the conventional ferry, the trip takes 4½ or 9 hours.

❷ Juneau. Mendenhall Glacier (p. 380, ⓫), near the airport and the ferry terminal, is among Alaska's most popular sights. The glacier descends through mountains to an iceberg-dotted lake. Besides the view—and the interesting exhibits in a U.S. Forest Service visitor center, and several enchanting hiking trails—the glacier parking lot also is Alaska's most accessible bear viewing area. During summer salmon runs, black bears gather under boardwalks a few steps from the cars, and within a few yards of visitors.

There is no road between Juneau and other Alaskan towns, but the Glacier Highway extends about 40 miles from town for access to hiking trails, beaches, and lovely views to the north. The highlight of the drive is a church 9 miles beyond the ferry dock.

The **Shrine of St. Thérèse** (p. 344, ❽) is a little chapel of rounded beach stones that sits peacefully on a tiny, wooded island at the

Getting to Gustavus

Alaska Airlines (p. 507) offers once-daily jet service to Gustavus in the summer, so you can fly from here back to Juneau and then home.

end of a causeway foot trail, surrounded by big trees, rocky shores, and waters where whales are often seen. It's a profoundly spiritual spot.

The **Alaska State Museum** (p. 374, **1**) contains extraordinary historic and cultural objects, and some that are both, such as the Abe Lincoln totem pole carved to mark one tribe's first encounter with white people. The museum isn't large, but the clever exhibits could hold your interest for hours.

Save time (and money) for a helicopter flight to a glacier with **Era Helicopters** (p. 381, **15**). After a shuttle ride to the airport, a chopper lifts you from sea level to the otherworldly landscape of the 1,500-square-mile Juneau ice field, where you can walk around or even enjoy a dog-sled ride. In good weather, this is among Alaska's most memorable experiences. Expect to pay $300 for a 1-hour outing, or $500 for 2 hours including sled dogs.

Juneau's many trails include choices for every ability level, from flat walks on the beach to challenging climbs up the mountains that rise behind town. The **Perseverance Trail** (p. 378, **8**), leading from the top of Basin Road a mile from the downtown area, leads gradually up a mountain valley thick with gold-rush history. ⏱ 2 days.

Begin Day 5 with a ride on a propeller aircraft from Juneau to Gustavus. The trip is only 90 miles, but neither community has a road link. You'll be spending the next 2 nights either in a relaxing full-service inn in Gustavus or 10 miles away at Bartlett Cove, the headquarters of Glacier Bay National Park.

3 Gustavus & Glacier Bay National Park.
Each of the communities on this itinerary has great sea kayaking, but nowhere are your chances of seeing whales and other wildlife better than on a guided beginner's paddle at Gustavus or Glacier Bay National Park. The experience of encountering a whale while sitting in a kayak is incomparable. Within the park, go with **Glacier Bay Sea Kayaks** (p. 408); Gustavus-based **Spirit Walker Expeditions** (p. 408) leads guided day trips to whale-watching grounds beyond park boundaries.

Bicycling in Gustavus opens up a peaceful countryside of quiet roads that pass through meadows and spruce forests, leading you

> The Perseverance Trail above Juneau leads to the remains of a late-19th-century mining community at Silverbow Basin.

along creeks and to sandy beaches. Gustavus is a place to relax. Most of the lodges and inns lend bikes to guests.

A boat from **Glacier Bay Lodge & Tours** (p. 406, **1**) voyages daily up the 65-mile fjord of Glacier Bay National Park to the prodigious glaciers dominating its head. You'll see how this retreating ice has carved the land over the past century, and you'll likely encounter plentiful wildlife, especially whales and other marine mammals.

If you're an angler, plan to spend at least 1 day fishing for halibut or salmon. A charter boat from Gustavus allows you to access rich waters in which to cast your hook—and also offers the good possibility of spotting some whales. Halibut are available all summer, and salmon are plentiful at certain times. Waves aren't rough here, so seasickness is rare. ⏱ 3 days.

Kenai Peninsula to the Arctic in 2 Weeks

If you want to visit some of Alaska's most memorable places and you'd like to do it on a budget, this is the trip for you. You'll get a chance to see the sea otters of Kachemak Bay, the glaciers of Prince William Sound, the big river valleys of the Interior, the Arctic and its indigenous people in Barrow, and the heights of Mount McKinley. By driving yourself most of the way rather than flying, you'll be able to make a grand circuit of Alaska's most scenic highways—and keep costs to a minimum.

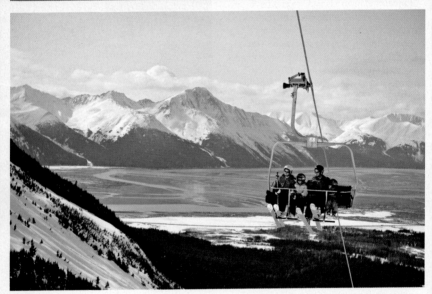

> The icy waters of Turnagain Arm spread below Alyeska ski resort, less than an hour south of Anchorage.

START Anchorage. Fly into Ted Stevens Anchorage International Airport. **TRIP LENGTH** 1,266 miles.

❶ Anchorage. For my suggestions on how to spend time in Anchorage, see p. 62. ⏱ **2 days.**

On the morning of Day 3, enjoy the 45-mile drive south from Anchorage to Whittier on the Seward Highway.

❷ Seward Highway. This is one of Alaska's most scenic routes (p. 250, ❶). Stop at the **Begich, Boggs Visitor Center** (p. 86, ❿),

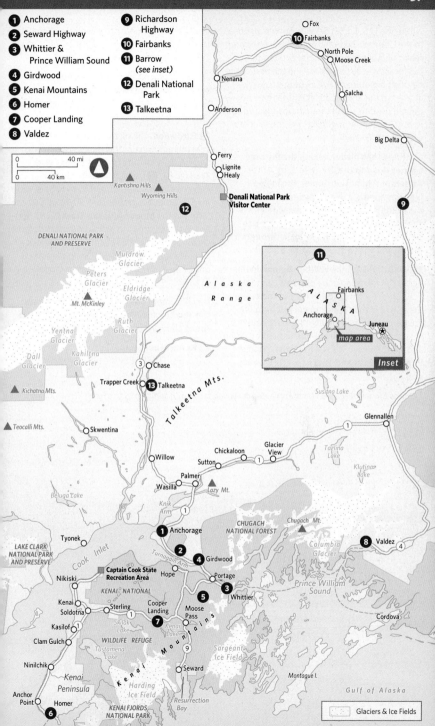

1 Anchorage
2 Seward Highway
3 Whittier & Prince William Sound
4 Girdwood
5 Kenai Mountains
6 Homer
7 Cooper Landing
8 Valdez
9 Richardson Highway
10 Fairbanks
11 Barrow (see inset)
12 Denali National Park
13 Talkeetna

where the U.S. Forest Service orients visitors to the Chugach National Forest, the enormous realm of mountains, glaciers, and temperate rainforest where you will spend the rest of the day. Get a picture by the iceberg-strewn lake in front of the center; a glacier that has mostly melted used to stand there imposingly, which is why the center originally was constructed on this site. ⏱ 2 hr.

Continue to Whittier, taking the Portage Glacier Road to the 2¾-mile-long Anton Anderson Memorial Tunnel, the longest highway tunnel in North America. Because the tunnel is only a single lane wide and is shared by railroad trains, it is common to wait as long as 45 minutes to go through. The tunnel will put you just outside of:

❸ **Whittier & Prince William Sound.** Whittier lies at the head of a Prince William Sound fjord, under a hanging glacier. But the real draw here is the chance to get out onto the Sound. Several competing tour boat companies make the voyage out to encounter wildlife and lots of big ice. To see the most, choose **Phillips Cruises and Tours** (p. 202), which

uses a fast catamaran to penetrate all the way up College Fjord—you'll see a total of 26 glaciers in 5 hours. ⏱ 1 day.

After the glacier tour, reverse your route back through the tunnel (toward Anchorage) and drive 20 miles to Girdwood, where you'll spend the night.

❹ **Girdwood.** Hiking trails weave through the coastal rainforest of this funky skiing town. Our family's favorite is the **Winner Creek Trail** (p. 87, ❼), which leads to a roaring river gorge with a hand-operated tram to help you across. From the grand Hotel Alyeska, you can also ride the **Mount Alyeska Tram** (p. 87, ❼) above the big trees to behold wonderful alpine views; at the top, enjoy summertime walks at an elevation of 2,300 feet. Or simply relax in one of the town's luxurious accommodations. ⏱ 1 day.

Day 4 is spent on the 184-mile drive along the Seward and Sterling highways to Homer. Along the way, you'll pass through the:

❺ **Kenai Mountains.** The road climbs in short order from the sea to the broad, alpine terrain

> *Phillips Cruises' 26-glacier tour of Prince William Sound comes with narration by U.S. Forest Service Rangers.*

of Turnagain Pass at 1,000 feet, 21 miles beyond Girdwood. Stop at the big parking lot for a stroll through the heather.

About 35 miles from Girdwood you can go rafting on Sixmile Creek with **Chugach Outdoor Center** (p. 232, ❷); it's the wildest spot I know of for a commercial rafting day trip, with class IV and V rapids. You'll find lots of other opportunities for casual stops in beautiful places along the drive, too. 🕐 **1 day.**

In the late afternoon, continue on the Sterling Highway to Homer, where you'll spend the night.

❻ **Homer.** Visit the unique **Pratt Museum** (p. 260, ❷), where the area's culture and natural history are on display, for an orientation to this maritime community and its active arts scene.

The **Alaska Islands & Ocean Visitor Center** (p. 260, ❶), operated by the U.S. Fish and Wildlife Service, presents Alaska's coastal environment through fascinating exhibits, nature walks, and programs.

Finish the day with a trip across Kachemak Bay to Halibut Cove aboard the wooden **Danny J passenger ferry** (p. 240, ❾). It puts you in the heart of the area's watery paradise. The artists' colony of Halibut Cove has only a natural ocean channel as a road; boardwalks connect houses and galleries. On the evening trip, dine at **The Saltry Restaurant,** which operates in tandem with the *Danny J;* if going in the afternoon instead, you can take a sack lunch and have more time to explore the walkways, beaches, and meadows of the island village.

Spend Day 5 in one of two ways, both of which involve a full day outdoors. If you're an angler, you're in luck: Homer is known for exceptional halibut fishing, and many boats are available to take you out. I recommend you book through **Inlet Charters Across Alaska Adventures** (p. 240, ⓫). Don't forget to buy a ticket for the Homer Jackpot Halibut Derby. The biggest fish of the summer, generally more than 300 pounds, wins the pot of more than $40,000.

If you're not an angler, join the **Center for Alaskan Coastal Studies** (p. 243, ⓮) for a day trip to learn about the marine environment at a field station in Peterson Bay, across the water from Homer. All-day trips begin with a boat ride and a visit to a bird colony, and

> *Complete a trip on the* Danny J *with dinner at Halibut Cove's only restaurant, The Saltry.*

usually include forest nature walks and tide-pool explorations.

On Day 6, before leaving for your next destination, Cooper Landing, you'll have time to explore the town a bit more. Homer is home to one of Alaska's most vibrant arts communities and you can buy anything from cheap crafts to fine art at its many galleries and gift shops. Don't miss the nonprofit **Bunnell Street Arts Center** (p. 260, ❸); the commercial galleries are along Pioneer Avenue and on Homer Spit. But anglers take note: If you're eager to try salmon fishing in Cooper Landing, you'll want to get an earlier start and spend more of your time there. 🕐 **2½ days.**

Midmorning on Day 7, take the Sterling Highway 120 miles north to Cooper Landing, where you'll spend the night. The drive should take about 2½ hours.

❼ **Cooper Landing.** The upper Kenai River at Cooper Landing and the tributary Russian River are legendary salmon fishing streams. If you know your stuff and a salmon run is in progress, you can achieve success with tackle purchased from any of the many shops along the highway. Otherwise, go with an experienced guide service that provides gear, such as **Alaska Rivers Company** (p. 238, ❺). If you're not into fishing, consider a river-rafting trip or an afternoon hike instead. 🕐 **Half-day.**

> *A sunflower salutes the day at Georgeson Botanical Garden in Fairbanks.*

Day 8 takes you from the Kenai Peninsula across Prince William Sound to Valdez. Drive 60 miles north on the Sterling and Seward highways and Portage Glacier Road in time to catch the ferry from Whittier to Valdez, where you'll spend the night. Your 89 mile trip across the Sound, which will take just under 3 hours, will offer spectacular sightseeing, so keep your camera handy.

8 Valdez. This oil-terminal town lies at the head of a long Prince William Sound fjord, a good spot for a sea kayaking outing on which to view wildlife and explore the rugged country. Go with **Pangaea Adventures** (p. 223, **2**).

Valdez also has a terrific museum, the **Valdez Museum and Historical Archive** (p. 224, **5**), that tells the story of the town's role as a threshold to the Interior. ⏲ 1 day.

Plan to spend much of Day 9 in the car, as you'll drive the 360 miles northeast from Valdez to Fairbanks, where you'll spend the next 3 nights. The drive, which will take about 8 hours, includes a stretch on the:

> *Tour bus passengers view Denali National Park from Stony Hill.*

9 Richardson Highway. Your drive to Fairbanks takes you through some of Interior Alaska's most unforgettable scenery, including this awesome passage over the Alaska Range. The little-used route once was the only road into the heart of Alaska, and several historic spots along the way are worth a stop for more than stretching your legs, including the **Wrangell–St. Elias National Park Visitor Center** at Copper Center (p. 191, **8**); the **Sullivan Roadhouse** in Delta Junction (p. 294, **3**), and **Rika's Roadhouse,** on the Tanana River (p. 294, **4**). ⏲ 1 day.

Plan to spend Day 10 exploring:

10 Fairbanks. Alaska's second-largest city has some rough-hewn (sometimes corny) charm, but you'll need your car to find the best of it. The most interesting attraction is the **University of Alaska Museum of the North** (p.

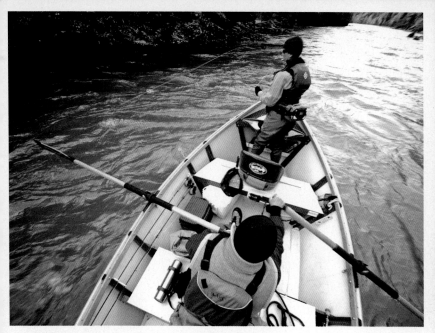

> *The upper Kenai River at Cooper Landing has legendary salmon fishing.*

317, **7**), containing the finest natural history collection in the state and nationally noted art and sound installations. Take some time for the rest of the campus, too, especially the **Georgeson Botanical Garden** (p. 317, **8**).

Fairbanks is a river city. The region's waterways were its original roads, and barges still move cargo to the area's smaller villages. Renting a canoe for a paddle on slow-moving brown water or on challenging white water is easy to arrange, with pickup and drop-off, through **Alaska Outdoor Rentals & Guides** (p. 299, **8**). ⏱ 1 day.

Day 11 is devoted to a day trip to the Arctic. You'll take a quick Alaska Airlines flight to Barrow in the morning and return to Fairbanks that night.

11 **Barrow.** The thousand-year-old Iñupiaq culture dominates this town on the edge of the Arctic Ocean, where family crews still pursue the bowhead whale in sealskin boats and schoolchildren learn to avoid polar bears. Most visitors go on a guided tour offered by

Alaska Airlines Vacations (p. 427). If you go on your own, make sure to visit the marvelous **Iñupiat Heritage Center** (p. 426). ⏱ 1 day.

On Day 12, get an early start out of Fairbanks and take the Parks Highway 120 miles south to Denali National Park, where you'll spend the next 2 nights. Be sure to stop at the Wilderness Access Center to pick up tickets for the buses that allow access into the park proper.

12 **Denali National Park.** For my suggestions on spending time in Denali, see p. 31, **6** . ⏱ 2 days.

Rise early again on Day 14 and drive 154 miles south on the Parks Highway to:

13 **Talkeetna.** Stop here for a quick flight up to one of Mount McKinley's glaciers—see p. 130, **1** , for more information. ⏱ 3 hr.

In the afternoon, continue on the Parks and Glenn highways another 114 miles back to Anchorage.

A DANGEROUS TIME

The fast and furious impact of climate change

BY CHARLES WOHLFORTH

THE IMPACT OF THE EARTH'S WARMING CLIMATE has been evident in Alaska for more than a decade, and it seems that every few months, some new record is set. Sadly, which those records are historic, they no longer make headlines because of their frequency. The cause of this warming is the accumulation in the atmosphere of carbon dioxide, primarily from the burning of fossil fuels. The effect is devastating on a land and an eco-system that relies on cold. The results are unexpected and heart-breaking—from bears that no longer hibernate as they should, and are therefore more vulnerable, to rivers that flood more severely in spring, destroying the fragile life that surrounds them in the process. Here are just a few key issues.

Saying Goodbye to Glaciers

Many of Alaska's glaciers have lost mass—thickness as well as length—at an astonishing rate. For example, the Portage Glacier has nearly vanished from view, and a 2007 study showed that glaciers near Juneau were receding more than 30 feet per year. Glaciers depend on cold and precipitation, and increased snowfall can offset melting in some cases. But, on balance, the loss of ice from Alaska's many snow-capped mountains is enough to significantly contribute to a rising world sea level. You'll still see glaciers on your visit, but know that you are potentially seeing the demise of these natural wonders.

Sea Ice: Slipping Away

The frozen ocean north of Alaska is thawing in summer to an extent that probably has not been seen in thousands of years. The Northwest Passage, the trading route that explorers sought for centuries in vain, is now a reality. Since 2007, the ice that once blocked the passage year-round has retreated enough in summer to allow vessels to pass over the top of the continent. This loss of ice threatens a wide range of Arctic animals, including polar bears, which depend on sea ice to survive. The earlier sea ice melts in the season, the shorter the bears' hunting season becomes. When they are forced to come ashore early, they are at risk of starvation. But polar bears aren't the only threatened species. Indeed, an entire ecosystem of specially adapted organisms depends on the ice, from tiny bacteria to seals that birth pups in ice-bound dens.

Eroding Shores & Melting Permafrost

While rising sea levels may ultimately affect low-lying areas in Alaska, the rapid erosion that threatens northern coastal communities is far from theoretical—it is already a major problem. The cause is the loss of ice. Sea ice that used to protect shores from storms is absent; at the same time, the frozen ground beneath the shoreline is melting, making the land soft and susceptible to collapse. As beaches disappear, towns and wildlife are threatened. Meanwhile, permanently frozen ground called permafrost lies beneath much of the state, and the warming climate has caused melting that, surprisingly, can force the land upward. A recent study showed that land in coastal Alaska had risen 10 feet over the last 200 years thanks to these frost heaves. That kind of disruption undermines roads, buildings, and even trees, impacting both people and wildlife.

Changes at Sea & on Land

AQUATIC IMPACT Increased ocean and river water temperatures are affecting aquatic life. Warmer streams can damage runs of salmon, while northward movement of warm ocean water means predatory fish newly able to enter northern waters can make short work of fish previously safe from such threats.

FORESTS UNDER FIRE A changing climate moves the optimal growing ranges for plants and trees; but trees can't move, so nature has ways of clearing them away. In Southcentral Alaska, warmer springs brought an enormous plague of spruce bark beetles that killed more than 4 million acres of forest over more than a decade (it stopped only when all the susceptible trees were dead). In Interior Alaska, a severe increase in forest fires, brought about by higher-than-normal temperatures that create hazardous conditions, has blackened millions of acres every summer.

The Best of Southeast & Southcentral Alaska

You'll need 2 weeks for this trip, but that will give you time to either dig in deeply in one part of Alaska or sample two different regions of the state. This tour combines the southern portion of Southeast Alaska—the zone of big rainforest trees, totem poles, and marine life—with the Southcentral region, including Alaska's largest city and access to its most famous national park (Denali) and the highest mountain in North America (McKinley).

START Ketchikan. **Fly into Ketchikan International Airport. TRIP LENGTH** 684 miles.

❶ **Ketchikan.** Explore the downtown area, squeezed between forested mountains and the sea. Don't miss the shops on **Creek Street** (p. 394, ❷) or the tour of the **Deer Mountain Tribal Hatchery and Eagle Center** (p. 397, ❾), where you can see salmon and eagles up close.

Ketchikan is full of totem poles. Historic poles are at the **Totem Heritage Center** (p. 396, ❼), within walking distance from downtown, while the most captivating outdoor setting for totem poles is the **Totem Bight State Historical Park** (p. 396, ❻).

For your second day, consider a fishing trip with a guide from **Ketchikan Charter Boats** (p. 398), going for salmon or halibut. If you're not interested in fishing, Ketchikan is a terrific base for hiring a floatplane to see bears or tour the spectacular terrain in **Misty Fjords National Monument** (p. 398, ⓫); I recommend **Island Wings Air Service** (p. 398). ⏱ 2 days.

> Ketchikan totem poles are traditionally painted in black, red, and turquoise.

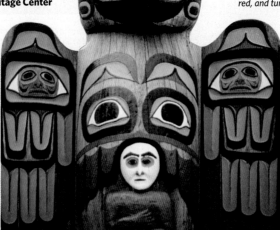

Take the slow (11-hour) but very scenic ride 148 miles to Petersburg aboard an Alaska Marine Highway System ferry. You can reserve a cabin if you will be on board overnight. If you'd prefer to save some time, you can fly into Petersburg (a 2-hour flight), where you'll spend the next 3 nights.

2 Petersburg. One of my favorite small towns, this fishing village has everything: friendly people, charming streets over the water, incredible hiking trails, fishing, sea kayaking, and some of the best whale-watching in Alaska. Leave time to wander the town, meet new friends, and try one of the splendid hikes.

Petersburg's Frederick Sound is among the most reliable spots in Alaska for whale-watching; the boats that take visitors are small and intimate. Some carry hydrophones that allow you to listen to the humpbacks as they spin their underwater webs of bubbles to entrap a meal of herring. Spend all day with **Kaleidoscope Cruises** (p. 404), captained by a retired marine biologist with a 10-year record of seeing whales on every trip.

Island-protected waters and fascinating landscapes nearby make Petersburg a wonderful spot for either a first sea kayaking excursion or a longer expedition for experienced paddlers. **Tongass Kayak Adventures** (p. 370) offers many options, including a half-day trip across to Kupreanof Island and up Petersburg Creek; those who make the trek often spot bears and deer along the shore. ⏱ 2½ days.

On **Day 6,** catch the once-daily, 45-minute flight from Petersburg to Juneau. When you arrive, rent a car at the airport. You'll only need it for the afternoon, so plan to return it the same day and then take the shuttle downtown for your 3-night stay.

3 Juneau. Explore the state's capital city, enjoying some of the activities described on p. 374. Plan to spend a day on a boat ride to the Tracy Arm–Fords Terror Wilderness with **Adventure Bound Alaska** (p. 381, **14**) to witness some of Alaska's most impressive scenery, including a huge tidewater glacier with seals lounging on bergs, floating in front of mile-tall mountains that rise straight up from the water. ⏱ 3 days.

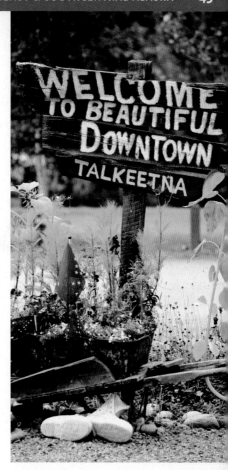

> *Quirky and beautiful—a sign welcomes McKinley climbers to Talkeetna.*

On **Day 9,** fly to Anchorage, where you'll spend the next 2 nights. Alaska Airlines offers several daily nonstop flights that take about 2 hours. Rent a car at the airport.

4 Anchorage. For my suggestions on how to spend your first day in Anchorage, see p. 68. On your second day, anglers should use the city as a base for an all-day fly-in fishing trip. Floatplane operators based at Lake Hood provide gear and guides, dropping clients on remote lakes and riversides for fishing experiences that can be extraordinary. Where you go will depend on where the fishing is hot. I recommend **Rust's Flying Service** (p. 75, **4**).

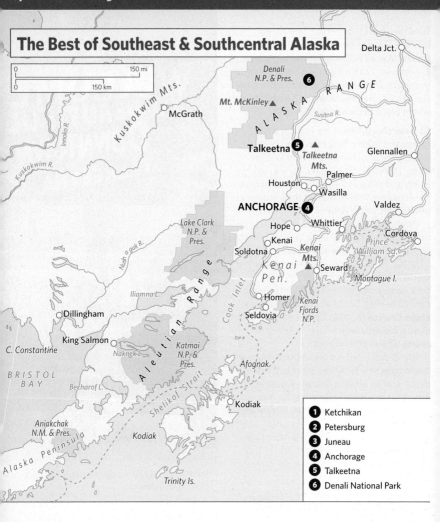

The Best of Southeast & Southcentral Alaska

Delta Jct.

Denali
N.P. & Pres. **6**

Mt. McKinley ▲

A L A S K A   R A N G E

Kuskokwim Mts.

McGrath

Susitna R.

Talkeetna **5**   ▲
Talkeetna
Mts.

Glennallen

Imloko R.

Kuskokwim R.

Houston   Palmer

Wasilla

ANCHORAGE **4**

Valdez

Hope   Whittier

Cordova

Lake Clark
N.P. &
Pres.

Kenai

Prince
William Sd.

Soldotna   *Kenai
Mts.*

Nush a gak R.

K e n a i
P e n.

▲ Seward

Montague I.

Iliamna L.

Homer

Kenai
Fjords
N.P.

Cook Inlet

Dillingham

Seldovia

King Salmon

Katmai
N.P. &
Pres.

Naknek L.

Afognak

C. Constantine

B R I S T O L
B A Y

Becharof L.

A l e u t i a n   R a n g e

Shelikof Strait

Kodiak

Aniakchak
N.M. & Pres.

Kodiak

Alaska Peninsula

Trinity Is.

0 ――― 150 mi
0 ――― 150 km

- **1** Ketchikan
- **2** Petersburg
- **3** Juneau
- **4** Anchorage
- **5** Talkeetna
- **6** Denali National Park

Non-anglers should head to the tundra-clad mountains within the enormous Chugach State Park. The **Glen Alps trailhead** (p. 56, **8**), high above the city, provides access to exciting climbs as well as easy rambles in the mountain valleys. Even the views from the parking lot are breathtaking.

Returning downtown from Glen Alps, you will pass the **Alaska Zoo** (p. 74, **2**), a fun stop for an hour or half a day. You'll see wildlife indigenous to Alaska, or at least to the North, along pleasant wooded paths. ⊙ **2 days.**

On **Day 11,** drive 114 miles north from Anchorage on the Glenn and Parks highways to Talkeetna, where you'll spend the night.

5 **Talkeetna.** This is a funny little town, full of mountain climbers preparing to assault Mount McKinley, but also filled with a lot of history. Don't miss the charming **Talkeetna Historical Society Museum** (p. 174, **3**), which recreates the feel of frontier days with a series of restored buildings.

Talkeetna lies near the confluence of three large, swift glacial rivers. You can get out on

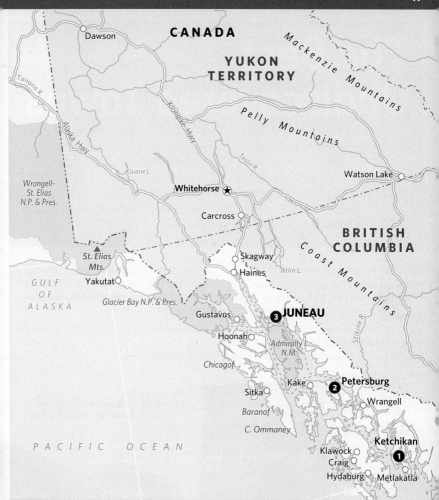

this intimidating water in a speedy and exciting jet boat for a tour or fishing excursion. **Mahay's Riverboat Service** (p. 175, ➏) has a long-standing reputation for great trips.

The highlight of a visit to Talkeetna is a flight to Mount McKinley, North America's highest peak, with a landing on one of its glaciers. You'll use the same planes that carry climbers to the mountain. Since you're staying in Talkeetna, it will be easy to go early in the morning, which greatly improves your chances of clear, smooth flying weather. Several good

operators offer flights, including **Talkeetna Air Taxi** (p. 130, ➊). ⏱ 1½ days.

Take the Parks Highway 154 miles north from Talkeetna to Denali National Park, where you'll spend the next 2 nights.

➏ **Denali National Park.** For my suggestions on exploring Denali, see p. 31, ➏. ⏱ 2½ days.

To return to Anchorage, drive 168 miles south on the Parks and Glenn highways.

The Best Undiscovered Towns

The great majority of visitors to Alaska go to the same collection of places, pretty much on the same timetable. They see good stuff, no doubt about it—Denali National Park is definitely worth the effort—but the emphasis on those spots is way out of balance. Many other places in Alaska are as majestic or as rich with wildlife but receive hardly any visitors at all. If you are the kind of traveler who likes making your own discoveries, here is an itinerary to put you in mind of the kind of adventure that's possible.

START **Palmer, a 40-mile drive on the Glenn Highway from Ted Stevens Anchorage International Airport. TRIP LENGTH 685 miles.**

❶ **Palmer.** This windswept little town grew out of a Depression-era program to colonize the surrounding Matanuska Valley with Dust Bowl farmers. There's just enough atmosphere on the main street, **Colony Way**, to warrant a visit, including interesting shops and the hip music scene at the **Vagabond Blues** coffee shop (p. 138, ③). ⏲1 hr.

Take the Glenn Highway 74 miles northeast to the Matanuska Glacier area, where you'll be spending the night.

> Kennicott, an abandoned mining town, is a tourist destination and backcountry hiking stopover.

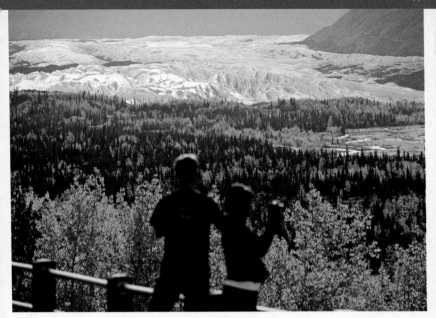

> *The icy expanse of Matanuska Glacier is visible over the tops of fall foliage from a park overlook.*

2 Matanuska Glacier area. The Glenn Highway is beautiful and scary, passing through a steep, rocky canyon by the glacier. Stop at Chickaloon to join a scenic rafting trip on the Matanuska River with **Nova Raft and Adventure Tours** (p. 221, **4**). They also offer hikes on the glacier. The access road to the huge **Matanuska Glacier** itself crosses private land; you can get to it self-guided for a fee, or just view it for free from a state park overlook (p. 220, **3**).

The **Sheep Mountain Lodge** (p. 221) has cozy cabins and a good restaurant—I suggest you spend the night here. If you get an early start the next morning, you can hike for a few hours on the lodge's own network of alpine trails. ⏱ 1 day.

After your morning hike on Day 2, drive the 88 miles to Copper Center, a journey that will take around 2 hours, where you'll spend the next 2 nights.

3 Copper Center. There's not much to this tiny Athabascan village (p. 191, **8**), but walking the dusty roads and skirting the riverside evokes an authentic sense of life in a rural Alaska Native community. Also stop in at the **Wrangell–St. Elias National Park Visitor Center** (p. 191, **8**) to learn about America's largest and most rugged park, where you will spend a full day tomorrow. ⏱ Half-day.

You'll be spending all of Day 3 in and around Kennicott and McCarthy. Rather than drive your rental car over the rough road leading there, you can take a bush plane or a van. The total trip from Copper Center is about 112 miles—for more information on your options, see p. 195.

4 Kennicott & McCarthy. Your journey into the wilderness has brought you to one of Alaska's most remarkable communities, the intact mining ghost town of Kennicott (p. 214) and its still-breathing but equally historic sister town of McCarthy (p. 217, **7**). Spend the day touring the old buildings and walking on the Root Glacier with **St. Elias Alpine Guides** (p. 214, **1**); save some time to soak up the frontier ambience of McCarthy. ⏱ 1 day.

On Day 4, take the Richardson Highway 105 miles south from Copper Center through Thompson Pass toward Valdez.

The Best Undiscovered Towns

1. Palmer
2. Matanuska Glacier area
3. Copper Center
4. Kennicott & McCarthy
5. Thompson Pass
6. Valdez
7. Cordova
8. Whittier
9. Portage Glacier area

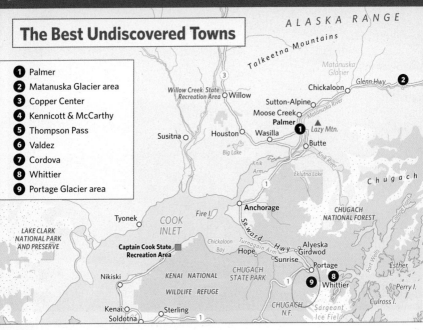

> You might see hundreds of sea otters while sea kayaking from Cordova's harbor into Prince William Sound.

5 Thompson Pass. The Richardson Highway descends to Valdez through extraordinary views within the towering pass. Stop at **Worthington Glacier** (p. 195, **5**), just before the pass, to get up close to ancient ice. ⏱ 1 hr. See p. 190, **7**.

Continue on to:

6 Valdez. ⏱ 2 hr. See p. 222.

In the afternoon, catch the ferry for the 3-hour, 84-mile ride across Prince William Sound to Cordova, where you'll spend the next 2 nights.

7 Cordova. No community in Alaska has more character or more first-rate outdoor opportunities than this historic little fishing town beyond the road network. Join a sea kayak outing with **Cordova Coastal Outfitters** (p. 212) to see marine wildlife just beyond the harbor, including sea lions and rafts of sea otters.

Devote the balance of your time to seeing the **Copper River Delta** (p. 209, **10**) and visiting **Childs Glacier** (see "Alaska's Best Glacier," on p. 212). Your route is the Copper River Highway, an unpaved road extending 48 miles east of town, passing over the immense Copper River and through Alaska's richest and most scenic bird-watching wetlands. It ends at the awe-inspiring glacier, which towers on the far side of the river from the viewing area, releasing ice with enormous roars and splashes of water. ⏱ 1 day.

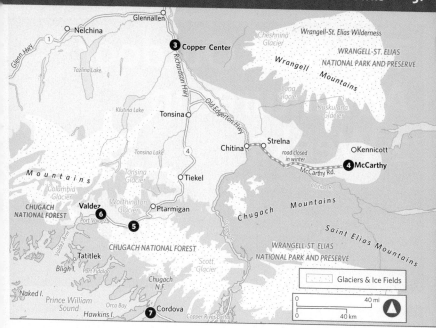

On the morning of Day 6, take the ferry for a 3¼-hour, 110-mile ride across the breadth of Prince William Sound to Whittier.

⑧ Whittier. Other than access to Prince William Sound, Whittier's primary attraction is its oddness. The town was built by the military in World War II as a port at the head of the Passage Canal fjord, and the great majority of the population still live in a single, 14-story concrete building. People get around via long pedestrian tunnels, one of which connects the building to the school and another that burrows under the rail yard that takes up most of the town's flat ground. Use Whittier as a base for getting out onto **Prince William Sound** (see "On the Water from Whittier," on p. 202). ⏱ At least 1 hr. See p. 201, ❸.

From Whittier, take the Anton Anderson Memorial Tunnel to the:

⑨ Portage Glacier area. Wrap up your time with a look at this spectacular glacier. ⏱ At least 1 hr. See p. 86, ⑪.

> A glacier creeps toward Prince William Sound near Whittier.

The Best Outdoor Adventures in 2 Weeks

For the avid outdoors enthusiast, few places compare to Alaska. At least, I've never found anywhere else like it. If your idea of paradise is a long, muscle-powered journey far beyond the bounds of civilization—a vacation without a single moment in a museum or gift shop—this tour may be for you. I've set it up without consideration for those who seek hard walls or indoor plumbing at the end of the day. Better yet, use this plan only for inspiration, and find your own version of outdoor heaven among Alaska's infinite choices.

> *Glacier Bay National Park, roughly the size of Connecticut, can only be seen by boat, plane, or sea kayak.*

START Gustavus, a 30-minute prop plane flight from Juneau International Airport. **TRIP LENGTH** 1,424 miles.

① Gustavus & Glacier Bay National Park. Most of the first week is a sea kayaking expedition in the park. Spend your first day exploring the village of Gustavus—renting a bike is a great way to get around—and spend the night in a cozy country inn at the village of Gustavus. You'll travel in a group with your guide from one of the state's best eco-tour operators, **Alaska Discovery** (p. 479), going by charter boat to remote West Arm, at the head of 65-mile-long Glacier Bay. The next 4 days are spent paddling in two-hatch kayaks in a pure wilderness of bedrock mountains and glacier ice, rich with marine mammals, and

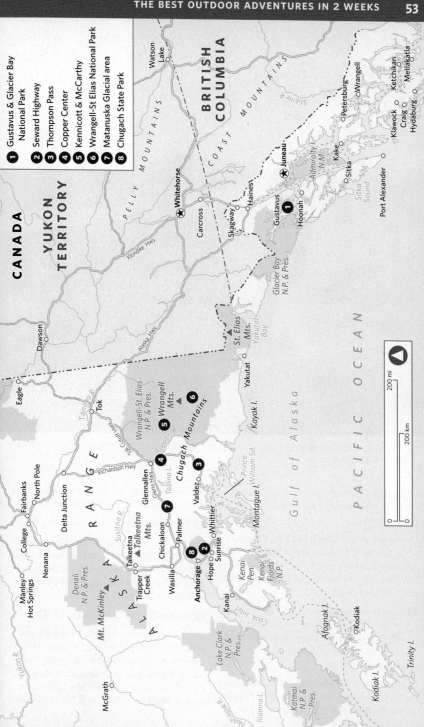

1. Gustavus & Glacier Bay National Park
2. Seward Highway
3. Thompson Pass
4. Copper Center
5. Kennicott & McCarthy
6. Wrangell-St Elias National Park
7. Matanuska Glacial area
8. Chugach State Park

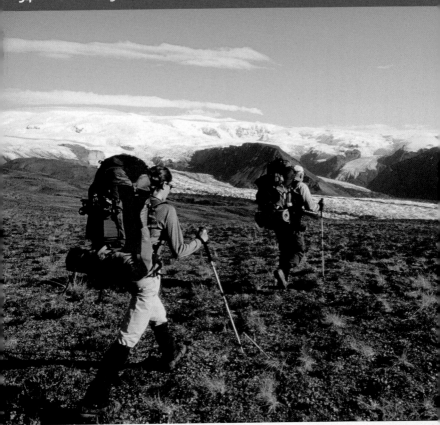

> *Wrangell-St. Elias, straddling the Alaska-Yukon (Canada) border, encompasses the second and fourth highest peaks in North America.*

hiking to the famous glaciers. At night you'll camp on the shore. ⏱ 1 day in Gustavus; 4 days on the water.

On the evening of Day 5, you'll be dropped off in Juneau in time to catch a flight to Anchorage, where you'll rent a car and spend the night. On the morning of Day 6, drive 43 miles on the scenic:

② **Seward Highway.** See p. 250, **①**, for more information on stops along the highway, and p. 86, **⑩**, for the **Begich, Boggs Visitor Center,** where you'll learn a bit about the terrain you're traversing. ⏱ Half-day.

Continue on to Whittier, where you will board the fast ferry for a nearly 3-hour trip 78 miles across the island-dotted waters of Prince William Sound to Valdez. From Valdez, take the Richardson Highway north through:

③ **Thompson Pass.** ⏱ 2 hr. See p. 190, **⑦**.

Continue on to Copper Center, where you'll spend the night. Plan to spend about 2 hours making the 105-mile drive, not including your stop in Thompson Pass. Spend the morning of Day 7 exploring:

④ **Copper Center.** ⏱ 2 hr. See p. 191, **⑧**.

In the late morning, head to Kennicott and McCarthy. Rather than drive your rental car over the rough road that leads through the national park, you can take a bush plane or a van from Copper Center (see "Getting to Kennicott & McCarthy" on p. 195 for details).

5 Kennicott & McCarthy. ⏱ 1 day. See p. 195, **4**.

Spend the night in McCarthy and meet up with St. Elias Alpine Guides on Day 8 for a 4-day backpacking expedition.

6 Wrangell–St. Elias National Park. Your trek explores part of the nation's largest and most rugged national park, which embraces four mountain ranges, including 9 of the 16 tallest peaks in the United States. With so many peaks to choose from, St. Elias Alpine Guides offers as part of its catalog summit expeditions of mountains that have never been climbed before. That takes weeks, however—given your time constraints, you'll want to take the **Donoho Peak Wilderness Exploration.** A perfect introduction to backpacking in the park, it includes hiking along the Root Glacier and crossing it in crampons, with the third day devoted to dayhiking to explore the mountains and the otherworldly phenomena created by ice and water. ⏱ **4 days.**

You'll arrive back in McCarthy late in the afternoon of Day 11, having earned a night in a warm bed. If you drove to McCarthy, stay there; if you flew or took the van, return to Copper Center for the night. On Day 12, take the Richardson and Glenn highways 88 miles from Copper Center (200 miles from Kennicott and McCarthy) to the Matanuska Glacier area, where you'll spend the night. You'll spend the rest of Day 12, and Day 13, exploring:

7 Matanuska Glacier area. After your two guided expeditions, now is the time for spontaneous, self-guided exploration. The Glenn Highway crosses high alpine country and a grand tundra plateau, where caribou can sometimes be seen from the road and good

> The Glenn Highway wends its way through tundra between Anchorage and Wrangell-St. Elias.

hiking trails branch off at various spots. You'll want to spend the night at the **Sheep Mountain Lodge** (p. 221) or the **Majestic Valley Wilderness Lodge** (p. 221). They're both terrific, and each has its own trails and friendly, outdoorsy folks to give advice.

For more information on how to spend your second day here, see p. 220. ⏱ 1½ days.

On Day 13, take the Glenn Highway toward Anchorage, where you'll spend your final night. It's a 114-mile trip that will take about 2½ hours.

8 Chugach State Park. Finish the trip in the mountains above Anchorage. Starting at the Glen Alps trailhead, hike to an area above the tree line, where the scenery opens up and you can follow Alaska's most popular mountain trails—or strike out on your own into untracked terrain. ⏱ 1 day.

Get a Guide

It takes skill and knowledge to safely plan and carry out the outdoor trips I've described here to **Glacier Bay National Park** and **Wrangell–St. Elias National Park,** beyond the abilities of most readers. But with the highly regarded guide services I recommend here, any fit person who enjoys camping can manage these trips.

Kenai Fjords & Denali, Car-Free

This plan takes you to most of the popular spots listed in this chapter's first itinerary—including the two premier national parks of Alaska's central region—but allows you to do it without a car or an escorted tour. Taking the Alaska Railroad to the parks costs more than renting a car to make the same journey, even for a single traveler, but adds a level of luxury and relaxation you don't get on a road trip. Moreover, the tracks pass through some gorgeous terrain you can't see any other way. Plan to spend a week exploring.

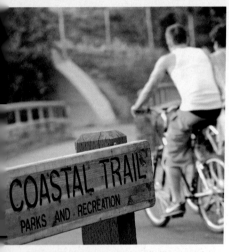

> Anchorage's 10-mile, bike-friendly Tony Knowles Coastal Trail is mostly wooded and wild.

START Anchorage. Fly into Ted Stevens Anchorage International Airport. **TRIP LENGTH** 731 miles.

1 Anchorage. There's plenty to do in downtown Anchorage on foot or by bicycle. The **Tony Knowles Coastal Trail** (p. 70, **6**) and the **Anchorage Museum at Rasmuson Center** (p. 68, **1**) are good examples. ⏲1 day.

On Day 2, board the Alaska Railroad's Coastal Classic train for the 127-mile, 3½-hour ride south from Anchorage to Seward.

2 Train ride through Spencer Glacier backcountry. The train is slow, but it's the only way other than with hiking boots or a snowmobile to see the extraordinary mountain country it passes through, including the **Spencer Glacier.** The ride itself is a trip highlight. ⏲Half-day. See p. 236, **1**.

You'll spend the next 2 nights in Seward, which is easily managed on foot with an occasional cab ride between downtown and the boat harbor.

3 Seward. ⏲Half-day. See p. 268.

On Day 3, get an early start and board a tour boat for a ride into Kenai Fjords National Park.

4 Kenai Fjords National Park. ⏲1 day. See p. 234, **5**.

You'll spend all of Day 4 aboard the Park Connection motorcoach for the 11-hour, 364-mile journey to Denali National Park, where you will spend the next 2 nights.

5 Denali National Park. ⏲1½ days. See p. 31, **6**.

On the afternoon of Day 6, take the Alaska Railroad's Denali Star train to Anchorage, where you'll spend your final night. It's a 240-mile trip that takes 7½ hours. Plan to stay near the airport.

6 Anchorage. Aviation, which plays a central role in Alaskan life, is the focus of a couple of great activities near the airport. See the **Alaska**

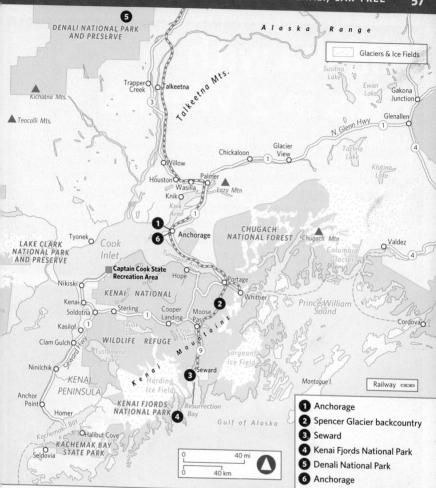

Glaciers & Ice Fields

1 Anchorage
2 Spencer Glacier backcountry
3 Seward
4 Kenai Fjords National Park
5 Denali National Park
6 Anchorage

Railway

Aviation Heritage Museum (p. 75, 3) before your departure; it contains an unsurpassed collection of historic aircraft and often affords the opportunity to see volunteers restoring recently acquired planes. The museum sits on the shore of Lake Hood, the world's busiest floatplane base, and if you haven't taken a flightseeing trip yet, this is the place to do it. Fly with **Rust's Flying Service** (p. 75, 4) to get a close-up look at feeding brown bears, fish a remote stream or lake, or just take a quick spin to observe the wilderness from the air. ⏲ Half-day.

To RV or Not to RV?

Many visitors tour Alaska in RVs and campers. The reasons are obvious: These vehicles combine the flexibility of camping with the comfort of a warm, dry bed. For a large family, an RV can make sense, since traveling gets expensive when you need to rent more than one room every night. However, renting a large RV is also expensive—around $1,500 a week, not counting gas and mileage charges—and driving the beast and servicing its toilet isn't much fun. In the end, I prefer tent camping, but then, I don't mind a little frost in the campsite on a chilly mountain morning.

Alaska with Kids in 2 Weeks

Alaska is a fabulous family destination. Some of our family's happiest memories are of camping together in its vast spaces—trips we made with our children from their earliest ages. There's no better way to tour the state with kids, and no more economical way of traveling. The challenges are manageable. As tent campers you can rent everything you need in Anchorage, touring in a hired car and setting up camp spontaneously when you find a good spot. Campgrounds are numerous, and most of the state is public land where camping is permitted anywhere. RV campers can rent a rig in Anchorage. This itinerary will work even if you decide to spend the night indoors.

> *The Alaska SeaLife Center in Seward, the state's only public aquarium and wildlife center, puts "research on display."*

START Anchorage. Fly into Ted Stevens Anchorage International Airport. **TRIP LENGTH** 1,240 miles.

❶ Anchorage. After arriving in Anchorage, tent campers should pick up a rental car and rent camping equipment (see "Gearing Up to Fly & Camp," on p. 157). RV travelers who choose **Alaska Motorhome Rentals** (p. 373) will be picked up at the airport and taken to a rig for orientation and checkout.

Then stock up on groceries and hit the road. ⏱ Half-day.

Drive 20 miles south of the city on the Seward Highway for your first night of camping.

❷ Seward Highway. For information on this drive, see p. 84. For your first night's campsite, choose the oceanside **Bird Creek Campground** (p. 115) in **Chugach State Park** (p. 55, ❽). ⏱ 1 day.

1. Anchorage
2. Seward Highway
3. Kenai Mountains
4. Seward
5. Kenai Fjords National Park
6. Kenai National Wildlife Refuge
7. Valdez
8. Richardson Highway
9. Fairbanks
10. Chena Hot Springs
11. Denali National Park
12. Talkeetna

0   40 mi
0   40 km

Railway

Glaciers & Ice Fields

> *Mew gulls nest in southern Alaska in late spring; here two chicks chill on an iceberg.*

On Day 2, continue 107 miles south on the Seward Highway to Seward, where you'll spend the next 2 nights. En route, you'll pass through the:

❸ Kenai Mountains. ⏱1 day. See p. 38, **❺**.

On Day 3, spend some time exploring:

❹ Seward. Kids will love the **Alaska SeaLife Center** (p. 268, **❶**), which not only exhibits marine birds and animals, but studies and rehabilitates them for release back into the wild. The center contains a broad range of seabirds, aquariums rich with Alaskan sea life, and marine mammals such as sea lions and seals. By planning ahead, you can join a behind-the-scenes tour to watch the scientists work.

Seward is a terrific place for a family sea kayaking expedition along the shores of Resurrection Bay, south of town. You can put a kid in the forward hatch of a two-hole kayak with a parent behind. Go with **Sunny Cove Sea Kayaking** (p. 252, **❹**). Plan to camp at **Primrose Landing Campground** (p. 251, **❷**). ⏱1 day. See p. 268.

Plan to spend all of Day 4 aboard a tour boat, departing from the Seward harbor, to Kenai Fjords National Park. Make sure everyone takes a seasickness remedy an hour beforehand, just in case.

❺ Kenai Fjords National Park. You can't count on seeing whales, but tour boats here often do, and otters, sea lions, and seabirds are quite likely. Even so, bring activities to keep kids happy, as the trip takes all day and the scenery, although impressive, passes slowly. To see a glacier, you need an all-day tour that goes at least to Aialik Bay. The largest operator with the most choices is **Kenai Fjords Tours** (p. 234, **❺**). ⏱1 day. See p. 234.

In the late afternoon, retrace your journey along the Seward Highway to Tern Lake; pick up the Sterling Highway going west and then south to the town of Sterling, where you'll spend the next 3 nights. It's an 83-mile trip that will take just under 2 hours. On the morning of Day 5, explore:

❻ Kenai National Wildlife Refuge. The refuge, which surrounds Sterling, comprises a great swath of lake-dotted wetlands and streams with some of the biggest salmon and trout in the world. Fish the river—Kenai or Moose—on your own with rented gear from **Alaska Canoe & Campground** (p. 249, **⓫**), or ask them to set you up with a guide.

I also recommend camping there and renting canoes and other equipment for our favorite activity in the area: paddling the connected lakes and slow-running streams of the **Swan Lake canoe route** (p. 252, **❺**). Tent campers can take their gear along for overnight journeys in this gentle wilderness. ⏱2 days. See p. 274, **❶**.

On Day 7, return on the Sterling and Seward highways the way you came. At Seward Highway mile 80, you'll turn right onto Portage

Glacier Road, taking the Anton Anderson Memorial Tunnel to Whittier. There, you'll board the ferry for the ride across Prince William Sound to Valdez, where you'll spend the night. The 83-mile drive will take 2 hours, and the 78-mile ferry trip is just under 3 hours.

7 **Valdez.** The trip across Prince William Sound is the real highlight of your visit to Valdez. But the town also hosts the **Valdez Museum and Historical Archive** (p. 224, **5**), a fun museum with recreated historic rooms and a collection of old firetrucks. You'll want to camp at **Blueberry Lake State Recreation Site** (p. 208). ⏲ Half-day. See p. 222.

On Day 8, drive north from Valdez on the:

8 **Richardson Highway.** For more information on this drive, see p. 190, **7**. I suggest you spend the night at the **Bureau of Land Management Paxson Lake Campground** (mile 175, no phone; $10 per night). ⏲ 1½ days.

Get a very early start on Day 9, as you'll spend part of the morning exploring stops along the Richardson Highway while en route to Fairbanks (190 miles from Paxson Lake), where you'll spend the next 2 nights.

9 **Fairbanks.** Alaska's second-largest city is great for children, with family-oriented attractions and many easygoing outdoor activities. ⏲ 1 day. See p. 316.

On Day 11, you'll drive 57 miles east of town to:

10 **Chena Hot Springs.** ⏲ 1 day. See p. 307, **12**.

On Day 12, drive 120 miles south to Denali National Park, where you'll spend the next 2 nights.

11 **Denali National Park.** After getting settled, visit the **Denali Visitor Center** to see the exhibits and sign up the kids for the **Junior Ranger Program** (p. 154, **3**). Start with the selection of nature trails out back, which make good, easy hikes for younger children, or challenge older kids with a 5-mile round trip up the steep **Mount Healy Overlook trail** (see p. 135, **8**).

You may have a hard time saying no to the wild white-water rafting that's extremely popular at Denali. The class III and IV rapids in the Nenana Canyon are too rough for preteens, but an easier float upriver can be done with younger children. Go with **Denali Outdoor**

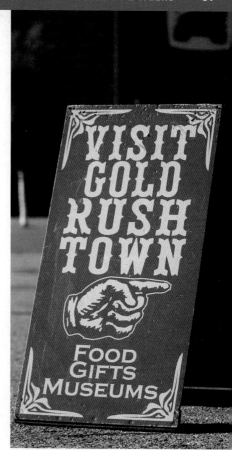

> *Alaska was a state built on gold—or at least the pursuit of it.*

Center (p. 169).

Rise early on Day 13 for your exploration of the Denali backcountry on a park shuttle bus (p. 149), which transports you closer to wildlife and scenery and drops you off for wilderness hikes. I've included advice for taking kids (p. 155), but the main rule is simple: Get off the bus and enjoy the outdoors. ⏲ 2 days. See p. 31, **6**.

Rise early again on Day 14, and take the Parks Highway 154 miles south to Talkeetna.

12 **Talkeetna.** ⏲ 3 hr. See p. 172.

After lunch, continue on the Parks and Glenn highways another 114 miles to Anchorage, where you can return your equipment before flying home.

4
Anchorage

My Favorite Anchorage Moments

Anchorage is my hometown. I could probably fill a whole book with favorite moments. But the city gets a bad rap from most travel writers, and many visitors treat it merely as a jumping-off point to begin a journey to the "real" Alaska. In response, I point out that this is a city where you can climb a mountain without catching sight of another person on the same day you dine in a gourmet restaurant. Visitors catch 40-pound salmon from a stream that is a 5-minute walk from high-rise downtown hotels. Wandering moose commonly disrupt traffic. As you'll discover, Anchorage is well worth your time.

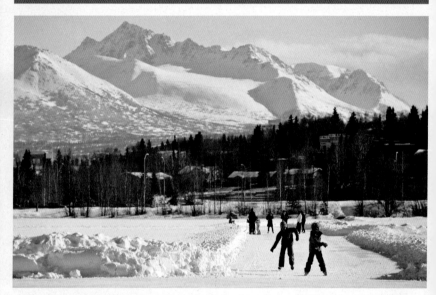

> PREVIOUS PAGE *Snowcapped mountains loom over downtown Anchorage.* THIS PAGE *Skaters come by the hundreds to get on the ice at Westchester Lagoon.*

❶ Seeing the city from above at Glen Alps. The mountains that stand behind Anchorage like a stage backdrop are good for more than scenery. You can drive into a high valley between the peaks of Chugach State Park to begin a variety of hikes or bike rides above the tree line. Turn around, and you'll behold the most striking view of the city and the mountains and ocean beyond. See p. 74, ❶.

❷ Walking in the woods at Eagle River Nature Center. The hiking trails of this educational center wrap around a beaver pond and offer lots of bird and wildlife viewing opportunities. The staff lead daily nature walks and present exhibits and programs inside. For the more ambitious, one 25-mile trail leads all the way over the Chugach Mountains, past glaciers and peaks, to Girdwood. See p. 72, ❷.

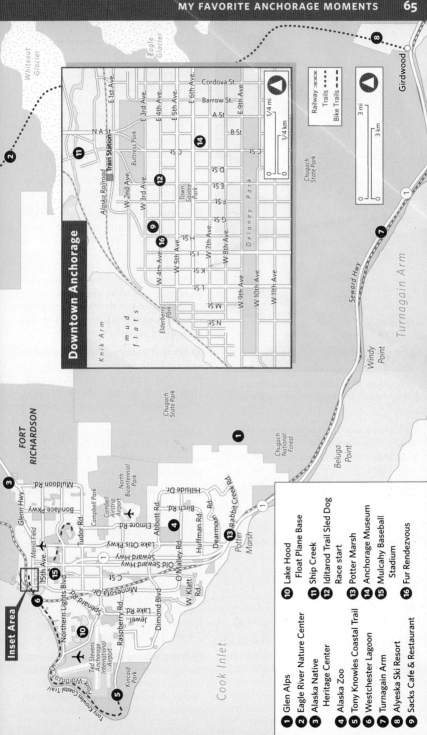

Downtown Anchorage

Cordova St.
Barrow St.
A St.
B St.
C St.
D St.
E St.
F St.
G St.
H St.
I St.
J St.
K St.
L St.
M St.
N St.

E 1st Ave.
E 3rd Ave.
E 4th Ave.
E 5th Ave.
E 6th Ave.
E 9th Ave.

N A St.
W 2nd Ave.
W 3rd Ave.
W 4th Ave.
W 5th Ave.
W 7th Ave.
W 8th Ave.
W 9th Ave.
W 10th Ave.
W 11th Ave.

Train Station
Alaska Railroad
Buttress Park
Town Square Park
Delaney Park
Elderberry Park

Knik Arm

m u d f l a t s

1/4 mi
1/4 km

Railway
Trails
Bike Trails

3 mi
3 km

Girdwood

Chugach State Park

Seward Hwy

Turnagain Arm

Windy Point

Beluga Point

Chugach National Forest

Chugach State Park

FORT RICHARDSON

Inset Area

Glen Hwy
Muldoon Rd.
Boniface Pkwy.
Tudor Rd.
Campbell Park
North Bicentennial Park
Campbell Airstrip Airport
Elmore Rd.
Birch Rd.
Abbott Rd.
Hillside Dr.
Huffman Rd.
Dearmoun Rd.
Rabbit Creek Rd.
Potter Marsh

Merrill Field
15th Ave.
Lake Otis Pkwy
Seward Hwy
Old Seward Hwy
O'Malley Rd.
C St.
Minnesota Dr.
W. Klatt Rd.
Dimond Blvd
Jewel Lake Rd.
Raspberry Rd.
Spenard Rd.
Northern Lights Blvd.

Ted Stevens Anchorage International Airport
Kincaid Park
Tony Knowles Coastal Trail
Point Woronzof Dr.

Cook Inlet

1. Glen Alps
2. Eagle River Nature Center
3. Alaska Native Heritage Center
4. Alaska Zoo
5. Tony Knowles Coastal Trail
6. Westchester Lagoon
7. Turnagain Arm
8. Alyeska Ski Resort
9. Sacks Cafe & Restaurant
10. Lake Hood Float Plane Base
11. Ship Creek
12. Iditarod Trail Sled Dog Race start
13. Potter Marsh
14. Anchorage Museum
15. Mulcahy Baseball Stadium
16. Fur Rendezvous

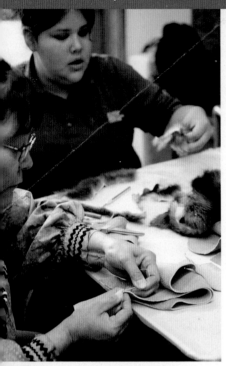

> *The Alaska Native Heritage Center offers art classes with instruction from Native artisans.*

❸ **Meeting an artisan at the Alaska Native Heritage Center.** Native groups built and manage this living museum, which hosts dance and interpretive sessions as well as traditional exhibits. Best of all, artisans create their wares in a series of stalls, welcoming visitors and talking one-on-one about their lives and work. See p. 72, ❶.

❹ **Getting up close to a bear at the Alaska Zoo.** The truth is, most bear sightings in the wilderness are from a distance (and that's how I like it!). This fun little zoo gives you the chance to see bears and other Alaska wildlife at a much closer range, in enclosures designed to match their natural habitat. See p. 74, ❷.

❺ **Riding a bike on the Tony Knowles Coastal Trail.** Many cities have their manicured waterfront promenade. In Anchorage, the coastal trail is appropriately wild and extreme—10 miles long, mostly wooded, and out of sight of roads, with ample opportunities to encounter moose, waterfowl, eagles, even beluga whales

and, near **Westchester Lagoon,** spawning salmon. See p. 70, ❻.

❻ **Skating on Westchester Lagoon.** Anchorage has many groomed outdoor ice rinks, including one in Town Square Park downtown, but the best is on the Westchester Lagoon pond, where city crews clear more than a mile of wide paths as well as casual rinks and hockey areas. Skaters come out by the hundreds, warming their hands around fires and buying hot chocolate and other treats from vendors. See p. 71, ❹.

❼ **Driving along Turnagain Arm.** The drive south from Anchorage follows the Seward Highway, which was chipped out of the sheer wall of the Chugach Mountains at the edge of a waterway with some of the world's largest tides. Scenic stops come at regular intervals, allowing you to climb those mountains or to stand at the edge of the Arm and simply observe the wildlife and the severe landscape. See p. 84.

❽ **Skiing at Alyeska Ski Resort.** Alaska's best ski resort, a steep mountain with challenging runs, is less than an hour south of town. It hosts international competitions and offers some of the best views you'll ever see from downhill runs; the shimmering water of Turnagain Arm spreads below you as you ski. Since the base is near sea level, the weather is temperate; since this is Alaska, the snow is plentiful and the season long. See p. 92.

❾ **Dining on fresh grilled salmon.** Alaska's best restaurants are in Anchorage. All specialize in doing their own thing—creative cuisine with lots of flavors drawn from many different ethnic influences, kind of like the cosmopolitan population of the city itself, where more than 90 languages are spoken in the schools. Anyway, you can always count on a good piece of fresh grilled salmon, which most folks here would agree is the world's best food. Anchorage's **Sacks Cafe & Restaurant** is one of the best places to indulge. See p. 108.

❿ **Flying into the wilderness on a floatplane.** Planes constantly buzz around **Lake Hood,** said to be the world's busiest floatplane base. An air taxi from here can take you virtually anywhere: to a remote and fish-packed river

> *Alyeska Resort has a reputation for "steep and deep" skiing, with an average snowfall of 631 inches and 2,500 feet of vertical terrain.*

or lake, to a habitat thick with bears, or over the top of spectacular mountains and glaciers. **Rust's Flying Service** is a reliable operator with many options. See p. 75, **4**.

11 Catching a salmon downtown. Among the many places to fish in or near Anchorage, none is more convenient than **Ship Creek,** right at the center of the original city and still only steps away from the downtown hotels. Equipment is for rent along the banks in season, making it easy to go after the sizable king and silver salmon. See p. 70, **8**.

12 Watching the last great race. The **Iditarod Trail Sled Dog Race** begins amid great festivities in early March, with sleds traveling from 4th Avenue through Anchorage, then restarting the next day in Willow for the long journey to Nome. If you come at that time, for the best of winter, you'll find Alaska at its liveliest, with town festivals, sports, and arts events peaking in activity. See p. 121.

13 Watching the birds at Potter Marsh. Boardwalks extend into the broad marsh at the south end of the city, near Turnagain Arm, where bird-watchers set up their scopes and glimpse a wide variety of species. Anchorage has several other types of bird habitats as well, and the active bird-watching community offers support to visitors. See p. 84, **1**.

14 Encountering Alaskan art at the Anchorage Museum. Alaska's largest museum houses the state's biggest collection of contemporary art, including work that uses modern techniques to express Alaska's beauty and magnitude. A new center run cooperatively with the Smithsonian is due to open as well, with a rich collection of Alaska Native artifacts. See p. 68, **1**.

15 Watching a baseball game under the midnight sun. Alaska's semipro league fields the nation's best college players, including many who have gone on to become big-league Hall of Famers. Tiny **Mulcahy Baseball Stadium** puts you nearly within touching distance of the action, and lights are unnecessary for the always bright (but seldom warm) night games. See p. 120.

16 Running with the reindeer at Fur Rendezvous. The city's winter festival, at the end of February and start of March, includes more than a week of fun, crazy, exciting activities, including the annual **Running of the Reindeer,** at 4th Avenue and H Street, in which a crowd runs down the street with a herd of reindeer—similar to the famous running of the bulls in Pamplona, Spain, except the reindeer are docile and gentle. See p. 484.

The Best of Anchorage in 1 Day

Many visitors allocate only a day for Anchorage. The reason: Anchorage is the place in Alaska that's most like anywhere else, with shopping malls and traffic jams—although the city *is* unique for having been plunked down in the middle of the wilderness. It's perfectly reasonable to spend just 1 day here if you're eager to hit the road (or rails) for wilder parts. But do try to spend at least a day—the cultural and outdoor highlights on this tour will orient you to the state and give you a much deeper insight into what you'll see on your travels. If your lodgings are downtown, you won't need a car for this single day on foot or bicycle.

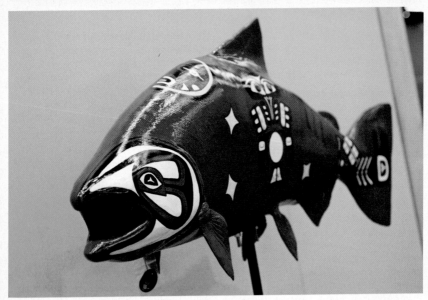

> *Alaska's natural heritage—earth, sea, and sky—inspires much of the art on display at the Anchorage Museum.*

START Museum Plaza, 6th Avenue and C Street.

① ★★★ kids **Anchorage Museum at Rasmuson Center.** Alaska's largest museum, recently expanded with a glass front, contains the state's largest collection of contemporary art; the Smithsonian's Arctic Studies Center, with its Native artifacts; a children's science museum called the **Imaginarium Discovery Center;** and an explanatory history exhibit, the Alaska Gallery. The Alaska Gallery is where most visitors go to absorb a simple, chronological survey of the state's anthropology and history; it gives a useful if outdated overview. Looking at Alaska's art will give you more profound

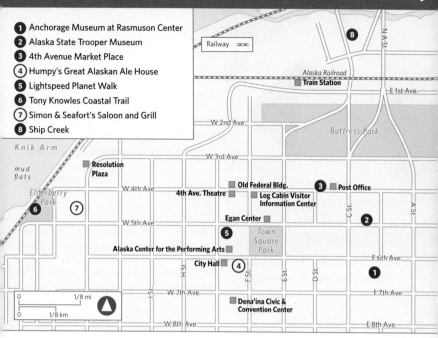

1 Anchorage Museum at Rasmuson Center
2 Alaska State Trooper Museum
3 4th Avenue Market Place
4 Humpy's Great Alaskan Ale House
5 Lightspeed Planet Walk
6 Tony Knowles Coastal Trail
7 Simon & Seafort's Saloon and Grill
8 Ship Creek

Railway

Alaska Railroad
Train Station

E 1st Ave.

Knik Arm

W 2nd Ave.

Buttress Park

W 3rd Ave.

mud flats

Resolution Plaza

Old Federal Bldg.

3 Post Office

Elderberry Park

W 4th Ave.

4th Ave. Theatre

Log Cabin Visitor Information Center

6   7

W 5th Ave.

Egan Center

2

5

Town Square Park

E 6th Ave.

Alaska Center for the Performing Arts

City Hall   4

1

0   1/8 mi
0   1/8 km

W 7th Ave.

E 7th Ave.

Dena'ina Civic & Convention Center

W 8th Ave.

E 8th Ave.

insight into the land and its people; the scenery and wildlife dominate almost every work, even nonrepresentational pieces. Children shouldn't miss the Imaginarium Discovery Center, which formerly occupied its own space and at this writing is moving to merge with the museum. The highlight has always been the touch tanks full of sea creatures; now it also has a planetarium. ⏲ 2 hr. 625 C St. ☎ 907-929-9200. www.anchoragemuseum.org. Admission $15 adults, $7 children 3–12, free for children 2 and under. Alaska residents $10 adults; $8 seniors 65 and over, students, or military. Summer daily 9am–6pm; winter Tues–Sat 10am–6pm, Sun noon–5pm.

② ★ **Alaska State Trooper Museum.** This proud little temple of frontier law enforcement makes for a fun and charming (and brief) stop. Officially called the Fraternal Order of Alaska State Troopers Law Enforcement Museum, its collection is heavy on insignia and uniforms, but also contains treasures such as a 1952 Hudson Hornet patrol car and a mug shot of Steve McQueen, arrested here in 1973 for spinning doughnuts in an Olds Toronado. ⏲ 20 min. 245 W. 5th Ave. ☎ 800-770-5050 or 907-279-5050. www.alaskatroopermuseum.com. Free admission. Mon–Fri 10am–4pm; Sat noon–4pm.

Organizing Anchorage's Geography

Anchorage has fewer than 300,000 people, but the physical area of the city is huge. The bowl, which is the central part where most of the people live, measures roughly 12 by 15 miles, but a drive from Eklutna, at the city's extreme northern boundary, to Portage, at its southern end, is 74 miles and could easily take 2 hours. Indeed, the city's boundaries contain a huge chunk of the Chugach Mountains, numerous glaciers, and even a slice of Prince William Sound. More relevant here is my philosophy on how to cover the populated area of the city: You shouldn't waste vacation time driving in traffic between attractions on opposite sides of town, so I've set up these 1-, 2-, and 3-day itineraries, each of which concentrates on one area. When planning your own days, take driving time into account, because it adds up fast.

> *The Lightspeed Planet Walk brings to human level the vastness of the solar system.*

❸ ★ 4th Avenue Market Place. Various shops here sell crafts by Alaska Natives, and artist demonstrations often happen in the summer. The building also contains a theater showing a variety of 3-D and large-format films, including shows about the Northern Lights and Alaska scenery. An exhibit about the 1964 Great Alaska Earthquake (see "Whole Lotta Shaking," on p. 208), the second strongest ever recorded on Earth, includes both informative exhibits and a shaking interactive component. ⏱ 1 hr. 411 W. 4th Ave. 907-272-9076. Alaska films $10, exhibit $6. Daily 10am–9pm.

④ 🍺 ★ Humpy's Great Alaskan Alehouse. You'll find lots of good places for lunch downtown. This is a popular tavern with a prodigious selection of craft beers on tap, including many you won't likely encounter again, from tiny Alaskan breweries. The food is good, too; burgers are a specialty. 610 W. 6th Ave. ☎ 907-276-BEER (276-2337).www.humpys.com $$. See p. 117.

❺ ★ kids Lightspeed Planet Walk. A sculpture of the sun and a multimedia kiosk that teaches about the solar system are the starting points for this stroll. From this point, going west on 5th Avenue and then continuing south on the **Tony Knowles Coastal Trail** (below), you will pass markers representing each of the planets of the solar system, placed at a distance in scale if you could walk at the speed of light. Pluto (still considered a planet when a high-school student conceived the project) is about 10 miles away in Kincaid Park. Sun Station at 5th Ave. and G St. www.anchorageplanetwalk.org.

SITE GUIDE PAGE 71

❻ ★★★ kids Tony Knowles Coastal Trail. This paved trail, which snakes along the shore more than 10 miles from downtown to the 1,500-acre Kincaid Park, is perhaps the best element of Anchorage's built environment. It manages to uniquely link the urban and the wild. For this is not a tame shoreline: For the most part, it looks as it did before people arrived here, and wildlife sightings are common. The closest place to rent bicycles is at **Pablo's Bicycle Rentals,** a booth at the corner of 5th Avenue and L Street (☎ 907-250-2871; www.pablobicyclerentals.com). ⏱ Half-day. Join the path at Elderberry Park, at the west end of 5th Ave.

⑦ 🍺 ★★ Simon & Seafort's Saloon and Grill. Just across the street from where you rent the bikes, this is a perfect spot for dinner—where you can look out across the coastal trail to Cook Inlet and the mountains beyond. Rather than dress for the dining room, eat in the more casual but still first-rate bar. 420 L St. ☎ 907-274-3502. www.simonandseaforts.com $$. See p. 108.

❽ ★★ Ship Creek. It's not too late to wrap up the evening with a bit of fishing. After all, it stays light until quite late. The walk is fairly short from downtown into the railroad area, where the creek runs between muddy banks. Sometimes a booth is in operation for renting gear, but more likely you will need your own rod and boots—and good timing—for the mud. King salmon run in June, silvers in August and September, and success is most common on a rising tide. For fishing licenses, updates, and advice, contact the Alaska Department of Fish and Game, ☎ 907-267-2218; www.sf.adfg.state.ak.us.

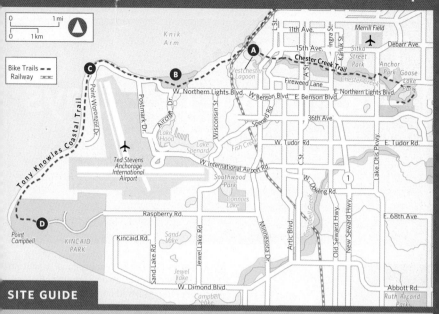

0 1 mi
0 1 km

Bike Trails - -
Railway ⊏⊐⊏⊐

Knik
Arm

11th Ave.
15th Ave.
Chester Creek Trail
Merrill Field
Debarr Ave.
Westchester
Lagoon
Fireweed Lane
Chester Creek
Sitka
Street
Park
Anchor
Park
Goose
Lake
Park

A
C
B

Point Woronzof Dr.
Postmark Dr.
Airport Dr.
W. Northern Lights Blvd.
W. Benson Blvd. E. Benson Blvd.
Wisconsin St.
E. Northern Lights Blvd.

Tony Knowles Coastal Trail

Lake
Hood
Lake
Spenard
Fish Creek
Spenard Rd.
C St.
36th Ave.
W. Tudor Rd.
E. Tudor Rd.
Lake Otis Pkwy.

Ted Stevens
Anchorage
International
Airport

W. International Airport Rd.
Southwood
Park
Connors
Lake

Arctic Blvd.
Minnesota Dr.
W. Dowling Rd.
Old Seward Hwy.
New Seward Hwy.
Campbell Creek
1

D

Raspberry Rd.
Kincaid Rd.
Sand
Lake
Sand Lake Rd.
Jewel Lake Rd.
Jewel
Lake
W. Dimond Blvd.
Campbell
Lake

E. 68th Ave.

Abbott Rd.
Ruth Arcand
Park

Point
Campbell
KINCAID
PARK

⑥ Tony Knowles Coastal Trail

After about a mile, the coastal trail drops under the railroad tracks to follow the edge of the dike around Ⓐ **Westchester Lagoon,** a large, man-made pond where ducks and geese paddle and nest and where muskrats can be seen in the swampy areas at the west end. The lagoon is drained by a salmon stream, beside which a platform allows viewing of the fish as they work their way up from Cook Inlet. A pretty ride of another 2.25 miles brings you to Ⓑ **Earthquake Park;** it commemorates the world's second-largest recorded earthquake, measuring 9.2 magnitude, which occurred on Good Friday, March 27, 1964 (see "Whole Lotta Shaking," on p. 208). The area now looks like a rugged, wooded land; before the quake it was a subdivision, but the shaking liquefied the land, which swallowed many houses as it slumped from the bluff down to the level of Cook Inlet. Signs explain the history and geology, and an abstract sculpture represents the event. It's a good stopping point if you've pedaled far enough.

Another 1.5 miles (4.75 miles total) brings riders to Ⓒ **Point Woronzof,** which sticks into Cook Inlet like Anchorage's prow. Next to the parking lot, a pathway leads down to the gravel beach, where a pleasant walk is to be had. The grassy overlook around the lot is a popular spot to watch the sun set over the mountains to the west or, in good weather, to view Mount McKinley to the north. For those with plenty of energy, the trail runs another 5 miles to Ⓓ **Kincaid Park.** This extraordinary stretch of paved trail runs through woods atop the ocean bluff, with occasional openings to climb down the bank to the beach and broad wetlands, where bird-watching can be exceptional. The trail enters the park at about mile 6.5, and at the end, around mile 10, rises to its hilly uplands—the site of the **Kincaid Outdoor Center,** with bathrooms, vending machines, tables, phones, and an information desk.

The Best of Anchorage in 2 Days

As I've already said, I think spending a few days in Anchorage is more than worthwhile. You'll need a car for this second day, which takes you north and east of the downtown area to the Alaska Native Heritage Center and up the Glenn Highway to Eagle River and Eklutna, where you'll find some of the area's best outdoor and informal cultural attractions. Since this is mostly an outdoor day in areas without restaurants, consider picking up a packed lunch before you leave downtown (try Dianne's Restaurant, p. 104).

> Moose sightings are not uncommon in Anchorage.

START From the Glenn Highway, take the North Muldoon exit. **TRIP LENGTH** 96 miles roundtrip.

❶ ★★★ kids Alaska Native Heritage Center. The center was built in first-class fashion by Native peoples with the goal of teaching about their diverse cultures. The experience is authentic, personal, and nonexploitative. A visit consists of several parts. After entering, see a dance or storytelling performance in the spectacular gathering place. Continue from there into expertly presented educational exhibits in the hall of cultures, the only aspect of the visit that resembles a traditional museum. Along one side of the hall, Native artisans work in a line of open stalls where you're welcome to sit down, talk, and learn. Outside, traditional village sites around a man-made pond represent each Native culture, with guides on hand to tell you about them. In large part, this is the only place you can find these traditional buildings. ⏲ 2½ hr. 8800 Heritage Center Dr. ☎ 800-315-6608 or 907-330-8000. www.alaskanative. net. Admission $25 adults, $21 seniors and military, $17 children 7-16, free for children 6 and under; Alaska residents $10 adult, $7 children. Summer daily 9am–5pm; call for winter hours.

Take the Glenn Highway north 12 miles to the Eagle River exit. Turn right on Artillery Road, then again on Eagle River Road, and continue 12.5 miles to the end.

❷ ★★ kids Eagle River Nature Center. The nonprofit center teaches about this lovely natural spot, partly with indoor exhibits and programs but mostly with a set of nature trails at the head of the Eagle River Valley; it covers biology and geology and even goes to a beaver pond, with wildlife sightings common. A challenging, 25-mile backpacking trek—the Crow Pass Trail—begins here, too. ⏲ 2 hr. At the end of Eagle River Rd. ☎ 907-694-2108. www.ernc. org. $5 parking fee. June-Aug daily 10am–5pm; May and Sept Tues-Sun 10am–5pm, closed Mon; Oct-Apr Fri-Sun 10am–5pm.

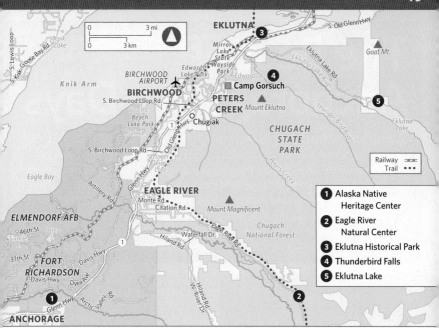

Return to the Glenn Highway and turn right, taking it 12 miles to the Eklutna exit, where you'll cross the overpass and bear to the left.

❸ ★ Eklutna Historical Park. The centerpiece of the park is the Eklutna people's remarkable cemetery, where Athabascan and Russian Orthodox traditions somehow combined to produce a tradition of doll-size spirit houses that are built over each grave. The park also includes the oldest building in the region, the log **St. Nicholas Orthodox Church,** dating to around 1870. ⏱ 30 min. Eklutna Village Rd. ☎ 907-688-6026. Admission $5 adult, $3 children 10–18, free for children 9 and under. Summer Mon–Fri 10am–4pm, Sat–Sun noon–4pm; closed in winter.

Drive back across the overpass and turn right onto Old Glenn Highway toward the trailhead parking lot, ½ mile down on the right.

❹ ★ kids Thunderbird Falls. An easy hike leads 1 mile to the waterfall, which seems to crash down 200 feet through the trees. By staying on the level path, you can see it from above, or climb down to its foot on a steeper trail. ⏱ 1 hr. Glenn Highway, Thunderbird Falls exit. $5 parking fee.

Return on the Old Glenn Highway toward Eklutna, turning right on Eklutna Lake Road and continuing 10 miles to its end.

❺ ★★ Eklutna Lake. The lake, at 1,000 feet in elevation within a steep mountain valley, gathers water from Eklutna Glacier, from which all of Anchorage ultimately drinks. Walk along the shore of the gray glacial water; you can easily find your own route, or follow the lakeside path on the north side for as long as your time and interest last. The setting of this big alpine lake is alone worth the visit.

An Outdoor Alternative

If you've had enough of indoor experiences, consider skipping the above itinerary and spending a full day at Eklutna Lake. Among other trails, a level path runs 7 miles to the head of the lake and then 6 more miles to the glacier. You can bike or hike the path, or even paddle one way in a kayak and bike back. At the lake, **Lifetime Adventures** (☎ 907-746-4644; www.lifetimeadventures.net) offers that option, as well as other gear rental and guiding.

The Best of Anchorage in 3 Days

Spending a third day in Anchorage will allow you to get out and explore the wilder side of Alaska's biggest city. The Chugach Mountains, which form a half-circle around the eastern side of the Anchorage bowl, are the city's alpine playground in both summer and winter. Trails lead up some of the front mountains, while other paths trace the valleys without as much elevation gain (although few hikes are truly easy). Innumerable ways without trails extend over the heather, too. Down below, visit the zoo and, at the airport, the aviation museum, finishing with a flightseeing trip to experience the scenery from above.

> A hiker scrambles the last leg of the climb up Flat-top Mountain.

START Glen Alps. From New Seward Highway, take O'Malley Road 3.6 miles east toward the mountains; turn right on Hillside Drive. Go 1 mile and turn left onto Upper Huffman Drive, then go .7 mile and turn right onto Toilsome Hill Drive. Continue 2 miles to the well-marked Glen Alps parking lot. **TRIP LENGTH 15** miles.

❶ ★★★ kids **Glen Alps.** The name Glen Alps refers to a trailhead with a parking lot; at 2,100 feet, it's a threshold to an enormous area for hiking and exploration above the tree line, with

stupendous views. The most famous trail goes up 3,500-foot Flattop Mountain, a gorgeous hike of a couple of hours with a scramble at the top. You can also bike among the mountains here, most simply on the Powerline Pass Trail. Navigation is easy and route choices many, as you can see a long way away. ⊕ Half-day. Chugach State Park. ☎ 907-345-5014. www.alaskastateparks.org. Parking fee $5.

Drive back down the mountain to O'Malley Road.

❷ ★★ kids **Alaska Zoo.** The zoo has a charming, small-town feel that is conducive to fun and relaxation. It occupies a spread of rural land left largely to its native vegetation, which suits the endemic wildlife in the enclosures. On a single visit you can see the full range of the most popular animals in Alaska, from bears to seals, and even some found at high latitudes in other parts of the world, such as a yak. The polar bear exhibit includes underwater viewing that showcases the animal's amazing swimming ability. Although it won't hold your attention as long as a big-city zoo would, it provides a good chance to encounter Alaskan animals up close—and maybe get the best wildlife pictures of your trip. ⊕ 2 hr. 4731 O'Malley Rd. ☎ 907-346-3242. www.alaskazoo.org. Admission $12 adults, $9 seniors and military, $6 children 3–17, free for children 2 and under. Daily 9am–6pm. Closed Thanksgiving and Christmas.

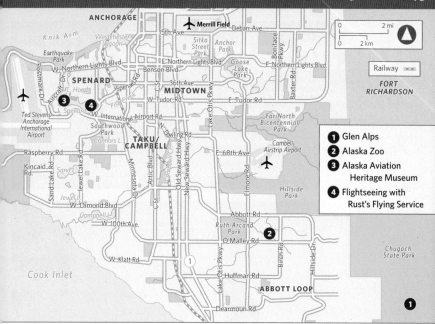

1 Glen Alps
2 Alaska Zoo
3 Alaska Aviation Heritage Museum
4 Flightseeing with Rust's Flying Service

From the zoo, drive west 3 miles on O'Malley Road as it widens into an expressway and becomes Minnesota Drive, which continues north another 3½ miles to the International Airport Road exit. Go west toward the airport 1½ miles before turning right on Postmark Drive, and right again shortly on Heliport Drive and finally on Aircraft Drive.

3 ★★ **Alaska Aviation Heritage Museum.** Flying opened Alaska as road or rail never could: Mail delivery went directly from dog sled to bush plane. The brave pilots who have connected communities over the years are memorialized here through their planes, and the collection also includes historic military aircraft. Visitors can try out a flight simulator and sometimes watch restoration work in progress. The museum is of greatest interest to those fascinated with mechanical things, but it teaches a lot about Alaska as well. The location is on the shore of the Lake Hood floatplane base, said to be the busiest in the world, and during a normal visit you'll notice all manner of aircraft operating. ⏱ 1 hr. 4721 Aircraft Dr. ☎ 907-248-5325. www.alaskaairmuseum. org. Admission $10 adults, $8 seniors, $6 children 5–12, free for children 4 and under. Summer daily 9am–5pm; winter Wed–Sun 9am–5pm.

4 ★★★ **Flightseeing with Rust's Flying Service.** Many of the best outdoor activities start from the docks at Lake Hood, where airplanes tie up. Consider **fly-in fishing** or **bear viewing** (p. 89) if you have time. On a budget or need to save time? Take a brief spin just to witness the grandeur from the air. You can enjoy a half-hour flight for as little as $100 per person.

As always with flightseeing, the more time (and money) you spend, the more you will see—a splurge here makes sense. Rust's pioneered the idea that you can fly from Anchorage to view some of Alaska's most spectacular scenery without first driving or taking a train to a closer starting point. Flights to Prince William Sound encounter glorious mountain islands with hidden lakes and waterfalls straight from a fairytale, or you can fly to Mount McKinley and soon be exploring the folds of its glacier-carved peaks. Do some research on Rust's website, but then be flexible; the pilot will know where the weather and the viewing are best when you are ready to fly. ⏱ At least 30 min. 4525 Enstrom Circle. ☎ 800-544-2299 or 907-243-1595; www. flyrusts.com. Prices and hours vary.

Anchorage with Kids

Keeping children entertained in Anchorage is easy. It is
an outdoor city full of young families who enjoy the opportunities afforded by bike
paths, nearby mountains, lakes, and hiking trails. Active folk have created great
indoor spaces for kids as well. Here are ideas for families (and really, for anyone
looking for fun) with 2 days to spend here in the summer; the winter can be even
better. See the "The Best of Anchorage Outdoors," on p. 88, for my suggestions.

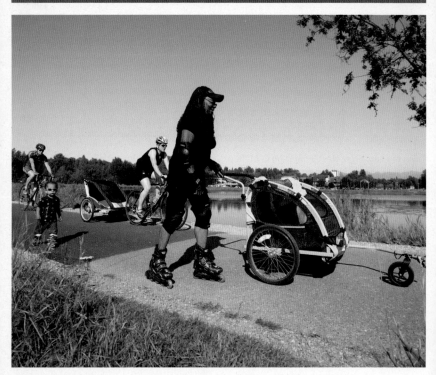

> Strollers and little skaters can navigate the Tony Knowles Trail near Westchester Lagoon.

START Elderberry Park, at the west end of 5th
Avenue in downtown Anchorage. **TRIP LENGTH**
42 miles.

❶ ★★★ **Tony Knowles Coastal Trail.** There's
nothing my kids enjoy more than going for
a bike ride with their parents. Anchorage's
award-winning trail system allows you to do it
with a sense of total safety, since road crossings all come with tunnels or bridges. Starting

the trail at Elderberry Park, you'll want to try
out the excellent playground equipment there.
And bring bread crumbs for the ducks at
Westchester Lagoon, a little over 1 mile south.
I've described the entire trail elsewhere, but
to save energy, I recommend you explore and
play for just a couple of hours, ending at the
lagoon. ⏱ 2 hr. See p. 70, ❻. For information on
bike rentals, see p. 89.

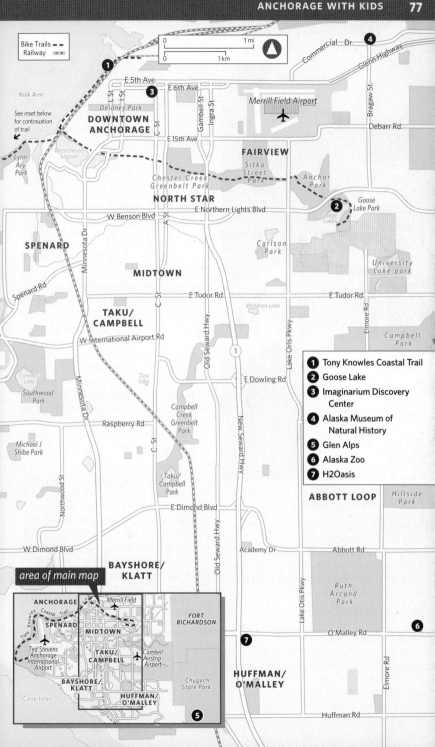

Bike Trails - -
Railway ===

0 —— 1 mi
0 —— 1km

DOWNTOWN ANCHORAGE

Knik Arm

See inset below for continuation of trail

Lynn Ary Park

Westchester Lagoon

Delaney Park

E 5th Ave.
E 6th Ave.
E 15th Ave.

L St.
I St.
C St.
Gambell St.
Ingra St.

Merrill Field Airport

FAIRVIEW

Sitka Street Park

Anchor Park

Goose Lake Park

Bragaw St.

Debarr Rd.

Chester Creek Greenbelt Park

NORTH STAR

W Benson Blvd
E Northern Lights Blvd

Goose Lake

Carlson Park

University Lake park

SPENARD

Minnesota Dr.

Spenard Rd.

MIDTOWN

A St.
C St.

E Tudor Rd.

E Tudor Rd.

Waldron Lake

TAKU/ CAMPBELL

W International Airport Rd

Campbell Park

Connors Lake

Southwood Park

Tina Lake

Old Seward Hwy

E Dowling Rd.

Lake Otis Pkwy

Elmore Rd.

Michael J Shibe Park

Northwood St.

Raspberry Rd.

Campbell Creek Greenbelt Park

New Seward Hwy

1 Tony Knowles Coastal Trail
2 Goose Lake
3 Imaginarium Discovery Center
4 Alaska Museum of Natural History
5 Glen Alps
6 Alaska Zoo
7 H2Oasis

Taku/ Campbell Park

ABBOTT LOOP

Hillside Park

W Dimond Blvd

BAYSHORE/ KLATT

E Dimond Blvd

Academy Dr

Abbott Rd.

Ruth Arcand Park

O'Malley Rd

Elmore Rd

area of main map

ANCHORAGE

Merrill Field

SPENARD

MIDTOWN

Ted Stevens Anchorage International Airport

Tony Knowles Coastal Trail

TAKU/ CAMPBELL

Cambell Airstrip Airport

BAYSHORE/ KLATT

HUFFMAN/ O'MALLEY

Cook Inlet

FORT RICHARDSON

Chugach State Park

HUFFMAN/ O'MALLEY

Huffman Rd.

> Native artifacts are on display at the Anchorage Museum at Rasmuson Center.

Pedal 4 miles east from the lagoon on Lanie Fleischer Chester Creek Trail to Goose Lake Park. Or by car, take Northern Lights Boulevard east from Lake Otis Parkway, turn right on UAA Drive, and make an immediate left (unmarked) into the park.

❷ ★★ Goose Lake. One of our favorite bike rides leads from the Coastal Trail at Westchester Lagoon to the lake, where you can swim, buy an ice cream, or rent a paddle boat for some explore time. Although the trail weaves through the city, it's wooded the entire way, and the lake itself is tucked into a large natural park so that it looks like it's out in the wilderness. ◷ Half-day.

Ride back downtown and return your bikes. If time permits, or if weather has shortened your time outdoors, go east on 6th Avenue just under 1 mile, to the museum.

❸ ★★ Imaginarium Discovery Center. This fun children's science museum, which became a part of the **Anchorage Museum at Rasmuson Center** in 2010, has long been one of the favorite places for Anchorage kids to play. The highlight has always been the seashore touch tanks, but the new location also adds a small planetarium and some 70 other exhibits. There's a special area for children age 5 and younger. ◷ 2 hr. See p. 68, **❶**.

On Day 2, you will need to pick up a rental car. Take the Glenn Highway to the Bragaw Street exit; turn left and go 2 blocks.

❹ ★ Alaska Museum of Natural History. Alaska is cold now, but dinosaurs once lived in its northern part in great numbers. Digs find more big bones every year. This small museum has a permanent exhibit of Alaskan fossils belonging to the Bureau of Land Management, including changing interactive features that children especially enjoy; past examples include simulated digs. ◷ 1 hr. 201 North Bragaw St. ☎ 907-274-2400. www.alaskamuseum.org. Admission $5 adult, $3 children 5–12, free for children 4 and under. Summer Mon–Sat 10am–5pm; winter Tues–Sat 10am–5pm.

Drive south on Bragaw Street 1¾ miles before turning right on Northern Lights Boulevard. Go about ½ mile to UAA Drive and turn left, then left again on Providence Drive. Then turn right on Elmore Road, continuing 3½ miles to Abbott Road. Turn left and go just under 3 miles on Hillside Drive, following signs to stay on it as it makes a series of turns. Turn left on Upper Huffman Road and then right on Toilsome Hill Road, continuing just under 2 miles to the marked trailhead parking lot.

❺ ★★★ Glen Alps. Some Anchorage children measure themselves by the Chugach Mountains: A first time up Flattop is a marker of growing up in many families. The trailhead at Glen Alps is the start of that hike and many easier routes starting at 2,000 feet in elevation. It's a terrific place for a family

> *If you want a guaranteed polar bear sighting, try the Alaska Zoo, or their Polar Bear Live Cam.*

mountain-biking outing, too, following the Powerline Pass Trail. Best of all, you can match your hike to your ability level, going up steeply, sitting back in the heather to pick berries, or taking a long, relatively level walk. ⏱ Half-day. See p. 74, ❶.

Retrace your drive back to the intersection of Hillside Drive and O'Malley Road, and take O'Malley heading west (downhill).

❻ ★★ **Alaska Zoo.** Anchorage's small zoo is perfectly scaled to children, with gravel paths that wind through native trees, giving them the sense that they are discovering the animals on their own. Besides the enclosures for every kind of Alaskan animal you might want to see, there is a petting zoo as well. ⏱ 2 hr. See p. 74.

Continue west on O'Malley Road to H₂Oasis, at the intersection of O'Malley and New Seward Highway.

❼ ★ **H₂Oasis.** This indoor water park may not impress kids from warmer locales, where water rides are outdoors in big amusement parks, but you'll find no better way to burn up youthful energy on a rainy day. There's lots of noise and plenty to do—the place claims to be the fifth-largest indoor water park in the country. ⏱ 2 hr. 1520 O'Malley Rd. ☎ 888-H2OASIS (426-2747) or 907-522-4420. www.h2oasiswaterpark.com. Admission $24 adults, $19 children 3–12, free for children 2 and under. Summer daily 10am–9pm. Winter Mon, Wed, Fri 3pm–9pm; Sat–Sun 10am–9pm.

A Stroll Through Downtown Anchorage

On a sunny summer day, the streets of downtown Anchorage come alive with visitors and street vendors, businesspeople between meetings, and a profusion of bright flowers planted in hanging baskets and in beds in Town Square Park. Spend an enjoyably low-key afternoon just walking around this modern, northern city. This walk covers a little more than 2 miles; to shorten it by half, skip from stop **12** to stop **19**.

> Politicians and firemen once rubbed elbows at Anchorage's Old City Hall; be sure to check out the old fire pole.

START 4th Avenue, between E and F streets.

1 ★ **Old City Hall.** Built in 1936, when the city had only about 4,000 residents, this modest two-story building was large enough to contain the city's offices and firehouse. The lobby contains a fun and illuminating free display on city history, including dioramas of the early streetscape, old photographs, and the fire bell and fire pole. ⏱ 15 min. 524 W. 4th Ave.

2 ★ **Iditarod Starting Area.** The Iditarod Trail Sled Dog Race (see "Going to Extremes," on p. 94) starts on 4th Avenue each March, and it is commemorated by a bronze dog and a topographic mural of the route on the building at 4th and D. The Wendler Building, with the CLUB 25 sign, is among the oldest in Anchorage, built in 1915, although it didn't stand here originally. In general, the buildings on the left or north side of 4th are more modern—everything on that side from E Street east for several blocks collapsed in the 1964 earthquake (see "Whole Lotta Shaking," on p. 208), when the street split in half lengthwise, with that side ending up a dozen feet lower. 4th Ave. between E and D sts.

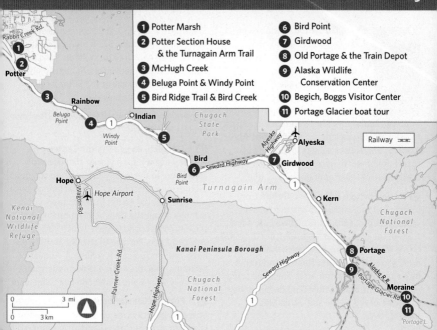

1 Potter Marsh
2 Potter Section House
  & the Turnagain Arm Trail
3 McHugh Creek
4 Beluga Point & Windy Point
5 Bird Ridge Trail & Bird Creek

6 Bird Point
7 Girdwood
8 Old Portage & the Train Depot
9 Alaska Wildlife
  Conservation Center
10 Begich, Boggs Visitor Center
11 Portage Glacier boat tour

Railway ×==×

Seward Hwy., south end of Potter Marsh. $5 parking fee at trailhead, no fee at Potter Section House.

3 ★ McHugh Creek. Here you'll find a picnic area with a nice path around the creek's waterfalls. A strenuous all-day hike leads 3,000 feet up the mountain, or you can join the **Turnagain Arm Trail** (**2**, left) here, at its halfway point. Mile 111, Seward Hwy. $5 parking fee.

4 ★★ Beluga Point & Windy Point. You'll want to choose at least one of the right-hand pullouts on this stretch of highway to appreciate the view and scan for wildlife. On the cliffs above, Dall sheep are often sighted quite low and near the road. It's possible to witness both beluga whales and death-defying windsurfers out on the water. Other pullouts along the way offer equal views, and some have interpretive signs about the area's nature and gold-rush history. Miles 110 and 106, Seward Hwy.

5 ★★ Bird Ridge Trail & Bird Creek. The trailhead comes first. It's a spectacular hike from early on, but very strenuous, working its way 3,000 feet straight up the mountain in

a little over a mile. The creek has good silver salmon fishing in the late summer and fall, and is well developed to provide places for anglers to park and dip a line. Pink salmon are here most of the summer in even-numbered years. The excellent **Bird Creek Alaska State Parks Campground** is described on p. 115. ⏲ 30 min.; longer for hike or fishing. Miles 102 and 101, Seward Hwy. $5 parking fee for trailhead and fishing area.

6 ★★ Bird Point. A nature trail, whale sculpture, and interpretive kiosk are all here, at one of the best spots to view Turnagain Arm. If its inhabitants haven't moved on, a beaver lodge may still be active right next to the path. Among the displays is an explanation of the unique phenomenon of bore tides and how to predict them. When conditions are right, the enormous tides here—up to 40 feet can separate high and low—will create an incoming wall of water that sweeps up the Arm. The nature trail is an easy 5-minute walk. ⏲ 30 min. Mile 96, Seward Hwy. $5 parking fee.

SITE GUIDE
PAGE 87

⑦ ★★ Girdwood. Although officially a part of Anchorage, Girdwood, 30 miles to the south, thinks of itself as its own town, with a streak of individuality that runs deep. It's a forest community of ski bums, backwoods folk, and affluent vacationers. Girdwood's main reason to exist is the excellent skiing at **Mount Alyeska** (p. 92), Alaska's biggest and best ski resort. But if you're here in the summer, there are a range of other options.

⑧ ★ Old Portage & the Train Depot. Continuing beyond Girdwood, the road passes a wooden depot; across the highway are a few ruins of the town of Portage left from the 1964 Great Alaska Earthquake, which lowered this area, allowing the sea to flood in and turn it into an enormous salt marsh. The dead trees you see in the marsh still stand because they were preserved by the saltwater. Mile 80, Seward Hwy.

⑨ ★★ Alaska Wildlife Conservation Center. A 200-acre compound houses orphaned deer, moose, owls, elk, bison, musk oxen, foxes, and caribou. A nonprofit organization houses rescued wildlife here. Visitors can drive through and see them in large enclosures; you can also get out of the car to look. ⏱ 2 hr. Mile 79, Seward Hwy. ☎ 907-783-2025; www.awcc.org. Admission $10 adults; $7.50 military, seniors, and children 4–12; free for children 3 and under; maximum of $30 per vehicle. Summer daily 8am–8pm (last vehicle in at 7:30pm); call for off-season hours, as they vary.

Continue on the Seward Highway to Portage Glacier Road.

⑩ ★★ Begich, Boggs Visitor Center. The center was built for a glacier that used to stand here in the lake (you can often still get a picture with an iceberg). The glacier has since receded, but the center includes fascinating exhibits about the Chugach National Forest, the nation's second largest, which surrounds you. ⏱ 30 min. Portage Glacier Rd. ☎ 907-783-2326. www.fs.fed.us/r10/chugach. Admission $3 adults, free for children 15 and under. Summer daily 9am–6pm; winter Sat–Sun 10am–5pm.

⑪ ★ Portage Glacier boat tour. A day boat operated by Gray Line of Alaska crosses the lake in front of Portage Glacier five times a day in summer to get a look at the ice, which you can barely see from the road. If this is your only chance to witness a glacier in Alaska, it's worth the look; otherwise, wait. ⏱ 1 hr. Portage Glacier Rd. ☎ 800-478-6388 reservations; 907-783-2983 at the lake. www.graylineofalaska.com. $29 adults, $15 children 12 and under.

Captain Cook Was Here

The name Turnagain Arm is a memorial to one man's annoyance. Captain James Cook anchored at Point Possession, which you can see to the right, and sent a boat up this way in search of a Northwest Passage to the Atlantic. He didn't think the passage would be found here, but his officers insisted on checking. The boat didn't make it far because of the shallows and enormous tidal current. The crew had to constantly turn the boat to avoid getting stuck—hence the name—before giving up. Explorer George Vancouver, who was on Cook's ship that day, was sent back here years later to check again for the passage, and groused in his log about how much trouble Cook would have saved if he had looked just a little longer and confirmed his belief that Turnagain Arm was of no use.

Train Ride to Mountain Adventures

Much of the glorious wilderness traversed by the **Alaska Railroad** (☎ 800-544-0552; www.alaskarailroad.com) between Seward and Anchorage remains inaccessible by any other means of transportation. In recent years, the railroad has recognized this remarkable asset and begun offering day-rail excursions from Anchorage to bring independent outdoors people and escorted tour groups to a pristine area around Spencer Glacier for hiking, canoeing, or rafting. The train leaves you for a bit less than 3 hours near a glacial lake before turning back. The basic Chugach Whistle Stop service costs $103 per person from Anchorage or Girdwood, $64 from Whittier or Portage.

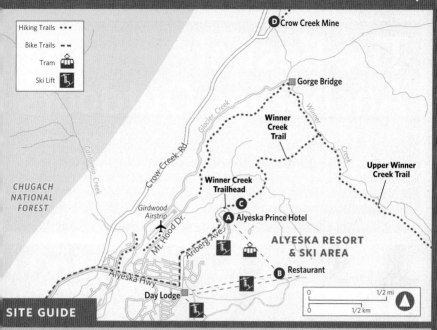

Legend:
Hiking Trails ···
Bike Trails --
Tram
Ski Lift

D Crow Creek Mine

Gorge Bridge

Winner Creek Trail

Upper Winner Creek Trail

CHUGACH NATIONAL FOREST

Glacier Creek

California Creek

Crow Creek Rd.

Girdwood Airstrip

Winner Creek Trailhead

C

A Alyeska Prince Hotel

ALYESKA RESORT & SKI AREA

Mt. Hood Dr.

Arlberg Ave.

Alyeska Hwy.

B Restaurant

Day Lodge

0   1/2 mi
0   1/2 km

SITE GUIDE

7 Girdwood

A The Alyeska Tram (pictured above) runs up the mountain with skiers in winter, with walkers in summer, and with diners headed for mountaintop resort restaurants year-round. If you're not planning to climb an Alaska mountain with muscle power, this is a good chance to experience the air and views up there. The ride takes 7 minutes, alighting at the 2,300-foot level of Mount Alyeska, well above the tree line. Dress warmly. The tram departs from the **Hotel Alyeska** (p. 113) daily between 9am and 9pm in the summer and whenever the lifts are running in the winter. The cost is $18 for adults; $15 for seniors 60 and over, or children 8 to 17; $9 for children 4 to 7; and free for children 3 and under. **B Glacier Express,** the cafeteria at the top of the tram, has fantastic views. Stop in for lunch or a snack to extend your visit at the mountaintop. **C Winner Creek Trail** is among the region's best family hikes. Starting from behind the Hotel Alyeska, the mostly level path weaves through huge spruce trees to a gorge where Winner and Glacier creeks join amid roaring waters. You can cross with a hand-operated tram. The hike is 4.5 miles to the tram and back. The Toohey family shows off picturesque pioneer life at their 1896 gold mine, **D Crow Creek Mine** (Crow Creek Rd., off the Alyeska Hwy.; ☎ 907-278-8060; www. crowcreekmine.com). Guests are provided a bag of dirt to pan, guaranteed to have at least some gold. Admission is $5 for adults and free for children, while gold panning is $15 for adults, $10 for seniors, and $5 for children 11 and under (includes admission). Hours are 9am–6pm daily. The mine is closed from mid-September to mid-May. ⏱ 2 hr.

The Best of Anchorage Outdoors

Having grown up in Anchorage, I didn't realize what was special about my hometown until I traveled elsewhere. The more I see of the world, the more my admiration for Anchorage grows. From our house near the airport we can be cross-country skiing in 5 minutes, trail hiking in 15, mountain climbing in 30. Moose and bald eagles are regular visitors at our cul-de-sac. These are the qualities that make the city unique and most worth your time.

> Kincaid is Anchorage's most popular cross-country ski park, but many neighborhoods have their own trails.

Summer
Biking & Mountain Biking

The network of paved bike trails, which follow greenbelts that span the city, are Anchorage's most notable man-made feature. The ★★★ **Tony Knowles Coastal Trail** (p. 70, **6**) follows the wooded shoreline for 10 miles; the ★★ **Lanie Fleischer Chester Creek Trail** leads from the coastal trail at Westchester Lagoon (p. 71, **A**) through town to Goose Lake (p. 78, **2**), where you can swim or buy an ice cream. For this sort of ride, you can rent bikes downtown at **Pablo's Bicycle Rentals** (p. 70, **6**).

Most trails in the area are open to mountain bikes, and Anchorage has some extraordinary ones. ★★★ **Kincaid Park** is connected to the bike trail system via the coastal trail and has 40 miles of challenging, hilly paths on 1,500 wooded acres. The park is at the west end of Raspberry Road; to get there from downtown or the airport, take Minnesota Drive south to the Raspberry exit and go right (west). ★★ **Eklutna Lake** (p. 73, **5**) features a long, flat path by a mountain lake, with a rental booth at the trailhead. ★★ **Glen Alps** (p. 74, **1**) opens up riding above 2,000 feet, on paths across alpine tundra. To rent mountain bikes, try **Downtown Bicycle Rental,** 4th Avenue and C Street (☎ 907-279-5293; www.alaska-bike-rentals.com).

Bird-Watching

Anchorage offers some of Alaska's most accessible birding, with many opportunities for birders from the other states to observe new species. Among the best spots are the tidal marshes along the southern part of the ★★★ **Tony Knowles Coastal Trail** (p. 70, ❻) near **Kincaid Park,** where you can sometimes see sandhill cranes; ★★ **Glen Alps** (p. 74, ❶) for alpine species, such as the hermit thrush and willow ptarmigan; and ★ **Potter Marsh** (p. 84, ❶) for waterfowl, terns, shorebirds, and others, including the Pacific loon, the red-necked grebe, and the Arctic tern.

For general information on birding, you can call the Anchorage Audubon Society's recorded hotline at ☎ 907-338-BIRD (338-2473), or visit www.anchorageaudubon.org.

Fishing

There's more natural fishing outside of town, but within Anchorage you can catch a large salmon if you don't mind company. ★ **Ship Creek** (p. 70, ❽) is right downtown. ★ **Campbell Creek** is a more natural setting, with silver salmon in August and September and trout and char all summer; to get there, take C Street just north from Dimond Boulevard—where the creek runs under the road you can join the adjacent bike trail for access all along it. For more information, contact the Alaska Department of Fish and Game (☎ 907-267-2218; www.sf.adfg.state.ak.us; recorded fish updates ☎ 907-267-2503).

The ultimate Alaska fishing experience is at the other end of a floatplane ride from Lake Hood, next to the Ted Stevens Anchorage International Airport. Anchorage is a great starting point, with experienced operators and many remote streams with productive salmon fishing within minutes by air. My personal pick is ★★★ **Rust's Flying Service** (p. 75, ❹), a firm with a long history and an impeccable safety record. Spend the day with a guide, all equipment provided, for around $500 per person, with a two-person minimum—they'll choose a spot with hot fishing that day. Or experienced salmon anglers can go without a

> *A floatplane takes off from Lake Hood in search of bears.*

guide and pay about $250 a day. Either way, you'll be in real wilderness.

Flightseeing & Bear Viewing

Air services based at **Lake Hood** take visitors through most of the summer to see bears or simply to witness the wilderness from above. Bears congregate on certain streams during salmon runs, limiting the times and places for the best viewing, and you won't likely have such a spot to yourself—but it's still a wild and remote experience. A flightseeing trip can be had for as little as $100 per person; expect to pay $600 to $800 per person for a full day of bear viewing. Again, I suggest you ride with ★★★ **Rust's Flying Service** (p. 75, ❹).

Hiking & Nature Walks

The Anchorage area is a hiker's paradise. I've mentioned many choices, including—south of town—the **Turnagain Arm Trail** (p. 84, ❷), **Bird Ridge Trail** (p. 85, ❺), and in Girdwood, **Winner Creek Trail** (p. 87, ❼). North of town, try **Thunderbird Falls** (p. 73, ❹) or **Eklutna Lake** (p. 73, ❺).

Closer to town, **Kincaid Park** (see above) has 40 miles of lovely wooded trails, a pond, and access to ocean beaches and tidal marshes. **Glen Alps** (p. 74, ❶) offers tundra mountainside above the city, within a half-hour of downtown. The **Eagle River Nature Center** (p. 72, ❷) has both interpreted nature trails and longer forest hikes. ***Note:*** There is a $5 parking fee at all but the Winner Creek and Kincaid Park trails.

The Best of Anchorage Outdoors

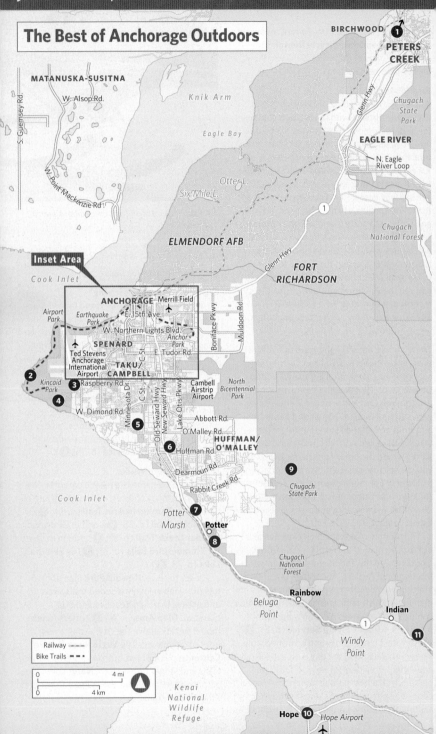

MATANUSKA-SUSITNA

S. Guernsey Rd.

W. Alsop Rd.

W. Point Mackenzie Rd.

Knik Arm

Eagle Bay

Otter L.

Six Mile L.

BIRCHWOOD

1

PETERS CREEK

Glenn Hwy.

Chugach State Park

EAGLE RIVER

N. Eagle River Loop

1

Glenn Hwy.

ELMENDORF AFB

Chugach National Forest

Cook Inlet

FORT RICHARDSON

Glenn Hwy.

Inset Area

ANCHORAGE Merrill Field

Airport Park

Earthquake Park

E. 15th Ave.

W. Northern Lights Blvd.

SPENARD

Ted Stevens Anchorage International Airport

E. Tudor Rd.

Anchor Park

TAKU/ CAMPBELL

Boniface Pkwy.

Muldoon Rd.

2

3 Raspberry Rd.

Kincaid Park

4

W. Dimond Rd.

Minnesota Dr.

C St.

Old Seward Hwy.

New Seward Hwy.

Lake Otis Pkwy.

Cambell Airstrip Airport

North Bicentennial Park

5

Abbott Rd.

O'Malley Rd.

6 Huffman Rd.

HUFFMAN/ O'MALLEY

Dearmoun Rd.

9

Chugach State Park

Rabbit Creek Rd.

Cook Inlet

Potter Marsh

7

Potter

8

Chugach National Forest

Rainbow

Beluga Point

Indian

1

11

Windy Point

Railway
Bike Trails

0   4 mi
0   4 km

Kenai National Wildlife Refuge

Hope **10** Hope Airport

Mount Eklutna
Ekutna Lake Rd.
Eklutna Lake

Chugach State Park

Eagle River Rd.

Eagle L.

Alpine Skiing
Mount Alyeska 16

Biking & Mountain Biking
Downtown Bicycle Rental 24
Eklutna Lake 13
Glen Alps 9
Kincaid Park 4
Laine Fleischer Chester Creek Trail 20
Pablo's Bicycle Rentals 21
Tony Knowles Coastal Trail 2

Bird-Watching
Glen Alps 9
Kincaid Park 4
Potter Marsh 7
Tony Knowles Coastal Trail 2

Cross-Country Skiing
Kincaid Park 4
Kincaid Outdoor Center 3

Fishing
Campbell Creek 26
Rust's Flying Service 5
Ship Creek 23

Flightseeing & Bear Viewing
Lake Hood 19
Rust's Flying Service 5

Hiking & Nature Walks
Bird Ridge Trail 11
Eagle River Nature Center 14
Eklutna Lake 13
Glen Alps 9
Kincaid Park 4
Thunderbird Falls 12
Turnagain Arm Trail 8
Winner Creek Trail 16

Ice Skating
Champions Choice 26
Town Square Park 22
Westchester Lagoon 20

Rafting & Sea Kayaking
Matanuska River 1
Prince William Sound 18
Sixmile Creek 10
Spencer Glacier 17

Snowmobiling
Glacier City Snowmobile Tours 15

Swimming
Goose Lake 25
H2Oasis 6

Downtown Anchorage

Knik Arm

W. 5th Ave.
Merrill Field
Debarr Ave.
FAIRVIEW
15th Ave.
Chester Creek Trail
Sitka Street Park
Anchor Park
W. Northern Lights Blvd.
Fireweed Lane
NORTH STAR
W. Benson Blvd.—E. Benson Blvd.
Goose Lake Park
36th Ave.
SPENARD
MIDTOWN
Spenard Rd.
W. Tudor Rd.
E. Tudor Rd.
Lake Hood
Lake Spenard
Fish Creek
W. International Airport Rd.
Ted Stevens Anchorage International Airport

0   1 mi
0   1 km

Alyeska
Seward Highway   Girdwood
Bird
Turnagain Arm

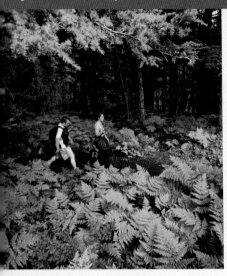

> *The Winner Creek Trail in Girdwood rewards hikers with a view of a roaring river gorge.*

Rafting & Sea Kayaking

Although rafting currently is not offered within Anchorage, several firms offer floats on day trips from the city, either to the north on the **Matanuska River** (p. 221, ❹) or to the south on **Sixmile Creek** (p. 232, ❷). Or for a calm, scenic ride in front of **Spencer Glacier,** take the Alaska Railroad's float tour option (see "Train Ride to Mountain Adventures," on p. 86).

There's little boating in the hazardous waters off Anchorage, but it's easy to do a sea kayaking day trip to **Prince William Sound** through Whittier and be back in the city in the evening (see "On the Water from Whittier," on p. 202).

Swimming

Outdoor swimming in Alaska is chilly, with air temperatures topping out in the low 70s, but we enjoy it. In town, a hot bike ride on the Lanie Fleischer Chester Creek Trail to **Goose Lake** (p. 78, ❷) is pleasantly followed by a cool dip. For kids, the **H₂Oasis** indoor water park (p. 79, ❼) may be just what you need.

Winter
Alpine Skiing

Mount Alyeska (☎ 800-880-3880; www. alyeskaresort.com) is in Girdwood, 30 miles south of Anchorage. Its slopes are challenging and the conditions can be glorious, with a

> *The waters off Anchorage are a little too wild for rafting, but several outfitters offer calmer floats on nearby rivers.*

long season, ample snow, plentiful light in the spring, and fabulous ocean views. The mountain reaches 3,939 feet and has 1,400 acres of skiing, beginning from a base elevation of only 250 feet and rising 2,500 feet. While it isn't as big as the huge resorts in the Rockies, it's still well worth the trip. All-day lift tickets are $60 for adults; $45 for children 14 to 17 and seniors 60 to 69; $40 for children 8 to 13; and $15 for children 7 and under and for seniors 70 and over.

Cross-Country Skiing

Anchorage has some of the nation's best cross-country trail networks; the most extensive is at **Kincaid Park,** with 40 miles of groomed trails, including about 10 miles that are lighted for night skiing. The park takes in 1,500 miles of rolling birch forest, with a pond and beautiful ocean views. Moose frequently show up. The large **Kincaid Outdoor Center** (☎ 907-343-6397) is open for warming up, with staff on-site, and is free to use. National championships were held here in 2009 and

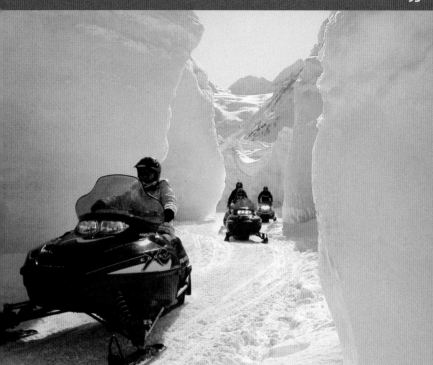

> *Glacier City Snowmobile Tours lets you explore the Alaskan backcountry, glaciers, and ice caves (weather permitting) on your own snowmobile.*

2010. The center is open Monday through Friday noon to 9pm, Saturday 10am to 9pm, and Sunday 10am to 5pm.

The short drive to Kincaid rewards you with the superb skiing there, but many Anchorage neighborhoods have their own trails, and there are four other major skiing parks. The bike trail network also becomes a skiing network in the winter. The **Nordic Ski Association of Anchorage** posts maps and other information about all the trails on its website (www.anchoragenordicski.com) and welcomes questions at ☎ 907-276-7609. For information on renting equipment, see "Outdoor Equipment (Rental & Sales)," on p. 101.

Ice Skating

Five lakes and many outdoor rinks attract hundreds of skaters on crisp winter days. Here's a chance to partake in the best of living in a northern city. **Westchester Lagoon** (p. 71, Ⓐ) has acres of groomed ice, including long paths and rinks, and often food vendors and

fires for warming. The rink at **Town Square Park** (p. 81, ❻) is small but more convenient to most visitors, in a charming urban setting. All of Anchorage's outdoor rinks and groomed lakes are free to use. For more information, including conditions, contact Anchorage Parks & Recreation (☎ 907-343-4355; www.muni.org/parks). To rent skates, head to **Champions Choice** (University Center Mall at Old Seward Hwy. and 36th Ave; ☎ 907-563-3503; www.championschoicehockey.com); the cost is $10 a day.

Snowmobiling

Based in Girdwood, **Glacier City Snowmobile Tours** (☎ 877-783-5566; www.snowtours.net) is a family that suits up clients—most of whom have never been on a snowmobile—to ride. Where the tour takes you is determined according to snow conditions, which sometimes allow groups to venture as far as beautiful Spencer Glacier. Groups are small and the attitude is casual. A 5½-hour outing costs $240.

GOING TO EXTREMES

In this state, extreme sports are a way of life

BY CHARLES WOHLFORTH

ALASKANS HAVE A REPUTATION for being hardy, independent, and adventurous. The best proof that the image is more than a stereotype can be found in the number of inexplicably tough competitions Alaskans engage in, often during the winter. Many of these contests are obscure and without glory, but what they have in common is that they involve either incredible tests of endurance, feats of daring, or dedication to full-time preparation (or all three). It may be difficult for visitors to understand the appeal of some of these sports—and I use the word loosely. But to Alaskans, it is all part of the same spirit that allows us to endure long, dark winters and bone-chilling weather without fleeing to warmer parts. Here are just a few of Alaska's more unusual competitions.

Iron Dog Snowmobile Race

This is the world's longest and toughest snowmobile race, running from Wasilla, to Nome, and then back again across the state to Fairbanks, covering about 2,000 miles in all. Racers on snowmobiles bounce through the wilderness at highway speeds, with a record finish (including mandatory stops) coming in just under 38 hours. For more information, call ☎ 907-563-4414 or visit www.irondog.org.

Iditarod Trail Invitational

Next time you hear someone bragging about running a marathon or even competing in an Iron Man, ask if they could handle this: A race in February's deep snow, in temperatures usually well below zero, over the Iditarod Trail 1,161 miles from Knik to Nome, camping along the way. Oh, and you're doing all of this on foot or bike. In 2010, Tom Jarding won on foot in a time of 20 days, 14 hours, completing the equivalent of two full marathons every day for three weeks. Now that's tough. For more information, visit www.alaskaultrasport.com

Tesoro Arctic Man Ski & Sno-Go Classic

This really is insane. A skier flies straight down a steep 1,700-foot slope, then grabs a rope and is pulled up the next slope by a snow machine going as fast as 88 mph, then skis down a 1,200-foot slope. It's all about speed: The record time for covering the 5½ mile course is 4 minutes, 1 second. This adrenaline-fest is held every April, and it has become an excuse for thousands of Alaskans to arrive in their RVs, briefly forming the fourth largest community in the state, right there in the wilderness off the Richardson Highway. For more information, call ☎ 907-456-2626 or visit www.arcticman.com.

The Iditarod Trail Sled Dog Race

The Iditarod—a 1,161 mile dog sled race from Anchorage to Nome—has become Alaska's biggest annual event, and a beloved symbol of what the state is all about. Over the course of more than a week (the record time is just under 9 days) starting the first Saturday in March, mushers and teams of 16 dogs make their way through ice, storms, and temperatures that dip well below freezing. This is the original extreme Alaskan event, and it has inspired many others, including the Iditabike race, which involves traversing 200 miles of the Iditarod's trail on bicycle. In the snow. See p. 121.

Anchorage Shopping Best Bets

Best Native Arts and Crafts
Alaska Native Arts Foundation Gallery, 500 W. 6th Ave. (p. 97)

Best Fishing Gear
B&J Sporting Goods, 2749 C St. (p. 99)

Best Furs
David Green Master Furrier, 130 W. 4th Ave. (p. 99)

Best for Gifts
Cabin Fever, 650 W. 4th Ave. (p. 100)

Best for Fine Art
Artique, Ltd., 314 G St. (p. 99)

Best Seafood You Can Ship Home
10th and M Seafoods, 1020 M St. (p. 100)

Best Outdoor Clothing
REI, 1200 W. Northern Lights Blvd. (p. 101)

Best Outdoor Equipment (Sales and Rental)
Alaska Mountaineering & Hiking, 2633 Spenard Rd. (p. 101)

> *Artique art gallery in downtown Anchorage.*

Anchorage Shopping A to Z

Alaska Native Arts and Crafts

★★★ Alaska Native Arts Foundation Gallery
DOWNTOWN This nonprofit devoted to elevating Native fine arts highlights individual artists in gallery shows and exhibits a variety of work in an adjoining room; the website also is worth a look. Work spans the range of expression by Alaska's best artists, from traditional carvings rooted in tribal heritage to cutting-edge contemporary work commenting on current issues, as in a recent show on Alaska Native art and politics. 500 W. 6th Ave. ☎ 907-258-ANAF (258-2623). alaskanativearts.org. AE, DISC,MC, V.

★★ Anchorage Museum at Rasmuson Center
DOWNTOWN This elegant gift store, tucked in the glass front of the museum, offers well-selected and reasonably priced Native art, books, and other items. 625 C St. ☎ 907-929-9262. www.anchoragemuseum.org/shop. AE, DISC, MC, V.

★★ 4th Avenue Market Place DOWNTOWN
Once a downtown shopping center, this spot is now a supermarket of Native craft work, such as carvings, jewelry, dolls, furs and other clothing, masks, prints, and the full range of visual art in the style of Alaska Native cultures. Demonstrations by carvers and other artists are sometimes given on summer afternoons. 411 W. 4th Ave. ☎ 907-272-9076.

★★★ Hospital Auxiliary Gift Shop EAST
ANCHORAGE Located within a hospital dedicated to serving Native villagers from all over Alaska—the de facto center of Native communities in the city—this surprising shop carries a vast array of authentic, traditional handmade items on consignment from patients and their families. Products include purely decorative pieces, such as masks and grass baskets, and useful items, including knives and outdoor clothing. In the Alaska Native Medical Center, 4315 Diplomacy Dr. ☎ 907-563-2662. www.anmc.org. No credit cards.

> *An authentic craft from the Alaska Native Medical Center gift shop.*

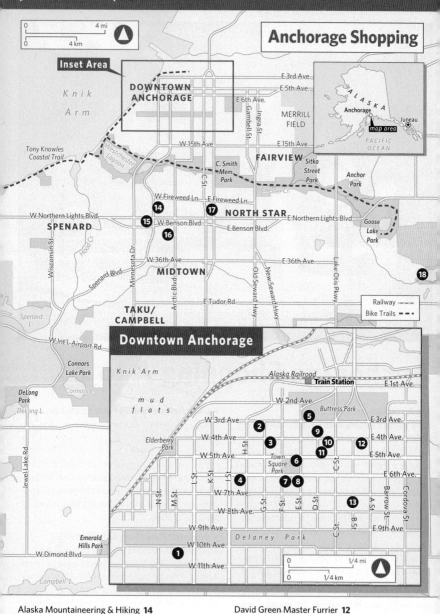

Anchorage Shopping

Knik Arm

DOWNTOWN ANCHORAGE

Inset Area

E 3rd Ave.
E 5th Ave.
E 6th Ave.
MERRILL FIELD
ALASKA
Anchorage
Juneau
map area
PACIFIC OCEAN

W 15th Ave.
E 15th Ave.
FAIRVIEW

Tony Knowles Coastal Trail
Westchester Lagoon
C. Smith Mem. Park
Sitka Street Park
Anchor Park

W Fireweed Ln.   E Fireweed Ln.
14   **17**
NORTH STAR
W Northern Lights Blvd.   E Northern Lights Blvd.
SPENARD
15   W Benson Blvd.
16   E Benson Blvd.
Goose Lake Park

W 36th Ave.
E 36th Ave.
MIDTOWN

Hood Cr.
Spenard Blvd.
Minnesota Dr.
Arctic Blvd.
Old Seward Hwy.
New Seward Hwy.
Lake Otis Pkwy.

TAKU/ CAMPBELL
E Tudor Rd.
18

Spenard L.
W Int'l. Airport Rd.

Railway
Bike Trails - - -

Connors Lake Park
Connors L.

DeLong Park
DeLong L.

Downtown Anchorage

Knik Arm
Alaska Railroad
Train Station
E 1st Ave.

mud flats
W 2nd Ave.
Buttress Park
E 3rd Ave.

Elderberry Park
W 3rd Ave.   **2**   **5**
W 4th Ave.   **3**   **9**   E 4th Ave.
W 5th Ave.   **10**   **12**
Town Square Park   **11**   E 5th Ave.
6
4   **7 8**   E 6th Ave.
W 7th Ave.
W 8th Ave.
13

Jewel Lake Rd.
N St.
M St.
L St.
K St.
I St.
H St.
G St.
F St.
E St.
D St.
C St.
B St.
A St.
Cordova St.
Barrow St.

Emerald Hills Park
W 9th Ave.
Delaney Park
W 10th Ave.   **1**
W Dimond Blvd.
W 11th Ave.
E 9th Ave.

Campbell L.

0   1/4 mi
0   1/4 km

Alaska Mountaineering & Hiking **14**
Alaska Native Arts Foundation Gallery **8**
Alaska Sausage and Seafood **16**
Anchorage Market and Festival **5**
Anchorage Museum at Rasmuson Center **13**
Army Navy Store **10**
Artique, Ltd. **2**
B&J Sporting Goods **17**
Cabin Fever **3**

David Green Master Furrier **12**
4th Avenue Market Place **9**
Hospital Auxiliary Gift Shop **18**
International Gallery of Contemporary Art **11**
Kobuk Coffee Company **6**
Oomingmak Musk Ox Producers' Co-operative **4**
REI **15**
6th Avenue Outfitters **7**
10th and M Seafoods **1**

Watch Out for Fakes

When shopping for Alaska Native arts and crafts, be aware that counterfeiting is a serious problem. What seems to be a bargain often isn't: Inexpensive items may be priced that way because they're actually Asian knockoffs. By making sure you are buying the real thing, you avoid getting cheated and ensure that your money goes to Alaska Native artists whose communities desperately need the cash income. The shops listed here are all legit, but it's always good to know the name of the individual artist who made a valuable piece, where it was made, and that the shop will vouch for its authenticity, preferably because they bought direct from the artist.

★★★ **Oomingmak Musk Ox Producers' Co-operative** DOWNTOWN You'll find just one thing at this unique shop: hand-knitted items made from the silky under-hair of the musk ox. The patterns used in the hats and scarves reflect the traditions of individual village masters, who do the work in the Alaska Bush. 604 H St. ☎ 907-272-9225; www.qiviut.com. AE, DISC, MC, V.

Fine Art

★★ **Artique, Ltd.** DOWNTOWN
This gallery shows dramatic oils and other serious works in one half (usually by only one or two Alaskan artists) and a large collection of inexpensive prints in the other half. 314 G St. ☎ 907-277-1663. www.artiqueltd.com. AE, DISC, MC, V.

★★ **International Gallery of Contemporary Art** DOWNTOWN This nonprofit gallery mounts large, one-artist shows for a month at a time, showcasing Alaska's artistic cutting edge in an uncompromising way. 427 D St. ☎ 907-279-1116. www.igcaalaska.org. MC, V.

Fishing Gear

★★ **B&J Sporting Goods** MIDTOWN
A business that has been serving practical outdoor needs for generations lives on in a basement under a Kentucky Fried Chicken. The location may seem strange, but the sales staff here really know their stuff. 2749 C St. ☎ 907-274-6113. www.bnjsg.com. AE, DISC, MC, V.

> An artisan at work at the Oomingmak Musk Ox Producers' Co-operative.

Furs

★★ **David Green Master Furrier** DOWNTOWN
If you're looking for fur, you've come to the source: a shop that's been making furs since 1922. Anchorage's lack of sales tax adds savings to a big purchase, too. 130 W. 4th Ave. ☎ 907-277-9595. www.davidgreenfurs.com. AE, DISC, MC, V.

Gifts

★★ **Anchorage Market & Festival** DOWNTOWN A large downtown parking lot becomes a big street market Saturdays and Sundays through the summer, with every kind of craft and gift that will fit on a card table or in a tent. 3rd Ave. and E St. ☎ 907-272-5634. www.anchoragemarkets.com.

> *The International Gallery of Contemporary Art is dedicated to local and edgy artists.*

★★★ Cabin Fever DOWNTOWN
This is a classy version of a kind of shop that dominates downtown Anchorage: gift shops with mass-produced items such as T-shirts, candles, and dolls. Here you'll find inventory of higher quality, along with a relatively calming atmosphere and a general sense of good taste. 650 W. 4th Ave. 907-278-3522. www.cabin feveralaska.com. AE, DISC, MC, V.

★★ Kobuk Coffee Company DOWNTOWN
Occupying one of the oldest and most authentic historic buildings in town, this is a nostalgic, old-fashioned shop full of teapots, fancy candy, soaps, and the like, with a tiny cafe in back. 504 W. 5th Ave. ☎ 907-272-3626. www.kobukcoffee.com. AE, DISC, MC, V.

Gourmet Food
★★★ Alaska Sausage and Seafood SPENARD
Famous for reindeer sausage gift packs and smoked salmon, this shop also will either smoke or vacuum-pack and freeze your own sport-caught fish for shipping home. 2914 Arctic Blvd. ☎ 907-562-3636. www.alaska sausage.com. MC, V.

★★★ 10th and M Seafoods DOWNTOWN
Few gifts from Alaska are as well appreciated as crab or salmon. Over decades, 10th and M has made an art of processing and delivering these gifts in perfect condition. 1020 M St. ☎ 907-272-1685. www.10thandmseafoods.com. AE, DISC, MC, V.

Outdoor Clothing
★★ Army Navy Store DOWNTOWN
For those few who are in the market for gear suitable for the high Arctic in midwinter, there is no better source than this well-stocked shop relied upon for half a century by oil-field workers and Eskimos. 320 W. 4th Ave. ☎ 907-279-2401. www.army-navy-store.com. AE, DISC, MC, V.

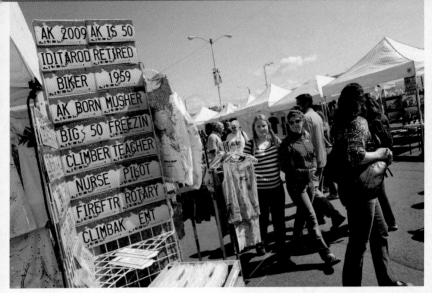

> *Souvenirs and bric-a-brac at the weekend market and festival.*

★★★ REI SPENARD
Visitors heading for the outdoors will want to stop here for the extensive selection of high-quality clothing and the comprehensive equipment sales and rental offerings, including camping gear, canoes, cross-country skis, and many other items. 1200 W. Northern Lights Blvd. ☎ 907-272-4565. www.rei.com. AE, DISC, MC, V.

★★ 6th Avenue Outfitters DOWNTOWN
A convenient downtown stop for a wide range of sturdy outdoor gear and advice. 524 W. 6th Ave. ☎ 907-276-0233. www.6thavenueoutfitters.com. AE, DISC, MC, V.

Outdoor Equipment (Rental and Sales)
★★★ Alaska Mountaineering & Hiking SPENARD
Elite athletes and climbers aren't the only folks who shop here. Anyone looking to buy or rent top-quality gear and get personal advice on planning an outdoor trip will find expert staff willing to help. 2633 Spenard Rd. ☎ 907-272-1811. www.alaskamountaineering.com. AE, DISC, MC, V.

★★★ REI SPENARD
See the listing above, under "Outdoor Clothing."

> *A traditional carving at Alaska Native Arts Foundation Gallery.*

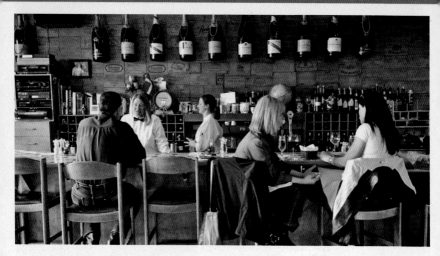

Anchorage Restaurant Best Bets

Best Burger Joint
★ **Arctic Road Runner,** 5300 Old Seward Hwy. or 2477 Arctic Blvd. (p. 103)

Best Cajun
★★★ **Double Musky Inn,** Mile 3, Crow Creek Rd., Girdwood (p. 104)

Best Casual Cafe
★ **Snow City Cafe,** 1034 W. 4th Ave. (p. 109)

Best Creative Cuisine
★★★ **Sacks Cafe & Restaurant,** 328 G St. (p. 108)

Best Diner
★ **City Diner,** 3000 Minnesota Dr. (p. 103)

Best Greek
★ **The Greek Corner,** 201 E. Northern Lights Blvd. (p. 105)

Best Halibut
★★★ **The Marx Bros. Cafe,** 627 W. 3rd Ave. (p. 107)

Best Inexpensive Lunch
★ **Dianne's Restaurant,** 550 W. 7th Ave. (p. 104)

Best International Cuisine
★★★ **Jens' Restaurant,** 701 W. 36th Ave. (p. 105)

Best Italian
★★ **Campobello Bistro,** 601 W. 36th Ave. (p. 103)

Best Japanese
★★ **Kumagoro,** 533 W. 4th Ave. (p. 105)

Best Pizza
★★ **The Moose's Tooth Pub and Pizzeria,** 3300 Old Seward Hwy. (p. 107)

Best Trendy Retro Hangout
★★ **Spenard Roadhouse,** 1049 W. Northern Lights Blvd. (p. 109)

Best Ski Bum Hangout
★ **Chair 5,** Lindblad Ave, Girdwood (p. 103)

Best Southwestern
★★ **Bear Tooth Grill,** 1230 W. 27th Ave. (p. 103)

Best Steak
★★ **Club Paris,** 417 W. 5th Ave. (p. 104)

> Jens' reliably inspired menu draws a regular crowd.

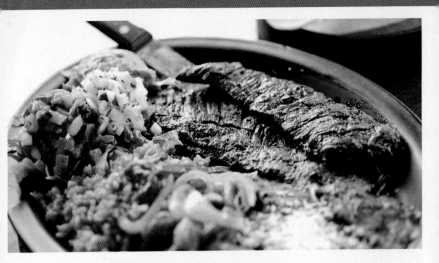

Anchorage Restaurants A to Z

★ kids **Arctic Road Runner** MIDTOWN *BURGERS* The "Local Burgerman," an Anchorage institution, serves big burgers with unusual toppings such as peppers, ham, and fried onion rings at two pleasingly old-fashioned joints. The Old Seward Highway location is decorated with photographs of local celebrities of the past. 5300 Old Seward Hwy. or 2477 Arctic Blvd. ☎ 907-561-1245 or 907-279-7311. Burgers $4–$7. No credit cards. Lunch & dinner Mon–Sat.

★★ **Bear Tooth Grill** SPENARD *SOUTHWESTERN* Casual, fun, noisy, and inexpensive—but with some menu choices even for sophisticated diners—the Bear Tooth matches Anchorage perfectly and is hugely popular. Count on a wait for a table. The menu includes excellent vegetarian choices, and fish is done well, too. 1230 W. 27th Ave. ☎ 907-276-4200. www.beartooththeatre. net. All items $6–$20. AE, DC, DISC, MC, V. Lunch & dinner Mon–Fri; dinner only Sat–Sun.

★★ **Campobello Bistro** MIDTOWN *NORTHERN ITALIAN* Although it's situated in a mini-mall storefront, walking through the door is surprisingly like stepping into Italy, with authentic, robust food and professional, jocular service. Prices are reasonable for some of the best food in Anchorage. 601 W. 36th Ave. ☎ 907-563-2040. Entrees $15–$25. DC, MC, V. Lunch Mon–Fri; dinner Tues–Sat.

★ kids **Chair 5** GIRDWOOD *AMERICAN* A great spot to take the family after skiing at Mount Alyeska or on a road trip, Chair 5—an hour south of the city—is rich with small-town warmth and ski-bum camaraderie. Although the bar dominates the entrance, children are treated especially well, and the menu includes a variety of dishes, from fast food to fine dining, that will please each member of the family. 5 Lindblad Ave. ☎ 907-783-2500. www. chairfive.com Entrees $18–$28. AE, DC, DISC, MC, V. Lunch & dinner daily.

★ kids **City Diner** SPENARD *DINER* Chrome, neon, and vinyl create an atmosphere like a movie set, a theme fully realized through the friendly service and the milk shakes presented in metal mixing cups. But the food is much better than at most diners, produced with excellent ingredients and a minimum of grease. 3000 Minnesota Dr. ☎ 907-277-CITY (277-2489). www.citydiner.org. Entrees $7–$19. AE, DISC, MC, V. Breakfast, lunch, and dinner daily.

> *Bear Tooth satisfies carnivores and herbivores alike.*

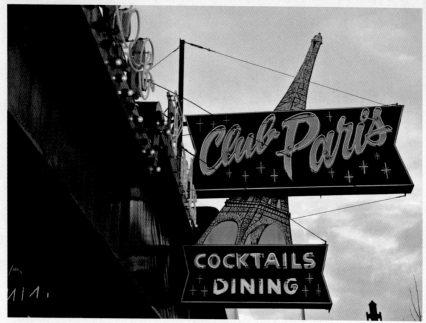

> *Bon appetit at the legendary, distinctly old-school, Club Paris.*

★★ Club Paris DOWNTOWN *STEAK*
An authentic oilman's steakhouse surviving from the cocktail era has become a treasure rare enough to be featured in the *New York Times*. Fame hasn't spoiled it. You can still get a strong cocktail in the dark confines of the restaurant and bar, and the steaks are done to perfection. 417 W. 5th Ave. ☎ 907-277-6332. www.clubparisrestaurant.com. Entrees $18–$44. AE, DC, DISC, MC, V. Lunch Mon–Sat; dinner daily.

★★ Crush DOWNTOWN *BISTRO*
This is a wine bar that also serves food, but the food is far from an afterthought. At dinner, most dishes are small plates of exotica to share around the table. At lunch, more traditional sandwiches and salads are served. The wine list, by the glass or bottle, is excellent. 343 W. 6th Ave. ☎ 907-865-9198. www.crushak.com Entrees $7–$14. AE, DC, MC, V. Lunch Mon–Fri, dinner Mon–Sat.

★ Dianne's Restaurant DOWNTOWN *CAFE*
You'll see more office workers than tourists here, but if you seek a healthy, hearty sandwich, a soup, or a hot special—and you want to save time—you'll do no better. Food is served from a cafeteria counter, and seating is in a light, airy dining room. 550 W. 7th Ave. ☎ 907-279-7243. www.diannesrestaurant.com. Entrees $5–$10. AE, DISC, MC, V. Breakfast & lunch Mon–Fri.

★★★ Double Musky Inn GIRDWOOD *CAJUN*
A perfect mix of noise, bold and expert cooking, and an ultra-casual ski bum atmosphere have made this Alaska's most famous restaurant. Some leave with raw nerves, others with euphoric energy. The location is an hour from the city. Since the restaurant doesn't take reservations, the best strategy to get a table is to grab seats in the bar and order appetizers there while waiting to move to the dining room. Mile 3, Crow Creek Rd., Girdwood. ☎ 907-783-2822. www.doublemuskyinn.com. Entrees $18–$37. AE, DC, DISC, MC, V. Dinner Tues–Sun. Closed Nov.

★★ Glacier Brewhouse DOWNTOWN *BREWPUB*
Decorated like a lodge and smelling pleasantly of wood smoke, the brewhouse packs in diners thanks to a broad price range, a lively atmosphere, and exceptional food. The convenient location and reasonably fast service make it a

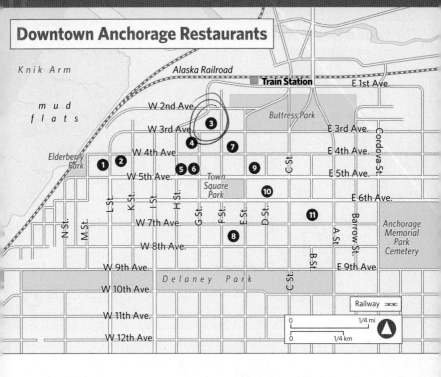

Downtown Anchorage Restaurants

Club Paris **9**
Crush **10**
Dianne's Restaurant **8**
Glacier Brewhouse **5**
Kumagoro **7**
The Marx Bros. Cafe **3**

Muse **11**
ORSO **6**
Sacks Cafe & Restaurant **4**
Simon & Seafort's Saloon and Grill **1**
Snow City Cafe **2**

622 W 3rd halibut

prime choice for visitors. 737 W. 5th Ave. ☎ 907-274-BREW (274-2739. www.glacier brewhouse.com Entrees $8–$34. AE, DC, DISC, MC, V. Summer lunch & dinner daily; winter closed for lunch Sun.

★ kids **The Greek Corner** MIDTOWN *GREEK*
This homey, unpolished family restaurant serves traditional Greek dishes as well as pizza and Italian food. The service is sincerely warm and accommodating. 201 E. Northern Lights Blvd. ☎ 907-276-2820. Entrees $10–$20. MC, V. Lunch & dinner Mon–Sat; dinner only Sun.

★★★ **Jens' Restaurant** MIDTOWN *INTERNATIONAL* Gifted owner-chef Jens Hansen

produces Alaska's most adventurous and memorable meals, inspired by his international travels. The menu changes continuously, with just a few constants (such as the much-loved pepper steak). Service is perfect, with broadly spaced tables and friendly, formally attired waiters. The restaurant incongruously occupies a mini-mall. 701 W. 36th Ave. ☎ 907-561-5367. www.jensrestaurant.com. Entrees $18–$39. AE, DC, DISC, MC, V. Lunch Mon–Fri; dinner Tues–Sat. Closed Jan.

★★ **Kumagoro** DOWNTOWN *JAPANESE*
The food, service, and dining room are authentically Japanese, and the location is

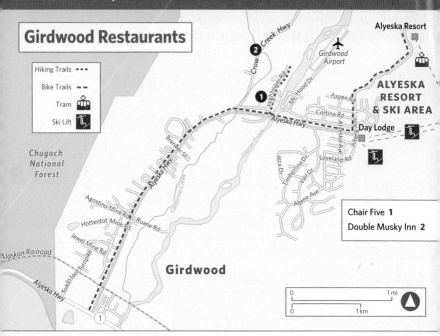

Girdwood Restaurants

Hiking Trails	•••
Bike Trails	– –
Tram	
Ski Lift	

Alyeska Resort

ALYESKA RESORT & SKI AREA

Crow Creek Hwy

Girdwood Airport

Mt. Hood Dr.

Highgrove Rd.

Aspen Rd.

Cortina Rd

Alyeska Hwy

Day Lodge

Chugach National Forest

Brentler St.

Alyeska Hwy

Glacier Creek

Alta Dr.

Timberline Dr.

Vail Dr.

Loveland Rd.

Alpine Ave.

Agostino Mine Rd.

Ruane Rd.

Hottentot Mine Rd.

Jewel Mine Rd.

Alaskan Railroad

Alyeska Hwy

Toadstool Turnpike

California Creek

Girdwood

Chair Five **1**
Double Musky Inn **2**

0 — 1 mi
0 — 1 km

> *An unlucky chicken at the Lucky Wishbone.*

> *The laid-back atmosphere at Snow City Cafe.*

town. Reserve a couple of days ahead for a table in the dining room at the height of the summer season, or eat in the bar, where the food and the view are still exceptional. 420 L St. ☎ 907-274-3502. www.simonandseaforts. com. Entrees $8–$42. AE, DISC, MC, V. Summer lunch Mon–Fri, dinner daily; winter lunch Mon–Thurs, dinner daily.

★ Snow City Cafe DOWNTOWN *CAFE*

Popular for excellent breakfasts, this large, cheerful, youthful spot with an idiosyncratic menu is a good choice for casual meals a cut above those from your typical storefront cafe. The youthful waitstaff strive to make a connection with guests. 1034 W. 4th Ave. ☎ 907-272-CITY (272-2489). www.snowcitycafe.com. All items $8–$12. AE, DISC, MC, V. Breakfast & lunch daily.

★★ Spenard Roadhouse SPENARD *CAFE*

The unique ambience here recreates suburban Alaska in the 1970s, with tater tots and other "after-school specials" on the menu (but the tots are served with smoked paprika aïoli, and the bar offers a broad selection of small-batch bourbons). It's fun, not over the top, and the menu is broad enough for many tastes and budgets. 1049 W. Northern Lights Blvd. ☎ 907-770-7623. www.spenardroadhouse.com. Entrees $9–$20. AE, DISC, MC, V. Lunch & dinner daily.

> *A seafood risotto at Sacks.*

Anchorage Hotel Best Bets

Best Full-Service Hotel
★★★ **Hotel Captain Cook,** 939 W. 5th Ave.
$$$$ (p. 113)

Best for Families
★★ **Residence Inn by Marriott,** 1025 35th
Ave. $$$$ (p. 115)

Best Alaskan Hospitality
Elderberry Bed & Breakfast, 8340 Elderberry
St. $ (p. 112)

Best Hostel
Alaska Backpackers Inn, 327 Eagle St. $ (p.
111)

Best Downtown Bargain
★★ **Susitna Place,** 727 N St. $$ (p. 115)

Best Historic B&B
★ **The Oscar Gill House Historic Bed &
Breakfast,** 1344 W. 10th Ave. $$ (p. 114)

Best Deal Near the Airport
★ **Lakeshore Motor Inn,** 3009 Lakeshore Dr.
$$ (p. 113)

Best Themed B&B
★★ **Lake Hood Inn,** 4702 Lake Spenard Dr.
$$$ (p. 113)

Best Location
★★ **Anchorage Grand Hotel,** 505 W. 2nd Ave.
$$$ (p. 111)

Best View Rooms
★★★ **Anchorage Downtown Marriott,** 820 W.
7th Ave $$$$ (p. 111)

Best Ski Resort
★★★ **Hotel Alyeska,** 1000 Arlberg Ave. $$$$
(p. 113)

Best Downtown Country Inn
★★ **Copper Whale Inn,** 440 L St. $$$ (p. 111)

Most Scenic Campground
Bird Creek Alaska State Parks Campground,
Mile 101, Seward Hwy. $ (p. 115)

> *The sign says it all: Copper Whale Inn.*

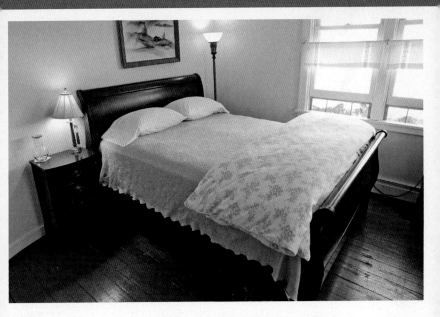

Anchorage Hotels A to Z

Alaska Backpackers Inn DOWNTOWN
This is a friendly, cheerful, well-equipped
hostel with a choice of bunks or private rooms.
In a town where decent economy lodgings
hardly exist, this is a place you'll feel safe and
welcome. 327 Eagle St. ☎ 907-277-2770. www.
alaskabackpackers.com. 37 units, 109 beds.
Doubles $50; shared bath, bunks $25. MC, V.

★★★ **Anchorage Downtown Marriott** DOWN-
TOWN The décor is bland, but this newest of
the high-rise, full-service downtown hotels
has a large pool and huge picture windows
that dominate each bedroom with amazing
views. 820 W. 7th Ave. ☎ 888-236-2427 or
907-279-8000. www.marriott.com/amcdt. 392
units. Doubles $290 high season; $180 low season. AE, DC, DISC, MC, V.

★★ **Anchorage Grand Hotel** DOWNTOWN
This is a comfortable, low-key, all-suite hotel
overlooking the port in the heart of downtown,
steps from the Alaska Railroad depot. Having
been converted from apartments, the suites
all have cooking facilities, but the housekeep-
ing has always been perfect on my many

visits, with nary a scent of food. *505* W. 2nd
Ave. ☎ 888-800-0640 or 907-929-8888. www.
anchoragegrand.com. 31 units. Doubles $205
summer; $105 winter. AE, DISC, MC, V.

★★ **Copper Whale Inn** DOWNTOWN
A pair of clapboard buildings with the look and
feel of a good country inn stand on some of
downtown Anchorage's best real estate, overlooking Cook Inlet and sitting a block from the
Tony Knowles Coastal Trail. A booth to rent
bikes for the trail is on-site. 440 L St. ☎ 866-
258-7999 or 907-258-7999. www.copperwhale.
com. 14 units. Doubles $185–$210 summer;
$85–$110 winter. AE, DISC, MC, V.

★★ **Courtyard by Marriott** AIRPORT
This is the nearest hotel to the airport, and as
such, it caters to business travelers, with a pool
and many other amenities. The airport's scenic
floatplane base is right across the street, but
you will need a car for the rest of the city. 4901
Spenard Rd. ☎ 800-314-0782 or 907-245-0322.
www.marriott.com/ANCCY. 154 units. Doubles
$199–$299 summer; $129–$179 winter. AE, DISC,
DC, MC, V.

> *Guestrooms are cozy but inviting at the Oscar Gill House B & B.*

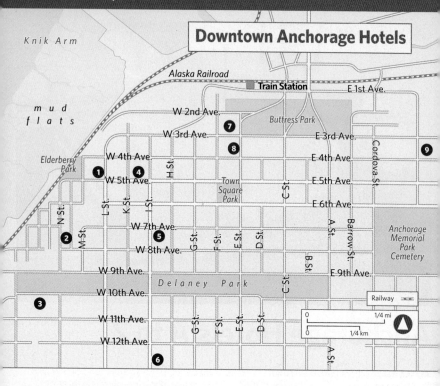

Downtown Anchorage Hotels

Alaska Backpackers Inn **9**
Anchorage Downtown Marriott **5**
Anchorage Grand Hotel **7**
Copper Whale Inn **1**
The Historic Anchorage Hotel **8**

Hotel Captain Cook **4**
The Oscar Gill House Bed and Breakfast **3**
Susitna Place **2**
Wildflower Inn **6**

★★ **Dimond Center Hotel** SOUTH ANCHORAGE
Although situated among big-box stores and a mall, this hotel has many elaborate, luxurious features. The location puts you near the Seward Highway and a short drive from Chugach State Park. 700 E. Dimond Blvd. ☎ 866-770-5002 or 907-770-5000. www.dimondcenterhotel.com. 109 units. Doubles $250–$300 summer; $130–$179 winter. AE, DC, DISC, MC, V.

Elderberry Bed & Breakfast SAND LAKE
Besides the low rates, the main attraction of this cozy home-stay B&B is the old-fashioned hospitality. Linda and Norm Seitz, a couple

with a long history in Alaska, treat guests as adopted family, telling stories and giving travel advice. 8340 Elderberry St. ☎ 907-243-6968. www.elderberrybb.com. 3 units. Doubles $95–$115 summer; $75 winter; w/breakfast. MC, V.

★ **The Historic Anchorage Hotel** DOWNTOWN
Among the city's oldest businesses, this concrete building preserves the scale of those days, and small-town walking distances—as it's right in the middle of the busiest tourist streets. Hospitality is warm and rooms, although modern in amenities, are decorated in an old-fashioned style, with Queen Anne

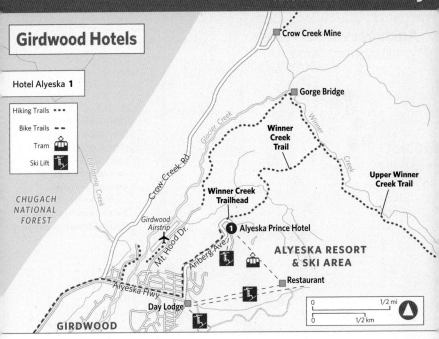

Girdwood Hotels

Hotel Alyeska 1

Hiking Trails · · ·
Bike Trails – –
Tram
Ski Lift

CHUGACH
NATIONAL
FOREST

Crow Creek Mine

Gorge Bridge

Winner
Creek
Trail

Glacier Creek

California Creek

Crow Creek Rd.

Winner Creek
Trailhead

Upper Winner
Creek Trail

Winner Creek

Girdwood
Airstrip

Mt. Hood Dr.

Arlberg Ave.

1 Alyeska Prince Hotel

ALYESKA RESORT
& SKI AREA

Restaurant

Alyeska Hwy.

Day Lodge

GIRDWOOD

0   1/2 mi
0   1/2 km

---

furniture and much patterned fabric. Ask for a room in the rear, as front rooms can be noisy. 330 E St., Anchorage, AK 99501. ☎ 800-544-0988 or 907-272-4553. www.historic anchoragehotel.com. 26 units. Doubles $189-$209 summer, $89-$159 winter; w/breakfast. AE, DC, DISC, MC, V.

★★★ Hotel Alyeska GIRDWOOD

A grand hotel with dormers and turrets, like an old-world château, stands among huge spruce trees in a Chugach Mountain valley, linked from its back door to the exciting ski slopes of Mount Alyeska by a tram and lift. The facilities and restaurants are excellent. 1000 Arlberg Ave. ☎ 800-880-3880 or 907-754-1111. www.alyeskaresort.com. 304 units. Double $275-$360 summer and Christmas; $145-$240 winter. AE, DC, MC, V.

★★★ Hotel Captain Cook DOWNTOWN

Royalty and movie stars stay here, in the city's original and reigning premier hotel. Built in the 1960s by Walter Hickel, one of the state's most interesting self-made men, it brought top-class lodging and dining to Alaska. The hotel's nautical theme is carried throughout, with dark, rich colors and custom teak

paneling and furniture. An excellent health club and pool are in the basement. Although rooms and bathrooms are smaller than current standards, the service, facilities, and restaurants are unmatched. 939 W. 5th Ave. ☎ 800-843-1950 or 907-276-6000. www.captaincook. com. 547 units. Doubles $255-$265 summer; $155-$165 winter. AE, DISC, MC, V.

★★ Lake Hood Inn AIRPORT

This cleanly appointed inn sits on the shore of a busy floatplane lake, with the owner's own aircraft pulled up front. The aviation theme continues throughout; headphones even allow guests to listen in on tower transmissions. Rooms are comfortable and airy. 4702 Lake Spenard Dr. ☎ 866-663-9322 or 907-258-9321. www.lakehoodinn.com. 4 units. Doubles $169-$189, w/breakfast. AE, DISC, MC, V.

★ Lakeshore Motor Inn AIRPORT

The concrete building's exterior, although dressed up by flowers, doesn't accurately reflect the inn's quality. Inside, comfortable rooms are well equipped and cost far less than comparable accommodations in the airport area. The style is hotel typical—the noteworthy thing is the low price. 3009 Lakeshore

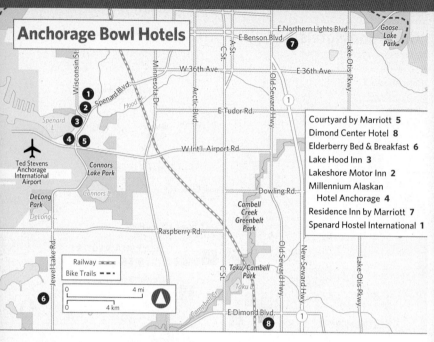

Anchorage Bowl Hotels

E. Northern Lights Blvd.

Goose Lake Park

E. Benson Blvd. **7**

Wisconsin St.

Spenard Blvd.

Hood St.

Minnesota Dr.

W. 36th Ave.

E. 36th Ave.

A St.

C St.

Lake Otis Pkwy.

1
2
3
4 **5**

Spenard L.

Arctic Blvd.

E. Tudor Rd.

Old Seward Hwy.

1

Ted Stevens Anchorage International Airport

Connors Lake Park

W. Int'l. Airport Rd.

Lake Hood Inn **3**

DeLong Park

Connors L.

Dowling Rd.

DeLong L.

Cambell Creek Greenbelt Park

Raspberry Rd.

Jewel Lake Rd.

Taku/Cambell Park

C St.

Taku L.

Old Seward Hwy.

New Seward Hwy.

Lake Otis Pkwy.

6

Railway ▬▬▬
Bike Trails ▬ ▬ ▬

0   4 mi
0   4 km

E. Dimond Blvd.

8

1

Courtyard by Marriott	**5**
Dimond Center Hotel	**8**
Elderberry Bed & Breakfast	**6**
Lake Hood Inn	**3**
Lakeshore Motor Inn	**2**
Millennium Alaskan Hotel Anchorage	**4**
Residence Inn by Marriott	**7**
Spenard Hostel International	**1**

> Dimond Center Hotel is conveniently located.

Dr. ☎ 800-770-3000 or 907-248-3485. www.lakeshoremotorinn.com. 44 units. Doubles $159 summer; $59 winter. AE, DC, DISC, MC, V.

★★ Millennium Alaskan Hotel Anchorage

AIRPORT This big, full-service hotel with a sportsman's lodge theme sits on the shore of the Lake Spenard floatplane base, convenient to the airport. Rooms along long corridors are large and attractively decorated, but mostly without views. The lobby and restaurant bustle with activity, since the hotel hosts many meetings. 4800 Spenard Rd. ☎ 800-544-0553 or 907-243-2300. www.millenniumhotels.com/anchorage. 248 units. Doubles $239–$319 summer; $99–$145 winter. AE, DC, DISC, MC, V.

★ The Oscar Gill House Bed & Breakfast

DOWNTOWN Friendly Mark and Susan Lutz host in the house they rescued and restored with their own hands—the oldest building in town. Although sized to more modest times, the accommodations are attractive and homey. Breakfast is ample and the hospitality warm and personal. 1344 W. 10th Ave. ☎ 907-279-1344. www.oscargill.com. 3 units. Doubles $115–$135 summer; $75–$85 winter; w/breakfast. AE, MC, V.

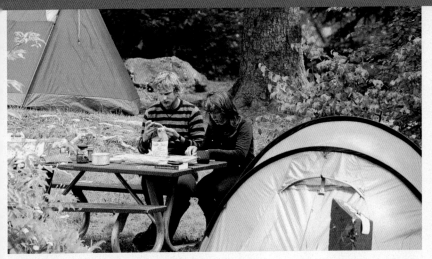

> *Bird Creek Campground is first come, first served.*

★★ kids **Residence Inn by Marriott** MIDTOWN
All units are suites with cooking facilities and sitting areas. Although the hotel lacks character, it is good for families, with a pool and outdoor courts for play, and it stands among trees in a commercial area near groceries and other utilitarian shopping. Rates are for any number of guests. 1025 35th Ave. ☎ 877-729-0197 or 907-729-0197. www.marriott.com/ancri. 148 units. Suites $239–$299 summer; $169–$205 winter; w/breakfast. AE, DC, DISC, MC, V.

Spenard Hostel International AIRPORT
Rather than the gritty and rules-oriented feeling of many hostels, this place feels more like well-kept communal housing, with guests respected and treated to good facilities. 2845 W. 42nd Ave. ☎ 907-248-5036. www.alaskahostel. org. Bunks $25–$27. MC, V.

★★ **Susitna Place** DOWNTOWN
This house overlooking Cook Inlet is within walking distance of downtown. The reasonably priced rooms (all but one cost $140 or less) are comfortable and well kept, and the hosts warm and interesting but not intrusive. 727 N St. ☎ 907-274-3344. www.susitnaplace. com. 9 units. Doubles $105–$195 summer; $65–$115 winter; w/breakfast. AE, DISC, MC, V.

★ **Wildflower Inn** DOWNTOWN
Two-bedroom suites with Mission-style furniture rent for a bargain rate in a cute clapboard house with a picket fence. The downtown core is a half-mile walk, but the bus stops in front and a gourmet deli is across the street. 1239 I St. ☎ 877-693-1239 or 907-274-1239. www.alaska-wildflower-inn.com. 3 units. Doubles $129–$139 summer; $79 winter; w/breakfast. MC, V.

Campgrounds

Anchorage Ship Creek RV Park DOWNTOWN
This is the most central place to park your rig, in a railroad and industrial area that is either a long walk or a short drive from the downtown sights. 150 N. Ingra St. ☎ 800-323-5757. www.bestof alaskatravel.com. 147 sites. Full hookups $46.

Bird Creek Alaska State Parks Campground
SEWARD HIGHWAY This state park campground lies along the surging waters of Turnagain Arm, and right across the road from one of the area's best salmon streams. Sites are nestled among big spruce trees. No reservations, so arrive early on weekends. Mile 101, Seward Highway. No phone. 28 sites. $15 per night.

Eagle River Campground EAGLE RIVER
Fourteen miles north of the city, this state campground, well managed by a contractor, is the closest to town to offer a natural camping experience, among thick trees beside the river. They take reservations and also rent a couple of tents with cots. Hiland Road. ☎ 800-952-8624 or 907-694-7982. www.lifetime adventures.net. 57 sites. DISC, MC, V.

Anchorage Nightlife & Entertainment Best Bets

Best Cocktails
★★ **Club Paris,** 417 W. 5th Ave. (p. 117)

Best Downtown Hangout
★★ **Bernie's Bungalow Lounge,** 626 D St. (p. 117)

Best Club for Dancing
★★ **Chilkoot Charlie's,** Spenard Road and Fireweed Lane (p. 117)

Best Brewpub
★ **Snow Goose Restaurant & Brewery,** 717 W. 3rd Ave. (p. 120)

Best Summer Spectator Sports
★★★ **Alaska League Baseball,** Mulcahy Stadium, 16th Avenue and A Street (p. 120)

Best Winter Spectator Sports
★★ **Alaska Aces Hockey,** Sullivan Arena, 16th Avenue and A Street (p. 120)

Best Winter Festival
★★★ **Anchorage Fur Rendezvous,** (p. 121)

Best Theater Pub
★★★ **Bear Tooth TheatrePub,** 1230 W. 27th Ave. (p. 120)

Best Live Theater
★★ **Cyrano's Off-Center Playhouse,** 4th Avenue and D Street (p. 120)

Best Performance Venue
★★★ **Alaska Center for the Performing Arts,** 631 W. 6th Ave. (p. 119)

Best Live Blues-Rock Club
★★ **Blues Central/Chef's Inn,** 825 W. Northern Lights Blvd. (p. 117)

Best Neighborhood Bar
★ **Darwin's Theory,** 426 G St. (p. 117)

Best Acoustic Music
★★ **Whistling Swan Productions,** www.whistlingswan.net (p. 119)

Best Classical Music
★★ **Anchorage Symphony Orchestra,** 631 W. 6th Ave. (p. 119)

> *One of the "quieter" corners of Chilkoot Charlie's.*

Anchorage Nightlife & Entertainment A to Z

Bars & Nightclubs

★★ Bernie's Bungalow Lounge DOWNTOWN
A hip, arty crowd convenes in the small rooms and the large, hedged backyard, sipping cocktails and attending wine tastings, music events, and parties. 626 D St. ☎ 907-276-8808.

★★ Blues Central/Chef's Inn MIDTOWN
Live music starts nightly at 9:30, with well-known blues acts imported from around the country and up-and-coming rock performers. It's also a steakhouse. 825 W. Northern Lights Blvd. ☎ 907-272-1341.

★★ Chilkoot Charlie's SPENARD
Alaska's largest and most famous club is an adult playground of many stages and dance floors riffing on a dark roadhouse theme. The club rocks hard, but there are quiet spots to steal away in its mazelike confines. Caution as you leave, however, as the area can be rough. Spenard Rd. and Fireweed Lane. ☎ 907-272-1010. www.koots.com.

★★ Club Paris DOWNTOWN
A dark, grown-up bar (and steakhouse) with classic cocktail atmosphere and strong drinks, this is the most authentically Alaskan place in town. 417 W. 5th Ave. ☎ 907-277-6332. www.clubparis.com.

★ Darwin's Theory DOWNTOWN
As unpolished as it is friendly, this little side-street tavern is a great place to meet people. 426 G St. ☎ 907-277-5322.

★ Glacier Brewhouse DOWNTOWN
The brewhouse, also listed under Anchorage Restaurants A to Z, serves excellent beer with a smile. It's on the quiet and genteel side, however, as the food operation dominates. 737 W. 5th Ave. ☎ 907-274-BREW (274-2739). www.glacierbrewhouse.com.

★ Humpy's Great Alaskan Alehouse DOWNTOWN This much-loved downtown bar serves a huge number of Alaska beers on tap, cooks good food, and has a small dance floor with local music most nights. It's got a friendly but boisterous atmosphere. 610 W. 6th Ave. ☎ 907-276-BEER (276-2337). www.humpys.com.

> A hookah at Bernie's Bungalow Lounge.

Anchorage Nightlife & Entertainment

Inset Area

DOWNTOWN
ANCHORAGE

Knik
Arm

E 3rd Ave.
E 5th Ave.
E 6th Ave.

MERRILL
FIELD

Bike Trails
Railway

Tony Knowles
Coastal Trail

W 15th Ave.

E 15th Ave.

FAIRVIEW

14

Sitka
Street
Park

12   **13**

Chester Cr.

Anchor
Park

W Fireweed Ln.   E Fireweed Ln.

W Northern Lights Blvd.

9   **10**

NORTH STAR

11

E Northern Lights Blvd.

Goose
Lake
Park

SPENARD

W Benson Blvd.

E Benson Blvd.

W 36th Ave.

E 36th Ave.

MIDTOWN

TAKU/
CAMPBELL

E Tudor Rd.

Downtown

Knik Arm

Alaska Railroad

Train Station

E 1st Ave.

mud
flats

W 2nd Ave.

1

Buttress Park

W 3rd Ave.

E 3rd Ave.

Elderberry
Park

W 4th Ave.

2

E 4th Ave.

W 5th Ave.

3

6   **7**

E 5th Ave.

Town
Square
Park

4

E 6th Ave.

5

8

W 7th Ave.

W 8th Ave.

E 9th Ave.

W 9th Ave.

W 10th Ave.

Delaney Park

W Dimond Blvd.

W 11th Ave.

Alaska Aces Hockey **13**

Alaska League Baseball **12**

Alaska Center for the Performing Arts **4**

Bear Tooth TheatrePub **9**

Bernie's Bungalow Lounge **8**

Blues Central/Chef's Inn **11**

Carrs/Safeway Great Alaska Shootout **13**

Chilkoot Charlie's **10**

Club Paris **6**

Cyrano's Off-Center Playhouse **7**

Darwin's Theory **2**

Glacier Brewhouse **3**

Humpy's Great Alaskan Ale House **5**

Out North Contemporary Art House **14**

Snow Goose Restaurant & Brewery **1**

> *Ballerinas await their entrance cue at the Alaska Center for the Performing Arts.*

★ **Snow Goose Restaurant & Brewery** DOWN-TOWN This place serves good food, brews good beer, and has a patio with terrific ocean views for sunny days. An attached theater presents visiting musical performers and other shows. 717 W. 3rd Ave. ☎ 907-277-7727. www.alaskabeers.com.

Music

★★ **Anchorage Concert Association** DOWN-TOWN Check the website for this nonprofit promoter's extensive season of traveling Broadway shows, classical music and dance, circus and humor, and some jazz and pop, all at the **Alaska Center for the Performing Arts.** 621 W. 6th Ave. ☎ 907-272-1471. www. anchorageconcerts.org.

★★ **Anchorage Symphony Orchestra** DOWN-TOWN The symphony performs popular clas-sical work and some new pieces with local and imported musicians at the **Alaska Center for the Performing Arts.** 621 W. 6th Ave. ☎ 907-274-8668. www.anchoragesymphony.org.

★★ **Whistling Swan Productions** VARIOUS This family-run operation brings an extensive schedule of folk, traditional, and alternative performers to venues across town, from coffeehouses to concert halls. www. whistlingswan.net.

Performing Arts

★★★ **Alaska Center for the Performing Arts** DOWNTOWN Alaska's premier performance venue has three auditoriums and the city's best ticket agency, called CenterTix. Every-thing goes on here: opera, symphony, theater, dance, country and rock music, magic shows, and comedians. 631 W. 6th Ave. ☎ 907-263-ARTS (263-2787). www.centertix.net.

> *Catch the annual Iditarod start on the first Saturday in March.*

Spectator Sports

★★ Alaska Aces Hockey MIDTOWN
Anchorage's minor-league professional hockey team, one of the best in the national ECHL, generates as much excitement and noise as you'll find in the city on a winter night. Sullivan Arena, 16th Ave. and A St. ☎ 907-258-2237. www.alaskaaces.com.

★★★ Alaska League Baseball MIDTOWN
The Anchorage Glacier Pilots and the Anchorage Bucs field teams of the nation's top college players for games under the midnight sun in an intimate park. Games are almost every day in June and July. Bring a coat for a night game, as it's always cool, and relax with a cold beer. Mulcahy Stadium, 16th Ave. and A St. Pilots ☎ 907-274-3627. www.glacierpilots.com. Bucs ☎ 907-561-BUCS (561-2827). www.anchoragebucs.com.

★★ Carrs/Safeway Great Alaska Shootout
MIDTOWN The University of Alaska Anchorage hosts men's and women's basketball tournaments with NCAA Division I teams over Thanksgiving weekend and the week before. Sullivan Arena, 16th Ave. and A St. ☎ 907-786-1250. www.goseawolves.com.

Theater

★★ Cyrano's Off-Center Playhouse DOWN-
TOWN Local actors bring to life award-winning

> *Margarita and a movie at Bear Tooth TheatrePub.*

★★★ Bear Tooth TheatrePub SPENARD
The theater presents second-run movies that sell out thanks to the terrific food and beer you enjoy while watching, and it occasionally puts on national touring musicians or art films. 1230 W. 27th Ave. ☎ 907-276-4200. www.beartooththeatre.net.

★ Snow Goose Restaurant & Brewery DOWN-
TOWN Besides the bar upstairs, there's a hall frequently used by local and visiting acoustic musicians. 717 W. 3rd Ave. ☎ 907-277-7727. www.alaskabeers.com.

> *An Alaska Goldpanner swings in a late-night game against the Anchorage Glacier Pilots.*

original theater in a performance space so intimate, you feel you've lived through it with them. 4th Ave. and D St. 907-274-2599. www.cyranos.org.

★★ Out North Contemporary Art House

EASTSIDE This theater specializes in the new, avant-garde, and outrageous; the organization also has a film series, an art gallery, and poetry readings. 3800 DeBarr Rd. ☎ 907-279-3800. www.outnorth.org.

Winter Festivals & Fun

★★★ Anchorage Fur Rendezvous DOWN-

TOWN At the end of February and beginning of March the city breaks winter's dreary hold with an explosion of activity, including dog-sled races, fireworks, a snow sculpture contest, arts and craft shows, and the Running of the Reindeer on 4th Avenue, a gentler and funnier version of the running of the bulls in Pamplona, Spain. For information on events, call 907-274-1177 or visit www.furrondy.net.

★★ Iditarod Trail Sled Dog Race DOWNTOWN

Alaska's biggest event of the year begins with a ceremonial start the first Saturday in March,

filling Anchorage with international visitors and excitement. 4th Ave. and D St. ☎ 907-376-5155. www.iditarod.com.

Arts Season vs. Visitor Season

Anchorage has a lively performing arts scene for a town its size (although nothing you'd make the trip for), but all that stuff happens in the wintertime. When the sun is out in the summer, Alaskans take to the mountains, rivers, and beaches, or get to work making money in the visitor or fishing industries. You'll find almost nothing happening in music, theater, or anything else requiring an audience, except for the schlock put on for the tourists. In summer, though, you can still go fishing under the midnight sun, or catch a baseball game, or hoist a glass (well, that you can do almost anytime!). For calendar listings of what's happening when you will be visiting, check the Friday edition of *Anchorage Daily News* or go to www.adn.com/play.

Anchorage Fast Facts

Accommodations Booking Services
Dozens of B&Bs are listed on a website maintained by the cooperative **Anchorage Alaska Bed and Breakfast Association** (www.anchorage-bnb.com). You can search by area of town or by preferred amenities, or browse alphabetically. Links go directly to the B&Bs' own sites. Many have online availability calendars. Those without computer access can call the association's hotline (☎ 888-584-5147 or 907-272-5909), which is answered by hosts at member properties, who offer referrals to places that meet callers' requirements.

ATMs
ATMs are ubiquitous, and you can pay for almost anything with plastic.

Currency Exchange
The only dedicated exchange desk is at a **Wells Fargo** bank branch in the 5th Avenue Mall, 5th Avenue and D Street, ☎ 907-263-2016.

Dentists & Doctors
Alaska Regional Hospital is at 2801 DeBarr Rd., ☎ 907-276-1131, www.alaskaregional.com; and **Providence Alaska Medical Center** is at 3200 Providence Dr., ☎ 907-562-2211, www.providence.org. The hospitals can refer you to an emergency dentist as well.

Emergencies
Dial ☎ **911** from any telephone.

Getting Around
The **People Mover** system makes sense for destinations that are served by direct routes from downtown. As with any city bus system, the buses pick up passengers at marked stops along their routes. Bus fares all over town are $1.75 for adults; $1 for children 5 to 18; 50¢ for seniors 60 and over, people with disabilities, or those carrying a valid Medicare card; free for children 4 and under. Pay the driver, or get change or tokens at the Transit Center at 6th Avenue and G Street. Buses generally come every half-hour; hourly on weekends. Plan your trip to match the schedule. For information, call ☎ 907-343-6543 or log on to www.peoplemover.org. Find the current location of buses at http://bustracker.muni.org/InfoPoint.

If you're driving yourself, always check road reports before taking Alaska highways in winter; in summer, verifying your route can mean avoiding construction delays that can last hours. Call ☎ 511 or go to http://511.alaska.gov for information.

Getting There
BY PLANE Ted Stevens Anchorage International Airport (ANC) is served by most major domestic carriers and receives a few international flights. Rental cars are available on-site, with taxes and fees around a third of the rental cost (you can save by renting off the airport premises). If you don't rent a car or ride a hotel courtesy van, a cab is the best option to get into the city from the airport. The fare downtown is $18 to $20. Use Alaska Yellow Cab, ☎ 907-222-2222. BY TRAIN The Alaska Railroad depot is downtown. BY CAR Only one road connects Anchorage to the outside world—the Glenn Highway, which enters the city at its northeast corner. The Seward Highway connects to the Glenn and runs south to the Kenai Peninsula. The drive to Anchorage from Seattle, the nearest major U.S. city, is 2,500 miles long and can take a week.

Internet Access
Free wireless hotspots are common. The entire airport is a free hotspot. Internet access also is widely available at coffee shops, including downtown at **Kaladi Brothers Coffee,** 6th Avenue and G Street.

Pharmacies
Pharmacies can be found in grocery stores, including the **Carrs/Safeway** store at 1650 W. Northern Lights Blvd., ☎ 907-339-0560. Like other grocery stores in Anchorage, it is open 24 hours; however, the pharmacy is open only until 9pm weekdays, 7pm Saturday and Sunday.

Police
The **Anchorage Police Department** has main offices at 4501 Elmore Rd., south of Tudor Road; for a nonemergency, call ☎ 907-786-8500. For nonemergency police business

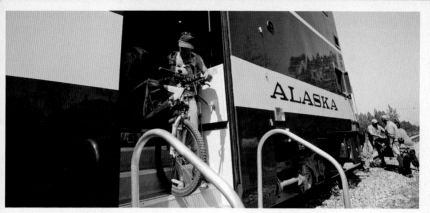

> *The bike-friendly Alaska Railroad has a depot in downtown Anchorage.*

outside the city, call the **Alaska State Troopers,** 5700 E. Tudor Rd. (☎ 907-269-5511). If you have an emergency, dial ☎ **911.**

Post Office
The city has many post offices. The downtown branch is downstairs in the 4th Avenue Market Place at D Street. The post office is open Monday through Friday from 10am to 5:30pm.

Safety
Rates of sexual assault are high in Anchorage and all over Alaska. Women should be careful leaving bars or walking alone in secluded places at night, even when the sun stays up late in the summer.

If you're planning to go skiing, snowmobiling, or hiking in the backcountry, you must be careful to check avalanche conditions. The **Chugach National Forest hotline** (☎ 907-754-2369) offers updated avalanche forecasts, maps, and educational material: www.cnfaic. org.

Taxis
You'll likely get around primarily on foot (if you're downtown) or by rental car (if you're going anyplace else). But should you need a taxi, try **Alaska Yellow Cab** (☎ 907-222-2222). Typically you cannot hail a cab from the street; you need to call one and wait, sometimes 10 minutes or more. Rates are $2 to start the meter and $2.50 per mile. A ride downtown from the airport is $18 to $20.

Telephones
Since practically everyone has a mobile phone, pay telephones are rare, but occasionally you can find one. Insert a quarter and dial the number. Mobile phones and smartphones will work in Anchorage the same as anywhere else in the United States.

Toilets
Public bathrooms are easy to find. They're available anywhere food is sold, including coffee shops, grocery stores, convenience stores, and gas stations, as well as in hotels, shopping malls, museums, office buildings, government buildings, outdoor centers, and other public places. Many restaurants reserve bathrooms for their guests only.

Tours
Gray Line of Alaska offers a bus tour of Anchorage highlights (☎ 800-544-2206; www. graylineofalaska.com), which lasts 3 hours and includes the Anchorage Museum and the Alaska Native Heritage Center. Prices are $49 for adults, half-price for children 12 and under (includes admission to the attractions).

Visitor Information
For general information, get in touch with the **Anchorage Convention & Visitors Bureau,** 524 W. 4th Ave., Anchorage, AK 99501-2212; ☎ 907-276-4118; www.anchorage.net. For outdoors information, contact the **Alaska Public Lands Information Center,** 605 W. 4th Ave., Suite 105, Anchorage, AK 99501; ☎ 866-869-6887 or 907-644-3661; www. alaskacenters.gov.

5
Denali & Mat-Su

My Favorite Denali & Mat-Su Moments

Denali National Park is the real thing. Not an amusement park. Not even a tourist attraction. It's a big swath of the wildest part of North America set aside and managed so that it stays wild. There are no cars, hardly any trails, no shortcuts to "do" the park quickly—not unless you're prepared to miss the main event. Instead, for those who invest the time and a little effort, Denali offers the opportunity to experience the world as it was before humankind dominated Earth. Here, on a short walk from your shuttle bus, you can leave behind everything you know and enter the real Alaska, with nothing between you and the wild.

> PREVIOUS PAGE *Mount McKinley reflected in the placid waters of Wonder Lake.* THIS PAGE *Caribou, which are plentiful in Denali National Park.*

1 Hiking trackless tundra. Even after a lifetime of visits, it's still exhilarating to climb down the steps of a shuttle bus into the real Denali, where a few strides over the tundra erase the world of man-made things. That moment, and the rest of the day spent walking off-trail, creates a special sense of freedom—and of humility. Start your adventure anywhere between the **Toklat River** and **Highway Pass.** See p. 148, **8**-**9**.

2 Encountering a grizzly bear. Because **Denali National Park** blocks private vehicles

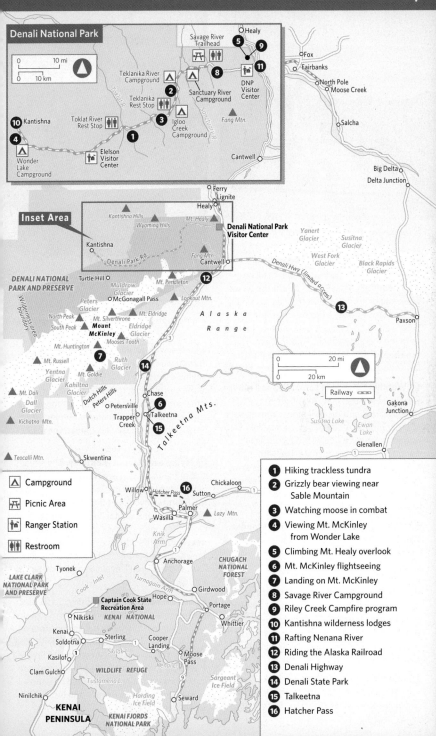

Denali National Park

0   10 mi
0   10 km

Healy
Savage River Trailhead
5
9
Fox
Fairbanks
8
North Pole
Moose Creek
Teklanika River Campground
2
DNP Visitor Center
11
Teklanika Rest Stop
Sanctuary River Campground
Salcha
10 Kantishna
Toklat River Rest Stop
3
Igloo Creek Campground
Fang Mtn.
1
Elelson Visitor Center
Cantwell
Big Delta
4
Wonder Lake Campground
Delta Junction

Inset Area

Ferry
Lignite
Healy
Kantishna Hills
Mt. Healy
Denali National Park Visitor Center
Yanert Glacier
Susitna Glacier
Wyoming Hills
Kantishna
West Fork Glacier
Black Rapids Glacier
Denali Park Rd.
Fang Mtn.
Cantwell
Denali Hwy (limited access)

DENALI NATIONAL PARK AND PRESERVE
Turtle Hill
Mt. Pendleton
12
Muldrow Glacier
13
Peters Glacier
McGonagall Pass
Lookout Mtn.
Paxson
North Peak
Mt. Silverthrone
Mt. Eldridge
A l a s k a
R a n g e
South Peak
Mount McKinley
Eldridge Glacier
Mooses Tooth
Mt. Huntington
7
Ruth Glacier
Gakona Junction
Mt. Russell
Mt. Goldie
14
Yentna Glacier
Kahiltna Glacier
Dutch Hills
Chase
Mt. Dall
Peters Hills
Petersville
6
Susitna Lake
Ewan Lake
Dall Glacier
Trapper Creek
Talkeetna
15
Kichatna Mtn.
T a l k e e t n a   M t s.
Glenallen
Teocalli Mtn.
Skwentina

0   20 mi
0   20 km

Railway

Wilderness area boundary

Campground
Picnic Area
Ranger Station
Restroom

Chickaloon
Willow
16
Sutton
Hatcher Pass
Palmer
Wasilla
Lazy Mtn.
Knik Arm
Tyonek
LAKE CLARK NATIONAL PARK AND PRESERVE
Anchorage
CHUGACH NATIONAL FOREST
Cook Inlet
Turnagain Arm
Girdwood
Hope
Portage
Captain Cook State Recreation Area
Whittier
Nikiski
KENAI NATIONAL
Kenai
Soldotna
Sterling
Cooper Landing
Kasilof
Skilak L.
Moose Pass
Clam Gulch
WILDLIFE REFUGE
Tustumena L.
Sargeant Ice Field
Ninilchik
KENAI PENINSULA
Harding Ice Field
KENAI FJORDS NATIONAL PARK
Seward

1 Hiking trackless tundra
2 Grizzly bear viewing near Sable Mountain
3 Watching moose in combat
4 Viewing Mt. McKinley from Wonder Lake
5 Climbing Mt. Healy overlook
6 Mt. McKinley flightseeing
7 Landing on Mt. McKinley
8 Savage River Campground
9 Riley Creek Campfire program
10 Kantishna wilderness lodges
11 Rafting Nenana River
12 Riding the Alaska Railroad
13 Denali Highway
14 Denali State Park
15 Talkeetna
16 Hatcher Pass

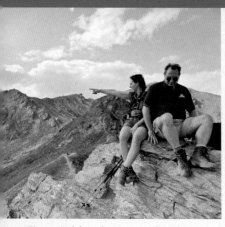

> *The overlook from the Mount Healy trail.*

> *Rafting class III and IV rapids on the Nenana River.*

from venturing much farther than the entrance, the wildlife within the park still behaves naturally. Passengers on shuttle buses often see bears without ever disembarking. On one visit I made, a mother bear and two cubs walked up to investigate the bus, looking us in the eye as we peered out at them. The area near **Sable Mountain Pass** is a particularly good spot for bear viewing. See p. 148, ⑥.

❸ **Watching moose in combat on red tundra.** Fall starts in August at Denali, when the tundra turns rust and the bull moose make use of their antlers. A pair of muscled bulls, 1,500 pounds apiece, collide with a terrific *crack,* fighting for the right to mate. I've witnessed this in **Denali National Park,** just yards away from one of the park shuttle buses. Watch for them along the Park Road, between miles 1 and 3. See p. 31, ⑥.

❹ **Viewing Mount McKinley from Wonder Lake.** North America's tallest peak is awesome from many vantages—we can see it clearly from Anchorage—but no perspective is lovelier than the one from across Wonder Lake, 90 miles from the park entrance. Visitors camp or stay at a Kantishna wilderness lodge (p. 166) to be here in the morning before the clouds form, when the white triangle of the mountain seems to fill half the sky, although it's still 27 miles away. See p. 151, ⑭.

❺ **Climbing Mount Healy Overlook.** Arriving at Denali National Park can be frustrating: You'd like to head into the park, but you must first deal with getting bus tickets and waiting your turn to climb aboard. But from right behind the visitor center, a trail leads up one of the surrounding mountains. A few minutes later, you're on your own in fresh mountain air with a series of spectacular, sweeping views. Frustrations magically disappear. See p. 135, ⑧.

❻ **Flying over Mount McKinley.** The sheer size of the mountain is difficult to grasp. One of its creases, the Ruth Gorge, is deeper than the Grand Canyon, and that's just from rim to ice surface—the ice itself is 4,000 feet deep. Only after one has flown among the massive ridges and cliffs does the mind begin to grasp the immensity of this feature, probably the largest object you'll ever see on Earth. See p. 130, ❶.

❼ **Landing on Mount McKinley.** Some bush pilots, mostly those who fly in from Talkeetna with mountain climbers, will land visitors on a glacier on the flank of Mount McKinley using aircraft with skis. It's an environment few will ever experience—searingly bright, intoxicatingly fresh and pure, surrounded by impossibly huge mountain terrain, and incredibly alone. See p. 172, ❷.

> *The Denali Star, Alaska Railroad's flagship train, crosses a gulch near the national park.*

8 Waking in a tent. Your body is warm, snuggled down in the sleeping bag, but your face can feel the cool morning air, your ears can hear the birds singing and a nearby stream tumbling, and your nose detects the mixed scents of last night's campfire and the morning's dew on delicate subarctic vegetation. You have slept in Denali National Park and are awakening as no hotel visitor can. Give the **Savage River Campground** a try. See p. 169.

9 Attending a campfire program. National parks were made for families, and I recall few moments of family entertainment more satisfying than sitting around a campfire at a spot like **Riley Creek Campground** for a rousing ranger program with my children before walking back to the tent in the cool twilight. If you want your kids to learn that they can live without electronics, this is how to do it. See p. 154, **3**.

10 Settling in at a wilderness lodge. Deep in the backcountry, a collection of wilderness lodges in an area called **Kantishna** allow the lucky few to sleep within Denali in beds and explore the park with guides. Guests experience the national park at their doorstep rather than on a long bus ride. See p. 166.

11 Rafting the Nenana River. The gray water, heavy with glacier silt, boils and froths as it rushes between the steep rock walls of the Nenana Canyon, just outside the park. It's a ferocious raft ride, with waves that wet passengers from head to toe. See p. 135, **7**.

12 Riding the Alaska Railroad. The scenery opens slowly, grandly, and without signs of humanity as the train works its way north from Anchorage to Denali National Park. Inside, travelers dine around white-clothed tables or sit below dome windows; outside, on balconies at the end of some cars, they feel the air rush by and watch for wildlife. See p. 151.

13 Exploring the Denali Highway. Nature didn't draw the line around Denali National Park, and many areas in the region are just as scenic and rich with wildlife as the park itself. The partially paved Denali Highway, which runs through the Alaska Range east of the park, is a rough but free access route into this wild country—no permit necessary. See p. 142, **15**.

14 Canoeing at Denali State Park. The state park, south of Denali National Park, has some of the best views of Mount McKinley and is more casual and easier to manage—for example, by stopping at a canoe rental shop and launching on **Byers Lake.** See p. 141, **9**.

15 Meeting the locals in Talkeetna. The whole main street of this funny little gold-rush town is a national historic landmark. On a summer day, international mountain climbers lounge outside the town's bars, artists create and sell their work in front of their cabins, boaters and rafters launch on the river, and airplanes lift for the glaciers of Mount McKinley. See p. 172.

16 Rambling in Hatcher Pass. A mountain road climbs and twists upward before emerging in a broad alpine valley high above the Mat-Su area. After a fascinating visit to the well-preserved old gold mine, the opportunities for beautiful hikes on trails or over the tundra are limitless. See p. 141, **6**.

Denali & Talkeetna in 3 Days

Because of Denali National Park's remoteness, size, and access restrictions, visiting the park is impractical for most visitors without spending two nights near the park entrance, and three days only begin to offer some breathing room. Don't go to Denali for a quick survey of the highlights— you'll be wasting your time. The tour I've outlined here will get you into the core of the park, with a good chance of observing wildlife and having a true wilderness experience. After all, that's what Denali is all about.

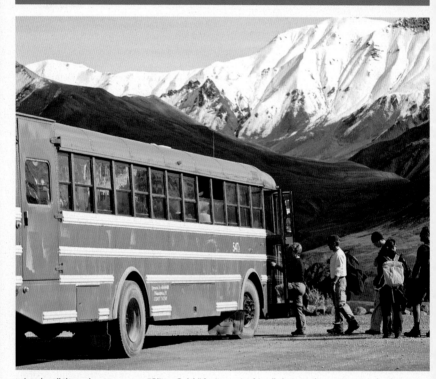

> Locals call the park entrance area "Glitter Gulch" for its tourist-friendly but not always attractive development.

START Talkeetna, 119 miles from Anchorage on the Glenn, Parks, and Talkeetna Spur highways. TRIP LENGTH 286 miles.

❶ ★★★ Talkeetna Air Taxi flightseeing trip over Mount McKinley. Climbers assaulting Mount McKinley fly from the airstrip in Talkeetna to the Kahiltna Glacier on the

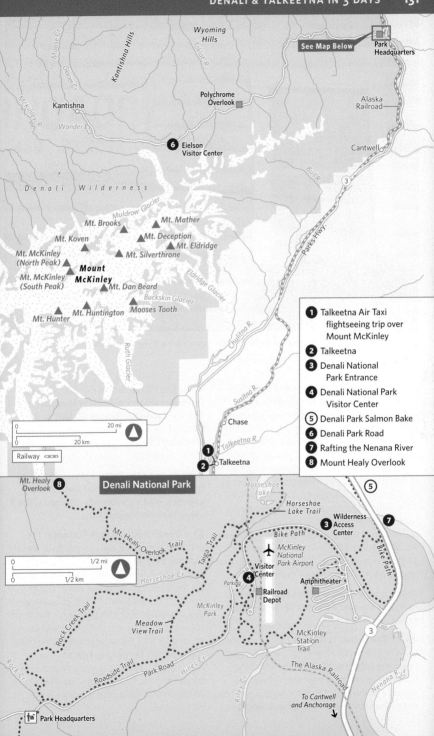

Moose Cr.

Glacier Cr.

Kantishna Hills

Wyoming Hills

Toklat R.

See Map Below

Park Headquarters

McKinley R.

Kantishna

Wonder L.

Polychrome Overlook

Alaska Railroad

Cantwell

6 Eielson Visitor Center

Denali Wilderness

Muldrow Glacier

Mt. Brooks

Mt. Mather

Mt. Koven

Mt. Deception

Mt. Eldridge

Mt. McKinley (North Peak)

Mt. Silverthrone

Mount McKinley

Mt. McKinley (South Peak)

Mt. Dan Beard

Eldridge Glacier

Buckskin Glacier

Mt. Hunter

Mt. Huntington

Mooses Tooth

Bull R.

Parks Hwy.

Chulitna R.

3

Ruth Glacier

Susitna R.

0 — 20 mi
0 — 20 km

Railway ▭▭

Chase

Talkeetna R.

1
2 Talkeetna

1 Talkeetna Air Taxi flightseeing trip over Mount McKinley

2 Talkeetna

3 Denali National Park Entrance

4 Denali National Park Visitor Center

5 Denali Park Salmon Bake

6 Denali Park Road

7 Rafting the Nenana River

8 Mount Healy Overlook

Mt. Healy Overlook 8

Denali National Park

Horseshoe Lake

5

Horseshoe Lake Trail

Mt. Healy Overlook Trail

Taiga Trail

Bike Path

3 Wilderness Access Center

7

Horseshoe Cr.

McKinley National Park Airport

✈

Parking

Visitor Center
4

Amphitheater

Bike Path

0 — 1/2 mi
0 — 1/2 km

Rock Creek Trail

Meadow View Trail

McKinley Park

Railroad Depot

Roadside Trail

Park Road

Hines Cr.

Riley Cr.

McKinley Station Trail

McKinley Park

3

The Alaska Railroad

Rock Cr.

🚻 Park Headquarters

To Cantwell and Anchorage
↓

Nenana R.

> *The historic Roadhouse welcomes visitors to Talkeetna's downtown with local brews and fresh-baked cookies.*

mountain's flank, and visitors can use the same flight services for the mind-blowing experience of soaring through the mountain's immense folds and below its miles-high cliffs. Nothing you'll do in Alaska will impress you more. Take the longest flight you can afford and, best of all, add on a glacier landing; the moment you step out of the plane and appreciate the size of everything, the awe you feel is magnified. Get an early start for the best chance of good viewing, since clouds pile up on the mountain as the day goes on. ⏱ At least 1 hr. ☎ 800-533-2219. www.talkeetnaair.com. $190 per person for 1 hr., $280 for 1½ hr.; glacier landing adds $75 and 30 min. to any flight.

Before driving onward to Denali National Park, you can spend the rest of the morning exploring:

❷ ★★ **Talkeetna.** This small, funky gold-rush town is well worth a morning spent taking in the scene—the mountain climbers waiting for their flights, the artists selling their creations, and the quaint, historic buildings. The entire downtown is on the National Register of Historic Places. Definitely stop in at the **Talkeetna Historical Society Museum** (p. 174, ❸); the **Talkeetna Ranger Station** (p. 174, ❹); and the town cemetery, with its **Mount McKinley Climbers' Memorial** (p. 175, ❺). ⏱ 3 hr. See p. 172.

Drive north on the Parks Highway 154 miles from Talkeetna to the Denali National Park entrance, arriving in the late afternoon. You'll spend the next 2 nights here.

❸ ★ **Denali National Park Entrance.** The entrance area sits at the eastern tip of Denali National Park, near Broad Pass, where the highway and rail line cross the Alaska Range. It's there because of access alone, not because it's the area you come to the park to see. Indeed, Mount McKinley is farther from the entrance than from Talkeetna. But by keeping all park development here, the U.S. National Park Service has kept the heart of the park wild. And this is a good place to learn about the park, to enjoy activities like rafting, and to arrange for further excursions into the park proper.

> *Life-size wildlife dioramas occupy an environmentally conscious building at the park visitor center.*

Once you arrive in the afternoon, your first task is to pick up tickets for the Denali shuttle bus or a tour bus, as you can't drive into the park (for more information, see "The Very Most Important Facts About a Denali Visit," on p. 143). ⏱ 1 hr. Mile 1, Denali National Park Road. Mar–Sept daily 5am–7pm (reservation desks open at 7am); closed Oct–Apr.

❹ ★★ kids **Denali National Park Visitor Center.** If time remains on the first day, visit this beautiful, environmentally innovative building, which is a fascinating and appropriately impressive museum of the park. Huge murals, life-size wildlife recreations, and even the carpet are designed to bring the outdoors inside. Cultural exhibits cover the Athabascan people, mining, tourism, and scientific research. Catch the award-winning 18-minute film *Heartbeats of Denali*. ⏱ 1 hr. Free admission. Mar–Sept daily 8am–6pm; closed Oct–Apr.

⑤ 🍴 **Denali Park Salmon Bake.** You've had a long day, and it's time to relax. Whether you choose to eat here or not, you can kick up your heels with a hot live band and catch the energy of the midnight sun with the area's summertime group of young people. Mile 238.5, Parks Hwy. ☎ 907-683-2733. $$. See p. 170.

On Day 2, get as early a start as possible for your shuttle ride into the park proper. Animals are more active, and Mount McKinley is less likely to be socked in by clouds, in the morning.

Going by Rail

Driving a car rented in Anchorage is the easiest and least expensive way to travel to Talkeetna and Denali National Park. But you can also get there on the **Alaska Railroad,** which adds an element of romance and relaxation to the trip. The downside is that you must allow more time and adjust where you will go, as trains are slow and run only once a day in each direction. But if you'd rather ride the rails than rent a car, see "Denali by Rail" on p. 151.

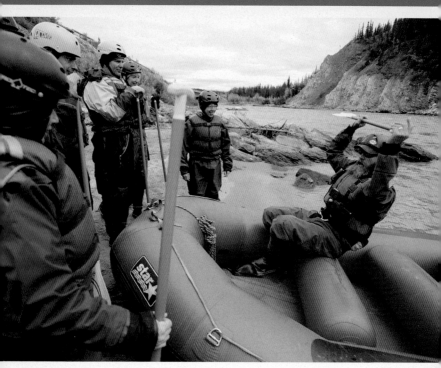

> *The minimum age for riding the more challenging lower portion of Nenana Canyon is 12; the upper portion is better for younger rafters.*

6 ★★★ **Denali Park Road.** The bus ride on the 90-mile Denali National Park Road is the centerpiece of a trip to the park. Your chances are good of seeing bears, caribou, or moose, and you might glimpse wolves or mountain goats. The scenery unfolds as you ride, and if you don't want to follow along with a map or book, you don't have to—you can just let it unfold around you. However, I've put together a mile-by-mile

Timing It Right

Denali National Park is completely seasonal—almost no one is there from October through mid-May. This chapter covers the summertime. You can assume anything mentioned here is closed in the winter, unless noted otherwise. Exceptions include cross-country skiing at **Hatcher Pass** (p. 141) and the **Iditarod Trail Sled Dog Race** (see "Going to Extremes," on p. 94).

road guide—"The Best of the Denali Park Road," beginning on p. 146—covering what you'll encounter, some good places to get off on the way, and what to bring.

There are several different buses you can take, but with a single day for the experience, I recommend the park shuttle bus. It provides the opportunity for a wilderness dayhike while still allowing you to see everything a tour bus would offer. After getting off at the wilderness spot of your choice, you can always catch another bus going back the other way. For more information, see "Denali Bus Choices" on p. 149.

When taking the shuttle bus, you can choose your destination according to your stamina and interests: The **Toklat River** (p. 148, **8**) is one of the best areas for level walking. If you travel to **Thorofare Pass** (p. 149, **11**) or the **Eielson Visitor Center** (p. 149, **12**), you may spy Mount McKinley, if weather permits. If you go all the way to the **Kantishna** area

(p. 151, **15**), you'll see pretty much everything, but you'll have spent 12 hours on the road.

Regardless of your choices, you'll spend the whole day in the park backcountry and sleep well when you return to your room. ☺ **Full day.**

On Day 3, have fun along the park's boundary. Take the free shuttle service to the launch point for the rafting trip.

❼ ★★ Rafting the Nenana River. Ride the Nenana River as it passes by the park, frothing wildly through a steep-walled canyon with class III and IV rapids. Everyone on the raft gets soaked with the silty gray water. Although operators dress everyone in rain gear or dry suits, it's a good idea to plan for a shower afterward, to get the silt out of your hair. A variety of companies offer these floats, charging $80 to $120, but I recommend the folks at the **Denali Outdoor Center,** with locations among the big hotels—at Mile 238.9, Parks Highway, and at Mile .5, Otto Lake Road, in Healy (☎ 888-303-1925; www.denali outdoorcenter.com). Despite the popularity of the outing, however, don't discount the risks; with children or your own doubts, choose to

raft the scenic and calmer upper portion of the river, or take a relaxed rafting trip in Talkeetna (p. 175, **❼**). ☺ **2½ hr.**

From the Nenana Canyon area, drive south less than a mile to enter the park; the visitor center is about a mile ahead on the right. The trailhead is behind the visitor center; take the Taiga Trail less than half a mile to the Mount Healy Overlook trail.

❽ ★★ Mount Healy Overlook. The trail rises quickly from the wooded park entrance area to break above the tree line, with a broad view of expansive, unpopulated land. Surrounded by the fresh air and extraordinary vista, you feel your head suddenly clear from the activity of the buses and crowds. The entire hike is a strenuous 5-mile round trip, but you can climb to good views in less than an hour. ☺ **Half-day** for the full hike. Trailhead is less than .5 mile along the Taiga Trail, which starts behind the visitor center.

McKinley or Denali?

The Alaska Native people of Interior Alaska, the Athabascans, called the tallest mountain Denali, meaning "the great one" or "the high one," and the Russian owners of Alaska marked it on an 1839 map with a name close to that. But after the United States bought Alaska, an American gold prospector "discovered" the mountain in 1896 and named it for the Republican party's presidential candidate, William McKinley.

Alaskans have pushed for many years to restore the name Denali to the mountain. In 1980, when Congress expanded the park, Alaskans won a name change from McKinley to Denali National Park. But since the 1970s, Ohio members of the House of Representatives have blocked changing the name of North America's tallest mountain. Why? McKinley was an Ohioan.

Whatever the law says, however, Denali is the more common name in Alaska—not Mount Denali or Denali Peak, just Denali.

Denali in Winter

The Denali region is spectacular in winter, not to mention spectacularly cold. Virtually all visitor facilities close, and venturing into the park proper is only for serious outdoors types who have well-developed winter skills. With the Park Road snowed in, the only way to get around the backcountry is by ski, snowshoe, or dog sled. But there is a pleasant way for visitors to see the unbelievable beauty of this country in deep snow and orange winter light: aboard an **Alaska Railroad** train. A single train with just a passenger car and a dining car runs from Anchorage to Fairbanks each Saturday, returning on Sunday. It's a whistle-stop train, perhaps the last of its kind in America, offering essential transportation for latter-day pioneers who live in the wilderness along the tracks. Meeting those folks is a part of the uniquely authentic Alaskan experience. The ride takes 12 hours; one-way tickets are $150 for adults and $75 children. For more information, contact the Alaska Railroad (☎ 800-544-0552 or 907-265-2494; www.alaska railroad.com).

Denali & Mat-Su in 1 Week

With a week to spend at Denali and its environs, you have the time to dig in and get to know some of your favorite places. That time is best spent within the park, where avid outdoors people would be happy to spend the entire week hiking or backpacking. But I've designed this tour to include stops at attractions in the Matanuska and Susitna valleys, universally known as Mat-Su, as they provide a broader picture of what you can experience on a relatively relaxed tour. You'll need to rent a car that you can take off paved roads. See "Driving Off-Pavement,"on p. 194 and "Renting the Right Car for Going Off-Pavement," on p. 509.

> *A farm for musk oxen, an ancient species of arctic mammal, is nestled in the Matanuska Valley, outside of Palmer.*

START Palmer, 40 miles north from Anchorage on the Parks and Glenn highways. **TRIP LENGTH** 775 miles.

❶ ★ Palmer. During the Great Depression, Dust Bowl farmers were moved to the fertile Matanuska Valley, which surrounds this windswept town. It has the feel of a community in farming country, with serrated mountains that ring the valley. Small-scale farming still goes on here, producing vegetables for Anchorage. The long, cool days and rich soil are perfect for root vegetables and broccoli, cabbage, and the like, which grow to world-record size (see "Land of Giants," on p. 138). ⏱ 30 min. See p. 48, ❶).

1 Palmer
2 Musk Ox Farm
3 Vagabond Blues
4 Wasilla
5 Independence Mine State Historical Park
6 Hatcher Pass Lodge
7 Talkeetna
8 Talkeetna Air Taxi flightseeing trip over
   Mount McKinley

9 Denali State Park
10 Wilderness Access Center &
   Denali National Park Visitor Center
11 Denali National Park Tundra Wildlife Tour
12 Cabin Nite Dinner Theater
13 Denali National Park wilderness experience
14 Denali National Park entrance activities
15 Denali Highway

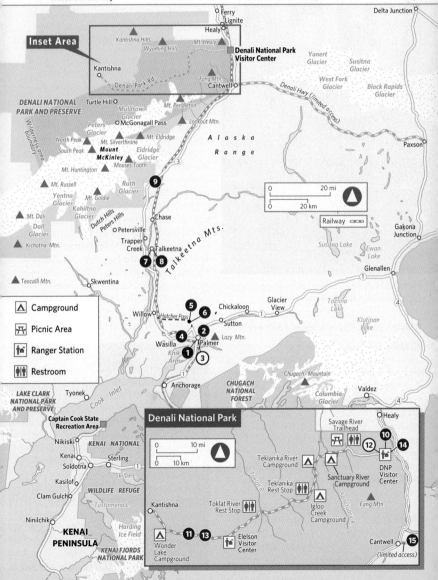

> *A faded plaque on a retired boxcar at the Museum of Alaska Transportation and Industry.*

Take the Glenn Highway about 1 mile north to:

❷ Musk Ox Farm. Just north of town, on the Glenn Highway, you can visit one of the oddest agricultural outfits you'll ever come across: the Musk Ox Farm, home to shaggy animals that look like they're from another planet. Wandering the Arctic tundra, they shed so much warm, soft fuzz that Alaska Natives learned to collect the stuff for knitting. The farm here supplies this wool, called *qiviut,* so knitters in the **Oomingmak Musk Ox Producers' Co-operative** can make it into exquisite hats and scarves (p. 99). Stop in to see the animals up close. ⏱ 1 hr. Glenn Hwy. just north of Palmer. ☎ 907-745-4151. www.muskoxfarm. org. Admission $8 adults, $7 seniors, $6 children 5–12, free for children 4 and under. Summer daily 10am–6pm; closed winter.

③ 🍺 **Vagabond Blues.** There are a number of signs of intelligent life in Palmer, and this hip coffeehouse is among the preeminent. Stop in for excellent light food at breakfast, lunch, or dinner. The live music sometimes features imported national folk artists. 642 S. Alaska St. ☎ 907-745-2233. $.

In the afternoon, take the Glenn Highway 1 mile north to Palmer-Fishhook Road. It will eventually turn into Trunk Road and then Bogard Road, bringing you to Wasilla, which is 14 miles west.

❹ Wasilla. Thanks to an anything-goes attitude toward community planning, the hometown of former governor Sarah Palin is among Alaska's least appealing communities. As a bedroom community to Anchorage, it transformed in a few decades from farms to shopping centers; it looks like one big highway frontage road. Palin's house is on Lake Lucille, which you can access at the **Best Western Lake Lucille Inn** (p. 139).

One interesting spot reflecting the pioneer spirit of the area lies just beyond town, northbound (west by the compass) at mile 47 on the Parks Highway: the **Museum of Alaska Transportation and Industry** (3800 W. Museum Dr.; ☎ 907-376-1211; www.museum ofalaska.org). Volunteers have mounted exhibits of 14 airplanes, 13 firetrucks, 7 locomotives, 2 steam cranes, and various other machines. This place is heaven for certain

Land of Giants

The **Alaska State Fair** (☎ 907-745-4827; www.alaskastatefair.org), held in late August and early September over the 10 days leading up to and including Labor Day, is the area's biggest annual to-do. It features music, rides, booths, contests—everything you'd expect at a rural fair—with one unique added attraction: weirdly huge vegetables. The climate and long summer days of the Matanuska Valley create perfect conditions for enormous cabbages and other similar vegetables, such as Brussels sprouts, turnips, or kale (oh, yum!). Just imagine a 42-pound beet. The fairgrounds are along the Glenn Highway, just south of Palmer.

> *Old ore car tracks still cross a wooden trestle overlooking Independence Mine State Historical Park in Hatcher Pass.*

guys and gals. You know the type: They like to fix machines, polish them up, and make them better than new—and the more complicated and obsolete the device, the better. Both the exhibits and the people add to the charm. The museum is open daily from 10am to 5pm May through September, and the rest of the year by appointment. Admission is $8 for adults; $5 for students, seniors, and military; and $18 for families. ⏱ **2 hr.**

From Wasilla, take Main Street, which soon becomes Wasilla-Fishhook Road, 11 miles north from the intersection with the Parks Highway. Bear left and drive another 11 miles as it continues under various names, mainly Hatcher Pass Road.

Not Interested in Wasilla?

Let's face it: The main reason to visit Wasilla is if you're interested in seeing the hometown of former vice presidential candidate and current conservative commentator Sarah Palin. If you'd rather skip Wasilla (a reasonable decision), continue on Palmer-Fishhook Road directly to ➏ Hatcher Pass.

➎ ★★ kids **Independence Mine State Historical Park.** Within Hatcher Pass's treeless valley, you'll find a well-preserved hard-rock gold mine open for tours. A few buildings have been restored, and you can take a self-guided tour or join a group led by a ranger. The paved trails are easily navigable by just about anyone, and the rugged half-mile Mill Trail leads up to some

An Alternative Plan

Not everyone wants to rough it, staying in a cabin at the end of an unpaved road, so here are two options for those who'd prefer a motel. Either backtrack to Wasilla and then drive north to Talkeetna (total trip: 93 miles), or spend the night in Wasilla at the **Best Western Lake Lucille Inn,** 1300 W. Lake Lucille Dr. (☎ 800-528-1234; www.best westernlakelucilleinn.com; 54 units; doubles $189–$224; AE, DC, DISC, MC, V). This hotel, on the same lake as former governor Sarah Palin's house, offers the best standard rooms in the valley, with good views, flightseeing trips, and self-guided canoeing offered from the dock below the lawn.

> *An air taxi can get you up close and personal with the crown jewel of the Alaska Range, Mount McKinley.*

picturesque ruins. Besides this interesting and photogenic site, the valley and surrounding mountains are a hiker's paradise, and even those who don't want to hike can enjoy walking over the tundra. Ask at the visitor center about longer routes. In winter the historical site is closed, but the park remains open for skiing, with both groomed loops for cross-country and limitless backcountry terrain (but check for avalanche conditions—see the Safety section of "Denali & Mat-Su Fast Facts," on p. 178). ⏲ 2 hr. ☎ 907-745-2827 or 907-745-3975. www. alaskastateparks.org. $5 day-use fee per vehicle. Afternoon guided tours, additional $5 per person. Visitor center open summer daily 10am–7pm; closed winter.

At the end of your first day, you'll spend the night at:

❻ ★★ kids **Hatcher Pass Lodge.** Up in the mountains, a mile from the mine, the Hatcher Pass Lodge is one of my favorite places to stay

with my family, and we've had several memorable skiing vacations here. The cabins lack running water, TVs, and phones—it's a true backcountry experience—but the lodge serves good meals, and the world outside your door is ample entertainment. In my opinion, this is the best place to stay in the area. If you'd rather overnight in a more traditional spot, see "An Alternative Plan," below. ⏲ Overnight. Hatcher Pass. ☎ 907-745-5897. www. hatcherpasslodge.com. 9 cabins, 3 lodge rooms. Doubles $100–$165. AE, DC, DISC, MC, V.

On the morning of Day 2, you could return to Wasilla and take the Parks Highway to Talkeetna. Or take Hatcher Pass Road 30 miles west (an hour's drive) to the Parks Highway at Willow; this mountain route is unpaved, open in summer only, and potentially unsuitable for your rental car, but it is lovely. From Willow it is 43 miles to Talkeetna, where you'll spend the night.

7 ★★ **Talkeetna.** This is a day to enjoy the charm of a backwoods gold-rush town that was adopted by mountain climbers and other outdoorsy folk. Stop in at Denali National Park's **Talkeetna Ranger Station** (p. 174, **4**) to learn about those who climb Mount McKinley.

Talkeetna's whole main street is on the National Register of Historic Places. It's a frontier town from a century ago. The best place to learn about the facts and the spirit behind the town's story is the **Talkeetna Historical Society Museum** (p. 174, **3**). Among my favorite small-town museums, this place truly reflects the funky spirit of Talkeetna while also telling its story clearly.

Save the last half of the day to get out on one of the major rivers that meet at Talkeetna. Steve Mahay has for decades navigated these fast-flowing glacial waters in powerful jet boats. Guests on **Mahay's Riverboat Service** (p. 175, **6**) go on thrilling tours in comfortable, enclosed boats. ⏱ Half-day. See p. 172.

Get an early start on Day 3 to go:

8 ★★★ **Talkeetna Air Taxi flightseeing trip over Mount McKinley.** Take one of the planes that fly climbers to Mount McKinley, for a tour through the vertical white kingdom of North America's highest mountain, including a landing on a high-altitude glacier. I can recommend nothing more impressive in all of Alaska.

Since you have an entire week for your Denali trip, you can arrange your schedule to optimize conditions for this, your best outing. Alaskans learn to organize their lives around sunny days. Predictions are often inaccurate here, so regardless of what the weatherman says, if you have clear skies, take your flight right away, even if you have to change other plans. If it's cloudy and dull, try to wait a day; bright, clear light will make an enormous difference in what you see. ⏱ 2 hr. See p. 130, **1**.

After your flight, take the Parks Highway 64 miles north to:

9 ★★ kids **Denali State Park.** Don't confuse this low-key state park with its similarly named neighbor. It's easy to zoom through this park along the highway south of the national park, but stopping is well worth your time. Mount McKinley is as close as it gets on any road, and the views from the south are dramatic. Check

> *The Talkeetna Ranger Station, the base for park management of McKinley climbers.*

out the several developed vantage points, some of which have campgrounds and trails. Definitely stop at **Byers Lake** to visit the peaceful Veterans Memorial and take a paddle in a canoe or kayak rented from **Denali Southside River Guides** (☎ 877-425-7238; www.denali riverguides.com), which also offers guided fly-fishing during the summer. A 2½-hour paddle costs $79 per person. An excellent campground and a couple of hiking trails are here as well. ⏱ 3 hr. Parks Highway, miles 135 to 164. Free admission. Park always open.

Continue 90 miles north to the entrance of Denali National Park, where you'll spend the next 4 nights. It will likely be late in the day, but pay a visit to the:

10 ★★ **Wilderness Access Center & Denali National Park Visitor Center.** The Wilderness Access Center is where you'll get tickets for the park buses (you can't drive into the park),

> *A visitor takes in the view from mile 53 of the Park Road, near the Toklat River.*

and the visitor center has ingenious and informative exhibits that explain the park's science, nature, and culture. ⏱ 1 hr. for both. See p. 132, ❸ and p. 133, ❹.

Park wildlife viewing and weather are best in the morning, so get an early start on Day 4.

⓫ ★★★ **Denali National Park Tundra Wildlife Tour.** This narrated ride is the perfect introduction to the park. ⏱ 1 day. See "Denali Bus Choices" on p. 149.

⓬ 🍷 **Cabin Nite Dinner Theater.** After a day sitting on the bus, you may enjoy spending a lively evening taking in a fun, corny, musical revue put on by one of the big cruise-line hotels. See p. 170.

Get up early again on Day 5 for another bus trip into the park.

⓭ ★★★ **Denali National Park wilderness experience.** On your second full day at Denali, take the shuttle bus into the park. Buy a ticket to go as far as Eielson Visitor Center, at mile 66 on the Park Road, but get off wherever you like for your hike. The **Toklat River** area (p. 148, ❽) is one of the best for level walking, and **Igloo Mountain** (p. 148, ❺) is a popular climb. For more suggestions, check out the tour described in "The Best of the Denali Park Road," starting on p. 146.

Basically, you can hike anywhere (although you won't be let off the bus when wildlife are close by, for obvious reasons). There's always another bus going back the other way when you're ready to return. Spend the whole day and sleep well tonight. If you feel uncomfortable heading off on your own from the shuttle, consider joining a ranger-led **Discovery Hike** (p. 160). ⏱ 1 day. See "Denali Bus Choices," on p. 149.

You've had 2 very full days at Denali—on Day 6, you can either take another shuttle bus trip into the park, or you can partake of the activities offered around the park entrance.

⓮ ★★ kids **Denali National Park entrance activities.** You can white-water raft, hike, or check out a dog-sled demonstration, among many other options. See "The Best Denali Adventures," starting on p. 158. ⏱ 1 day.

Spend your final day exploring the remote and beautiful Denali Highway, which runs 133 miles east to the tiny town of Paxson. Take the Parks Highway 27 miles south to Cantwell and turn left onto the highway.

SITE GUIDE PAGE 145

⓯ ★★ **Denali Highway.** The scenery along this partly unpaved road over the Alaska Range is at least as impressive as what you encounter inside the park, but here access is uncontrolled and the land is open to casual exploration. The expansive alpine views make wildlife sightings likely, and I find it hard to resist hopping out of the car for a ramble over the tundra. Just be prepared before you go—you'll need a rental car that you can take off paved roads, and you should be sure you're well stocked with supplies, as you won't find much along the way.

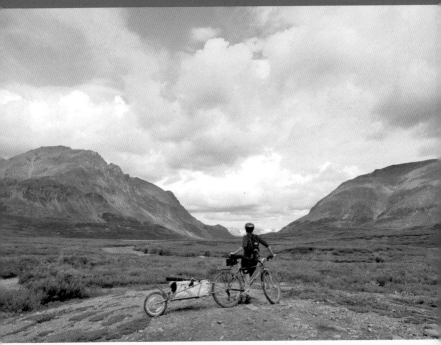

> *A biker enjoys the alpine vista on the more freewheeling, partly gravel Denali Highway.*

The Very Most Important Facts About a Denali Visit

Denali National Park has remained wild, despite high demand for visits, through a rationing process, which is better known as the bus transportation system. You need to book well ahead to get the most coveted bus tickets: those for the early morning shuttles, which afford the best opportunity of seeing wildlife and majestic Mount McKinley. Here's the lowdown on how to work the system.

- **Whom to Contact. Doyon/ARAMARK,** ☎ 800-622-7275 or 907-272-7275, www.reservedenali.com. This concessionaire handles bus and campground reservations along with its own hotels and activities outside the park boundary. Within the park, contact Doyon/ARAMARK at the Wilderness Access Center (p. 132, ❸).

- **When to Reserve.** The reservation system for the whole summer is available by phone or online starting the previous December 1. Phones are answered 7am to 5pm daily Mountain Standard Time. Make your reservations as soon as you know the date of your vacation.

- **What to Reserve.** Prime bus times and campsites are the important "gets" for a great visit and should be booked as soon as possible. Hotel rooms are easier to obtain, but reserving well ahead is wise—unless you want to gamble on grabbing a last-minute bargain.

- **What If You Don't Reserve?** The park's system holds back 35% of shuttle bus seats for walk-in sales, available in-person only at the Wilderness Access Center beginning 2 days before the ride. If you're lucky, you can snag a good ticket the day before an outing, but sometimes you have to be at the window when it opens in the morning to get one for 2 days later.

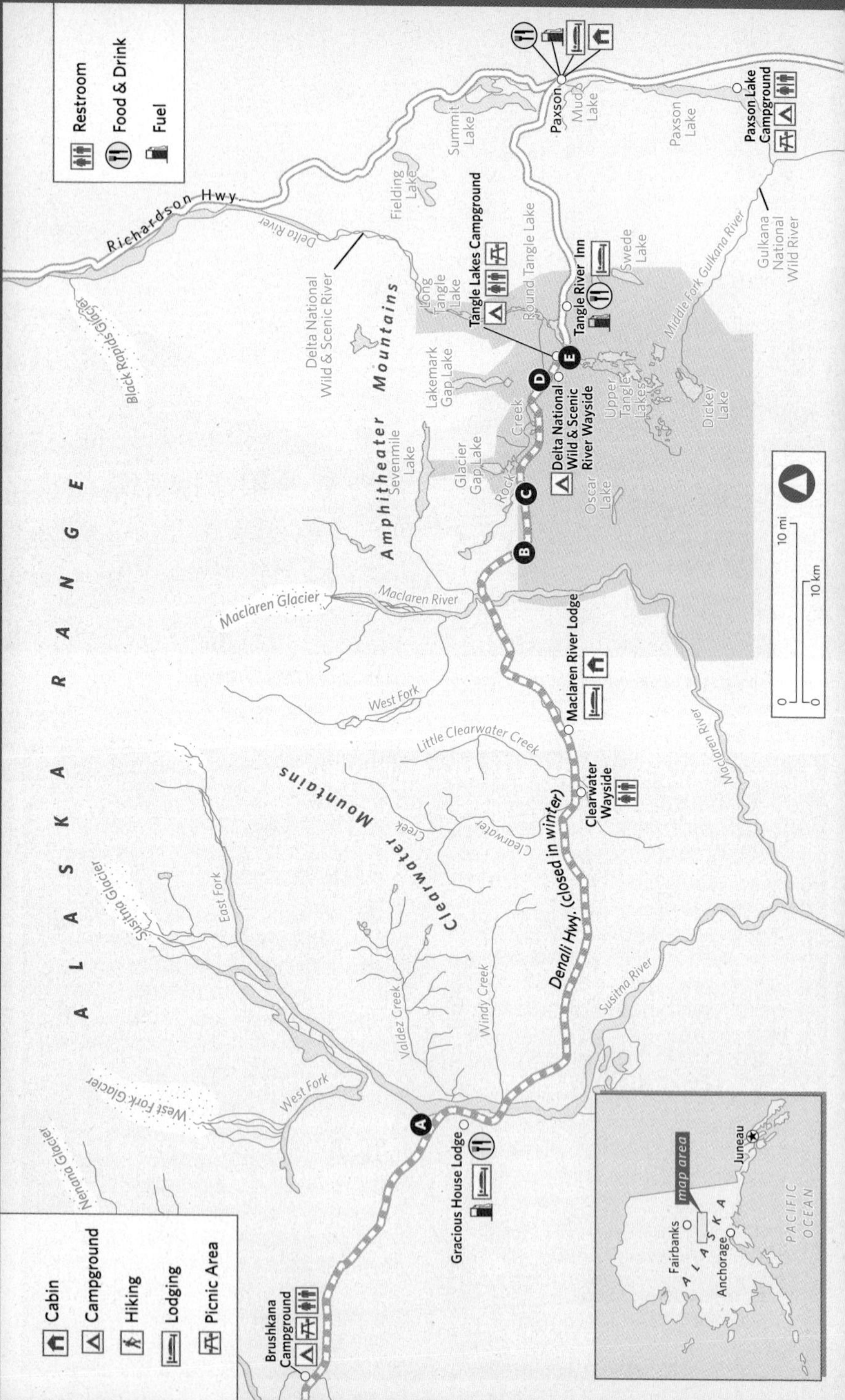

Restroom
Food & Drink
Fuel

Cabin
Campground
Hiking
Lodging
Picnic Area

Richardson Hwy.

Black Rapids Glacier

Delta River

A L A S K A   R A N G E

Nenana Glacier

West Fork Glacier

Susitna Glacier

East Fork

West Fork

Voldez Creek

Windy Creek

Clearwater Creek

Clearwater Mountains

Amphitheater Mountains

Summit Lake

Fielding Lake

Long Tangle Lake

Round Tangle Lake

Tangle Lakes Campground

Tangle River Inn

Delta National Wild & Scenic River

Delta National Wild & Scenic River Wayside

Lakemark Gap Lake

Sevenmile Lake

Glacier Gap Lake

Rock Creek

Upper Tangle Lakes

Oscar Lake

Dickey Lake

Swede Lake

Middle Fork Gulkana River

Gulkana National Wild River

Paxson

Mud Lake

Paxson Lake

Paxson Lake Campground

Maclaren Glacier

Maclaren River

Maclaren River Lodge

Little Clearwater Creek

Maclaren River

Clearwater Wayside

Denali Hwy. (closed in winter)

Susitna River

Gracious House Lodge

Brushkana Campground

B **C** **D** **E**

A

10 mi

10 km

Fairbanks

Anchorage

Juneau

A L A S K A

map area

PACIFIC OCEAN

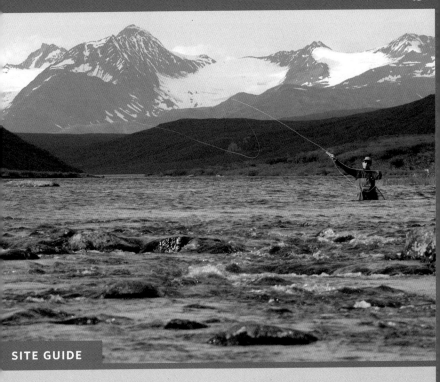

SITE GUIDE

⓯ Denali Highway

The Denali Highway leads 133 miles (allow at least 3 hours) to Paxson, but be advised that you won't find food, lodging, or services there. Indeed, you'll likely either turn around and return to Denali, or else continue on the Richardson Highway to Fairbanks (p. 40, ⑨), 180 miles north, or to Copper Center (p. 191, ⑧), in the Copper River Country, 90 miles south. But really, this trip is all about the drive itself. Around the 40-mile mark, there is an interpretive sign about the Alaska Range; at mile 49.5, stop for a short climb up a hill on the north side of the highway to fantastic Ⓐ **views of the mountains** and Susitna Valley. *Note:* The milepost markers count backward starting from Cantwell.

At spectacular Ⓑ **Maclaren Pass,** 98 miles into the drive, you'll get an even more amazing sight. You'll be at an elevation of 4,086 feet, and the Alaska Range, Maclaren Glacier, and Maclaren River are arrayed before you. Wildflowers bloom on the tundra in June and July.

From mile 86 to mile 119 of your drive, you're within the Ⓒ **Tangle Lakes Archaeological District,** which is interesting to know about, although there's nothing particularly to see. With more than 500 archaeological sites, reaching back as far as 10,000 years, it is among the richest ancient cultural finds in the subarctic. Glaciers cut Ⓓ **Landmark Gap** into the mountains; caribou use it as a migration route. The best viewpoint is 112.5 miles into the drive.

Finally, stop in at one of my favorite canoeing spots: Ⓔ **Tangle Lakes.** At mile 113, the waters are rich in waterfowl, including trumpeter swans, sandhill cranes, and loons. You can rent a canoe there from the **Tangle River Inn** (☎ 907-822-3970; www.tangleriverinn. com) for $5 an hour or $35 for 24 hours. ⊕ 1 day. For information on the highway and its stops, contact the Bureau of Land Management, Glennallen Field Office. ☎ 907-822-3217. www. blm.gov/ak.

The Best of the Denali Park Road

A bus ride on the single unpaved road that cuts 90 miles through the center of Denali National Park is the centerpiece of most visits. There's no other route for witnessing the best of the park's wildlife and scenery, and private vehicles are not allowed (although you can go on a mountain bike— see p. 162). Your choice of bus determines your style of travel, although not necessarily what you see; I've covered those considerations under "Denali Bus Choices," p. 149. But how far you go does make a difference in your chances of laying eyes on wildlife and taking in dramatic views. Here I've laid out what to expect mile by mile as you ride, including spots to get off for a hike, if you are on a shuttle bus that allows it. For the best landscapes, sit on the left side of the bus as you head into the park.

> The Savage River runs through a glacier-carved valley; a trail through the area can be accessed from mile 15 on the Park Road.

START Wilderness Access Center, at the entrance to Denali National Park. **TRIP LENGTH** At least 1 day, up to 180 miles.

❶ ★ Mile 9. The first spot with a view of Mount McKinley. Look for moose, especially during the fall rutting season.

❷ ★ Savage River Bridge. Pavement ends here, at mile 14, and a Park Service checkpoint stops private vehicles. From the parking lot by the bridge, a simple climb over dry tundra leads to Primrose Ridge, also known as Mount Margaret.

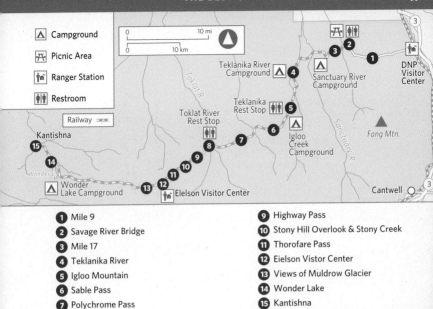

Legend	
🏕	Campground
🧺	Picnic Area
🛖	Ranger Station
🚻	Restroom

Railway ══

1 Mile 9

2 Savage River Bridge

3 Mile 17

4 Teklanika River

5 Igloo Mountain

6 Sable Pass

7 Polychrome Pass

8 Toklat River

9 Highway Pass

10 Stony Hill Overlook & Stony Creek

11 Thorofare Pass

12 Eielson Vistor Center

13 Views of Muldrow Glacier

14 Wonder Lake

15 Kantishna

3 Mile 17. This is the end of the line for the Natural History Tour bus.

4 ★★ Teklanika River. After 70 minutes, the bus has covered 27 miles and reached a large rest stop overlooking the Teklanika River, with flush toilets, the last plumbing along the road. The Teklanika is a braided river—a stream wandering in a massive gravel streambed that's much too big for it—created by water from fast-melting glaciers at the end of the last ice age. The river's constantly changing course spreads the glacier's debris of rock and dust. Flat plains in glacial terrain usually are laid down by this mechanism.

Getting Ready to Ride

Besides reserving spots on an early morning shuttle bus well in advance (see "The Very Most Important Facts About a Denali Visit," on p. 143), there are some other must-have items for a day in the backcountry: good walking shoes, rain gear and layers of clothing in case of cold or wet weather, binoculars or a spotting scope, lunch and snacks, plenty of water, and insect repellent.

> If you're lucky, you may see wolves, particularly along the Toklat River.

> *Tundra hillsides of varying shades of red and green add to the spectacular visual splendor of Polychrome Pass.*

❺ ★★ Igloo Mountain. Keep your binoculars close at hand, because this is an excellent place to spot distant Dall sheep. Manageable climbs on Igloo, Cathedral, and Sable mountains take off along the road in the section from Igloo Creek to Sable Pass, beginning at mile 34. Routes like these have casual trails at best, so you will have to find your own way and stay within your limits.

❻ ★ Sable Pass. As lovely as it is to look at, the area from mile 38 to mile 43 is a critical habitat area for bears, and is therefore usually closed to people. A half-eaten sign helps explain why. This is the start of the road's broad alpine vistas, so be sure to get your camera ready.

❼ ★★★ Polychrome Pass. After a nail-biting climb on the narrow gravel road, the bus surmounts 5-mile-wide Polychrome Pass at mile 46, the most scenic point on the ride. The toilet break here comes at 2 hours and 25 minutes into the trip. The valley below is known as the Plains of Murie, after Adolph Murie, a

biologist who pioneered study here beginning in the 1920s and helped develop the National Park Service's scientific ethic (the name does not always appear on maps, however). Note how the mountains of colored rock on either side of the plain match up—they once were connected before glacial ice carved this valley. Huge rocks on its floor are glacial erratics, plucked from the bedrock by moving ice and left behind when the ice melted.

❽ ★★ Toklat River. This braided river provides a flat plain of gravel for easy walking. For many visitors, this is the best choice for a backcountry hike, but stick to dry land and don't try to cross the glacial water. Visibility is terrific for seeing wildlife (and avoiding bears). You can get advice and use a toilet at the roadside station here before getting under way. I enjoy walking upriver; the route can take you much farther than most will want to attempt. The glaciers that feed the river are 10 miles upstream; the river bottom is habitat for bears, caribou, and wolves, and a good place for picnics. There is no food or water, but there are outhouses at a stop at mile 53, just up the road.

9 ★★ **Highway Pass.** The highest point on the road, at mile 58, has dramatic views of Mount McKinley. The alpine tundra from here to the Eielson Visitor Center is inviting for walking. If you do take a hike, go slowly, as tundra is soft underfoot and can conceal holes that can twist an ankle.

10 ★★ **Stony Hill Overlook & Stony Creek.** The Tundra Wildlife Tour turns around here, at mile 62, after taking in a great McKinley view in clear weather. Amazingly, the peak is still 36 miles away. At mile 60, Stony Creek, rising to the right (north) side of the road, is a popular hiking route.

11 ★★ **Thorofare Pass.** The road narrows further as it winds its way over the mountains. This area near mile 64 is prime territory for bears and caribou. Bus drivers know best where the animals are on any particular day, since they talk to fellow drivers by radio.

12 ★★★ **Eielson Visitor Center.** Reconstructed in 2008, the center is a model of environmentally sensitive construction and sustainable design, and one of the most advanced buildings in the national park system. Check out the viewing areas, exhibits, and interpretive programs. There's also a place to eat your sack lunch. The facilities and the fine vantage for beholding McKinley make this the best turnaround point for most shuttle bus riders, 66 miles into your trip. By turning around here,

Denali Bus Choices

Four basic kinds of bus rides take visitors into the backcountry. Choosing which bus ticket to buy decides a lot about your park experience. I've listed them here in order of my recommendation; all four can be booked through concessionaire Doyon/ARAMARK (p. 143), except as noted.

- **Shuttle Bus.** These buses, similar in construction to school buses but somewhat more comfortable, are the basic element of the Denali transportation system. They don't serve food or offer scripted commentary, but riders can get off and on anywhere in the park. This is the only way for most visitors to enjoy backcountry hiking. There are plenty of opportunities to talk to the driver; just get his or her attention when you want to stop. The **camper bus** is a shuttle bus intended for those staying in backcountry campgrounds. Tickets $25–$47 adults (depending on bus turnaround point), half-price for children 15–17, free for children 14 and under.

- **Tundra Wildlife Tour.** Using somewhat better-appointed buses than the shuttles, these narrated tours offer lunch and closed-circuit viewing equipment to display real-time animal sightings on board. The bus goes about 60 miles into the park

and returns, an 8-hour journey. The tour includes various stops, but riders can't get off on their own. Tickets $104 adults, half-price for children 14 and under.

- **Kantishna Experience.** This 13-hour guided tour (which does not allow riders to get off the bus on their own) traverses the entire 90-mile road to the Kantishna area, a private settlement of lodges within the park. This round-trip, park-sponsored tour, arranged via the same process as the rest of the transportation system, includes a ranger-guided hike at the far end. Two competing firms also offer similar tours for about the same cost, but with gold panning or a dog-sled demonstration at the destination rather than a hike; they are **Kantishna Wilderness Trails** (☎ 800-230-7275) and **Denali Backcountry Adventure** (☎ 888-560-2489). Tickets $155 adults, half-price for children 14 and under.

- **Natural History Tour.** These buses traverse only the edge of the park, penetrating 17 miles down the Park Road, short of the area with the best scenery and wildlife viewing opportunities. The 5-hour tour concentrates instead on presentations. Tickets $62 adults, half-price for children 14 and under.

> *Eielson Visitor Center is an accessible way to see the park for families with small children or individuals whose activity is limited.*

> *You may see a beaver on your tour; they live in ponds near Eielson Visitor Center and Horseshoe Lake.*

you save time for hiking rather than riding onward and spending the entire day in the seat of a bus. Shuttle staff operate a dispatch office and can find you a seat on a returning bus if you leave yours.

The area's wild geology is evident all around the center. Seismic measurements show McKinley continuously growing, about an inch every three years. A short trail and ranger-led hikes around the center can get you closer to the scenery, although for a longer hike some of the less vertical areas you passed earlier might be more appealing. A good strategy is to pick out an area for a hike while on the bus outbound to Eielson, and then get off for your ramble on the return trip. Buses come frequently, and you can always flag one down after hiking.

⓭ ★ Views of Muldrow Glacier. At mile 68.5 the incredibly rugged terrain visible to the north is not the ground, but the ice of a glacier covered by soil and vegetation. The Muldrow Glacier descends from McKinley's peak and was used by early climbers. Today, most fly to a base camp at 7,200 feet in elevation on the Kahiltna Glacier, on the south side. The Park Road comes within a mile of the Muldrow's face and then continues through wet, rolling terrain past beaver ponds, finally descending into a small spruce patch near mile 82.

14 ★★★ **Wonder Lake.** The most famous photographs and paintings of Mount McKinley look across the peaceful lake, less than 30 miles from the peak, at mile 86 of the road. The reason the mountain looks incredibly massive from this considerable distance is simply that it is: Rising from only 2,000 feet in elevation to a height of 20,320 feet, it stands on lower ground than other great peaks, and therefore appears larger to viewers. Wonder Lake Campground, with the park's most coveted sites, is on the far side of the road.

15 ★ **Kantishna.** An old gold-mining community preceded the 1917 creation of the park, and that private property remains at its heart. The Kantishna area has no natural attraction for day-trippers, although you can join daylong tours that stop here for meals and activities such as gold panning (see "Denali Bus Choices," p. 149). A better reason to go, for those who can afford it, are the wilderness lodges at Kantishna, which host visitors willing to spend a few nights beyond the park's access barriers (see "The Denali Lodge Experience," p. 166).

Denali by Rail

The **Alaska Railroad** (☎ 800-544-0552 or 907-265-2494; www.alaskarailroad.com) pioneered tourism to Denali National Park decades before a road ever reached its entrance, and a large number of visitors still get there by rail. The advantages of taking the train are the scenic route, which avoids highway development, and the luxurious and stress-free style of travel. You can ride in full-dome cars decorated with fine art and experience an extraordinary class of service, with gourmet, white-tablecloth dining. On the downside, taking the train is slow and quite expensive, and without a car you'll be restricted to activities in the park and near its entrance. Hotels in the Nenana Canyon area near the entrance all offer courtesy shuttles to get you around, but these are the most expensive lodgings at Denali. Hotels and lodges with lower rates and more character in Healy or Carlo Creek don't make sense if you come by train.

The Denali Star train leaves Anchorage at 8:15am for a 3:45pm arrival at the Denali National Park entrance area. That's 7½ hours to cover 240 miles, for an average speed of about 32 miles an hour. This isn't practical transportation, but the slow speed enhances views of the countryside and occasional wildlife sightings, and the trip is relaxing. The other impractical aspect is the fare, which costs more than renting a car for your entire trip to the park, even for a single passenger. You can save something over posted fares by booking a package. I'm usually skeptical of packages for Alaska travel because I think you need to make your own discoveries, but the Alaska Railroad offers some unique, self-guided package deals that save considerable money.

You can stop in Talkeetna for a Mount McKinley glacier flight, even if you take the train. The train stops there on the way to the park, and you can get the same train going north the next day (this hop-off, hop-on approach increases the train fare by about 15 percent).

Although cruise lines also offer luxurious cars on the same train, I recommend the Alaska Railroad cars, which come in two types: standard service, called *Adventure Class,* and first-class, *Gold Star* service. The Adventure Class seats are first-rate: clean and classy, with big windows, access to dome seats, and good dining. The Gold Star cars offer luxury at a level I've encountered on no other train, with gourmet dining, full dome seats for every passenger, beautifully appointed cars, and large outdoor balconies (because the train is so slow, standing outdoors is delightful). The Adventure Class fare is $146 one way, while Gold Star fares are $231. All fares are half-price for children.

A Denali Camping Adventure

Thanks to the cruise ship lines, Denali National Park has more $250-a-night hotel rooms next to it than any other park in the country, but there are no lodgings on park land itself—that special territory is reserved for campers, who pay a tenth as much. The park campgrounds are well designed to suit a variety of travelers—from retired campers driving RVs to backpackers preparing to venture into the trackless wilderness—and they're particularly good for families. Here I've suggested a plan for those interested in a tenting trip, but with an eye to keeping clean and within comfort zones. You will need to start from a city where you can rent gear; I recommend Anchorage. Reserve Denali campsites as far ahead as possible, using the system explained on p. 143.

> If you plan on camping in the park, come prepared with the proper equipment, including lots of warm layers and a proper tent.

START Anchorage. TRIP LENGTH 1 week, 572 miles.

Campers will need to gear up and shop in the city before heading to the park by road.

❶ **Anchorage.** It will take at least half a day to rent and buy the equipment and food you'll need for your trip (see "Gearing Up to Fly & Camp," on p. 157). Spend the night just up the road from the city, at the **Eagle River Campground** (p. 115). ⊕ Half-day.

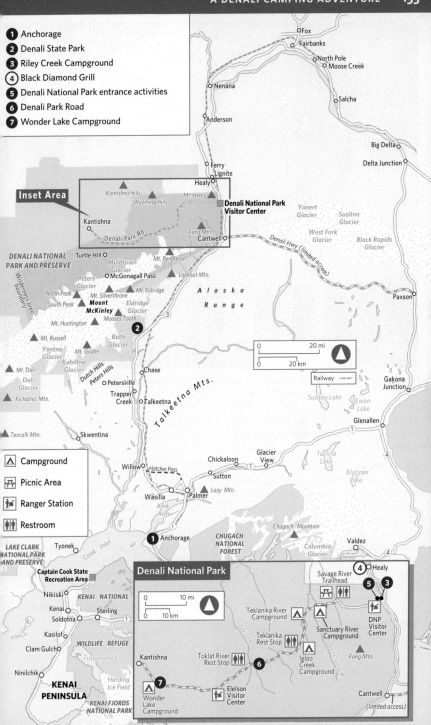

1. Anchorage
2. Denali State Park
3. Riley Creek Campground
4. Black Diamond Grill
5. Denali National Park entrance activities
6. Denali Park Road
7. Wonder Lake Campground

Inset Area

Denali National Park Visitor Center

DENALI NATIONAL PARK AND PRESERVE

Wilderness Area Boundary

Kantishna Hills
Wyoming Hills
Mt. Healy
Kantishna
Denali Park Rd.
Fang Mtn.
Cantwell
Turtle Hill
Muldrow Glacier
Mt. Pendleton
McGonagall Pass
Lookout Mtn.
Peters Glacier
Mt. Silverthrone
Mt. Eldridge
North Peak
South Peak
Mount McKinley
Eldridge Glacier
Mt. Huntington
Mooses Tooth
Ruth Glacier
Mt. Russell
Mt. Goldie
Yentna Glacier
Kahiltna Glacier
Dutch Hills
Peters Hills
Mt. Dali
Dall Glacier
Chase
Kichatna Mtn.
Teocalli Mtn.
Skwentina
Petersville
Trapper Creek
Talkeetna

Fox
Fairbanks
North Pole
Moose Creek
Nenana
Salcha
Anderson
Big Delta
Delta Junction
Ferry
Lignite
Healy
Yanert Glacier
Susitna Glacier
West Fork Glacier
Black Rapids Glacier
Denali Hwy (limited access)
Paxson
Alaska Range
Gakona Junction
Railway
Susitna Lake
Ewan Lake
Glenallen
Chickaloon
Glacier View
Tazlina Lake
Sutton
Klutina Lake
Willow
Hatcher Pass
Lazy Mtn.
Wasilla
Palmer
Knik Arm
Chugach Mountain
Columbia Glacier
Valdez
CHUGACH NATIONAL FOREST
Anchorage
Tyonek
Cook Inlet
LAKE CLARK NATIONAL PARK AND PRESERVE
Captain Cook State Recreation Area
Nikiski
KENAI NATIONAL
Kenai
Sterling
Soldotna
Skilak L.
Kasilof
WILDLIFE REFUGE
Tustumena L.
Clam Gulch
Ninilchik
KENAI PENINSULA
Harding Ice Field
KENAI FJORDS NATIONAL PARK

Talkeetna Mts.

Campground
Picnic Area
Ranger Station
Restroom

20 mi
20 km

Denali National Park

Savage River Trailhead
Teklanika River Campground
Teklanika Rest Stop
Sanctuary River Campground
Igloo Creek Campground
Kantishna
Toklat River Rest Stop
Elelson Visitor Center
Wonder Lake Campground
Fang Mtn.
Cantwell
(limited access)
DNP Visitor Center
Healy

10 mi
10 km

> *Local brews on tap at Black Diamond Grill, a destination in and of itself north of the park.*

On Day 2, drive 111 miles north on the Parks Highway to Denali State Park, where you'll spend the night.

2 ★★ kids **Denali State Park.** The park along the highway south of the national park has a low-key feel that makes it conducive to relaxation and spontaneity in ways that the national park, so planned and regulated, is not. You won't get closer to Mount McKinley on any other road, even within the national park, and the views are spectacular in clear weather. If you spend the night here, your chances of seeing the mountain in the morning are as good as they get. Check out the several developed vantage points, some

More Information

Note that commercial campgrounds near Denali are covered under "Where to Stay," which starts on p. 164. Find additional details about camping within the park at Denali's website, www.nps.gov/dena.

of which have campgrounds and trails. Your highlight today will be **Byers Lake,** to see a quietly inspiring Veterans Memorial and, best of all, venture on the lake in a rented canoe or kayak. The campground here is a great place to spend the night. ⏱ 1 day. See p. 141, **9**.

On Day 3, continue 90 miles north on the Parks Highway to Denali National Park's Wilderness Access Center to pick up the camping and bus permits you've reserved well in advance (see "The Very Most Important Facts About a Denali Visit" on p. 143). You'll spend the next 2 nights at the:

3 ★★ kids **Riley Creek Campground.** This campground is handy to a lot that you'll want to do, including casual fun along the river (but keep kids close by, as the water is fast), evening ranger programs, and classic pleasures around the campfire. The campground has a post office and a store with a deli, showers, laundry, a dump station, and Wi-Fi.

You'll also have time on the day you arrive for activities to learn about and become oriented to the park. Make a point of visiting the **Denali National Park Visitor Center** (p. 133, ❹). It's a fascinating museum of the park, and a good place to pick up a Junior Ranger Program packet if you're traveling with children. Kids complete activities, geared toward either ages 4 to 8 or ages 9 to 14, along with parents while visiting the park. When the booklet is completed, the child can turn it in and say a pledge to receive a certificate and badge. The materials are available as well at the **Murie Science and Learning Center** (p. 163) and the **Talkeetna Ranger Station** (p. 174, ❹). ⏲ 2 hr.

❹ 🍴 **Black Diamond Grill.** This restaurant north of the park entrance near Healy is a good spot for kids, with a 9-hole golf course, GPS treasure hunts, and covered-wagon rides with full camp meals. The wagon-ride meals are $79 per person and available for breakfast, lunch, or dinner. Mile 247, Parks Hwy., at Otto Lake Rd. $$. See p. 170.

On Day 4, take advantage of what the park environs have to offer.

❺ ★★ kids **Denali National Park entrance activities.** Knowing the best of your park visit is ahead—the shuttle bus ride into the park's core—take a full day now for the fun activities at the park entrance. Two of the best half-day

> A moose calf and his mother near Riley Creek Campground.

Seeing Denali with Kids

The biggest challenge of taking children to Denali National Park is the amount of driving involved. It takes most of a day to get there, and once you're there, the only way into the heart of the park is on a long bus ride. Even adults get restless on the buses, but the prospect of seeing wildlife makes up for much. Children, however, sometimes have trouble catching a glimpse of distant animals and often aren't good at using binoculars. It's not at all like a zoo, and it could leave them underwhelmed. That said, I've also witnessed a 10-year-old become a shuttle bus celebrity by being the best wildlife finder on board. And there's a solution

to getting antsy on the shuttle bus: Just get off and go for a walk. You can always get on another bus as it passes. Finally, note that if your child normally needs a car seat, you will need one on the bus as well.

If you do plan a family vacation to Denali—and we've had some great ones there—I recommend using this camping itinerary for your trip. Staying in hotels is expensive, and you're too cooped up. The setting of some of the area's hotels is not conducive to unstructured play because of high-speed traffic on the nearby highway, but (at least to my kids) campgrounds are just big playgrounds.

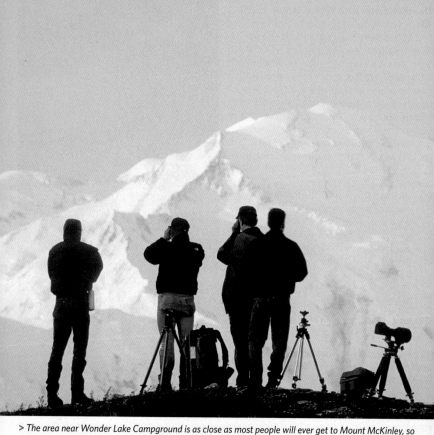

> The area near Wonder Lake Campground is as close as most people will ever get to Mount McKinley, so have a camera ready.

activities for energetic people are **rafting on the Nenana River** (p. 135, ❼) and **climbing the Mount Healy Overlook** (p. 135, ❽). If either of those is too strenuous for children in your group, other hiking options include the network of very easy nature trails behind the visitor center; the best of these is the **Horseshoe Lake Trail,** 1.5 miles round trip. If that's unsatisfying, as it likely will be for some, the 2-mile **Savage River Loop** is more interesting and hardly more difficult. That trailhead is at mile 15 of the Park Road. You can drive or take a free shuttle bus. The trail leads downstream along the river, crosses a bridge, and returns on the far side.

Other activities to consider: a ranger program or guided walk, the dog-sled demonstration, bicycling, or riding an all-terrain vehicle. All are described in "The Best Denali Adventures," starting on p. 158. ⏱ 1 day.

On Day 5, get an early start—the morning is the best time to find animals and observe Mount McKinley, which often gets socked in by clouds later in the day. You'll be spending the next 2 nights at a campsite in the park.

❻ ★★★ **Denali Park Road.** Break camp early and board the **camper bus** (see "Denali Bus Choices," on p. 149) for an 86-mile ride on Denali National Park Road to Wonder Lake, where you will make camp. Although the kids may go nuts on the full-day ride, it's your best chance of seeing bears, caribou, or moose, and you might spy wolves or mountain goats. The scenery is amazing, too (see "The Best of the Denali Park Road," p. 146). Some of the best views come at Polychrome Pass and later. ⏱ 1 day.

7 ★★★ 🄺🄸🄳🄸 **Wonder Lake Campground.** This legendary campground is as near as most people ever get to Mount McKinley, in the coveted center of the park. It's also the deepest wilderness all but a few Americans will ever experience. Bring bug dope, as the mosquitoes are legendary, too. Some campers wear head nets or netted shirts. Tent sites are separated, but everyone cooks in a central area to avoid attracting bears to individual camps. This is an opportunity to play in a beautiful setting far from man-made things; you can spend all of Day 6 here, hiking the trail to the McKinley Bar (a braided river bed) and following that level ground as far as you like. Mile 85, Denali Park Rd. See "The Very Most Important Facts About a Denali Visit," on p. 143, for reservation information. ⏱ 1 day.

On Day 7, break camp at Wonder Lake and take the camper bus back to the park entrance. If you're like our family, you'll be ready for a hotel room with a shower and a soft bed for the night. Choices are listed on p. 164.

Gearing Up to Fly & Camp

Traveling by air to go camping with a family is no joke, especially in the era of baggage fees and Transportation Security Administration rules, but don't give up on one of the best ways to see Alaska because of that. There are ways to manage the difficulties.

If you're backpacking, you don't have to worry about the bulk of your equipment, because you'll already be traveling light, but camp stoves can be a problem, which I'll address below. If you will rent an RV in Alaska, packing isn't a special problem, as most of what you need will be on the rig (but get a list from the rental agency to avoid surprises). If, however, you plan to go car camping—family-style, with relatively bulky gear—bringing everything from home may be expensive due to baggage fees, and a hassle, too.

I recommend flying into Anchorage to rent a car and then driving to **REI** (p. 101) or another sporting goods store to rent camping equipment, and to buy much of what you cannot rent. Planning ahead is the key. Make a list of exactly what you'll need. From that list, bring from home only items that are expensive and easy to transport. When you arrive, buy cheap items and rent bulky items. Call ahead to reserve the rental gear or make sure it will be available.

Camp stoves are a special case. They're difficult to take on an airplane, even in checked baggage. Officially, you can pack one if it has no fuel tank and no odor of fuel, but odors are subjective and you could lose the stove. This is an item to rent, or you can buy a cheap propane stove in Alaska and then give it away or mail it home without the fuel tank when you're done with it.

You can rent a tent, sleeping bags and pads, backpacks, and paddling gear. You should bring your own cooking outfit, first-aid kit, binoculars, electronics, and other personal gear. You'll need rain gear, sweaters, and synthetic long underwear, and you may want knit caps, wool socks, and gloves. Unexpectedly cold nights in the 30s can come at any time of year. If you'll be on the water, also bring or buy rubber boots or water shoes.

Some items you cannot bring or rent—you'll have to buy them. TSA regulations prohibit bear-deterrent spray in effective sizes; it's not an essential, but if it will make you feel more secure, you can buy it at any sporting goods store in Alaska for around $50. Likewise, matches, lighters, and flares should be bought in Alaska and properly discarded or given away before you leave. For complete TSA rules on camping equipment, go to www.tsa.gov and enter the search term "camping."

The Best Denali Adventures

While the vast majority of Denali National Park is reserved for hiking, backpacking, and wildlife viewing, and those are the premier activities, there's plenty to do at the park entrance and just outside. Some of the businesses offering these outings are here only because the people are—for example, there are many better places to go fishing in Alaska. But river rafting and flightseeing are at their best here.

> *The braided bed of the Toklat River is easily accessible for hiking and offers fantastic views.*

All-Terrain Vehicles

Although they're not allowed in the park, ATVs are popular with hunters and remote residents in the region—they travel much faster and can carry heavier loads than one can manage on foot. **Denali ATV Adventures** (☎ 907-683-4288; www.denaliatv.com) offers rides north of the park, in the Otto Lake area and on the Stampede Trail, for scenery and wildlife viewing. Commentary is delivered through radio headsets inside riders' helmets. Rates are $95 for those driving and $45 for passengers. Drivers must be 18 if going solo, 21 if carrying a rider; children can ride on a parent's unit.

Backcountry Hiking

The opportunity for a casual hike in trackless wilderness is Denali's most unique quality. But while the terrain may be unfamiliar, it needn't be scary. Trackless wilderness, by definition,

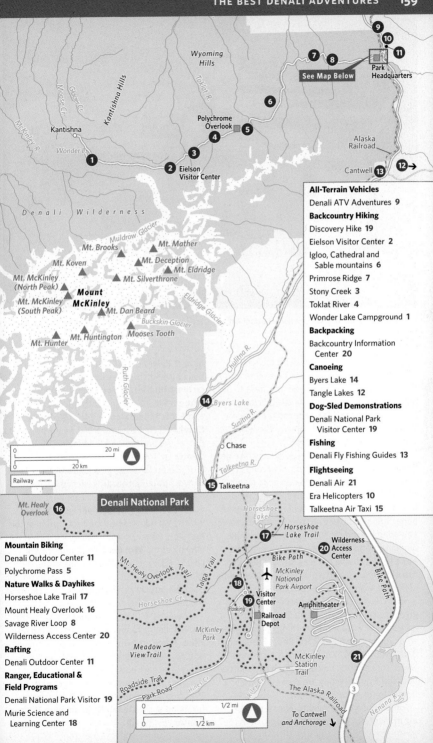

All-Terrain Vehicles
Denali ATV Adventures 9

Backcountry Hiking
Discovery Hike 19
Eielson Visitor Center 2
Igloo, Cathedral and
  Sable mountains 6
Primrose Ridge 7
Stony Creek 3
Toklat River 4
Wonder Lake Campground 1

Backpacking
Backcountry Information
  Center 20

Canoeing
Byers Lake 14
Tangle Lakes 12

Dog-Sled Demonstrations
Denali National Park
  Visitor Center 19

Fishing
Denali Fly Fishing Guides 13

Flightseeing
Denali Air 21
Era Helicopters 10
Talkeetna Air Taxi 15

Mountain Biking
Denali Outdoor Center 11
Polychrome Pass 5

Nature Walks & Dayhikes
Horseshoe Lake Trail 17
Mount Healy Overlook 16
Savage River Loop 8
Wilderness Access Center 20

Rafting
Denali Outdoor Center 11

**Ranger, Educational &
Field Programs**
Denali National Park Visitor 19
Murie Science and
  Learning Center 18

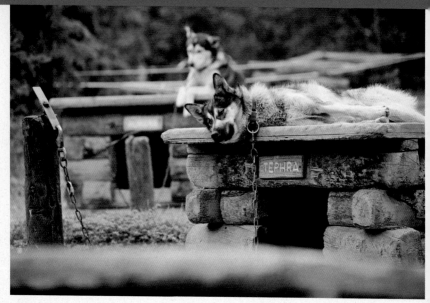

> *Park dogs nap on their kennels near the park entrance; rangers use sled teams to patrol the backcountry.*

doesn't have trails. Happily, with the shuttle bus system, you don't have to be a backcountry expert to hike off-trail, you only have to be able to find the road. The shuttle bus drops hikers off wherever they like and picks them up again when flagged down anywhere on the 90-mile route.

How you prepare for a backcountry hike depends on what you plan to do. Everyone going into the backcountry needs rain gear, layers of both warm and cool clothes, sturdy walking shoes, water, lunch, insect repellant, toilet paper, and plastic bags to carry out everything you bring in (and most people will also want binoculars and a camera). If you plan to hike more than a couple of miles, bring a detailed map, a compass, and a plan, leaving word with someone as to where you are going.

In the absence of trails, naturally I cannot give mileage and hiking time. Both are up to you. But I've included something of a menu of what you can do under "The Best of the Denali Park Road" (p. 146). You needn't be fixated on any of these spots, however. From the shuttle bus, you'll notice many areas of gently rolling tundra for exploration on foot.

Here are some highlights: For steep hiking or climbing, try **Primrose Ridge,** from the Savage River Bridge (which you can reach by bus or car) on the Park Road near mile 14—or, farther into the backcountry, the area beginning at mile 34 that includes **Igloo, Cathedral** and **Sable Mountains** (p. 148, **⑤**); **Stony Creek,** which leads upward at mile 60 (p. 149, **⑩**); or the area around the **Eielson Visitor Center** (p. 149, **⑫**).

If you prefer a less strenuous hike and want to avoid potential hazards such as tundra holes, the braided river beds are best. Most accessible is the **Toklat River** (p. 148, **⑧**), which also has a ranger contact station at the bus stop, where you can get advice. For those staying at the **Wonder Lake Campground** (p. 151, **⑭**), you can do a day hike along the McKinley River, but you wouldn't have time for both the bus ride and a hike if you're staying at the park entrance area.

Travelers with doubts about hiking on their own can join a ranger-led, full-day **Discovery Hike.** There are two a day in the peak season, one around the visitor center and the other nearer the park entrance. Your cost is merely the price of the shuttle ticket to get to the hike. You'll need to sign up at least a day beforehand at the **Denali National Park Visitor Center** (p. 133, **④**).

Backpacking

Trekking in Denali National Park is famous—and rationed. The National Park Service sets aside 43 large backcountry units and allocates a limited number of backpacking permits to each. Permits are available only in person at the **Backcountry Information Center,** and only 2 days before the hike; thus, you may need to get to the park 2 days before you start your trek. Rangers will provide orientation, but read up in advance on what to bring and how to be safe in Alaska's wilderness, including hypothermia, stream crossings, wilderness medicine, and bear avoidance. The Backcountry Information Center is adjacent to the **Wilderness Access Center** (p. 132, ❸) and is open from 9am to 6pm daily in season; it is closed October through April.

Canoeing

Canoeing isn't a major activity at the national park, and no equipment rental is available. Denali State Park has gorgeous canoeing at **Byers Lake** (p. 141, ❾), where you can camp and rent a canoe. Likewise at the **Tangle Lakes** area (p. 145, ❶❺) on the unpaved Denali Highway, east of the park.

Dog-Sled Demonstrations

Rangers still use dog teams to patrol the backcountry in winter, and in summer the dogs earn their keep by showing off to visitors at the kennels a few miles beyond the park entrance area. The popular free program happens as often as three times a day in the summer. Check times and get the free shuttle bus to the kennels at the **Denali National Park Visitor Center** (there is no parking at the kennels).

Fishing

The cold climate and opaque glacial water make fishing poor in the national park; it makes more sense to fish at another point on your Alaska trip. However, outside the park, you can join Rick McMahan of **Denali Fly Fishing Guides** (☎ 907-768-1127; www.denaliflyfishing.com), who takes clients fishing (mostly for Arctic grayling) at a private lake or on a stream near the park, at a rate of $150 for a half-day and $300 for a full day, lunch included.

Flightseeing

The sight of Mount McKinley up close from

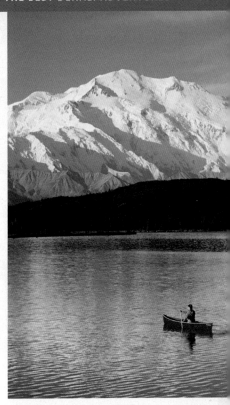

> *You can't canoe in the park, but you can get out on the water at nearby Tangle Lakes.*

a small plane is something I'll never forget. I prefer flying from Talkeetna, where flights are generally less expensive and pilots spend much of their time ferrying climbers to McKinley's glaciers; I recommend **Talkeetna Air Taxi** (p. 130, ❶). But you can also fly directly from the park with **Denali Air** (☎ 907-683-2261; www.denaliair.com). Either way, budget at least an hour, and $200 to $400 per person, depending on the tour you choose. Be sure to plan your trip so you can make the flight early in the morning, when the skies are more likely to be conducive to good viewing. Consider building in an extra day just in case the weather doesn't cooperate.

Flying by helicopter offers an entirely different experience. These tours, which leave from near the park entrance, don't go to Mount McKinley, but they do land visitors in scenic alpine spots or atop a glacier for hiking. They cost more than fixed-wing flights,

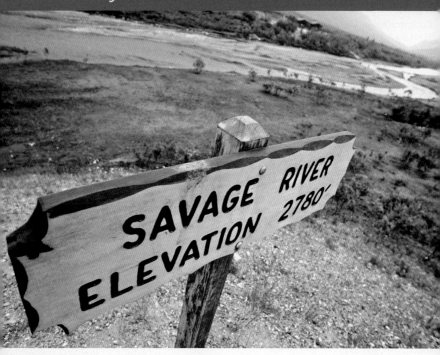

> *The elevation of Denali National Park ranges from about 2,000 feet to 20,320 feet at the peak of Mount McKinley.*

around $475 per person. I suggest you go with **Era Helicopters** (☎ 800-843-1947; www.eraflightseeing.com), a reliable operator.

Mountain Biking

For vigorous outdoors people, touring Denali National Park by bicycle offers special freedom, since bikes can bypass the checkpoint that keeps private vehicles off the Park Road. By reserving campsites along the way, a party could travel well into the park at will. However, bikes aren't allowed off road, and the road itself is dusty, with buses passing frequently. You can take bikes on camper buses, but space is quite limited, so it's a good option only on the leg outbound into the park, when your reservation will assure room. Plan to bus in and ride out. But bear in mind that in order to reach the most scenic spots on a day trip, you'd have to be a strong rider and get an early start: **Polychrome Pass** (p. 148, **7**) is 32 miles past the checkpoint. The best rental operation is **Denali Outdoor Center** (☎ 888-303-1925; www.denalioutdoorcenter.com).

Rates are $40 for 24 hours, $25 for 6 hours, with discounts for longer rentals.

Nature Walks & Dayhikes

The Denali entrance area has several short, easy trails that introduce visitors to the nature of the area, generally linking at the Denali National Park Visitor Center, including the 1.5-mile **Horseshoe Lake Trail** (p. 156, **5**). The only strenuous hike of the group is a steep, 5-mile round trip to the **Mount Healy Overlook** (p. 135, **8**). An easy trail a bit farther into the park is the 2-mile **Savage River Loop;** you'll have to drive or take a free shuttle to the starting point (p. 143). A map and trail descriptions are in the park's *Alpenglow* newspaper. Rangers offer guided hikes in the entrance area several times a day; check at the visitor center or the **Wilderness Access Center** (p. 132, **3**) for times.

Rafting

The Nenana River has some of the best commercial rafting in Alaska, and the only rafting at the park. I recommend going with **Denali Outdoor Center** (p. 135, **6**).

Ranger, Educational & Field Programs

Few activities add as much to the depth and humanity of a national park visit as a ranger-led walk, campfire program, or talk; you not only learn much more about the park, but also can slow down and connect with a person who knows and loves the area. The four larger campgrounds have campfire programs nightly at 7:30 in the high season; check the **Denali National Park Visitor Center** (p. 133, ④) for other current ranger offerings.

The Park Service and its partner organizations offer educational exhibits and programs based out of the **Murie Science and Learning Center** (☎ 866-683-1269 or 907-683-1269; www.murieslc.org) at the park entrance. Programming includes evening lectures, morning walk-in science presentations, youth camps, and natural history field seminars for adults and for families with children. Three-day courses are around $320 per person. Check topics and register well in advance on the website. The center is just north of the Denali visitor center and is open daily—in the summer from 9:30am to 5:30pm, and in the winter from 9am to 4pm.

Climbing Mount McKinley? Maybe Not

Besides its height, size, and steepness, the severe weather and cold on Mount McKinley make it among the world's most challenging climbs. Even in summer, temperatures can fall to –40°F. Experts have equated it to climbing in Antarctica.

Climbers train many months to get ready and usually plan to spend three weeks on the mountain. Guides charge around $7,000 per person. Most climbs happen in the spring and early summer, when the weather is more predictable and comparatively warm, the sky is light all night, and the snow is firmer than later in the summer.

Climbs usually begin with a flight by ski plane from Talkeetna to the 7,200-foot level of the Kahiltna Glacier. If you fly over the mountain, you can see the seasonal village of tents on the glacier there. Each year about 1,200 climbers in 300 parties start the climb, so it's not about being all alone.

On average, only about half the parties make it to the top. And every year, it seems, some people die trying—more than 100 climbers have perished in all. And that doesn't count the rescuers, pilots, and support personnel killed in this extreme environment. You can visit memorials to climbers and pilots in Talkeetna, at the town cemetery's **Mount McKinley Climbers' Memorial** (p. 175, ⑤), and learn more about the climbers and the mountain's history at the **Talkeetna Ranger Station** (p. 174, ④) and the **Talkeetna Historical Society Museum** (p. 174, ③).

The first successful party to summit Mount McKinley made it in 1913, organized by Episcopal archdeacon Hudson Stuck, a remarkable adventurer and humanitarian who traveled Alaska by dog sled, and led by Harry Karstens, who became the park's first superintendent. The first person to stand at the peak was an Alaska Native with the group, Walter Harper.

Climbers attempting the mountain over the next five decades were few and lonely. But in the 1970s and 1980s, the numbers exploded. Today more than 100 may summit the mountain in a single day. The number of climbers has created new problems, including the expense of rescue and support and the challenges of garbage and human waste disposal.

During the climbing season, the Park Service stations rescue rangers at an emergency medical clinic at the mountain's 14,200-foot level—and a helicopter is ready to go after climbers in trouble. A climbing fee of $200 a head defrays only a small portion of rescue costs.

The concentration on Mount McKinley is interesting in a state with so many mountains that have never been climbed or even named. Visitors can find many safer and easier climbs to test themselves. If you want to learn technical mountaineering, consider a climbing program such as **Alaska Mountaineering School** (☎ 907-733-1016; www.climbalaska.org), in Talkeetna.

Where to Stay Near Denali

> *The communal kitchen at Denali Mountain Morning Hostel and Lodge.*

★ Cedar Hotel at Denali Grizzly Bear Resort
SOUTH OF THE PARK Buildings constructed since 2006 stand over the Nenana River with comfortable, modern rooms decorated in an Alaska rustic motif with lots of cedar. They open onto balconies from which you can see and hear the river. Mile 231.1, Parks Hwy. ☎ 866-583-2696. www.denaligrizzlybear.com. 105 units. Doubles $179. DISC, MC, V.

★★ Denali Bluffs Hotel NENANA CANYON
Rectangular buildings cling to a steep mountainside looking down on the Nenana Canyon area. Rooms are light, comfortable, and expensive. Several other large, pricey hotels with good rooms are in this area, but mostly they fill with guests on escorted tours offered by the cruise lines. Mile 238.4, Parks Hwy. ☎ 800-276-7234 reservations; 907-683-7000 local. www.denalialaska.com. 112 units. Doubles $256–$291. AE, DISC, MC, V.

★ kids Denali Crow's Nest Log Cabins NENANA CANYON Five tiers of authentic log cabins climb the side of Sugarloaf Mountain, offering lodgings more fitting for a national park than the area's other anonymous hotel rooms, and at more reasonable rates. Don't stay here if you have problems with stairs, as the site is steep and it's quite a climb to some cabins. Mile 238.5, Parks Hwy. ☎ 888-917-8130. www.denalicrowsnest.com. 39 cabins. Doubles $159. MC, V.

More Information

There are no accommodations in the park—they're all outside its boundaries on pockets of private land. The most expensive hotels are within a mile or two of the park entrance, in the **Nenana Canyon** (aka Glitter Gulch) area; stay there if you come by train. **Healy** and **Stampede Road** lodgings are 10 miles or more to the north. Other lodgings are in the **South of the Park** area, 7 miles south; around **Carlo Creek,** 14 miles south; and near **Denali State Park,** 90 miles south.

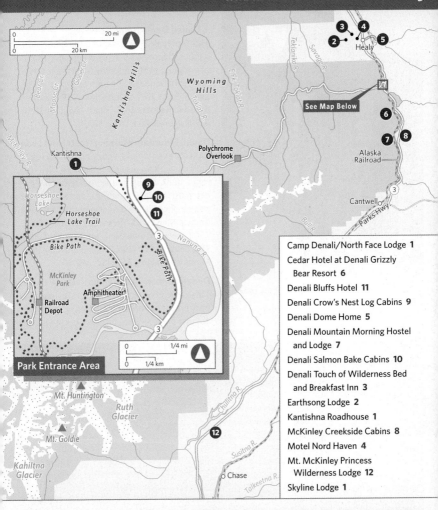

Camp Denali/North Face Lodge **1**
Cedar Hotel at Denali Grizzly
 Bear Resort **6**
Denali Bluffs Hotel **11**
Denali Crow's Nest Log Cabins **9**
Denali Dome Home **5**
Denali Mountain Morning Hostel
 and Lodge **7**
Denali Salmon Bake Cabins **10**
Denali Touch of Wilderness Bed
 and Breakfast Inn **3**
Earthsong Lodge **2**
Kantishna Roadhouse **1**
McKinley Creekside Cabins **8**
Motel Nord Haven **4**
Mt. McKinley Princess
 Wilderness Lodge **12**
Skyline Lodge **1**

Cruising for a Room?

A pair of enormous hotels catering mainly to cruise-line passengers dominate Nenana Canyon, but they have few rooms for guests who aren't on package trips, and when they do, expect to be quoted high prices. They are the **Denali Princess Lodge** (pictured); (☎ 800-426-0500 reservations, 907-683-2282 local; www.princesslodges.com) and the **McKinley Chalet Resort** (☎ 800-276-7234, or 907-683-8200 local; www.denaliparkresorts.com). To stay there economically, grab a last-minute deal when the flow of cruise-ship passengers has receded, or book a land-tour package with the Princess or Holland America cruise lines or with the Alaska Railroad.

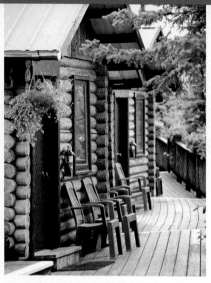

> *One of Denali Crow's Nest's authentic log cabins.*

★ Denali Dome Home HEALY

This family B&B occupies a large house and geodesic dome on 5 acres in the year-round community of Healy, away from the touristy atmosphere nearer the park entrance. Mile 248.8, Parks Hwy. ☎ 800-683-1239. www. denalidomehome.com. 7 units. Doubles $170–$190, w/breakfast. DISC, MC, V.

Denali Mountain Morning Hostel and Lodge

CARLO CREEK This is a cozy hostel in a log building with an organic food store. You can rent a bunk, a wall tent, a private room, or a cabin. All share a bathhouse and kitchen. A couple of good, inexpensive restaurants are nearby. Mile 224.5, Parks Hwy. ☎ 907-683-7503. www.hostelalaska.com. 14 units. Bunks $32; doubles $80–$95. 2-night minimum in rooms and cabins. AE, DISC, MC, V.

Denali Salmon Bake Cabins NENANA CANYON

This is the economical place to stay near the park entrance without camping. The cabins are just basic shelter, but they're clean and

The Denali Lodge Experience

The unique geography of Denali National Park places an area of private land called Kantishna right in the middle, near Mount McKiley, and safely beyond the transportation bottleneck of the park entrance and the bus system. Visitors at the lodges have a natural experience away from ticky-tacky highway development—like campers, but with indoor comforts, good food, and in some cases, expert guiding. Hikes and other activities in the park are at your doorstep. However, staying at a lodge requires a significant investment of time and money—at the best places, this means minimum stays of 3 days, with rates that could bring the tab for a couple to more than $3,000.

★★★ **Camp Denali/North Face Lodge.** Camp Denali is the pioneer and still the standout among the Kantishna lodges, and the only one with views of Mount McKinley from the rooms, which are cute log cabins with outhouses. The cooking and guiding are expert, and the whole place is run with a strong environmental ethic. The sister property, North Face, is somewhat less appealing, but the rooms have running water and

toilets. P.O. Box 67, Denali National Park, AK 99755. ☎ 907-683-2290. www.camp denali.com. 33 units. $505 per person per night; sessions of 3, 4, or 7 nights only. Rates include all meals, guided activities, and transportation from park entrance. No credit cards.

★★★ **Kantishna Roadhouse.** This lodge has more of the feel of a hotel than the others, with proper bathrooms in each cabin, a bar, and an emphasis that varies from the eco-aspects of the setting—they offer less strenuous activities such as gold panning, too. Mailing address: 1 Doyon Place, Suite 300, Fairbanks, AK 99701. ☎ 800-942-7420. www. seedenali.com. 32 units. $405 per person per night; minimum stay 2 nights. Rates include all meals, guided activities, and transportation from park entrance. AE, DISC, MC, V.

★★★ **Skyline Lodge.** This is the lowest-cost Kantishna alternative, without guiding, and you pay extra for meals other than breakfast. It's friendly, simple, and casual, with sleeping cabins and a central building for bathrooms and dining. P.O. Box 46, Denali Park, AK 99755. ☎ 907-683-1223. www.katair.com. 4 units. Doubles $225, w/breakfast. DISC, MC, V.

> *Knotted wood paneling in a cabin at Earthsong Lodge.*

they stand near the restaurant of the same name (p. 135, ⑤). Young people who would enjoy the music and camaraderie there will probably be happiest in the cabins as well. **Mile 238.5, Parks Hwy.** ☎ 907-683-2733. www.denaliparksalmonbake.com. 12 cabins. Doubles $69–$135. AE, DC, DISC, MC, V.

★ **Denali Touch of Wilderness Bed and Breakfast Inn** HEALY This cozy inn has immaculate rooms and common areas that create a warm feeling and offer expansive mountain views. The location is about 3 miles off the highway in an area north of the park, well away from the busy park entrance. **Mile 2.9, Stampede Rd.** ☎ 800-683-2459. www.touchofwildernessbb.com. 9 units. Doubles $179–$189, w/breakfast. 2-night minimum. AE, DISC, MC, V.

★★ **Earthsong Lodge** HEALY Solid-log buildings command sweeping views over the open tundra, 4 miles off the highway. Year-round hosts Jon and Karin Nierenberg share their frontier lifestyle, which includes a working sled-dog kennel. Guests stay in individual cabins and dine in a lodge building. **Stampede Trail Rd.** ☎ 907-683-2863. www.earthsonglodge.com. 12 cabins. Doubles $155–$195. MC, V.

★ **kids McKinley Creekside Cabins** CARLO CREEK Cabins sit by the creek with decks and private bathrooms. They're simple but reasonably priced accommodations. Families save money in these units, which sleep up to 6, and there are outdoor areas for visiting and playing. **Mile 224, Parks Hwy.** ☎ 888-5DENALI. www.mckinleycabins.com. 30 units. Cabins for 4, $139–$199. DISC, MC, V.

Travel Tip

Since hardly anyone goes to Denali in the winter, I've listed only summer rates. In fact, all these hotels are closed in the winter except the four hotels and B&Bs in Healy.

> *More budget-friendly accommodations at Motel Nord Haven.*

Lodges Deep in the Wilderness

To get way off the Denali beaten track, consider spending a few days at a fly-in wilderness lodge. Below I've described two of the best, each with a very different flavor. What they have in common is that they are far from any road, reachable only by float plane, and not really near Denali National Park either, except in spirit.

★★ **Caribou Lodge.** This truly remote spot 20 miles east of Talkeetna gives visitors an authentic experience of life on a homestead deep in the Alaska Bush. Mike and Pam Nickols built it and live here year round, sharing a lifestyle of complete self-reliance and isolation. The setting is perfect, on an alpine lake surrounded by rounded mountains of tundra, where guests can hike off trail, see wildlife and Mount McKinley, and paddle on the lake. In winter Mike teaches dog mushing. There is room for only three small parties a time. Bathing is in a shared shower house and each cabin has an outhouse for a toilet. Talkeetna. ☎ 907-733-2163. www.cariboulodgealaska.com. 3 cabins. $310 per person per day. Rates include meals and guiding and are based on double occupancy; air charter to lodge extra. 2-day minimum. No credit cards.

★★★ **Winterlake.** This is the most luxurious remote lodge I've visited. The cabins are as rustic as you would want them to be at this location on a lake west of Cook Inlet, at an Iditarod Trail checkpoint, but the service is more like a first-class hotel, with amenities included like massage, yoga groups and cooking classes with the hostess, Kristen Dixon, who is one of Alaska's most accomplished chefs. Even the wine selection is extraordinary. Outdoors, summer or winter visits are well outfitted. There's a dog team for guest instruction and use, or go cross-country on skis or snowmobiles. During summer, paddle on the lake, float a river, hike trails from the lodge, or use the lodge's helicopter for glacier or mountain-top excursions or remote fishing (with an additional charge). Airfare from Anchorage is included in the rates. Anchorage. ☎ 907-274-2710. www.withinthewild.com. 5 cabins. 2 nights $1,999 per person; 4 nights $3,535 per person. Some guided activities included in rate. AE, MC, V.

★★ **Motel Nord Haven** HEALY
Stay here for standard hotel rooms in a friendly, immaculately kept establishment with many amenities; you'll save as much as $100 over renting an equivalent room at the park entrance. Rates are for up to four guests in a room. The Nordmark family that owns and operates the motel is warm and hospitable. Mile 249.5, Parks Hwy. ☎ 800-683-4501. www. motelnordhaven.com. 28 units. $138–$164, w/ breakfast. AE, DISC, MC, V.

★★★ **Mount McKinley Princess Wilderness Lodge** DENALI STATE PARK On a wooded hillside 100 miles from the park entrance, this luxurious hotel has a striking view of the mountain, which is only 42 miles away, as close as any major hotel gets. The Princess cruise line runs it like a resort, with a full set of activities and good hiking trails on-site, since nothing else is nearby. The rooms are beautifully appointed and fit the setting. Mile 133.1, Parks Hwy. ☎ 800-426-0500 or 907-733-2900. www.princesslodges.com. 460 units. Doubles $189. AE, DC, DISC, MC, V.

Camping In & Around Denali

I've mentioned two of the best campgrounds of the six within the park: **Riley Creek** (p. 154, ❸), by the entrance, and **Wonder Lake** (p. 157, ❼), at the far end, reached only by the camper bus. Only one other is normally accessible by private vehicles: **Savage River,** a loop on the taiga 13 miles within the park. **Teklanika River** is 29 miles down the Park Road, accessible via the camper bus. Reserve sites at any of those four through the system described on p. 143, and do it as early as possible. Camping permits are $20 to $28 per night.

Two small, primitive backcountry campgrounds don't take reservations: **Igloo** and **Sanctuary River;** for those, you'll need to get permits in person at the **Wilderness Access Center** (p. 132, ❸) when you arrive.

Commercial campgrounds are located north and south of the park entrance. Here are three, in order of my preference:

★ **Denali Outdoor Center Otto Lake Campground and Cabins.** Mile ½, Otto Lake Road (turn west at Mile 247, Parks Hwy., 10 miles north of the park entrance). ☎ 888-303-1925. www.denalioutdoorcenter.com.

★ **Miners Market and Deli/McKinley RV and Campground.** Mile 248.5, Parks Hwy. (10 miles north of the park). ☎ 907-683-1418; http://mckinleyrv.com.

★ **Denali Grizzly Bear Cabins and Campground.** Mile 231.1, Parks Hwy. (6 miles south of the park entrance). ☎ 866-583-2696. www.denaligrizzlybear.com.

Where to Dine Near Denali

> Overlook Bar & Grill also has a fantastic sun deck.

★★★ 229 Parks Restaurant and Tavern

SOUTH OF PARK *INTERNATIONAL* A talented chef and her family make this the area's best restaurant, in a beautiful post-and-beam building 8 miles south of the park. The cuisine is distinctively Alaskan in its ingredients and eclectic in its preparation. Waits for a table are common in the summer; it's often open winter weekends, but call ahead. Mile 229, Parks Hwy. ☎ 907-683-2567. www.229parks. com. Entrees $18–$33. MC, V. Summer breakfast and dinner Tues–Sun; call ahead in winter.

★★ kids Black Diamond Grill HEALY *GRILL*

A restaurant with Northern Italian influences is part of a complex of fun attractions on the taiga, with a unique 9-hole golf course, all-terrain vehicle tours, GPS treasure hunts, minigolf, and covered wagon rides with full-service, camp-style meals. Mile 247, Parks Hwy., at Otto Lake Rd. ☎ 907-683-4653. www. blackdiamondgolf.com. Entrees $8–$24. AE, DISC, MC, V. Breakfast, lunch, and dinner daily.

★ Cabin Nite Dinner Theater NENANA

CANYON *DINNER REVUE* The show about a gold-rush woman is the epitome of touristy entertainment, but it is fun and well produced by young professional singers and dancers who serve platters of salmon and ribs while in character. At the McKinley Chalet Resort, Mile 238.5, Parks Hwy. ☎ 800-276-7234; www. denaliparkresorts.com. Tickets $62, half-price for children 2–12, free for children 2 and under. Nightly shows 5:30 and 8:30. AE, DISC, MC, V.

★★ Denali Park Salmon Bake NENANA CAN-

YON *GRILL* This is a rollicking local hot spot for beer, music, and good food within a broad price range—not only the $20 grilled salmon, but also pulled pork sandwiches, Tex-Mex options, and fancy seafood entrees. Touring music acts come through regularly during the summer, often with a cover charge. Mile 238.5, Parks Hwy. ☎ 907-683-2733. www. denaliparksalmonbake.com. All items $8–$37. AE, DC, DISC, MC, V. Breakfast to midnight daily.

★★ King Salmon Restaurant NENANA CAN-

YON *SEAFOOD* At the edge of the canyon, where rafters float by, this is a place for a special night of dining, with excellent food by the Princess cruise line, mainly steak and salmon. In the Denali Princess Lodge, Mile 238.5, Parks Hwy. ☎ 907-683-2282; www.princesslodges. com. Entrees $20–$40. AE, DC, DISC, MC, V. Breakfast, lunch, and dinner daily.

★ kids McKinley Creekside Cafe CARLO CREEK

STEAK/SEAFOOD This is a friendly and casual little place with food consistently good enough

More Information

Other than the restaurants listed here, casual food places sprout up every summer near the park entrance, in and between the big hotels, where you can find pizza, fish and chips, sandwiches, or a buffet for lunch or dinner. Except as noted, all restaurants are open during the summer visitor season only.

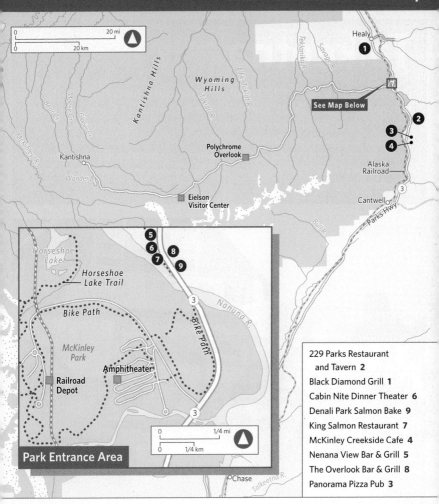

229 Parks Restaurant
  and Tavern **2**

Black Diamond Grill **1**

Cabin Nite Dinner Theater **6**

Denali Park Salmon Bake **9**

King Salmon Restaurant **7**

McKinley Creekside Cafe **4**

Nenana View Bar & Grill **5**

The Overlook Bar & Grill **8**

Panorama Pizza Pub **3**

to bring in the locals. There is a playground outside and a kid's menu, and they pack substantial sack lunches for the park shuttle-bus ride. Mile 224, Parks Hwy. ☎ 888-533-6254. www.mckinleycabins.com. Entrees $6–$21. DISC, MC, V. Breakfast, lunch, and dinner daily.

★ **Nenana View Bar & Grill** NENANA CANYON GRILL This comfortable restaurant overlooks the river, serving delicious pizza and great firegrilled steaks. At the McKinley Chalet Resort, Mile 238.9, Parks Hwy. ☎ 907-683-8200. www.denaliparkresorts.com. All items $12–$28. AE, DISC, MC, V. Lunch and dinner daily.

★ **The Overlook Bar & Grill** NENANA CANYON GRILL Up the steep mountain above the highway, the dining room and bar of rough-cut lumber are a cheerful, noisy setting for a beer and dinner. Mile 238.5, Parks Hwy., up the hill. ☎ 907-683-2641. Entrees $9–$44. MC, V. Lunch and dinner daily.

★ **Panorama Pizza Pub** CARLO CREEK PIZZA By the highway, this popular spot for pizza and beer also has a bakery/deli that packs lunches in cloth tote bags for the park bus. Local music often happens in the evening. Mile 224, Parks Hwy. ☎ 907-683-2623. Pizzas $13–$32. MC, V. Dinner daily till midnight.

Talkeetna

Talkeetna is a fun little town to visit in its own right, with its downtown strip of historic gold-rush buildings, a museum loaded with town spirit, and the mountaineering culture that gathers here, focused on Mount McKinley. But Talkeetna also works as part of a trip to Denali, allowing the outside-the-park portion of a visit to happen in a place with authenticity and character, unlike the touristy highway strip best known as Glitter Gulch near the national park entrance.

> Nagley's General Store has coffee and ice cream; founded in 1921, its motto is "Established Before Most of You Were Born."

START Talkeetna is 99 miles north of Anchorage and 138 miles south of Denali National Park

1 ★★ **Talkeetna Aero Services Denali National Park tour.** The downside to basing your Denali National Park visit in Talkeetna is that you could miss the most important part of the Denali experience—the bus ride to encounter the wildlife and scenery within the park. Talkeetna Aero Services solves that problem by offering a daily round-trip plane to the park

entrance, a package that includes ground transfers, a box lunch, and a park bus tour. My only reservation about this approach is that it may not allow enough time for a full appreciation of Denali. ⏱ 1 day. Village Airstrip, a half-block south of Main St. ☎ 888-733-2899. www.talkeetnaaero.com. Packages $395 per person.

2 ★★★ **Talkeetna Air Taxi flightseeing trip over Mount McKinley.** The best reason to come to Talkeetna is to fly over Mount McKinley and land on one of its glaciers. Since I've

MATANUSKA-
SUSUTNA

Beaver Rd

Gliska St

TALKEETNA

N Main St

Front St

Talkeetna Easy St

Railroad Ave

N Main St

Talkeetna Spur Rd

1st St

1st St

2nd St

2nd St

3rd St

3rd St

Denali St

2nd St

*Talkeetna
Village Strip
Airport*

Veterans Way

S Terminal Ave

*Talkeetna
Airport*

Talkeetna Spur

Alaska Railroad-Talkeetna

1. Talkeetna Aero Services Denali
   National Park tour
2. Talkeetna Air Taxi flightseeing trip
   over Mount McKinley
3. Talkeetna Historical Society Museum
4. Talkeetna Ranger Station
5. Mt. McKinley Climbers' Memorial
6. Jet boat tour with Mahay's
   Riverboat Service
7. Talkeetna River Guides rafting
   floats and fishing

Where to Stay & Dine
Café Michele **8**
Swiss-Alaska Inn **9**
Talkeetna Alaskan Lodge **10**

A L A S K A
Fairbanks
Talkeetna
Anchorage
Juneau
PACIFIC
OCEAN

*Susitna
River*

Talkeetna Spur

0   1/4 mi
0   1/4 km

> *For the best views and photo opportunities, ask for the copilot's seat on a flightseeing trip to Mount McKinley.*

already enthused about what you'll see, here are some of the important details: All flights depart from the airstrip across the railroad tracks from downtown Talkeetna. The air services are in small buildings on the perimeter of the strip. They all have good reputations, but I have personal experience with Talkeetna Air Taxi, which is why I'm recommending it. You'll most likely fly in a small, single-engine plane with just a few seats. If you want to take pictures, ask for the copilot's seat, which has the most window space. I recommend taking

A Bit About Talkeetna

The history of Talkeetna is among the richest in the region. The town began as a trading post and gold-rush center a century ago. When President Woodrow Wilson chose the route for the Alaska Railroad, Talkeetna became an important construction camp for the rails to the Interior. With World War I and the completion of the railroad, Talkeetna declined, a quiet backwater populated by backwoods folks, until the growth of mountain climbing and visitation to Denali National Park in the 1980s. Today its residents are visitor industry workers, mountain guides, and those backwoods folks who still simply love the rural life here.

the longest flight you can afford, including a glacier landing. This will be the best outing of your trip, and it's not the time to economize. ⏲ At least 1 hr. See p. 130, ❶.

❸ ★★ **Talkeetna Historical Society Museum.** This is quite a museum for such a small town. There are five buildings: first, one with artifacts on local mining history, including biographies of individual characters; second, a re-creation of the old railroad depot; third, a building with climbing displays and a fascinating model of Mount McKinley; and fourth and fifth, old trappers' cabins with period artifacts. ⏲ 1 hr. On the Village Airstrip, a half-block south of Main Street. ☎ 907-733-2487. www.talkeetna historicalsociety.org. Summer daily 10am–6pm; generally closed in winter. Admission $3 adults, free for children 12 and under.

❹ ★ **Talkeetna Ranger Station.** Besides being a useful information stop for your visit, the station offers a glimpse into the elite world of high-altitude mountaineering. It is the base for the national park's management of Mount McKinley climbers, and you can soak up the atmosphere here while learning about climbing. ⏲ 30 min. 1st and B sts. ☎ 907-733-2231. www.nps.gov/dena. May–Labor Day daily 8am–6pm; rest of the year Mon–Fri 8am–4:30pm.

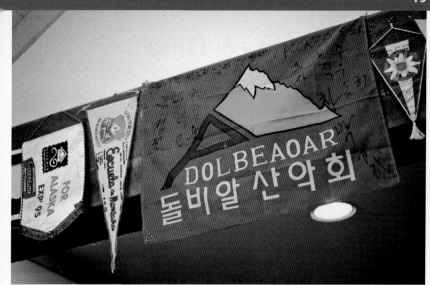

> *International climbing expedition flags decorate the rafters of the Talkeetna Ranger Station.*

⑤ ★ Mount McKinley Climbers' Memorial.
A visit to the town cemetery is interesting and sobering, as you take in the international monument to lost mountaineers and the markers and propellers for individual climbers and pilots. Some memorialize people who are not even buried here: More than three dozen climbers who have died on Mount McKinley remain frozen in its eternal snows. ⏱ 30 min. East of the railroad tracks, near the airstrip.

⑥ ★★ Jet boat tour with Mahay's Riverboat Service. Steve Mahay's speedy boats navigate the swift, glacial rivers that meet in Talkeetna, providing fun and exciting explorations on comfortable vessels. ⏱ At least a half-day. Near the Talkeetna River boat launch. ☎ 800-736-2210 or 907-733-2223. www.mahaysriverboat. com. $60 to $145 per person.

⑦ ★★ Talkeetna River Guides rafting floats and fishing. Rides from Talkeetna, run by **Talkeetna River Guides,** seek wildlife sightings, not white water. It's an easy and relatively inexpensive way for a family to get out into the wilderness and away from roads, without motors. The firm also offers nonmotorized fishing excursions. ⏱ 2 hr. Main St. ☎ 800-353-2677 or 907-733-2677. www.talkeetnariverguides.com. $69 adults, $49 children 10 and under.

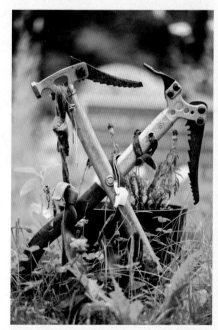

> *A climber's ice tools honor fallen comrades at the Mount McKinley Climbers' Memorial in the Talkeetna cemetery.*

Where to Stay & Dine

> Cafe Michele was voted one of the top ten restaurants in Alaska by the Food Network.

★★ **Café Michele** *BISTRO* In this bistro occupying a quaint little house downtown, sandwiches on homemade focaccia bread are served for lunch, and dinners have gained a wide reputation. Specialties include soy-ginger salmon and pesto cream seafood pasta. Don't miss the desserts. Talkeetna Spur Rd. and 2nd St. ☎ 907-733-5300. www.cafemichele.com.

More Information

Casual meals are easy to come by in downtown Talkeetna. You'll also find restaurants in the hotels listed here.

Entrees $24–$34. MC, V. Lunch and dinner daily. Closed Oct–May.

★ **Swiss-Alaska Inn** This is a friendly family business offering basic lodgings at reasonable rates. All rooms are clean and comfortable, but some are quite small. The restaurant serves familiar American meals, plus a few German dishes. F St., near the boat launch. ☎ 907-733-2424. www.swissalaska.com. 20 units. Doubles $132. AE, DISC, MC, V.

★★ **Talkeetna Alaskan Lodge** The hotel, beautifully built out of big timbers and river rock, stands on a bluff 2 miles from Talkeetna with

> *A river rock fireplace dominates the lobby at Talkeetna Alaskan Lodge.*

a remarkable view of Mount McKinley and the Alaska Range. Rooms are well appointed and common areas sumptuous, but the rates are high, even given the quality of the place. Dining options include a restaurant and a bistro.

Mile 12.5, Talkeetna Spur Rd. ☎ 888-959-9590 reservations; 907-733-9500 local. www.talkeetnalodge.com. 212 units. Doubles $265–$395. AE, DISC, MC, V. Closed Oct–Apr.

What Is a Glacier?

It took scientists a long time to figure out how glaciers work and how they shape the landscape. One of the most important clues was the mysterious presence of huge boulders in Europe's Alps, boulders that were nowhere near the rock outcroppings they had originally come from. The answer to the mystery lay in the extinct glaciers from long ago—from the last ice age—which had plucked the rocks from the original places they were created and moved them great distances before setting them down when the ice melted.

A glacier is a powerful machine for eroding mountains. It begins at high elevation, where air temperature is cool enough and precipitation heavy enough that the winter's snows never melt in the summer. As the snow grows deeper and heavier through decades and millennia, it compresses into dense ice. Eventually, the pressure is great enough that the ice begins sliding slowly downhill. With the immense force behind such a pile of ice, the glacial flow can bulldoze bedrock out of the

way. Underneath the glacier, the freeze-thaw cycle of super-pressurized water can crack bedrock and pluck chunks for further movement and pulverizing.

The glacier continues flowing downhill until it reaches an elevation where the face melts as fast as new snow and ice is being added up above. For hanging glaciers, that happens up in the mountains. For tidewater glaciers, it happens when the ice meets the ocean. In either case, the melting zone is where the glacier leaves all the rocky refuse it has carved out of the mountain on its passage, including big boulders (called *glacial erratics*), long damlike berms of gravel (called *moraines*), and table-flat plains, created by silt-laden streams of melt called *braided rivers*, which spread the material as they switch channels. Once you learn to recognize these features around the active glaciers in Alaska, you can pick them out all over the northern United States and Canada, where the glaciers of earlier ice ages once shaped the land.

Denali & Mat-Su Fast Facts

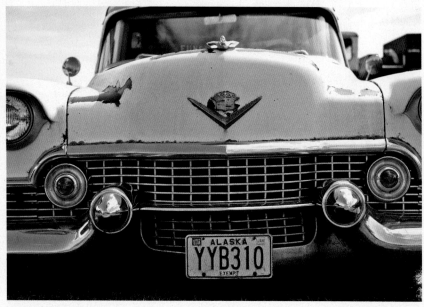

> *An old school ride at the Museum of Alaska Transportation and Industry.*

ATMs

Cash machines are scattered through the Nenana Canyon area, including at Lynx Creek Market Store and Deli, on the Parks Highway.

Dentists & Doctors

DENALI The seasonal Canyon Clinic, ☎ 907-683-4433, is near the park entrance, daily 9am to 6pm with help on call 24 hours. **HEALY** Year-round, 12 miles north of the park entrance, is Community Interior Health Center, ☎ 907-683-2211, Monday through Friday 9am to 5pm. **TALKEETNA** Talkeetna Denali Family Medical Clinic, 125 1st St., ☎ 907-733-2708. **PALMER** or **WASILLA** Mat-Su Regional Medical Center, 2500 S. Woodworth Ln. in Palmer, ☎ 907-861-6000.

There are no dental clinics in these communities—if you have a problem, check in with a doctor at one of the above health centers for advice on finding a dentist.

Getting There & Getting Around

Denali National Park can be reached by road or rail. The only road is the Parks Highway, which connects Fairbanks and Anchorage; the park is about 240 miles north of Anchorage and 120 miles south of Fairbanks. The **Alaska Railroad** (☎ 800-544-0552 or 907-265-2494; www.alaskarailroad.com) parallels the Parks Highway and also serves the park. Service details are on p. 151.

Shuttle buses run within the park, and hotel shuttles connect the park entrance area to nearby hotels. Rail passengers should choose those close accommodations. If you drive to Denali, you can stay and eat at farther-flung places. Taxis aren't a good option here, and there is no public transportation.

Emergencies

Dial ☎ **911.** In the national park backcountry, you won't find telephones or cellular service, but bus drivers do have radio contact.

Internet Access

Connections and Wi-Fi are widely available, even in some lodgings that don't have telephones.

Pharmacies

It's wise to stock up, including at pharmacies, before departing the city for Denali National Park. Since the park is seasonal, stores there mainly carry convenience groceries and camping items. The nearest major pharmacies are in large grocery stores in Wasilla, Palmer, Anchorage, and Fairbanks.

Police

DENALI The Alaska State Troopers, ☎ 907-683-2232 or 907-768-2202, have posts in **Healy**, 12 miles north of the park, and in **Cantwell**, 28 miles south. TALKEETNA The Alaska State Troopers, ☎ 907-733-2256, are based near the Parks Highway on the Talkeetna Spur Road. PALMER/WASILLA The Alaska State Troopers can be reached at ☎ 907-745-2131, 453 S. Valley Way (in Palmer), and the Palmer Police Department can be reached at ☎ 907-745-4811, 423 S. Valley Way. The Wasilla Police Department can be reached at ☎ 907-352-5401, 1800 E. Parks Hwy.

Post Office

DENALI NATIONAL PARK This post office is just within the park entrance, near the Riley Creek Campground. TALKEETNA It's on the left side of the Spur Highway as you enter the town.

Safety

Other than the constant concern in Alaska about sexual assault, crime is not a particular problem in the Denali region. Important tips for driving rural highways and maintaining outdoor safety are covered in chapters 2 and 14. Always check road reports before driving Alaska highways in winter; in summer, verifying can mean avoiding construction delays that can last hours. Call ☎ 511 or go to http://511.alaska.gov.

Be aware of avalanche conditions. Only experienced and properly equipped backcountry users should go off-trail in the winter. To check current avalanche conditions in Hatcher Pass, go to http://dnr.alaska.gov/parks/asp/curevnts.htm.

Toilets

At the park entrance area, public bathrooms are plentiful—in the hotels, visitor centers, campgrounds, and other public facilities. Within the park, the shuttle and tour buses frequently stop at outhouses along the way.

Visitor Information

DENALI Try the Denali National Park Visitor Center, at the park entrance, P.O. Box 9, Denali National Park, AK 99755 (☎ 907-683-2294; www.nps.gov/dena). TALKEETNA Denali National Park Talkeetna Ranger Station, at 1st and B streets (P.O. Box 588), Talkeetna, AK 99676 (☎ 907-733-2231) has information on Talkeetna. PALMER/WASILLA Check out the Mat-Su Visitors Center, 7744 E. Visitors View Court, Palmer, AK 99645 (☎ 907-746-5000; www.alaskavisit.com).

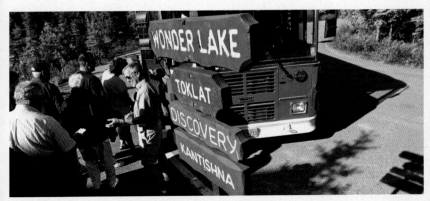

> *Visitors get ready for the ride of a lifetime in Denali National Park.*

Prince William Sound & the Copper River Country

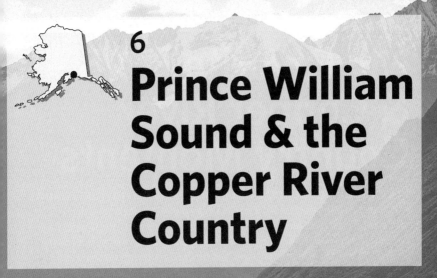

My Favorite PWS & Copper River Country Moments

Prince William Sound is an inland sea with myriad islands and fjords, an intricately folded shoreline, high mountain peaks, and thick rainforest timber shrouded in mist. Its opposite in many ways, the Copper River Country lies beyond the first ring of mountains and glaciers that surrounds the Sound; this is a dry land of small trees and tundra, bright with sunshine and traversed by long highways and rivers. Although they contrast in so many ways, the two regions are linked by geography and natural transportation routes. In visiting both, you encounter much of the broad range of what Alaska has to offer, and do it in off-the-beaten-track places that are not overrun with other visitors.

> PREVIOUS PAGE *Matanuska Glacier is 4 miles wide and 27 miles long.* THIS PAGE *The Chenega ferry plies the waters of Prince William Sound.*

❶ Crossing Prince William Sound by ferry.
The state ferries that cross the Sound are everyday transportation for the people who live here, but for visitors they show off the scenery of islands and snowy mountains almost as well as a tour boat. That means you don't pay a lot to see a huge swath of the Sound, with the bonus of ending up at the next step on your journey. See p. 189, ❸.

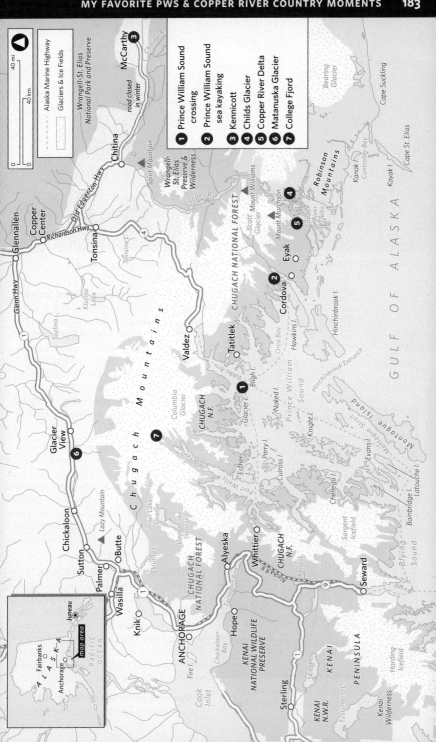

1 Prince William Sound crossing
2 Prince William Sound sea kayaking
3 Kennicott
4 Childs Glacier
5 Copper River Delta
6 Matanuska Glacier
7 College Fjord

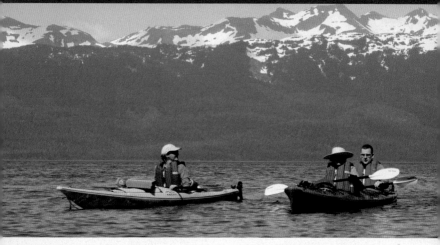

> *Cordova Coastal Outfitters rents bikes, kayaks, skiffs, canoes, and fishing and camping gear.*

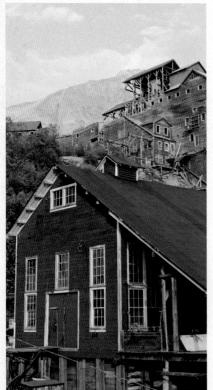

> *The Alaska Syndicate founded Kennicott as a copper mining town in 1911, and abandoned it 27 years later.*

2 Sea kayaking in Prince William Sound. You can do it from Whittier, Valdez, or Cordova—it's all good—but if I had a choice, I'd paddle with **Cordova Coastal Outfitters** from that town's harbor to the largest rafts of sea otters that I've ever seen (they're counted in the hundreds). Besides offering access to wildlife and scenery, a sea kayak also lets you land on the shore and explore untracked places at will, creating a feeling of complete freedom. See p. 212, **4**.

3 Touring the mining ghost town at Kennicott. A century ago the richest men in the world built a complete town and industrial facility here in a place that remains remote wilderness. Then one day, when the copper was running out, suddenly they closed it, leaving breakfast dishes on tables and invoices on desks. Walking through more than 70 years later takes you back in time in a unique way. See p. 214, **1**.

4 Feeling the chill from Childs Glacier. The region is Alaska's most heavily glaciated, but none of the giant frozen monsters is more impressive than this one, 48 miles east of Cordova. Viewers see it from across the Copper River, which cuts the glacier's face to leave a wall of ice that fills your field of vision. You can feel both the cold on your face and the grinding rumble of moving ice in your gut. See p. 212.

5 Canoeing on the Copper River Delta. The delta is among the hemisphere's most

> *Sea otters share their shellfish—you may see them floating past if you kayak on Prince William Sound.*

important migratory stopovers and breeding grounds for a huge variety of birds. Its networks of streams and ponds make for wonderful wilderness paddling, especially along Alaganik Slough, where you can have a canoe delivered for your use. See p. 209, 10.

6 Rafting at Matanuska Glacier. The glacier lies like a sleeping beast in the canyon it carved. The great Matanuska River flows from its melt, producing rapids wild enough for the most daring river riders as well as more relaxed floating suitable for families with kids. **Nova Raft and Adventure Tours** has the experience to keep you safe and ensure a fun outing. See p. 221, 4.

7 Exploring College Fjord. The boats that voyage from Whittier make the great glaciers and narrow passages of western Prince William Sound remarkably accessible, even for a day trip from Anchorage. For the best all-day tour, ride to Whittier on a comfortable Alaska Railroad train and enjoy the scenery of Turnagain Arm before going through the tunnel to the Sound and boarding a boat to take in as many as two dozen glaciers. See p. 201, 2.

> *The rising sun creeps over the Matanuska Glacier.*

THE SECRET LIVES OF WHALES

A look at Alaska's magnificent sea life

BY LINDA BARTH

ALASKA MAY BE KNOWN FOR ITS MOUNTAINS AND GLACIERS, but one of the greatest natural wonders you'll see here is the whale. There are 11 species living off the coast of Alaska (Beaked, Beluga, Blue, Bowhead, Fin, Humpback, Gray, Orca, Minke, North Pacific Right, and Sperm), and if you spend any time on the coast, the odds are that you'll see at least one of them. Whales are incredibly intelligent and playful, and they live in groups called pods that can range in size from just a few to over a hundred. These communities are tight knit, but the closest relationships are between calves (as the babies are known) and their mothers. To keep in touch as they travel vast expanses of ocean, whales communicate using echolocation, sending out noises ranging from clicks to what, in the case of humpback whales, sounds like singing. Some guides carry equipment that allows them to amplify whale sounds—ask about it when you're booking a whale-watch.

Getting Lucky: Four Whales You're Most Likely to See

ORCA

The killer whale earned its name by killing and eating other whales. An adult male can grow to up to 27 feet in length, weighing in at 13,300 pounds (twice as much as adult female). But orca can be almost playful, coming in close to check out boats—kayaking amid orca is an extraordinary experience. They are fairly easy to see off the coast of Southeast Alaska and in the Aleutian Islands from early spring through the late summer.

BELUGA

These relatively small (males can grow up to 16 feet), toothed whales can live in

extremely cold water — it doesn't have a dorsal fin, which allows it to swim under ice without getting stuck. They're hard to miss, both because they're white—the word "beluga" comes from the Russian word for white—and because they gather near shore to feed and calve during the summer.

GRAY

Every year, the gray whale makes one of the animal kingdoms longest migrations, traveling up to 14,000 miles from coastal Alaska to Baja California, where they mate and calve before

heading back up north. Because they prefer relatively shallow waters, the gray whale is fairly easy to spot from shore. These giants (a male can grow to 46 feet in length and weigh up to 40 tons) are particularly sociable, and have been known to swim right up to boats to say hello.

HUMPBACK

At birth, humpbacks weigh 1.5 tons, and females can grow up to 49 feet long and weigh 35 tons (males are a bit smaller). They're really fun to watch leaping out of the water, slapping their tails, and generally cavorting.

Unfortunately, they are endangered thanks to years of hunting and entanglement in fishing and boat lines.

Alaska's Best Whale-Watching

Coastal Southeast Alaska offers some of the best whale-watching in the state—you can get great whale-watching trips out of Seward (p. 268), Whittier (p. 189, ❷), and Homer (p. 260). From Valdez, Stan Stephen's boat tour of Prince William Sound (p. 222, ❶) offers a glimpse of lots of sea life, including humpbacks. Cordova's Orca Inlet (p. 212, ❹) is an excellent place to rent a kayak and possibly get up close with (what else?) killer whales (and even the occasional humpback), as does Icy Strait, off of Gustavus (p. 367). Kenai Fjords National Park (p. 234, ❺) offers some of the state's best whale-watching, and you're likely to see orca, humpback, fin, and minke whales in the summer, and gray whales in the spring. Frederick Sound (p. 404) is also a good place to spot orca and humpback whales. Finally, Cook Inlet (p. 83, ⓮) is the best place to spot beluga whales.

The Best of PWS & the Copper River Country in 3 Days

The loop by ferry and highway across Prince William Sound and through the Copper River Country is a classic long-weekend trip from Anchorage, and makes all kinds of sense for visitors. Besides viewing the Sound from the ferry, you'll have the opportunity to get out on the water, from either Whittier or Valdez. The drive onward from Valdez takes you over the coastal mountains, through some of Alaska's most spectacular highway scenery, and into the Interior, a region that differs in weather, terrain, and culture from the coastal areas. There, you'll have plenty of opportunities for hiking or rafting. Plan to rent a car in Anchorage.

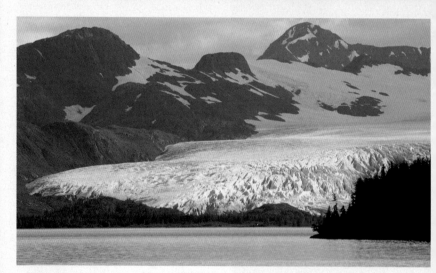

> *A tidewater glacier creeps into Prince William Sound; in the background alpine glaciers are visible.*

START Anchorage. **TRIP LENGTH** 428 miles.

1 ★★★ **Seward Highway.** This lovely stretch of road is an excellent introduction to Alaska. ◷ 90 min. See p. 250, **1**.

You'll need to pass through the 2¾-mile-long Anton Anderson Memorial Tunnel en route to your next stop. Because the tunnel is used by both trains and cars, there can be a wait, so be prepared, and give yourself at least 90 minutes to get from Anchorage to:

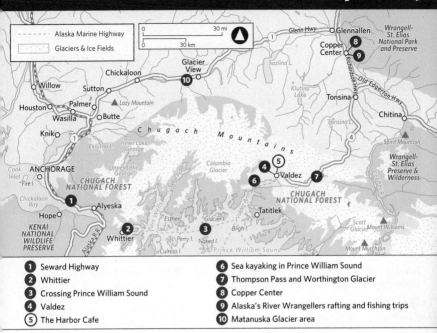

Legend:
- - - - Alaska Marine Highway
☐ Glaciers & Ice Fields

0   30 mi
0   30 km

1. Seward Highway
2. Whittier
3. Crossing Prince William Sound
4. Valdez
5. The Harbor Cafe
6. Sea kayaking in Prince William Sound
7. Thompson Pass and Worthington Glacier
8. Copper Center
9. Alaska's River Wranglers rafting and fishing trips
10. Matanuska Glacier area

2 ★ **Whittier.** Other than access to Prince William Sound, Whittier's primary attraction is its oddness. If it looks like a military outpost, that's because it once was. During World War II, Whittier's ice-fee port, at the head of the Passage Canal fjord, became a critical route for bringing defense materials into Alaska. The military built both a tunnel through the mountain to make getting here easier, and a 14-story concrete building to house personnel. The military is long gone, but the townspeople still live in that one big building. Whittier has more railroad yard and port than road, and people get around more through lengthy pedestrian tunnels than on sidewalks. ⏱ 1 hr. See p. 201, **3**.

You'll need to be at the waterfront ferry terminal in time to catch the ferry across Prince William Sound. It runs almost every day in summer, and it's usually possible to book space for a car with little advance notice. But for peak periods, and to be on the safe side, reserve your place as early as possible. Walk-on passengers don't need reservations.

3 ★★★ kids **Crossing Prince William Sound.** The 78-mile ferry ride on the Alaska Marine Highway System's *Chenega* is a highlight of the trip. Children love this boat, where they can explore the decks and passageways while other vessels and unfamiliar shores speed by outside the windows. Although the ship is too fast for seeing much wildlife, you'll pass the wooded islets and deep fjords of Prince William Sound, and even glimpse Bligh Reef, where the tanker *Exxon Valdez* grounded in 1989, causing North America's largest oil spill, at least 11 million gallons in size. Chugach National Forest encompasses the entire region, and a ranger is often aboard, offering interpretive talks and answering questions. ⏱ 3 hr. Alaska Marine Highway System. ☎ 800-642-0066. www.ferryalaska.com. $89 one-way, half-price for children 6–11, free for children 5 and under; additional $105 for a 15-foot car.

More Information

See p. 225 for more information on hotels and restaurants in Valdez; for Copper Center, see p. 191; and for the Matanuska Glacier area, see p. 221.

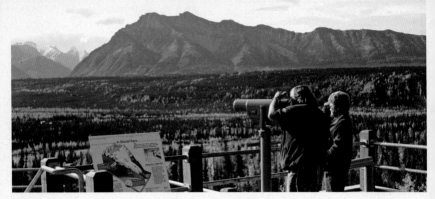

> *The Matanuska Glacier State Recreation Site is easily accessible from the Glenn highway and provides fantastic views, campgrounds, and restrooms.*

Take the rest of your very busy first day to explore Valdez, where you'll spend the night.

④ ★★ kids Valdez. The ferry puts you in Valdez in the afternoon. It's is not a beautiful town, but the setting, on the water below steep, snowy mountains, certainly is. The 1964 Great Alaska Earthquake (see "Whole Lotta Shaking," on p. 208) completely destroyed the town, which has a gold-rush pedigree, and it has been rebuilt on the current site since then. There are three fascinating little museums that you could see in an afternoon. The **Valdez Museum and Historical Archive** (p. 224, ⑤) tells the town's story in a way that combines small-town charm and professional skill. The museum's **annex** is essentially another museum, in a building next to the ferry dock; it contains the Remembering Old Valdez Exhibit, a scale model of the town before the earthquake. The **Maxine & Jesse Whitney Museum** (p. 224, ⑦) houses the large and miscellaneous collection of a pair of Alaska pioneers, and captures the spirit of a bygone time in this offbeat region.

If you'd prefer to spend the rest of your first day outdoors, there are several excellent hiking trails in Valdez, including a short walk through seaside woods at **Dock Point** (p. 223, ④) or the 12-mile-long **Shoup Glacier trail** (p. 223, ③). The latter provides access along the way to wilderness beaches decorated with wild irises. ⏱ Half-day. See p. 222.

⑤ 🍽 **The Harbor Café.** This is the prime stop in Valdez for lunch or a snack, with the best food I've ever encountered at a place with picnic tables and a menu posted on the wall. 225 N. Harbor Dr. ☎ 907-835-4776. $$. See p. 225.

Get an early start on Day 2.

⑥ ★★★ **Sea kayaking in Prince William Sound.** Set aside most of your second day to get out on the water, on a sea kayaking day trip with **Pangaea Adventures** (p. 223, ②) to experience Shoup Glacier. A boat will carry you to spectacular **Shoup Glacier State Park,** where you'll launch your kayaks. You will paddle in calm water and get a close look at the ice, eating lunch on the shore near the glacier's face. If you prefer, Valdez is also a good place to take a fishing charter (see **Fish Central** on p. 202) or a raft ride (p. 223, ②). ⏱ 1 day.

Wrap up Day 2 by taking the Richardson Highway 105 miles north into the mountains behind Prince William Sound.

⑦ ★★ kids **Thompson Pass and Worthington Glacier.** The Richardson Highway, the first route into Alaska from the sea, was originally a dog-sled path, and it winds its way up into the mountains along the rock corridor of Keystone Canyon and over the dizzying alpine scenery of Thompson Pass. You'll want to stop along the road to take it all in. The pass receives an average annual snowfall of 47 feet; all that snow piling on these coastal mountains creates glaciers, and 30 miles out of Valdez, one comes near the road. Park at **Worthington Glacier State Recreation Site** and walk a 1-mile trail to the glacier's face. ⏱ **3 hr. for the drive, with stops.**

Continue on the Richardson Highway to Copper Center, where you'll spend the night.

❽ ★ **Copper Center.** The small houses and dusty roads of this tiny Athabascan village offer a glimpse of rural Alaskan life. The poverty and simplicity of things may surprise you, but remember that people here live close to the land and their traditions; it's a heritage many value more highly than urban comforts. You can also get a small taste of **Wrangell–St. Elias National Park** (p. 55, ❻)—its prodigious mountains are in the distance. You would need at least a full day to get into the nation's largest national park, but stop at the park's visitor center and headquarters in Copper Center, which has displays, ranger programs, and a short nature trail. ⏱ **1 hr. Mile 106, Richardson Hwy. ☎ 907-822-7250. www. nps.gov/wrst. Summer daily 8am–7pm; winter Mon–Fri 8am–4:30pm.**

Spend Day 3 on the water. If you're not interested in fishing, take the shorter float trip. If you do go fishing, it's an all-day trip, so you'll need to skip stop ❿.

❾ ★★ **Alaska's River Wrangellers rafting and fishing trips.** Before leaving Copper Center, consider a river rafting or fishing trip. The area is huge and little used, so your experience will be in the midst of real wilderness. Alaska River Wrangellers offers a schedule that allows clients to choose a trip for the level of risk, adventure, and remoteness they are comfortable with, or to combine white-water rafting with salmon fishing. ⏱ **At least a half-day for float, 1 day for fishing. Copper Center landing strip. ☎ 888-822-3967. www.riverwrangellers. com. Float from $99, full-day Tonsina River fishing trip from $299.**

In the afternoon, drive 88 miles north on the Richardson Highway and west on the Glenn Highway to the Matanuska Glacier area, before your evening drive back to Anchorage.

❿ ★★ 🅺🅸🅳🆂 **Matanuska Glacier area.** The Glenn Highway crosses high alpine country and a grand tundra plateau, where caribou can sometimes be seen from the road. Good hiking trails branch off at various spots, and each of the two lodges here has its own trails and friendly, outdoorsy folks to give advice. In wintertime, the area is a cross-country skier's paradise, with many miles of groomed trails at the lodges and limitless backcountry skiing.

If you have a hankering to see another glacier, the huge **Matanuska Glacier** is visible from the highway to the west (onward toward Anchorage). The **Matanuska Glacier State Recreation Site** overlooks it and has a nature trail and campground. To get closer, in the summer only, you can take a rough, 3-mile side road to **Glacier Park** (p. 220, ❶). ⏱ **1 hr. for the drive, 2 hr. for the nature trail.**

Spending the Night near Copper Center

The best place to stay and eat near Copper Center is the **Copper River Princess Wilderness Lodge,** built to resemble the historic red mining buildings in the park. Owned by the cruise line of the same name, the lodge combines its location in the heart of beautiful, remote country with accommodations and food at the company's high standards. 1 Brenwick-Craig Rd. (at Mile 102, Richardson Hwy.), Copper Center. ☎ 800-426-0500 or 907-822-4000. www.princesslodges.com. 85 units. Doubles $179. AE, DISC, MC, V.

The Best of PWS & the Copper River Country in 1 Week

Adding just a few days to a tour of this region makes a huge difference, as it allows you to visit two of the state's most appealing and out-of-the-way spots: Kennicott and Cordova. Your friends may question your decision to spend a week of your vacation in these relatively obscure towns—you can just smile. We're better off keeping these secrets to ourselves. Like the 3-day tour above, this trip begins and ends in Anchorage, using both highway and ferry, but it differs in that you're traveling the loop in the opposite direction. Depending on the days of travel you choose, you can arrange passage on the Prince William Sound ferry to go either way; the first step of your planning should be to study the ferry schedule, which doesn't offer rides in every direction every day.

> *The 328-mile Glenn Highway shrinks from a six-lane road in downtown Anchorage to two lanes in Tok.*

START Anchorage. TRIP LENGTH 667 miles.

Drive north on the Glenn Highway.

1 ★ **Glenn Highway.** The drive on the Glenn Highway, beyond Palmer to the Matanuska Glacier area, is among the most dramatic—and scariest—in Alaska, as the highway traces the edge of a canyon over the river and glacier. Allow some time for spontaneous stops at rural roadside spots that may catch your interest. ⏰ 2½ hr.

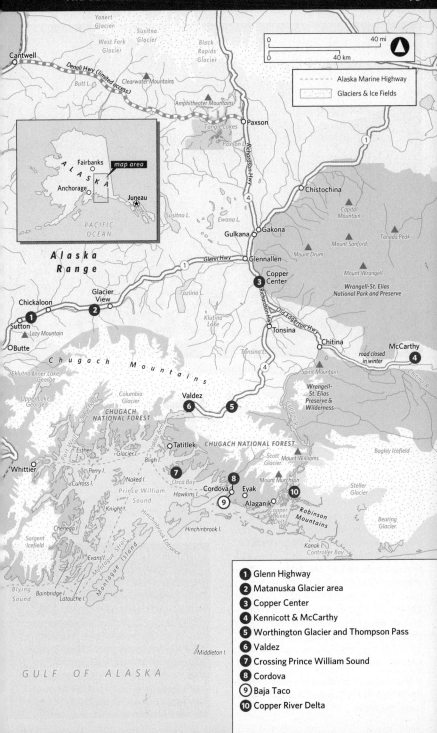

1 Glenn Highway
2 Matanuska Glacier area
3 Copper Center
4 Kennicott & McCarthy
5 Worthington Glacier and Thompson Pass
6 Valdez
7 Crossing Prince William Sound
8 Cordova
9 Baja Taco
10 Copper River Delta

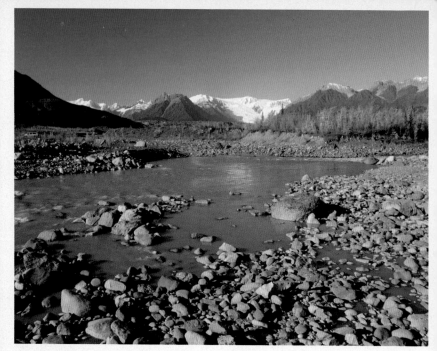

> *The road ends at the Kennicott River, but a footbridge will take you farther in to McCarthy.*

Continue on the Glenn Highway 114 miles from Anchorage.

② ★★ kids **Matanuska Glacier area.** The huge Matanuska Glacier itself lies below the road, and you can see it as you drive. The best road-side spot for a really good look is the **Matanuska Glacier State Recreation Site** (p. 220, **③**) on the canyon rim above the ice and with a nature trail and campground. To approach the glacier at its own level, take a rough, 3-mile side road, summer only, to **Glacier Park** (p. 220, **①**). A guide service with 3 decades of experience, **Nova Raft and Adventure Tours,** offers both daily hikes on the glacier to see its crevasses and strange ice formations (p. 221, **④**) and raft rides on the water that comes from it, which forms the Matanuska River (p. 204, **①**, for a family-friendly run; p. 221 for a more daring ride). Reserve your raft ride in advance. ◷ Half-day.

In the afternoon, continue 88 miles along the Glenn Highway to Copper Center, where you'll spend the night.

③ ★ **Copper Center.** You'll drive one of Alaska's most spectacular sections of road, the Glenn Highway eastward from the Matanuska Glacier, as it crosses the high alpine country and a tundra plateau with long sight-lines that allow you to view caribou from the road. From several pull-outs along the way hiking trails climb over the mountains along the way—if you have the time, by all means stop and explore. Copper Center itself is a tiny

Driving Off-Pavement

Unpaved roads create a significant consideration in traveling this region, since most rental car contracts prohibit driving on them. Follow the work-arounds I've included at each place where pavement ends; or rent a car from a local company that allows driving on unpaved roads. In Anchorage, one such company is **High Country Car and Truck Rental** (☎ 888-685-1155; www.highcountry anchorage.com) See "Renting the Right Car for Going Off-Pavement," on p. 509.

Athabascan village and will give you a taste of rural Alaskan life. Get your orientation to the park at the **Wrangell–St. Elias National Park Visitor Center and Headquarters** (p. 191, ⑧). ◷ Half-day for the drive and visitor center.

Get an early start on Day 2 for your journey to Kennicott and McCarthy, where you'll spend the next 2 nights. Getting there is half the adventure—see "Getting to Kennicott & McCarthy," at right for details.

④ ★★★ Kids **Kennicott & McCarthy.** I've brought you all this way to see an extraordinary and unique place, where history survives with crystal clarity amid a wilderness that has never been conquered. In 1911 the Alaska Syndicate, owned by the age's wealthiest Wall Street barons, finished building a railroad from the port of Cordova to this spot: a copper find of such richness that its discoverer at first mistook its bare rocks for grass where he could feed his horses. The syndicate built the town of Kennecott (the misspelling is long-standing), only to abandon it when copper prices fell in 1938—with everything left in place. Now part of the national park, the ghost town is a window on that time. The sister town of McCarthy was where the miners went on rare partying breaks, and it remains a fun and welcoming rural outpost. Spend your first afternoon in the area exploring casually.

The outdoor opportunities are many, but no one should miss a guided tour through the ghost town buildings of Kennicott. **St. Elias Alpine Guides** (see "Getting the Most out of the Great Outdoors," on p. 218) leads these tours with remarkable professionalism and verve. To complete a wonderful day, join their Root Glacier hike in the afternoon. ◷ 1½ days. Tour $25; half-day hike on Root Glacier $65.

On Day 4 leave Kennicott and McCarthy for the 178-mile drive (118 from Chitina, or 105 from Copper Center) to Valdez, much of it on the Richardson Highway.

⑤ ★★ Kids **Worthington Glacier and Thompson Pass.** The Richardson Highway traces the silver skein of the Trans-Alaska Pipeline through the mountains toward Valdez. Before the steep descent to the fjord where the town lies, stop at the **Worthington Glacier State Recreation Site** and walk the 1-mile trail to the glacier's face; there is no fee, and the site is

Getting to Kennicott & McCarthy

You have three choices for making the trek from Copper Center to the historic Kennicott and McCarthy area within Wrangell–St. Elias National Park.

The **Backcountry Connection van** (☎ 866-582-5292 in Alaska, or 907-822-5292; www.kennicottshuttle.com) is a good compromise between ease and reasonable cost. It leaves Copper Center and nearby towns early in the morning, taking 3½ hours for the one-way trip and arriving at 11:30am. The return trip departs at 4:30pm; they also offer the option of flying one way. Round-trip van fare is $99 per person on the same day, or $139 if you return on a different day.

Going by air both ways is the easiest and quickest route. Just take the Richardson and Edgerton highways 52 miles to Chitina (the road is paved) and fly with **Wrangell Mountain Air** (p. 218). The half-hour trip, departing three times a day, includes glacier viewing. Luggage is limited, and tickets cost $229 round trip.

By parking your car and taking the van or plane, and then picking it up on the return ride, you avoid the complication of finding a rental car that you can permissibly drive on unpaved roads. But you *can* drive yourself there, if you don't mind the rough road. From Copper Center take the Richardson Highway south 17 miles to the Edgerton Highway, which you'll follow east for its full 35 paved miles to the hardly-there town of Chitina. Continue from Chitina on the 60-mile, dirt McCarthy Road, which ends at the Kennicott River and is crossed by a **footbridge** (p. 217). Under normal summer conditions, any reliable vehicle can make the trip; the road is closed off-season.

More Information

See p. 221 for more information on hotels and restaurants in the Matanuska Glacier area; for Kennicott and McCarthy, see p. 219; and for Cordova, see p. 213.

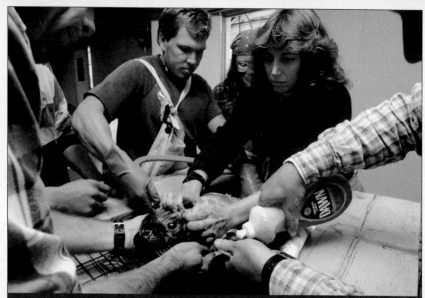

An Environmental Disaster: The Wreck of the *Exxon Valdez*

Oil has brought great wealth, development, and job opportunities to Alaska, but it also lies at the root of one of the United States' worst environmental disasters. Just after midnight on March 24, 1989, the *Exxon Valdez*—freshly loaded with oil from the Alaska pipeline—ran aground on the clearly marked Bligh Reef while trying to avoid icebergs in the Valdez Narrows. Later investigations blamed both Exxon and the U.S. Coast Guard for cost-cutting and complacency. When the ship wrecked, an unqualified third mate was handling the job of two officers; Captain Joe Hazelwood had left the bridge after a night of drinking and other officers were recovering from round-the-clock work shifts. The damage was colossal. At

least 11 million gallons (257,000 barrels) of oil hemorrhaged into Prince William Sound. The spill impacted 1,300 miles of shoreline and, according to state estimates, killed more than 250,000 seabirds, 2,800 sea otters (a lucky one gets cleaned, above), 300 harbor seals, 250 bald eagles, 22 orcas, and billions of salmon. Despite a cleanup effort that cost over $2 billion, oil could still be found buried in some beaches on the Sound 21 years later, although visitors won't see signs of damage. Some species never returned to their pre-spill numbers, but the passage of time makes it difficult to identify the cause of problems. The Sound's important Pacific herring fishery crashed after the spill and has never re-opened.

always open. It's as close as roadside glacier encounters get. This ice exists due to the immense snowfall that piles up here, an average of 47 feet a winter. The vertical scenery of Thompson Pass comes next, then rock-walled Keystone Canyon. ⏱ 4 hr. for the drive from Kennicott and McCarthy, 2 hr. from Chitina or Copper Center; 1 hr. total for stops.

In the afternoon, you'll arrive in Valdez, where you'll spend the night.

❻ ★★ kids Valdez. After Kennicott, the museums in Valdez may hold special interest, helping you put together the region's story. There are three. **The Valdez Museum and Historical Archive** (p. 224, ❺) presents a walk through time with a series of exhibits and recreated rooms. In a separate **annex,** essentially a different museum, you can see a scale model of Valdez from before its destruction in the 1964 Great Alaska Earthquake (see "Whole Lotta Shaking," on p. 208). The **Maxine & Jesse Whitney Museum**

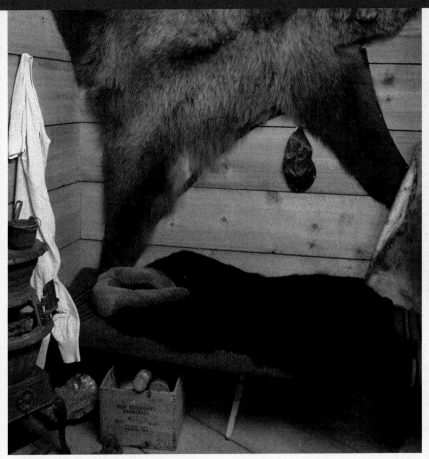

> *A recreated prospector's cabin at the Valdez Museum and Historical Archive helps visitors imagine what life must have been like during the gold rush.*

(p. 224, **7**) recaptures the time of Alaska pioneers half a century ago. ⏱ Half-day.

Once again, get an early start on Day 5, catching the ferry for the 84-mile voyage across Prince William Sound to Cordova.

7 ★★★ kids **Crossing Prince William Sound.** ⏱ 3 hr. See p. 189, **3**.

Spend what's left of Day 5 and Day 6 exploring Cordova, where you'll spend the next 2 nights.

8 ★★★ kids **Cordova.** This little fishing town combines the best qualities of coastal Alaska. Off the road network and small enough to have retained the feel of old-time America, before McDonald's or Wal-Mart, Cordova is in a remote corner of special beauty. The outdoor opportunities are unmatched, and there are plenty of friendly folks to guide you. **Cordova Coastal Outfitters** (p. 212, **4**) is run by enthusiasts who want to show off their home. Their sea kayaking outings from the harbor encounter sea lions and rafts of sea otters. ⏱ 2½ days. See p. 210.

⑨ 🍴 **Baja Taco.** The bus with the restaurant that grew up around it, near the harbor, is probably the best place to eat in town, and it definitely has the best coffee and milk shakes. **South end of the boat harbor.** ☎ 907-424-5599. $–$$. See p. 213.

> *An aerial view of Cordova shows the town's harbor, Eyak Lake, and the Chugach National Forest.*

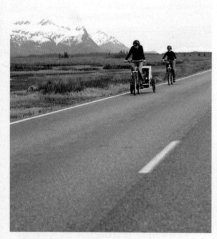

> *Bikers on the Copper River Highway.*

On the last day of your tour, spend at least a few hours in the Copper River Delta. The Copper River Highway, the only road out of Cordova, runs through it.

🔟 ★★★ kids **Copper River Delta.** The delta's enormous wetlands are a migratory bird stopover of global importance, and one of the loveliest places I know for bird-watching and scenic driving; if you can't drive your car on this gravel route because of your rental agreement, you can rent an older-model car, van, or SUV from **Northern Nights Inn** (p. 213). The Copper River Highway is the old bed of the railroad to Kennicott. It extends only 48 miles these days, ending near **Childs Glacier** (see "Alaska's Best Glacier," on p. 212). You can feel the rumbling of the ice in your bones and occasionally see great chunks crash into the water. ⏱ At least a half-day. See p. 209, 🔟.

Heading for Home

The fastest way to return to Anchorage from Cordova is by taking the ferry back across Prince William Sound to Whittier and driving the scenic Seward Highway. If you catch the 8:30am boat, you'll be back in Anchorage by 2pm.

Teddy Roosevelt & the Battle for Alaska

The remote and sleepy towns of Kennicott and Cordova played a crucial role in an environmental battle a century ago that seized the nation and helped bring down a president.

In 1906, President Theodore Roosevelt (above) stopped the sale of coal lands in the region, and in 1907 created Chugach National Forest, on the advice of his conservation chief, Gifford Pinchot. In 1909 Roosevelt handed over the White House to his handpicked successor, William Howard Taft, with the understanding that Taft would keep Pinchot on board and honor his conservation philosophy.

But Taft appointed Pinchot's enemy, Seattle judge Richard Ballinger, as Secretary of the Interior. Ballinger had worked as an attorney for men claiming coal resources near the Bering River, in Chugach National Forest just east of Prince William Sound. His former clients hoped to sell mining rights to the Alaska Syndicate, which needed coal for the railroad from Cordova to the Kennicott copper mine. The syndicate was controlled in turn by J. P. Morgan and the Guggenheim family.

When Ballinger tried to approve coal mining despite Roosevelt's previous order, Pinchot blew the whistle in the national press and was fired by Taft. Dramatic congressional hearings produced months of headlines and finally an embarrassing admission by Taft that he had lied about aspects of the controversy. Roosevelt, disenchanted with Taft, decided to run against him in 1912.

But Taft now controlled the Republican Party machine. Despite losing the primaries to Roosevelt, he won the nomination at a crooked party convention in Chicago. Roosevelt responded by starting his own Bull Moose Party to run for president, thus splitting the Republican vote in the general election. Democrat Woodrow Wilson came in first, Roosevelt second, and Taft third.

Some historians point to that 1912 election as the dividing line—the point at which Democrats took over the progressive and conservation issues that Roosevelt had championed as a Republican president, and the Republicans instead became known as a pro-business party.

Conservation battles continued for decades more in Alaska—and continue to this day. In the end, foes were unable to abolish Chugach National Forest, although they did shrink it enough to allow room for the city of Anchorage, founded in 1914 on former national forest land. The coal eventually got into private hands—in the 1970s—but has never been mined. The railroad to the copper mine ran on oil instead of coal, operating from 1911 to 1938. When it closed, the town of Kennicott was suddenly abandoned and left much as we find it today.

For more on this history, see my book *The Fate of Nature: Rediscovering Our Ability to Rescue the Earth* (Thomas Dunne/St. Martins).

Prince William Sound, Car-Free

The towns of Prince William Sound face the sea, not the land. That's a good thing, in that you can see the grand mountains and fjords, and absorb the region's fascinating history, without long drives or the impracticality of infrequent bush plane flights or long-haul bus service. The same can't be said for many other parts of the state. This tour makes use of trains and ferries, and gets you close to a Prince William Sound glacier on a comfortable tour boat rather than in a sea kayak. If you're not eager to get behind the wheel, and you prefer your outdoor experiences to be comfortable, this may be the right trip for you.

> The Green Star-certified Alaska Railroad is one of the best—and most environmentally friendly—ways to get around the Prince William Sound area.

START Anchorage. **TRIP LENGTH** 5 days, 368 miles.

❶ The Alaska Railroad. Take the Alaska Railroad on the 62½ mile scenic ride to Whittier. The train's arrival is timed to coordinate with tour boats leaving out of Whittier. ☉ 3 hr.

☎ 800-544-0552. www.alaskarailroad.com. One-way fare $65 adults, $33 children 17 and under.

The docks are a short walk from the train station, and departures are timed to the arrival of the train.

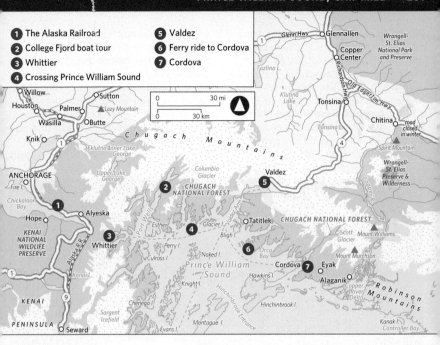

1 The Alaska Railroad
2 College Fjord boat tour
3 Whittier
4 Crossing Prince William Sound
5 Valdez
6 Ferry ride to Cordova
7 Cordova

2 ★★★ **College Fjord boat tour.** The deep and entirely pristine fjords of northwestern Prince William Sound receive the flow of dozens of glaciers, which were named after Ivy League colleges by an expedition that came on a luxury yacht in 1899. The best way to see them is on a fast tour boat that can get to these remote spots relatively quickly. The distances are great, but on these protected seas, the water is smooth and seasickness rare. ⏱ At least a half-day. See "On the Water from Whittier," on p. 202, for more information.

3 ★ **Whittier.** Other than access to Prince William Sound, Whittier lacks attractions, but it is interesting for its very strange lifestyle and urban design. Most of the flat ground in the steep fjord is taken up by a huge railroad yard, and most of the residents live in a single, 14-story building called Begich Towers, which

More Information

See p. 225 for more information on hotels and restaurants in Valdez; for Cordova, see p. 213.

was left over from World War II. That's also where I recommend you stay (see "Spending the Night in Whittier," below). ⏱ 1 hr. See p. 189, 2.

Get an early start on Day 2 and take the ferry to Valdez, where you'll spend the next 2 nights.

4 ★★ kids **Crossing Prince William Sound.** The ferry ride to Valdez will take you to a different part of the sound than you saw on the College Fjord boat ride. The 78-mile route passes the many wooded islands that dot the central sound, as well as Bligh Reef, where the tanker *Exxon Valdez* grounded (see "An Environmental Disaster: The Wreck of the *Exxon Valdez*," on p. 196). If you're lucky, a ranger from Chugach National Forest will be hosting a free interpretive talk in the observation lounge. ⏱ 3½ hr. See p. 189, 3.

5 ★★ **Valdez.** The town of Valdez isn't particularly interesting to walk around—the whole thing was built after the 1964 earthquake destroyed the original site (see "Whole Lotta Shaking" on p. 208)—but the community has

three small museums within walking distance that are worth your time. The **Valdez Museum and Historical Archive** (p. 224, ➎) covers the area's history. Its **annex,** near the ferry dock, shows a complete scale model of Valdez as it looked before the earthquake (p. 224, ➏). The **Maxine & Jesse Whitney Museum** (p. 224, ➐) contains miscellany evocative of pioneer days, which weren't that long ago.

On your second day in Valdez, take

advantage of the town's prime location for halibut and salmon fishing. I suggest you check in with **Fish Central** (☎ 888-835-5002 or 907-835-5002; www.fishcentral.net), which is based on the harbor docks and offers both charters and rentals. Halibut and other bottom fish are available all summer—those charters last 12 hours and cover a lot of water, for a cost of around $300 per person. Silver salmon run in August and can be caught much

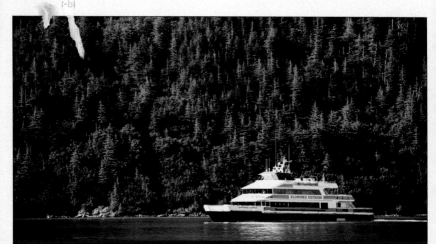

On the Water from Whittier

The harbor in Whittier opens a spectacular part of Prince William Sound for boat tours, fishing, and sea kayaking. There are lots of ways to spend time on the water. Here are some recommended operators:

Phillips Cruises and Tours (☎ 800-544-0529 or 907-276-8023; www.26glaciers.com) operates a large, high-speed catamaran for its 26 Glacier Cruise. This 5-hour tour costs $139 for adults and $79 for children 11 and under; fees and fuel surcharge are $17 per passenger.

Honey Charters (☎ 888-477-2493 or 907-472-2493, www.honeycharters.com) and **MJ's Bread N Butter Charters** (☎ 888-472-2396 or 907-472-2396; www.breadnbuttercharters.com) both offer halibut and salmon fishing charters, as well as water-taxi service and tours to see the sound or for kayaking drop-offs. Taking a small boat for a tour costs more (prices

depend on your group size, the tour length, and other factors), but it creates a more individual and spontaneous outdoor experience, with the opportunity to explore and to emphasize what interests you most.

If you'd rather get a little closer to nature, consider sea kayaking—you can kayak from the harbor or take a longer tour in the sound. **Alaska Sea Kayakers** (☎ 877-472-2534 or 907-472-2534; www.alaskaseakayakers.com) and **Prince William Sound Kayak Center** (☎ 877-472-2452 or 907-472-2452; www.pwskayakcenter.com) are both good operators.

Finally, if you're an experienced mariner, consider renting your own boat. **Whittier Boat Rentals** (☎ 907-232-2783; www.alaska-boat-rentals.com) can arrange for you to head out for a day of fishing or an extended, sleep-aboard trip. Full-day trips cost from $550 to $950.

Spending the Night in Whittier

The best place to stay in Whittier is high in the one big building that dominates the town, with the same fabulous views the residents enjoy. **June's Whittier Condo Suites** offers 12 condo units on the top two floors, each a spacious and well-appointed apartment. ☎ 888-472-6001 or 907-472-6001. www.whittiersuitesonline.com. Doubles $145–$450. AE, MC, V.

closer to the town—expect to pay around $200 for most of a day. If you're experienced, you can also rent your own boat and gear (p. 202), and spend some time exploring if fishing doesn't hold your interest all day. ⏱ 1½ days. See p. 222.

On Day 4, board the ferry bound for Cordova.

Alternative Travel: A Yacht Cruise

Perhaps the best way to see Prince William Sound sidesteps the towns, hotels, and ferries. Board a classic wooden yacht with only about a dozen guests and a skipper who knows all the secret places in the 3,500 miles of the sound's folded coastline. The *Discovery* is a special vessel, comfortable but nautical, with a mahogany saloon where a friendly crew serves expertly prepared meals and good wine. The boat carries kayaks and small boats so passengers can get ashore, but the biggest treat is the opportunity to cruise the best of this incredible marine wilderness for a week in total comfort. Discovery Voyages, ☎ 800-324-7602, www.discoveryvoyages. com. 7-day itinerary, including 5 nights aboard and 2 at a B&B in Anchorage, starts at $3,900 per person, double occupancy.

6 ★ kids **Ferry ride to Cordova.** Enjoy another scenic voyage on Prince William Sound—trust me, it is nearly impossible to get enough of this lovely terrain. ⏱ 3 hr. $50 adults, $25 children 6–11, free for children 5 and under.

You'll spend the next 2 nights in:

7 ★★ **Cordova.** Although Cordova is best known for its vigorous outdoor activities, the town's history and culture are fascinating, too. First there's the beautiful, old-fashioned community itself: safe, sociable, and free of franchises or chains—on the main street, business owners are the ones behind the counters. The town's two museums are small but allow visitors to meet locals and learn about their lives: The **Native Village of Eyak's Ilanka Cultural Center** (p. 211, **3**) exhibits old and contemporary art and objects representing several Native tribes that live here, and has a fully reconstructed killer whale skeleton. The **Cordova Historical Museum** (p. 211, **2**) is densely packed with items from the town's rich past.

Cordova is a great place to try something new, with excellent guides and incredible places to visit, on the water or the **Copper River Delta.** For more details on what the town has to offer in terms of the great outdoors, see p. 210.

The one thing you must not miss is flight-seeing: The combination of ocean, mountains, glaciers, river, and delta—and nothing manmade—can create the illusion that the land below is a giant work of abstract art. I recommend taking a ride with **Gayle Ranney's Fishing & Flying** (p. 212). She'll figure out a tour that fits your interests and budget; you'll be able to go for as little as $100 per person with at least three passengers. ⏱ At least 1 day.

Heading for Home

To save time (and money), don't retrace your steps back to Anchorage. Instead, fly from Cordova on **Alaska Airlines** (☎ 800-426-0333; www.alaskaair.com) back to Anchorage or onward to wherever you're going next. Alaska serves Cordova with one northbound and one southbound flight daily. It is the only Prince William Sound community with jet service.

A PWS and CRC Outdoor Adventure

Our family has spent some of our happiest days in this region: camping out on tiny islands in Prince William Sound, canoeing on the Copper River Delta, exploring the old mine buildings at Kennicott, hiking on the Root Glacier, and much more. This is the best of Alaska for those who enjoy getting outdoors. There's more to do, and a greater sense of freedom and the open wilderness, than anywhere else I know of. And if your kids can handle long car rides, this is the perfect tour for families. You'll need to rent a car that you can take off paved roads—see "Driving Off-Pavement," on p. 194.

> The dizzying but scenic Glenn Highway will deliver you to the Matanuska Glacier area.

START Matanuska Glacier area. Take the Glenn Highway 115 miles north from Anchorage. **TRIP LENGTH** 8 days, 663 miles.

① ★★ Matanuska Glacier area. The drive from Anchorage to the glacier, especially the section beyond Palmer, is one of my favorites. The road wraps around cliffs over the canyon created by the glacier and river, popping out from birch trees to confront extraordinary vistas. You'll find several spots to stretch your legs, including trails and historic sites along the road.

The huge Matanuska Glacier fills the bottom of the canyon. The best views are from the state recreation site, on the easy 1-mile nature trail. Getting closer means taking a steep side road and paying a fee (p. 221, **①**). **Nova Raft and Adventure Tours** (p. 221, **④**) offers a **Glacier Run,** which goes right by the glacier; it has mild white water, but is appropriate for children as young as 5 (those 4 and under are not allowed). The trip costs $75 for adults and $40 for kids 11 and under. ⏱ 2½ hr. for the raft trip. See p. 221, **①**.

1. Matanuska Glacier area
2. Sheep Mountain Lodge
3. The ride to Kennicott & McCarthy
4. Kennicott & McCarthy
5. Chitina and the Copper River
6. Liberty Falls
7. Worthington Glacier and Thompson Pass
8. Valdez
9. Cordova
10. Copper River Delta

> *A seal enjoys a fish released by the Solomon Gulch Hatchery.*

> *Caribou pick their way across the tundra.*

② 🚍 **Sheep Mountain Lodge.** The log main building contains the friendliest roadside restaurant you could find, with good casual meals, lots of flowers, and a fascinating family hosting—they're competitive dog mushers who host a race here in the winter. Mile 113.5, Glenn Hwy. ☎ 877-645-5121. $–$$. See p. 221.

On Day 2, be ready for a long, adventurous, and scenic drive which will take you all the way to Kennicott and McCarthy. Take Glenn Highway east 88 miles to the Richardson Highway, then head south to Copper Center. From there, follow the directions in "Getting to Kennicott & McCarthy," on p. 195.

❸ **The ride to Kennicott & McCarthy.** The Glenn Highway leads across a plateau above the tree line, where you have a good chance of seeing caribou. After turning south on the Richardson Highway, stop for a break and orientation to the area at the visitor center for **Wrangell-St. Elias National Park** (p. 191, ❽), in Copper Center. 🕐 2 hr.

Spend the balance of Day 2 exploring the area around Kennicott and McCarthy, where you'll be staying for 2 nights.

More Information

You're likely to need gear for this trip, and I strongly suggest you rent it in Anchorage. The issues of managing luggage and renting camping equipment are covered in "Gearing Up to Fly & Camp," on p. 157.

❹ ★★★ **Kennicott & McCarthy.** You're here to see one of the nation's best-preserved ghost towns, which you should do in the best way: on a half-day tour with **St. Elias Alpine Guides** (see "Getting the Most out of the Great Outdoors," on p. 218). The same firm organizes hikes right over the ice of the Root Glacier; these can be combined with the tour for a fantastic full day of learning and adventure. 🕐 Full day. $25 tour, $65 glacier hike.

On Day 4, you will drive 95 miles back to the Richardson Highway and take it 60 miles south to Blueberry Lake, making the stops listed below along the way.

❺ ★ **Chitina and the Copper River.** At Chitina you'll see a 100-year-old town that has almost dried up. You can pick up picnic supplies at the general store. The ranger station is worth a stop, and check out the rotating fish wheels, which scoop up fish from the prodigious run of red salmon that pass this way. 🕐 30 min. At the end of the unpaved McCarthy Rd. and the start of the Edgerton Hwy., 60 miles from Kennicott and McCarthy.

9 miles west of Chitina on the Edgerton Highway, you'll find:

❻ ★ **Liberty Falls.** This waterfall comes right down through a lovely campground at the Liberty Falls State Recreation Site, making a nice spot for a break or picnic. A 2.5-mile trail from the recreation site leads to excellent mountain views. 🕐 3 hr. for the round-trip hike.

7 ★★ **Worthington Glacier and Thompson Pass.** The Richardson Highway traces the Trans-Alaska Pipeline through the mountains, descending to the fjord where Valdez lies. You'll be camping beyond the summit, before reaching Valdez. Just before you get to the campground, stop at **Worthington Glacier State Recreation Site.** An easy 1-mile trail leads to the glacier's face. Drive on a few miles to the campground at **Blueberry Lake State Recreation Site** (which offers good grayling fishing), in the alpine tundra of Thompson Pass. If you're continuing on to Valdez for the night, you'll complete your trip with dizzying views of the descent toward town and the rock walls of Keystone Canyon, which begins just around the corner from the campground. If you're camping here, you'll get to see it in the morning. ⊕ 1 hr. to hike the glacier trail.

Get an early start on Day 5, and continue on 24 miles past Blueberry Lake to:

8 ★★ **Valdez.** This is an outdoor trip, but kids will love a couple of indoor attractions here, such as the **Valdez Museum and Historical Archive,** which has neat, recreated old rooms and a collection of antique firetrucks (p. 224, **5**), and its **annex** (p. 224, **6**).

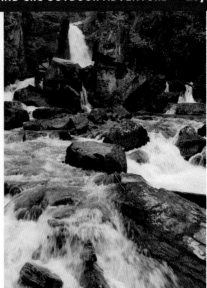

> *Liberty Falls State Recreation Site, along the Edgerton Highway near Wrangell-St. Elias National Park.*

Across the Valdez Harbor from town, take in the **Solomon Gulch Hatchery** (on Dayville Road, en route to the tanker terminal; ☎ 907-835-1329), which releases more than 200 million salmon each year. The pink salmon return from late June to early August in astounding numbers, attracting seals and birds that feed on them, which you can observe from shore (when this is happening, kids will surely enjoy fishing). A free, self-guided tour of the hatchery starts from the parking lot near the Solomon Creek bridge. The hatchery is open from 7am to 10pm, so you shouldn't have trouble working it into your schedule. ⊕ 1 day. See p. 222.

In the late afternoon, take the ferry on an 84-mile, 3-hour voyage across Prince William Sound to Cordova, where you'll spend the next 2 nights.

Long-Distance Playground

The Matanuska Glacier area attracts families in winter for cross-country skiing and snowmobiling weekends, reaching a peak in the late winter, when the air is warmer, the days are longer, and the snow is still deep. When our children were younger, we would go to the **Majestic Valley Wilderness Lodge** (p. 221) for an Easter celebration with friends, including an egg hunt on skis. The **Sheep Mountain Lodge** (p. 221)—whose owner, Zack Steer, is an admired Iditarod musher—hosts a 150-mile dog-sled race in December. In July a huge bike race starts there, pedals 200 miles to Valdez, and returns; it's called the **Fireweed 400** (www.fireweed400.com), and it does have heats of 50, 100, and 200 miles for those who don't fancy the idea of climbing back into the mountains after descending to Valdez.

Spending the Night near Kennicott

You'll be spending 2 nights in the area, so be sure to arrive in time to set up camp at the **Glacier View Campground** (p. 219). If you'd prefer to stay indoors, see my suggestions for where to stay, on p. 219.

⑨ ★★★ kids **Cordova.** We once spent a week-long family vacation in Cordova, and I don't know when my kids have been happier. They felt as though they had been transported into a movie—it was closer than they'd ever been to a classic small town with a main street of family businesses. Moreover, Cordova is so safe, with no road link to the outside world, that they were able to roam on their own unsupervised, shopping and exploring as they couldn't do at home.

Whole Lotta Shaking

Alaska is a land of extremes, but that hardly prepared residents for what happened on March 27, 1964. At 5:36pm on Good Friday, the ground began to shake with tremendous force—and it didn't stop for a full 4 minutes. The Great Alaska Earthquake, as it came to be known, registered a staggering magnitude 9.2, making it the second-strongest quake ever registered. The epicenter near College Fjord (p. 201, **②**), was just 43 miles from Valdez, which was swept away by a tsunami wave and had to be rebuilt at a new location.

The quake was caused by the slippage of the Pacific tectonic plate beneath Alaska's continental plate. Land moved 60 feet sideways and see-sawed, with areas in Prince William Sound rising at much as 38 feet and parts of the Kenai Peninsula sinking 10 feet. This was the largest land movement ever recorded, covering a block of the earth's crust 600 miles long and 250 miles wide.

But while the quake itself caused tremendous damage, including nearly destroying 30 blocks of downtown Anchorage, the tsunamis triggered by the disruption were even worse. Of the 131 people who perished, 119 were killed by waves. A landslide-driven wave threw sand 220 feet up the shore of Valdez Harbor. A third of the residents of the Prince William Sound village of Chenega were killed in a wave, and 16 people died on the coasts of California and Oregon.

The earthquake transformed the land and shore of Alaska permanently, and changed life for a generation of Alaskans. The Earth has been relatively quite in nearly 50 years since, but geologists says we should always be ready—it will eventually happen again.

Aside from the town's friendliness, the outdoor opportunities make it a great destination. Join a sea kayaking outing with **Cordova Coastal Outfitters** (p. 212, **④**) to see marine wildlife just beyond the harbor, including sea lions and rafts of sea otters. Or put the whole family in the same boat, potentially saving money and easing concerns about young ones, by renting a skiff from Cordova Coastal for fishing or to explore the waters around town on your own. A half-day beginners' kayaking trip costs $75 per person, concentrating on wildlife sightings. Boats rent for $150 to $225 a day; fishing gear is extra.

You can use the other half of your first full day in Cordova to go on a hike. I love the **Tripod Mountain trail** because it leads right from the city streets, ascending the mountain behind the town and coming to spectacular views quickly. It's steep—1,255 feet in about 1 mile—so allow half a day. To get to the trailhead, take Browning Street to 6th Street at the foot of the ski hill. Get information on hikes from the **Chugach National Forest Cordova Ranger Station** (p. 210, **①**). ⏱ 2 days. See p. 210.

You'll want to get an early start on Day 7, as you'll want plenty of time in the:

SITE GUIDE PAGE 209

⑩ ★★★ kids **Copper River Delta.** Set aside an entire day to explore the delta and visit **Childs Glacier** on the Copper River Highway. The unpaved road is only 49 miles (it's more of the abandoned railroad line that you drove along to Kennicott), but there are many places to stop and a lot of wonderful scenery and wildlife to see. You may want to camp near the glacier if it won't put you too far from the ferry when you need to leave.

Spending the Night at Blueberry Lake

The campground at the **Blueberry Lake State Recreation Area** is among Alaska's most scenic, near a pond on the alpine tundra of Thompson Pass. The campground has water, pit toilets, and 25 campsites. Sites are $12 per night. If you'd rather not camp, plan to stay in Valdez (p. 222).

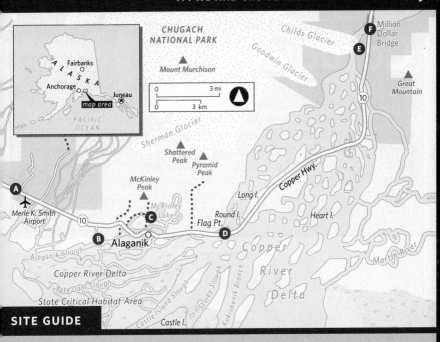

SITE GUIDE

⑩ Copper River Delta

The entrance to the delta's flat wetlands comes just before ⓐ **Ten-Mile.** This geographically named spot, near the airport, features a bird-watching area erected by the U.S. Forest Service, complete with interpretive signs introducing visitors to one of the continent's most important waterfowl wetlands.

At mile 17, turn right onto the 3-mile side road to the ⓑ **Alaganik Slough Boardwalk.** This 1,000-foot span leads over a pond with bird-watching blinds; a separate trail runs 1 mile along the river. This is the best spot for an easy but wild and remote canoe outing. If you make arrangements in advance, **Cordova Coastal Outfitters** (p. 212, ④) will have a boat waiting for you at the slough.

Your next stop is ⓒ **McKinley Lake** (pictured). The lake sits back in the lap of the mountains, surrounded by big trees and near ruined mine workings of gold-rush provenance. You can get there on an easy 2.25-mile trail, starting at mile 21 of the highway, or a canoe paddle of about the same length from Alaganik Slough.

Around mile 27, the road crosses a 10-mile-long set of bridges that hop island to island

across the vast, silty ⓓ **Copper River.** Pull over and walk down to the river, where endless sandy beaches are suitable for sand castles and play. On the left at mile 48, a viewing area looks across the river to the awesome face of ⓔ **Childs Glacier,** which in summer drops big hunks of ice. Consider camping here (see "Alaska's Best Glacier," on p. 212).

At the end of the road, a mile beyond the glacier, the road crosses the ⓕ **Million-Dollar Bridge,** an engineering marvel of its day, which was built at lightning speed as workers raced encroaching glaciers. You can drive across, but the road on the other side soon gives out. Don't get stuck! ⊙ 1 day.

Cordova

The little fishing town of Cordova sits in one of Prince
William Sound's loveliest spots (and that's really saying something). It feels
like a living time capsule. The people are friendly and interesting, and the
opportunities to get outdoors—as a beginner or an expert—are without equal.
All that, and still the town is a little-known backwater which receives few
visitors. Yet it's not hard to get there, with daily service by fast ferry and Alaska
Airlines jet. You have to take some initiative to enjoy the best of Alaska; if you
want to try, this is the place to do it. This is *the* place to base yourself if you're
looking to explore the Copper River Delta—plan to spend at least 2 days here.

> Cordova is home to the Eyak, a small but linguistically and ethnographically distinct people, who started the
  Ilanka Cultural Center.

START Cordova is 145 miles east of Anchorage
as the crow flies, and is accessible only by air
or ferry.

**❶ ★ Chugach National Forest Cordova
Ranger District.** The whole region is within
the Chugach National Forest. The rangers' office has a few modest exhibits, but the rangers
behind the desk are the bigger asset. They'll

help you plan outdoor activities that match
your interests and abilities, and they have
maps and other information on all the trails
and attractions. Since so few visitors come,
you'll probably get their undivided attention.
⏱ 1 hr. 612 2nd St. (at Browning Street). ☎ 907-
424-7661. www.fs.fed.us/r10/chugach. Free
admission.

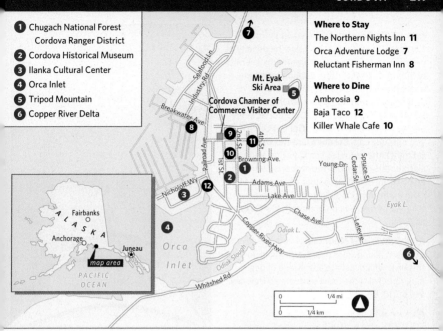

1. Chugach National Forest Cordova Ranger District
2. Cordova Historical Museum
3. Ilanka Cultural Center
4. Orca Inlet
5. Tripod Mountain
6. Copper River Delta

Where to Stay
The Northern Nights Inn **11**
Orca Adventure Lodge **7**
Reluctant Fisherman Inn **8**

Where to Dine
Ambrosia **9**
Baja Taco **12**
Killer Whale Cafe **10**

Mt. Eyak Ski Area
Cordova Chamber of Commerce Visitor Center

Fairbanks
A L A S K A
Anchorage
Juneau
map area
PACIFIC OCEAN

Orca Inlet

Seafood Ln.
Industry Rd.
Breakwater Ave.
Railroad Ave.
1st St.
2nd St.
4th St.
Browning Ave.
Young Dr.
Cedar St.
Spruce St.
Adams Ave.
Lake Ave.
Nicholoff Wy.
Chase Ave.
Lefevre
Copper River Hwy.
Odiak L.
Eyak L.
Odiak Slough
Whitshed Rd.

0   1/4 mi
0   1/4 km

❷ ★ **Cordova Historical Museum.** This crowded little museum contains objects of real interest among other items kept here as the town's favorite bric-a-brac. Cordova's history is eventful and multifaceted, and has produced a variety of objects: a historic lighthouse lens, a Linotype machine, the interior of a fishing boat, a parka made of bear gut, basketry, and photographs of fishing and historic scenes. ⏱ 1 hr. 622 First St. ☎ 907-424-6665. www.cordovamuseum.org. Summer Mon–Sat 10am–6pm, Sun 1–5pm; winter closed Mon. Donation is $1.

❸ ★ **Ilanka Cultural Center.** The Eyak people of Cordova built this center to preserve and teach about their own culture and that of the other Native peoples who live here. There's a small gallery of traditional and contemporary art, the most famous and intense of which is the "shame pole" directed at Exxon for the oil spill: In an ancient tradition of calling the powerful to account, a fisherman who lost his livelihood after the spill carved it as an act of protest. The cultural center also has the skeleton of a killer whale and, best of all, friendly people who want to talk about their heritage.

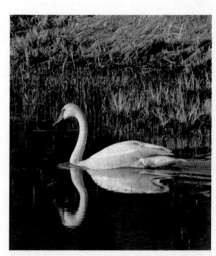

> Every spring, more than five million birds, including swans, flock to the tidal flats of the Copper River Delta.

⏱ 1 hr. 110 Nicholoff Way, across from the Fishermen's Memorial at the small boat harbor. ☎ 907-424-7903. www.ilankacenter.org. Donations encouraged. Summer Tues–Sat 10am–5pm; closed in winter.

❹ ★★★ kids **Orca Inlet.** The water in front of Cordova is well named, because the density of wildlife is astounding. It's common to see rafts of hundreds of sea otters floating together, a rare phenomenon anywhere else, and I've also encountered humpback whales and sea lions not far from town. And, of course, keep an eye out for killer whales. Get out there if you possibly can. **Cordova Coastal Outfitters** (at right) offers guided sea kayaking tours and skiff rentals right from the harbor; nowhere else in Prince William Sound can you get to such appealing paddling waters without first taking an expensive boat charter. ⏱ At least a half-day.

❺ ★★ kids **Tripod Mountain.** There are several excellent hiking trails near Cordova, including this one, which has the advantage of beginning right from the town's streets. ⏱ Half-day. See p. 210, ❶.

❻ ★★★ kids **Copper River Delta.** This 700,000-acre wetland within the Chugach National Forest is home to some of Alaska's best bird-watching and to its best glacier. Don't forget to bring your binoculars. ⏱ At least 1 day. See p. 208, ❿, and "Alaska's Best Glacier," below.

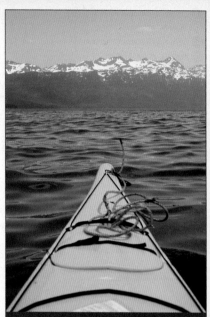

Alaska's Best Glacier

It's only my opinion, of course, that **Childs Glacier** is tops among Alaska's 100,000 glaciers, but it is certainly the most exciting one that you can drive to. Chugach National Forest built an elevated viewing platform in the picnic area across the Copper River from the glacier's face, which towers 300 feet above. You might wonder why, since the glacier's blue ice fills your field of vision from wherever you stand. The reason isn't to get a better look; it's to provide high ground when a piece of ice that's large enough to create a wave falls off and floods the picnic area. At times, fish have been found high in the trees. You likely won't encounter that sort of event, but getting this close to a glacier this big is something you won't forget. You can feel the ice rumbling in your gut, and some say the noise keeps them awake in the campground. It's at mile 48 on the Copper River Highway.

Getting Outdoors in Cordova

I've mentioned some of the spectacular places around Cordova to give you a taste of what you can see and do. But this is a place where you go to explore the wilderness on your own, and that takes equipment and local knowledge. These businesses make it possible:

Cordova Coastal Outfitters. These real enthusiasts lead sea kayak outings and rent kayaks, skiffs, canoes, and bicycles. More important, they'll help you figure out where to go, and they'll take the equipment to you where you need it. At the boat harbor near the grocery store. ☎ 800-357-5145 or 907-424-7424. www.cordovacoastal.com.

Fishing & Flying. Pilot Gayle Ranney knows the area intimately and can get you to remote beaches and cabins, to incredible fishing (with a guide or on your own), or simply aloft for the scenery. At the airport. ☎ 907-424-3325.

Alaska River Expeditions. These folks offer remote floats and other expeditions in the wild country around Cordova. ☎ 800-776-1864 or 907-424-7238. www.alaskarafters.com.

Where to Stay & Dine

★ kids **Ambrosia** ITALIAN
This is the kind of solid family restaurant that stays in business in a small town, with reliable food, large portions, and friendly, helpful service. 410 First St. ☎ 907-424-7175. All items $10–$21. MC, V. Lunch and dinner daily.

★★ kids **Baja Taco** MEXICAN
On the basis of terrific food, this hot spot grew from a bus to the current restaurant (which still includes the bus). Try the salmon tacos with a beer from Mexico or Alaska. South end of the boat harbor. ☎ 907-424-5599. www.bajatacoak. com. All items $5–$15. No credit cards. Breakfast, lunch, and dinner daily. Closed Oct–Mar.

★ **Killer Whale Cafe** DINER
Every little town like this has a diner where folks meet their neighbors for coffee; here in Cordova, it's a vegetarian-friendly place that also serves halibut sandwiches. First St. ☎ 907-424-7733. Entrees $8–$11. MC, V. Breakfast and lunch daily.

★ kids **Northern Nights Inn**
This big 1906 house was thoughtfully renovated and decorated with period furniture. Rooms are generally spacious and present an extraordinary value at these rates. Hostess Becky Chapek is a delight—and your best source for trip-planning advice. She also rents cars that can be driven along the unpaved Copper River Highway. 500 3rd St. ☎ 907-424-5356. www.northernnightsinn.com; for car rentals, www.chinookautorentals.com. 5 units. Doubles $85–$110. AE, DISC, MC, V.

★ **Orca Adventure Lodge**
Simple rooms occupy a renovated cannery on a gravel beach north of town, where guided activities begin every day, by sea kayak, fishing boat, or floatplane. For $155 per person per night, you can stay as you would at a wilderness lodge, with all meals and outdoor equipment included. 2500 Orca Rd. ☎ 866-424-ORCA (424-6722) or 907-424-7249. www. orcaadventurelodge.com. 40 units. Doubles $155. AE, MC, V.

> A viewing deck at the Reluctant Fisherman Inn.

★★ **Reluctant Fisherman Inn**
This up-to-date hotel sits at the top of the harbor, with decks and big windows to look out upon the boats. It's one of the central spots in town and Cordova's closest thing to "upscale," but still homey and family-run. 407 Railroad Ave. ☎ 907-424-3272. www.reluctant fisherman.com. 40 units. Doubles $120–$165, w/breakfast. AE, MC, V.

Camping in Cordova

Alaska River Expeditions (p. 212) offers a campground 12.5 miles out of town on the Copper River Highway, on the left just past the airport. Sites are among the trees; the charge is $15 a night. It has pit toilets and an office. There's also a U.S. Forest Service campground at **Childs Glacier,** 49 miles from Cordova. Sites are $10; reserve at www.recreation.gov.

Kennicott & McCarthy

Two towns were founded here, way out in the wilderness, for copper mining a century ago, then abandoned and left mostly untouched for 50 years before being rediscovered. Now within Wrangell–St. Elias National Park, by far the nation's largest and most mountainous, the towns offer an extraordinary mix of wild country and history, but they remain—at residents' insistence—hard to get to. The road is rough, and the final leg of the trip requires use of a footbridge. But that adds to the magic of a visit and the pristine qualities of the outdoors. You'll want to spend at least a full day here. *Note:* The towns are entirely seasonal, and hardly anyone is here in the wintertime. Businesses often have separate winter contact information. All information here is valid only for the visitor season, mid-May to mid-September.

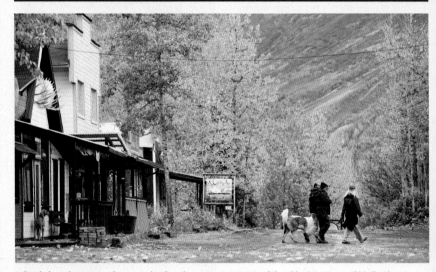

> *Brothels and raucous saloons used to line the now-quiet streets of the old mining town of McCarthy.*

START Kennicott and McCarthy are 300 road miles from Anchorage.

❶ ★★★ kids St. Elias Alpine Guides Tour of Kennecott Mill Town. What was formerly the Kennicott industrial community, at the Kennicott Glacier area (the spelling difference carries on a century-old error), is among America's best-preserved ghost towns. The red buildings stand crisply on the mountainside above the dirty Kennicott Glacier, preserved by the dry weather. When the mine closed in 1938, everything was left as is, and you can still find ore in the machinery and, at least the last time I checked, invoices in

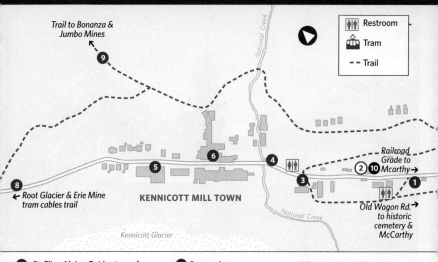

Legend:
- Restroom
- Tram
- Trail

Trail to Bonanza &
Jumbo Mines

⑨

Railroad
Grade to
Mcarthy →

⑤

⑥

④

③

②⑩

①

⑧
← Root Glacier & Erie Mine
tram cables trail

KENNICOTT MILL TOWN

National Creek

Old Wagon Rd. →
to historic
cemetery &
McCarthy

Kennicott Glacier

① St. Elias Alpine Guides tour of
   Kennicott Mill Town
② Kennicott Glacier Lodge
③ General store and park
   visitor center
④ Train depot

⑤ Power plant
⑥ Concentration Mill
⑦ McCarthy
⑧ Root Glacier trail
⑨ Bonanza Mine hike

Where to Stay & Dine

Glacier View Campground **12**

Kennicott Glacier Lodge **10**

Kennicott River Lodge
   and Hostel **11**

McCarthy Lodge **13**

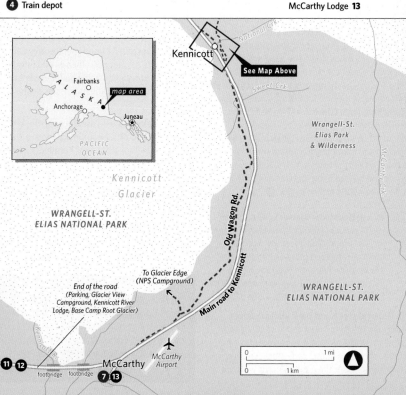

ALASKA

Fairbanks
map area
Anchorage

Juneau

PACIFIC
OCEAN

Kennicott

See Map Above

Kennicott
Glacier

**WRANGELL-ST.
ELIAS NATIONAL PARK**

*Wrangell-St.
Elias Park
& Wilderness*

Old Wagon Rd.

Main road to Kennicott

To Glacier Edge
(NPS Campground)

End of the road
(Parking, Glacier View
Campground, Kennicott River
Lodge, Base Camp Root Glacier)

**WRANGELL-ST.
ELIAS NATIONAL PARK**

⑪ ⑫
footbridge   footbridge

McCarthy
⑦ ⑬

*McCarthy
Airport*

0   1 mi
0   1 km

> *Take in the views with a cup of tea or a family-style dinner at Kennicott Glacier Lodge.*

the desk drawers. The Alaska Syndicate (see p. 195, ❹) built the mine, the miners' bunk houses way up on the mountain above, and family housing for the technical and managerial workers here, and kept it all in proper order. McCarthy, 5 miles down the road, was where the miners spent their rare days and nights off, playing pool, partying, and visiting prostitutes. You can walk around Kennicott's mostly abandoned buildings (the recreation hall is now used by the National Park Service)—if you'd like to do so on your own, follow bullets ❸–❻ below. But I cannot recommend more strongly signing on for the tour, which will take you inside the mill building. It's a truly enlightening adventure. ⏱ 2½ hr. See p. 195, ❹.

② 🏨 ★★ **Kennicott Glacier Lodge.** Even if you're not staying in this wonderful lodge, nestled among the ghost town buildings, take the time for a glass of iced tea or a beer on the veranda overlooking the glacier and the other red buildings. ☎ 800-582-5128 or 907-258-2350. $. See p. 219.

❸ **General store and park visitor center.** Although at the farthest reach of civilization, families lived a remarkably normal life in Kennicott, shopping in this well-stocked store. Now it's an essential contact point with the National Park Service; exhibits and a film teach about the area, and rangers give advice. ⏱ 20 min. ☎ 907-960-1105. Daily 9am–5:30pm.

❹ **Train depot.** Here ended the Copper River and Northwestern Railroad line, the only connection in its day between the sea and Interior Alaska. It's amazing how the builders were able to thread the glaciers and mountains as they erected it.

❺ **Power plant.** Inside are the enormous generators and other equipment, with a solid 19th-century look, that kept Kennicott going.

❻ **Concentration mill.** Kennicott's iconic building, the 14-story mill, leans into the mountain. Ore processing used gravity to bring rock from the mountain above to the top of the mill, then through the machinery as it was purified and readied for loading on trains at the bottom.

More Information

These towns are the definition of isolated, in part because they're not easy to get to. But not to worry—it's not all that hard, either. For everything you need to know, see "Getting to Kennicott & McCarthy," on p. 195.

> *What's left of the once-booming copper mining operations of Kennicott and McCarthy.*

the trail, just continue on the road through the ghost town. A better plan is to join a guided hike with **St. Elias Alpine Guides** (p. 218) and go out on the glacier; best of all, make this an add-on to their ghost town tour (p. 214, ❶). ⏲ Half-day. Tours $65 per person for half-day on the glacier, $100 for all-day hikes, $125 for ice-climbing lessons.

Crossing the Footbridge

It can be discouraging to reach the end of your long journey at the parking lot along the Kennicott River, where a metal footbridge prevents you from driving any farther. Don't despair. This barrier is part of what keeps Kennicott and McCarthy special.

When you arrive, call your lodging from the phone that is conveniently located on the near side of the footbridge. They'll send someone to pick up you and your luggage. If you'd rather do it yourself, there are carts available to help you move your gear across the bridge, at which point you can pick up one of the vans that run between the two towns—the ride will cost $5 per person. If you're traveling light and want to stretch your legs after your journey, just make the 15-minute walk into McCarthy. For advice on all this, and on planning your visit, stop at the ranger station just short of the parking areas.

❼ ★★ **McCarthy.** The contrast of McCarthy to the company town of Kennicott remains startling: One was neat and orderly—almost prim—while the other was a rip-roaring frontier town of log saloons and brothels. The miners came here during off-duty hours, and unlike its neighbor, McCarthy never died completely. But while it may not be a true ghost town, the look of those early days remains, as does the casual, friendly attitude of the people. Most of the area's businesses, lodgings, and restaurants can be found here. ⏲ 2 hr.

❽ ★★ kids **Root Glacier Trail.** This is the best hike for most visitors, a scenic and gently rising walk that parallels glacial ice, then crosses it. Unguided, you can do the hike to the ice edge (but don't go onto it); depending on where you turn around, that hike is 3 to 7 miles round trip, doable in a half-day. To find

9 ★★ **Bonanza Mine Hike.** This is a hike only for the physically fit, but it offers astounding views and a fascinating destination: the mine high on the mountain above Kennicott, where the copper came from and where the miners lived their harsh existence in bunkhouses. The Bonanza has the feel from before the Park Service domesticated Kennicott years ago, with artifacts still lying around (don't take anything—that's stealing). The trail rises 3,800 feet over 4.5 miles. ⏱ 1 day. The trailhead is .5 mile from the visitor center on the way to the Root Glacier; turn right and head uphill.

Getting the Most out of the Great Outdoors

Wrangell–St. Elias National Park is much more than Kennicott and McCarthy. The whole park is six times larger than Yellowstone, and it contains 9 of North America's 16 highest peaks in four different mountain ranges. McCarthy is a great spot to access some of that wilderness on a scenic flight; a base camp expedition; or a backpacking, mountain climbing, or rafting excursion. Here are two key businesses that can make it happen.

St. Elias Alpine Guides. These highly regarded mountaineering guides regularly climb peaks that have never been summited before, but they also offer dayhikes, ghost town tours, and rafting rides for the rest of us. A spectacular rafting day trip, returning via a glacier viewing flight, costs $275 per person. Kennicott. ☎ 888-933-5427 or 907-345-9048. www.steliasguides.com.

Wrangell Mountain Air. Flight services are the keys to the Wrangell–St. Elias backcountry, and this is one of the best. Use them for transportation to McCarthy, to fly out for fishing, to reach a base camp for camping and dayhikes, or to set up a backpacking expedition. They'll help you plan and rent some of the equipment you need, but remember: This is deep wilderness and only for those with appropriate outdoor experience. McCarthy. ☎ 800-478-1160 or 907-554-4411. www.wrangellmountainair.com.

Where to Stay & Dine

> *The long verandah of Kennicott Glacier Lodge.*

Glacier View Campground FOOTBRIDGE
This is a handy spot on the road-accessible side of the footbridge. Besides campsites, they offer showers, rent mountain bikes for $25 a day, and have a cafe serving barbecue for lunch and dinner. **McCarthy Rd.** ☎ 907-554-4490; 907-243-6677 in off season. www.glacierviewcampground.com. Campsite $20. DISC, MC, V.

★★ Kennicott Glacier Lodge KENNICOTT
This wonderful lodge blends in with the other red buildings right in the middle of the ghost town, and is the most convenient place for most of what you want to do. The rooms are comfortable, the food excellent, and the hospitality friendly. Ten rooms have private bathrooms (the only ones in the area). This is also the only place to eat in the ghost town. Dinners are served family-style on a fixed menu, by reservation only. Package rates are available. ☎ 800-582-5128 or 907-258-2350; 907-554-4477 in season only. www.kennicott lodge.com. 35 units. Doubles $199–$259. AE, DISC, MC, V. Breakfast $12–$18, lunch $10–$18, dinner $35–$45.

Kennicott River Lodge and Hostel FOOT-BRIDGE This is a simple, inexpensive place to lay your head in attractively rustic rooms. It has a common kitchen, a lounge, a sauna, and showers, and you can drive to it. **McCarthy Rd.** ☎ 907-554-4441; 941-447-4252 winter. www.kennicottriverlodge.com. 4 cabins, 2 rooms. Bunks $28; doubles $70–$90. MC, V.

★★ McCarthy Lodge MCCARTHY
Although just 5 miles distant from the ghost town, this lodge puts you in a charming, living community where you can meet many inter-esting characters among the historic build-ings. Rooms are full of period charm; none has a private bathroom. ☎ 907-554-4402. www.mccarthylodge.com. 20 units. Doubles $159. MC, V. Entrees $15–$32.

More Information

Various casual and changeable eateries are located at the footbridge and in McCarthy. I've also mentioned dining options at the places to stay. The only place to eat in the Kennicott ghost town is the Kennicott Glacier Lodge.

Matanuska Glacier Area

This sparsely settled area along a steep and dramatic stretch of the Glenn Highway doesn't seem at first like a place that should be featured; other than the glacier and the canyon it has carved through the mountains, there's nothing much there—just vertical terrain, birch trees, and rock. But the glacier and the river that flow from it are attractions in themselves, and a couple of terrific wilderness lodges provide a peaceful place to stay, with long trails and wonderful people as hosts.

> Matanuska is the largest glacier accessible by car in Alaska.

START The Matanuska Glacier Area is 114 road miles from Anchorage.

❶ ★★ Matanuska Glacier area. The glacier lies like an immense animal on the floor of the Talkeetna Mountains canyon it has carved, visible intermittently from the highway that clings to the cliff above. It's the largest in Alaska that you can drive to, with a face 4 miles wide. You can walk 15 minutes to the glacier's terminus by taking a bumpy, 3-mile side road off Glenn Highway, at mile 102, and paying your admission fee to the land-owner, a family business called Glacier Park. ⏱ 1 hr. ☎ 888-253-4480. www.matanuskaglacier.com. Admission $15 adults, $13 seniors, $10 students and military, $5 children 6–12, free for children 5 and under.

❷ ★★ Nova Raft and Adventure Tours glacier hike. I highly recommend that you sign up for a hike on the ice. You'll get to visit weird formations, crevasses, caves, and surface ponds. The glacier's face is gradual, creating routes that are safe with the proper equipment and guidance. Nova offers two daily trips, in which guests are grouped by ability level and the hiker-to-guide ratio is five to one. You can combine a hike with rafting, too (see ❹ below). Children 10 and younger are not allowed. ⏱ Half-day. ☎ 800-746-5753 or 907-745-5753, http://novalaska.com. $85 per person, including park entrance fee.

❸ ★ kids Matanuska Glacier State Recreation Site. Besides a campground, there's a 1-mile nature trail here leading to the best overlooks of the glacier anywhere along the highway. ⏱ 1 hr. Mile 101, Glenn Hwy. Day-use fee $5.

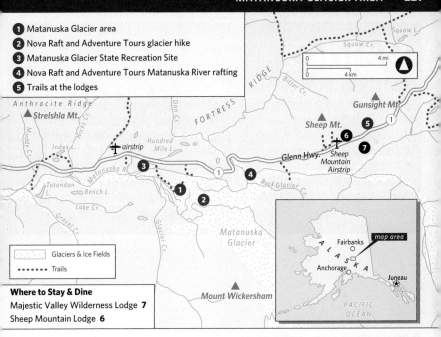

1. Matanuska Glacier area
2. Nova Raft and Adventure Tours glacier hike
3. Matanuska Glacier State Recreation Site
4. Nova Raft and Adventure Tours Matanuska River rafting
5. Trails at the lodges

Glaciers & Ice Fields

Trails

Where to Stay & Dine
Majestic Valley Wilderness Lodge **7**
Sheep Mountain Lodge **6**

4 ★★ kids **Nova Raft and Adventure Tours Matanuska River rafting.** The Matanuska runs through a mountain canyon in a broad bed, creating impressive wilderness terrain. The **Glacier Run** (p. 204, ❶) is a scenic ride that is not too scary for kids as young as 5, but has enough white water to keep it interesting. The **Lion Head** run involves wild, class IV rapids between the glaciers' side pile of gravel, called a lateral moraine, and the massive rock cliff known as Lion Head; it is for teens and adults only. ⏱ Half-day. ☎ 800-746-5753 or 907-745-5753. http://novalaska.com. Lion Head run $75–$90 adults; children 12 and under not allowed.

5 ★ kids **Trails at the lodges.** The **Sheep Mountain Lodge** and the **Majestic Valley Wilderness Lodge** (at right) both offer remarkable networks of trails and access to long, challenging hikes nearby. Since the lodges specialize in winter visits, the trails are groomed for cross-country skiing. But non-guests can walk the trails, too, perhaps after a meal or drink at the lodge; it's polite to stop in and say hi before using them. Sheep Mountain's 12 miles of trails even have interpretive signs. ⏱ At least 1 hr.

Where to Stay & Dine

Majestic Valley Wilderness Lodge
The setting in these mountains and the grandeur of the main log building bring many wedding parties. Guests can enjoy a range of rooms and cabins, and big family-style dinners are the norm. Mile 114.9, Glenn Hwy. ☎ 907-746-2930. www.majesticvalleylodge.com. 12 units, 2 cabins. Doubles $120–$165. MC, V.

Sheep Mountain Lodge
Delightful cabins sit on a hillside above the highway, with great views. The restaurant, in operation since 1946, occupies the log lodge building and serves good, healthy meals. The dog-mushing family who lives here provides wonderful hospitality. Mile 113.5, Glenn Hwy. ☎ 877-645-5121. www.sheepmountain.com. 11 cabins. Doubles $159–$189 summer; $99–$149 winter. MC, V. Lodge closed 1 month each in spring and fall (call ahead). Entrees $20–$28. Mid-May to mid-Sept breakfast, lunch, and dinner daily.

Valdez

The town of Valdez doesn't have the charm, beauty, or outdoor activities of Cordova, but it's more convenient to link with your other destinations, and there is plenty to do, including sea kayaking, museums, rafting, hiking, and glacier tours. The town's utilitarian look comes from its unfortunate history: The Great Alaska Earthquake of 1964, which centered just west of here, swept the waterfront with a huge wave and left the site uninhabitable. The existing town was laid out and reconstructed by military engineers. That's just one chapter of an eventful history that makes the museum particularly interesting.

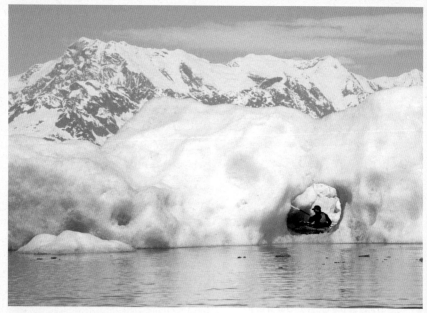

> On a "mothership" trip with Pangaea Adventures, you'll sleep on a boat and make paddling, hiking, and fishing excursions.

START Valdez is 300 road miles from Anchorage.

1 ★★ **Stan Stephens glacier and wildlife cruise of Prince William Sound.** Tour boats from Valdez harbor travel out the fjord and to glaciers westward in the Sound, including the huge Columbia Glacier and, for those who go farther, the active Meares Glacier, which allows a closer look and which sometimes drops big pieces of ice. There's an excellent chance of seeing wildlife on these trips, too—keep an eye out for humpback whales and sea lions. Founder Stan Stephens is legendary here. He was fighting for better protection from oil spills on the very eve of the *Exxon Valdez* spill. ⊙ 6 hr. or 9 hr. Valdez harbor, near the entrance. ☎ 866-867-1297.

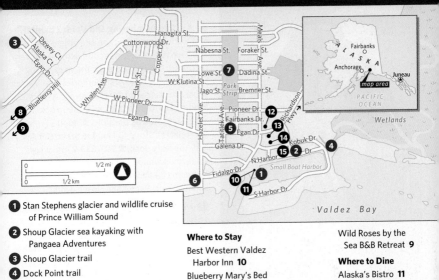

1 Stan Stephens glacier and wildlife cruise of Prince William Sound

2 Shoup Glacier sea kayaking with Pangaea Adventures

3 Shoup Glacier trail

4 Dock Point trail

5 Valdez Museum and Historical Archive

6 Remembering Old Valdez Exhibit

7 Maxine & Jesse Whitney Museum

Where to Stay

Best Western Valdez Harbor Inn **10**

Blueberry Mary's Bed and Breakfast **8**

Mountain Sky Hotel and Suites **12**

Totem Inn **13**

Wild Roses by the Sea B&B Retreat **9**

Where to Dine

Alaska's Bistro **11**

Fu Kung Chinese Restaurant **14**

The Harbor Cafe **15**

---

www.stanstephenscruises.com. $112 Columbia Glacier, $147 Meares Glacier; half-price for children 2–12; free for children 2 and under. Lunch included.

2 ★★ **Shoup Glacier sea kayaking with Pangaea Adventures.** The trip begins with a boat ride that takes you near the glacier; then you paddle into the smooth, reflective lagoon in front of its face, landing on a beach near the ice for lunch and a hike. The guide service, Pangaea Adventures, has a great deal of experience and offers many other choices, too; these include short paddles right next to Valdez or, farther afield, expeditions and "mother ship" trips, where you sleep on a yacht but paddle during the day. ☉ 1 day. 107 N. Harbor Dr. ☎ 800-660-9637. www.alaskasummer.com. Tours $179 for 8 hr.; shorter tours begin at $59.

3 ★★ kids **Shoup Glacier trail.** This is an easy trail running along the edge of the Port Valdez fjord, with many spots where you can get to a rocky beach that will be all your own. The 12-mile (one way) trip leads to the lagoon in front of Shoup Glacier and three primitive Alaska State Parks cabins that can rent for the

night; you need a reservation and camping equipment for that (☎ 907-269-8400; www.alaskastateparks.org). Most folks will want to hike an hour or two and then find a picnic spot before returning. ☉ Half-day for partial hike; at least 2 days for entire trail. Trailhead at the west end of town, at the end of W. Egan Dr.

4 ★ kids **Dock Point trail.** This is an easy, short trail handy to downtown Valdez. The .75-mile route circles a point east of the small boat harbor amid woods, wildflowers, and ocean views. ☉ 1 hr. Trailhead at the end of N. Harbor Dr.

Fun Fact

After Captain James Cook first marked Prince William Sound on a chart in 1778, a stream of explorers and traders came to learn more and to exploit the sea otter for its valuable pelt. Explorers from Spain gave the area a number of names, including Port Valdez, which much later became the site of the town. No Spanish people settled here, and the pronunciation of the word was Americanized long ago: Folks say, "Val-*deez*."

> *The lens from the Cape Hinchinbrook Lighthouse, which marked the entrance to Prince William Sound, at the Valdez Museum.*

⑤ ★★ kids Valdez Museum and Historical Archive. History has been busy in this little town, with the gold-rush hoax that birthed it, the early road link that gave it life, the 1964 earthquake that leveled it, the oil pipeline that enriched it, and the *Exxon Valdez* oil spill that made it infamous. The museum makes the most of it all with a walk that leads you through time using recreated rooms that spark the imagination. ⏱ 2 hr. 217 Egan Dr. ☎ 907-835-2764. www.valdezmuseum.org. Admission $6 adults, $5.50 seniors over 65, $5 children 14–17, free for children 13 and under. Summer daily 9am–5pm; winter Mon–Sat 1–5pm.

Camping In & Around Valdez

The best campground in the area is the state parks system's **Blueberry Lake Campground** (p. 208), 24 miles out of town. To camp closer, choose the **Sea Otter RV Park,** which is on the outer breakwater of the small boat harbor, ☎ 907-835-2787. Full-hookup RV sites are $30 a night.

⑥ ★ kids Remembering Old Valdez Exhibit. Not a stick remains at the site where the 1964 earthquake, the second-strongest ever recorded, swept Valdez off the map. Using records and old-timers' memories, the Valdez Museum recreated the old town in a tabletop model of 400 buildings, as close to how it actually looked as possible. A good 37-minute film tells the story. ⏱ 1 hr. 436 S. Hazelet Ave., near the ferry dock. ☎ 907-835-2764. www.valdezmuseum.org. Admission to Valdez Museum (⑤ above) covers both buildings. Summer daily 9am–5pm; closed winter.

⑦ ★★ kids Maxine & Jesse Whitney Museum. This unique museum is full of Alaskan objects out of context—at first it seems a mishmash of arrow heads, animal trophy mounts, Native crafts, and much else—but there is a unifying theme. Everything was collected by the Whitneys, a pioneer couple who owned a roadside rock shop, and the exhibit here skillfully evokes their bygone world. ⏱ 1 hr. 303 Lowe St. ☎ 907-834-1690. www.pwscc.edu. Admission $5 adults, $4 seniors, $3 children 5–12, free for children 4 and under. Summer daily 9am–7pm; winter by appointment.

Settling Down on the Sound

You need to get out of town to truly connect with the peaceful nature of Prince William Sound. One of the best places for that is **Prince William Sound Lodge**, a remote wilderness lodge near the abandoned community of Ellamar (☎ 907-440-0909 or 907-248-0909; www.princewilliamsound.us). Life slows to the pace of the tides where guests for decades have walked the beach, watched wildlife, and climbed without trails through meadows and forests. You never get the feeling, as you do at some lodges, that you're supposed to be busy doing something. The facilities are very comfortable and the food excellent. The location, not far from the Chugach Native village of Tatitlek, makes access easy via scheduled air service from Anchorage. Rates are $325 per person per day, including all meals and some guiding, with a 2-day minimum, and the lodge takes no credit cards.

Where to Stay & Dine

★ **Alaska's Bistro** HARBOR *MEDITERRANEAN*
The dining room in the Best Western has good views from every table. The menu includes lots of local seafood prepared in Northern Italian and similar styles, or get a grilled steak or pizza. 102 N. Harbor Dr. ☎ 907-835-5688. Entrees $10–$30. AE, MC, V. Breakfast, lunch, and dinner daily.

★★ **Best Western Valdez Harbor Inn** HARBOR
This attractive hotel commands the best location in town, right on the harbor entrance, with a grassy area from which to watch the boats come in. Rooms are nicely decorated and have lots of amenities. 100 N. Harbor Dr. ☎ 888-222-3440 or 907-835-3434. www.valdezharborinn. com. 88 units. Doubles $159–$169 summer; $99–$109 winter; w/breakfast. AE, DISC, MC, V.

★ **Blueberry Mary's Bed and Breakfast** WEST OF TOWN Interesting people with a beautifully situated waterfront house invite guests into handcrafted rooms with handmade quilts, feather beds, and a hypnotic ocean view. 810 Blueberry Hill Rd., off W. Egan Dr. ☎ 907-835-5015. www.blueberrymarys.com. 2 units. Doubles $110–$125, w/breakfast. No credit cards. Closed Sept 15–June 1.

★ kids **Fu Kung Chinese Restaurant** HARBOR *CHINESE* This family-run restaurant has survived small-town changes for decades on the strength of its plentiful, tasty food and fast service. Local seafood is used in Chinese and Thai dishes, and they serve some sushi, too. 207 Kobuk Dr., 1 block from boat harbor. ☎ 907-835-5255. Entrees $9–$16. AE, DISC, MC, V. Lunch and dinner daily.

★★ kids **The Harbor Cafe** HARBOR *CAFÉ*
Although it looks like a boat-harbor burger joint, the food produced by the Peruvian owner is nothing short of amazing, even if it comes in a basket at lunch. In the evening, the cafe is more formal (read: not as good with kids), with just a few sophisticated items on the menu. 225 N. Harbor Dr. ☎ 907-835-4776. Entrees $30–$56. MC, V. Summer lunch and dinner Mon–Sat 11am–8pm, lunch only Sun; winter lunch and dinner Tues–Sat.

> *A mounted grizzly bear greets guests at the Best Western Valdez Harbor Inn.*

★★ kids **Mountain Sky Hotel and Suites** HARBOR Here you'll find good standard rooms with all the features familiar to anyone who has stayed in a midscale name-brand chain. Family suites comfortably sleep six, and there is a small pool. 100 Meals Ave. ☎ 800-478-4445 or 907-835-4445. www.mountainskyhotel.com. 102 units. Doubles $169–$199 summer; $99 winter; w/breakfast. AE, DISC, DC, MC, V.

★ kids **Totem Inn** HARBOR
The motel's appearance from the street is uninspiring, but the rooms inside provide a good value, and those in the two-story building include full kitchens. Avoid the cottages. 114 E. Egan Dr. ☎ 888-808-4431 or 907-835-4443. www.toteminn.com. 69 units. Doubles $129 summer; $80 winter. AE, DISC, MC, V.

★ **Wild Roses by the Sea B&B Retreat** WEST OF TOWN Large, elegant rooms are filled with light from the water, and a spacious, private suite has the qualities of an apartment. 629 Fiddlehead Ln. ☎ 907-835-2930. www.alaska bytheseabnb.com. 3 units. Doubles $134–$177 summer; $79 winter. MC, V.

PWS & the CRC Fast Facts

Emergencies

For all emergencies, dial ☎ **911**.

Internet Access

CORDOVA Some hotels will offer Wi-Fi, but if yours doesn't (or you're camping), you can get free Wi-Fi and access to computers at the public library (☎ 907-424-6667) and at Orca Book and Sound (☎ 907-424-5305), both on First Street. VALDEZ The Valdez Consortium Library (☎ 907-835-4632), at 260 Fairbanks St., offers computers and free Wi-Fi.

Doctors & Medical Services

CORDOVA Cordova Community Medical Center and Ilanka Community Health Center, located together on Chase Street (☎ 907-424-8000), off the Copper River Highway near the Odiak Slough. VALDEZ Providence Valdez Medical Center (☎ 907-835-2249), 911 Meals Ave.

Pharmacies

I highly recommend getting what you need before you leave Anchorage or Palmer, and definitely bring prescriptions with you. Should you need anything, your best bet is the grocery stores in Cordova and Valdez.

Police

For nonemergencies, call the **Alaska State Troopers** in Palmer (☎ 907-745-2131), the **Cordova Police Department** (☎ 907-424-6100), or the **Valdez Police Department** (☎ 907-835-4560).

Post Office

CORDOVA There is a post office at the corner of Railroad and Council avenues. VALDEZ You'll find one at Galena Drive and Tatitlek Avenue, 1 block back from Egan Avenue.

Road Conditions

Always check road reports before driving Alaska highways in winter; in summer, verifying can mean avoiding construction delays that can last hours. Call ☎ 511 or go to http://511.alaska.gov.

Safety

Important tips for driving rural highways and outdoors safety are covered in chapter 2. Crime is not a problem in this part of the state.

Visitor Information

COPPER RIVER COUNTRY Copper Valley Chamber of Commerce and Visitor Center, Richardson and Glenn highways (P.O. Box 469), Glennallen, AK 99588, ☎ 907-822-5555, www.traveltoalaska.com. CORDOVA Cordova Chamber of Commerce Visitor Center, 404 First St., north of Council Avenue (P.O. Box 99, Cordova, AK 99574), ☎ 907-424-7260, www.cordovachamber.com. MATANUSKA GLACIER AREA Mat-Su Visitors Center, 7744 E. Visitors View Court, Palmer, AK 99645, ☎ 907-746-5000, www.alaskavisit.com. VALDEZ Visitor Information Center, 104 Chenega St., at the corner of Egan Drive (P.O. Box 1603), Valdez, AK 99686, ☎ 907-835-4636, www.valdezalaska.org. WHITTIER Whittier Chamber of Commerce, ☎ 907-677-9448; www.whittieralaskachamber.org. WRANGELL St. Elias National Park, P.O. Box 439, Copper Center, AK 99573, ☎ 907-822-5234, www.nps.gov/wrst.

> *Northern exposure: Moose crossing.*

My Favorite Kenai Peninsula Moments

I love the Kenai Peninsula. It's not as exotic as other parts of Alaska, but it has everything you come here for: cute coastal towns, big trees, and tidewater glaciers as in Southeast Alaska; tundra-clad high country with hiking that rivals the best at Denali National Park; and practically unequalled fishing and opportunities to see the broad range of Alaska's wildlife. The peninsula surpasses other areas in ease of travel: You can get around without all-day drives, expensive flights, or inconveniently scheduled ferries. Distances are not so great, good hotels and restaurants are plentiful, and there's a lot you can do yourself, saving money on guides and pilots.

> PREVIOUS PAGE *The Alaska SeaLife Center.*
> THIS PAGE *A pod of killer whales take a breather.*

❶ Driving the Seward Highway. It's tough to pick out a best spot on this drive, among the nation's most scenic byways (an official designation, by the way). But I'll highlight the drive through Turnagain Pass, because there you have the opportunity to enter into the scenery rather than just driving past. Park your vehicle and walk across the alpine heather as far as you like, up the mountains or through the pass. See p. 250, ❶.

❷ Seeing killer whales at Kenai Fjords National Park. The tour boats that leave from Seward always enjoy amazing scenery and frequently encounter pods of killer whales slicing through the water with their high dorsal fins and smooth black-and-white bodies. See p. 234, ❺.

❸ Riding the Alaska Railroad past Spencer Glacier. The rails from Anchorage to Seward pass through sublime mountain scenery you can't get to any other way in the summer. The views that pass by those big windows—of the Spencer Glacier area's canyons and ice—are unforgettable. See p. 236, ❶.

❹ Dining on a boardwalk in Halibut Cove. This artists' colony across Kachemak Bay from Homer has no roads, only docks and boardwalks upon which to reach the gallery, the studios, the big houses, and the restaurant alongside the placid waters of a narrow channel. Take the wooden passenger ferry over for dinner or lunch, and enjoy the setting as much as the great food. See p. 240, ❾.

❺ Sea kayaking on Kachemak Bay. The Kenai Peninsula has many sea kayaking options, but I've never enjoyed a day of paddling more than when I joined a lazy trip with True North Kayak Adventures around the bay's Yukon Island. The intimate encounter with the sea otters, the cliffs and rock arches, and the company of my companions made me feel a part of the place. See p. 240, ⓫.

❻ Flying to a bear camp from Sterling. Many people pay a fortune to fly out to brown bear

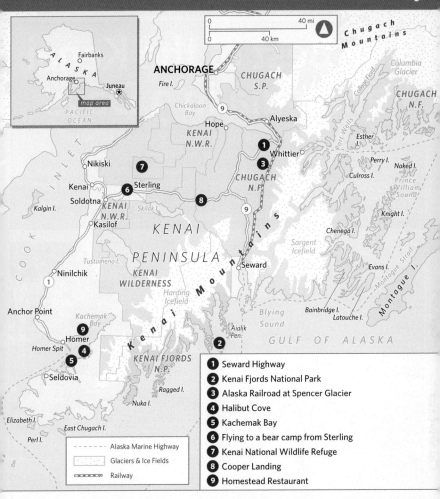

1 Seward Highway
2 Kenai Fjords National Park
3 Alaska Railroad at Spencer Glacier
4 Halibut Cove
5 Kachemak Bay
6 Flying to a bear camp from Sterling
7 Kenai National Wildlife Refuge
8 Cooper Landing
9 Homestead Restaurant

--- --- Alaska Marine Highway
Glaciers & Ice Fields
Railway

viewing sites and spend only a few hours. It makes more sense to spend just a bit more and overnight at a camp where you're likely to see bears more than once and to experience their habitat. The Lake Clark Bear Camp offered by Great Alaska Adventure Lodge in Soldotna is the place to do it. See p. 243, **15**.

7 **Canoeing on the Kenai National Wildlife Refuge.** This is Alaska's gentlest wilderness experience, suitable as a self-guided outing even for families with kids. Rent what you need at Alaska Canoe & Campground in Sterling, and then float on a series of lakes or a slow-moving river in lovely, pristine backcountry. See p. 249, **11**.

8 **Hooking a salmon on the Kenai River in Cooper Landing.** Salmon make the world go 'round in these parts. In Cooper Landing you can fish them on a float trip or from shore, and stay in lodgings among trees and mountains that will remind you why you came to Alaska. See p. 238, **5**.

9 **Enjoying grilled salmon at the Homestead Restaurant.** This dinner house among the woods and meadows east of Homer produces some of Alaska's best meals, and the atmosphere of good cheer is perfect after a day on the water. Local oysters, simply grilled seafood and steaks, a terrific wine list—paradise. See p. 267.

The Best of the Kenai Peninsula in 3 Days

The Kenai Peninsula is a microcosm of Alaska—with glaciers, mountains, marine wildlife, fishing, and interesting towns—and as in the rest of Alaska, it takes time to get around and see everything. With 3 days, you have time only for one main destination, Seward, and from there, the boat access to Kenai Fjords National Park. Fortunately, this brief trip will expose you to each of the elements of that Alaskan microcosm.

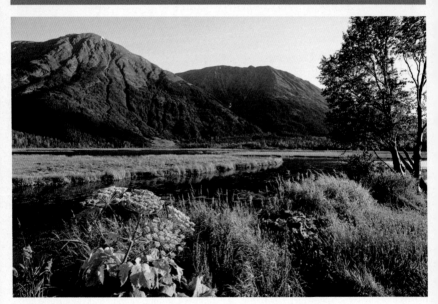

> A stop off the Seward Highway at Tern Lake promises excellent bird-watching.

START Anchorage. **TRIP LENGTH** 307 miles.

Take the Seward Highway out of town, and be sure to get a very early start, as the first day is a busy one.

➊ ★★★ Seward Highway. The Seward Highway is among the nation's most scenic—particularly the first 40 miles. Give yourself time to enjoy the drive. ⏱ 2 hr. See p. 250, ➊.

After 65 miles on the Seward Highway, turn off onto the Hope Highway.

➋ ★★ Sixmile Creek rafting with Chugach Outdoor Center. After passing through the glorious alpine valley of Turnagain Pass, the Seward Highway comes to a bridge high over Canyon Creek and the intersection with the Hope Highway. Floats down the ferocious waters of Sixmile Creek begin near here and head toward Hope. This is the wildest commercial rafting I know of, in class IV and V water, and you will be asked to prove your swimming ability before you can go (you wear a dry suit over

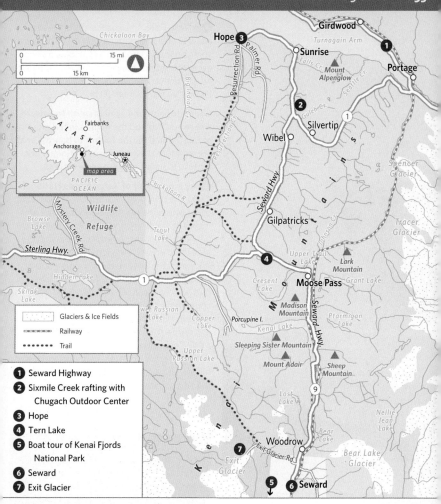

1 Seward Highway
2 Sixmile Creek rafting with
   Chugach Outdoor Center
3 Hope
4 Tern Lake
5 Boat tour of Kenai Fjords
   National Park
6 Seward
7 Exit Glacier

your clothing). If that's too scary for some in your party (or if you have children), the center also offers a scenic ride in Turnagain Pass, without rapids; your group can split up from the same starting point and meet at the end. ⏲ Half-day. Chugach Outdoor Center. Mile 7.5, Hope Hwy. ☎ 866-277-RAFT (277-7238). www.chugachoutdoorcenter.com. Sixmile Creek trip $99–$149, Turnagain Pass trip $80.

Take the Hope Highway 18 miles to the town of Hope.

Travel Tip

The Kenai Peninsula gets a lot of visitors, so it's wise to make reservations for outdoor activities and tours at least a few days in advance, and preferably as soon as you know your trip dates. Showing up for a raft ride, glacier boat tour, or sea kayaking paddle without a reservation might work, but only if you're lucky. Plan ahead.

More Information

For my suggestions on where to stay and dine in Seward, see p. 268.

> *Glaciers "calve" icebergs into Holgate Arm in Kenai Fjords.*

❹ ★ **Tern Lake.** The shallow pond lies in a circle of steep mountains, one of the prettiest spots on the highway. Bird-watching here is excellent—hence the name. There's a pullout on the highway, or go to the west end of the lake to the picnic area. ⏱ 1 hr.

Continue another 43 miles south to Seward, where you'll spend the night. On the morning of Day 2, head for the harbor to board a boat for your tour of Kenai Fjords National Park. Be sure to make advance reservations.

❺ ★★★ **Boat tour of Kenai Fjords National Park.** The park takes in a stretch of the Pacific coast where the sea meets mountains a mile high. The fjords are flooded glacial valleys cut between the peaks, and the glaciers that created them are still here, dropping icebergs in the water. Besides the extraordinary scenery, the concentration of wildlife is astounding. Bird-watchers can see many species rarely encountered except on such rocky outer shores, some in cloudlike flocks: puffins (both tufted and horned), murrelets (marbled, ancient, and Kittlitz's), cormorants (red-faced, pelagic, and double-crested), murres (common and thick-billed), and auklets (rhinoceros and parakeet). It's also common to glimpse humpback or killer whales, porpoises, sea lions, and sea otters. The only practical way to get there is

❸ ★★ **Hope.** This tiny gold-rush town at the end of the 18-mile Hope Highway is a lovely backwater, a trip back in time—well worth a casual walk. There's an interesting little museum, the **Hope and Sunrise Historical and Mining Museum** (p. 245, ❸). Get an ice cream across the street at **Sweet Mo's Simple Pleasures Ice Cream** (no phone), which occupies the town's old post office. ⏱ 1 hr. As you enter the village, look on your right for the museum and ice cream shop; the road is unnamed.

Return via the Hope Highway to the Seward Highway, and turn right to continue going 19 miles south.

Seward's Murals

Artists have decorated Seward like no other town in Alaska, a particular point of pride for the locals. You can see the evidence in the central business area, around Adams Street and 4th Avenue. The town's most noteworthy wall art is behind the altar in **St. Peter's Episcopal Church,** at 2nd Avenue and Adams Street (☎ 907-224-3975), a sweet little chapel under the mountains dating from 1906. The 1925 mural by Dutch artist Jan van Emple shows the Resurrection as if it had happened at Seward's Resurrection Bay, with apostles who look like real Alaska Natives and pioneers living in town at the time. Services are Sunday morning at 8 or 11; at other times, you can ask for the key at the **Seward Museum** (p. 269, ❸) or at the **Van Gilder Hotel** (p. 273).

on a large boat, and only full-day trips have time to make it into the park and back. That requires a sojourn into the ocean on the way, and many visitors get seasick. Take a remedy before starting.

Among the many good operators, **Kenai Fjords Tours** (the largest) is the one I recommend; you can visit and dine at their beachfront lodge on the otherwise uninhabited Fox Island, far out in Resurrection Bay (see "Fox Island: A Special Getaway," below). ⊙ 1 day. Small Boat Harbor. ☎ 800-478-8068. www.kenaifjords.com. Full-day cruise to the park $139.

If you've spent the night on Fox Island, you'll be returned to Seward in the afternoon. To make up some time, skip ❻ and go straight to the Exit Glacier ❼. Otherwise, begin your morning by exploring:

❻ ★★ **Seward.** This is a fun little seaside town to visit, easy to manage and with plenty to see. Besides being the threshold to Kenai Fjords National Park (see ❺ above), the other main attraction is the **Alaska SeaLife Center** (p. 268, ❶), a research aquarium that also has

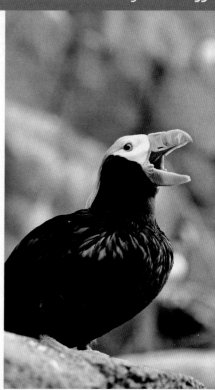

> Get within a few feet of a tufted puffin at the Alaska SeaLife Center.

Fox Island: A Special Getaway

Fox Island, 10 miles from Seward, stands like a defensive tower at the mouth of Resurrection Bay. It's an inspiring spot; painter Rockwell Kent made his career capturing these vistas. Kenai Fjords Tours built the ★★ **Kenai Fjords Wilderness Lodge** on a crescent-shaped cobble beach, where guests stop for a lunch of grilled salmon as part of a national park tour (see above)—or add to the tour an overnight in one of the cute log cabins at the edge of the trees above the beach. This is an easy way to reach quiet and remote wilderness on a quick trip; most lodges charge more, have longer minimum stays, and cost more to get to. If staying overnight, be sure to join a sea kayaking tour. By starting at this remote site, you'll have a better paddle than if you begin in town. Kenai Fjords Wilderness Lodge, part of Kenai Fjords Tours (p. 241). A 1-night package, including all meals, boat transportation from Seward, and a national park tour, is $379 per person; a 3-hr. sea kayaking tour is $109.

wonderful exhibits for visitors. It's where you can observe animals up close—in the case of the birds, you're within their enclosure, standing right next to them—that you'll encounter later in the park from a distance. ⊙ 2 hr. See p. 268.

On your way back to Anchorage, take the Seward Highway 3½ miles and take a left at the clearly marked entrance to Exit Glacier. The glacier is another 9½ miles farther on.

❼ ★ **kids Exit Glacier.** You'll have seen some very impressive glaciers by this point, but a stop at Exit Glacier is worthwhile anyway. You can get right up to it and feel the cold that rolls off. The glacier is part of the national park, and rangers at the nature center there lead walks three times daily. The short, level path to the glacier's face is easy on your own as well. ⊙ 1 hr. Nature Center open summer daily 9am–8pm; Sept daily 9am–5pm; closed winter. Free admission.

The Best of the Kenai Peninsula in 1 Week

A week on the Kenai Peninsula makes a complete Alaska vacation, with some of the best of what you want to see, all in a reasonably compact area with relatively simple transportation links. Since I know that everyone who visits Alaska wants to check out a glacier, I've included a rail link from Anchorage to Seward, where you can rent a car. The train passes a glacier on this ride, but the rest of the scenery can leave you speechless, too— and there's no other way through that backcountry without embarking on a wilderness expedition. If the cost and relative complication of taking the train doesn't appeal to you, simply rent a car in Anchorage and follow the first day of "The Best of the Kenai Peninsula in 3 Days" (p. 232) for your travel to Seward.

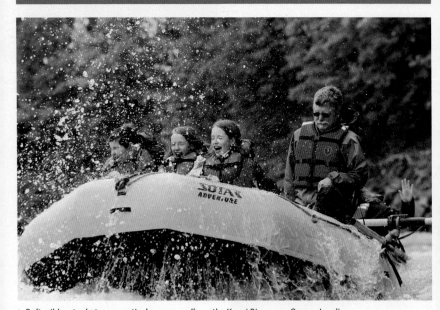

> Raft wild water between vertical canyon walls on the Kenai River near Cooper Landing.

START Anchorage. **TRIP LENGTH** 550 miles.

Board the Alaska Railroad's Coastal Classic in Anchorage, bound for Seward, a 127-mile journey that takes 3 hours.

1 kids ★★★ **Spencer Glacier backcountry.** The Alaska Railroad is the only transportation route through the most spectacular glacial backcountry between Anchorage and Seward. It's amazing to see what the builders accomplished in bringing rails through the canyons and past the ice. Even in the less expensive seats, this train is a comfortable and calming way to take in all this beauty through big,

Map legend:

1. Spencer Glacier backcountry
2. Seward
3. The Ranting Raven
4. Exit Glacier
5. Cooper Landing
6. Kenai's Old Town
7. Veronica's Old Town Cafe
8. Homer
9. Halibut Cove
10. The Saltry Restaurant
11. Kachemak Bay
12. Homer's museum and galleries
13. Cosmic Kitchen
14. The Homer Bench
15. Lake Clark Bear Camp

Map key:
- - - - Alaska Marine Highway
Glaciers & Ice Fields
Railway

0 ——— 40 mi
0 ——— 40 km

clean windows as it passes by at slow speed. The only other way to enjoy such an unfolding panorama is with a backpack. ⏱ 3 hr. ☎ 800-544-0552. www.alaskarailroad.com. One-way fare $75 for basic service, $130 for Gold Star service. For more information on the railroad, see "Denali by Rail" on p. 151.

Pick up a rental car in Seward and spend the day exploring the town.

2 ★★ **kids** **Seward.** Spend some time in the small, charming downtown, which has some of the best views you'll ever see from city streets. The **Alaska SeaLife Center** (p. 268, **1**) is the Kenai Peninsula's best indoor attraction. ⏱ 2 hr. See p. 268.

More Information

For detailed information on sights and recommended hotels and restaurants, see individual town tours later in this chapter.

Travel Tip

You'll be starting your journey aboard Alaska Railroad's Coastal Classic.

> *The Russian Orthodox Church is still a presence in Kenai's Old Town.*

③ 🍵 **The Ranting Raven** is a fun little coffee shop and art gallery that also carries locally made jewelry. It's right on 4th Avenue, the main street, which you can stroll along before or after visiting the SeaLife Center. 228 4th Ave. ☎ 907-224-2228. $.

Take the Seward Highway 3½ miles and take a left at the well-marked turnoff for Exit Glacier. The glacier is another 9½ miles farther on.

④ ★ kids **Exit Glacier.** Wrap up your day with a quick visit to Exit Glacier for an easy and interesting walk around its face. Like most glaciers in Alaska, Exit is retreating rapidly, and you can see how the vegetation has regrown in its wake. It takes time for soil to accumulate and plants to pioneer bare ground; signs show where the glacier stood at various times. ⏱1 hr. See p. 235, ➐.

Get an early start on Day 2, and drive 49 miles west on the Seward and Sterling highways to:

➎ ★★ **Cooper Landing.** More than anything else, this forest community along the Kenai River is a base for a variety of outdoor activities. Cooper Landing is a magnet for anglers, with some of Alaska's best salmon fishing. There are many shops on the highway where you can get advice and gear, or go with a guide such as **Alaska Wildland Adventures,** at the Kenai Riverside Lodge see p. 421), or **Alaska Rivers Co.,** Mile 50, Sterling Hwy. (☎ 907-595-1226; www.alaskariverscompany.com). They're both long-experienced operators, with Alaska Wildland the more upscale and expensive. A half-day of fishing with Alaska Rivers only costs $105, and a full day is $195 to $275.

If fishing isn't for you, Cooper Landing also is a good starting point for a hike or a river-rafting outing. There are many good trails here of varying difficulty levels; the most famous is the **Resurrection Pass Trail,** which was the original gold-rush transportation route through these mountains. The whole trail makes a fantastic backpacking trip to Hope, 39 miles away, but a good, all-day hike of medium difficulty goes 4.5 miles (one way) to Juneau Falls from the trailhead at mile 52 on the Sterling Highway.

The same firms mentioned above for fishing also offer raft rides through the frothing water of **Kenai Canyon,** which take all day, or scenic 2-hour floats on the upper river without rapids. The scenic floats run from $49 to $54, while the canyon float will cost $135 to $140. ⏱ At least half-day for fishing; full day for round-trip hike to Juneau Falls; at least 2 hr. for rafting.

Begin Day 3 with a side trip to Kenai. Take the Sterling Highway 45 miles to the Kenai Spur

Saving on a Rental Car

The prices for renting a car in Seward are higher than you're used to paying, and drop-off charges apply for returning the car in Anchorage. But because the car rental taxes are so high in Anchorage (over a third of the cost), you won't pay much more for the vehicle than if you picked it up and returned it at the Anchorage airport.

> *Thanks to the Alaska Maritime National Wildlife Refuge, admission to the Alaska Islands & Ocean Visitor Center is free.*

Highway in Soldotna, then 11 miles west to Kenai. Give yourself a bit more than an hour to get to:

6 ★ **Kenai's Old Town.** The city of Kenai grew up during the oil years from a Russian America village, the core of which still remains. Stop at the **Kenai Visitors and Cultural Center** to take a look at its museum, which has changing exhibits on the area's history and art, and to pick up a map of numbered stops in the historic area, two blocks away via Main Street and Overland Avenue. (Leave your car here and walk.) The centerpiece of the Old Town area is the Holy Assumption of the Virgin Mary Russian Orthodox Church, a little onion-domed chapel built of logs in 1895 for a parish that has been here since 1845. Make a small donation to go in and see the icons. Several buildings nearby have the same unusual construction as the church of interlocking logs, now deeply weathered and shifted but still holding together like good cabinetry.

Across Alaska Street from the church, the Kenai River bluff presents an extraordinary view of the river's mouth and the broad, silty waters of Cook Inlet. A footpath leads from between the apartment building and professional offices down to the long, sandy beach and dunes—a lovely spot for a walk. But don't park on Alaska Street and block the residents and businesses. ⊕ 2 hr. Kenai Visitors and Cultural Center, 11471 Kenai Spur Hwy. ☎ 907-283-1991. www.visitkenai.com. Summer Mon–Fri

9am–7pm, Sat–Sun 10am–6pm; shorter hours off-season. Admission $5 to museum portion, free for students through high-school age.

⑦ 🍽 **Veronica's Old Town Cafe.** This tiny coffeehouse and eatery occupies one of the ancient log buildings across from the church in Kenai's Old Town, and just going inside is cool. The food is good, especially the quiche on polenta crust, and the cafe is open long hours, with acoustic music on weekends. 602 Pederson Way. ☎ 907-283-2725. $.

Return less than a mile on Kenai Spur Highway to Bridge Access Road and cross the Kenai River. The views from the bridge and nearby wildlife viewing area can be lovely. On the far side, turn right on Kalifornsky Beach Road and follow it 16 miles back to the Sterling Highway. Turn right and continue 61 miles to Homer, where you'll spend the next 3 nights.

8 ★★ kids **Homer.** The town has developed in relation to the marine riches of 40-mile-long Kachemak Bay, first as a fishing village, then as a destination for artists, retirees, and visitors inspired by the extravagant beauty of the place. Any visit, whether on the water or in the galleries, focuses on the bay. On your first afternoon, stop at the remarkable **Alaska Islands & Ocean Visitor Center** (p. 260, **1**), run by the U.S. Fish and Wildlife Service, which is like a museum of the coastal

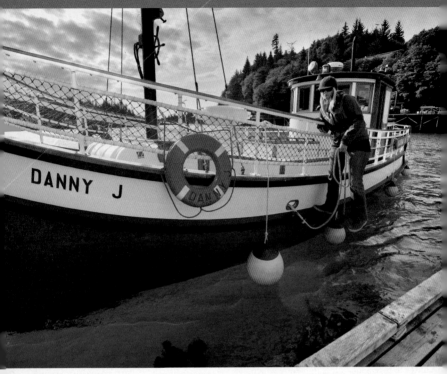

> *Halibut Cove's Saltry Restaurant operates the* Danny J *ferry between Homer and the artists' colony.*

environment, with high-tech exhibits that recreate the feeling of being on a volcanic Pacific Island surrounded by a flock of birds, and which teaches about the history and nature of these places. You can join a guided nature hike or tide-pool exploration here, or walk self-guided on a marsh trail that leads about .3 miles to Bishops Beach, where ocean waves pound the shore and you can walk for miles. ⏱ 2 hr. See p. 260.

❾ ★★★ Halibut Cove. On your first evening in Homer, board the wooden *Danny J* passenger ferry at the boat harbor for a 6-mile voyage across the bay to the village of Halibut Cove. The boat is operated by the restaurant to bring over diners, but guests can also explore while there. The village is an artists' colony and retreat of the well-off, without roads or cars—instead there is a placid channel, and everyone gets around by skiff or by walking the wooden boardwalks between houses. ⏱ 4 hr. See "The Saltry Restaurant," below.

⑩ 🍽 The Saltry Restaurant's location would make it a delight even without good food, but the grilled fish and whole-grain bread are terrific. Those who don't want fish can order buffalo—beef isn't on the menu. The boat leaves Homer at 5pm, with just enough time for a leisurely dinner and to soak up the village ambience. Halibut Cove. ☎ 907-296-2223. www.halibut-cove-alaska.com. Reserve at least 2 days ahead. $30 boat fare; entrees $25–$34. MC, V.

⑪ ★★★ Kachemak Bay. Spend Day 4 on the bay, whether angling, kayaking, or exploring nature.

If you're interested in fishing, you're in luck: These waters are famous for halibut. The winner of the summer-long derby in Homer always gets a fish topping 300 pounds (and a check for well over $30,000, so be sure to buy your ticket at the booth on Homer Spit before you fish). Halibut are bottom fish that can live

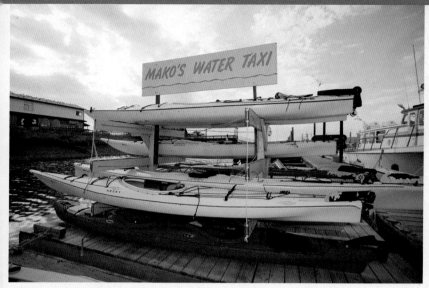

> One of the many sea kayaking outfits in Kachemak Bay State Park.

50 years, and lunkers over 100 pounds are common. Charter boats from Homer usually spend a full day to get to waters with the biggest halibut. The trips are not for easily bored kids or for those susceptible to seasickness. Also, pack lunch and drinks the night before. I suggest you book through **Inlet Charters**

Across Alaska Adventures (☎ 800-770-6126; www.halibutcharters.com), a reliable local agent for the charter fleet. A full-day trip will cost about $275 per person.

The bay is famous as well for sea kayaking, and plenty of guides will vie to take you out. Your outing will begin with a boat ride to the

Spending the Night in Cooper Landing

Cooper Landing is a tiny town, but it has a few excellent places to stay. The **Kenai Princess Wilderness Lodge,** a luxurious hotel on a forested hill above the Kenai River, has the feel of an authentic wilderness lodge. Rooms occupy a series of buildings on the compound, the best of them fixed up like cabins but with every comfort. The on-site restaurant is first-rate. Frontier Cir. ☎ 800-426-0500. www.princesslodges.com. 86 units. Doubles $249–$309. AE, DC, DISC, MC, V. Closed mid-Sept to mid-May.

A cheaper option, is the **Hutch Bed and Breakfast,** a family-run inn on grounds where evening campfires are common and rabbits hop around. Mile 48.5, Sterling Hwy., ☎ 907-595-1270. www.arctic.net/~hutch. 12 units. $89–$119, w/breakfast. MC, V.

Finally, across Skilak Lake by boat, a collection of cabins and tent cabins hides among the trees, a peaceful and comfortable retreat. If you can extend your Cooper Landing visit to 2 nights, consider staying there, at the **Kenai Backcountry Lodge.** Fishing isn't the focus; nature is, with lake kayaking, mountain hiking, and peaceful quiet. Showers and toilets are in a central bathhouse, and dining is on the wilderness lodge plan, with everyone eating together. Alaska Wildland Adventures, Skilak Lake. ☎ 800-478-4100 or 907-783-2928. www.alaskawildland.com. 10 cabins. $975 per person for the minimum 2-night stay, includes meals and guiding. DISC, MC, V.

> *The non-profit Bunnell Street Arts Center in Homer is one of the state's best galleries.*

rocky islands and narrow fjords on the far side of the bay from Homer, as the town side's low beaches aren't appealing for kayaking. I recommend **True North Kayak Adventures** (☎ 907-235-0708; www.truenorthkayak. com), which takes clients to Yukon Island and the surrounding waters, where natural rock arches and islets transform through the changing of the tide into slowly evolving fanciful shapes. The outing lasts 8 hours, but it isn't taxing, as there are plenty of breaks and time to simply drift in calm places. Plan to spend $150 per person.

A local nonprofit, the **Center for Alaskan Coastal Studies** (p. 243, ⓮), offers daily excursions across the bay for wildlife viewing, nature walks, and tide pooling, and you can add a short sea kayaking excursion, too. ⏱1 day for each option.

⓬ ★★ kids **Homer's museum and galleries.** You've spent the previous day outdoors, so consider spending at least half of Day 5 indoors. The **Pratt Museum** (p. 260, ❷) is the town's remarkable natural history and art museum. It has mounted touring exhibits and

has created technology that has spread far beyond Homer. A visit conveys the best of the town and its environment from the local perspective. Outside, don't miss the garden for a chance to learn about local botany.

Homer is an arts-oriented community, and there are many galleries. These aren't snooty shops, though—all contain work within the price range of a typical visitor. Don't miss the **Bunnell Street Arts Center** (p. 260, ❸), Homer's nonprofit art space in a transformed hardware store and trading post. Most other galleries are on **Pioneer Avenue,** and a few are among the boardwalks on Homer Spit. ⏱2 hr. for the museum, 1 hr. for the galleries and arts center.

Alternative Ending

Unfortunately, bear viewing is rather expensive. If it's not within reach of your budget, skip the next (and final) stop and instead try the canoeing trip detailed on p. 249, ⓫, for a more affordable wilderness experience.

> *Emerald Air Service, based out of Homer, takes passengers to view Alaskan coastal brown bears, which are genetically identical to, but larger than, grizzlies.*

⑬ 🍴 kids **Cosmic Kitchen.** This bright, inexpensive eatery is considered a treat by everyone in our family. Make a delicious, wholesome, and speedy lunch of their burritos or wraps by eating on the deck, which is shielded from the wind by glass panels. 510 E. Pioneer Ave. ☎ 907-235-6355. www.cosmickitchenalaska.com. $. See p. 266.

In the afternoon, follow East End Road east from Homer, then turn left on Easthill Road and follow it to the end, where you'll take a right and go 1½ miles on E. Skyline Drive.

⑭ ★★ kids **The Homer Bench.** Atop the big bluff at the back of downtown Homer, 1,000 feet above the town, rolling hills of meadows with patches of forest extend many miles, often with sweeping views of the distant mountains and sea. It's a favorite area for hiking, mountain biking, or (in season) cross-country skiing. An excellent starting point is the **Carl E. Wynn Nature Center,** with a variety of trails for the fit or the disabled, and naturalists on hand who lead nature walks and offer daily programs. Check ahead to time your visit with events. ⏱ 2 hr. Center for Alaskan Coastal Studies, Carl E. Wynn Nature Center. Mile 1.5, Skyline Dr. ☎ 907-235-6667. www.akcoastalstudies.org. Admission $7 adults, $6 seniors, $5 children 17 and under. Mid-June through Labor Day daily 10am–6pm.

On Day 6, take the Sterling Highway 86 miles north to Sterling, where you will join an overnight bear-viewing expedition.

⑮ ★★★ **Lake Clark Bear Camp.** The pristine wild lands on the far side of Cook Inlet, with two large national parks—Katmai and Lake Clark—contain an enormous population of brown bears fattened on the area's prodigious salmon runs. The Great Alaska Adventure Lodge in Sterling maintains a private camp in the area, near Mount Iliamna, where bears come to feed on grass in the early summer; later in the year, this makes a good base for trips to see them feeding on salmon. Guests fly by small plane and spend the night in beds in the big, heated tents; by staying in the camp overnight, you much improve your chances of good bear viewing. ⏱ 1 day. Great Alaska Adventure Lodge, 33881 Sterling Hwy., Sterling. ☎ 800-544-2261 or 907-262-4515. www.greatalaska.com. 1-night all-inclusive package $1,095 per person. AE, MC, V.

Fjord-free?

I've set up this tour without a day spent taking a boat tour to **Kenai Fjords National Park** (p. 271, ⑥). This deserves an explanation. You'll be boating and likely seeing marine wildlife from Homer instead, where seasickness is less common. But should you manage to find the time, doing both is a great idea, too.

The Best of the Kenai Peninsula with Kids

If you want to learn about taking kids to the Kenai Peninsula, you've come to the right author. I've been doing it for 18 years with my children (Robin, 18; Julia, 15; Joey, 10; and Becky, 9), and my parents took me there when I was a tot. This is the best Alaska region for a family vacation because there's a lot to do without expensive guides or air charters—and because the distances, although they seem long enough, are shorter than on road trips elsewhere in the state. I've set up the tour to keep drives short and included lots of energy-burning time outdoors. You could make it even more memorable by camping as you go. You're rarely far from a campground in this region, and I've described some of the best campgrounds with the town tours, starting on p. 260. For advice on getting gear, see "Gearing Up to Fly & Camp," on p. 157.

> Kids can handle starfish and other tide-pool denizens in the touch tank at Alaska SeaLife Center.

START Anchorage. **TRIP LENGTH** 7 days, 550 miles.

Take the Seward Highway south en route to Hope, 90 miles away.

❶ ★★★ Seward Highway. Begin your trip with a 40-mile drive along this astonishingly scenic route. Your first day driving from Anchorage is an easy one with plenty of time for spontaneous stops. The Seward Highway route along Turnagain Arm will present plenty of good opportunities for them. ⏱ 2 hr. See p. 250, ❶.

Stop 50 miles from Anchorage at Turnagain Pass.

❷ ★★ Turnagain Pass. The highway rises rapidly from the salt marshes of Turnagain Arm to the pass, at 1,000 feet, which is a crease in mountains 4,000 feet high. A couple of parking lots on the alpine tundra are here, allowing you to indulge the urge to get out of

Map Legend:

1. Seward Highway
2. Turnagain Pass
3. Hope
4. Seward
5. Caines Head State Recreation Area and Fort McGilvray
6. Exit Glacier
7. Tern Lake
8. Sal's Klondike Diner
9. Homer
10. Peterson Bay & China Poot Bay
11. Kenai National Wildlife Refuge canoe routes

- - - - - Alaska Marine Highway
··········· Glaciers & Ice Fields
⚬⚬⚬⚬⚬ Railway

0   40 mi
0   40 km

the car and run around a bit. Trails here are casual, and you can go any direction you like; with the absence of trees, it's easy to find your way back. But keep track of kids, who can get lost in the brush.

You can join an easy rafting outing here, offered by **Chugach Outdoor Center,** based in Hope (p. 232, ❷). Their Sixmile Creek run

is much too rough for children, but their alternate float here in the pass is easy. ⏱ 1 hr. for the drive; half-day for the rafting trip.

Drive 12 miles on the Seward Hwy. to the Hope Hwy, and follow it 18 miles to Hope, where you'll spend the night.

❸ ★★ **Hope.** Founded during a minor gold rush in the 1890s, this sleepy little town of fewer than 150 survives on its attitude and dusty authenticity: Hope feels and looks like the friendly frontier community you would dream up if you sat down to imagine one. Park the car and wander. Children will enjoy the **Hope and Sunrise Historical and Mining**

> *Tern Lake, a shallow pond encircled by steep mountains and fed by streams, is one of the prettiest spots off the Seward and Sterling highways.*

Museum (☎ 907-782-3740), which includes a compound of pioneer buildings you can poke around—a barn, a blacksmith's shop, a miner's bunkhouse, and an old-time schoolhouse. The museum is open noon to 4pm daily from Memorial Day to Labor Day, and admission is free

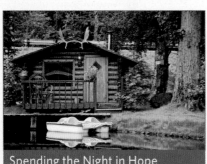

Spending the Night in Hope

Stay in Hope at **Bowman's Bear Creek Lodge and Dinner House**. The cute log cabins stand around a little pond with a canoe, next to a rushing stream—the scene looks like a child's crayon drawing, and any kid who doesn't experience love at first sight is hopelessly jaded. Each cabin is stocked with firewood for the wood stove. Bathrooms are in a pleasant shower house. Eat here, too; the tiny restaurant is as charming and friendly as the rest of the place. On the Hope Hwy. ☎ 907-782-3141. www. bowmansbearcreeklodge.com. 5 cabins. Doubles $150 summer; $100 winter. DISC, MC, V. Entrees $22–$26. Dinner Tues–Sun summer; Thurs–Sun winter.

(though donations are accepted). Right across from the museum, stop at **Sweet Mo's Simple Pleasures Ice Cream** (no phone), in the old post office.

On Day 2, spend some time getting outdoors. ★ **Resurrection Creek** runs along the west side of the community. All five Pacific salmon species enter it, but it's especially known for pinks, which come in enormous numbers from early July to mid-August; they bite readily and fight with all their 4 pounds of muscle. Scorned by many Alaska anglers as too easy to catch and not as tasty as their larger cousins, they're nonetheless the perfect quarry for children. You'll need to bring gear with you.

If you're not into fishing, try hiking ★★ **Gull Rock Trail.** Beginning just beyond the creek and continuing through the Chugach National Forest's spectacular Porcupine Campground, the trail is a perfect family hike: well maintained, mostly level, and with many good views of Turnagain Arm. The entire trail is about 5 miles one way to the overlook at Gull Rock, but a rewarding hike can be had without going so far. ⏱ 1½ days.

In the late afternoon of Day 2, get back on the Seward Highway for the 70-mile drive to Seward, where you'll be spending the next 2 nights. On the morning of Day 3, plan to spend some time exploring:

❹ ★★★ **Seward.** This is a fun town to walk around in, with its murals and its old-fashioned main street. Most visitors come for the boat tours to **Kenai Fjords National Park** (p. 271, ❻). I leave it up to you to decide if that trip is a good idea with your children. It's a long boat ride, with seasickness common, and the animals can be too far away for kids to get a satisfactory look.

On the other hand, I know children will enjoy the **Alaska SeaLife Center** (p. 268, ❶), with its dramatic exhibits and its important function: rescuing stranded and injured animals. Although not as large as a big-city aquarium, it will hold kids' interest for at least an hour. Best of all, join a behind-the-scenes tour to learn how scientists and animal rescuers at the center do their work. Check times and reserve your spot for tours on the website. 🕐 2 hr. See p. 268.

In the late morning, drive 3 miles south of town to Miller's Landing on Lowell Point, where you'll board a water taxi to:

❺ ★★ **Caines Head State Recreation Area and Fort McGilvray.** I can report from experience that kids can't believe this adventure is even allowed. You'll take a small boat to a remote beach, hike a forest trail to a World War II fort on a high ocean overlook, and then explore the fort's dark underground corridors with flashlights. The Caines Head trail in total is too long for kids, and parts are accessible only at low tide, so take a water taxi to North Beach from Miller's Landing. Hike the wide, gradually rising trail from North Beach 1 mile, then take a left-hand fork 1 mile more to Fort McGilvray. Beware of the cliffs at the fort; stay on the concrete. The fort commands a towering view of the ocean, 650 feet straight down; it was built to stop the Japanese, who had captured two Alaskan islands, from invading the bay. With a flashlight and plenty of caution, you can go into the excitingly scary and utterly black maze of passages and rooms. Afterward, retrace your steps and wait for the boat back from North Beach (or camp out there for the night). 🕐 At least a half-day. Water taxis: ☎ 866-541-5739. www.millerslandingak.com. $43 per person (round trip). Park information: Alaska State Parks. (907) 262-5581. www.alaskastateparks.org.

Much of Day 4 will be spent en route to Homer, 165 miles away. To begin, take the Seward Highway 3½ miles, and take a left at the well-marked turnoff for Exit Glacier. The glacier is another 9½ miles farther on.

> *Taking a break on the Harding Ice Field Trail, overlooking Exit Glacier.*

❻ ★ **Exit Glacier.** This is the only glacier you'll encounter on the trip as I've planned it here, but it's a good one to see with kids because they can run around on the gravel plain left behind by the glacier and get close enough to feel the icy cold. Don't let them go closer than indicated by the signs, however, as the ice can fall off and cause injury. 🕐 1 hr. (p. 235, ❼).

Continue 43 miles north from Seward to Tern Lake, turning left to continue toward Homer on the Sterling Highway. As you pass beyond

Travel Tip

The trip from Seward to Homer would normally take about 3 hours to drive, but there's much you would miss. Instead take your time, as there are many pretty spots, hikes, and tiny towns along the way. Make your own discoveries, and plan to spend the whole day.

> *The One Big Ocean exhibit at the Islands & Ocean Visitor Center teaches visitors how essential a healthy North Pacific is to the entire globe.*

the lake, a driveway on the left leads to a Chugach National Forest picnic ground.

❼ ★ Tern Lake. Stretch your legs, play by the water, enjoy the scenery, watch for birds and wildlife. You know the drill. See p. 234, **❹**.

Continue 57 miles on the Sterling Highway to Soldotna.

⑧ 🍴 Sal's Klondike Diner, in Soldotna, may look like something from your own childhood: a classic Western highway diner under a movie-style false front, with big portions, fast service, cheap prices, and a model train. It's open 24 hours a day, all year. 44619 Sterling Hwy. ☎ 907-262-2220. $–$$.

Continue 75 miles to Homer, where you'll be spending the next 3 nights. Spend the morning of Day 5 exploring:

❾ ★★ Homer. There's plenty to do in Homer that children and their parents will enjoy, some indoors and more outdoors. For the indoors, check out the **Alaska Islands & Ocean Visitor Center** (p. 260, **❶**), with its exhibits,

films, and programs, and the **Pratt Museum** (p. 260, **❷**), where the models of boats and the marine life exhibit are highlights.

Outdoors, drive up onto the bench above Homer to the **Wynn Nature Center** (p. 243, **❿**) and join a walk with one of their charismatic young guides. If you still have time and energy left, another wonderful, scenic family hike called the **Homestead Trail** is also on the bench. From the nature center, drive back the way you came, but stay to the right rather than descending the hill, so you reach the reservoir, 3¾ miles away. The trail is an old wagon road leading over the rolling hills with their meadows of wildflowers, with sweeping ocean views. It's too far to hike the entire trail; go as far as you like and then return to the car. ⏱1 day. See p. 260.

On Day 6, you'll head to Peterson Bay on a guided nature tour boat ride.

❿ ★★★ Peterson Bay & China Poot Bay. The field station program at Peterson Bay, operated, like the Wynn Center, by the **Center for Alaskan Coastal Studies** (p. 243, **❿**), introduces families to the shoreline and forest of this extraordinary land and creates new lovers

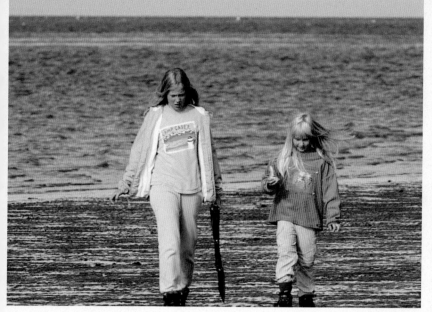

> *Younger travelers will enjoy exploring the rich variety of habitats around China Poot and Peterson bays.*

of nature. The day begins with a boat ride across to the station's dock on a wooded isthmus between Peterson and China Poot bays, near a remarkable variety of habitat types: rocky beach, estuary, rich intertidal pools, forests, meadows, and more. Guides skilled in environmental education lead groups over the trails and through the tide pools; back at the station, they show off creatures kept in touch tanks. In the later afternoon, add a bargain-priced sea kayaking excursion from the center for a couple of hours. Bring lunch, warm clothing, and sturdy footwear for the trails and beach—you'll be tired but happy on the boat ride back to Homer (or plan for an overnight in a yurt at the center). ⏱1 day. $105 adults, $73 children 12 and under. $155 with sea kayaking included (adult or child). Yurt $80 for up to 6.

On Day 7, get an early start and take the Sterling Highway 86 miles back toward Anchorage, stopping en route at the town of Sterling, gateway to the:

⓫ ★★★ **Kenai National Wildlife Refuge canoe routes.** The big, flat region on the west side of the peninsula is pockmarked by innumerable lakes and laced with slow, winding rivers. It's a paradise for family canoeing, where the land and waters are gentle but also big and remote enough to allow a true wilderness experience. To get oriented, stop at the **Kenai National Wildlife Refuge Visitor Center** as you pass through Soldotna (p. 274, ❶).

In Sterling, a business called **Alaska Canoe & Campground,** 35292 Sterling Hwy. (☎ 907-262-2331, www.alaskacanoetrips.com), is the key to accessing the refuge. The Max and Annette Finch family rents canoes and camping gear, and offers shuttles to take paddlers to the starting point and endpoints of their routes, if necessary. The trip you plan depends on your group and interests; to do one of the long routes—through the lakes of the Swan Lake Canoe Route or down the Swanson River—you would have to camp in the backcountry, but there are plenty of pretty places to paddle for just the day, too. Max and Annette also offer advice and even lessons and a guide, although that's not really necessary. They have a couple of nice cabins with kitchens that sleep up to 8 (they rent for $150 per night), or you can backtrack to Soldotna for the night. ⏱1 day.

A Kenai Peninsula Outdoor Adventure

The tours throughout this chapter contain many adventures, but here I have in mind a trip for folks who love being vigorous outdoors and don't want to go back inside even at night. You have a great advantage over those who are tied to beds and cars, because the best of Alaska is found beyond the end of the road, and usually there's no one else there when you arrive. The four major outings here will take you to such places over the course of 10 days, while minimizing cost by avoiding use of bush planes, wilderness lodges, and, where possible, guides. You will need to rent your equipment. That's covered under "Gearing Up to Fly & Camp," on p. 157.

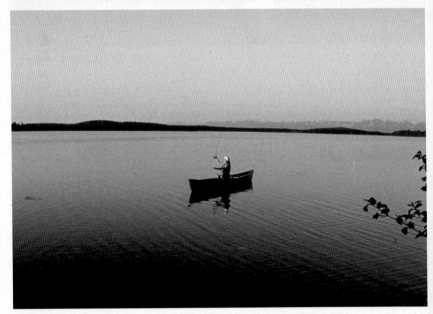

> The Swan Lake Canoe Route connects 30 lakes by waterways and short walking paths.

START Anchorage. **TRIP LENGTH** 519 miles.

Take the Seward Highway 127 miles to Seward.

❶ ★★★ Seward Highway. If you get an early start, you may have time for some of the extraordinary trails, alpine rambles, and river-raft rides to be had along the spectacular highway from Anchorage to Seward. The first 40 miles are along scenic Turnagain Arm (p. 84). Take a mountain walk at **Turnagain Pass** (p. 244, ❷), shoot the rapids on **Sixmile Creek** (p. 232, ❷), or go bird-watching on **Tern Lake** (p. 234, ❹).

Seward Highway
1. Seward Highway
2. Primrose Landing Campground
3. Primrose Creek Trail
4. Northwestern Fjord's sea kayaking trip
5. Swan Lake Canoe Route
6. Homer
7. Kachemak Bay State Park

--- Alaska Marine Highway
Glaciers & Ice Fields
Railway

Stop 17 miles short of Seward at the well-marked turnoff for Primrose Landing Campground, where you'll spend the next 2 nights.

2 ★★ **Primrose Landing Campground.** This small U.S. Forest Service campground on the shore of Kenai Lake is among our family's favorites for its setting. It also provides access to one of Alaska's most beautiful trails, the **Primrose Creek Trail,** which you can hike for a whole day. Chugach National Forest, Seward Ranger District. ☎ 907-224-3374. www.fs.fed. us/r10/chugach. Campsites $11 per night.

Get an early start on Day 2.

Getting Geared Up

I've assumed you will rent your equipment in Anchorage and drive to the Kenai Peninsula in a rented car, but you can also fly to Kenai to rent your car, and rent equipment in Sterling at **Alaska Canoe & Campground** (p. 249, **11**). When comparison shopping, look at the total cost of each option, including car rental taxes, which are sky-high in Anchorage. And if you do decide to fly to Kenai, simply skip stops **1**–**4** and begin your tour at stop **5**.

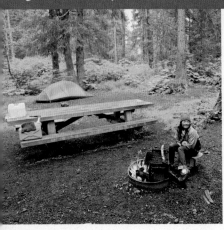

> *Primrose Landing Campground on Kenai Lake.*

③ ★★ **Primrose Creek Trail.** You'll need a full day for this hike, or you can backpack it, as there are ample areas for camping. The entire route, including the connecting **Lost Lake Trail,** leads 16 miles to Seward; an annual run for cystic fibrosis covers that distance in late August. But I recommend you hike to the high country and then return to your campsite. The trail rises steeply through spruce forest for nearly 5 miles before breaking into an airy alpine space with extraordinary views. Go at least that far before turning back; if time and energy permit, hike the full 8 miles to Lost Lake, returning the same distance. ⏱1 day. Chugach National Forest, Seward Ranger District. ☎ 907-224-3374. www.fs.fed.us/r10/chugach.

On Day 3, drive the 17 remaining miles of the Seward Highway into Seward, and join up with your guides at Sunny Cove Sea Kayaking for a 3-day adventure.

④ ★★★ **Northwestern Fjords sea kayaking trip.** This is the financial splurge of the trip, but it's worth it to paddle for 3 days in the overwhelming glacial scenery of this remote **Kenai Fjords National Park** area, with its abundant wildlife and tidewater glaciers. Few park visitors will go so far, and those who do will see the area only briefly from the deck of a crowded tour boat; you'll be able to live there for a couple of days. **Sunny Cove Sea Kayaking** takes small groups out by boat through exposed ocean waters to the fjords, where the seas remain calm among the steep, protective

mountains. I recommend the 2-night paddle to Northwestern Fjord to make the most of the journey, but the firm offers 1-night trips to Aialik Bay—also spectacular and glaciated, but nearer—for less money. You can also save by bringing your own camping gear and food; otherwise, Sunny Cove will provide everything and cook for you. ⏱3 days. Sunny Cove Sea Kayaking, Seward. ☎ 907-224-4426. www.sunnycove.com. Northwestern Fjord 3-day $1,199 per person fully outfitted, $949 with client's own camping gear and food; Aialik Bay 2-day $699 per person fully outfitted, $599 with client's own camping gear and food.

After returning from sea kayaking on Day 5, you will have been camping for 4 nights. Spend a night in Seward to clean up, and then set off on the morning of Day 6 for the 83-mile drive on the Seward and Sterling highways to the town of Sterling. From there, take Swanson River Road north and turn right on Swan Lake Road. The entrance is at mile 3½.

⑤ ★★ **Swan Lake Canoe Route.** The broad, flat west side of the **Kenai National Wildlife Refuge** (p. 249, ⑪) includes a congressionally designated wilderness of thousands of lakes, more than 100 of which are connected by short paths that allow canoeists to travel lake to lake; you'll relax after carrying your gear by lying back on the water, listening to the wind in the birches, and feeling for the tug of a trout on your line. By getting a shuttle ride on the area's unpaved roads, you can set up a long journey without having to cover the same ground or water twice. Anyone with a bit of camping and canoeing skill can do it, given the willingness to carry the boat over portages that are usually about .25 mile and rarely as long as a mile.

Your choices of routes are myriad, and picking which way to go is part of the fun. Most canoeists simply travel a few lakes into the system, then return the way they came. But an excellent one-way journey covers 11 lakes: 9.5 miles from the west entrance on unpaved Swan Lake Road to Swan Lake, then 17 miles of floating down the gentle and fish-rich Moose River (8 to 10 hours) to where it meets the Kenai River, at the Izaak Walton State Recreation Area, in Sterling. Allow at least 3 nights for a relaxing trip. Primitive campgrounds are

> *The Swan Lake Canoe Route will get you into the thick of the Kenai National Wildlife Refuge.*

scattered along the shore of the lakes and river, and you can camp whenever you're ready. Start at **Alaska Canoe & Campground** (p. 249, **11**) to rent a canoe and other equipment and to arrange for a shuttle ride. They also offer a campground, showers, cabins, and important advice. Get advance information, much of which is on the Web, from the refuge headquarters in Soldotna (p. 274, **1**). ⏱ 3 days.

In the late afternoon of Day 8, drive south 86 miles on the Sterling Hwy from Sterling to Homer, where you'll spend the night.

6 ★★ **Homer.** Take some time to get oriented to this outdoorsy town and its great artistic output. You should definitely stop at the **Alaska Islands & Ocean Visitor Center** (p. 260, **1**). The **Pratt Museum** (p. 260, **2**) is also well worth your time. ⏱ Half-day. See p. 260.

On the morning of Day 9, head to Homer's harbor to pick up a water taxi.

7 ★★ **Kachemak Bay State Park.** This huge shoreline park takes in most of the amazing mountainous vista on the far side of the bay from Homer. Although it can be reached only by boat, the park has 25 miles of trails, many campsites, and several public-use cabins (which are famous, but which I won't cover here since they are extremely difficult for

non-Alaska residents to reserve). Pack food and gear for 2 days of camping, and board a water taxi at the harbor to be dropped off in this roadless wilderness at the starting point of your choosing. Experienced paddlers can rent kayaks from the water taxi for an added degree of freedom in your exploration. If you don't want to camp, many day trips are possible, or consider renting a yurt through **Alaskan Yurt Rentals** (☎ 907-235-0132; www.alaskanyurtrentals.com; $65 a night). These are much easier to reserve than the cabins.

An excellent trip starts in **Halibut Cove Lagoon,** where the state park maintains a dock and a ranger station. The lagoon sits like water in a bowl between the mountains. Several of the park's trails connect there, and you can camp near the ranger station or, if you carry your stuff, at China Poot Lake, 2.6 miles up the trail. Setting up your base for 2 nights, plan a hike for the second day: either the relatively easy 5.5-mile Coalition Loop to lovely China Poot Bay or the challenging 4.6-mile climb of Poot Peak. You can't get to the very top without mountaineering equipment, but the views along the trail are incredible. Check on trail conditions before picking a route. ⏱ 2 days. Kachemak Bay State Park. ☎ 907-235-7024. www.alaskastateparks.org. Mako's Water Taxi: ☎ 907-235-9055. www.makoswatertaxi.com. $75 per person.

SALMON

Alaska's most revered fish

BY MIKE DUNHAM

SALMON IS SUCH A STAPLE OF THE ALASKAN DIET that the fish is honored in both cuisine and culture. Superstitious skippers kiss and release the first fish of the season. Chefs compete to create original recipes. Charter planes rush the early catch to gourmets around the world. Each summer, Anchorage hosts an annual "Wild Salmon on Parade" art show.

And every season, thousands of anglers troll in fishing derbies or stand shoulder-to-shoulder along the banks of wild rivers and urban streams, striving to catch a year's supply of "subsistence" salmon—enough fish to keep them sated until the next season. Indeed, many Alaskans eat salmon almost every day. And while salmon are near extinction in much of the western U.S., Alaska's population has managed to survive, thanks in part to the lack of dams on the state's major rivers. Salmon runs here remain robust, which is a good thing, given how popular wild salmon's nutritional benefits (and tastiness) have made it.

The Circle of Life

BEGINNINGS
Laid in gravel at the head of freshwater rivers in the late summer, eggs hatch under the ice during the cold months of early spring. The newborn *alevin* carry an egg sack with them, which provides nourishment. Five to 10 weeks later they become *fry*, recognizable as fish, feeding on insects and other aquatic life—some of which also feeds on them!—as they grow into *parr*. After 1 to 3 years in fresh water, they become *smolt*, adapting to life in saltwater and swimming downstream to the sea.

AT SEA
In their adult form, most salmon range far and wide in the ocean, though silvers tend to stay closer to shore. They eat, grow, and dodge predators that include seals and sharks. But after 1 to 3 years at sea, they stop eating and return to fresh water, usually trying to get back to the same place where they were hatched. Scientists aren't in agreement about what drives salmon back to the place of their birth, with some believing that smell, or the magnetic pull of the earth, are responsible.

SPAWNING
To reproduce, salmon must swim upstream for hundreds of miles and more, over rapids, past anglers, bears, and even fish-hungry wolves. The few that reach the headwaters seek gravel patches deep enough to avoid freezing during the winter. Using her tail, the female digs a *redd* in the gravel and lays thousands of eggs, which the male fertilizes by discharging his *milt*. Both parents die soon after (Pacific salmon are unique in this regard). Their rotting bodies contribute nutrients to the food chain that will sustain the infant salmon when they hatch in the spring.

Which Is Which? Getting to Know Salmon

CHUM, OR DOG
The second largest of Alaska's salmon, the chum has the lowest fat content, making it leaner than other species, though still delicious. Nonetheless, old timers used them for dog food. Spawning males sprout formidable fangs—another reason why they're called "dogs."

◀ SILVER, OR COHO
Anglers love this spectacular, leaping fish for its spunk and size—33 pounds is the record. Silvers have a reputation for striking at flies and lures, making them a favorite among anglers.

KING, OR CHINOOK
The largest species of salmon, kings can reach 100 pounds or more, though most adults top out at 25 pounds. Yukon River kings migrate up to 2,000 miles to reach their breeding grounds.

PINK, OR HUMPY
The most abundant species of salmon, pinks are known to breed in any spot that feels right. During spawning, the male develops a large hump on its back, hence the name.

RED, OR SOCKEYE
With its bright flesh and robust flavor, the smallest Alaska salmon species, averaging 4 to 7 pounds, lives longer than other salmon, up to six years. It is the most valuable salmon to the canning industry.

The Best Kenai Peninsula Fishing in 1 Week

The Kenai Peninsula is Alaska's most popular region for fishing because of its remarkably rich rivers and ocean waters, combined with easy, relatively inexpensive access. This tour is for the fishing fanatic who wants to focus on some of the most famous areas but who isn't necessarily wealthy. If you are prepared to spend more freely (around $1,000 per person per day, all-inclusive), even better fishing is found in remote areas with lodges in southwest Alaska, including the amazing salmon runs and trophy-sized trout of the Bristol Bay drainage. For more information, see "Fishing at a Remote Wilderness Lodge" on p. 259.

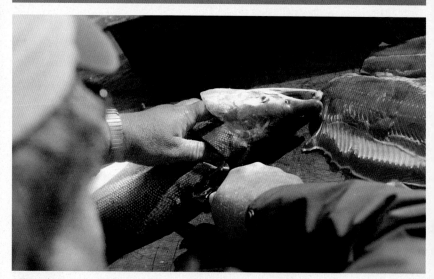

> King salmon are the big catch along the Kenai River.

START Kenai. Take the 25-minute flight from Anchorage to Kenai, and rent a car. **TRIP LENGTH** 254 miles.

❶ ★ **Kenai & Soldotna.** The few hours of sightseeing in **Kenai's Old Town** (p. 239, ❻) alone wouldn't justify the big tourism infrastructure here; everyone comes in pursuit of the world's largest king salmon. But the area is worth a look. ⏱ 2 hr.

Get an early start on Day 2.

❷ ★★★ **Lower Kenai River.** The world's largest sport-caught king salmon, at nearly 100

① Kenai & Soldotna
② Lower Kenai River
③ Cooper Landing
④ Homer

pounds, came from the Kenai River and is on display at the **Soldotna Visitor Center** (p. 274, ①). In fact, big fish are so common here that trophy-class kings have to be over 75 pounds, as opposed to 50 pounds anywhere else. As always in fishing, but even more when fishing for kings, success depends on timing, patience, skill, and luck. I can't help you with luck, but the other three elements are controllable.

Timing means coming when the fish are in the river, for the smaller run that peaks mid-June or the main run during July. Silvers peak in mid-August and reds from late July to early August (you can check exact dates—for more information, see "Fishing Intelligence" on p. 258).

Patience means the average angler fishes 29 hours and gets 12 strikes before landing a king.

Skill means going with a guide in a boat. Many are available in Kenai and Soldotna, often at a savings as a package with lodgings (see "All in One," p. 258). For the a la carte option, contact the friendly folks at the **Sports Den,** 44176 Sterling Hwy., Soldotna (☎ 907-262-7491;

More Information

For detailed information on sights, and my recommendations for lodging and dining, see the individual town tours later in this chapter.

> *Cleaning the salmon catch on the Kenai River.*

www.alaskasportsden.com), who offer a full menu of fishing trips. In general, expect to pay $150 to $170 for a 6½-hour trip, or $250 to $265 for a full day. ☉ **1 day.**

All in One

To fish the lower river at an all-inclusive lodge, consider a stay at the **Great Alaska Adventure Lodge** (p. 276) in Sterling, 12 miles north of Soldotna at the confluence of the Kenai and Moose rivers, a legendary fishing spot. The lodge has a long riverfront; after a day fishing in a boat with one of their guides, you can cast all night in the midnight sun right outside your room. You can also combine fishing with other activities, such as bear viewing, or split up during the day so some in your group can concentrate on fishing while others do something else. The cost of a 2-day package is $1,195 per person.

On Day 3, take the Sterling Highway 45 miles from Soldotna to Cooper Landing, where you'll spend the next 3 nights.

❸ ★★★ **Cooper Landing.** The tiny town is strung along miles of the two-lane Sterling Highway and the upper Kenai River to its headwaters, Kenai Lake, and the confluence of the red-salmon–packed Russian River. The fishing can be so hot on the Russian that anglers stand shoulder to shoulder, waiting turns for a spot, which we call "combat fishing" around here. The differences between the upper Kenai and the lower are its mountain beauty, faster flow, and shallower depth; fishing here is primarily in drift boats or from shore, instead of the motorized boats in the broad, deep lower river.

I recommend you stay at a fishing lodge, where you can get away from competition and enjoy the expertise and camaraderie of guides. The best is the **Kenai River Sportfishing Lodge,** which has a long river frontage, cute cabins, and good food, and which owns permits to guide all along the river. A 2-day, 3-night stay will cost $1,525 per person. However, if their rates are too much for your budget, there are less expensive choices for getting on the river with a guide for the day and staying at a B&B. See "Spending the Night in Cooper Landing," on p. 241, for more information. ☉ **3 days.** See p. 238, ❺.

Fishing Intelligence

Salmon runs are brief and intense, with peaks that can last only a matter of days. Successful salmon anglers concentrate first on *when* to fish, not where. It used to be you needed your own network of informants, but now the Alaska Department of Fish and Game publishes weekly fishing reports and even real-time counts of fish in certain rivers, based on sonar measurements. The department's website is an invaluable place to begin learning about fishing in Alaska in general—not just about salmon—and you can buy your license online, although virtually every grocery store, tackle shop, and guide also sells licenses. Go to the site at www.adfg.state. ak.us, then navigate to "Sport Fish" and the region you are interested in.

After 3 full days of fishing the Kenai, get an early start on Day 6 and take the Sterling Highway 116 miles south and west to Homer.

4 ★★ **Homer.** The art and outdoors of Homer make it a fun place to visit, with plenty to do—a particular plus if members of your party are not avid anglers. The famous fishing attraction of Homer is its halibut fleet, which heads out early each morning for long days on Kachemak Bay and beyond to hook the enormous bottom fish. The advantages of **halibut fishing** (see "Getting Outdoors In & Around Homer" on p. 263) are the long season, which doesn't vary much through the summer, the reliability of the catch, and the delectable flesh of the fish. The best times to go are during biweekly periods of mild tidal changes, when currents are weaker, making it easier to keep your bait down on the bottom. Ask about that when you reserve, and if possible, adjust your schedule accordingly.

Homer is one of only a few places in Alaska with developed wintertime sportfishing.

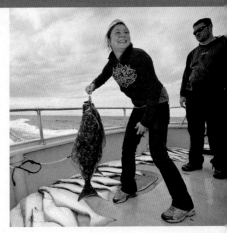

> Halibut is an easy and tasty catch off Homer's waters.

Salmon feed in Kachemak Bay and lower Cook Inlet even when they're not spawning. Charter boats target winter kings, and a big derby takes place in the early spring, when cross-country skiing is still going on. To plan such a trip, contact **Inlet Charters Across Alaska Adventures** (p. 240, **11**). ⏱ At least 1½ days.

Fishing at a Remote Wilderness Lodge

Flying a small plane to a remote lodge in the Bristol Bay region puts you in the middle of some of the world's best fishing, far from any crowds. It's possible to catch 10-pound native rainbow trout—not one, but several in a day. A fishing journalist told me of catching 30 king salmon in a day (catch and release, of course). An extraordinary ecosystem and a lack of human presence create this abundance—and the absence of people is because of the cost. Lodges in the region are reached only by small plane. Their staff, food, materials, and everything else must be carried a flight at a time. Expect to spend $1,000 a day, with daily prices going down somewhat for additional days. Rather than profile a particular lodge, I prefer to point you to a booking agency that can send you where the fishing is best at the time you are traveling; otherwise, you could spend a lot of money to go to a lodge outside peak run times. I recommend the Anchorage-based **Sport Fishing Alaska,** 9310 Shorecrest Dr. (☎ 888-552-8674; www.alaskatripplanners.com), run by a longtime Alaskan who does only this and charges a $95 upfront fee.

Getting Your Fish Home

You probably won't be able to eat all the halibut or salmon you catch on vacation (many anglers release salmon after a photo, but most keep their halibut). Eat as much fresh as possible; many lodges and some restaurants will cook it for you, and some lodgings have outdoor grills for guests' use. To get the rest home in good condition, it should be processed, vacuum-packed, and frozen as soon as possible. Guides and charter operators typically make these arrangements for clients, although you will have to pay separately, around $1.25 a pound. If fishing on your own, you can find businesses offering this service in most fishing towns, and some hotels provide freezers as a guest amenity. For shipping, have your processed, frozen catch packed in sturdy cardboard fish boxes with cold packs. Do some research to find the cheapest way of getting the boxes home: second-day express shipping or with your luggage, incurring airline baggage fees.

Homer

Homer is among my favorite towns, though not for the buildings and urban design, which are even quite ugly in places. What I like is that Homer remains truly itself despite being full of visitors. You get to be like the locals, which is much more interesting than being a tourist. There are guides to take you on amazing outdoor adventures, but in Homer you don't need one, and people tend to go across the bay on a water taxi and guide themselves. For a community its size, the town has an exceptional museum, supported and attended by towns-people—unlike many Alaskan museums that are merely tourist attractions. Homer is alive and real. You'll want to spend at least 2 days here if you plan on fishing.

> *The shoreline of Kachemak Bay is ideal for strolling and exploring tide pools.*

START Homer is 235 miles from Anchorage.

1 ★★ kids **Alaska Islands & Ocean Visitor Center.** Grandly and specially built for the Alaska Maritime National Wildlife Refuge, which essentially wraps the island shores of the state, the center impresses, educates, and orients. Drop in for the exhibits, a film, a path, programs, and ranger walks, which include guided tide-pool tours. ⏲ At least 1 hr. 95 Sterling Hwy. ☎ 907-235-6961. www.islandsandocean.org. Free admission. Summer daily 9am–6pm; check website or call for low-season hours, as they vary.

2 ★★ kids **Pratt Museum.** The museum covers history and art, but is strongest in natural history, including Homer's relationship with the sea, and the practical matters of learning to recognize the marine and land plants and animals you'll see. ⏲ 1 hr. 3779 Bartlett St. (at Pioneer Ave.). ☎ 907-235-8635. www.prattmuseum.org. Admission $8 adults, $6 seniors, $4 children 6–18, free for children 5 and under; $25 family rate. Summer daily 10am–6pm; winter Tues–Sun noon–5pm. Closed Jan.

3 ★ **Bunnell Street Arts Center.** The community's nonprofit gallery, among the state's

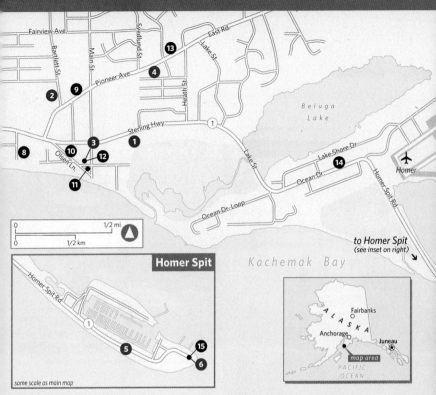

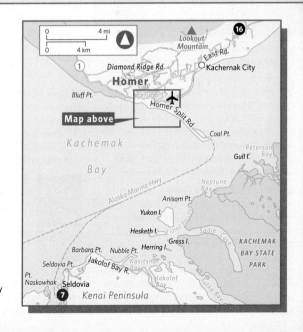

1 Alaska Islands & Ocean
   Visitor Center
2 Pratt Museum
3 Bunnell Street Arts Center
4 Pioneer Avenue galleries
5 Homer Spit
6 Land's End Resort
7 Trip to Seldovia

Where to Stay

Driftwood Inn **11**
Land's End Resort **15**
Ocean Shores Motel **8**
Old Town Bed and Breakfast **12**

Where to Dine

Café Cups **9**
Cosmic Kitchen **13**
Fat Olives **10**
Fresh Sourdough Express Bakery
   and Restaurant **14**
The Homestead Restaurant **16**

> *Shorebird sculptures outside the Islands & Ocean Visitor Center.*

> *Land's End Resort offers waterfront dining.*

best, occupies a perfect space, in a former hardware store and trading post with undulating wood floors and light from nearby Bishops Beach. Serious art shows happen monthly, and the center also hosts concerts. ⏱ 30 min. 106 W. Bunnell Ave. ☎ 907-235-2662. www.bunnell streetgallery.org. Summer daily 10am–6pm; winter, Mon–Fri 10am–5pm, Sat noon–4pm.

④ ★ Pioneer Avenue galleries. Many artists live and create in Homer and in the tiny communities around Kachemak Bay, taking their inspiration from the sea and mountains. At least eight galleries line Pioneer, most with affordable work, and others are easily found with a widely distributed map (download it at www.fireweedgallery.com/cs4.pdf). They're generally open from 11am to 6pm in the summer, with shorter hours Sunday. ⏱ 1 hr.

⑤ ★ Homer Spit. The town's most important feature is the 5-mile-long tendril of land extending into Kachemak Bay, which provides its access to the sea. You'll go there anytime you take a boat, and it's also a fun place to walk, shop, and camp, despite the crowding and cheap tourist development.

⑥ Land's End Resort. This is the town's most expensive hotel, but you don't have to stay there to enjoy the incredible location, at the very end of Homer Spit, where fishing boats and whales go by. Get a table on the glass-walled deck for a drink or appetizer. See p. 267.

SITE GUIDE PAGE 265

⑦ ★★ Trip to Seldovia. The tiny fishing town of Seldovia once was the commercial center for all of Cook Inlet. Today it's a sleepy retirement community and portal to remote ocean waters and mountain biking routes. You can get a feel for the town and go sea kayaking or biking on a day trip. Make sure you reserve your activities before you leave Homer, checking that your schedule fits with the boat's.

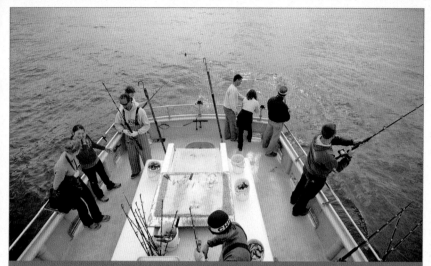

Getting Outdoors In & Around Homer

Fishing. The famous halibut fishing is one of Homer's main draws. You can also fish for salmon right on Homer Spit in the Nick Dudiak Fishing Lagoon (better known as the Fishing Hole), which was carved from the shore for the purpose. The Alaska Department of Fish and Game stocks king and silver salmon here, which return in the early and late summer, respectively. For gear and advice, head to **Ulmer's Drug and Hardware,** 3858 Lake St.

Hiking. Both sides of Kachemak Bay offer great hikes. On the Homer side, hike on the bench above town to the **Wynn Nature Center** (p. 243, ⑭) or the **Homestead Trail** (p. 248, ⑨). Across the bay, take a water taxi to **Kachemak Bay State Park** (p. 253, ⑦).

Sea Kayaking. Waters perfect for kayaking are found all along the south side of Kachemak Bay, reachable by water taxi. Those needing a guide can go with **True North Kayak Adventures** (p. 242, ⑪); experienced paddlers can rent equipment and get dropped off by **Mako's Water Taxi** (p. 253, ⑦). If you take a boat to the village of Seldovia, you can do a less expensive sea kayaking tour right from the harbor there (p. 265, ⑦).

Tide Pooling. Families especially shouldn't miss the opportunity to encounter the undersea world in the low-tide zone around Kachemak Bay. You can go with a guide at the **Alaska Islands & Ocean Visitor Center** (p. 260, ❶) or at **China Poot Bay** (p. 248, ❿), or go on your own. Get a pair of rubber boots and stop at the center for an identification key and advice. The nearest tide pools to town are at Coal Point, at least a half-hour walk west on Bishops Beach from the park at the end of Beluga Place. You will need a tide of at least 1 foot below mean low water to see much of anything—the lower the tide, the better.

Mountain Biking. Many unpaved bike routes beckon around Kachemak Bay, but the best way to get away from cars and into wild country is to explore the roads and abandoned routes connecting to **Seldovia** (p. 262, ⑦) and **Jakolof Bay.** Taking Mako's Water Taxi to the dock in Jakolof Bay is the most direct way to the best biking routes. The road there leads west 7 miles to Seldovia, or south many miles more, over stream crossings and washouts, for a long wilderness journey clear across to the far side of the Kenai Peninsula. You can rent a bike in Homer to take across, at **Homer Saw and Cycle,** 1532 Ocean Dr. (☎ 907-235-8406); call ahead to reserve and to get advice.

A Wilderness Lodge Experience

An extraordinary array of wilderness lodges lie on the south side of Kachemak Bay, reached only by boat from Homer. Like wilderness lodges anywhere in Alaska, these places are destination where guests settle in for a few days and have all their meals and activities provided by their hosts. Below I've described the least and most expensive choices. Many more are linked on the website of the Homer Chamber of Commerce: www.homeralaska.org (click "Accommodations," then "Across Kachemak Bay").

★ **Across the Bay Tent and Breakfast.** Accessed from Homer by water taxi, this lodge has the special quality of being affordable for normal people. Cabins and tent cabins are among the trees on a steep hill overlooking lovely Kasitsna Bay, but the location isn't too remote, as a dirt road leading to the village of Seldovia and some great mountain biking routes is at the back of the property. Guests can take advantage of the hosts' hospitality to the degree they choose, cooking most of their own food or joining in the meals grilled by the shore. The lodge is laid back and charming, a paradise for outdoorsy families. On Kasitsna Bay, Seldovia. ☎ 907-235-3633; winter ☎ 907-345-2571). www.tentandbreakfastalaska.com. 6 units. $75 per person with breakfast; $110 per person with all meals. Half price for children 6–11, free for those 5 and under. MC, V. Closed mid-Sept to Memorial Day.

★★★ **Kachemak Bay Wilderness Lodge**. This is one of the original eco-lodges (pictured), and still among the best. It has three special qualities no one else does as well. One, although the accommodations are luxurious, they don't look it; the place fits perfectly into its setting; like the collection of historic seaside cabins (pictured above) it is. Second, the setting, on rich China Poot Bay, where the wealth and accessibility of the marine and coastal environment are unmatched. Third, the charisma and practices of the hosts and guides, who are not only real Alaskans, but also leading experts on the nature and history of the region, and leaders for its protection. The food is famous and guiding is included. That works simply enough: each morning, each party's own guide asks what they want to do, and that's how they spend the day. Homer. ☎ 907-235-8910. www.alaskawildernesslodge.com. 5 cabins. $1,700 per person for a 2-night stay, $2,400 3-night, $3,500 5-night; children 7–17 half price, those 6 and under free. Rates all-inclusive, including boat transportation from Homer. Boating, kayaking, and all guiding included. 2-, 3- or 5-night package only. V. Closed Sept 15–May 25.

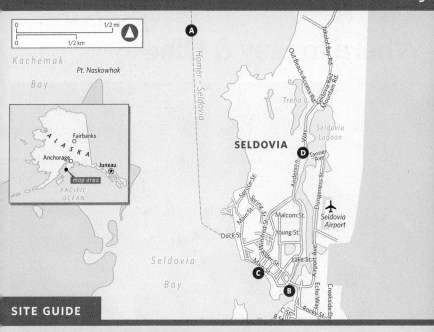

SITE GUIDE

⑦ Trip to Seldovia

Day trips to Seldovia begin in Homer Harbor, where tour boats carry passengers across Ⓐ **Kachemak Bay,** stopping to take in the lovely island scenery and marine wildlife. The boat ride is a highlight of the trip. You have various choices and times; I've always been happy with **Rainbow Tours** (see below). Before the 1964 earthquake (see "Whole Lotta Shaking," on p. 208), most of the town was on a boardwalk along placid Ⓑ **Seldovia Slough.** Most of it is gone, but the little bit that's left is lovely and deeply evocative of the past. There's also good king salmon fishing from the shore of the slough, peaking in mid-June.

Two longtime residents (a couple) lead Ⓒ **kayak tours** on Seldovia Bay under the name **Kayak'atak,** starting right from the town (☎ 907-234-7425; www.alaska.net/~kayaks). A 3-hour tour costs $80 per person.

One main thoroughfare, Ⓓ **Jakolof Road,** leaves Seldovia and doesn't go much of anywhere. It leads 7 miles through the countryside to Jakolof Bay, and thence on across the peninsula for many miles more of unmaintained dirt track. These are great routes for a

mountain bike. Call ahead for the availability of bikes; if you can't line one up, you may be able to bring one from Homer. Get information, and the boat ride, from **Rainbow Tours** (☎ 907-235-7272; www.rainbowtours.net). A round-trip passage to Seldovia, with wildlife viewing on the way, costs $50 for adults, $45 for seniors, and $40 for children. ⊕ 1 day.

Where to Stay & Dine

> *Café Cups pleases the sophisticated palate.*

★★★ **Café Cups** DOWNTOWN *SEAFOOD* A funny old building transformed into a work of art is the site of a restaurant that serves both mainstream food and a list of daily specials using local seafood and sophisticated preparation. 162 W. Pioneer Ave. ☎ 907-235-8330. www.cafecupsofhomer.com. Entrees $18–$30. MC, V. Dinner Tues–Sat.

★★ **kids** **Cosmic Kitchen** DOWNTOWN *MEXICAN* This casual, order-at-the-counter eatery is a local favorite for tasty, filling dishes produced quickly and inexpensively, and for the pleasant indoor and outdoor dining areas. 510 E. Pioneer Ave. ☎ 907-235-6355. www.cosmic kitchenalaska.com. Entrees $5–$11. MC, V. Breakfast, lunch, and early dinner Mon–Fri; no dinner Sat; closed Sun.

More Information

Wilderness lodges on the south side of Kachemak Bay are covered in "A Wilderness Lodge Experience" (p. 264).

★ **Driftwood Inn** DOWNTOWN This cozy old place near Bishops Beach has two parts: the original building, with inexpensive little rooms that are a bit like Pullman compartments, and the newer buildings next door, with big, beautifully appointed rooms and suites overlooking the water. 135 W. Bunnell Ave. ☎ 800-478-8019 or 907-235-8019. www.thedriftwoodinn.com. 33 units. Doubles $65–$195 summer; $49–$99 winter. MC, V.

★★ **Fat Olives** DOWNTOWN *MEDITERRANEAN* Magnificent pizza and much fancier dishes come from the Italian brick oven in a remodeled bus garage. It's the trendiest and most popular eatery in Homer. 276 Olson Lane. ☎ 907-235-8488. Lunch $7–$12; dinner entrees $16–$26. MC, V. Lunch and dinner daily.

★ **kids** **Fresh Sourdough Express Bakery and Restaurant** NEAR HOMER SPIT *CAFÉ* This warm and lively place was organic and Earth-friendly decades ago, with lasting success thanks to tasty meals, wonderful baked goods, and friendly touches like the kids' play area in front. Stop here for a box lunch before a day on the water. 1316 Ocean Dr. ☎ 907-235-7571. www.freshsourdoughexpress.com. Entrees $10–$25. DISC, MC, V. Summer breakfast, lunch, and dinner daily; no dinner in winter.

★★★ The Homestead Restaurant EAST OF HOMER SEAFOOD
This white-tablecloth restaurant in a log building in the countryside east of town offers some of Alaska's best meals in a warm, exuberant atmosphere—perfect after a day on the water. Mile 8.2, East End Rd. ☎ 907-235-8723. www.homesteadrestaurant.net. Dinner only. Entrees $21–$39. AE, MC, V. Summer daily; winter Wed–Sat. Closed Jan–Feb.

★★★ Land's End Resort HOMER SPIT
This nautical hotel enjoys perhaps Alaska's best location (which is really saying something), at the very end of Homer Spit, 5 miles out in Kachemak Bay. Room choices are many, with a broad selection of sizes, styles, and prices. There's a good seafood restaurant on site called the Chart Room, with a riveting water view across the beach to where otters loll on the waves and boats pass by within yards. Entrees are $16 to $38, but the best of the menu is the appetizers, of which you can make a meal. 4786 Homer Spit Rd. ☎ 800-478-0400 or 907-235-0400. www.lands-end-resort.com. 95 units. Doubles $125–$245 summer; $85–$145 winter. AE, DC, DISC, MC, V.

> *Old buoys decorate the front of the Driftwood Inn.*

★ Ocean Shores Motel DOWNTOWN
These are comfortable standard rooms on a grassy compound just above Bishops Beach, and a short walk to the downtown sights and restaurants. 451 Sterling Hwy. ☎ 800-770-7775 or 907-235-7775. www.oceanshoresalaska.com. 38 units. Doubles $129–$204 summer; $69–$79 winter. AE, DISC, MC, V.

★ Old Town Bed and Breakfast DOWNTOWN
Situated above the Bunnell Street Arts Center, the cockeyed, historic building drips with charm, artfully enhanced by handmade quilts, antiques, and original paintings. There are no TVs or in-room phones, and the entry is up a steep, narrow staircase. 106 W. Bunnell Ave. ☎ 907-235-7558. www.oldtownbedandbreakfast.com. 3 units. Doubles $95–$115 high season; $56–$75 low season; w/breakfast. MC, V.

Camping by the Sea

The classic Homer camping spot is nestled amid the sand and pebbles of **Homer Spit,** where you can hear the sea and the wind flaps your tent. In addition to being a great spot, it's also a great deal. The city charges $8 for tents, $15 for RVs—payable at the Camp Fee Office, located in a small log cabin on the spit, across the road from the fishing hole (☎ 907-235-1583, summer only). For RV hookups, the **Driftwood Inn** (p. 266) has a nice, enclosed campground with good facilities near Bishops Beach, charging $29 to $49 for a site.

Seward

The town of Seward lies at the head of Resurrection Bay

and below one of the few inland passages through the mountains for many miles, a strategic position recognized early on by Russian invaders and still important for the steady stream of cruise-ship visitors and railroad passengers who come through here. Most travelers who make Seward a destination use it as a base for day trips to Kenai Fjords National Park, the best of which is reached only by boat. But the town in its own right is worthy of a day of sightseeing and hiking, and the autumn silver-salmon fishing is legendary. You'll want to spend at least 2 days here if you plan to explore the park.

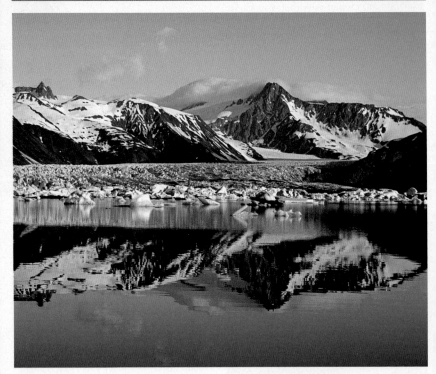

> *Bear Glacier Lake is a popular sea kayaking destination in Kenai Fjords National Park.*

START Seward is 127 miles from Anchorage.

1 ★★ kids **Alaska SeaLife Center.** This is a research institution and public aquarium of exceptional quality, and Seward's one must-see attraction. Built with government money won from Exxon after the 1989 oil spill that soiled more than 1,000 miles of the coast, the center combines research of Alaska's ocean ecology, rehabilitation of injured seabirds and marine mammals, and breathtaking wildlife exhibits. You can step into the aviary and walk among

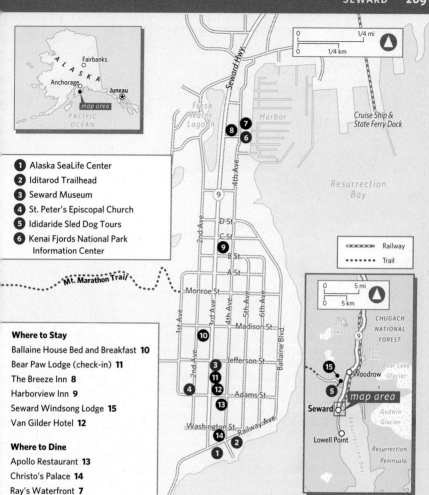

1 Alaska SeaLife Center
2 Iditarod Trailhead
3 Seward Museum
4 St. Peter's Episcopal Church
5 Ididaride Sled Dog Tours
6 Kenai Fjords National Park
   Information Center

Where to Stay

Ballaine House Bed and Breakfast **10**

Bear Paw Lodge (check-in) **11**

The Breeze Inn **8**

Harborview Inn **9**

Seward Windsong Lodge **15**

Van Gilder Hotel **12**

Where to Dine

Apollo Restaurant **13**

Christo's Palace **14**

Ray's Waterfront **7**

---

the sea birds; from a floor below, you can spy them through glass as they "fly" underwater, beating their wings as if in the air. ⏲ 2 hr. 301 Railway Ave. ☎ 888-378-2525. www.alaskasealife.org. Admission $20 adults, $15 students (12–17 or with ID), $10 children 4–11, free for children 3 and under. Summer daily 9am-6:30pm; winter daily 10am–5pm.

❷ **Iditarod Trailhead.** This spot, on the water just east of the SeaLife Center, is where pioneers entered Alaska. The broken concrete and twisted metal you see while walking north on the beach are the last ruins of the Seward

waterfront, which was destroyed during the Great Alaska Earthquake of 1964 (see "Whole Lotta Shaking," on p. 208). Keep an eye out for sea otters swimming offshore. ⏲ 15 min.

❸ ★ **Seward Museum.** The town's tiny museum contains clippings, memorabilia, and curiosities of its eventful history, and some art produced by talented people who have passed through. ⏲ 1 hr. 3rd Ave. and Jefferson St. ☎ 907-224-3902. Admission $3 adults, 50¢ children 17 and under. Summer daily 10am–5pm; call ahead in winter.

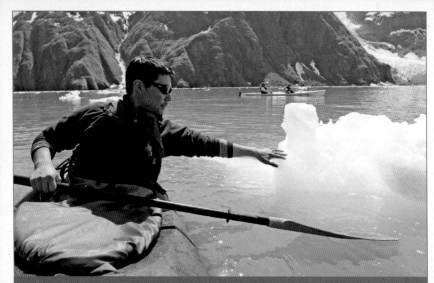

Getting Outdoors in Seward

Hiking. The spectacular and rewarding hike up to the top of **Mount Marathon,** which looms right behind the town, entails a 3,022-foot rise over a bit less than 4 miles. It is strenuous and takes a full day to make the round trip—the trailhead is at 1st Avenue and Monroe Street. Whether or not you're up for the hike, consider this: The mountain is most famous for the Independence Day footrace from downtown to the summit and back (runners use a shorter trail), which has been run annually since 1908. Thousands line the streets to see bloody, muddy finishers come in after tumbling down the mountain in as little as 10 minutes (it takes them about 40 to get to the top).

Caines Head State Recreation Area (p. 247, **5**), which has a lovely coastal trail that leads to the abandoned Fort McGilvray, is an excellent choice for families. You'll want to catch a ride with a **Miller's Landing water taxi** (p. 247, **5**) in order to get there, as parts of the trail are underwater at high tide. Bring flashlights so that you can poke around the ruins of the World War II defensive emplacement. You can easily spend half a day here.

Fishing. Hard-fighting **silver salmon** invade Resurrection Bay in late August and September. The town goes wild with anglers coming to catch them and enter the annual derby. Some cast from shore, but your best chance is to go on a 1-day boat charter. I prefer the small boats known as *six-packs,* which hold six or fewer passengers, but the 12-person boats have the advantage of being a bit more stable on the waves. If you tend to get seasick, that's the way to go. I like **Crackerjack Sportfishing Charters,** on the boardwalk at the top of the harbor ramps (☎ 800-566-3192; www.crackerjackcharters.com). If you book the whole boat, you can add in sightseeing or whale-watching; multiday tours are also available. Another very good operator is **The Fish House** (☎ 800-257-7760 or 907-224-3674; www.thefishhouse.net), a store and local booking agency located at the Small Boat Harbor. Rates for salmon charters tend to run about $175 per person, including gear.

Sea Kayaking. Seward is a fabulous place to give sea kayaking a try. Check in with **Sunny Cove Sea Kayaking** (p. 252, **4**) for their guided tours, suitable for beginners, which leave right from town. If you're lucky, you'll see sea otters, seabirds, and maybe even schools of salmon. Plan to pay $65 for 3-hour paddles, $130 for 8-hour tours. They offer plenty of other options as well.

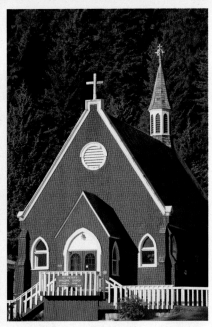

> *St. Peter's Episcopal Church, ca. 1906, in Seward.*

4 ★ **St. Peter's Episcopal Church.** ⏲ 20 min. See "Seward's Murals" on p. 234.

5 ★ 📷 **Ididaride Sled Dog Tours.** Want to give sled-dog mushing a try? An Iditarod racing family—the father, Mitch Seavey, is a past champion, and his sons are coming up in his footsteps—shows off their kennel and offers

> *Visitors to the Alaska SeaLife Center learn a bit about salmon, the state's favorite fish.*

rides on a wheeled sled pulled by 12 dogs; it's a fun, popular event. ⏲ 90 min. Ididaride, Old Exit Glacier Rd. off Herman Leirer Rd. ☎ 800-478-3139. www.ididaride.com. $59 adults, $29 children 11 and under.

6 ★★★ 📷 **Kenai Fjords National Park.** The heart of the park is reached by **tour boat;** many go on this trip daily from the Seward Small Boat Harbor. A 20-minute drive north from Seward, the park's **Exit Glacier** (p. 235, **7**) is an easy and interesting way to encounter big ice. The **Kenai Fjords National Park Information Center,** located at the Seward Small Boat Harbor (☎ 907-224-7500; www. nps.gov/kefj), is your best stop for information about the park and anything else you want to do outdoors while in the area. It is open daily from 8:30am to 7pm in the summer, with shorter hours in the spring and fall; it's closed October through April. ⏲ At least 1 day.

The Real Deal: Summertime Snow Mushing

While the **Ididaride** tour (**5**) is a quick and easy way to get a feel for dog-sled racing, it's not quite the same thing as riding a real dog sled through the snow. For that unique experience, the folks at **Godwin Glacier Dog Sled Tours** (☎ 888-989-8239; www. alaskadogsled.com) will take you to a glacier above Seward for a real dose of mushing. You'll get there by helicopter, enjoying the flightseeing sights on the way, and once you're on the ice, you'll meet the dogs. You can even drive the sled yourself. Trips cost $450 per person for adults and $430 for children 12 and under.

Where to Stay & Dine

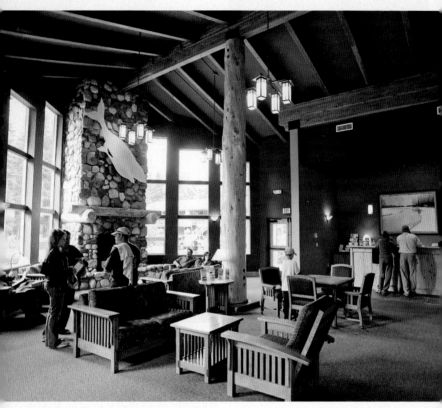

> *The spacious lobby at Seward Windsong Lodge.*

★ kids **Apollo Restaurant** DOWNTOWN
MEDITERRANEAN/SEAFOOD With fast, flexible
service, this is a good place to take children,
and the food is surprisingly good for a small-
town restaurant with campy Greek decor. 229
4th Ave. ☎ 907-224-3092. www.apollo
restaurantak.com. Entrees $10–$24. AE, MC, V.
Lunch and dinner daily.

Ballaine House Bed and Breakfast DOWN-
TOWN Here's an old-fashioned B&B in a 1905
house with a fun, accommodating hostess
and bargain rates. Rooms are small and don't
have private bathrooms, and children under 8
are not allowed. 437 3rd Ave. ☎ 907-224-2362.

www.superpage.com/ballaine. 5 units. Doubles
$99 double, w/breakfast. No credit cards.

★ **Bear Paw Lodge** NORTH OF SEWARD
This log house in a forest outside of town has
four comfortable rooms with active, interesting ourdoorsy hosts with active lives and lots
of enthusiasm. You need a car to stay here.
Check in at the kayaking office. 328 3rd Ave.
☎ 907-224-3960. www.sewardbearpawlodge.
com. 4 units. Doubles $125–$185, w/breakfast.
MC, V. Closed Oct-Apr.

★ **The Breeze Inn** HARBOR
This hotel in the harbor parking lot offers inexpensive but nicely kept older motel rooms,

and good upscale hotel rooms in a wing built in 2008. 1306 Seward Hwy. ☎ 888-224-5237 or 907-224-5237. www.breezeinn.com. 100 units. Double $139–$269 high season; $49–$119 low season. AE, DC, DISC, MC, V.

★ **Christo's Palace** DOWNTOWN *SEAFOOD/ ITALIAN* The long menu here includes something for everyone, from pizza to rack of lamb. Service is excellent, and you can get a good meal quickly. 133 4th Ave. ☎ 907-224-5255. www.christospalace.com. Entrees $8–$38. AE, DC, DISC, MC, V. Lunch and dinner daily.

★ kids **Harborview Inn** DOWNTOWN
This comfy inn, midway between the Small Boat Harbor and downtown, puts both within (long) walking distance. Rooms are reasonably priced, especially the large suites and apartments that can house an entire family. 804 3rd Ave. ☎ 888-324-3217 or 907-224-3217. www.sewardhotel.com. 35 units. Doubles $149; apartments $169–$299. AE, DISC, MC, V. Closed Oct to mid-May.

★★ **Ray's Waterfront** HARBOR *STEAK/ SEAFOOD* This may be Alaska's best waterfront seafood restaurant, overlooking the boat harbor and serving local fish done simply and well. The noisy dining room contributes to the sense of fun at the end of a day on the water. At the boat harbor. ☎ 907-224-5606. www. rayswaterfrontak.com. Lunch $8–$15; dinner entrees $15–$30. AE, DISC, MC, V. Lunch and dinner daily. Closed Oct to mid-Mar.

★★ kids **Seward Windsong Lodge** NORTH OF SEWARD This is Seward's best hotel. Stay here to feel as though you're at a national park; you're near Exit Glacier, among spruce trees on the broad valley of the Resurrection River, with a big lobby that could be at Yellowstone. Family suites have TVs and video games in the kids' room. The lodge has a good restaurant. Mile .5, Exit Glacier Rd. (also known as Herman Leirer Rd.). ☎ 888-959-9590; 907-224-7116 local. www.sewardwindsong.com. 180 units. Doubles $249–$299. AE, DISC, MC, V. Closed Oct–Apr.

> Grilled Alaskan salmon at Ray's Waterfront.

★ **Van Gilder Hotel** DOWNTOWN
A 1916 building restored with authentic period details has small bedrooms and bathrooms but feels cozy and real. The community kitchen on the main floor allows guests to stop for a free hot drink at any time, or even to cook their own meals. 308 Adams St. ☎ 800-204-6835 or 907-224-3079. www.vangilderhotel. com. 23 units. Doubles $119–$169 high season; $59–$79 low season. AE, DISC, MC, V. Closed Oct–Mar.

Kenai & Soldotna

Although these towns are the population center of the Kenai Peninsula, they're short on visitor activities other than salmon fishing (even if that is some of the best around). You should, however, consider using Kenai and Soldotna as a base for further exploration of the Kenai National Wildlife Refuge and the rest of the peninsula. By flying from Anchorage to Kenai and renting a car there instead, you save three hours of driving each way and a third of the cost of your vehicle rental, as taxes are that much lower here. You'll want to spend a few days here if you plan to fish.

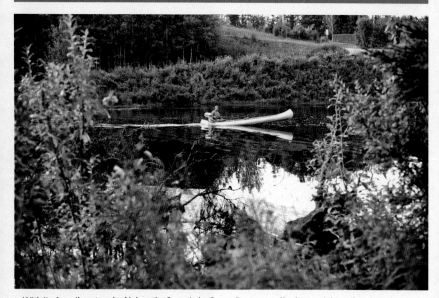

> With its 60-mile network of lakes, the Swan Lake Canoe Route can afford several days of exploring.

START Kenai and Soldotna are 158 and 147 miles from Anchorage, respectively.

❶ ★ Kenai National Wildlife Refuge Visitor Center. The refuge covers a huge swath of the peninsula, most of it quite remote, but also includes much of the Kenai River and the wilderness lakes of the **Swan Lake Canoe Route** (p. 252, ❺). The visitor center sits atop a wooded hill just south of Soldotna, with a 3-mile nature trail, exhibits, and trip-planning information. The website is handy, too. ⏱ 1 hr. Ski Hill Road, Soldotna (turn left just south of the Kenai River Bridge, and take a right turn in front of the building-supply store). ☎ 907-262-7021. http://kenai.fws.gov. Summer Mon–Fri 8am–5pm, Sat–Sun 9am–5pm; winter slightly shorter hours, closed Sun.

❷ ★ Kenai Visitors and Cultural Center. Besides being an information stop, the center contains a small museum. ⏱ 1 hr. See p. 239, ❻.

❸ ★ Old Town. Of the peninsula's modest historical sites, this may be the best: a collection of buildings echoing Kenai's development as part of Russian America. ⏱ 1 hr. See p. 239, ❻.

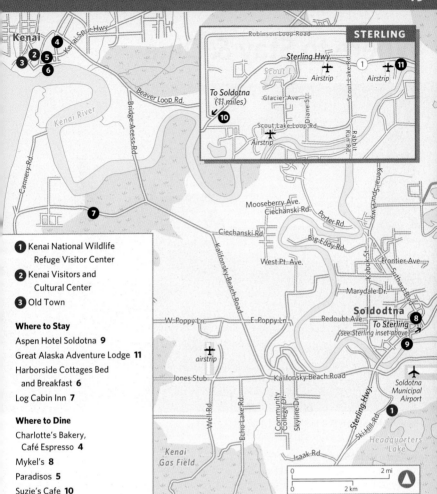

STERLING

To Soldotna
(11 miles)

1 Kenai National Wildlife
Refuge Visitor Center

2 Kenai Visitors and
Cultural Center

3 Old Town

Where to Stay

Aspen Hotel Soldotna **9**

Great Alaska Adventure Lodge **11**

Harborside Cottages Bed
and Breakfast **6**

Log Cabin Inn **7**

Where to Dine

Charlotte's Bakery,
Café Espresso **4**

Mykel's **8**

Paradisos **5**

Suzie's Cafe **10**

Getting Outdoors in Kenai & Soldotna

Let's face it—there are better places to go if you'd like to hike, sea kayak, or bike. But if you're interested in salmon fishing, this is the spot. Angling for salmon in the **Kenai River** overwhelms all other attractions in the area during the summer runs. See p. 256, **1** for more details.

Where to Stay & Dine

> *Harborside Cottages Bed and Breakfast fronts the Kenai River.*

★★ **Aspen Hotel Soldotna** SOLDOTNA
This nondescript rectangular building just off the highway strip contains the area's best standard hotel rooms, packed with amenities. 326 Binkley Cir. ☎ 888-308-7848 or 907-260-7736. www.aspenhotelsak.com. 63 units. Doubles $169–$179 summer; $99 winter; w/breakfast. AE, DC, DISC, MC, V.

★ **Charlotte's Bakery, Café Espresso** KENAI
CAFÉ Local regulars fill the light, cheerful little dining room for some of the best sandwiches I've ever tasted, and terrific salads and baked goods, too. 115 S. Willow St. ☎ 907-283-2777. All items $5–$12. MC, V. Breakfast and lunch Mon–Sat.

★★ **Great Alaska Adventure Lodge** STERLING
Those coming to fish should consider staying at this full-service lodge, which has extensive Kenai River frontage, guides, and many other outdoor activities. 33881 Sterling Hwy. ☎ 800-544-2261 or 907-262-4515. www.greatalaska.com. 2 day all-inclusive package $1,195 per person. AE, MC, V.

★ **Harborside Cottages Bed and Breakfast**
KENAI Clean, bright cottages with country decor make the most of a scenic site atop the bluff of the Kenai River's mouth in the Old Town area. 13 Riverview Dr. ☎ 888-283-6162 or 907-283-6162. www.harborsidecottages.com. 5 cottages. Doubles $185. AE, DISC, MC, V. Closed winter.

★ **Log Cabin Inn** SOUTH OF KENAI
A family hosts in a huge log building (like a wilderness lodge) on wooded grounds south of the Kenai River, offering comfortable rooms and cabins for bargain rates. 49860 Eider Dr. ☎ 907-283-3653. www.alaskalogcabininn.com. 7 units, 3 cabins. Doubles $110–$125 summer; $79 winter; w/breakfast. AE, MC, V.

★★★ Mykel's SOLDOTNA *SEAFOOD*

This traditional fine-dining restaurant offers exceptional food and extremely friendly service. No one else even competes for "the best in town." 35041 Kenai Spur Hwy. ☎ 907-262-4305. www.mykels.com. Lunch $8–$18, dinner entrees $15–$35. V. Summer lunch and dinner daily; winter lunch and dinner Tues–Sun.

★ Paradisos KENAI *GREEK*

This is an old-fashioned family restaurant with big portions of familiar food; reasonable prices; and speedy, friendly service. Besides Greek cuisine, you can get Italian or Mexican food, pizza, steaks, and crab. Main St. and Kenai Spur Hwy. ☎ 907-283-2222. Entrees $8–$38. AE, DC, DISC, MC, V. Lunch and dinner daily.

Suzie's Cafe STERLING *DINER*

The specialty here is comfort food, and it's brought cheerfully and done right, with big portions. Mile 87.2, Sterling Hwy. ☎ 907-260-5751. Entrees $7–$25. MC, V. Lunch and dinner daily. Closed mid-Sept to May.

> *Fine dining at Mykel's.*

Camping In & Around Kenai & Soldotna

Izaak Walton State Recreation Area is at the hot-fishing confluence of the Moose and Kenai rivers, at mile 81 on the Sterling Highway. Sites are $10 per night. Across the road, **Alaska Canoe & Campground** (p. 249, ⓫) is a good choice for showers, laundry, and partly wooded sites.

In Soldotna, the wooded **Centennial Park Campground** (no phone) lies on the Kenai River bluff next to the visitor center and close to fishing and stores. From the Sterling Highway, turn right on Kalifornsky Beach Road just south of the bridge. Camping costs $16 a night.

In Kenai, you can park your RV with a fantastic view on the bluff next to Old Town, at **Beluga Lookout Lodge and RV Park,** 929 Mission Ave. (☎ 907-283-5999; www.belugalookout.com). Full hookups are $35 to $60 a night.

> Kayaks at Kachemak Bay
Wilderness Lodge.

Kenai Peninsula Fast Facts

Accommodations Booking Services

SEWARD Alaska's Point of View Reservation Service (☎ 907-224-2323, www.alaskasview.com).

Getting There & Getting Around

BY PLANE Kenai and Homer have airports served from Anchorage daily by Era Alaska (☎ 800-866-8394; www.flyera.com), which partners with Alaska Airlines. BY TRAIN The Alaska Railroad (☎ 800-544-0552; www.alaskarailroad.com) connects Seward with Anchorage, with stops or connections at Girdwood, Portage, and Whittier. BY CAR Most visitors drive to the peninsula from Anchorage via the Seward Highway.

You'll want to rent a car in order to get around—be sure to check on road conditions (see Safety, below).

Emergencies

Dial ☎ **911.**

Doctors & Dentists

If you need emergency dental care, your best bet is to go to the local hospital. HOMER South Peninsula Hospital, Bartlett Street, off Pioneer Ave. (☎ 907-235-8101). KENAI/SOLDOTNA Central Peninsula General, 250 Hospital Place, Soldotna (☎ 907-262-4404); from the Sterling Highway, take Binkley Street to Marydale Avenue. SEWARD Providence Seward Medical Center is at 417 1st Ave. (☎ 907-224-5205).

Internet Access

HOMER Tech Connect Computer Sales and Services, 432 E Pioneer Ave. (☎ 907-235-5248). KENAI Kenai public library, 163 Main St. Loop (☎ 907-283-4378). SEWARD Free at the Seward Public Library, 5th and Adams. SOLDOTNA Soldotna public library, 235 Binkley St. (☎ 907-262-4227).

Police

HOMER Homer Police Department (☎ 907-235-3150); outside the city, Alaska State Troopers (☎ 907-235-8239). KENAI/SOLDOTNA Kenai Police Department (☎ 907-283-7879); Soldotna Police Department (☎ 907-262-4455); outside city limits, Alaska State Troopers (☎ 907-262-4453). SEWARD Seward Police Department (☎ 907-224-3338) or, outside the city limits, the Alaska State Troopers (☎ 907-224-3346).

Safety

Road safety is a major issue in this part of Alaska. The two-lane highways of the Kenai Peninsula are often congested in the summer, especially on weekends. Be patient, as passing will usually save little time and horrible head-on collisions are shockingly frequent. The law requires vehicles with more than a few cars following to pull over and let them pass, regardless of speed—a sensible provision that prevents passing and saves lives. Always check road reports before driving Alaska highways in winter; in summer, verifying can mean avoiding construction delays that can last hours. Call ☎ 511 or go to http://511.alaska.gov for updates.

If you're heading into the backcountry, you should keep apprised of **avalanche conditions,** which are updated regularly on the Chugach National Forest hotline (☎ 907-754-2369). You'll find also updated avalanche forecasts, maps, and educational material at www.cnfaic.org.

Visitor Information

KENAI PENINSULA Kenai Peninsula Tourism Marketing Council (☎ 800-535-3524 or 907-262-5229; www.kenaipeninsula.org). HOMER Homer Chamber of Commerce Visitor Information Center, 201 Sterling Hwy. (☎ 907-235-7740; www.homeralaska.org). KENAI Kenai Visitors and Cultural Center (p. 239, ❻). Seward: Seward Chamber of Commerce, Seward Hwy. (☎ 907-224-8051; www.seward.com). SOLDOTNA Soldotna Visitor Information Center, 44790 Sterling Hwy. (☎ 907-262-9814 or 907-262-1337; www.visitsoldotna.com).

8
Fairbanks & the Interior

My Favorite Fairbanks & the Interior Moments

So many of my favorite moments in Interior Alaska have in common a sense of peace and simplicity. The small towns move at the pace of the slow, wide rivers and the gradually developing display of the aurora, and the city of Fairbanks is just an overgrown version of this. Long highways cross enormous spaces with a benign kind of loneliness, leading you to where you can watch the weather change on a mountain range as if it were all your own. In a sense, there's not much here. But the quiet moments seem full.

> PREVIOUS PAGE The Aurora borealis (northern lights). THIS PAGE Famed Granite Tors.

❶ Climbing to the Granite Tors. After a long, hot hike up from Chena Hot Springs Road on the **Granite Tors Trail,** you emerge in the oddest place: a tundra plateau called the Plain of Monuments, where towering granite outcroppings stand like surreal statues, defying the eye to place them in scale. You can explore at will; no one else is around. See p. 288, ❼.

❷ Watching the aurora over Chena Hot Springs. Late on a deeply black, deeply cold winter night, you float outdoors in a hot springs pond near Fairbanks while unearthly lights swirl in the dome of sharp, bright stars above you. The aurora can go on for half an hour without a break—an awesome and even emotional show of weird waves of swirling color. See p. 289, ❽.

❸ Walking along Galbraith Lake. Far into the Arctic, along this stretch of the rugged Dalton Highway, the northern foothills of the Brooks Range sensuously undulate beneath a blanket of tundra, like the hips and shoulders of sleeping giants. Pull over anywhere, start walking, and you can cross great open spaces, seeing only the brutally chiseled mountains and enormous sky above, and the tiny, delicate shapes in the heather below. See p. 315, ❾.

❹ Floating along the Chena River to the Pump House. The slow, brown water of the Chena meanders its way through Fairbanks, mostly past wooded shores, but with stops along the way that remind you you're in a city. Pulling up to a dock, you walk into the

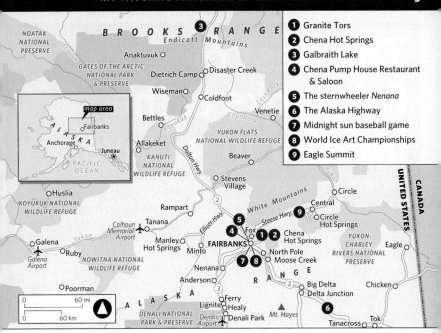

1. Granite Tors
2. Chena Hot Springs
3. Galbraith Lake
4. Chena Pump House Restaurant & Saloon
5. The sternwheeler *Nenana*
6. The Alaska Highway
7. Midnight sun baseball game
8. World Ice Art Championships
9. Eagle Summit

excellent **Pump House Restaurant & Saloon** for a cocktail and sumptuous dinner before a shuttle picks you up and returns the canoe. See p. 299, **4**.

5 Letting children play on the stern-wheeler *Nenana*. After its time on the Yukon River was done, this ship—not much different than the Mississippi River version that Mark Twain learned to steer—was saved and set up in Pioneer Park. Children can climb its decks, past the mahogany and brass passenger salons to the wheelhouse, and take the wheel. See p. 309, **7**.

6 Marveling at the sky over the Alaska Highway. Hours pass between strange little towns like Tok and Delta Junction along the Alaska Highway, while scenery slowly reels by—mountains, rivers, forests both green and burned. The sky above is so big and unobstructed, you can see weather systems unfolding—lightning in the distance one direction, sunshine in another. See p. 293.

7 Cheering on a baseball game under the midnight sun. The summer sun is still aloft when the baseball game begins at 10:30pm on the summer solstice, typically on June 21, but you'd better have a coat and a blanket as you settle in with a cold beer on the bleachers. The quality of the play is good, but the best part is the sense of tradition—of young men and the game, of the sounds and smells of a minor-league ballpark—and the more than a century of playing in the middle of the night, without lights. See p. 307.

8 Taking in the World Ice Art Championships. The Fairbanks community annually builds a park with a sculpture garden full of huge, crystal clear statues carved with great art and mastery. They will last only a month, until the warmth of spring melts them. Until then, people stream through to admire the work and to enjoy their ephemeral civic space, celebrating winter. See p. 320, **11**.

9 Enjoying the view from Eagle Summit. The gravel Steese Highway climbs rounded mountains with a rhythmic repetition that's hypnotic, until suddenly you've arrived at the summit, where you can look seemingly forever over soft shapes receding to the horizon. You're high enough, and far north enough, that on the longest day of the year, the sun will never set. See p. 303, **14**.

The Best of Fairbanks & the Interior in 3 Days

The land of the Interior region may not match your preconceptions about Alaska. You'll find it typically warm and dry in the summer (and very cold in winter), with long, wide river valleys, flatlands of trees kept small by the northern climate, and rounded mountains. A few narrow highways, with many unpaved miles, link tiny towns separated by hours of driving. Most visitors focus on the central city of Fairbanks, as I have done in this tour. There, without too much time on the road, you can get a feel for life in this friendly country of gold mining, river travel, and backwoods freedom lovers. Although you can explore downtown Fairbanks on foot, you'll want to rent a car to get around.

> The paddle-wheel riverboat Discovery plies the lazy waters of the Chena.

START **Fairbanks. Fly into Fairbanks via Anchorage, and rent a car.** TRIP LENGTH **122 miles.**

1 ★★ **Downtown Fairbanks.** This is Alaska's second-largest city, but it has many qualities of a small town, both good and bad. On the good side, it's friendly, low-key, and easy to manage. On the bad side, the underwhelming urban environment could make you wonder why you're here. The key to Fairbanks is to use your car to get around to the widely scattered attractions and outdoor activities, seeking out your fun, as it may not come to you.

Start at the **Morris Thompson Cultural and Visitors Center** (p. 316, **1**), and check out the exhibits and information sources inside. This is a critical stop, especially if you need advice about outdoor activities. Once you're well-stocked with information, stroll across the long, beautifully arched footbridge over the Chena River. Stop into the lobby of **Doyon, Limited** (p. 317, **4**), to see this Native regional corporation's exhibit of traditional artifacts and modern art.

The 1904 **Immaculate Conception Church** (p. 317, **5**) is an interesting historic building, decorated with authentic gold-rush decor, including a pressed-tin ceiling.

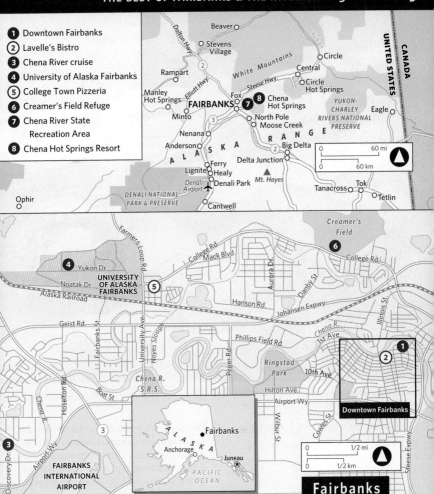

Legend:

1. Downtown Fairbanks
2. Lavelle's Bistro
3. Chena River cruise
4. University of Alaska Fairbanks
5. College Town Pizzeria
6. Creamer's Field Refuge
7. Chena River State Recreation Area
8. Chena Hot Springs Resort

Fairbanks

Next, stop in at the **Yukon Quest Sled Dog Race Headquarters** (p. 317, 6), in a log building with a sod roof. The Quest, an even more difficult race than the Iditarod, runs in February between Fairbanks and Whitehorse, Yukon Territory (Canada). Here, you can see mushing equipment and an exhibit about the race.

Visit **Golden Heart Park** (p. 317, 6) for its fountain and bronze statue of a Native family. Fairbanks's community pride is as strong as that of any place I've ever visited, and this plaza shows it off. You can learn more about the city at the **Fairbanks Community Museum** (p. 316, 3), a fun collection of historical exhibits and miscellany representing the town's funky frontier identity. At the **Fairbanks Ice Museum** (p. 320, 11) you can see what the city is most famous for: cold. Ice sculptures stand in four glass freezers, and a slide show presents images of the famous World Ice Art carving contest that happens in Fairbanks each March. ⏱ Half-day.

---

② 🍴 **Lavelle's Bistro.** This is among Alaska's best restaurants, but it's not too formal for a snack. Stop in for an appetizer and a glass of wine. 575 1st Ave. ☎ 907-450-0555. $$-$$$. See p. 325.

> *Vintage patches from the 1,161-mile Yukon Quest sled dog race are sold as souvenirs at the race headquarters in downtown Fairbanks.*

Get down to the waterfront in time for a:

❸ ★★ kids **Chena River cruise.** Through Fairbanks winds the river, lazy and brown—a theme for the casual feel of the city. There are plenty of ways to get on the water, but the most popular for visitors is the *Discovery,* a day cruise on a real paddle-wheel riverboat; it's offered by the Binkley family, whose generations have operated riverboats in Alaska since the Klondike gold rush. Although designed for buses of escorted tourists (and highly scripted), the excursion is still entertaining and lively. The boat makes a stop at a mock Athabascan village and passes shoreline exhibitions, including a mushers' dog yard, as it travels from near the airport to the confluence with the mightier Tanana River, where the Chena's brown water mixes with glacial gray. ⊕ Half-day. 1975 Discovery Dr. ☎ 866-479-6673 or 907-479-6673. www.riverboatdiscovery.com. $55 adults, $38 children 3–12, free for children 2 and under. Mid-May to mid-Sept daily at 8:45am and 2pm.

On Day 2, drive to the west side of the city, to College, once a separate town and still the site of Alaska's most important campus. The main entrance is at College Road and University Avenue. Park near the museum at Yukon and Sheenjek drives.

❹ ★★★ kids **University of Alaska Fairbanks.** The top college in Alaska is also Fairbanks's best tourist attraction, with the UA Museum of the North (p. 317, ❼), the Georgeson Botanical Garden (p. 317, ❽), and the Large Animal Research Station (p. 305, ❸). Choose one (or all) for a visit, or you can join a free, student-led walking tour of the campus. ⊕ 2 hr. Tour meets at Signers' Hall, 402 Salcha St., off Tanana Loop on the east side of campus. ☎ 907-474-7021. www.uaf.edu/visituaf. Summer Mon–Fri 10am.

Walk down Yukon Street, then turn downhill on the footpath to the garden.

The Interior in Winter

More visitors come to the Interior in the winter than to much warmer regions of Alaska. It makes sense. Southeast Alaska is damp and gloomy in the winter—maybe not that different from home. Interior winters are the real thing: always snowy, cold that sinks as low as −40°F, inky black skies with sharp stars, and frequently, the rippling colors of the aurora. The towns come to life, too, with winter festivals, skiing, and dog mushing, although a snap of extreme cold can put a damper on those activities.

The best time for a winter visit is in March, when the coldest temperatures are over with and some light has returned, but there's still plenty of snow. In Fairbanks, the incredible **World Ice Art Championships** (pictured); (☎ 907-451-8250; www.icealaska.com) happen in late February and last through the first half of March. Ice carvers come from all over the globe to work with huge, clear ice cubes cut from a nearby lake. Some of their highly detailed creations stand as tall as a building. At around the same time, Fairbanks puts on the **North American Sled Dog Championships** (☎ 907-457-MUSH (457-6874); www.sleddog.org), races with up to two dozen dogs in a team speeding around a course that starts downtown.

Good aurora viewing can happen anytime the sky is dark and the sun is casting off a lot of charged particles to interfere with the Earth's magnetic field—which, during the winter, is most of the time. There's nothing like seeing a bright, colorful aurora. The scientists at the University of Alaska's Geophysical Institute have the world's top program for studying the phenomenon, using rockets and lots of other advanced equipment. You can see their predictions and other interesting and helpful information at www.gi.alaska.edu. The short version is this: Come when the sky is dark and the moon is dim; stay outside the city, away from city lights, perhaps at **Chena Hot Springs Resort** (p. 289, ⑧) or **A Taste of Alaska Lodge** (p. 322); and be ready from 10pm to 2am. At Chena Hot Springs you can request a wake-up call for aurora activity. For more information on this phenomenon, see "The Amazing Aurora" on p. 290.

Downhill skiing in Fairbanks is strictly of the community variety—there are small ski areas, but no resort—but the cross-country skiing is excellent at **Birch Hill Recreation Area** (p. 299, ⑩) or the **University of Alaska trails** (p. 286, ④). You can rent equipment in town (see "Outdoor Gear," on p. 317). Find current information, including events, trail conditions, and maps, at the **Nordic Ski Club of Fairbanks** website (www.nscfairbanks.org).

> *Creamer's Field, a 2,000-acre migratory waterfowl refuge, is a prime stopover point for Canada geese, pintails, and golden plovers.*

⑤ 🍕 **College Town Pizzeria.** Every campus needs great pizza pie nearby, and this super-casual order-at-the-counter place (just across the road) fits the bill. The crust is terrific, and you can get regular American pizza or Italian gourmet-style. College and University roads. ☎ 907-457-2200. $.

From the University of Alaska campus, drive 5 miles east on College Road to Creamer's Field, on the left.

⑥ ★★ kids **Creamer's Field Refuge.** The refuge is ideal for bird-watching and nature walks. The large, open pasture of the former dairy farm is a migratory stopover, and you can see bird capture and banding taking place at the associated **Alaska Bird Observatory** (p. 320, ⑭). ⏱ At least 2 hr. See p. 320, ⑬.

On Day 3, you'll go east of town to the Chena River State Recreation Area and the hot springs, 57 miles from Fairbanks, where you can visit and perhaps swim for the day or, if you care to add a day to the tour, spend the night. From Fairbanks, take the Steese Highway 6 miles north to Chena Hot Springs Road and turn right.

⑦ ★★ kids **Chena River State Recreation Area.** A paved road leads an hour into un-spoiled country, where you'll find small mountains with rewarding trail hikes and the headwaters of the Chena River, which sparkles and froths past roadside campgrounds. I love the riverside stops to enjoy the scenery and the water, especially Rosehip Campground, at mile 27. Red Squirrel Campground, at mile 42.8, has a picnic ground with a placid swimming pond.

The rounded mountains are studded with odd granite outcroppings, some of them

> *A Christmas tree makes the atmosphere festive in the geothermal pools at Chena Hot Springs Resort.*

towering like monolithic statues. These tors make excellent destinations for hikes. The best are on a taxing all-day hike—15 miles round trip—on the Granite Tors Trail, which starts at mile 39.5 of the road. The Angel Rocks Trail is easier, reaching an outcropping that's not as oddly wonderful; that 4-mile round-trip hike begins at mile 48.9 of the road. ⏲ At least a half-day.

8 ★★★ kids **Chena Hot Springs Resort.** The geothermal hot springs come to the surface in a steep-walled valley at the end of the road, beyond the state recreation area. An ingenious Fairbanks entrepreneur's unique resort stands here, with a museum made entirely of ice; greenhouses heated with geothermal water, producing food for the restaurant; and an innovative electrical system powered by the springs. Best of all, a series of steaming pools are open for swimming, including a rock-rimmed outdoor pool where you can float in hot water under cold skies. Kids can paddle in the indoor swimming pool. To stay overnight, choose either the best rooms, which are quite good, or the yurts; the midrange rooms aren't great, and service can be inconsistent. The restaurant and bar are fun and quirky. The resort offers many activities as well. ⏲ At least 1 hr. Mile 56.5, Chena Hot Springs Rd. ☎ 907-451-8104. www.chenahotsprings.com. Swimming facility open daily 7am–midnight. Day pass $10 adults, $8 seniors 60 and over, $7 children 6–17, free for children 5 and under. Towel rental $5. Ice museum tour $15 adults, $7.50 children 6–12, free for children 5 and under. Chena Hot Springs Resort: 80 units. Doubles $189–$249; yurts $65 (available mid-May to mid-Sept only). AE, DC, DISC, MC, V.

THE AMAZING AURORA

Nature's spectacular light show

BY MIKE DUNHAM

TRICKY TO PREDICT, difficult to photograph, and nearly impossible to describe, the mysterious Northern Lights—or aurora borealis— seem out of this world. And, in a way, they are. The sun sends out a constant storm of subatomic particles, electrons, and protons, known as the "solar wind." Most solar wind bounces off the magnetic field around the planet. But at the poles, these magnetic lines curve earthward, providing a portal through which solar wind enters the atmosphere. There, the wind's particles collide with oxygen and nitrogen atoms, releasing energy that we see as a bright glow. The colors range from pale greens to brilliant reds, and at times, seem to fill the sky from horizon to horizon. Aurora activity doesn't stop when the sun comes up, but you'll only be able to see the lights at night.

The Lore of the Lights

Eskimo legends consider the aurora a gateway to the afterlife, where ancestors celebrate or light the way for their relatives. Nordic mythology supposed the lights to reflect the violence of distant battles. Sourdoughs imagined the bright glow might indicate the location of gold fields. The Japanese believe that children conceived under the Northern Lights will be exceptionally favored—or so say some Alaskans. Japanese visitors have said they're not familiar with that belief. Nonetheless, interior Alaska is a coveted destination for winter honeymooners from Japan. Others insist that whistling at the lights will make them come closer. There's no proof of that either, but it's hard to test; when the lights are out, one's lips are usually too numb to pucker.

Getting a Front Row Seat

The best time to see the aurora in Alaska is from mid-August to mid-April, and the best locations are north of the Alaska Range and

away from the coast. Fairbanks is a prime viewing spot, especially if you can get away from the glare of the city. Chena Hot Springs (p. 289, ❽), an hour from Fairbanks by road, offers an accessible site where visitors can watch the lights from a steaming hot tub.

Viewing the lights requires no special gear, but you'll want to dress warmly for temperatures that may reach well below zero—once a display begins, it can continue for hours. And prepare to be amazed. Even jaded Alaskans form telephone trees to call one another when the lights are out. Some hotels will ring guests when a good display takes place in the middle of the night—be sure to ask when you check in. And if you want to plan ahead, the University of Alaska Geophysical Institute issues aurora forecasts, which are available at www.gedds.alaska.edu/autoraforecast. You can also *hear* auroras year-round; a display at the University of Alaska Museum of the North in Fairbanks takes readings of the electromagnetic energy, plus weather and seismic activity, and translates them into sound.

The Best of Fairbanks & the Interior in 1 Week

If you enjoy road trips, crossing the heart of Alaska is a rare opportunity. It's a chance to drive through country that would be considered pure wilderness but for the road you're traveling on. Rather than seeing towns, billboards, or even farms pass by, you watch the shape of the land evolve, with the changing mix of trees or tundra, rivers, and sometimes glimpses of wildlife. But there are also plenty of boring stretches, and the distances between your destinations are long. This trip is for those who enjoy the freedom of the truly open road and have the patience for the many miles to be covered.

> *A lifelike diorama of nesting trumpeter swans at the Tetlin National Wildlife Refuge Visitor Center.*

START Alaska Highway near the Tetlin National Wildlife Refuge. Drive 357 miles from Haines via the Haines and Alaska highways; 415 miles from Skagway via the Klondike and Alaska highways; or 2,000 miles from Seattle via British Columbia and the Alaska Highway. TRIP LENGTH 695 miles.

❶ ★ **Tetlin National Wildlife Refuge.** The refuge encompasses the highway for the first 65 miles of your drive after entering the U.S. from Canada. It's a giant wetland and forest area used by thousands of migratory birds in the spring and fall, and it's the summer home for 30 resident and 96 migratory species, including trumpeter swans and lesser sandhill

> *The still-intact 10-acre compound of Rika's Roadhouse shows what stopovers on the Valdez–Fairbanks route were once like.*

cranes. You may also see caribou along the way. A visitor center has exhibits, a 1-mile nature trail, and an observation deck. ◷ At least 1 hr. Visitor center: Alaska Hwy. Mile 1,228. ☎ 907-883-5312. http://tetlin.fws.gov. Free admission. Daily 8am–4:30pm. Closed Sept 15–May 15.

Drive 84 miles west on the Alaska Highway to Tok.

❷ ★ Tok. Every town has to be best at something. Tok brags of being the coldest community in North America. The average low is –25°F in January. For summer visitors, Tok serves as an entrance to Alaska, with cafes, motels, stores, and visitor centers.

The **Alaska Public Lands Information Centers** (☎ 907-883-5667; www.alaskacenters. gov) is a team project of the various federal and state agencies that own most of Alaska. Anyone interested in outdoor activities should take a look. The Tok center is located at mile 1,314 on the Alaska Highway, and is open daily in the summer from 8am to 7pm; in the winter, it's open Monday through Friday from 8am to 4:30pm.

The Tok Chamber of Commerce takes seriously the town's role as a portal into Alaska, and its **Main Street Visitor Center** (☎ 907-883-5775; www.tokalaskainfo.com) is packed with information on anywhere you might go on the highways. The center is open daily in the summer from 8am to 7pm. ◷ 1 hr.

Begin Day 2 by continuing 108 miles northwest to Delta Junction.

More Information

I've started this trip plan on the Alaska Highway, at the east side of the state; you could have come up from Haines or Skagway, though, or even have driven all the way from the Lower 48. Make sure to review border-crossing details (p. 508) closely before you leave home; there's no town anywhere near the border crossing, so it's not easy to fix oversights. If you are in Anchorage, you'll want to start this itinerary at Tok (❷ at left) and skip the earlier stops.

The Best of Fairbanks & the Interior in 1 Week

3 ★ Delta Junction. This little highway town has a bit more to it than Tok, but it's not a destination. Delta Junction is named for a huge confluence of rivers but is more famous today for Fort Greely, site of the national missile defense system. Next to the visitor center at the intersection of the Alaska and Richardson highways, the official end of the Alaska Highway, stop in at the **Sullivan Roadhouse** (☎ 907-895-4415; www.deltachamber.org/sullivan. html). Before cars could drive Alaska's rough routes, travel was by sled-dog teams in winter and horse teams in summer. Roadhouses were spaced along the way. Sullivan's was one of the places where travelers could dine, sleep, and rest their animals. It was in business until 1922, but is as primitive as if from the previous century. Take a look for yourself in the summer from Monday to Friday, 9am to 5pm; admission is free. ⏱ 30 min.

Continue 16 miles northwest on the Alaska Highway.

4 ★★ kids Rika's Roadhouse. This roadhouse within the Big Delta State Historical Park operated from 1909 to 1947. Like the Sullivan Roadhouse, mentioned at the previous stop, Rika's supported the pre-automobile route

FAIRBANKS

1. Tetlin National Wildlife Refuge
2. Tok
3. Delta Junction
4. Rika's Roadhouse
5. North Pole & Santa Claus House
6. Downtown Fairbanks
7. University of Alaska Museum of the North
8. Chena River and Pioneer Park
9. Pump House Restaurant & Saloon
10. Birch Hill Recreation Area
11. Gold Dredge No. 8
12. Chena River State Recreation Area
13. Chena Hot Springs Resort
14. Steese Highway
15. Nenana

from Valdez to Fairbanks, but there's much more to see. The entire pioneer world of the roadhouse is intact on a 10-acre compound on the banks of the Tanana River, with outbuildings, a vegetable garden, and livestock pens. The site was particularly important because a ferry operated here, across the river. Now you can see an amazing suspension bridge crossing the Tanana from which hangs the silver Trans-Alaska Pipeline. A concessionaire operates a restaurant offering simple meals. ⊙ 2 hr. Mile 275, Richardson Hwy. ☎ 907-895-4201. Free admission. Grounds and museum open summer daily 8am–8pm.

Continue 74 miles northwest on the Alaska Highway.

5 ★ kids **North Pole & Santa Claus House.** Of course a town named North Pole has to have a big Christmas shop. **Santa Claus House** could strike you as either charming or campy, with its 40-foot Santa statue out front and live reindeer. It's a long-standing Alaska tradition, dating to the 1950s, and still run by the pioneering Miller family. Letters from North Pole, with the town's postmark, impress kids at Christmastime, and you can arrange at the shop for one with personal details to come at the right time. They also *receive* a lot of letters to Santa, some

A Canadian Detour: Dawson City, Eagle & the Rough Road into History

If you're driving from Canada or the Lower 48, you may want to consider taking a detour off the Alaska Highway and checking out Dawson City (in Canada) and Eagle (in Alaska). The trip will add an extra 127 miles to your journey, but those extra miles are well worth the effort. Not only will you get to see two true gold-rush towns, but you'll be traveling the Top of the World Highway, which offers spectacular mountain scenery.

Begin your journey by taking the Klondike Highway to **Dawson City**—the destination of the 1898 Klondike gold rush. This once-tiny Yukon town boomed, briefly becoming the second-largest city on the west coast of North America, after San Francisco. Today, it is a well-preserved example of gold-rush living. There are museums, historic buildings, a riverboat, a gold dredge tour, and even a nonprofit casino. For travel information, contact the **Klondike Visitors Association** (☎ 867-993-5575; www. dawsoncity.ca). For information on the historic sites, contact **Parks Canada** (☎ 867-993-7200; www.parkscanada.gc.ca, click on "National Historic Sites").

After seeing the historic sites in Dawson for a day or two, take the ferry across the Yukon River and drive west on the scenic **Top of the World Highway,** which will take you across the border into the United States (remember, you'll need a passport). As long as you're on this odyssey, turn north on to the charitably named Taylor Highway and make a side trip to the historic and unpolished bush community of **Eagle.** Be prepared: Name aside, the Taylor Highway (pictured) is more of a narrow dirt road. That 65-mile, one-way drive takes about 2 hours. But as a result, Eagle is the real deal—a former gold-rush town filled with century-old buildings and artifacts. And it's relatively tourist-free (in fact, the only motel was wiped out by a flood in 2009, so spending the night may require a tent). Be sure to take the 3-hour historic walking tour with the **Eagle Historical Society and Museums** (☎ 907-547-2325; www.eagleak.org). The walks begin daily at 9am, from Memorial Day to Labor Day, and the cost is $7 per person. You can also launch a float trip from Eagle, through the Yukon-Charley Rivers National Preserve. Call the **National Park Service office** in Eagle for information (☎ 907-547-2233; www.nps.gov/yuch).

To join up with the Fairbanks/Interior itinerary, simply retrace your drive on the Taylor Highway and continue south to the Alaska Highway (161 miles in about 4 hours), which intersects 12 miles east of Tok.

> *Watch world-class ice carvers at work through the freezer windows of the Fairbanks Ice Museum.*

of which you can view at www.kidssantaletters.com. ⏱1 hr. Santa Claus House, 101 St. Nicholas Dr. ☎907-488-2200. www.santaclaushouse.com. Summer daily 8am–8pm; Sept–Dec daily 10am–6pm; Jan–Apr 10am–6pm Sat-Sun only.

Continue northwest on the Alaska Highway another 15 miles.

6 ★★ **Downtown Fairbanks.** Entering a city after such a long drive through the wilderness can come as a shock to the system. Spend a couple of days taking in the attractions of this northern outpost of American culture, but also take advantage of the big Alaskan spaces nearby.

Spending the Night in Delta Junction

Should you decide to take a break here, the best (but still quite modest) choice is **Kelly's Alaska Country Inn,** at the intersection of Richardson and Alaska highways. ☎907-895-4667. www.kellysalaskacountryinn.com. 20 units. Doubles $139 summer; $109 winter.

Begin with a walk **downtown** (p. 284, **1**). If time allows, pay a visit to the **Fairbanks Ice Museum** (p. 320, **11**). This is one of two attractions in Fairbanks aimed at bringing the experience of the city's intense winters to summer visitors (the other is **40 Below Fairbanks** (p. 309, **7**). Perhaps surprisingly, the ice museum is more than a gimmick. Ice-carving artists do amazing work in walk-in freezers that serve as studios, and there's a good slide show. ⏱1½ hr. See p. 316.

On Day 3, drive to the University of Alaska campus on the west side of Fairbanks, about 4 miles from downtown.

7 ★★★ **University of Alaska Museum of the North.** The Museum of the North is among Alaska's best, with excellent sections on natural history and culture; it draws from the rich intellectual life of the state's main university campus, which is renowned for Arctic science and archeology. ⏱3 hr. See p. 317, **7**.

In the afternoon take University Avenue south and turn left on Airport Way. Pioneer Park is at the intersection with Peger Road.

The Strange Story of Fairbanks

The wild story of Fairbanks's founding is hard to believe, but hardly less likely than the decision to build Alaska's second-largest city on the shore of a meandering little stream in this cold Interior Valley, close to nothing. And besides, historians attest to it.

A flimflam man by the name of E. T. Barnette (pictured) saw during the gold-rush years that the men who made easy money were those running real estate scams. A number of towns, some still surviving, were built on false rumors of gold, with the developer the only one to get rich as stampeders rushed to his new town. Some developers also got lucky or made shrewd guesses about where the next gold rush would happen.

In 1901 Barnette bought the materials to build a new trading post and sailed up the Tanana River on a steamer, having made a deal that he would get off with his heavy luggage if the boat got stuck. The boat did get stuck, and when it tried an ill-fated detour up the Chena, the captain left Barnette, with his gear, fuming on the bank.

But Barnette wasn't beat. On word of gold in the area, he dispatched his Japanese cook, Jujiro Wada, to Dawson City, some 700 miles upriver via the Tanana and Yukon. Wada's grossly exaggerated account made the paper in Dawson City and, a few days later, the *New York Times*. Hundreds of men rushed to Barnette's trading post through winter weather as cold as –50°F.

When the rushing prospectors arrived, they found little chance of obtaining gold—and Barnette's trading post, with a monopoly on food, charging outrageous prices. Wada escaped lynching only when Barnette confronted his customers with a group of riflemen.

But Barnette's scam turned into a legit deal. An Italian named Felix Pedro, prospecting before Barnette arrived, found gold for real—a lot of it. Large-scale works to exploit the finds were built. Major industrial mining continues near Fairbanks to this day.

The naming of the town nicely fits politics into the sordid tale. Judge James Wickersham had set up the federal court in Eagle, just downriver from Dawson City. Barnette offered to name his new town for Wickersham's sponsor in Congress, Senator Charles Fairbanks, of Indiana, who later became Theodore Roosevelt's vice president. In exchange, Wickersham abandoned Eagle, loaded his files in his dog sled, and moved the courthouse to Fairbanks.

A century later, one might expect to find many local landmarks named for Barnette. But he didn't change his ways. After Barnette's arrest for bank fraud, townspeople burned their founder in effigy, and he left Alaska for good.

> *Rent mountain bikes in the summer, or cross-country ski in the winter, at Birch Hill Recreation Area.*

8 ★★ **kids** **Chena River and Pioneer Park.**
Rivers tie together the history and geography
of this region. The gentle Chena, which runs
through Fairbanks, gives you a chance to experience river life firsthand. Pioneer Park lies alongside it and collects Fairbanks history in one
charming, corny place; for a full tour, see p. 309,
7. The highlight, by far, is the riverboat *Nenana*,
a wooden stern-wheeler that navigated the
Yukon and Tanana rivers for the Alaska Railroad
until 1952. Guided tours go through mahogany
and brass rooms of that other era, including
the wheelhouse and engine room, and on the
cargo deck you can see models of all the river
towns the ship visited. In the summer, the free,
hour-long tours leave between noon and 8pm
whenever a group has congregated (the ship is
closed in the winter).

At the park's river landing, you can rent a
canoe to drift down the Chena past wooded
shores, perhaps to stop or land at a restaurant
(or maybe at your own lodgings) on the way.
Ask at the riverbank at **Alaska Outdoor Rentals & Guides,** 1101 Peger Rd. (☎ 907-457-2453;
www.2paddle1.com), about where you have

time to go. When you're done, they'll pick up
you and the canoe. If you were to paddle to the
restaurant mentioned next, 5.5 miles downstream, you would pay $37 for the canoe and
$19 for pickup. The same company can help
you set up a more ambitious canoe or kayak trip
anywhere in the region, and they rent bikes, too.
🕑 Half-day.

⑨ 🍴 **Pump House Restaurant & Saloon.** If
you've floated to one of Fairbanks's best
restaurants in your canoe, you might as
well stop in for a drink or a meal. It's a
fun place in a historic gold-rush building, but with award-winning fine dining
thrown in. Mile 1.3, Chena Pump Rd.
☎ 907-479-8452. $$. See p. 325.

**On Day 4 take the Steese Highway 3 miles
north of town.**

❿ ★★ **kids** **Birch Hill Recreation Area.** The
cross-country ski trails wind 15½ miles
through birch forest, starting near the top of
the hill. It's a peaceful setting for a bike ride
or a walk, with a choice of either challenging

> *Tourists hope to strike it rich, panning for the precious yellow metal at historic Gold Dredge No. 8.*

or relatively flat paths that all network from the same starting point, a clearing known as "the stadium." The steep trails are on the west, while the much easier White Bear loop is to the east, totaling 6 miles with cut-offs to shorten the distance to as little as a mile or so. If you're here in winter, it's a wonderful ski area, with a big ski center building. To rent mountain bikes, check in with **Alaska Outdoor Rentals & Guides** (p. 299, ❽). ⏱ Half-day. 101 Wilderness Dr. ☎ 907-459-1070. www. co.fairbanks.ak.us/parksandrecreation. Free admission. Daily 7am–10pm.

Drive 7 miles north on the Steese Highway, turn left on Goldstream Rd, and then left again on Old Steese Highway.

⓫ ★★ **Gold Dredge No. 8.** Fairbanks was built on gold mining, which entailed using water to sort gold from enormous quantities of gravel excavated from frozen ground. Dredges like the five-story monster at this commercial historic site marked a technological leap. Starting in 1927, the machine floated on a pond of its own making, digging gravel from

Spending the Night near Chena River

Service at the **Chena Hot Springs Resort** can be spotty, and the good rooms are expensive. Instead, I recommend you check into **A Taste of Alaska Lodge** (p. 322), where you'll get a good room and a sense of frontier life in the region.

> The Taku Chief, *once a tugboat on the Tanana River now rests in drydock behind the town of Nenana's log cabin Visitor Center.*

one end, processing it, and spitting out the refuse behind to fill in the pond again; in this way it crept 4½ miles across the countryside, leaving a trail of waste you can still see. The bare gravel piles north of Fairbanks are all mining spoils. The dredge itself is fascinating, and there's a museum recreating the life of the miners. Tours are well presented, but are timed for lunches of stew served to large groups of visitors on buses; consequently, you must time your visit to when lunch is served. The admission price is a bargain, as it includes the meal. ⏱ 2 hr. Gold Dredge No. 8, 1755 Old Steese Hwy. ☎ 907-457-6058. www.golddredgeno8.com. Admission $15. One tour daily; call to confirm time. Closed mid-Sept to mid-May.

On Day 5 take the Steese Highway 5 miles north from Fairbanks to Chena Hot Springs Road, continuing 57 miles through Chena River State Recreation Area to Chena Hot Springs. You will spend the next 2 nights in the area.

⑫ ★★ kids Chena River State Recreation Area. On the lovely drive upriver, you'll pass several spots to enjoy the river and the area's best trail hikes. There are many places for spontaneous exploration, or follow the ideas I've offered here. ◷ Half-day. See p. 288, ❼.

⑬ ★★★ kids Chena Hot Springs Resort. Day visits are wonderful here; stay for lunch and

An Alternative: Driving to the Arctic Circle

Rather than exploring the Steese Highway, you can spend the day making a long and wearying drive on the Dalton Highway to the Arctic Circle north of Fairbanks. It's a 10-hour round trip, but those who do it mostly make the trip in a single day from Fairbanks. This, frankly, is something I would not do, but many are itching to check "Reach the Arctic Circle" off their so-called bucket list. It's also possible to spend the night on the way, camping or staying at crude lodgings. If that sounds appealing to you, see "Extreme Driving: A Dalton Highway Road Trip" starting on p. 310.

On the plus side, the 200-mile drive to the Arctic Circle (followed by a 200-mile drive back) exposes you to the region's most dramatic highway scenery. There are extraordinary mountain vistas, the only bridge over the 2,000-mile-long Yukon River (an amazing, wood-decked span), and at the turnaround spot, a stop at the Arctic Circle for a picture.

It's a tough trip, mostly off pavement, and the road is extremely remote and lightly traveled (it's the same road highlighted on the History Channel TV show *Ice Road Truckers*). Read up and be prepared before you go.

spend the afternoon swimming in the hot springs pools. The hot water and beautiful setting are truly relaxing. The ice museum (it's a museum made of ice and filled with ice sculptures) is possible thanks to the free energy that comes from the geothermal springs. A tour inside includes a cocktail in a glass of ice. ◷ Half-day. See p. 289, ❽.

You'll spend Day 6 on the road, on the Steese Highway, which runs north out of Fairbanks, before returning to the Chena Hot Springs area.

SITE GUIDE PAGE 303

⑭ ★★ Steese Highway. Spend Day 6 exploring this route into the Alaska bush on a round-trip drive that you can tailor to your endurance—and your ability to subject your car to unpaved road. (If renting, see "Renting the Right Car for Going Off-Pavement," on p. 509.) The entire route is 162 miles one way, ending at the bank of the wide Yukon River, but I don't recommend you go that far, as there is little to greet you.

On your final day in the region, before you head for home or for other parts of Alaska, take the Parks Highway 52 miles south from Fairbanks to:

⑮ ★ Nenana. This little town where the Alaska Railroad crosses the Tanana River is worth a stop for its lazy ambience, suitable for a northern Tom Sawyer. I'm not recommending you do anything special here, just walk around and soak it up. The first stop off the highway is a log cabin visitor center where they keep a big book of guesses for the Nenana Ice Classic, a game that has gone on since 1917 to predict the exact minute the ice will go out on the river in the spring. Tickets are $2.50, and the prize is usually around $300,000. Walk down to the river to see where barges load up to carry goods on the Tanana and Yukon rivers; take a look at St. Mark's Episcopal Church on Front Street, a log cabin built in 1905; peek into the local tribe's cultural center; and drop by the old depot, where trains haven't stopped in many years, with an outdoor display of the golden spike driven by President Warren G. Harding in 1923. ◷ 1 hr. Nenana Ice Classic. ☎ 907-832-5446. www.nenanaakiceclassic.com.

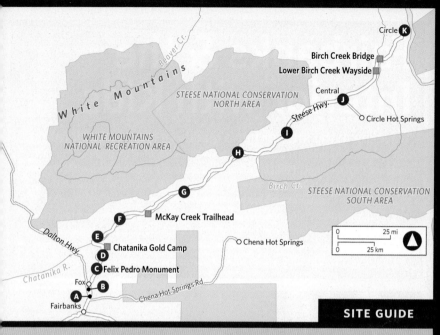

⑭ Steese Highway

The highway begins as a four-lane road leaving Fairbanks but rapidly dwindles, becoming a gravel road at mile 60 and a dirt one near its end. You'll see a lot of the **Ⓐ Trans-Alaska Pipeline,** but the best spot to get up close is at mile 8.4 of the Steese, where there is a pullout. You'll pass **Ⓑ Gold Dredge No. 8** at mile 9.5 (p. 300, ⑪). At mile 16.5 there is a **Ⓒ Monument to Felix Pedro,** the prospector whose find put Fairbanks on the map (see "The Strange Story of Fairbanks," p. 298).

From **Ⓓ Cleary Summit,** at mile 20.3, you can see the White Mountains to the north. Tours are infrequent at the **Ⓔ University of Alaska Poker Flat Research Range,** at mile 29.5, where scientists launch rockets to research the aurora. One of the area's best all-day canoe floats, on the **Ⓕ Chatanika River** (see "Outdoor Gear," on p. 317) starts at mile 39. **Ⓖ Davidson Ditch** is partly visible with its big pipes just past mile 57. It doesn't look like much, but miners found it worthwhile to build an aqueduct from way out here to Fairbanks to sluice gold. **Ⓗ Twelvemile Summit,** at mile 85.5, has wonderful views, and you can

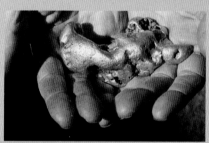

sometimes see caribou. **Ⓘ Eagle Summit,** at mile 107, is a good turnaround point. The views from the 1-mile trail here are fantastic, so be sure to get out of the car and stretch your legs.

If you decide to keep going, **Ⓙ Central,** at mile 128, is a tiny gold mining town, as close to the real old-time frontier as you're likely to find. Visit the **Circle District Historical Society Museum** (☎ 907-520-1893; www.cdhs.us), exhibiting mining equipment and history. Summer hours are Thursday to Sunday, noon to 5pm—the museum is closed in the winter. Finally, **Ⓚ Circle** is the Yukon River village at the bitter end of the road, with little to see; I don't recommend going that far on a day trip. ⊙ 1 day.

Fairbanks & the Interior with Kids

Traveling in the Interior has a quality of low-key exploration that I particularly enjoy, and that my kids loved before their teen years. You can wander a day in Pioneer Park or drift down a river, or you can drive a rural highway and stop at some random spot to take in the view and find out what's over the nearest hill. On the other hand, we've also had a legendary day of misery on a long road trip with a young one strapped into a car seat long after her breaking point. From this experience comes my advice: Do take kids to the region, but base yourself in Fairbanks and enjoy the fun activities in and near the city rather than tackling long drives to sites whose subtle charms may escape young eyes.

> It's Christmas year-round at North Pole & the Santa Claus House, a hokey but fun stop off Richardson Highway.

START Fairbanks. Fly to Fairbanks and rent a car. If you drive from Anchorage, the trip is 359 miles and takes more than 7 hours without stops. TRIP LENGTH 4 days, 170 miles.

① ★★★ University of Alaska Museum of the North. The extravagant design of the building itself will interest kids: Is it an iceberg or a swooping aurora? The natural history section contains many amazing items, organized by region of Alaska. The auditorium offers frequent presentations on the aurora (the university leads the world studying it), on winter, and on other subjects. ⏲ 2 hr. See p. 317, **⑦**.

② ★ Georgeson Botanical Garden. This enchanting spot, located at the bottom of the campus (about half a mile from both the museum and the trailhead), includes a children's garden with a big maze in the shape of a flower. You can also walk through the barn to see farm animals and reindeer in a paddock. ⏲ 1 hr. See p. 317, **⑧**.

From the east side of campus, take Farmers Loop Road to Ballaine Road, then make a quick left on Yankovich Road—the station is 1¼ miles down the road.

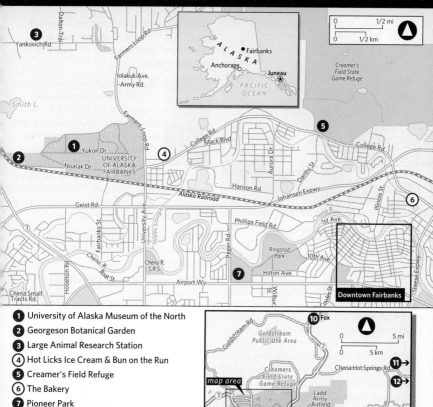

1 University of Alaska Museum of the North
2 Georgeson Botanical Garden
3 Large Animal Research Station
4 Hot Licks Ice Cream & Bun on the Run
5 Creamer's Field Refuge
6 The Bakery
7 Pioneer Park
8 North Pole and Santa Claus House
9 Chena Lake Recreation Area
10 El Dorado Gold Mine
11 Chena River State Recreation Area
12 Chena Hot Springs

3 ★ **Large Animal Research Station.** Known as LARS, this research station is actually a sizable farm, where scientists raise musk oxen, caribou, and reindeer for study. You can sometimes see the animals from the road, but I highly recommend joining a tour if at all possible. You'll have the chance to get up close to the animals and their babies, and to learn a lot about these ice-age creatures. ⏱1½ hr. Yankovich Rd. ☎ 907-474-7207. www.uaf.edu/lars. Tours $10 adults, $9 seniors, $6 students, free for children 6 and under. Tours depart daily Memorial Day through Labor Day every hour 10am–4pm. Call ☎ 907-474-5724 to confirm times.

4 🍦 **Hot Licks Homemade Ice Cream & Bun on the Run.** The best cones in Fairbanks come from Hot Licks, with blueberry and cranberry ice cream made with local wild berries. Across the street, in a travel trailer in the parking lot of the sporting goods store, Bun on the Run produces fantastic cinnamon rolls and, if you must be a grown-up, big sandwiches, too. Eat outdoors and let the kids have fun in the playground behind the Radio Shack. 3453 College Rd. ☎ 907-479-7813. www.hotlicks.net. $.

Start Day 2 outdoors, watching wildlife and learning about birds. To get to Creamer's

> *UA's Georgeson Botanical Garden.*

Field, take College Road from downtown or the university area.

⑤ ★★ Creamer's Field Refuge. Besides the big, open areas where you can see birds, the refuge has some interesting nature trails with guide booklets and a visitor center with exhibits. Kids may also be interested in the look of this former dairy farm. If possible, time your visit to watch researchers from the Alaska Bird Observatory catch, band, and release birds. ⏱ At least 1 hr. See p. 320, **⑬**.

⑥ 🍴 The Bakery. Stop in for wonderful sourdough pancakes or a filling lunch in this classic down-home diner. Kids can be themselves around the motherly waitstaff, who call everyone—from little tykes to burly miners—"hon" or "sweetie." 69 College Rd. ☎ 907-456-8600. $$.

Travel Tip

You can do this entire tour while staying at one hotel in Fairbanks. Consider **Wedgewood Resort** (p. 324) for its two-bedroom apartments with living rooms and full kitchens, which you can make into home for your stay (saving money on restaurants). But my favorite way to visit Fairbanks is camping. It's warm in the summer, and campgrounds are plentiful. I've listed some in town and nearby. See "Camping In & Around Fairbanks," on p. 323.

In the afternoon (your next stop opens at noon), take the Johansen Expressway to Peger Road, which reaches the park entrance at Airport Way.

SITE GUIDE PAGE 308

⑦ ★★ Pioneer Park. Fairbanks built the park, originally called "Alaskaland," in 1967 for the centennial of the Alaska purchase, and it still reflects the outlook of that simpler time, when folks installed carousels and miniature trains to entertain kids, as well as seven small museums and various other attractions. The place has real charm and valid educational qualities, and even jaded 21st-century children still enjoy it.

On Day 3, it's time to get out of the city. Take the Richardson Highway 15 miles east of Fairbanks to:

⑧ ★ North Pole & Santa Claus House. Even though you're going to "North Pole" to visit "Santa Claus House," don't expect any but the youngest children to think they're going to the *real* North Pole. Santa does not live on a suburban highway near an oil refinery. But the huge Christmas store, with massive statues of Santa as well as a live Santa and reindeer and such, will surely entertain. ⏱ 1 hr. See p. 295, **⑤**.

Take St. Nicholas Street east to the underpass, pass beneath the Richardson Highway, and turn right on the far side. Follow the street paralleling the highway and turn left on Laurance Road.

⑨ ★★ Chena Lake Recreation Area. The lake seemed a family paradise when we camped there with our young children: swimming and playing on the beach, paddling a canoe, camping in a well-made campground, watching the fish in the river, and walking the 2.5-mile nature trail. A boat rental concession offers canoes, rowboats, and paddleboats, and the 80-site campground even has sites on one of the lake's islands, reachable only by boat. Trout and salmon are stocked in the lake, which has several islands and bays; gentle and safe, but mysterious enough to be exciting, this place is just right for adventuring in a canoe with children. Should you decide to spend a night here, tent sites cost $10 while RV sites cost $12. ⏱ 1 day. Laurance Rd., North Pole. ☎ 907-488-1655. www.chenalakes.com. Day use $4 per vehicle

> *Several species of loons, known for their distinctive cry, summer on lakes all over Alaska.*

On Day 4, take the Steese and Elliott highways 9 miles north of Fairbanks to the El Dorado Gold Mine. Be sure to make a reservation in advance.

⑩ ★ El Dorado Gold Mine. This professionally produced tour teaches about mining, with the promise that guests can pan the concentrate they've seen gathered and get to keep their own gold. It's quite fun, if corny. The tour

begins with a ride on a train through a tunnel in the permafrost, where you learn about mining and the soils in which gold is found, followed by a demonstration of a sluice by a married couple of gold miners who are authentic and well-known Alaskan characters. ⏱ 2 hr. Mile 1.3, Elliot Hwy. ☎ 866-479-6673 or 907-479-6673. www.eldoradogoldmine.com. Tours $35 adults, $23 children 3–12, free for children 2 and under. Tours daily mid-May to mid-Sept; call for times. Reservations required.

Retrace your drive from Fairbanks, turning from the Steese Highway onto Chena Hot Springs Road. The Chena River State Recreation Area stretches along the second half of the 57-mile road.

⑪ ★★ Chena River State Recreation Area. The rounded mountains and clear river of the recreation area, with its trails and campgrounds, make this a rewarding family outdoor destination. After you break a sweat on a trail, you can visit the hot springs, described next, for a swim. If you're not up to a hike, just enjoy the river, easily accessed along the road or at the Rosehip Campground. If you do want to stretch your legs, the best family hike is a moderate climb 4 miles round trip to the Angel Rocks, a group of granite outcroppings on a wooded mountainside. ⏱ Half-day. See p. 288, **❼**.

⑫ ★★★ Chena Hot Springs. Plan to give yourself time for a swim and a meal at this unusual resort, where steaming hot water from the ground helps grow vegetables and powers machinery that keeps the ice museum frozen. ⏱ At least 1 hr. See p. 289, **❽**.

Celebrating the Summer Solstice

Because you're so far north, the sun barely sets in the summer in the Interior, and not at all some nights north of Fairbanks. Even if it slips below the horizon in the middle of the night, the sky stays bright and starless from May to August. On the longest day of the year—typically June 21, the summer solstice—Fairbanks gets almost 22 hours of direct sunlight. That's a very big deal, and cause for public and private celebration. The **Midnight Sun Run** (☎ 907-452-6046; www.midnightsunrun.us) starts at 10am on the solstice (or a day near it) with thousands of runners and walkers. It is a 6-mile event from the university campus to Pioneer Park that you can win for speed or for wearing a funny costume. The **Midnight Sun Baseball Game** (☎ 907-451-0095; www.goldpanners.com) starts at 10pm on the solstice and goes on for nine innings without artificial lights. It has been played annually since 1906, and for the last 50 years has been hosted by the semipro Alaska Goldpanners.

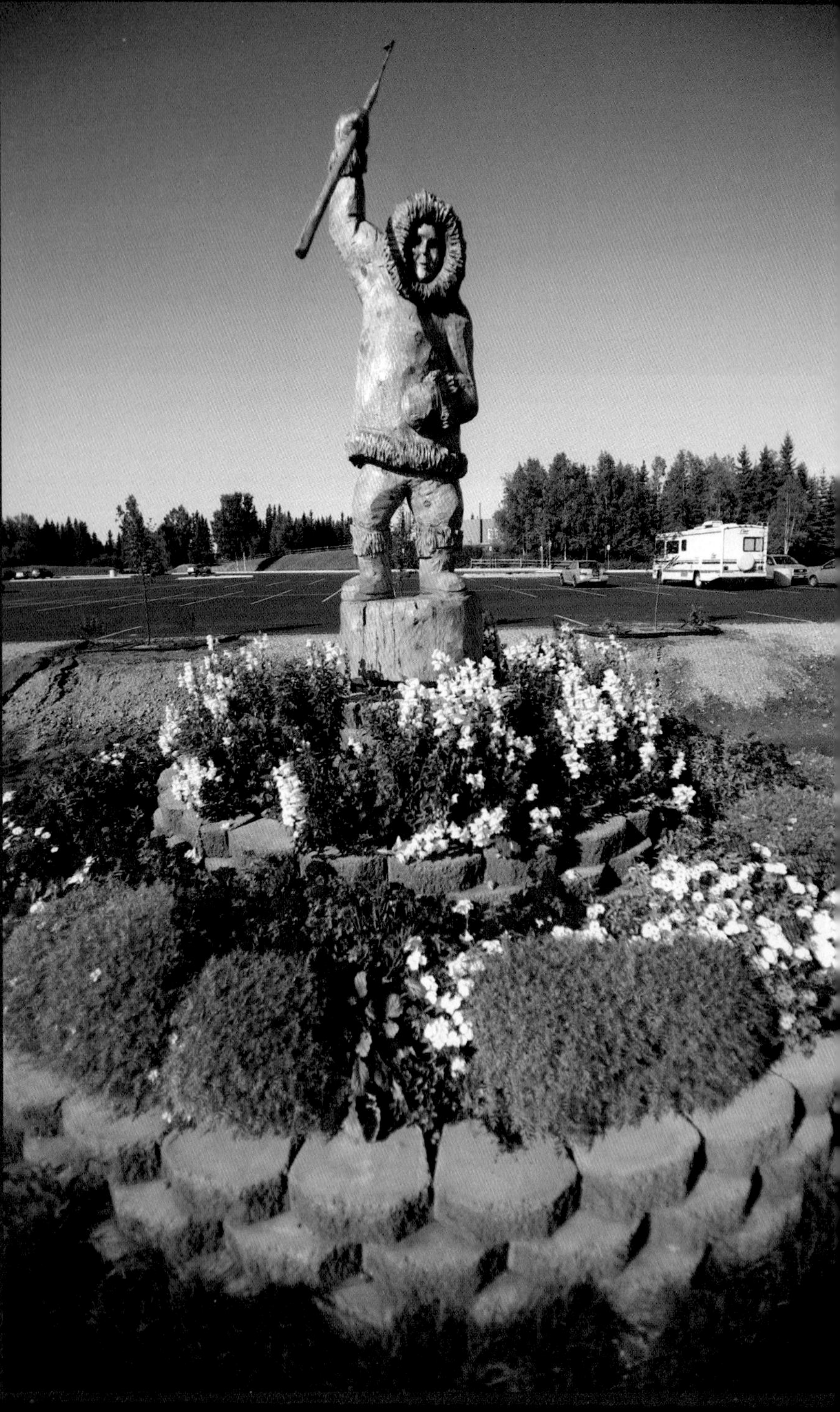

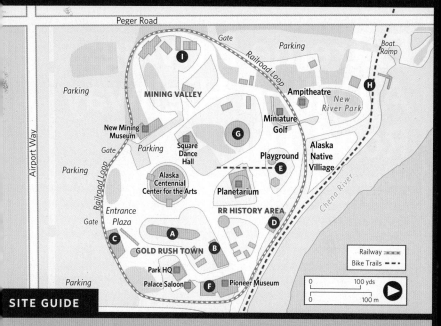

SITE GUIDE

7 Pioneer Park

There is much to do here, so take your time. Unless otherwise mentioned, all the attractions are free. The stern-wheeler **A** *Nenana* (p. 299, **8**) dominates the center of the park. The whole family will enjoy the **B** **Gold Rush Town** of cabins and old houses, which is home to shops, small eateries, and a restored-house museum.

Kids used to traveling in cramped back seats will marvel at **C** **President Harding's rail car.** It is the very same car he rode while in Alaska to drive the gold spike on the Alaska Railroad in 1923. If you'd like to take a train trip of your own, catch a ride on the **D** **Crooked Creek and Whiskey Island Railroad,** which circles the park while a tour guide points out the sights. Younger children particularly love it, and may demand multiple rides. The fare is $2 for adults, $1 for children. The **E** **children's area** has an old-fashioned merry-go-round ($2.50 per ride); two 18-hole miniature golf courses ($4.50 adults, $3 children 5 to 12, $1 children 4 and younger); and a well-equipped playground.

If your kids (or you) have been wondering what it feels like to experience some of the area's more extreme winter weather conditions, **F** **40 Below Fairbanks** will give you the chance.

In a room chilled to 40° F below zero, you can pound a nail with a rock-hard banana and toss a cup of water into the air to see it flash away. Admission is $8.50, a good investment if you're considering moving here.

G **The Pioneer Air Museum,** in the building with the gold geodesic dome, contains 14 vintage aircraft, mostly from Alaska's early days. Admission is $2 for adults, free for kids 12 and under. At the **H** **Chena River,** running along the edge of the park, you can rent a canoe or bike from **Alaska Outdoor Rentals & Guides** (p. 299, **8**). If you're done with the park, a canoe float can take you downriver to a restaurant for dinner. And speaking of dinner, the **I** **Alaska Salmon Bake,** near the mining display on the west side of the park, serves outdoor all-you-can-eat meals of prime rib and Alaskan fish, which you can combine with the fun and corny Golden Heart Revue at the park's **Palace Theatre.** The show, at 8:15 nightly, costs $18 for adults, $9 for children. Dinner is $31 for adults, $15 for children 3-12 (or $6.50 for child's hot dog plate). ⏱ At least a half-day. Airport Way and Peger Rd. ☎ 907-459-1087. www.co.fairbanks.ak.us/pioneerpark. Park attractions summer daily noon-8pm.

Extreme Driving: A Dalton Highway Road Trip

Alaska's only Arctic highway is the Dalton Highway, a gravel road built to carry materials 500 miles north from Fairbanks to the oil fields at Prudhoe Bay. Conditions here can be extreme, and travelers should take the journey seriously. Plan to camp, as lodgings are few along the way. Indeed, there are stretches of over 200 miles with scant sign of human habitation. But this is the ultimate Alaska road trip, through scenery so vast and extraordinary it can be a revelation. Even after a lifetime in Alaska, I was shocked by the beauty, and shocked again when it went on and on, miles flipping by like the pages of a 1,000-page book. ***Note:*** All my advice assumes you are going in the summer. Don't consider driving the Dalton in the winter.

> *The 4-foot-wide Trans-Alaska Pipeline carries oil under the 2,295-foot long E.L. Patton Yukon River Bridge.*

START Fairbanks. Take the Steese Highway north, joining the Elliott Highway until you reach the beginning of the Dalton Highway.

The drive from Fairbanks is 84 miles and will take around 2 hours. **TRIP LENGTH** 4 days, 1,000 miles.

❶ Dalton Highway start. The scenery on the roads leading to the start of the Dalton Highway is not particularly exciting. The Steese and Elliott highways cross wooded mountains. Pavement ends. Radio reception and cell phone coverage give out. After the 84-mile drive to the start of the Dalton, the mileposts start at zero, so add 84 to the numbers to get the distance from Fairbanks.

Continue 56 miles to the Yukon River.

❷ ★★ Yukon River Bridge area. The Yukon is one of the world's great rivers, running 2,000 miles from Canada across Alaska. This is its only bridge. It is long, high, and quite steep, and it has a wooden deck. The 4-foot-wide Trans-Alaska Pipeline crosses the river as part of the bridge. The oil pipeline is truly an impressive engineering achievement, and your appreciation for it only grows as you drive along its silver skein, elevated above the frozen ground on insulated pilings, for hour after hour. The pipeline carries oil from North America's two largest fields, Prudhoe Bay and Kuparuk, 900 miles from the Arctic Ocean to Valdez, where tankers take the oil onward, primarily to the west coast of the U.S.

Beyond the bridge are a couple of businesses, the last until Coldfoot, 119 miles on. A word on highway lodgings: Although I mention them, I don't recommend them. Except for the B&B in Wiseman, they are all retired construction camp dormitories, with tiny rooms and big communal bathrooms, and the quality ranges from serviceable to grungy. I prefer to do the trip by camping.

Plan Ahead

For many people who drive the length of the Dalton Highway, the big payoff is getting to see the Arctic Ocean at the end of the road. Unfortunately, because of the local oil company's security concerns, the shoreline is accessible only via a tour run by the **Arctic Caribou Inn** (see p. 315, ❿). You must pass the oil company's security screening in order to take it. Since that screening takes 24 hours, call in advance to give them your information. Otherwise, you may not be able to go.

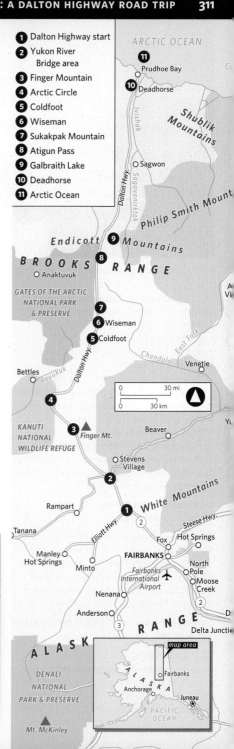

1. Dalton Highway start
2. Yukon River Bridge area
3. Finger Mountain
4. Arctic Circle
5. Coldfoot
6. Wiseman
7. Sukakpak Mountain
8. Atigun Pass
9. Galbraith Lake
10. Deadhorse
11. Arctic Ocean

> *The aurora lights the sky over a cabin in the village of Wiseman, on the south side of the Brooks Range.*

Just past the river, **Yukon River Camp** (☎ 907-474-3557; www.yukonrivercamp. com) has a gift shop, fuel (usually), and tire repair as well as food and lodging. It is open daily 9am to 9pm, and is closed from mid-September to mid-May.

Five miles beyond the river, the **Hotspot Café** (☎ 907-451-7543) similarly offers dining, lodging, a gift shop, gas (again, usually), and tire repair. It is open daily 10am to midnight from mid-May to mid-September.

A **Bureau of Land Management visitor contact station** near the bridge has volunteers to answer questions, but no phone. It is open in summer daily from 9am to 6pm.

Continue 42 miles to Finger Mountain Wayside, at Mile 98.

❸ ★★ **Finger Mountain.** You're now into the highway's wonderful views. It seems almost silly for me to point them out, as they can go on for hours, but this is a particularly good stop, with a half-mile nature trail and access to dry alpine tundra for further walking. ⏲ 1 hr.

Continue 17 miles to the pullout for the Arctic Circle, at Mile 115.

❹ ★ **Arctic Circle.** This is the terminal destination for many drivers on the Dalton. The Arctic Circle is the imaginary line around the globe at 66 degrees, 33 minutes north latitude. North of this point, the sun never sets at least one day a summer, and never rises at

least one night a winter. By driving here you can say you've been in the Arctic, and take a picture next to a sign that proves it. There is a primitive campsite here, should you choose to spend the night. ⏲ 30 min. Camping $8 fee.

Continue 60 miles to Coldfoot, at Mile 175; this part of the road is paved.

❺ ★★ **Coldfoot.** If you want to take a day for activities while along your drive, Coldfoot is the place to do it. **Coldfoot Camp** (☎ 866-474-

Know the Road

Road conditions vary, so it is difficult to predict the time needed to cover any given part of the highway. You can expect to average 40 miles per hour, and sometimes you can get up to 60 miles per hour. Here are one-way driving times from Fairbanks, assuming prime conditions and minimal stops: Yukon River, 3 hours; Arctic Circle, 5 hours; Coldfoot, 6 hours; Atigun Pass, 8 hours; Deadhorse, 13 hours.

For more information about the Dalton Highway, including an extremely useful booklet with maps and lots of detailed advice, go to the **Bureau of Land Management's** website: www.blm.gov/ak/dalton. In person, get advice and the booklet at the **Alaska Public Lands Information Center** in Fairbanks (p. 316, ❷).

3400 or 907-474-3500; www.coldfootcamp. com), an aptly named truck stop, is the largest collection of buildings on the highway, and it can be a relief to see people and businesses after a long day (or more) on the road. Besides the 24-hour gas station and friendly highway diner, there are lodgings, laundry, RV hookups, a post office, and a saloon. *Note:* If you're looking for rooms, consider going onward to Wiseman—see "Be Prepared," on p. 314; if camping, choose Marion Creek, just beyond Coldfoot.

While you're here, try a glorious flightseeing trip with **Coyote Air** (☎ 800-252-0603 or 907-678-5995; www.flycoyote.com), a family business with a married couple for pilots, at the airstrip across the road from the truck stop. They mainly fly adventurers out for wilderness trips, but you can also arrange for a charter just to take a spin, the cost depending on your interests and budget.

Before leaving Coldfoot, stop at the **Arctic Interagency Visitor Center** (☎ 907-678-5209 or 678-2014), on the west side of the highway. It's a remarkable facility to find so deep in the wilderness. Check out the award-winning exhibits about the North and consider attending one of the nightly educational programs in the theater. The center is open daily from 10am to 10pm from late May to early September. ☺ 1 hr. each for Coldfoot Camp and the visitor center; at least 1 hr. for flightseeing.

The **Marion Creek Campground** is 5 miles past Coldfoot, at mile 180, and it is the only developed campground on the highway. It has potable well water and outhouses and some sites big enough for large RVs. A 2-mile trail leads to a small waterfall. 27 sites, $8 per night.

Drive 7 miles north and take the 3-mile side road, at Dalton Highway mile 188, to Wiseman.

❻ ★★ Wiseman. This century-old gold-rush town lives on as a subsistence community where people feed themselves by hunting and gardening. It's a window into the frontier past, with friendly folks who sell furs and crafts from their homes, and an old-fashioned trading company that operates on the honor system. But do respect people's privacy—this is not a museum.

If you'd like to spend the night here but would prefer not to camp, you'll find cozy log

Off-Road: Exploring the Scenery—Safely

You can stop anywhere on the Dalton to take a walk or just enjoy the views, and you should do so whenever you feel the urge. Just remember to get your vehicle off the highway. Given the isolation, drivers tend to forget themselves and stop in the middle of the road to look at wildlife and scenery, and that's very dangerous given the fast-moving trucks that use the highway. Indeed, the tires on these heavy-duty trucks can throw rocks up to 30 feet off the road. Pipeline access roads are good places to pull over without having to worry about getting stuck, but don't block them, and camping on them is not allowed.

A Dalton Highway Checklist

This is not a drive for the ill-prepared. The odds are good that you'll see few other vehicles (besides enormous trucks) on the Dalton Highway, and there are long stretches (up to 200 miles) where there are virtually no services. I can't stress enough the need for advance planning. Bear in mind the following:

What is *not* available on the highway:
- No cell phone coverage
- No emergency medical facilities
- No way to call ☎ 911 (see "Fairbanks & the Interior Fast Facts," p. 326)
- No banks or ATMs
- No grocery stores
- Gas stations are up to 239 miles apart

What you'll need for a safe and happy trip:
- A reliable vehicle you can drive on gravel (need not be four-wheel-drive)
- Two full-sized spare tires and tools
- Warm and waterproof clothing
- A first-aid kit
- Insect repellent
- Food and camping supplies
- 5 gallons of fresh water
- A reservation for access to the Arctic Ocean (p. 315, ⓫)
- A road report from ☎ 511 or http://511.alaska.gov

> An aerial view of the James Dalton Highway as it comes down a mountain, having crossed Atigun Pass and the Brooks Range.

cabins and friendly hosts at **Arctic Getaway Bed and Breakfast.** On the main road. ☎ 907-678-4456. www.arcticgetaway.com. 3 cabins. Doubles/quads $95-$195. No credit cards. ☉ 1 hr.

Return to the Dalton Highway and continue 15 miles to:

❼ ★★ Sukakpak Mountain. If you thought the views yesterday were amazing, today your mind will truly be blown. The rock monolith of this mountain is only one of the extraordinary sights along this stretch. You will pass beyond the farthest-north trees and onto the plateau of the Chandalar Shelf, climbing towards the Brooks Range and broad alpine terrain with limitless sightlines, suitable for hiking.

Continue into the Brooks Range to Atigun Pass, at mile 244.

❽ ★★★ Atigun Pass. The highway cuts through the Brooks Range in a pass that looks like a moonscape. At this altitude, and this far north, nothing grows, and snowstorms arrive even in the middle of July. Where you can find a walkable route, the range has extraordinary mountain hiking; its high, rocky valleys, where life is so sparse, always seem to me barely of this world. ☉ 2 hr.

Continue on the highway down the steep north side of the Brooks Range. Galbraith Lake is 31 miles on, at mile 275.

Be Prepared

Once you leave Wiseman heading north, there are no businesses until the end of the road—227 miles ahead, in Deadhorse. Make sure you are well stocked with plenty of gas and supplies before you depart.

9 ★★★ **Galbraith Lake.** This part of the drive struck me as among the most beautiful, as the road lay like a ribbon over the rounded foothills of the Brooks Range, all clothed in tundra. Staying to the hilltops, it's possible to hike a long way here and see wildlife for a great distance. Caribou antlers are often found in the heather. The last official camping area on the road is at the lake (the overnight fee is $8), but there is no potable water there. ⏱ 2 hr.

Drive onward 139 miles through the treeless North Slope and Coastal Plain to the end of the road, in the industrial area of Deadhorse. If tent camping, pick out a spot as you approach the town, perhaps on the wide bed of the Sagavanirktok River.

10 **Deadhorse.** The community is a rather depressing industrial camp. But thanks to the local oil company's security measures, you cannot get to the Arctic Ocean without stopping here and joining a van tour (see **11**), so you will have to spend some time here. Other than the airstrip, hotels, general store, auto parts store, and gas station, there's really nothing for you in Deadhorse. Rooms, food, and the tour can be found at the main hotel, the **Arctic Caribou Inn,** at the airstrip (☎ 907-659-2368; www.arcticcaribouinn.com). Rooms have two twin beds in construction camp style and cost $240 a night (the inn takes major credit cards). The restaurant offers breakfast ($15), lunch ($18), and dinner ($20).

11 ★★★ **Arctic Ocean.** The road is blocked by security gates before reaching the ocean, but for most people, driving this far without going to the end is inconceivable. The **Arctic Caribou Inn** (**10**) offers 2-hour bus tours

> *A view of Galbraith Lake, on the north side of the Brooks Range.*

through the oil field, with a 15-minute stop at the shore. **Note:** The key issue is that you have to pass an oil company security screening at least 24 hours in advance, which means you should do it by phone from Fairbanks before starting. They will need each passenger's name and identification information, such as a driver's license or passport number. ⏱ 2 hr. Tour 4 times daily; advance reservations required. $40 per person.

Another Way to Do the Dalton

If this 1,000-mile wilderness drive sounds too daunting, there is an easier way to experience the Dalton Highway. **Northern Alaska Tour Company** (☎ 800-474-1986 or 907-474-8600; www.northernalaska. com) offers escorted tours that drive the highway by bus one way and fly the other way. It takes half as long and requires less than half as much planning. The firm has interesting add-ons as well, including flightseeing, dayhikes, and village visits. A basic 3-day, 2-night tour costs $989 per person.

Camping in Deadhorse

There is no tent camping area within Deadhorse, as the abundance of heavy equipment and grizzly bears makes it dangerous. When camping outside of town, the garbage-seeking bears are less of a problem, but you can avoid attracting them by keeping a clean campsite, with all food and other pungent items (such as soap) stored away from your tent, preferably inside your car.

Fairbanks

Fairbanks is home base for enjoying Interior Alaska, and in the tours in this chapter I've covered much of what there is to do there. This section will help you both find what you're interested in seeing and choose lodgings, campgrounds, and restaurants. The city is a transportation hub, and you can get there by air, train, or car.

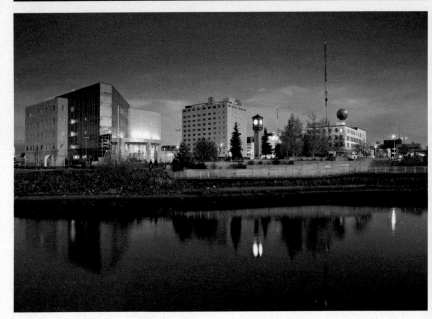

> The city of Fairbanks is surrounded by wilderness.

START **Fairbanks is 325 miles from Anchorage.**

❶ ★ Morris Thompson Cultural and Visitors Center. Besides containing the town's main visitor center, this Alaska Native–owned facility has a bookstore, exhibits, and a theater with free films and naturalist programs. ⊕ 1 hr. 101 Dunkel St. ☎ 800-327-5774 or 907-456-5774. www.morristhompsoncenter.org. May to mid-Sept daily 8am–9pm; rest of the year 8am–5pm.

❷ ★ Alaska Public Lands Information Center. This is an important stop if you plan to do outdoor activities or to drive one of the region's long rural highways, especially the Dalton Highway. ⊕ 1 hr. In the Morris Thompson Cultural and Visitors Center, 101 Dunkel St. ☎ 907-459-3730; www.alaskacenters.gov. Summer daily 9am–6pm; winter Mon–Sat 9am–5pm.

❸ ★ Fairbanks Community Museum. This is the town attic, where all kinds of interesting and whimsical stuff is exhibited in the crowded spaces of the former city hall. It's a maze you can enjoyably lose yourself in, as if wandering into the community's collective memory. ⊕ 1 hr. 104 Cushman St. ☎ 907-457-3669. Free admission, donations accepted. Summer Tues–Sat 10am–6pm; call for winter hours.

4 Doyon, Limited, lobby. If you're walking downtown along the river near the visitor center and footbridge, check out the beautiful display of Alaska Native art in the lobby of this office building. ⊙ 15 min. 1 Doyon Place. No phone. www.doyon.com.

5 ★ Immaculate Conception Church. The white, wood-frame church was built in 1904, just two years after E. T. Barnette landed to found the town (see "The Strange Story of Fairbanks," on p. 298), and it is decorated partly in the gold-rush style of the era. It is often open for a look inside. ⊙ 15 min. 115 N. Cushman St. ☎ 907-452-3533. www.alaska. net/~icc. Rectory open Tues–Fri 8:30am–4pm.

6 ★ Yukon Quest Sled Dog Race Headquarters. A big log building with a sod roof contains the offices for this 1,000-mile race, which is run between Fairbanks and Whitehorse, Yukon, across the border in Canada, changing directions in alternate years. Inside, you can see a free exhibit on mushing and get souvenirs. Right next door is **Golden Heart Park.** ⊙ 15 min. 550 1st Ave. ☎ 907-452-7954. www.yukonquest.com. Summer and race season Mon–Fri 10am–7pm, Sat–Sun 11am–4pm; spring and fall hours vary. Free admission.

7 ★★★ kids University of Alaska Museum of the North. The Museum of the North is among the state's best indoor attractions. It's a striking, dramatic building, and the curators' unconventional approach mixes culture and science throughout to create fresh, unexpected connections for viewers. A section mostly oriented to natural history shows discoveries from the university's exceptional research programs in geophysics and Arctic science, including jaw-dropping objects such as the huge, mummified steppe bison known as Blue Babe.

A newer section is a spectacular setting for Alaskan contemporary and traditional Native art. A sound and light installation by Fairbanks composer John Luther Adams has received intense national praise. It creates a hypnotic visual and aural environment in a special room, with music that changes along with changing real-time Earth measurements such as seismic vibrations and the aurora. ⊙ 3 hr. 907 Yukon Dr. ☎ 907-474-7505. www.uaf.edu/

museum. Admission $10 adults, $9 seniors 60 and over, $5 children 7–17, free for children 6 and under. Summer daily 9am–9pm; winter Mon–Sat 9am–5pm, closed Sun.

8 ★ kids Georgeson Botanical Garden. This delightful garden mixes science and pleasure. I enjoy looking at the experimental plots, but there also are many peaceful spots for contemplation or picnicking. A new children's garden includes a large maze in the form of a flower. ⊙ 1 hr. 117 W. Tanana Dr. ☎ 907-474-1944. www.uaf.edu/salrm/gbg. Admission $2. Summer daily 9am–8pm, store 9am–5pm, free guided tours Fri at 2pm; closed in winter.

9 ★ kids Large Animal Research Station. If you're interested in getting an up-close look at reindeer and musk oxen, this is the place to come. ⊙ 1½ hr. See p. 305, **3**.

10 ★★ kids Pioneer Park. Much of the history of Fairbanks was relocated to this big city park, and much of the innocent fun is concentrated

Outdoor Gear

It is unlikely that you'd come to Fairbanks just to see the city itself—it is best used as a base for exploring the Interior. And for that, you may need some help. Here are some of the best ways to gear up for hitting the great outdoors: You can rent camping gear, bikes, and canoes at **GoNorth Alaska Adventure Travel Center** (see "Renting the Right Car for Going Off-Pavement" on p. 509), which also has SUVs, campers, and motor homes for rent. If you're staying in the city, head to Pioneer Park, where you can rent canoes and bikes and get a shuttle ride for one-way trips from **Alaska Outdoor Rentals & Guides** (p. 299, **8**).

If you're planning to hit the slopes or cross some country, rent skis at **Beaver Sports**, 3800 College Rd. (☎ 907-479-2494; www.beaversports.com). And if you're really serious about getting out into nature, the **University of Alaska's Outdoor Adventures Program** at the Wood Student Center rents camping equipment, including high-quality expedition gear. On campus, Yukon Dr. near Chandalar Dr. ☎ 907-474-6027. www.uaf.edu/outdoor.

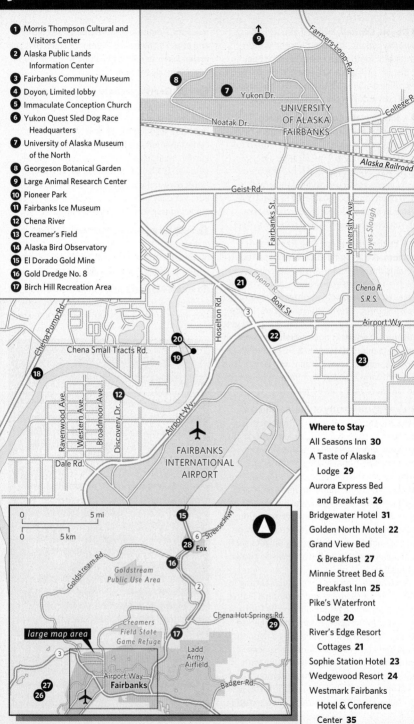

1. Morris Thompson Cultural and Visitors Center
2. Alaska Public Lands Information Center
3. Fairbanks Community Museum
4. Doyon, Limited lobby
5. Immaculate Conception Church
6. Yukon Quest Sled Dog Race Headquarters
7. University of Alaska Museum of the North
8. Georgeson Botanical Garden
9. Large Animal Research Center
10. Pioneer Park
11. Fairbanks Ice Museum
12. Chena River
13. Creamer's Field
14. Alaska Bird Observatory
15. El Dorado Gold Mine
16. Gold Dredge No. 8
17. Birch Hill Recreation Area

Where to Stay

All Seasons Inn **30**
A Taste of Alaska Lodge **29**
Aurora Express Bed and Breakfast **26**
Bridgewater Hotel **31**
Golden North Motel **22**
Grand View Bed & Breakfast **27**
Minnie Street Bed & Breakfast Inn **25**
Pike's Waterfront Lodge **20**
River's Edge Resort Cottages **21**
Sophie Station Hotel **23**
Wedgewood Resort **24**
Westmark Fairbanks Hotel & Conference Center **35**

Fairbanks

Where to Dine

Gambardella's Pasta
Bella **32**

Lavelle's Bistro **33**

Pike's Landing Riverside
Dining **19**

The Pump House Restaurant
and Saloon **18**

Thai House **34**

The Turtle Club **28**

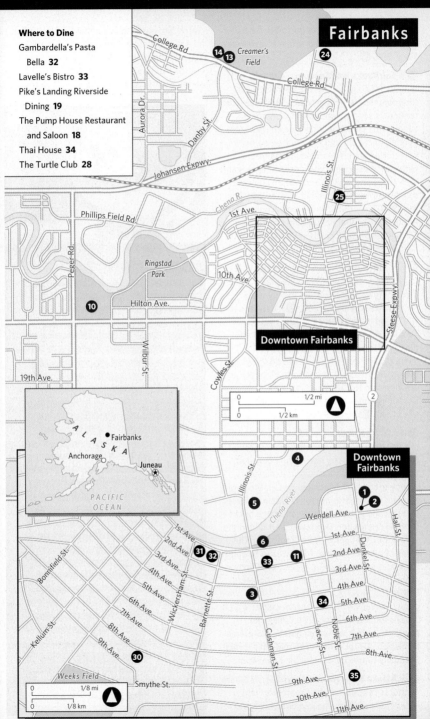

Downtown Fairbanks

Downtown Fairbanks

here, too, including the opportunity for a canoe paddle down the Chena River. ⏱ Half-day. See p. 299, ⑧.

⑪ ★ **Fairbanks Ice Museum.** Fairbanks is famous for cold, and for the World Ice Art Championships, held in March. Because winter here is so frigid and so long, organizers can harvest glass-clear lake ice chunks large enough to carve huge sculptures—some are two stories high. The museum has freezers with windows, where you can see carvers and their creations, and an auditorium showing a slide show of the real thing. ⏱ 1 hr. 500 2nd Ave. ☎ 907-451-8222. www.icemuseum.com. Admission $12 adults, $11 seniors and military, $6 children 6–12, $2 children 5 and under. Daily 10am–8pm. Closed Oct–Apr.

⑫ ★★ kids **Chena River.** There are many ways to get out on the lazy Chena River as it passes through town, but these are my favorites. First, the *Discovery* (p. 286, ❸), a riverboat which carries hundreds of tourists at a time on a trip downstream. Crowds aside, it still manages to be both fun and educational. Second, for those who prefer to do things on their own, floating a canoe from Pioneer Park downstream to a riverside restaurant is pure Fairbanks. For rental and dining information, see p. 299, ⑧. ⏱ Half-day.

⑬ ★★ kids **Creamer's Field Refuge.** As the city of Fairbanks grew, this dairy farm was saved from development by community contributions in 1966. It remains a prime migratory stopover and bird-watching spot. In the spring and fall, its pastures are full of Canada geese, pintails, and golden plovers, and large flocks of sandhill cranes and swans are common in the spring. Birds are fewer midsummer, but the 3 miles of pleasant nature trails weave through the area's various habitat types—pick up one of the complimentary explanatory booklets before you begin your walk, and return it when done. The farmhouse is a visitor center with wildlife exhibits. ⏱ 2 hr. 1300 College Rd. ☎ 907-452-5162. www.creamersfield.org. Free admission. Visitor center open mid-May to mid-Sept daily 10am–5pm; winter Sat noon–4pm.

⑭ ★ **Alaska Bird Observatory.** The staff here conducts research at the Creamer's Field Refuge, and visitors can join bird walks and watch bird banding, where tiny bands are put on a bird's leg to help scientists track migration, among other things. You can also check out the exhibits at the observatory building on the west side of the refuge, on the grounds

Fairbanks Shopping

The shopping scene is decidedly sparse in Fairbanks, with far fewer galleries or opportunities to find Native crafts than in other Alaska cities you will likely visit.

Downtown, the **Arctic Traveler's Gift Shop,** 201 Cushman St. (☎ 907-456-7080; www.arctictravelersgiftshop.com), is the place to look for Native art and crafts. It carries expensive artwork and affordable, authentic gifts. Next door, **If Only . . . ,** 215 Cushman St. (☎ 907-457-6659; www.ifonlyalaska.com), is a fine store that caters to locals with charming gifts, stationery, and the like. For an even bigger slice of local interest, though perhaps nothing you will take home, **Big Ray's Store,** 507 2nd Ave. (☎ 800-478-3458 in Alaska only or 907-452-3458; www.bigrays.com), carries equipment and clothing for both work in the Arctic and the rugged outdoor trips made by people around here. You may never have seen such warm clothing.

Near the airport, the **Great Alaskan Bowl Company** (pictured), 4630 Old Airport Rd. (☎ 800-770-4222 or 907-474-9663; www.woodbowl.com), uses local birch to make nested sets of bowls and other carved items. You can see the workshop behind glass; some of the items they make are amazing.

The shop at the **UA Museum of the North** (p. 317, ❼) is not large, but carries some well-chosen Alaska Native art.

of Wedgewood Resort (p. 324). It's the continent's farthest-north bird-banding observatory. 🕐 1 hr. 418 Wedgewood Dr. ☎ 907-451-7159. www.alaskabird.org. Free admission. Mon–Fri 9:30am–5pm. Call for banding times.

15 ★ kids **El Dorado Gold Mine.** A little on the corny side but still informative and certainly fun, this gold mining tour includes a participatory element that kids enjoy. 🕐 2 hr. See p. 307, **10**.

16 ★★ **Gold Dredge No. 8.** The authenticity of this monstrous earth-eating machine makes it Fairbanks's best historic site. You can go inside the dredge and learn how it worked, see the miners' grim quarters, and pan for gold. 🕐 2 hr. See p. 300, **11**.

17 ★★ kids **Birch Hill Recreation Area.** The hilly park just north of town has 15½ miles of trails for mountain biking or walking in summer and for the region's best cross-country skiing in winter. 🕐 Half-day. See p. 299, **10**.

Fairbanks Nightlife & Entertainment

If you're not worn out by your busy days spent in and around Fairbanks, you may want to hit the town in the evening. While Fairbanks doesn't offer the depth or variety of, say, Anchorage, there are some fun places to check out. To find out what's going on when you visit, call the city's 24-hour events line at ☎ 907-456-INFO or get a copy of the *Fairbanks Daily News-Miner.* You can also check the "Downtown Guide" and "Events" website pages of the **Downtown Association of Fairbanks** (☎ 907-452-8671; www.downtownfairbanks.com) for goings-on in that part of town.

★★ **The Blue Loon,** 2999 Parks Hwy. (☎ 907-457-5666; www.theblueloon.com) is a high-brow nightclub showing art films as well as hosting comedy nights and traveling musical acts. There are many beers on tap, and the burgers are good. On the other hand, the summer-only ★ **Howling Dog Saloon,** 2160 Old Steese Hwy. (☎ 907-456-4695; www.howlingdogsaloon.alaskan savvy.com) is known as the place to cut loose and drink a lot of beer. You'll find live music from Wednesday to Saturday, and there is a volleyball court out back. It is closed from October to April.

Folk musicians from the area and imported acts passing through perform regularly at the ★ **College Coffeehouse,** 3677 College Rd. (☎ 907-374-0468; www.collegecoffee housefairbanks.com). Dates are listed on the website. The ★ **Palace Theatre** (p. 309, **7**), in Pioneer Park, features a live nightly revue covering the city's fascinating history.

Thanks to the composers and musicians at the University of Alaska, Fairbanks has a rich classical music scene, despite the city's small size and rough edges. The ★★ **Fairbanks Symphony,** 312 Tanana Dr. (☎ 907-474-5733; www.fairbankssymphony.org), performs during a winter season.

Finally, if you'd really rather just spend a relaxing night at the movies, you can head for the **Regal Goldstream 16,** 1855 Airport Way (☎ 800-326-3264 movie listings, 907-456-1882 office). It's a typical multiplex movie theater showing Hollywood output.

Where to Stay

> *Grand View Bed & Breakfast.*

★ All Seasons Inn DOWNTOWN

This is a cozy country inn with a warm and conscientious owner, Mary Richards, on a residential street within walking distance of the downtown attractions. As it is a converted house, rooms are not large, but they are cheerful and have private baths. Guests visit with Mary and one another in the gracious common rooms, often over her extensive breakfasts. 763 7th Ave. ☎ 888-451-6649 or 907-451-6649. www.allseasonsinn.com. 8 units. Doubles $165–$215 summer; $89–$109 winter; w/breakfast. DC, DISC, MC, V.

★ A Taste of Alaska Lodge NORTH OF FAIR-BANKS

This is the homestead of a charismatic Alaskan family, with a log building atop a hillside on 280 acres, facing Mount McKinley. The location off Chena Hot Springs Road, less than half an hour from Fairbanks, makes it an excellent choice if you want a feeling of wilderness or a winter stay with aurora viewing. It's also a good alternative to the spotty service at Chena Hot Springs Resort (p. 289, ❽). 551 Eberhardt Rd. ☎ 907-488-7855. www.atasteofalaska.com. 8 units. Doubles $185, w/breakfast. AE, MC, V.

★★ Aurora Express Bed and Breakfast

CHENA RIDGE This is a family B&B made up of railroad cars and, just for decoration, a locomotive, all of which they've hauled up a mountain 6½ miles from town. You can stay in a vintage Pullman sleeper, a caboose, or a cute compartment on a historic theme in a remodeled car. Breakfast is served in the dining car. Ask before bringing young children, who may not be allowed. 1540 Chena Ridge Rd. ☎ 800-221-0073 or 907-474-0949. www.fairbanksalaskabedandbreakfast.com. 7 units.

Travel Tip

The cruise lines bring huge, escorted tour groups through Fairbanks, filling up the large hotels, including the Westmark, Pike's Waterfront Lodge, Sophie Station, River's Edge Resort, and Wedgewood Resort. Those dates may be booked up far in advance, but the flow of passengers differs among the companies, so while one hotel is full, another may have many vacancies. Shop around, as you can snag a good deal on those "off" nights.

Doubles $145–$160, w/breakfast. MC, V. Closed mid-Sept to mid-May.

★ **Bridgewater Hotel** DOWNTOWN
An older concrete building offers reasonably priced lodgings in a prime location on the Chena River. The rooms are light and feminine—comfortable if not luxurious. Look for vacancies and bargains on the weekends. 723 1st Ave. ☎ 800-528-4916, 907-452-6661, or 907-456-3642. www.fountainheadhotels.com. 94 units. Doubles $129–$169. AE, DC, DISC, MC, V. Closed mid-Sept to mid-May.

Golden North Motel AIRPORT
Find budget rooms at the airport in this family-operated motel. Lodgings are strictly functional but clean, and have good amenities. The hospitality is top-notch. Rates include a business center, a courtesy van, and snacks. 4888 Old Airport Rd. ☎ 800-447-1910 or 907-479-6201. www.goldennorthmotel.com. 62 units. Doubles $89–$106 summer; $62–$66 winter; w/ breakfast. AE, DC, DISC, MC, V.

★ **Grand View Bed & Breakfast** CHENA RIDGE
This big log house, 15 minutes out of town, overlooks a panorama of the Tanana Valley and Alaska Range. Hosts are members of an interesting, well-traveled family with three young children. All bedrooms have great views and private bathrooms. 915 Ridge Pointe Dr. ☎ 907-479-3388. www.grandview-bb.com. 4 units. Doubles $125 summer; $100 winter; w/ breakfast. MC, V.

★★ **Minnie Street Bed & Breakfast Inn**
DOWNTOWN This B&B, in a residential area near downtown and the rail depot, has luxurious features and the privacy you would expect in a bigger place, along with the friendly qualities of a small, owner-operated property. 345 Minnie St. ☎ 888-456-1849 or 907-456-1802. www.minniestreetbandb.com. 16 units. Doubles $139–$179 summer; $75–$89 winter; w/breakfast. AE, DISC, MC, V.

★★ **Pike's Waterfront Lodge** AIRPORT
Rooms in this riverside hotel are packed with

Camping In & Around Fairbanks

Tent camping is a good way to go in Fairbanks, with its mild summers and ample public lands, but stock up on mosquito repellent. There are plenty of RV parks, too. Here are my picks.

Chena River State Recreation Site. This public campground is right in the city, on a bend in the river among birch and spruce trees. Do not confuse it with the Chena River State Recreation Area, which is outside of town. Arrive early for a riverside site. Bathrooms have plumbing, and 11 sites are available with water and power hookups for RVs. On University Avenue by the river bridge. 56 sites. Walk-in sites $10; drive-in $17; RV $25.

River's Edge RV Park and Campground. On attractive land along the Chena, near the resort of the same name (p. 324), this commercial park has lots of services, including free shuttles. 4140 Boat St., off Airport Way and Sportsman Way. ☎ 800-770-3343 or 907-474-0286. www. riversedge.net. Full hookups $35; tent camping $21. AE, DISC, MC, V.

Chena Lake Recreation Area. About 30 minutes out of town, in North Pole, the campground has a variety of sites around a swimming and boating lake (p. 306, ❾).

Rosehip Campground (pictured). The rushing upper river passes by this beautifully forested campground in the Chena River State Recreation Area, 32 miles from the city. 37 sites, 6 suitable for RVs (no hookups). $10 per night.

> *The bustling lobby of Pike's Waterfront Lodge.*

amenities, and common areas have a lot of unique features, such as a greenhouse, an ice cream parlor decorated with a real airplane, solar panels, and a huge collection of wildlife art. 1850 Hoselton Dr. ☎ 877-774-2400 or 907-456-4500. www.pikeslodge.com. 208 units. Doubles $149–$225 summer; $69–$99 winter. AE, DC, DISC, MC, V.

★★ kids River's Edge Resort Cottages WEST SIDE

A trim little village of pastel cottages sits on a grassy lawn at a bend in the Chena, an idyllic setting that brings the best of Fairbanks to your doorstep. Families will enjoy having their own unit, without worries about noise and with lots of room to play outside. Inside, the cottages are identical to a good hotel room. 4200 Boat St. ☎ 800-770-3343 or 907-474-0286. www.riversedge.net. 94 units. Doubles $219 summer; $149 winter. AE, DISC, MC, V. Closed Oct–Apr.

★ Sophie Station Hotel WEST SIDE

The units all include full kitchens and separate living rooms and bedrooms, and the site is near grocery stores and the airport—making this spot ideal for business travelers or longer stays. The in-house cafe, called Zach's, is exceptionally good for a place tucked away in such a quiet hotel. 1717 University Ave. ☎ 800-528-4916 reservations or 907-479-3650 and 907-456-3642. www.fountainheadhotels.com. 148 units. Doubles $169–$205 summer; $89–$120 winter. AE, DC, DISC, MC, V.

★★ kids Wedgewood Resort EAST SIDE

The hotel consists of eight large buildings on 23 acres adjoining the Creamer's Field Refuge (p. 320, ⓭); the Alaska Bird Observatory is on the grounds, as is an antique auto museum. For families, the units of converted apartments make all kinds of sense, with large living rooms, separate dining areas, and fully equipped kitchens, and there is unlimited play space outside. 212 Wedgewood Dr. ☎ 800-528-4916 (reservations), 907-452-1442, or 907-456-3642. www.fountainheadhotels.com. 462 units. Doubles $185 summer; $75–$120 winter. AE, DC, DISC, MC, V.

★★★ Westmark Fairbanks Hotel & Conference Center DOWNTOWN

The city's traditional central hotel and meeting place, covering a full block and with one of the town's tallest towers, is stylishly decorated and offers many services and amenities. Because it is owned by the Holland America Line, service is up to cruise ship standards. 813 Noble St. ☎ 800-544-0970 (reservations) or 907-456-7722. www.westmarkhotels.com. 400 units. Doubles $225 summer; $84 winter; w/breakfast in winter only. AE, DC, DISC, MC, V.

Where to Dine

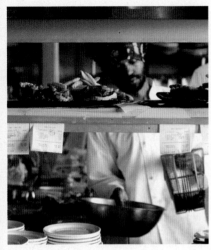

> Order up at Lavelle's Bistro.

★★ kids **Gambardella's Pasta Bella** DOWN-TOWN *ITALIAN* The food in this longtime local favorite is far better than you would expect for a provincial family restaurant, especially items such as the chicken rustico, sitting on polenta, and the lasagna, made with sausage, thin noodles, and a rich, dusky sauce. The ambience is authentic and intimate, with narrow, segmented dining rooms and constant bustle. 706 2nd Ave. ☎ 907-456-3417. www.nvo. com/gambardellas. Lunch $7–$13; dinner main courses $14–$28. AE, MC, V. Lunch Mon–Sat; dinner daily.

★★★ **Lavelle's Bistro** DOWNTOWN *BISTRO* The large, sleek dining room in the base of the Marriott SpringHill Suites is the first to bring sophisticated urban dining to Fairbanks. In the mode of Alaska's best restaurants, the cuisine is eclectic, with Southwest, Italian, Northwest, Asian, and French influences. Despite the quality, you can dine economically as well as grandly. 575 1st Ave. ☎ 907-450-0555. www. lavellesbistro.com. Entrees $11–$40. AE, DC, DISC, MC, V. Summer lunch Mon–Sat, dinner daily; winter dinner daily.

★ **Pike's Landing Riverside Dining** AIRPORT *STEAK/SEAFOOD* The somewhat dated dining room overlooks the Chena River with tiered levels to assure views for everyone. Menu highlights include the spicy crab-stuffed mushrooms appetizer and the salmon Caesar salad. Portions are large. For a casual meal, choose a burger or sandwich on the deck. 4438 Airport Way. ☎ 907-479-6500. www. pikeslodge.com. Entrees $10–$40. AE, DC, DISC, MC, V. Lunch and dinner daily.

★★ **The Pump House Restaurant & Saloon** WEST SIDE *STEAK/SEAFOOD* A restaurant in a historic, corrugated tin building on the riverside might be expected to be touristy, but the food here is award-winning and locals love the place. The pistachio halibut and seafood chowder are exceptional, or try exotic dishes such as reindeer or elk. You can canoe to the restaurant, and the riverboat *Discovery* (p. 286, ❸) paddles by, too. Mile 1.3, Chena Pump Rd. ☎ 907-479-8452. www.pumphouse. com. Entrees $18–$37. AE, DISC, MC, V. Summer lunch and dinner daily; winter dinner daily, brunch Sun.

★★ **Thai House** DOWNTOWN *THAI* Fairbanks has many authentic Thai restaurants. This one is centrally located, very good, and quite inexpensive. Formally attired servers advise diners on the food and how spicy to order it, and meals come quickly, done to a turn. 412 5th Ave. ☎ 907-452-6123. Entrees $7–$15. MC, V. Lunch and dinner Mon–Sat.

★ **The Turtle Club** FOX *AMERICAN* North of Fairbanks, in a nondescript, windowless building, no one is trying to entertain tourists. Instead, they slap down huge plates of prime rib, king crab, lobster, or prawns (that's the entire menu), and no one worries about loud voices or spilled beer. It's the energizing essence of a burly frontier culture. Mile 10, Old Steese Hwy., Fox. ☎ 907-457-3883. www.alaskanturtle.com. Entrees $20–$32. AE, DISC, MC, V. Dinner daily.

Fairbanks & the Interior Fast Facts

Accommodations Booking Services

The **Fairbanks Association of Bed and Breakfasts** lists about 20 B&Bs on its website at www.ptialaska.net/~fabb. The **Fairbanks Convention and Visitor Bureau** also provides B&B information and up-to-date vacancy data, in person at the Morris Thompson center (p. 316, ❶) or by calling ☎ 907-459-3785.

Dentists & Doctors

If you're in need of emergency dental care, check in at the local hospital or medical center. The only hospital in the region is **Fairbanks Memorial**, at 1650 Cowles St. (☎ 907-452-8181). With a dental emergency, contact the hospital for a referral. The smaller communities have clinics or no medical facilities at all. **Tok Clinic** is on the Tok Cut-Off across from the fire station (☎ 907-883-5855). In Delta Junction, the **Family Medical Center** is at Mile 267.2, Richardson Highway—1½ miles north of the visitor center (☎ 907-895-4879 or 907-895-5100).

Emergencies

Dial ☎ **911**. However, the number may not work on the Dalton Highway or in other rural areas; in that case, if you can find a phone or you have a satellite phone, call the Alaska State Troopers, ☎ **800-811-0911** or **907-451-5100.**

Getting Around

The layout of Fairbanks almost demands you rent a car. Staying in the walkable downtown area will expose you to few of the community's attractions. Buses are infrequent, and taxis are expensive to cover the widespread city. Car rental agencies are at the airport, including Avis, Hertz, Dollar, Budget, Payless, Alamo, and National. The Fairbanks North Star Borough's MACS bus system (☎ 907-459-1011; www.co.fairbanks.ak.us) links the university, downtown, shopping areas, and some hotels. Service is every 30 minutes at best, worse Saturday, and nonexistent Sunday. All buses connect at the transit park downtown, at 5th Avenue and Cushman Street. The

fare is $1.50 for adults; 75¢ for seniors, children, teens, and people with disabilities; free for children 4 and under. For a taxi, call Yellow Cab (☎ 907-455-5555). A cab downtown from the airport is $18 to $20.

Getting There

BY PLANE Alaska Airlines (☎ 800-252-7522; www.alaskaair.com) flies jets to Fairbanks, mostly through Anchorage, but also with some nonstops to Seattle, Barrow, and Prudhoe Bay. Flying to Fairbanks from Anchorage can be the cheapest way to get there, with round trips as low as $260. **BY TRAIN** The Alaska Railroad (☎ 800-544-0552; www. alaskarailroad.com) line ends in Fairbanks, with service from Denali National Park and Anchorage. The high-season one-way Denali fare is $64 and Anchorage is $210; first-class, Gold Star service is $149 and $320, respectively. **BY CAR** The 359-mile Parks Highway comes from Denali National Park and Anchorage, a drive of more than 7 hours. The Richardson and Alaska highways connect Fairbanks to the border, Canada, and the rest of the world.

Internet Access

Access is common in lodgings in populated areas, even in some places that don't have phone service. In Fairbanks, use the Internet and find business services at FedEx Copy Center, 418 3rd St. (☎ 907-456-7348). You can check e-mail for free at the Morris Thompson Cultural and Visitors Center at 101 Dunkel St.

Pharmacy

You will find pharmacies located in large grocery stores. The pharmacy in the Fred Meyer store at 3755 Airport Way (☎ 907-474-1400) is open Mon–Sat 9am–9pm; Sun 11am–5pm.

Police

FAIRBANKS For nonemergency police business within city limits, call the Fairbanks Police Department, ☎ 907-459-6500. **OUTSIDE CITY LIMITS** Call the Alaska State Troopers; near Fairbanks ☎ 907-451-5100; Tok ☎ 907-883-5111; Delta Junction ☎ 907-895-4800.

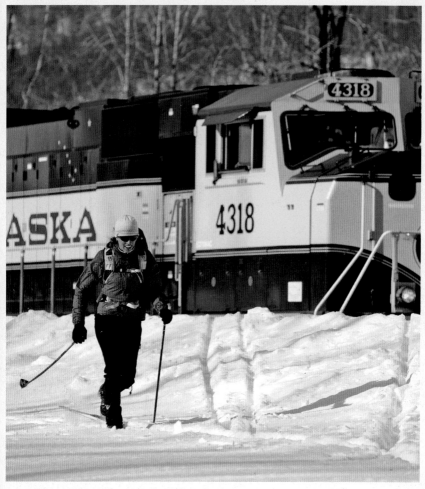

> *A cross-country skier tries to outrun the Alaska Railroad.*

Safety

Before driving Alaska's rural highways, check on construction or other delays, washouts, or warnings by calling ☎ 511 or going to http://511.alaska.gov. In winter, the Interior's rural highways are extremely lightly traveled, most services are closed, and temperatures can drop to levels where vehicles cannot be shut down lest they rapidly freeze. Most visitors should fly or take the train in winter; if you decide to drive, see "Renting the Right Car for Going Off-Pavement" on p. 509 for special preparations.

Visitor Information

FAIRBANKS Fairbanks Convention and Visitors Bureau (☎ 800-327-5774 or 907-456-5774; www.explorefairbanks.com); Alaska Public Lands Information Center (☎ 907-459-3730; www.alaskacenters.gov). **TOK** Tok Chamber of Commerce (☎ 907-883-5775; www.tok alaskainfo.com); Alaska Public Lands Information Center (☎ 907-883-5667; www.alaska centers.gov). **DELTA JUNCTION** Delta Chamber of Commerce (☎ 877-895-5068 or 907-895-5068; summer only 907-895-5069; www. deltachamber.org).

9 Southeast Alaska

My Favorite Southeast Moments

Southeast Alaska is a world of its own. Steep mountains fall straight into the sea on long, narrow fjords. Huge rainforest trees cloak the shores in mossy darkness. At the end of a long boat ride between walls of misty forest islands, you reach a little town of boardwalks and clapboard houses, accessible only by water or air, as are most towns in the region. Here you'll find gentle, small-town life akin to the magical Brigadoon—lost in time, undisturbed by the pressures of corporate America—and surrounding it, wilderness full of bear, deer, and whales, and few signs of people.

> PREVIOUS PAGE *The Stikine River.* THIS PAGE *A floatplane landed at Misty Fjords National Monument.*

1 Landing at Misty Fjords. The cliffs and glaciers of Misty Fjords National Monument unfold outside the window of a floatplane from Ketchikan, overwhelming the mind's ability to take it all in. You start to see it all as some kind of incredible movie. Then, when the plane lands and you get out on a wilderness beach, you appreciate the reality of it—that you are a minute speck amid an entire world of rock, ice, and sea. See p. 398, **11**.

2 Walking on Hammer Slough. The town of Petersburg melds smoothly into ocean waters on long docks and boardwalks, and on Hammer Slough the ocean snakes into the town. Houses have two doors: one that opens on the wooden boardwalk roadway, and the other on the watery roadway of the slough. Which is the front door is unclear. See p. 402, **1**.

❸ Riding the ferry through Peril Strait.
The ferries of the Alaska Marine Highway System are small enough, and their captains experienced enough, to weave through long, narrow channels that other large ships do not attempt. Going through Peril Strait to Sitka is like riding a forest trail on the water, with the trees so close you can sometimes see deer in among them. See p. 370, ❺.

❹ Experiencing the Tracy Arm–Fords Terror Wilderness. South of Juneau, vessels penetrate the steep, glacial mountains through a twisting fjord bounded by immense cliffs, where waterfalls crash from high above. At the head of the fjord, seals lounge on icebergs that float outward after falling from the faces of the glaciers. See p. 381, ⓮.

❺ Whale-watching on Frederick Sound.
Small boats from Petersburg seek humpback and killer whales in the Sound and are rarely disappointed. Some vessels carry underwater microphones so you can hear the whales calling to one another. Often, they're coordinating complex behaviors, such as when humpbacks spin nets of bubbles so as to concentrate schools of herring before lunging through the surface to devour them. See p. 404.

❻ Making friends in Wrangell. All the Southeast's isolated little towns are friendly (when not overrun by cruise ship visitors), but Wrangell is especially so. It seems innocent of the world: free of crime and of large businesses, with earnest folks who love their community and want to show it off to newcomers. I've been befriended on every visit, and even invited home to dinner by brand-new companions. See p. 349, ❺.

❼ Admiring the Sitka National Historical Park totem poles. The context gives special meaning to the totem poles at Sitka. This is where the Tlingit and the invading Russians fought a desperate battle for control of Southeast Alaska in 1804. Poles commemorating the events gaze down solemnly as you walk among the huge trees and hear the waves and the call of the raven. See p. 388, ❷.

❽ Seeing an eagle learn to fly again. The **Alaska Raptor Center** in Sitka nurses injured eagles. When the birds are ready to try out

> *Towering totem poles commemorate the battle between the Russians and the Tlingit here in 1804.*

their wings again, they practice in a flight training center, a huge aviary where visitors can see them at close range from behind one-way glass. See p. 390, ❼.

❾ Riding a train through the White Pass.
A herculean 2-year construction effort completed a narrow-gauge railroad in 1900, rising from the dock in Skagway over the extraordinarily steep and rocky pass to carry gold seekers into Canada. Using some antique cars, and occasionally pulled by steam engines, the trains still run, balancing on the cliffs like mountain goats. See p. 416, ❺.

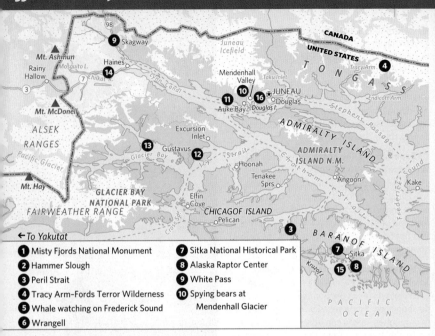

CANADA
UNITED STATES

9 Skagway

Mt. Ashmun
Rainy
Hallow
Mosquito L.
Haines

Mt. McDonell

ALSEK
RANGES

Pacific Glacier

Mt. Hay

GLACIER BAY
NATIONAL PARK
FAIRWEATHER RANGE

← To Yakutat

Juneau
Icefield

Mendenhall
Valley
Taku Inlet

11 **10** **16** ★ JUNEAU
Auke Bay Douglas I.

13 Gustavus **12**
Glacier Bay

Excursion
Inlet

Hoonah
Tenakee
Sprs.

Elfin
Cove
Pelican

CHICAGOF ISLAND

TONGASS

Tracy Arm **4**

Endicott Arm

Stephens Passage

ADMIRALTY ISLAND

ADMIRALTY
ISLAND N.M.

Angoon

Kake

BARANOF ISLAND

3

7 Sitka
15 **8**

Kruzof

PACIFIC
OCEAN

Frederick Sound

1 Misty Fjords National Monument	**7** Sitka National Historical Park
2 Hammer Slough	**8** Alaska Raptor Center
3 Peril Strait	**9** White Pass
4 Tracy Arm–Fords Terror Wilderness	**10** Spying bears at
5 Whale watching on Frederick Sound	Mendenhall Glacier
6 Wrangell	

> *A calving glacier in summer on Glacier Bay.*

10 Spying black bears at Mendenhall Glacier.
A group of mama black bears have decided
the safest place for themselves and their cubs
is among the throngs of tourists who come to
see the glacier in a Juneau suburb. A few steps
from the parking lot, you can watch them from
a boardwalk as they harvest spawning salmon
just yards away, cubs constantly in tow. See
p. 380, **11**.

**11 Feeling peaceful at the Shrine of St.
Thérèse.** North of Juneau, a lovely chapel
of rounded beach stones stands among big,
mossy trees on a little island reached by a
footpath. The chapel takes its sense of peace
and mystery from the natural beauty that
surrounds it. Stepping from the drowsy cool
among the trees, you'll feel the sun as it shines
on Favorite Channel, where whales can sometimes be seen. See p. 344, **8**.

12 Having dinner at Gustavus Inn. After a day
on the water, inn guests gather for sushi and
wine, followed by big platters of fresh sable-
fish or Dungeness crab, vegetables from the
huge garden outside, and the comradeship of
other adventurers. The Lesh family, famous for
their cuisine, creates the best of Alaskan hospitality with their inn's warmth. See p. 409.

13 Sea kayaking in Glacier Bay. Paddling in
misty weather, your group quickly finds itself
alone—until the sound of disturbed water

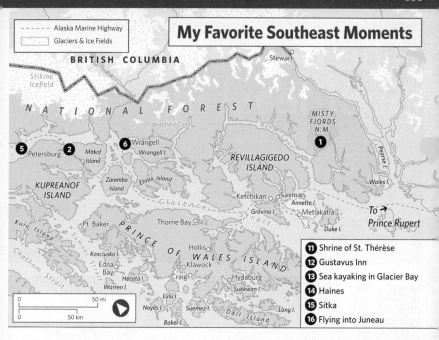

My Favorite Southeast Moments

- - - - - Alaska Marine Highway
. . . . . . Glaciers & Ice Fields

BRITISH COLUMBIA

Stewart

Stikine
Icefield

N A T I O N A L   F O R E S T

Bradfield Canal

MISTY
FJORDS
N.M.

Behm Canal

5 Petersburg **2** Mitkof
Island

6 Wrangell
Wrangell I.

1

REVILLAGIGEDO
ISLAND

Pearse I.

Wales I.

**KUPREANOF
ISLAND**

Zarembo
Island

Etolin Island

Ketchikan   Saxman
Annette I.

Kuiu Island

Pt. Baker

P R I N C E

Thorne Bay

C l a r e n c e

S t r a i t

Gravina I.   Metlakatla

Duke I.

To →
Prince Rupert

Chatham Strait

Kosciusko I.

Sumner Strait

Edna
Bay

Heceta I.

Klawock

Hollis

Craig

O F

W A L E S   I S L A N D

Hydaburg

Sukkwon I.

Warren I.

Lulu I.

0   50 mi

Noyes I.   Suemez I.

Dall Island

Long I.

0   50 km

Baker I.

11 Shrine of St. Thérèse
12 Gustavus Inn
13 Sea kayaking in Glacier Bay
14 Haines
15 Sitka
16 Flying into Juneau

reaches you. Humpback whales are surfacing nearby, breaking the surface with shining, dark skin before raising their flukes to submerge with a wave of the tail. Sitting quietly at water level, you're amazed at the encounter—it is yours alone. See p. 407, **3**.

14 Floating past eagles in Haines. Eagles concentrate on a stretch of the Chilkat River outside of town, where salmon last late into the winter. The giant raptors perch in gnarled cottonwood trees and on snags of driftwood along the broad gravel banks. Riding a raft downstream, you quietly slide by one after another. See p. 353, **14**.

15 Hooking into a salmon near Sitka. The boat ride among the islands of the Inside Passage is hypnotically beautiful, until a big hunk of muscle grabs your trolling line and the fight begins to land a wild, silver-bright salmon. You can have this sort of experience anywhere in the region. See p. 369, **4**.

16 Flying into Juneau. The views of Southeast Alaska from an Alaska Airlines jet can be spectacular as you approach the capital city. Before landing, the plane threads its way down

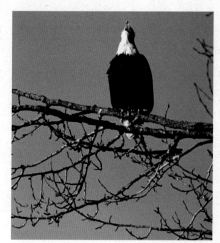

> *A bald eagle perches at the Chilkat Bald Eagle Preserve near Haines.*

Gastineau Channel and makes a sharp turn just above the treetops, before dropping to the seaside airport. The moment can be scary, but the feeling of being carefully inserted into this special world is a perfect start to your visit. See p. 376.

The Best of the Southeast in 3 Days

It's quite difficult to choose a best 3 days for Southeast Alaska, because the region is so full of beautiful and interesting places, and because getting from place to place can be a rewarding but time-consuming part of visiting. You can't drive between towns, because there are no roads. The ferry is inexpensive but slow. Since time is at a premium, it's best to fly from town to town—if you go by small propeller plane, you'll get a flightseeing ride in the bargain. This tour contains both the best in-town historic and cultural sites and some of the most spectacular scenery.

> Walk amongst history and the spruce trees of Sitka National Historical Park's temperate rain forest.

START Sitka, 600 miles southeast of Anchorage. Fly to Sitka via Seattle or Anchorage. TRIP LENGTH 150 miles.

❶ ★★★ **Sitka.** The former capital of Russian America is Alaska's most historic town, among the best in which to encounter Alaska Native culture, and among the state's most attractive communities. The town retains many historic buildings and an old-fashioned, walkable layout of narrow streets. It sits on Sitka Sound, full of whales and little islands, and is surrounded by deep green forest.

A good starting point is the Sitka tribe's community house, called the Sheet'ka Kwaán Naa Kahídi (p. 390, **❻**). It's a Tlingit clan house re-imagined with modern technology: A fire still burns in the middle of the floor, but

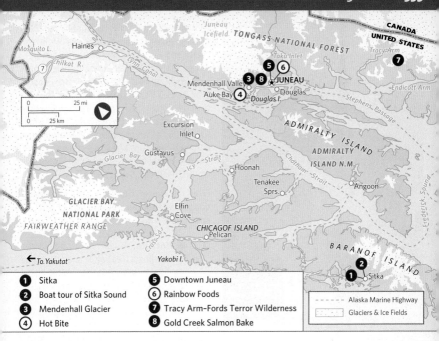

1. Sitka
2. Boat tour of Sitka Sound
3. Mendenhall Glacier
4. Hot Bite
5. Downtown Juneau
6. Rainbow Foods
7. Tracy Arm–Fords Terror Wilderness
8. Gold Creek Salmon Bake

- - - - - Alaska Marine Highway
.... Glaciers & Ice Fields

a modern ventilation system keeps the air clear. Half-hour dance and storytelling performances in this dramatic room are an excellent introduction to the area.

From there, stroll along Sitka's delightful waterfront to the Sitka National Historical Park (p. 388, ❷), which carries the deepest significance of any historical site in Alaska. Here the Tlingit made their stand against the invading Russians in 1804. The indoor part of the park includes an interesting museum, workshops where you can meet Native artisans, and Alaska's best exhibit of historic totem poles. More poles—true masterpieces—are outdoors and along the path to the battlefield.

Wrap up your morning with a visit to the **Alaska Raptor Center** (p. 390, ❼), a rehabilitation facility for injured eagles, hawks, owls, and other birds of prey. ⏱ Half-day.

In the afternoon, take a boat tour of the surrounding waters.

❷ ★★ kids **Boat tour of Sitka Sound.** The waters facing Sitka are rich in seabirds, sea otters, seals, sea lions, and whales. You don't need to go on a long cruise to see wildlife, so it's possible to fit in a tour after the sightseeing I've already described above. For the most part, this is an outing you will need to reserve in advance. ⏱ 3 hr. See "Sitka Sound Tour Options," on p. 389.

On Day 2, take the early-morning Alaska Airlines flight to Juneau (only 40 minutes), where you'll spend the night. Pick up a rental car from the airport, and take the Mendenhall Loop Road 4½ miles to:

❸ ★★★ kids **Mendenhall Glacier.** The glacier is among Alaska's top attractions, for a few reasons: Access is very easy; you can see the glacier right from the Forest Service's parking lot. The visitor center, trails, and campground are first-rate. And in August and September,

Travel Tip

You will not need to rent a car for your time in Sitka. Walking to the attractions mentioned here will cover 2¾ miles. You can shorten that by taking taxis, or rent a bike from **Yellow Jersey Cycle Shop** (p. 388).

> *Lincoln Street in downtown Sitka.*

with zero effort, you can encounter black bears feeding—just walk the boardwalks off the parking lot and you'll see them catching salmon.

Spend the balance of the morning on an awe-inspiring hike. The East Glacier Loop Trail leads 3.5 miles round trip from the visitor center through the forest; take in the view of a waterfall above the glacier (about half a mile from its face), and see parts of an abandoned dam and rail tram. There are steep sections, but it's doable for any fit adult or school-age child. ☉ Half-day. See p. 380, ⓫.

From the glacier, turn right on Mendenhall Loop Road (not the way you came) and continue 5½ miles to the Auke Bay Harbor.

④   🍔 **Hot Bite.** You can hardly be blamed for needing a treat after an early-morning flight and hike. Stop in at this burger shack—a local secret, with charcoal-broiled burgers and halibut and great milk shakes. Prices are a bit high, but the site on the Auke Bay Harbor is worth seeing in its own right. Auke Bay. ☎ 907-790-2483. $.

Cruise Ship Crowding

The Southeast Alaska towns most accessible to cruise ships are overcrowded by their passengers. The industry added ships year after year until the economic downturn caused a leveling off beginning in 2008, but by that time ports such as Ketchikan, Juneau, and Skagway commonly had five ships in port at a time. The arrival of 10,000 or more people every day overwhelms visitor attractions and even streets, as traffic can grind to a halt with wall-to-wall pedestrians. Near the docks, expensive gift shops catering to cruise passengers have pushed out local or authentically Alaskan businesses, leaving seasonal dead zones in certain communities.

Here are some tips to avoid crowding:

• Do downtown or tourist-oriented activities in the late afternoon, evening, or early morning, when many passengers are on the boats.

• Concentrate on activities not designed specifically for the cruise-ship trade. Hikes and historic sites have fewer big groups than aerial trams, zip-lines, or bus tours. Also, many outdoor guides offer different versions of their activities for independent travelers; these are typically longer, more intimate, and less expensive than the cruise passenger offerings.

• Focus on towns without so many ships. Sitka isn't as badly affected, because it has no dock for large ships; they anchor offshore and passengers come ashore in smaller boats, limiting the surge. Haines and Wrangell receive fewer cruise visits, and Gustavus and Petersburg are inaccessible to ships of that size.

• Plan your trip around the heaviest days in the busy ports. There are patterns to when the most ships come through. Since many cruises start and end on weekends, those days are lightest at these ports along the way. You can check individual dates on port schedules posted by Cruise Line Agencies of Alaska at www.claalaska.com.

Leaving the harbor, turn right onto Glacier Highway, which becomes Egan Drive, and drive southeast 12 miles to downtown Juneau. Turn left at Whittier Street, and park at the Alaska State Museum.

5 ★★★ Downtown Juneau. The original part of Juneau was packed into this little pocket in the mountains along Gastineau Channel, because this is where Joe Juneau and Richard Harris found gold in 1880. You could easily while away half a day at many of the places here, but since your time is limited, be judicious in how you choose to spend it.

Begin at the **Alaska State Museum** (p. 374, **1**), which captures the state in microcosm better than any other museum. Especially see the clan house downstairs, the eagle tree within the spiral stairway ramp, and the chronological history exhibit upstairs.

To get to the rest of downtown, which is atop a high cliff, head for the **State Office Building** (Main and 4th streets) and ride the elevator to the main lobby. Take time to check out exhibits from the historical collections of the Alaska State Library, located just off the lobby.

The **capitol building** (p. 376, **2**) is a rather unimpressive brick cube that houses some interesting displays on local history, while nearby **Juneau-Douglas City Museum** (p. 376, **3**) is a delight, with well-made exhibits on mining, town history, and Tlingit culture.

If you have time, you may also want to take a quick peek at the 1912 **Alaska Governor's Mansion** (p. 377). Finally, visit tiny **St. Nicholas Orthodox Church** (p. 378, **6**). You can also take a stroll along **Gold Creek** (p. 377), which runs through Cope Park and was the site of the original gold find that gave rise to the city of Juneau.

Finally, check out some of Juneau's best shopping. Generally, the stores get more tourist-oriented as you go down the hill toward the cruise ship dock. See "Shopping in Juneau," on p. 399, for more details. ⏱ Half-day.

⑥ 🍷 **Rainbow Foods.** This spot is a community meeting place as well as an organic grocery. Stop in for a healthy snack from the bakery or deli. 224 4th Street. ☎ 907-586-6476. $.

> An Alaskan salmon bake is a must.

Spend your third and last day on the water. The boat leaves early from the dock downtown at Marine Park. Make advance reservations.

7 ★★★ Tracy Arm–Fords Terror Wilderness. These fjords south of Juneau are less famous than Glacier Bay or Kenai Fjords and receive far fewer visitors, but the scenery certainly isn't second best, and the getting there is considerably easier. The boat leaves from the downtown waterfront. ⏱ Full day. See p. 381, **14**.

Make advance reservations for the next stop, and a bus will pick you up at your hotel.

8 ★ kids Gold Creek Salmon Bake. For your last evening in Juneau, if the weather's nice, consider this fun (if touristy) activity. Buses running continuously carry guests from the base of the Mt. Roberts Tram on S. Franklin St. to a picnic at Salmon Creek, where fish can be seen spawning (in season) and cooks grill salmon for dinner over a wood fire. Picnic tables sit under an outdoor dome, and a local musician performs. You can try gold panning or roasting marshmallows, and take a short walk to a waterfall. ⏱ 1½ hr. Alaska Travel Adventures. ☎ 800-323-5757 or 907-789-0052. www.bestofalaskatravel.com. $39 for adults, $26 for children 12 and under.

The Best of the Southeast in 8 Days

This plan covers highlights from the south to the north of the Southeast Alaska Panhandle, including totem poles, glaciers, whales, bears, boat rides, airplanes, and cute little isolated towns. The pace is fast, and adding days in each place is a good idea, even if it means you need to drop other stops I've recommended. Since the region lacks roads, you will need to get from town to town by ferry or air. I've included flights where they will save time or hassle, but the ferry is a great part of experiencing the region, so a day is allocated to traveling one of the most spectacular water routes.

> *You'd never think that the quaint Creek Street boardwalk in Ketchikan was once a hotbed of debauchery.*

START Ketchikan. Fly into Ketchikan International Airport from Seattle or Anchorage. **TRIP LENGTH** 188 miles.

1 ★★ **Ketchikan.** The downtown area, when not overrun by cruise-ship passengers, is compact and full of character. Until the demise of the timber industry, this was a muscular logging town. Buildings were fit in willy-nilly, here and there between the waterfront and the mountain cliffs of Revillagigedo Island, in a pragmatic way that somehow could not have had more beautiful results if planned.

A logical starting point is the impressive **Southeast Alaska Discovery Center** (p. 394, ❶), with its smart exhibits that tell the story of Tongass National Forest in natural history and culture. The forest, the largest in the U.S., encompasses all of Southeast Alaska.

Creek Street (p. 394, ❷) is a shop-lined boardwalk that was the town's red-light district until 1952, when prostitution was made illegal. Keep an eye out for the **Married Man's Trail**—once an inconspicuous route to Creek Street—which passes by a small waterfall that salmon try to leap over during runs. The trail is next to the **Soho Coho** at 5 Creek St. (☎ 800-888-4070; www.trollart.com), the lair of Ray Troll, who is known for his prints and paintings—in books and fine art and on T-shirts—full of science humor, often from the perspective of certain fish. Adjacent at the same address is **Alaska Eagle Arts** (☎ 800-308-2787; www.alaskaeaglearts.com), showing graphically powerful contemporary Alaska Native work.

Dolly's House (p. 396, ❸) was the home and workplace of Dolly Arthur, a prostitute who set up shop in 1919 and stayed until her death in 1975. It is a mildly amusing, slightly sad little museum. **Cape Fox Lodge** (p. 399) is reached by a funicular car that climbs 211 feet up the cliff alongside Creek Street. The hotel's cafe has good food and an elegant dining room with wonderful views.

Beyond Creek Street, be sure to visit the fascinating **Deer Mountain Tribal Hatchery and Eagle Center** (p. 397, ❾). Upstream from there on Ketchikan Creek you'll find lovely City Park and the **Totem Heritage Center** (p. 396, ❼). This museum of historic totem poles—up to 160 years old—shows and interprets them in a spiritual and educational setting absent elsewhere in this city of totem poles. ⏱ Half-day.

❷ ★★★ **Bear-viewing flight.** A couple of air taxis in Ketchikan offer flights to see groups of black bears in remote settings. The time of day you take your flight is not important, but you need to reserve well ahead and plan the rest of your visit around this highlight. I recommend it not only for the opportunity to see plenty of bears, but because the scenery from the air on the way is so spectacular. Where you will go and how much you will pay depends on the time of the summer—bears follow fish—and the flight service you choose. ⏱ Half-day. See p. 365, ❿ .

---

③ 🍔 ★ **Burger Queen.** Ketchikan has several great casual eateries on the waterfront, so you might well overlook this one. Don't. The food is remarkable—not only the burgers and shakes, but items like cornmeal-breaded halibut and Asian grilled chicken salad. There's little room to sit, but delivery is free—or dine at the park across the street. 518 Water St. ☎ 907-225-6060. $.

The Southeast Travel Puzzle

Many people think they have to take a cruise to see Southeast Alaska. Why? Because they're used to driving everywhere, and there are no roads connecting these towns to the rest to the world. Even some travel writers seem to dismiss the alternative of traveling as local people do, on the ferry and by short-hop flights. The ferry is treated by some writers as a grubby backpackers' way to get around. Not so. The boats are large and comfortable and are used by everyone here. With some advance planning, you can get your own compartment if you want privacy or will travel overnight. During the day there are lots of places to relax, watch the scenery pass slowly by, and enjoy presentations by forest rangers. Walk-on passengers don't need reservations, so you can travel spontaneously, stopping over in towns along the way without increasing the cost. Bring a bike for extra flexibility. If the schedule works out wrong, and a run would waste time or require you to sleep in a chair, just fly that leg. If you would consider riding a train while visiting Europe, don't rule out riding the ferry on a trip to Alaska.

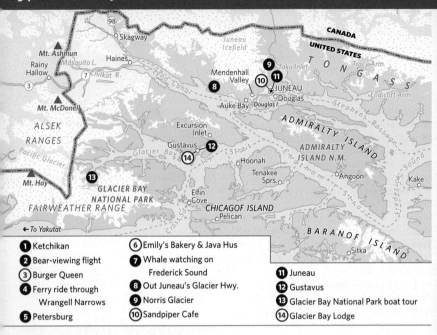

1. Ketchikan
2. Bear-viewing flight
3. Burger Queen
4. Ferry ride through Wrangell Narrows
5. Petersburg
6. Emily's Bakery & Java Hus
7. Whale watching on Frederick Sound
8. Out Juneau's Glacier Hwy.
9. Norris Glacier
10. Sandpiper Cafe
11. Juneau
12. Gustavus
13. Glacier Bay National Park boat tour
14. Glacier Bay Lodge

Day 2 is dedicated to a 148-mile ride on the ferry to Petersburg. Ferries run between the two towns most days of the week, and generally during the day, although some departures are at inconvenient times.

4 ★★ kids Ferry ride through Wrangell Narrows. The ferry ride from Ketchikan to Petersburg includes many stunning vistas, but the slalom up Wrangell Narrows as you approach Petersburg is extraordinary. The passage between Mitkof and Kupreanof islands is almost 25 miles long and so narrow and shallow that no other vessel the size of the 400-foot ferries attempts it. You can see the ship's displacement affect the water on shore. Alaska's ferries are a fun way to travel, with lots of space to move, fantastic views, comfortable seating, and interpretive rangers from the Tongass National Forest onboard. Kids are in their element, exploring the ship and looking over the rail. ⏱ 9 hr., including a 45-min stop in Wrangell. ☎ 800-642-0066. www.ferryalaska.com. $60 adults, $30 children 6–11, free for children 5 and under.

In the evening, you'll arrive in Petersburg, where you'll spend the next 2 nights. A rental car is not necessary, but is useful for exploring the scenic and little-used roads extending beyond the town, on Mitkof Island.

5 ★★ Petersburg. Of Alaska's many small coastal towns, none is more alluring or richer in local character than this healthy little enclave of Norwegian fishing families. Beyond the reach of cruise ships and otherwise off the beaten path, the island community lives according to the rhythms of the sea and the boundless, forested outdoors. Streets meld seamlessly into docks among old clapboard houses and fishing boats.

Explore on foot along the main street, Nordic Drive, and down Sing Lee Alley, which turns from pavement to wooden dock before passing the **Sons of Norway Hall** and the **Fisherman's Memorial Park** (also a dock), with plaques and a statue honoring lost mariners. Stop in at the charming small-town shops along the way, and explore the waterfront—an endless maze of piers and harbor floats—to absorb the energy of the salmon season, as crews fix nets, load boats, and deliver fish, and as hordes of summer workers pack the catch. **Eagle Roost Park** (on Nordic Dr.) is a pleasant place to watch the constant aerial activity of

The Best of the Southeast in 8 Days

> Petersburg is a charming, off-the-beaten track fishing village with strong Norwegian ties.

> Helicopters offer an unparalleled opportunity to get up close and even land on some of the southeast's most breathtaking glaciers.

bald eagles, more common than pigeons, that congregate for cannery waste.

Like everything in Petersburg, **Clausen Memorial Museum** (p. 403, ❷) is for those who live here, and that makes it far more authentic and interesting for visitors. ⏱ 1 day.

From the museum, walk down the hill back to Nordic Drive to:

⑥ 🍞 **Emily's Bakery.** Emily's produces whole-grain pastries and cookies that you'll yearn for once you're gone, as well as wonderful quiche and other memorable lunch items. There's nowhere to sit, but don't let that stop you from paying a visit here. 1000 Nordic Dr. ☎ 907-772-4555. $.

You will need reservations for the whale watching trip you'll take on Day 4. When you make the arrangements, you'll get directions about where to find your boat.

❼ ★★★ **Whale watching on Frederick Sound.** Humpback whales feed all summer in the waters off Petersburg, but their presence reaches its peak in midsummer, when it's common to see them bubble-feeding: spinning webs of bubbles to contain herring, then lunging upward through the surface to gobble them up. The whales sometimes "spy hop" high above boats

to look down into them, and once, in 1995, a whale jumped right into a boat, presumably accidentally (everyone fell in the water, but no one was injured). ⏱ 1 day. See p. 404.

On Day 5, take a late-morning, 45-minute flight to Juneau, where you'll spend the next 2 nights. Once there, rent a car for the afternoon to explore the road north of town; you may want to return the car the same day, as you won't need it for the rest of your stay.

❽ ★★ **Out Juneau's Glacier Highway.** The road that runs 40 miles north of Juneau— essentially, to nowhere—is known locally simply as "out the road." As little practical purpose as the route has, however, it's a wondrous way to explore some of the region's prettiest places on a self-guided outdoor experience. With an afternoon to spend after the flight from Petersburg, I recommend a quick trip out the road. ⏱ Half-day.

SITE GUIDE PAGE 344

After your hike, reverse your drive to return the car at the airport and then take a shuttle or taxi downtown, or keep the car and drive 40 miles downtown. On Day 6, you will not need a car to get to your glacier helicopter flight, as the operator picks up at hotels; get an early start for a full day.

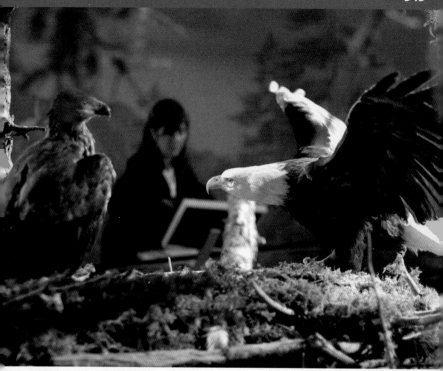

> *A nesting tree diorama at the Alaska State Museum shows both young and mature bald eagles.*

9 ★★★ **Norris Glacier.** This activity is a splurge, but it's an unforgettable experience that should not be missed if you can afford it. Fly with **Era Helicopters** (p. 381, **15**) over the vast Juneau Ice Field, a sea of glacier ice that lies behind the mountains and feeds the many glaciers that descend. You land on Norris Glacier, where the company maintains a camp of sled dogs. ⏱ 20 hr. See p. 381, **15**.

The Era shuttle will drop you at your hotel. The cafe and museum below are downtown, near the waterfront.

10 🍴 **Sandpiper Cafe.** Before the museum, stop in for lunch next door at this immaculate little restaurant done up as if it were at the beach. Although the menu is a little pricy—a burger is $12—the service and comfort food are excellent, and your burger could be game, such as caribou or yak, while your eggs might be duck. 429 Willoughby Ave. ☎ 907-586-3150. $$.

11 ★★★ **Juneau.** The city's best indoor attraction is the **Alaska State Museum** (p. 374, **1**), where the natural history and cultural exhibits offer both "wow" power and an orientation to Alaska's nature and people.

From there you have a choice: You can check out highlights of **downtown Juneau** (p. 374, **1**), which, along with the museum, can easily take the rest of your day. Or you can take a rewarding historic hike into the mountains behind Juneau, on the **Perseverance Trail** (p. 378, **8**). ⏱ Half-day.

On Day 7, take an early-morning Wings of Alaska flight from Juneau to Gustavus, where you'll spend the night. Taking a small plane rather than the afternoon jet service will give you more useful time and better views on the way. The flight takes less than an hour.

12 ★★★ **Gustavus.** This is among Alaska's most relaxing and enjoyable towns to visit, and ideally could extend your stay to a few days. The country inns are set on grassy

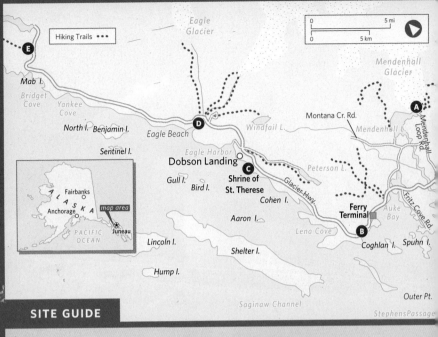

Hiking Trails •••

E

Mab I.

Bridget Cove

Yankee Cove

North I. Benjamin I.

Sentinel I.

Gull I.

Bird I.

Eagle Glacier

Mendenhall Glacier

D

Eagle Beach *Windfall L.*

Eagle Harbor

Dobson Landing

Shrine of St. Therese

C

Cohen I.

Aaron I.

Lena Cove

Peterson L.

Montana Cr. Rd.

Mendenhall

Glacier Hwy.

Ferry Terminal

Auke Bay

B

Coghlan I.

Spuhn I.

Mendenhall Loop Rd.

Fritz Cove Rd.

A

Lincoln I.

Shelter I.

Hump I.

Saginaw Channel

Outer Pt.

StephensPassage

ALASKA

Fairbanks

Anchorage

map area

Juneau

PACIFIC OCEAN

SITE GUIDE

❽ Out Juneau's Glacier Highway

Your first stop is the fascinating ❹ **Mendenhall Glacier** (p. 380, ⑪). Unless you choose to skip other stops on this tour, you won't have time for a hike here, but that's okay. You will have time to check out the ice, the visitor center, and, in season, the bears. Your next stop is the ❸ **Auke Village Recreation Area,** which sits on the north side of Auke Bay. It's a pleasant picnic spot and a good place for beach walks; there is also a good Forest Service **campground** (p. 384) here. Under the big trees, one can easily imagine the pleasant life of the indigenous people who lived here for centuries. Next, head to the ❻ **Shrine of St. Thérèse** (pictured); (☎ 907-780-6112; www.shrineofsainttherese. org), which is dedicated to St. Thérèse of Lisieux, a young 19th-century saint. The shrine is a vaguely Gothic chapel that was built in the

1930s of locally gathered beach stones; it sits on a tiny island among huge rainforest trees, reachable via a footbridge. It's a supremely peaceful spot, with the chapel complementing the spiritual calm: the hush of the mossy forest, the sound of ravens calling, and the sea caressing the rocky shore. Liturgy services are held summer Sundays at 1:30pm. This is also a good spot for tide pooling and seeing whales offshore in Favorite Channel.

The nearby ❹ **Eagle Beach State Recreation Area** is a good place to watch birds as you walk in the tall beach grass or, at low tide, on the flats of white sand. You can wander far. Walking to the left, explore the flats and the forest; to the right, the beach is backed by cliffs of fascinating rocks with ancient pebbles embedded in them. Finally, ❺ **Point Bridget State Park** has an easy and very scenic trail, 3.5 miles round trip, through a meadow of wildflowers and along the beach to the point. It's one of Juneau's best hikes because it is easy and little used, and because it passes through a variety of habitat types before reaching a seaside spot with a lovely beach and wonderful views.

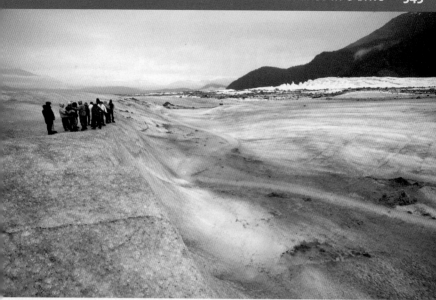

> Mendenhall Glacier is one of 38 large glaciers that extend from the Juneau Ice Field.

meadows, along creeks, or in the woods, offering full-service stays with meals included. Using the bikes provided by the inns, you can head to the sandy beach (where we've watched killer whales romping), go stream fishing, or just explore on your own.

Gustavus is a prime area for charter boat **fishing** and **sea kayaking** if you're of a mind for a more active day. The waters near the town are protected from large waves, so you're less likely to get seasick here while fishing halibut than in some ports. The easiest way to plan a trip to Gustavus is to choose your inn (see my recommendations on p. 408) and then have your host set up your activities, especially for fishing.

The allure of sea kayaking here is that the wilderness is so close at hand— from the first stroke of your paddle, you're into unspoiled waters rich with marine mammals. It's possible to see whales on a kayak trip from the Gustavus dock or even at Bartlett Cove, the threshold to Glacier Bay National Park. Half- or full-day trips that cost $100 to $150 per person are available. **Spirit Walker Expeditions** takes kayakers by boat for surefire whale-watching in Icy Strait for $435 per person. See "Getting Outdoors in Gustavus," on p. 408, for more information on all of these activities. ⊙ 1 day.

Glacier Bay National Park's Bartlett Cove headquarters, where the boat tour leaves, is just down the road from Gustavus, reachable by taxi or by the courtesy vans offered by some inns. You'll spend all of Day 8 onboard a tour boat to the head of Glacier Bay, and be back in time to catch the evening flight to Juneau.

⓭ ★★ Glacier Bay National Park boat tour. Most visitors who aren't on a cruise ship make it to the heart of the park on a tour boat offered by concessionaire **Glacier Bay Lodge & Tours** (p. 406, ❶). Leaving early each morning, the boat navigates to the big glaciers at the head of the bay, usually with plenty of wildlife sightings on the way. Lunch is provided. **Note:** I've found the 8-hour voyage too long for some kids. ⊙ 1 day. See p. 406, ❶.

⓮ 🍺 Glacier Bay Lodge. If you find yourself waiting at the national park headquarters for a ride or a boat, you're in a perfect place to kill time. On a nice day, get your beer and nachos on the deck and watch the whales go by in Bartlett Cove. In rainy weather, order a hot chocolate and sit around the huge stone fireplace in the lobby. See p. 409.

The Southeast with Kids

We have wonderful memories of touring Southeast Alaska by ferry with small children. My older daughter, now 15, learned to stand up on one of these trips, and I remember my older son, now 18, chasing a little girl all over the ferry when he was 4. Small towns are good places for kids, with their human scale, safe streets, and friendly people. The Southeast's towns provide the natural playgrounds of hiking trails and ocean shores, always handy. This tour covers a lot of territory, but you can slow it down and concentrate on fewer towns to reduce the traveling.

> A Great Horned Owl, also called a Tiger Owl, at the Deer Mountain Tribal Hatchery and Eagle Center.

START Ketchikan. Fly into Ketchikan International Airport from Anchorage or Seattle. TRIP LENGTH 7 days, 314 miles.

❶ ★★ Ketchikan. Start your exploration of Ketchikan at the **Southeast Alaska Discovery Center** (p. 394, ❶). The children will enjoy the exhibits, which recreate the forest indoors, among other effects, and here you can learn

a lot about the region as you begin your visit. Stroll down **Creek Street** (p. 394, ❷), an enchanting boardwalk of shops perched above a salmon stream, worth a walk even if you don't mention to the children its seedy past as the former red-light district. Stop in at Ketchikan's excellent **public library,** at the far end of Creek Street. The children's section downstairs is among the best we've visited, partly because

> *Ketchikan has one of the world's largest collections of totem poles, located at several parks and scattered throughout town.*

of the setting—looking out over the waterfall on Ketchikan Creek—and the small **Tongass Historical Museum** (p. 396, ❺) is upstairs. It features changing exhibits focused on the community.

The **Deer Mountain Tribal Hatchery and Eagle Center** should be next on your list. It's a remarkable little facility standing over Ketchikan Creek, scaled for kids. Salmon swim up the creek and into pools, where they are sorted and harvested for eggs to produce the next generation. You can get close to this real-life biology lesson and, at the right time of year, even feed schools of tiny fish. Best of all,

visitors can pass through an enclosure housing a pair of flightless eagles. You are within a few yards and can occasionally see the birds catching salmon from the creek.

City Park (p. 397, ❿), just up the creek from the hatchery, is an enchanting place. The creek breaks into multiple channels as it crosses the park, with pathways weaving among the trees and crossing the water on little bridges. Take time for relaxed play around the water. ⏱ **Half-day.**

② 🍴 **Halibut Hole.** Stop for lunch on the Creek Street boardwalk at the Halibut Hole, with fantastic halibut, salmon, clams, and shrimp fried in batter. 7 Creek St. ☎ 907-225-5162. $.

❸ ★★ **North Tongass Highway.** A two-lane road leads north of town about 18 miles, the farthest away you can drive on the island. It traces Tongass Narrows, and then Clover Pass, a sparkling body of water with many islands.

Ward Lake Recreation Area comes 8 miles out the highway; turn right at Revilla Road and

Travel Tip

The Ketchikan airport is on an island with no bridge, so take a water taxi to your hotel. If you will be camping or staying somewhere other than downtown, you can rent a car at the airport and ride the ferry across to the road. If you will bring a car, come on the ferry from Prince Rupert, B.C., Canada (see "Ferry All the Way," on p. 373).

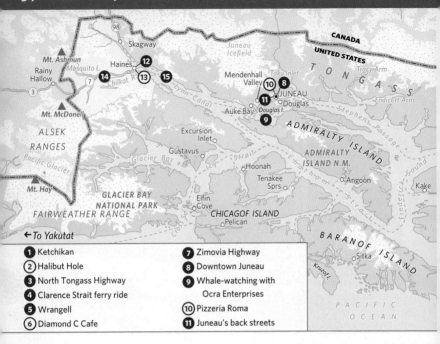

1. Ketchikan
2. Halibut Hole
3. North Tongass Highway
4. Clarence Strait ferry ride
5. Wrangell
6. Diamond C Cafe
7. Zimovia Highway
8. Downtown Juneau
9. Whale-watching with Ocra Enterprises
10. Pizzeria Roma
11. Juneau's back streets

follow the signs. The Forest Service maintains a picnic area and campground here, by the lake and a stream bearing trout and silver salmon. A 1.3-mile trail that circles the lake is perfect for children—it's flat and easy, yet interesting enough to be adventurous, with enormous rainforest trees on the way.

My favorite place to see totem poles in Ketchikan, and definitely the best with kids, is **Totem Bight State Historical Park** (p. 396, **6**), 10 miles out along the highway. Excellent signs and educational material add depth to the experience not found at most similar totem parks.

The end of the road, 18 miles out, reaches **Settlers Cove State Recreation Site.** It's

another pretty spot with easy trails and fun places to play, but here with a sandy beach on the ocean, at Clover Pass, rather than at a lake in the woods. The **Lunch Falls Loop Trail** is a short route through the big trees to an overlook on the pretty falls. The **Lunch Creek Trail** is 3.5 miles one way, following the creek upstream—probably farther than families want to go. ⏲ Half-day.

On Day 2, board the ferry for the 101-mile ride to Wrangell, where you'll spend the next 2 nights. You can arrange to drop off your rental car by parking it at the ferry terminal for the rental agency to pick up later. The boat schedule varies each day, so check departure times.

4 ★ **Clarence Strait ferry ride.** For children, the ferry ride may be the most memorable part of the trip. I know I remember my Alaska ferry rides from a young age, but not much about where we went. The ships are great fun to explore, and the passing views are hypnotic. Each vessel has a restaurant; the food is adequate, although there can be lines. Consider packing a picnic at a deli before boarding, and bring snacks and drinks to keep everyone

Travel Tip

You can rent a car wherever you are for the afternoon, even if you didn't rent one at the airport. **Alaska Car Rental** (☎ 800-662-0007 or 907-225-5000; www.akcarrental.com) offers free pickup, and you can arrange to leave the car anywhere in town when you're done with it.

The Southeast with Kids

- - - - - Alaska Marine Highway
☐ ☐ ☐ ☐ Glaciers & Ice Fields

BRITISH COLUMBIA

Stewart

Stikine Icefield

NATIONAL FOREST

MISTY FJORDS N.M.

Bradfield Canal

5 Wrangell
6
Petersburg Mitkof Island
7 Wrangell I.

REVILLAGIGEDO ISLAND

KUPREANOF ISLAND

Zarembo Island Etolin Island

2
3 Saxman
Ketchikan Annette I.
4 Gravina I. Metlakatla
1 Duke I.

Wales I.

To →
Prince Rupert

Pt. Baker PRINCE OF WALES ISLAND

Thorne Bay

Kuiu Island

Kosciusko I.
Edna Bay
Heceta I. Craig
Warren I. Klawock
Hollis
Hydaburg
Sukkwan I.

Lulu I.
Noyes I. Suemez I. Dall Island Long I.
Baker I.

0   50 mi
0   50 km

- **12** Haines
- **13** Mountain Market & Cafe
- **14** River float through Chilkat Bald Eagle Preserve
- **15** Lynn Canal ferry ride

happy. ⏲ 6 hr. ☎ 800-642-0066; www.
ferryalaska.com. $37 adults, half-price for
children 6–11, free for children 5 and under.

If you arrive early enough, you can get a
jump-start on exploring. Otherwise, plan
to get an early start on Day 3 so that you
can spend the morning checking out what
Wrangell has to offer.

5 ★★ **Wrangell.** Think of yourselves not
as tourists but as anthropologists exploring
a culture from the past. Certainly, few of us
have seen a town like Wrangell outside of old
movies, where folks all know each other and
greet strangers in the street, crime is almost
unknown, and teens heading off to the big city
dream of eating at McDonald's for the first
time. Our kids especially enjoy the freedom
that these isolated little communities create
for them. In fact, you may end up moving here!
You won't need a car while in Wrangell, but
you may want to rent bikes, and you can do
so at **Klondike Bike** (☎ 907-874-2453; www.
klondikebike.com) for $35 a day.

The **Nolan Center Museum,** at 296
Campbell Dr. (☎ 907-874-3770), is your best

Spending the Night in Wrangell

You have a few places to pick from, but I
recommend the waterfront **Stikine Inn,**
which is easy walking distance from the
ferry terminal. It's the town's main hotel:
comfortable and convenient, if not grand.
The on-site restaurant is clean and bright
and does simple food well. 107 Stikine Ave.
☎ 888-874-3388 or 907-874-3388. www.
stikineinn.com. 35 units. Doubles or quads
$114–$140. AE, DC, DISC, MC, V.

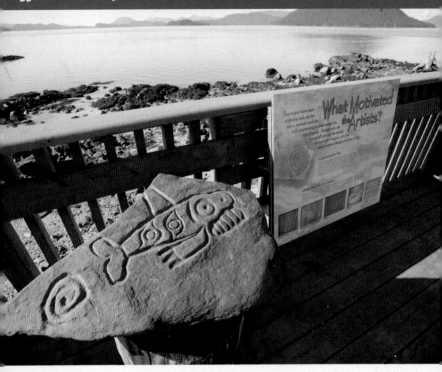

> *Make up your own story to go with the mysterious rock carvings known as petroglyphs on a beach north of Wrangell.*

starting point. Wrangell is among Alaska's oldest and most historic towns, and the museum contains some remarkably vivid treasures from the past, including the house posts from the Tlingit clan house that once stood in Wrangell. Kids—and anyone else—will be impressed about the story behind a huge gash in one of these exquisitely carved poles: When a guest admired one of the images, the chief chopped it off and handed it to him as a gift. All family members should also enjoy the exhibits on the area's natural history.

The museum is also the town visitor center, and the shop has an exceptional selection of books and Native crafts for bargain prices. It is open Monday through Saturday from 10am to 5pm in the summer, and Tuesday through Saturday from 1pm to 5pm in the winter. Admission is $5 for adults, $3 for seniors, $2 for children 6 to 12, and free for children 5 and under.

Any kid who isn't entranced by **Chief Shakes Island** needs an imagination transplant. A wooden bridge leads to the tiny island in the middle of the harbor (look for the otter that lives underneath), where a collection of totem poles and a Tlingit clan house stand. The original Chief Shakes conquered the region and made slaves of his enemies, handing down power through the mother's line for seven generations. When word of President Lincoln's Emancipation Proclamation finally got here, the family was relieved of some of its power. Descendents of Chief Shakes VII take care of the island and clan house, which is a scaled-down replica built in 1940, and will show you around if you make

Travel Tip

If you'd rather skip a formal lunch, consider picking up a picnic for your afternoon ride (see below). You can have one packed (and pick up ice cream cones while you're at it) at **Bob's IGA,** near the Nolan Center at 223 Brueger St. (☎ 907-874-2341).

advance arrangements; call Tish Peterman (☎ 907-874-3097; www.shakesisland.com). The cost is $5 per person, or $25 total if she has to make a special trip.

Petroglyph Beach State Historic Site on Grave Street, 1 mile north of the ferry dock (unstaffed; no phone), is exciting for its mystery and informality. No one knows what the rock pictures mean or exactly who made them, and finding them is like an Easter egg hunt, as they lie exposed on the beach in no particular order. The images are recognizable and quite distinct despite their age. The petroglyphs on the deck above the beach are replicas created so visitors can take rubbings, since people were damaging the originals. Don't go at high tide. ⏲ Half-day.

⑥ 🍴 **Diamond C Cafe.** Every small town needs one great diner, and this is Wrangell's. The menu is long, with familiar food done right for reasonable prices and some standouts, like grilled halibut. The dining room is clean and bright. **215 Front St.** ☎ 907-874-3677. $.

⑦ ★★ **Zimovia Highway.** Dedicate the afternoon to a bike ride south on the Zimovia Highway, the only route out of town, and to a fun hike. You can also explore the highway by car; rent from **Practical Rent A Car** at the Wrangell Airport (☎ 907-874-3975). From Front Street, go a block uphill to Church Street, turn right, and continue to the highway. The first stop is in less than a mile, at **City Park,** with a nice picnic area surrounded by big trees. This beach is good for tide pooling when the water is low. From there to **Shoemaker Bay Recreation Area,** about 5 miles out of town, you can follow a flat, paved bike trail of which the town is justifiably proud. It traces the beach the whole way and is entirely separated from traffic. Shoemaker Bay has another picnic ground, as well as the trailhead for the **Rainbow Falls Trail,** which climbs 500 feet over less than a mile, with many stairs; at its end, a waterfall seems to tumble through the branches of huge Sitka spruce and western hemlock trees. If you still have some remaining energy, Institute Creek Trail continues steeply, 2.75 miles more up the mountain. ⏲ Half-day.

On Day 4, depart for Juneau, where you will stay 2 nights. Alaska Airlines has one flight a day; at this writing, it leaves at 11am and takes under 2 hours, including a stop in Petersburg. If you'd rather save money than time, you can take the ferry. It takes 12 hours direct or 21 hours via Sitka (quicker if you can get a fast ferry). For convenience, it's easiest to rent a car at the Juneau airport, although you won't be using it much. In the afternoon, explore downtown.

⑧ ★★ **Downtown Juneau.** The **Mount Roberts Tramway** (p. 377, ④) is expensive and touristy, but in decent weather it will be a memorable and active outing to start a visit to Juneau with kids. The views are great, but the real benefit is to get to that invigorating alpine environment without an all-day climb that many kids couldn't manage.

The **Alaska State Museum** (p. 374, ①) has many great features for kids, including the clan house downstairs and the natural history exhibit, with an eagle in a tree circled by a spiral ramp to the second floor. The children's area on the second floor is outstanding, with a square-rigged ship to play in. ⏲ Minimum 2 hr.

On Day 5, plan to spend half the day on the water—make your reservations in advance, and Orca Enterprises will pick you up at your hotel.

⑨ ★★★ **Whale-watching with Orca Enterprises.** Humpback whales reliably feed in the summer near Juneau, and the competition of many small boats taking visitors to see them creates relatively reasonable prices within the

---

Wrangell on a Rainy Day

It rains a lot here, but just put on a raincoat and try not to let it spoil your fun. Still, should the weather be too much to take, consider taking the kids to the town's indoor pool and gym. Children love the giant inflatable dinosaur in the pool during open swim, and there's a good chance of making friends with other families. The **Wrangell Municipal Pool** (☎ 907-874-2444) is at 321 Church St., next to the high school, and is open Monday to Friday from 6:30am to 8pm, and Saturday from noon to 4pm. Admission is $2.50 per person.

> *Orcas, more commonly known as killer whales, feed and play in the quiet waters of Stephens Passage.*

reach of families. Besides humpbacks, you have a chance of seeing killer whales, Steller sea lions, harbor seals, and the thrilling Dall's porpoise, which looks like a killer whale but swims like a torpedo. A note to parents: Most children will lose interest in watching wildlife before you do, so bring something to keep them occupied. Orca Enterprises has four large vessels and will pick you up at your hotel. ⏱ Half-day. ☎ 800-733-6722 or 907-789-6801; www.alaskawhalewatching.com. $114 adults, $84 children 5–12, $54 children 4 and under.

⑩ 🍴 **Pizzeria Roma.** This is a casual, noisy place on the waterfront, with no need for good behavior. Besides that, the pizza and calzones are quite good. **2 Marine Way.** ☎ 907-463-5020. $.

In the afternoon, wander Juneau's back streets.

⑪ ★★ **Juneau's back streets.** This is one of my favorite family strolls, and it will keep both adults and young ones happily engaged for most of the afternoon. ⏱ Half-day. See "A Back-Streets Walk," on p. 377.

Early on Day 6, catch the Wings of Alaska flight to Haines on a small, prop-driven plane that will thrill most kids. It's an inexpensive way to see the region from the air—far better than viewing it from a jet. However, you can save money (but lose time) by taking the ferry, a 77-mile ride that takes 5 hours. You will spend 1 night in Haines.

⑫ ★★ **Haines.** This is another great town for kids. It's low-key and quirky, with lots of odd aspects, such as an old army fort with a Tlingit clan house in the middle and a museum dedicated to hammers. You should do some casual exploration.

The main feature is **Fort William Seward** (p. 410, ①), which mostly retains the look of a century ago, with big white buildings surrounding parade grounds. Among the good stops is the totem-pole carving studio at the **Alaska Indian Arts cultural center** (see p. 410, ①) in the old fort hospital on the south side of the parade grounds.

Two museums in Haines will particularly interest children. One is the **Hammer Museum** (p. 411, ④), a house containing more than 1,800 different kinds of hammers. Who knew?

The other is the **American Bald Eagle Foundation Natural History Museum** (p. 411, ④), with an enormous walk-through diorama of 180 eagles and other mounted wildlife. A facility holding three live eagles opened in 2010, too. ⏱ Half-day.

---

⑬ 🍴 **Mountain Market & Cafe.** This is a natural foods store and community center where they make hearty sandwiches, wraps, and soups for lunch. Prices are reasonable, and they can pack it all up for you to take out for a picnic in the myriad great spots for one around town. **3rd Ave. and Haines Hwy.** ☎ 907-766-3340. $.

In the afternoon, you'll be picked up at your hotel for a river trip. Note that if you're

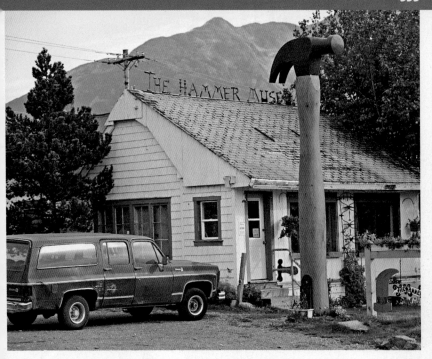

> *Hammers, hammers everywhere: There are 1,800 kinds at the Hammer Museum in Haines.*

traveling with children ages 6 and under, you'll need to skip this stop.

⓮ ★★ **River float through Chilkat Bald Eagle Preserve.** The largest concentration of eagles comes in the late fall, but there are plenty along the shores of the Chilkat River in the summer, too. The opportunity to see them on a float trip through the preserve feels right—quiet and nondisruptive. The rafting is not at all wild and is appropriate for children 7 and older. **Chilkat Guides** makes it fun, and scanning for eagles adds to the interest. Buses pick up clients. ☉ Half-day. Mile 1, Haines Hwy. ☎ 888-292-7789 or 907-766-2491. www.raftalaska.com. $89 adults, $62 children 7–12. Children 6 and under are not allowed.

On Day 7, board a ferry for the 4½-hour return trip to Juneau, where you can catch a flight home. En route, you'll experience one last bit of wonder.

⓯ ★★ **Lynn Canal ferry ride.** You'll spend most of the voyage to Juneau on the 90-mile-long Lynn Canal fjord, one of the most impressive runs on the ferry system. The mountains tower above you, amazingly steep. Way up near the top, almost a mile above, you can see the marks where ice reached during the most recent ice age. Below, the rock is smooth; above, sharp. ☉ 4½ hr. See p. 359, ❹.

Afternoon Alternative

If your kids are restless, consider skipping the previous stop and getting out of town on the Old Glacier Highway. For more information, see the minitour "Out Juneau's Glacier Highway," on p. 342, ❽.

Travel Tip

You don't need a car to get around Haines, but bikes will help. Rent from **Sockeye Cycle Co.,** on Portage Street in the Fort William Seward area (☎ 907-766-2869; www.cyclealaska.com). Bikes rent for $14 for 2 hours or $35 for 8 hours.

TOWERING TOTEMS

Alaska's ancient and
inspiring art form

BY MIKE DUNHAM

TOTEM POLES ARE ONE OF ALASKA'S LOVELIEST INDIGENOUS ART FORMS, and they serve many purposes. Because they can be seen at a distance, they helped guide travelers to villages, while their imagery identified the clans who lived there. For example, the Tlingit tribe is divided into two primary groups, designated as Raven and Eagle, while subdivisions are further indicated by Bear, Wolf, Killer Whale, and other animals. Human figures typically depict specific people, and poles were also used as memorials, grave markers, and even to ridicule those who owed debts. In the 19th century, government agents suppressed Native customs, and fewer poles were built. But in the 1890s, when the city of Seattle used a stolen totem to advertise itself as the gateway to Alaska's gold fields, interest in poles was reborn. Tourists wanted to see them, museums acquired them, and selling miniature poles became a cottage industry. In the 1930s, the federal government hired carvers to replicate historic poles and create new ones.

Getting a Good Look

Totems orginated in a narrow band of coastal rain forest in British Columbia and Southeast Alaska, where large spruce and cedar trees flourish. Not surprisingly, the greatest number of well-made poles can still be seen there. Here are a few of the state's best spots.

KETCHIKAN

In Ketchikan, you'll find totems all over town, but the best place to learn about what you're seeing is at the Totem Heritage Center (p. 396, ❼). Here, ancient poles are preserved and displayed, while modern carvers work in an adjacent shed. The nearby village of Saxman (p. 396, ❽), to the south, is home to many famous poles, and just to the north, Totem Bight State Park (p. 396, ❻) has reproductions of 14 historic poles.

SITKA

This town is well-known for its totems, and Sitka National Historical Park (p. 388, ❷) is home to 15 famous poles, including the Abraham Lincoln Pole, honoring—or perhaps ridiculing, depending on your perspective—the Great Emancipator, and the K'alyaan pole celebrating the Tlingit chief who fought the Russians and safely evacuated his tribe during a siege.

WRANGELL & HAINES

These two towns (p.349, ❺, and p. 410) are also traditional centers of totem making. They're both excellent places to see the poles.

The Art of Making a Totem Pole

The past 50 years has brought a revival of totem-making among Native artists and others, with fine poles now found in places where they were not traditionally raised, including Anchorage, Fairbanks, and Juneau. Before work can begin, a master carver creates a design to express a patron's intent, often honoring an individual or historic event. Then an appropriately sized tree, usually spruce or cedar, is harvested and stripped of its bark and the design is drawn onto the log. A team of carvers gets to work, usually using hand adz (an ax-like tool used to shape wood), chisels, or, on occasion, chainsaws. Once the carving is complete, the pole is painted, and traditional colors include black, blue, yellow, and red.

When a pole is ready, a *potlatch*, or raising ceremony, is held. These are day-long affairs, complete with traditional drumming, dancing, and speeches. Ropes and levers are used to tilt the pole into an awaiting hole and hold it in place until the hole can be filled. Afterward, a feast is shared and gifts are handed out to visitors.

Totem Trivia

> It's a common misconception that totems were worshipped—they weren't. They were intended to designate territory and convey information about history, a community, or prominent people.

> Totems are primarily a visual art form, but they can't be read like a book. Their meaning can only be understood by hearing the story or message from someone familiar with it.

> Many visitors to Alaska expect the top figure on a totem to have large wings. But totems in movies, television, or ads are often more garish than authentic poles. The wide wings on "Hollywood" poles are exaggerations of the more modest, often folded, wings on genuine Alaska pieces.

The Southeast's History & Culture

The historic sites of Southeast Alaska represent an alternate flow of events that is oddly unfamiliar to most of us who've been steeped in the mainstream American story. This is a place where the frontiersmen and conquistadors came from the west, speaking Russian; where the Natives were never finally defeated or forced from their land; and where an appreciable non-Native population arrived only with the dawn of the 20th century, and then with dreams of quick riches rather than settlement. In Southeast Alaska, the conservation movement arrived before the pioneers did, and so nearly the entire region is public land. If this different tale interests you, it's easy to see where it happened in towns largely preserved from their early years. I've set the tour up generally to march chronologically through history.

> Young and old alike participate in a performance at the Sitka tribe's community house, Sheet'ka Kwaán Naa Kahídi.

START Sitka. Fly in via Anchorage or Seattle.
TRIP LENGTH 7 days, 275 miles.

❶ ★★★ **Sitka.** Alaska's most historic community, with by far its best historic sites, Sitka is a place to immerse yourself in a dramatic and little-known story: the Russians' conquest of Alaska and the ambiguous results of their conflict.

It makes sense to begin with the Alaska Native perspective, as they were here first.

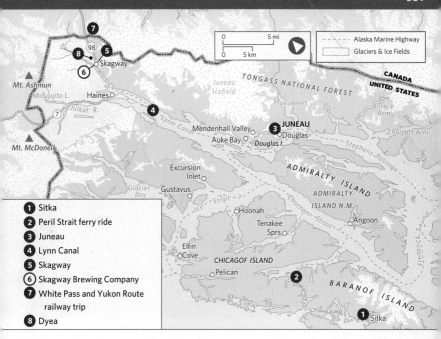

1 Sitka
2 Peril Strait ferry ride
3 Juneau
4 Lynn Canal
5 Skagway
6 Skagway Brewing Company
7 White Pass and Yukon Route railway trip
8 Dyea

The Sitka tribe's community house, **Sheet'ka Kwaán Naa Kahídi** (p. 390, 6), is also a good place to be reminded who ultimately won the war: Alaska Natives own 44 million acres of the state and control its largest corporations.

On Day 2, head 7½ miles out of town to the ★ **Old Sitka State Historic Site** (p. 386, 1), where Alexander Baranof, an agent for Russian businessmen, built a fort in 1799 after making himself the de facto ruler of Russian America. The Tlingit fought back and in 1802 overran the fort. As Baranof readied for a massive counterattack, the Tlingit dug in at the ★★★ **Sitka National Historic Park** (p. 388, 2). The National Park Service does a magnificent job of interpreting the site, which was the scene of a decisive battle.

Spend the rest of your afternoon exploring, beginning at the octagonal ★★ **Sheldon Jackson Museum** (p. 389, 4) which contains an extraordinary collection of Alaska Native artistic and historic objects, expertly presented.

As you near the far end of the boat harbor, you'll see the 1843 ★★ **Russian Bishop's House** (p. 389, 3), the best building surviving from Russian America. It's a fascinating window into

that distant and unfamiliar time, especially the upstairs tour, which shows off period furnishings and some original religious relics of Bishop Innocent Veniaminov, now a saint, who humanized the Russians' rule in Alaska.

Another two blocks will bring you to ★★ **St. Michael's Cathedral** (p. 389, 5), the church Veniaminov built. It was the first Russian Orthodox cathedral in the New World—the existing building precisely recreates the 1848 structure, which burned in 1966, though the icons and some furnishings are original.

Getting There & Around

As the flight schedule has stood for several years, you can fly into Sitka no earlier than midday. Flights going up and down the coast originate in Seattle or Anchorage, with a stop before Sitka in Juneau (from the north) or Ketchikan (from the south). Rent a car at the airport, unless you drop the **Old Sitka State Historic Site** (p. 386, 1) from your tour; then you won't need one and can get around on foot, bike, or taxi.

> *Perseverance Trail is a lovely half-day, 3-mile hike up to the mines that made Juneau.*

Castle Hill (p. 390, **8**), formally known as Baranof Castle Hill State Historic Site, has steep sides and a flat, oval top, perfect for defense, which was its purpose under Tlingit, Russian, and American control. In 1867 on this site, the Russians handed over to U.S. soldiers their title to Alaska. ⏱ **2 days.**

On Day 3, return the car to the airport and get a cab to the ferry dock for the trip to Juneau. If no taxis are waiting, you can call **Hank's Cab** (☎ **907-747-8888;** www.hankstours.com); if you ask, Hank will sing for you (he is a talented blues musician). The

10-mile ride from airport to ferry terminal takes less than 30 minutes.

2 ★★★ **Peril Strait ferry ride.** The trip takes 9 hours on a conventional ferry, about half that on the fast catamaran *Fairweather*. Both are part of the **Alaska Marine Highway System** (p. 373). The 150-mile passage involves a series of extraordinarily narrow passages, the most famous of which is Peril Strait; for a good deal of the long ride, the shore seems to pass by the ship just barely out of reach. Before aviation, steamers were the only form of public transportation around Alaska, and the challenges of navigating waters like these led to several catastrophic shipwrecks. ⏱ **1 day. See p. 370, 5.**

In Juneau, where you'll spend the next 2 nights, you can again get by without a car, but having one will make it easier to reach certain historic sites. To rent a car, take a cab from the ferry dock to the airport.

3 ★★★ **Juneau.** To continue Alaska's story where we left off in Sitka, visit the history exhibit on the second floor of ★★ **Alaska State Museum** (p. 374, **1**). It carries on the tale chronologically, using key artifacts, such as the desk where Secretary of State William

A Taste of History

Backdoor Cafe. For a quick, simple lunch, this coffee shop popular with the artistic crowd fits the bill, with daily specials, bagels, and the like. It's across the parade ground from the community house. Indulge your interest in history, as the cafe is located in the back of a great browser's hunting ground, Old Harbor Books. 104 Barracks St. (bookstore portion faces Lincoln St.) ☎ 907-747-8856. $.

Seward completed the treaty that bought the territory for 2¢ an acre. Even at that price, the Alaska purchase remained something of a joke for more than a decade—Americans thought it was a frozen waste. A photograph a bit farther on was taken to counter that impression: It shows miners from Juneau with a pile of newly mined gold worth more than the U.S. had paid for all of Alaska.

After the museum, stop for a snack at the **Silverbow Inn** (p. 384), Alaska's oldest continuously operating bakery, which has been in business in the same building since 1898. Then head to the ★★ **Juneau-Douglas City Museum** (p. 376, ➌), a small spot that helps put the town's history, including the amazing Treadwell mining town (see p. 379), in context. Make sure to get a copy of the walking tour map of the Treadwell Mine Historic Trail, which will be your final stop.

But before you get there, pay a visit to the ★★ **Perseverance Trail** and **Silverbow Basin** (p. 378, ➑). In 1880 Joe Juneau and Richard Harris found gold in the Silverbow Basin, a 3-mile, one-way walk up a well-maintained, gradually rising trail from the end of Basin Road, following Gold Creek between Mount Juneau and Mount Harris. A mining town was up there for 40 years a century ago.

In the chronology of this history tour, the ★ **Last Chance Mining Museum** (p. 378, ➐) comes after your walk to the gold discovery site (below), since the museum is itself a building from the mine's peak years, with massive iron equipment and other relics of heavy industry. The live-in staff know everything there is to know about Juneau history.

Wrap up your day with a visit to the ★★ **Treadwell Mine Historic Trail** (p. 379, ➒) where carpenter John Treadwell built the largest gold mine in the world. ⏰ 1 day.

On Day 5, board the ferry for the 7-hour ride up the Lynn Canal fjord to Skagway, where you'll spend the next 2 nights.

Spending the Night in Juneau.

A stay at **Alaska's Capital Inn** would enhance the historic theme of the trip; it's a restored mansion from gold-mining days. See p. 383 for more details.

➍ ★★ **Lynn Canal.** The ferry works its way up the Lynn Canal fjord, some 90 miles long in total, below the walls of mountains nearly a mile high. Taking the boat is the best way to get an idea of how the gold-rush greenhorns must have felt as they rode steamers from Seattle, San Francisco, and even as far away as Australia; they were headed to Skagway and Dyea, new camps at the foot of trails over these mountains, and on a 400-mile wilderness journey to Dawson City, Yukon—a journey few were qualified to attempt. The 1898 gold rush is Alaska biggest historic moment and its biggest producer of stories of heroism, fraud, and futility. See "Gold!," on p. 454, for more information. ⏰ 7 hr. $50 adults, $25 children 6–11, free for children 5 and under.

Gold & Conservation

The discovery of gold in 1880 brought people and industry to Juneau, but not much changed beyond this small coastal area. The big gold rush that populated Alaska happened in 1898, as you'll see when you visit Skagway. As those gold rushers spread across the territory and development began, President Theodore Roosevelt came into office in 1901 with his conservation agenda, and put limits on what they could do. Among other actions, he created Tongass National Forest in 1907; it is still by far the nation's largest, at 17 million acres encompassing essentially all of Southeast Alaska. The preeminent Alaska politician at the time was Judge James Wickersham, a great outdoorsman, who arrived in 1900 to help bring order to the corruption and fraud that plagued the gold-rush years. When Wickersham entered Congress as a nonvoting delegate, he took up Alaskans' cries against Roosevelt's conservation measures, with limited practical success, but helping set a pattern of bashing the federal government that remains a staple of Alaska politics today. You can see Wickersham's retirement home and personal effects at the **Wickersham House State Historic Site** in Juneau (p. 378, ➎).

> *Statue of a Tlingit guide and Stampeder at the Klondike Gold Rush historical park.*

> *The old White Pass and Yukon Route railway still operates.*

You won't need a rental car in Skagway; the town is compact and easy to get around on foot, and shuttles or buses can carry you to outlying attractions. On Day 6, get an early start so you can explore the town.

5 ★ **Skagway.** Locals recognized the tourism opportunity presented by Skagway's Wild West story within a few years of its heyday. Almost as soon as the gold rush ended, promoters began restoring and enhancing the buildings along Broadway with that image in mind. Unfortunately, the cruise industry's concentration on the town has spoiled it in the last 2 decades, with some of the most interesting historic businesses converted to gift shops. Enjoy your visit with the knowledge that tourism has a long history here, too, and try to get out of the overcrowded center of town.

Start at the **Klondike Gold Rush National Historical Park Visitor Center** (p. 414, **1**), which has an interesting museum. Check in there to get free tickets for the ranger-led walking tour, which is the best way to see the historic sites downtown. An excellent map is available for a self-guided tour, too. By using a guide, or at least the map, you get the stories behind the buildings, which otherwise aren't so interesting. The walking tour ends at its best stop, the **Moore House** (p. 415, **2**), home of Captain William Moore, who predicted gold would be struck in Yukon and founded Skagway, only to have his land stolen by the stampeding gold seekers.

Finally, be sure to stop in at the **Skagway Museum and Archives** (p. 415, **3**), where the collection includes the best of the town's gold-rush memorabilia. ⏲ 1 hr.

From the museum, go one block northwest to:

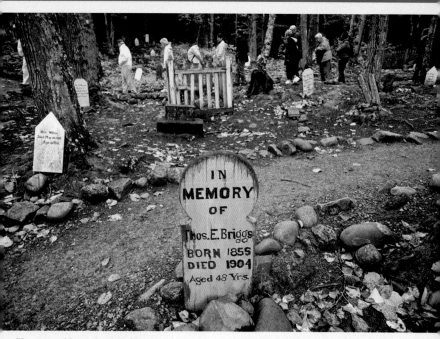

> The graves of Soapy Smith and Frank Reid, casualties of a shoot out, are big attractions at the Gold Rush Cemetery, in Skagway.

⑥ 🍺 **Skagway Brewing Company.** While the brewpub isn't historic, the experience of quaffing a local brew in the middle of the day is certainly fitting with the spirit of the gold rush. The constant partying of those days helped make Skagway so wild and dangerous (but surely you will keep things well in hand). The menu includes lots of sandwiches, soups, and appetizers. 7th Ave. and Broadway. ☎ 907-983-2739. $$.

❼ ★★ **White Pass and Yukon Route railway trip.** The narrow-gauge railroad that conquered the pass above Skagway to carry gold-rush travelers still operates summer excursion trains, some of them using historic equipment. Catching a ride is a real treat. ⏱ Half-day. See p. 416, ❺.

Travel Tip

Most Alaska towns quiet down in the wintertime, but Skagway nearly empties. Next to nothing is open off-season, and visits then are not recommended.

On Day 7, take a morning bike ride to Dyea. Ride 2 miles out of Skagway on Klondike Highway 2 and turn left on unpaved Dyea Road, following it for 8 miles; the ride takes less than an hour each way.

❽ ★★ **Dyea.** Skagway's sister ghost town is at the trailhead of the famous Chilkoot Pass. Rangers lead interesting walks here, explaining the area's history in great detail. Along the way, you'll visit an abandoned cemetery, Slide Cemetery (p. 416, ❻) that hauntingly captures the hopelessness most gold rushers faced. ⏱ Half-day. See p. 416, ❻.

Travel Tip

The trip to Dyea is best made by bicycle. Rent bikes at **Sockeye Cycle Co.,** on 5th Avenue off Broadway (☎ 907-983-2851; www.cyclealaska.com). Good mountain bikes rent for $14 for 2 hours. If you prefer transportation that's less strenuous, see "Getting Around Skagway," on p. 415.

The Southeast's Best Wildlife & Scenery

There is a sumptuous richness to the coastal rainforest on the grand, steep mountains of the Inside Passage. At times it seems everything really is alive, as Native cultural traditions maintain. You're never far from giant glaciers, towering cliffs, salmon-eating bear, and thick gatherings of birds. But hitting all the highlights is expensive. The few roads are short, and trails barely scratch the surface of the area around each town, so most visitors need the help of an expensive guide with a small plane or boat. The very best spots, such as the top bear-viewing areas, are rationed with permits, a system that drives prices up even more. In this plan, I've assumed you're ready to spend for the ultimate wildlife and scenery; to economize, mix and match the ideas here with other tours in this chapter.

> *Deer Mountain Trail, behind downtown Ketchikan, is a steep but rewarding climb up through large, mossy evergreens to great views.*

START Ketchikan. Fly into Ketchikan International Airport from Seattle or Anchorage. **TRIP LENGTH** 7 days, 90 miles.

❶ ★ Ketchikan. The **Southeast Alaska Discovery Center** (p. 394, ❶) makes the perfect first stop for your trip, as it offers a wide

> *Some of the world's foremost totem pole carvers work at Saxman Native Village Park.*

and detailed look at the region's wildlife and scenery.

One of the most scenic spots in Ketchikan is close at hand, but requires a strenuous upward hike on the mountain directly behind the town. If you're up for it, you're in for some of the region's most spectacular scenery on the **Deer Mountain Trail** (p. 397, **9**). But you don't have to do the entire hike; you can turn back when energy runs low, because the rewards start early. The first mile rises 1,000 feet to a sweeping ocean view, south of Tongass Narrows; the next mile rises another 1,000 feet to a fantastic view of Ketchikan; and a third mile goes up a final 1,000 feet to the alpine summit. ☺ Half-day.

Returning from the hike, turn right off Deermount Street on Stedman Street to the cafe on the right.

② 🍵 **Diaz Cafe.** Ketchikan's vibrant Filipino community revolves around this bright, friendly center of authentic food, which remains unchanged in some 60 years of operation. Ask for the "large guy," and a hearty, delicious bowl of sweet-and-sour rice and meat will appear before you instantaneously, for the price of $5.25. They don't take credit cards. 335 Stedman St. ☎ 907-225-2257. $–$$.

Drive south on Stedman, which becomes South Tongass Highway, 2½ miles to Saxman.

③ ★★ **Saxman Native Village Totem Pole Park.** Although this is a scenery and wildlife tour, no visitor to Ketchikan should skip the totem poles entirely. ☺ 1 hr. See p. 396, **8**.

Continue southward on the South Tongass Highway, pausing to enjoy the many ocean views along the way. Herring Cove is 2½ miles beyond Saxman.

④ ★ **Herring Cove.** A fish hatchery on the creek here attracts black bear, which you can often see from the safety of the highway bridge. In addition, a local business has developed bear viewing here into a full tourist experience called the **Alaska Rainforest Sanctuary** (☎ 877-847-7557; www.alaskarainforest.

Getting the Most Out of Gustavus

While you're here, you'll want to stay at an inn or wilderness lodge. Most provide transportation while you're there, and will meet you on arrival at the airport and pick you up following your glacier flight. Generally, the inns will set up your entire trip, including booking activities and taking care of transfers, and that is the easiest way to plan a visit. Talk over with them what you want to do.

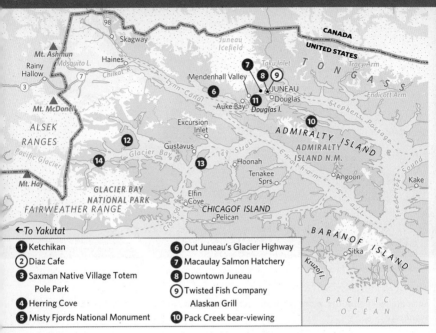

1 Ketchikan
2 Diaz Cafe
3 Saxman Native Village Totem
    Pole Park
4 Herring Cove
5 Misty Fjords National Monument

6 Out Juneau's Glacier Highway
7 Macaulay Salmon Hatchery
8 Downtown Juneau
9 Twisted Fish Company
    Alaskan Grill
10 Pack Creek bear-viewing

com), with guided walks on well-built trails and other interesting things to see, including captive reindeer and bald eagles. The cost is $80 for adults and $50 for children 12 and under. Call ahead for tour times, which depend on cruise-ship landings. The same folks offer a forest canopy zip-line tour, which takes 3½ hours and costs $175 per person; it's a less strenuous way to see the forest than the **Deer Mountain Trail** (p. 397, **9**), and you could substitute it for that stop. ⏱ 20 hr.

On Day 2, go to Misty Fjords National Monument. The all-day outing goes one way by boat, the other by air, and must be reserved in advance. If you go with Alaska Cruises (p. 398), they'll pick you up at the visitor center on the cruise ship dock. Otherwise, get directions on where to board your plane or boat when you reserve.

5 ★★★ **Misty Fjords National Monument.** You won't see much wildlife here, but the topography is so stunning, you really won't mind. ⏱ 1 day. See p. 398, **11**.

In the evening, fly 1 hr nonstop to Juneau, where you'll spend the next 3 nights, and rent a car at the airport. On Day 3, get an early start and drive north from the city on the Glacier Highway.

6 ★★ **Out Juneau's Glacier Highway.** The 40-mile route along the water north of Juneau is packed with beautiful scenery and walks. You can do it in half a day, but since you have the time, slowing down and spending the whole day is a better plan. Just be sure to pack a picnic, as you won't find much along the road. ⏱ 1 day. (p. 342, **8**).

Give yourself time to stop in at the Macaulay Salmon Hatchery on your way back to downtown Juneau; turn right from the highway at Channel Drive.

7 ★★ **Macaulay Salmon Hatchery.** The hatchery presents an exceptional opportunity for wildlife viewing, despite being just outside of town. When salmon are returning, from mid-June into the fall, seals and other predators often gather just offshore for the easy meal. The salmon, returning to their birthplace, traverse up a 450-foot fish ladder that has windows so you can see them swim. Inside the building, take a look at the saltwater

The Southeast's Best Wildlife & Scenery

BRITISH COLUMBIA

Stewart

- - - - Alaska Marine Highway

Glaciers & Ice Fields

Stikine Icefield

NATIONAL FOREST

Bradfield Canal

Behm Canal

MISTY FJORDS N.M. **5**

Petersburg

Mitkof Island

Wrangell

Wrangell I.

REVILLAGIGEDO ISLAND

Pearse I.

Wales I.

KUPREANOF ISLAND

Zarembo Island

Etolin Island

Clarence Strait

1 **2** **4**

Ketchikan

Saxman

Annette I.

3 Gravina I. Metlakatla

To → Prince Rupert

Pt. Baker

Thorne Bay

PRINCE OF WALES ISLAND

Duke I.

Kuiu Island

Summer Strait

Chatham Strait

Kosciusko I.

Edna Bay

Heceta I.

Warren I.

Hollis

Klawock

Craig

Hydaburg

Sukkwan I.

Lulu I.

Noyes I.

Suemez I.

Baker I.

Dall Island

0 — 50 mi

0 — 50 km

11 Mendenhall Wetlands State Game Refuge

12 Flightseeing trip to Glacier Bay

13 Icy Strait whale-watching

14 Glacier Bay National Park boat tour

---

aquariums, which realistically exhibit the underwater life of the area. Before the fish run starts, a visit isn't as exciting. ⏱ 1 hr. 2697 Channel Dr. ☎ 877-463-2486 or 907-463-5114. www.dipac.net. Admission $3 adults, $2 children 12 and under. Summer Mon–Fri 10am–6pm, Sat–Sun 10am–5pm; call ahead in winter.

Spend what's left of your afternoon and evening strolling through the city.

8 ★ **Downtown Juneau.** See p. 374.

9 🍽 **Twisted Fish Company Alaskan Grill.** Enjoy dinner at this lively place with huge windows on Gastineau Channel; it makes a perfect end to your day. 550 S. Franklin St. ☎ 907-463-5033; http://twistedfish. hangaronthewharf.com. $–$$. See p. 385.

Day 4 is dedicated to bear viewing in an area reached by small plane.

10 ★★★ **Pack Creek bear viewing with Alaska Fly 'N' Fish Charters.** The extraordinary brown bear viewing area in the Kootznoowoo Wilderness of Admiralty Island, 25 miles from Juneau, is the region's coveted opportunity for the ultimate encounter with huge bears at close range. *Kootznoowoo,* Tlingit for "fortress of bears," is said to have the highest concentration of brown bears on earth. The animals at the creek have become accustomed to people being nearby since hunting was prohibited in the 1930s, and in July and August they come close to viewing towers while feeding on salmon in the creek. To avoid crowding, the Forest Service limits visitors with a permit system. Longtime pilot Butch Laughlin offers permits for guests of his Alaska Fly 'N' Fish Charters and provides expert naturalist guiding along with everything else you need. ⏱ 5½ hr. ☎ 907-790-2120. www.alaskabyair. com. $600 per person. Call for departure times.

11 ★★ **Mendenhall Wetlands State Game Refuge.** The protected grassy estuaries covering 4,000 acres of Gastineau Channel are fed by the tide and by streams that flow from the mountains at many points (most notably the Mendenhall River), creating fresh and saltwater marsh habitats, ponds, sedge meadows, pockets of beach rye grass, and sandy islands and beaches. Shorebirds and waterfowl come through mostly during migrations in April and May, and begin passing on their southward journey again in late July. In midsummer many feeding birds are present, with 140 species counted during the course of the year. Check the tides before going, to make sure you can get onto the flats and won't get trapped by rising water. ⊕ 2 hr. No phone. www.wildlife. alaska.gov (click on "Refuges"). Free admission. Always open.

On Day 5, fly less than an hour from Juneau to Gustavus. By taking a small plane with Wings of Alaska (p. 419) or Air Excursions (below), you can go early enough to make the most of your day.

⑫ ★★★ Flightseeing trip to Glacier Bay. Begin your visit to Gustavus and Glacier Bay National Park with a flight over the enormous glaciers and impossibly steep mountains that you can see in their entirety only from above. The terrain is like something from another world, and only expert mountain climbers can access the great majority of it without an aircraft. If you fly a plane equipped with skis, you can include a glacier landing as part of the trip. Prices are difficult to pin down, because they depend on the length of the flight you choose, your starting point, and how many are onboard;

Seeing Bears in Southeast Alaska

Black bears can be annoyingly common in Southeast towns, which sometimes struggle with their presence at the town dump or their neighborhood patrols for unsecured trash. If you ask around, there's often a spot where you can find bears without great expense. Black bears (pictured above) are smaller than brown bears (which are also called grizzlies) and less dangerous, although they certainly can be intimidating when you meet one. And they can be just as interesting to watch.

Part of the allure of **Pack Creek,** on Admiralty Island, is the likelihood of seeing brown bears during salmon runs. An additional benefit is the permit system that keeps the area from being overrun by people. But it's not the only place to see bears. Many black bears and some brown bears visit the **Anan Wildlife Observatory** near Wrangell from mid-July to mid-August. Go with the marine

guide service there, called **Alaska Vistas** (☎ 866-874-3006 or 907-874-3006; www. alaskavistas.com). Several good bear-viewing spots also are accessible from **Ketchikan** by air (p. 398).

But focusing on a particular place to go may not be the best strategy. Bear viewing, like fishing, changes through the season, because bears congregate where fish are abundant. Every town in the region has flight services that carry clients to bear-viewing hot spots. Ask them where the bears are and how much it would cost to fly out and spend a few hours.

Finally, don't get hung up on seeing brown bears unless you have money to spend. You need time to watch bears. They don't show up on a schedule, and airplane charters are expensive by the hour. If you're on a budget, be satisfied to see black bears, which are so much easier and less expensive to find.

expect to pay at least $200 per person, and you will get a better flight if you pay more. You may be able to combine your transportation from Juneau to Gustavus with flightseeing, potentially saving some money. **Air Excursions** (☎ 907-697-2375; www.airexcursions.com), based in Gustavus and with a Juneau office, flies over the park daily. **Alaska Mountain Flying and Travel,** based in nearby Haines (☎ 800-954-8747 or 907-766-3007; www.flyglacierbay.com), specializes in flying adventurers to remote spots and offers glacier and beach landings as part of its tours. ⏱ 2 hr.

Plan to spend 2 nights at an inn or wilderness lodge in Gustavus, and spend Days 6 and 7 exploring the area. Be sure to include a whale-watch in your itinerary.

⑬ ★★★ Icy Strait whale-watching with Cross Sound Express. Icy Strait, just outside Glacier Bay, may have the most reliable whale-watching in Alaska, with killer whales and humpbacks seen pretty much without fail. Of the many, many times I've encountered whales, the most memorable have been here, including leaping humpback whales that smash down right next to the boat. Tod Stebens's company, Cross Sound Express, has never failed to see whales on its years of twice-daily trips. Check out the website for hundreds of photos of spectacular sightings. The boat, the 45-foot *Taz,* is well designed for viewing from inside or out and is equipped with hydrophones to listen to the

> *A view of Misty Fjords National Monument.*

animals' underwater communication. ⏱ Half-day. Cross Sound Express. ☎ 888-698-2726 or 907-766-3000. http://taz.gustavus.com. $120 per person, $60 children 4–6, free for children 3 and under.

On Day 6, get a ride from your inn or a taxi early in the morning to the headquarters of Glacier Bay National Park in Bartlett Cove for the boat ride into the bay.

⑭ ★★ Glacier Bay National Park boat tour. The all-day boat ride explores the geologically brand-new fjord and visits its giant glaciers. Even if you've already seen the ice from the air, approaching the face of a glacier from the water gives an awesome sense of scale. Wildlife sightings are common, too.

In the late afternoon, sip a beer on the deck of the Glacier Bay Lodge or take a walk on one of the trails. The **Forest Loop Trail** is a mile long, and it takes less than an hour to pass through the seaside rainforest and continue along the beach. The trailhead is at the Glacier Bay Lodge. ⏱ 1 day. See p. 406, ❶.

Seeing Birds

Landing at the airport's floatplane pond on your return from Pack Creek, you are well positioned for a bird-watching walk in the game refuge that surrounds the airport and includes much of Gastineau Channel. The **Airport Dike Trail** is about 2.5 miles round trip, with access to the wetlands near the Mendenhall River. If you're not already at the floatplane pond, take Old Glacier Highway onto Berner's Avenue just beyond the airport, turn left on Radcliffe Road and follow it to the end. Low tide is best for exploring the flats and marshes; if you prefer to watch from a platform, one is located on the right side of Egan Drive as you return downtown.

Where to Watch Whales

Various Southeast Alaska towns have reliable whale-watching waters, with **Gustavus** (p. 406), **Petersburg** (p. 402), **Juneau** (p. 374), and **Sitka** (p. 386) being top on the list. I think Icy Strait near Gustavus is probably the champion, but if you don't want to make the expensive trip and stay in Gustavus, your chances of seeing whales on boat tours from any of the other towns are also excellent.

A Southeast Camping Adventure

The camping experience in Southeast Alaska has magical qualities. Many of the campgrounds are simply inspiring, down at the base of enormous trees and near the sea or a lake, and generally are lightly used. The towns are small and easy for visitors to manage. The transportation between towns, by ferry, is casual and unlimited in luggage capacity, and you can even set up your tent on deck to create your own little compartment. Camping also saves a lot of money, which you can instead invest in activities to get out on the water or up in the air. Of course, there are also negatives, although they're manageable with quality, lightweight equipment. The Southeast is rainy—hence the rainforest—and you need good gear to stay dry. Moreover, unless you have lots of time to drive and take ferries, you will have to fly to your starting point, which means your luggage must be light and compact. Rental isn't an option, since you'll be doing a one-way tour. (See "Gearing Up to Fly & Camp," p. 157.)

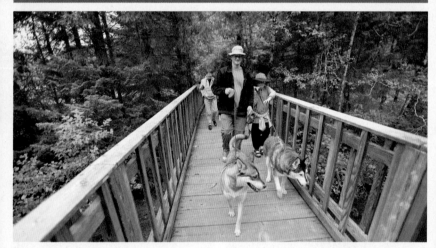

> You might spot ducks, geese, songbirds, or even the occasional great blue heron on the Estuary Life Trail.

START Sitka. Fly in via Anchorage or Seattle.
TRIP LENGTH 10 days, 375 miles.

1 ★★ **Starrigavan Recreation Area.** There are three campground loops here, all with large, well-separated sites; huge trees; and verdant surroundings. Some sites are right on Starrigavan Bay, with the feel of true seaside wilderness. The recreation area offers plenty to occupy the rest of your first day, after you make camp. The **Estuary Life Trail** and **Forest and Muskeg Trail** lead about 1 mile through a prime bird-watching area to the **Old Sitka State Historic Site** (p. 386, **1**), where Alaska Natives captured a Russian fort in 1802. The

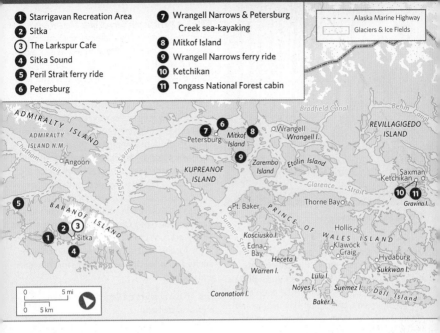

1. Starrigavan Recreation Area
2. Sitka
3. The Larkspur Cafe
4. Sitka Sound
5. Peril Strait ferry ride
6. Petersburg
7. Wrangell Narrows & Petersburg Creek sea-kayaking
8. Mitkof Island
9. Wrangell Narrows ferry ride
10. Ketchikan
11. Tongass National Forest cabin

- - - - - Alaska Marine Highway
‧‧‧‧‧ Glaciers & Ice Fields

Mosquito Cove Trail goes from the campground along the shore and through the forest to a pleasant beach. If you time that walk for low tide, you can explore the tide pools. ⏱ 1 day. Camping fees $12– $30 a night; some sites can be reserved through www.recreation.gov.

Spend part of the morning of Day 2 taking in a bit of town history. Drive into Sitka from the campground, and turn left on Lincoln Street to get to the historical park.

❷ ★★★ **Sitka.** Although your trip is outdoors-oriented, don't miss the historic and cultural attractions of downtown Sitka, especially the **Sitka National Historical Park** (p. 388, ❷), with its historic totem poles and contemporary Native artists at work. The trail through the woods to the battlefield combines history and an inspiring natural setting to put the story deeply in context. The other must-not-miss historical site is the **Russian Bishop's House** (p. 389, ❸), the best remaining structure from Russian America and a virtual time warp to that period. ⏱ 3 hr.

Return the way you came, on Lincoln Street; the next stop is on the right.

❸ 🍴 **The Larkspur Cafe.** This historic seaside coffeehouse and cafe is a great place to eat lunch, with wholesome, handcrafted local food and a festive, outdoorsy scene featuring live music and enthusiastic people. 2 Lincoln St. ☎ 907-966-2326. $. See p. 393.

❹ ★★★ **Sitka Sound.** Fishing is excellent for halibut or salmon in season, and the boat doesn't have to go far from town to reach productive spots—a situation that makes relatively economical half-day charters practical. If you're not a committed fish-slayer, you can include wildlife viewing on your charter; you'll

Travel Tip

After landing in Sitka, your life will be easier if you rent a car at the airport. The campground where you'll spend your first 2 nights is 7½ miles out of town. If you want to do it by bike, take a cab to **Yellow Jersey Cycle Shop** (p. 388) to rent. After buying what you need in Sitka, proceed north on Halibut Point Road to the Forest Service's **Starrigavan Recreation Area** and set up camp.

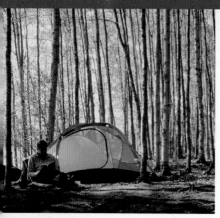

> *A peaceful campsite makes for a pleasant stay.*

likely see otters, seabirds, eagles, and often humpback whales. Or skip the fish entirely and concentrate on looking at animals. **Sitka's Secrets** (p. 389), run by a married couple of marine biologists, offers half-day fishing and wildlife tours for under $150 per person for either. You'll find many other options through a longtime booking agency, **Alaska Adventures Unlimited** (☎ 907-747-5576), or on the Web with the **Sitka Convention and Visitors Bureau** (www.Sitka.org/grid.html), which lists charter rates and offerings side by side. If you feel confident running a boat yourself, you can save money and do whatever you like with a rented skiff from **BJ Boat Rentals** (☎ 907-752-6375), from around $100 per day.

On Day 3, break camp and drop your rental car at the airport before boarding the ferry for the 177-mile ride to Petersburg, where you'll spend the night. Sitka Tours (☎ 907-747-8443) offers bus service to the ferry dock for $8 one way. The ferry to Petersburg runs several days a week; you will have to plan around that schedule (or choose to fly instead).

Spending the Night in Petersburg

Petersburg has plenty of places for wilderness camping but lacks a tent campground near town, so you may need to check into lodgings (listed on p. 405) for at least your first night, depending on the timing of your ferry.

⑤ ★★★ Peril Strait ferry ride. The ferries navigate a series of incredibly scenic narrow passages for hours to get around the east side Baranof Island to Juneau or Petersburg; this itself is a memorable part of your trip. The ferry leaves at a different time each day, so you may need to spend the night aboard. In midsummer you'll be able to see much of the scenery even at night, bedding down in your tent when tired. The trick of camping on the ferry is to pitch your tent on deck space that isn't directly exposed to the wind, which is found on the aft, especially behind the top-deck solarium. Locating your place as soon as you get onboard is prudent to assure a good spot. Bring duct tape to attach the tent to the steel deck. Once you've set up, you can roam the ship, storing valuables in the lockers that are provided. ⓧ 10 hr. $45 adults, half-price children 6–11, free for children 5 and under.

Get an early start on Day 4 so you can explore the town.

⑥ ★★ Petersburg. The town is well worth several hours of exploration. Besides a walk on the **waterfront** (p. 402, ❶), get to know the community by walking or biking north on Nordic Drive, around the north end of the island, and continuing along the shore to Sandy Beach, a peaceful spot with good bird-watching and tide pooling. Return on Haugen Road, making a circle of about 4 miles. ⓧ Half-day.

In the afternoon, join a sea kayak outing you have reserved in advance. You will be launching from the waterfront, which is within walking distance of the town's hotels.

⑦ ★★★ Wrangell Narrows & Petersburg Creek sea kayaking with Tongass Kayak Adventures. The water-road of Wrangell Narrows, between Mitkof Island (home to Petersburg) and neighboring Kupreanof Island, has many watery branches, even calmer and more protected than the Narrows, that lead into meadows and forests on each side. In your sea kayak, explore from Petersburg's harbor across the Narrows and up Petersburg Creek, on Kupreanof, a realm of salmon, deer, and bears. Experienced local guides lead the trips. ⓧ Half-day. ☎ 907-772-4600. www.tongass kayak.com. $85 per person.

> *Sandy Beach, along the shore north of Petersburg, also has tidal pools and excellent bird-watching.*

After returning from your kayak outing, pick up your reserved rental car at the Tides Inn (p. 405) or Scandia House (p. 405), and drive 22 miles south of Petersburg on the Mitkof Highway to Ohmer Creek Campground, setting up camp for 2 nights. Spend Day 5 exploring the island and hiking.

8 ★★ **Mitkof Island.** The island, 22 miles long and 16 miles wide, is inhabited only at the northernmost tip, the site of Petersburg, with the balance preserved in forest, meadow, mountain, and lake. Thanks to the active people of Petersburg and the Tongass National Forest rangers here, the island hosts an extraordinary range of outdoor activities. **Ohmer Creek Campground,** where I've recommended that you camp, has a mile-long hiking trail, a beaver pond, and good fishing. A swimming pond is 1½ miles up the road.

For an easy day of hiking and exploring, drive about 2 miles north from the campground to Three Lakes Road and continue 6 miles to the **Three Lakes Trail.** The 4.5-mile trail is a figure-eight loop, all on level boardwalk, surrounding a series of marshy lakes

(actually more than three) that are rich with waterfowl, including sandhill cranes. There are several shelters along the way, and three of the lakes have public rowboats that are free for use. If you're more ambitious, a relatively rough 1.5-mile trail continues to an ocean beach at Ideal Cove. ⏲ 1 day.

On Day 6, board a ferry for the 148-mile ride to Ketchikan, where you'll spend the night.

9 ★★ **Wrangell Narrows ferry ride.** Your second ferry ride takes you again on one of the system's most spectacular runs, down the length of the skinny corridor of Wrangell

Spending the Night near Petersburg

Ohmer Creek Campground has 10 sites among big trees along the creek. The camping fee is $6 per night. For more information, contact the U.S. Forest Service at the Petersburg Ranger District offices at 12 N. Nordic Dr. (☎ 907-772-3871; www.fs.fed.us/r10/tongass/districts/petersburg).

> *Fly fishing takes skill and patience, but the rewards are well worth the effort.*

Narrows (p. 340, **9**). ⏰ 9 hr. Fare $60 adults, $30 children 6–11, free for children 5 and under.

Arriving in Ketchikan, check into a hotel for the night. That will simplify your

transportation as you prepare for Day 7's trip to a remote cabin.

10 ★ **Ketchikan.** Your main purpose in coming to Ketchikan is its access to the outdoors beyond the town, at a U.S. Forest Service public use cabin, and you'll need part of a day to prepare. But some of that day is available for fun, or you can split up while one person handles logistics and the rest enjoy themselves.

The **Southeast Alaska Discovery Center** (p. 394, **1**) is a critical stop to make contact with Forest Service folks who can answer last-minute questions about your outdoor plans.

A firm called **Southeast Exposure** (p. 398) offers its Rainforest Ropes and Zipline Park, a half-day course (one of three in Ketchikan) that's particularly adventurous, with a fifty-foot climbing tower and room for self-directed activity on rope bridges, suspended logs, and the like. The zip-lines circle the property high in the trees. ⏰ At least 2 hr. See p. 394.

Later in the day, fly out with Island Wings Air Service (see "Cabin Preparations," below) to a wilderness cabin for the 3-night stay. The length of the ferry depends on the cabin you choose, and will be a key to your cost. The nearest cabins are within about 15 minutes by air.

Cabin Preparations

Imagine having a huge swath of the Southeast Alaska rainforest to yourself, along with a cabin, perhaps a rowboat or a trail, a lake or an ocean beach, great fishing, and limitless opportunities for unstructured exploration. You and your companions are on your own in the wilderness. The scores of Forest Service public use cabins near Ketchikan and other Southeast communities make it possible.

Planning ahead is essential. Get on the **Tongass National Forest** website (www.fs.fed.us/r10/tongass) to learn about cabin rentals and individual places you might like to go. But don't make a decision until you've contacted a flight service. The cabin only costs $25 to $45 a night, but getting there can easily cost more than $1,000, depending

on where you go. Michelle Madsen's **Island Wings Air Service** (☎ 888-854-2444 or 907-225-2444; www.islandwings.com) makes a specialty of flying to the cabins; her website is full of valuable advice, and she'll help you over the phone, too. After you've contacted her and figured out where you might like to go, reserve your cabin at www.recreation.gov, the **National Recreation Reservations Service** (☎ 877-444-6777).

You will need to bring sleeping bags and pads, rubber boots, and other personal gear, but you can rent almost everything else in a handy kit delivered to the plane from **Alaska Wilderness Outfitting and Camping Rentals** (☎ 907-225-7335; www.latitude56.com/camping/index.html).

⑪ ★★★ **Tongass National Forest cabin.** The 17-million-acre Tongass National Forest, by far the largest in the U.S., takes in all of Southeast Alaska, with untold miles of shoreline, lakeshore, and riverside that's never been altered from its natural state. The least expensive and most authentic way for most people to get into this wilderness is to rent a public use cabin from the U.S. Forest Service. The cabins are simple shelter, without plumbing, light, cooking facilities, or automatic heat; it's like camping, but indoors. What's special about each cabin is its location, each with its own lake or seashore—spectacular places that virtually belong to the cabin users during their stay. Many of the lake cabins have boats you can use. It's a journey into deep wilderness, and not to be taken lightly (see "Cabin Preparations," p. 372). But the experience is the best Alaska has to offer.

Ferry All the Way

If you have the time, traveling from the Lower 48 or Canada to Alaska by road, rail, and ferry is a great adventure. But you'd need a month to do the trip both ways, and you wouldn't save money or reduce your carbon footprint over flying. It's possible to bring your own car straight from home, but you can have a better trip if you take the train to the ferry, ride it as a foot passenger, and pick up a car for a one-way rental at the other end, flying home when your trip is done.

Step one is getting to the southern end of the ferry system, in **Bellingham, Washington,** or **Prince Rupert, BC.** Bellingham is connected to the rail network by **Amtrak** (☎ 800-USA-RAIL (872-7245); www.amtrak.com), but only one ferry runs there, with service just once a week. A better choice is to take Canada's **VIA Rail** (☎ 888-VIA-RAIL (842-7245); www.viarail.ca) by way of Jasper to Prince Rupert, which has four ferry sailings a week.

Long lead time is required for vehicle reservations on the ferry; that means you don't have flexibility along the way if you bring a car. Yet there's usually plenty of room for foot passengers without reservations. You can sleep in a recliner onboard the ferry, set up a tent on deck, or rent a cabin, which is similar to a compartment on a train. You usually need to make cabin reservations well in advance, but sometimes you can grab one as a standby (approach the purser as soon as you board). Cabins are cheap, under $100 for most overnight runs.

The voyage from Prince Rupert back to the highway blacktop in Haines or Skagway takes about 30 hours. From Bellingham, it takes 62 hours. I do not recommend just sitting on the ferry for that trip. Instead, get off in the ports along the way and enjoy the towns. If you don't require a car reservation or cabin, you can catch a ferry onward spontaneously, whenever you're ready. If the schedule isn't convenient, fly a short hop to the next town. The ferries charge no penalty fare for stopovers or one-way trips.

The passenger fare from Prince Rupert to Haines is $160; from Bellingham it's $363. It's inexpensive to bring a bicycle along, and very useful. Taking a car from Bellingham to Haines costs $800. Contact the **Alaska Marine Highway System** at ☎ 800-642-0066, www.ferryalaska.com.

You can rent a car in Haines, or rent a car or RV in Skagway. Avis has rental locations in both towns, with an add-on fee of about $300 extra to go one way to Anchorage. **Alaska Motorhome Rentals** (☎ 800-323-5757; www.bestofalaskatravel.com) rents RVs for the one-way trip to Anchorage. The rental costs around $230 a day, with a drop-off fee of between $795 and $995, plus gas and the cost of mileage.

The drive from Haines to Fairbanks is 655 miles; to Anchorage it's 777. From Skagway, add about 60 miles. At the other end of the ferry system, Prince Rupert is about 1,000 miles from Seattle, 2,500 miles from Chicago. If you drive all the way from home, it is still possible to make it a one-way trip; ship your car or RV back from Anchorage to Tacoma, Washington, while you fly and meet it there. That service is offered on relatively empty southbound cargo ships by **Totem Ocean Trailer Express** (☎ 800-234-8683 in Anchorage, or 800-426-0074 in the Lower 48; www.totemocean.com)

Juneau

Alaska's unique capital city cannot be reached by road and has little industry other than government and tourism. Its growth has done little harm to its spectacular setting on the side of the mountains along narrow Gastineau Channel, but it's also a big enough town to have some good restaurants and interesting lodgings, three museums worth attention, and a variety of sights to see. If you seek scenery, wildlife, and outdoor activities, Juneau's location and compactness put some extraordinary opportunities close at hand. Taking into account the full range of qualities that fulfill most visitors' checklists, Juneau is the most complete town in Southeast Alaska—and perhaps the entire state. You'll want to spend 2 to 3 days here.

> *The ethnographic floor of the Alaska State Museum highlights the traditional culture of the Aleut, Eskimo, Athabaskan, and Northwest Coast peoples.*

START Juneau. The capital city is 570 miles southeast of Anchorage, 900 miles northwest of Seattle.

① ★★★ **kids Alaska State Museum.** The museum isn't large, but what you learn here sticks with you because it carries off its effects so well. Cultural exhibits on the ground floor use remarkable Alaska Native artifacts to show what life was like long ago. The natural history exhibits are limited but vivid, capturing the feel of the rainforest. The history exhibit upstairs is the state's best, using priceless objects to tell Alaska's story. Be sure to check out the clan house downstairs, the tree and eagle within the spiral stairway ramp, and the chronological history exhibit upstairs. There's a good kids' section, too, and changing art exhibits. ⏱ 2 hr. 395 Whittier St. ☎ 907-465-2901. www.museums.state.ak.us. Admission summer $5 adults , free for children 18 and under; winter $3 adults. Summer daily 8:30am–5:30pm; winter Tues–Sat 10am–4pm.

Hiking Trails •••

Mt. Roberts Trail

Where to Stay

Alaska's Capital Inn **22**
Baranof Hotel **28**
The Driftwood Lodge **20**
Frontier Suites Airport Hotel **18**
Goldbelt Hotel Juneau **26**
The Historic Silverbow Inn **23**
Juneau International Hostel **21**
Pearson's Pond Luxury Inn and
Adventure Spa **17**

Where to Dine

Chan's Thai Kitchen **16**
The Gold Room **28**
The Hangar **27**
Island Pub **19**
Tarentino's **25**
Twisted Fish Company Alaskan Grill **29**
Zen **26**
Zyphyr Restaurant **24**

1 Alaska State Museum
2 Alaska capitol building
3 Juneau-Douglas City Museum
4 Mount Roberts Tramway
5 Wickersham House State Historic Site
6 St. Nicholas Orthodox Church
7 Last Chance Mining Museum
8 Perseverance Trail
9 Treadwell Mine Historic Trail
10 Macaulay Salmon Hatchery
11 Mendenhall Glacier
12 Glacier Gardens
13 Out the Road
14 Tour of Tracy Arm–Fords Terror Wilderness
15 Norris Glacier flightseeing

Juneau Visitor
Information Center

Gastineau Channel

Gastineau Ave.

S. Franklin St.

Marine Wy.

1/8 mi
1/8 km

Basin Rd.

Kennedy St.
East St.
Harris St.
Gold St.
Front St.
1st St.
2nd St.
3rd St.
Seward St.
N. Franklin St.
4th St.
5th St.
6th St.
7th St.
Main St.
Goldbelt Ave.
Dixon St.
Calhoun Ave.
Willoughby Ave.
W. Willoughby Ave.
Village St.
Whittier St.
Egan Dr.
Distin St.
12th St.
B St.

DOUGLAS ISLAND

TONGASS NATIONAL FOREST

Heintzleman Ridge

Nugget Cr.

Mendenhall Valley

Mendenhall Lake

Auke L.
Auke Bay
Lake Cr.

Mendenhall Loop Rd.

Glacier Hwy.

Montana Cr.

JUNEAU INT'L AIRPORT

West Juneau

N. Douglas Hwy.

Egan Dr.

Gastineau Channel

Blackerby Ridge

Salmon Creek Res.

Lemon Cr.

Salmon Cr.

Fritz Cove

Douglas

Juneau

TONGASS NATIONAL FOREST

2 mi
2 km

> *The Mount Roberts tram: 6 minutes to the top of the world.*

❷ ★ Alaska capitol building. The building is not grand; it began life in 1931 as a federal building and was transferred to Alaska when statehood was granted in 1959. But the capitol makes for an interesting stop thanks to the corridors hung with historic photos and to the old-fashioned woodwork with carved fish, gold-mining picks, and the like. You can wander freely in the building, and free guided tours start from the guard's desk in the lobby, whenever groups gather. The legislature is in session January to April, and the galleries are open for visitors if you'd like to see the state's government at work. ⏱ 1 hr. 4th and Seward sts. ☎ 907-465-3800. Free admission. Tour hours Mon–Fri 8:30am–5pm, Sat–Sun 9:30am–4pm; mid-May to mid-Sept only.

❸ ★★ kids Juneau-Douglas City Museum. This charming and well-presented museum is housed in a former library across from the capitol building. It makes Juneau's history wonderfully personal and vivid, and there's some very cool stuff to see as well, including an ancient fish trap and many-layered glass maps of the gold-mine tunnels. Stop in as well to buy useful guide maps for seeing the city's historic buildings, the **Evergreen Cemetery** (p. 377), and the **Treadwell Mine Historic Trail** (p. 379, ❾). In the summer season, the museum offers 1-hour historic walking tours Tuesday, Thursday, and Saturday at 1:30pm; tickets are $10 for adults and $7 for those 18 and under (museum admission is included). The tour leaves from the museum and is limited to the first 10 people to arrive—call ahead for reservations. ⏱ 2 hr. including walking

Mysteries of Juneau International Airport

The corkscrew maneuvers that airliners make to fly into Juneau can be impossible if visibility is too poor. Modern navigation equipment has alleviated the situation somewhat, but it's still quite possible to get stuck in Juneau or to be unable to land there due to clouds. Locals are so familiar with the situation that they have dedicated cable TV channel 19 to constantly show the view across the Gastineau Channel, so they can judge the visibility and the likelihood of flying for themselves; it's called "the Channel Channel." If possible, build extra time into your trip to Juneau so important plans won't be ruined by cancelled flights. Also, buy travel insurance to cover any deposits for activities you can't get to (p. 511).

Juneau's Gold-Mining History

Sitka remained as Alaska's capital after the United States bought the territory from Russia in 1867. A German mining engineer there, George Pilz, offered a reward to any Indian who would bring him evidence of gold in the region. Chief Cowee of the Auk Tlingits produced promising ore found near Gastineau Channel, and in 1880 Pilz sent two prospectors to look for its source, Joe Juneau and Richard Harris. They followed Gold Creek up between Mount Harris and Mount Juneau to the Silverbow Basin, and there found quartz laced with gold: Alaska's first major find. Recovering the gold veins here required massive investment in deep hard-rock mines, and Juneau rapidly became Alaska's largest and most urban town. The territorial capital moved here in 1906.

tour. 4th and Main sts. ☎ 907-586-3572. www.
juneau.org/parkrec/museum. $4 adults (free in
winter), free for children 18 and under. Summer
Mon–Fri 9am–5pm, Sat–Sun 10am–5pm; winter
Tues–Sat 10am–4pm.

❹ ★ kids **Mount Roberts Tramway.** The aerial
tram ride lasts only 6 minutes, rising from near
the cruise ships on Franklin Street to the tree
line on Mount Roberts, 1,760 feet up. The tram
offers great views and, more important, access
to alpine terrain that would otherwise require
effort beyond the physical means of many
visitors. Once at the top, a variety of trails go
higher, head downward, or just circle around
the facility. The top of Mount Roberts is 3 miles
away and 2,000 feet higher (too challenging a
climb for most); the hike back down to Juneau
is 2.5 miles. There's also a theater with a film on
Tlingit culture. ⏱ 1½ hr. 490 S. Franklin St.
☎ 888-461-8726 or 907-463-3412. www.mount
robertstramway.com. Full-day pass $27 adults,
$14 children 6–12, free for children 5 and under.
Daily 9am–9pm. Closed Oct–Apr.

A Back-Streets Walk

Begin at the intersection of 4th and Main
streets, between the **capitol building** (❷,
at left), the **State Office Building,** the **State
Court House** (look for the much-beloved
bronze bear statue in front), and the **Juneau-
Douglas City Museum** (❸, at left). The
museum is packed with interesting things to
look at from Juneau's past, offering a real immersion in history. While you're here, pick up
a map of Evergreen Cemetery and the historic
walking tour map of downtown Juneau. When
you're done, walk a block up Main and turn
left on 5th Street, crossing the pedestrian
bridge and descending the stairs to Calhoun
Street, thence turning right—the **Governor's
Mansion** is on the left. The wooden overpass
you crossed is the same one the governor
uses to get to work at his or her office in the
capitol building. Continue on Calhoun to
Cope Park, where you can take a moment to
relax in the shadows of the big trees along
the banks of roaring Gold Creek. This is the
stream where, in 1880, Juneau's founders
struck gold.

Return to Calhoun Street, which becomes
Irwin Street, and you'll come to **Evergreen
Cemetery.** The cemetery, sloping beautifully
down to Gastineau Channel, has its open
look because the markers are all flat to the
ground. Using the map you got at the museum, hunt for the graves of Juneau's founders and other interesting folks. Back at the
top of the cemetery, turn into Hermit Street
and take the public stairs next to house 430,
which leads to the bottom of Pine Street.
Climb Pine to Evergreen Avenue (great
views!) and turn right, walking it to the end.
A wooded trail leads to the **Flume,** a wooden
aqueduct once used to carry water to Juneau. Now it's a level boardwalk into the
forest of huge trees, bridging the gaps in the
mountainside. At the end of the Flume, keep
going along the creek upstream to the **Last
Chance Mining Museum** (p. 378, ❼). The
big machinery and other odd old stuff inside
should hold everyone's attention, especially
if you get to talk to the interesting historians
who live in the building.

> *Services are still sung in several languages at the St. Nicholas Russian Orthodox Church.*

⑤ Wickersham House State Historic Site. Judge James Wickersham was the most important political figure of Alaska's pre-statehood era. An adventurer, opportunist, judge, and congressional delegate, he brought order and development to the territory, but also contributed to its bare-fisted politics. He even punched a congressman on the floor of the U.S. House of Representatives. Among his accomplishments were the creation of Denali National Park (and he was the first non-Native to attempt to climb Mount McKinley), the start of the Alaska Railroad, and the charter for Alaska territorial legislature. See "Gold & Conservation," on p. 359, for more information on his fascinating life. The 1898 house where he retired contains many of Wickersham's belongings, including his assignment to Alaska, signed by Theodore Roosevelt. ⏱ 30 min. 213 7th St. ☎ 907-586-9001. www.alaskastateparks.org (click "Individual Parks"). Free admission. Summer Tues–Sat 10am–4pm; closed winter.

⑥ ★ St. Nicholas Orthodox Church. The tiny octagonal church was built in 1893, largely by Tlingit Indians who chose the Russian Orthodox faith when missionaries with governmental backing compelled them to become Christians. The Russian church at least allowed them to worship in their own language.

Services are still sung in many languages, and Alaska Natives make up many Russian Orthodox parishes all over the state. A donation is requested, and there is a small gift shop. 326 5th Ave. ☎ 907-586-1023. www.stnicholasjuneau.org. Daily 9am–5pm.

⑦ ★★ kids Last Chance Mining Museum. On the site where the gold that made Juneau was first discovered, this museum preserves old mining buildings and huge machines, their original equipment. This was once a nerve center for one of the world's biggest hard-rock mines, and the tunnels that honeycomb the mountains behind Juneau are still intact. Even in those early days, the town had electric lights, plumbing, and all other modern conveniences; Juneau's Alaska Electric Light and Power Company was founded in 1893. The industrial equipment at the museum helps you imagine that bygone world on the bank of the river that yielded the gold discovery, which built the town and began the modern development of Alaska.

A visit makes a perfect prelude to a half-day hike up the 3-mile **Perseverance Trail** (below), the route to the mountain site of the mine in the Silverbow Basin. ⏱ 1 hr., not including the hike. 1001 Basin Rd. ☎ 907-586-5338. Admission $4. Daily 9:30am–12:30pm and 3:30–6:30pm. Closed Oct to mid-May.

⑧ ★★ Perseverance Trail. This route follows the valley between Mount Juneau and Mount Harris, the two peaks upon which Juneau rests, on the route to the mines up in the high country that produced the gold that made the city. The well-constructed trail rises gently 3 miles one way and takes half a day. At the trailhead on Basin Road, the fascinating Last Chance Mining Museum preserves the massive equipment that supported the mine, along with the layered glass maps of the tunnels that are still intact inside the mountain. You can take a cab, walk, or bike (rent at the **Driftwood Lodge,** p. 383) to the museum and trailhead, a little over 2 miles from the Alaska State Museum. ⏱ Half-day.

You'll need to head out of town for the next stop. Cross the Juneau-Douglas Bridge. On the far side turn left and follow Douglas Hwy, staying on the same route through the town

of Douglas until bearing left on Savikko St. Park at the lot beyond the ball fields.

⑨ ★★ Treadwell Mine Historic Trail. Carpenter John Treadwell came to Juneau in the rush after the first gold discovery and quickly bought up promising mining claims on Douglas Island, on the far side of Gastineau Channel. There he built the largest gold mine in the world and became a millionaire in a few years (though he later lost the money in another investment and died a pauper). This large-scale development helped make Juneau Alaska's economic center, and Congress moved the capital here from Sitka.

The beach where you picked up the trail was created by refuse from the mine. During operation, until it collapsed and a flood destroyed it in 1917, the mine employed more than 2,000 men living in lavish conditions, considering the time

Shopping in Juneau

Juneau's best shops are all on Franklin Street and its side streets. Generally, the fancier, more tourist-oriented shops are nearest the water, where the cruise ships dock. But some of those have no connection to Alaska. To go deeper into local art and interests, walk up the hill.

Starting from the docks, you'll find that **Taku Store,** 550 S. Franklin (☎ 800-582-5122 or 907-463-3474; www.takustore. com), is interesting, even if you don't want to buy the fancy fish they sell; looking through the windows, you can see workers doing the processing.

Going up the hill a bit, you'll come to **Decker Gallery,** at 233 S. Franklin (☎ 907-463-5536), which carries the fanciful watercolors of Juneau's Rie Muñoz, one of Alaska's most popular artists. Find more local art at **Juneau Artists Gallery,** in the Senate Building at 175 S. Franklin (☎ 907-586-9891; www.juneauartistsgallery.com), which is a co-op of artists selling their own work in many media, much of it inexpensively.

Back on the left side of the street, upstairs at 174 S. Franklin, Bill Spear shows enamel pins and zipper pulls at his studio, **Wm Spear Design** (☎ 907-586-2209; www. wmspear.com). The variety of bright, vivid pins makes them addictive to collectors, and they're a terrific, original souvenir or gift from Alaska. They cost from $5 to $20 each.

Turning left on Front Street, walk half a block to **Annie Kaill's** fine art and craft gallery at 244 Front St. (☎ 907-586-2880). It's a richly stocked shop full of meaningful gifts. Turn right on Seward and continue a block to **The Urban Eskimo,** at 217 Seward St. (☎ 907-796-3626; www.urbaneskimo.com), which specializes in historic materials, such as gold-rush era photographs, books, and ephemera, and regional art and antiques.

The Observatory (☎ 907-586-9676; www.observatorybooks.com), an accredited dealer in rare charts, maps, and prints, is at 299 N. Franklin, with great browsing; **Foggy Mountain Shop** (☎ 907-586-9676; www. observatorybooks.com) is a good outdoors store, with clothing and equipment, including cross-country ski rentals, at 134 N. Franklin.

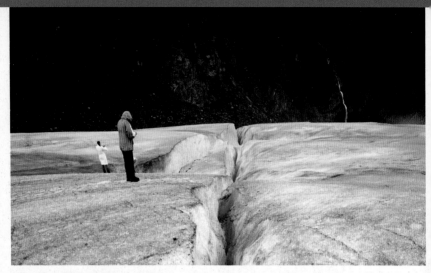

> *A small crevasse in the Mendenhall Glacier—don't get too close to it or the resident family of bears.*

and place, with a company swimming pool, theater, bowling alley, and more. The trail is level and can be covered in as little as half an hour. It goes among the ruins of the buildings and rails, now entangled with substantial trees that add to the mystery of the place, until it reaches the glory hole where the mine caved in after yielding 100 tons of pure gold. The walk is enhanced by taking along the brochure you can pick up at the **Juneau-Douglas City Museum** (p 376, ❸). ⏱ 1 hr. Free admission.

🔟 ★★ kids **Macaulay Salmon Hatchery.** When salmon are returning, see predators such as seals and eagles gather to feast just offshore, and watch the fish through windows in the fish ladder that leads to the building. Or take in the big saltwater aquariums with local marine life at any time. ⏱ 1 hr. See p. 364, ❼.

⓫ ★★★ kids **Mendenhall Glacier.** Several reasons make the glacier at the head of the suburban Mendenhall Valley a can't-miss part of a visit to Juneau. First is the glacier itself, looming blue-white across the lake from the visitor center and parking lot—it's as accessible as a glacier gets, and no less impressive for that. Next, the bears: A group of black bears have decided they like being surrounded by people while feeding on the salmon in Steep Creek, which runs past the parking lot. The female

bears apparently use tourists as a screen to protect their cubs from males, and during salmon runs, beginning in August and lasting into September, you can watch them come within yards, from the safety of the boardwalk. And then there's the visitor center, a fascinating glacier museum built into bedrock that as recently as 1935 was under ice. Finally, don't miss the trails, which are among the best in the area, especially the 3.5 mile **East Glacier Loop,** which starts behind the visitor center. ⏱ Half-day including hike. Glacier Spur Rd. (from Egan Dr., take a right on Mendenhall Loop to Glacier Spur). ☎ 907-789-0097. Visitor center admission summer $3 adults (free in winter), free for children 15 and under. Summer daily 8am–7:30pm; winter Thurs–Sun 10am–4pm.

⓬ **Glacier Gardens.** Greenhouses and outdoor plantings explode with the showy flowers that grow in this damp climate. Cruise-ship passengers often marry here. But the main attraction is the hour-long guided tour through the rainforest on open motorized carts, providing an opportunity for people with limited mobility to see the big trees and the steep ground they grow on. ⏱ 1½ hr. 7600 Glacier Hwy. ☎ 907-790-3377. www.glaciergardens.com. Admission $22 adults, $16 children 6–12, free for children 5 and under. Summer daily 9am–6pm. Closed Oct–Apr.

13 ★★ **Out the Road.** The drive 40 miles north from Juneau on the Glacier Highway, better known locally as "out the road," leads to little other than an outdoor wonderland of ocean and forest scenery, beach walks, many trails, and a peaceful Catholic shrine. See p. 342, **8**.

14 ★★★ **Tour of Tracy Arm–Fords Terror Wilderness with Adventure Bound Alaska.** These fjords south of Juneau are less famous than Glacier Bay or Kenai Fjords and receive far fewer visitors, but the scenery certainly isn't second best, and the getting there is considerably easier. The Adventure Bound Alaska tour boat leaves from downtown Juneau at 8am (but you must be onboard 15 minutes earlier) for an all-day voyage that covers approximately 150 miles round trip. The trip is too long for most children, and they don't take kids under 5. The boat is 56 feet, with lots of deck space for outside viewing. The crooked fjord of Tracy Arm penetrates many miles into the coastal mountains, through peaks a mile high that rise right out of the ocean, with waterfalls cascading thousands of feet down their faces. The destination: the Sawyer Glacier and South Sawyer Glacier, which calve chunks of ice. Seals commonly lounge up on the bergs in front of the glaciers, and the boat often encounters whales and other wildlife on the trip. ⏱1 day. 76 Egan Dr. ☎ 800-228-3875 or 907-463-2509. www.adventureboundalaska. com. $150 adults, $95 children 5–17; children 4 and under are not allowed.

15 ★★★ **Norris Glacier flightseeing.** This activity is a splurge, but it's an unforgettable experience. Fly with **Era Helicopters** over the vast Juneau Ice Field, a sea of glacier ice that lies behind the mountains and feeds the many glaciers that descend. You land on Norris Glacier, where the company maintains a camp of sled dogs. With a little training, you can drive a team for 25 minutes on the snow and ice. The whole tour takes 2¾ hours, with an hour on the glacier, 35 minutes in the air, and the rest transferring to the airport and such. It costs $489 per person. If you leave off the mushing, you can do just the flight and a 20-minute glacier landing for $279 per person. ⏱2O hr. Era Helicopters. ☎ 800-843-1947 or 907-586-2030. www.eraflightseeing.com.

Juneau Nightlife & Entertainment

Juneau's nightlife scene may not be sizzling, but there are still some fun things to do here. I've listed a few of my favorites below.

★ **Gold Creek Salmon Bake.** On a nice evening, it can be fun to join this picnic on Salmon Creek, where you can see fish spawning in season. Alaska Travel Adventures buses pick up diners and bring them for wood-grilled salmon and to hear local musicians, try panning for gold, or take a walk to a waterfall. See p. 337, **8**.

★ **The Hangar.** This is a big waterfront bar, with many brews on tap, pool tables, darts, and live music Friday and Saturday nights. The food is good, too. See p. 385.

★★★ **Perseverance Theatre.** Alaska's largest and most successful professional theater has gained a national reputation through alumni who went on to bigger things, including playwright Paula Vogel, who won a Pulitzer Prize for work done here. Other than youth theater and workshops, performances take place only during the winter season. 914 3rd St., Douglas. ☎ 907-364-2421. www. perseverancetheatre.org.

★ **Red Dog Saloon** The style of this barroom near the cruise-ship dock is Wild West, with sawdust on the floor, and tourists are generally the intended clientele, but it's still a fun place for a beer. 278 S. Franklin St. ☎ 907-463-3858, www.reddogsaloon.com.

20th Century Twin Theater Juneau still has an old-fashioned downtown movie theater, showing first-run Hollywood fare. 222 Front St. ☎ 907-586-4055.

Getting Outdoors near Juneau

Bear Viewing. At the **Mendenhall Glacier** (p. 380, ⑪) you can see black bears a few yards from your car in the late summer. But one of Alaska's most famous bear observatories, at **Pack Creek** (p. 365, ⑩) on Admiralty Island, is only 25 miles from Juneau by floatplane; there, from close at hand, visitors watch huge brown bears fishing in a remote setting where crowding is controlled by a permit rationing system. Go for the day by floatplane with **Alaska Fly 'N' Fish Charters** (p. 365, ⑩). Or go for a couple of nights of camping, kayaking, and bear watching to really get into this abundant wilderness; those trips cost $995 per person and are offered by **Alaska Discovery** (☎ 800-586-1911; www.alaskadiscovery.com).

Bird-Watching. The accessible wetlands of the **Mendenhall Wetlands State Game Refuge** (p. 365, ⑪), spanning Gastineau Channel around the Juneau airport, are a busy migratory stopover and summer feeding grounds for scores of species of waterfowl, seabirds, shorebirds, and songbirds.

Fishing. Harbors in Juneau are full of boats ready to take guests out salmon or halibut fishing, with skippers to teach you how to do it and all gear provided. **Juneau Sportfishing and Sightseeing,** 2 Marine Way (☎ 907-586-1887; www.juneausportfishing.com) is a large, long-established operator. Expect to pay $395 per person for a full day of salmon fishing (or $205 for 4 hours) or $425 for halibut and salmon.

Glacier Flights. Helicopters rise from the Juneau airport to the glaciers and ice field that fill in the land behind the mountains. The scenery is awesome, and you can land on the ice and get a close look. Better yet, fly to a sled-dog camp set up on a glacier and take a ride on the sled. I recommend **Era Helicopters** (p. 381, ⑮); a mushing outing with the company costs $489 per person; a flight and a 20-minute glacier landing is $279.

Hiking. There is no shortage of hiking near Juneau. My favorites include the historic and gradually rising **Perseverance Trail** (p. 378, ⑧); the historic, level, and easy **Treadwell Mine Historic Trail** (p. 379, ⑨); the challenging alpine hikes starting at the top of the **Mount Roberts Tram** (p. 377, ④); a rewarding hike near **Mendenhall Glacier** (p. 380, ⑪); and the peaceful seaside hikes at **Point Bridget State Park** (p. 344, ⑧).

Sea Kayaking. For a short paddle to get introduced to the sport, go with **Alaska Travel Adventures** (☎ 800-323-5757; www.bestofalaskatravel.com), which takes groups to North Douglas Island, across the channel from Auke Bay, with the chance of seeing wildlife on the way. About half the 3½-hour trip is spent on the water, with the rest devoted to the included transfer from downtown, suiting up, briefing and safety tips, and so on. The cost is $89 for adults and $59 for children 6 to 12. Not appropriate for children under age 6.

Juneau is the starting point for much more ambitious sea kayaking trips, too. **Alaska Discovery** (☎ 800-586-1911; www.akdiscovery.com) has lengthy experience operating from here and has earned an unequaled reputation (it is now owned by Mountain Travel Sobek). With them, you can paddle from inn to inn, sleeping and dining in complete comfort on a tour of the region; or explore to the very end of Glacier Bay National Park while camping on shore; or explore and camp a few days in waters near Juneau. Their bear-viewing kayak trips to Pack Creek are described on p. 365, ⑩. But these trips are not cheap: A 5-night inn-to-inn trip runs $3,000 per person.

Whale-Watching. Humpback whale sightings are quite reliable in waters off Juneau, and so many boats take visitors to see them that the whales sometimes hold out a flipper for tips (not really). I've recommended one of the larger operators, **Orca Enterprises** (p. 351, ⑨) earlier in the chapter. Also consider going on a six-passenger boat for a more intimate experience. Find choices through the **Juneau Convention and Visitors Bureau** (☎ 888-581-2201; www.traveljuneau.com). **Harv & Marv's Outback Alaska** (☎ 866-909-7288 or 907-209-7288; www.harvandmarvs.com) is run by a couple of local characters still going by the nicknames they earned as buddies in high school. They're known for making their trips fun and personal. They charge $149 per person, with discounts for larger groups.

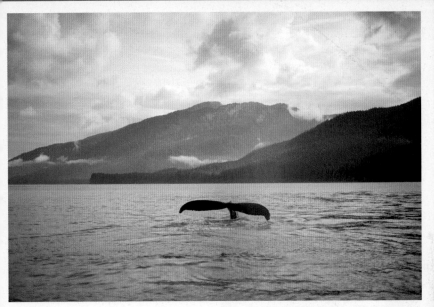

> *Don't miss a chance to see the mighty humpback whales that frequent the waters off Juneau.*

Where to Stay

★★★ Alaska's Capital Inn DOWNTOWN
The owners poured themselves into a detailed restoration of this gold rush–era mansion. Staying here would be like living in a luxurious museum if not for this couple's extraordinary hospitality and warmth and wonderful breakfasts. Their deep knowledge of the community is another big plus. 113 W. 5th St. ☎ 888-588-6507 or 907-586-6507. www.alaskacapitalinn.com. 7 units. Doubles $259–$339 high season; $139–$259 low season; w/breakfast. AE, DC, DISC, MC, V. Children under 11 not permitted.

★ Baranof Hotel DOWNTOWN
The Baranof has been a branch of the capitol building for decades—the concrete building dates from 1939—and history continues to be made here. The rooms tend to be small, but many have great views; the best have retained their old-fashioned details, while others are rather anonymous. The restaurant, the Gold Room, is described below. 127 N. Franklin St. ☎ 800-544-0970 or 907-586-2660. www.westmarkhotels.com. 196 units. Doubles $149–$189 high season; $129–$139 low season. AE, DC, DISC, MC, V.

The Driftwood Lodge DOWNTOWN
Stay here for a bargain on a basic room right downtown, next door to the Alaska State Museum. The building is made of cinderblocks with old-fashioned motel entrances, but rooms are clean and the rates and courtesy van save significant money. They rent bicycles, too. 435 Willoughby Ave. ☎ 800-544-2239 or 907-586-2280. www.driftwoodalaska.com. 63 units. Doubles $95–$110 high season; $68 low season. AE, DC, DISC, MC, V.

★ Kids Frontier Suites Airport Hotel AIRPORT
This is where to stay if you want a good room for a reasonable price and don't need to be in walking distance of the sights. Every unit is large and has a full kitchen. Pizza and pasta restaurants are on-site, as well as outdoor recreation areas, including a playground and a basketball court. 9400 Glacier Hwy. ☎ 800-544-2250 or 907-790-6600. www.frontiersuites.com. 104 units. Doubles $129–$179; $119 low season. AE, DISC, MC, V.

★★ Goldbelt Hotel Juneau DOWNTOWN
A business hotel of concrete and glass, the

> *Native artwork in the Goldbelt Hotel lobby.*

silverbowinn.com. 11 units. Doubles $149–$208 high season; $88–$148 low season; w/breakfast. $20 surcharge for 1-night stays in high season. AE, DISC, MC, V.

Juneau International Hostel DOWNTOWN This volunteer-operated nonprofit hostel is exceptionally well built and cared for. Guests pay little, but are expected to pitch in with chores and are locked out during the day. Reservations must be prepaid by mail or phone for a 5-night maximum stay. Shoes are removed at the door. 614 Harris St. ☎ 907-586-9559. www. juneauhostel.net. 47 beds. $10 adult, $5 children 6–17 (with parent), free for children 5 and under. MC, V. Closed intermittently Nov–Mar; check website.

★★★ Pearson's Pond Luxury Inn & Adventure Spa MENDENHALL VALLEY No longer recognizable as the suburban house it began as, the inn is a retreat of rooms with every conceivable amenity—a collection of honeymoon suites all in one building. The private pond and elaborately manicured grounds suggest the Alaska wilderness while dishing out the sensual comfort that is the constant theme. 4541 Sawa Circle. ☎ 888-658-6328 or 907-789-3772. www.pearsonspond.com. 5 units. Doubles $299–$499 high season; $149–$299 low season; w/breakfast. AE, DC, DISC, MC, V.

Goldbelt provides an airtight level of quality hard to find elsewhere in Juneau. Despite the owners' Tlingit art in the lobby, however, the building doesn't have much local character. The restaurant off the lobby, Zen, is described below. 51 W. Egan Dr. ☎ 888-478-6909 or 907-586-6900. www.goldbelttours.com. Doubles $189–$199 high season; $114–$169 low season. AE, MC, V.

★★ The Historic Silverbow Inn DOWNTOWN This quirky and charming downtown hotel in a 1914 building, with uneven wood floors, bare brick, and rooms of various sizes, is also a center of community social life, with a popular bagel deli and evening films and events. The hospitality is casual but thoughtful. 120 2nd St. ☎ 800-586-4146 or 907-586-4146. www.

Camping near Juneau

The Forest Service operates two remarkably good campgrounds in the summer. The **Mendenhall Glacier Campground,** next to the Mendenhall River and overlooking the lake and glacier, is beautifully constructed and has bathrooms with showers. The 69 sites are huge and broadly separated; nine have full RV hookups, and another nine have electricity and water. To get there, turn north on Montana Creek Road from Mendenhall Loop Road. Tent sites are $10, RV sites $26 and $28. The 11-site **Auke Village Campground,** 1¾ miles north of the ferry dock, is among large trees on an ocean beach. Sites are $10 per night. For reservations at both, use www.recreation.gov.

Where to Dine

> The dramatic dining room at Zephyr.

★★ Chan's Thai Kitchen AUKE BAY *THAI*
The delicious, authentic cuisine is served in a simple setting that somehow adds to the experience of discovery: a small, overlit dining room in a half-basement. Few tourists make it here. 11820 Glacier Hwy. ☎ 907-789-9777. Entrees $11–$14. MC, V. Dinner Tues–Sun.

★★ The Gold Room DOWNTOWN *CONTINENTAL* Juneau's most traditional fine-dining establishment is in the Baranof Hotel, long an annex to the capitol for legislators and lobbyists. The intimate dining room is decorated in an opulent art deco style, and the menu includes various cuts of beef, and seafood such as scaollops in pomegranate butter sauce. 127 N. Franklin St. ☎ 800-544-0970 or 907-586-2660. www.westmarkhotels.com. Entrees $25–$62. AE, DC, DISC, MC, V. Daily dinner.

★ The Hangar DOWNTOWN *GRILL*
This lively bar and grill occupies a converted airplane hangar overlooking Gastineau Channel. The food is above average, prices are reasonable, service is quick, and the noisy atmosphere and broad selection of beers are conducive to a good time. 2 Marine Way. ☎ 907-586-5018. www.hangaronthewharf.com. Entrees $13–$30. AE, MC, V. Daily lunch and dinner.

★ Island Pub DOUGLAS *PIZZA*
Locals cross the bridge from Juneau for a night out and surprisingly good food at this rough-and-ready pub with a brick oven. The menu doesn't stop at pizza but offers a variety of interesting choices. The water view is terrific. 1102 2nd St. ☎ 907-364-1595. www.theislandpub.com. Entrees $10–$12; pizza $13–$19. AE, DC, DISC, MC, V. Lunch and dinner daily.

★ [kids] Tarentino's DOWNTOWN *ITALIAN*
Right amid the sights downtown, this traditional family restaurant offers big meals prepared well for reasonable prices, mostly taken from the familiar list of Italian dishes. 140 Seward St. ☎ 907-523-0344. Entrees $9–$20. MC, V. Lunch and dinner daily.

★★ Twisted Fish Company Alaskan Grill
DOWNTOWN *SEAFOOD* This summer-only restaurant is next to the cruise-ship dock, but it's no tourist trap—the dining room is gorgeous, with high ceilings, interesting decoration, and great views. The menu contains good, unexpected choices, such as salmon in pastry or in a taco, and the service is excellent. 550 S. Franklin St. ☎ 907-463-5033. http://twistedfish.hangaronthewharf.com. Entrees $7–$30. AE, DISC, MC, V. Lunch and dinner daily. Closed Oct–Apr.

★★ Zen DOWNTOWN *ASIAN FUSION*
Off the lobby of the Goldbelt Hotel, the dining room is decorated in shades of green with an elegant Asian theme and the fine dining cuisine, such as ginger halibut and black cod, are consistently excellent. 51 W. Egan Dr. ☎ 907-586-5075. www.goldbelttours.com. Entrees $10–$42. AE, MC, V. Daily breakfast, lunch, dinner.

★★★ Zyphyr Restaurant DOWNTOWN *MEDITERRANEAN* This traditional fine-dining establishment has a magnificent sense of style, with wooden floors, very high ceilings, and tables widely separated in dim light for extra privacy. The service is expert and full of character, and the food has been memorable and flawless on each of my visits. 200 Seward St. ☎ 907-780-2221. Entrees $13–$32. MC, V. Summer dinner Tues–Sun; winter dinner Tues–Sat.

Sitka

The combination of qualities present in Sitka makes it the single-best town to visit in Alaska. The history of Russian America evident here is more interesting and better presented than Alaska's other, more modest historical assets. Encounters with Alaska Native culture, including dance performances and visual art, are easily found and rewarding. The totem poles are spectacular. And the outdoor activities are exceptional, too, out on the water or on the trails of Baranof Island, where the town is located. Plan to spend 2 days here.

> Once a Tlingit then Russian fort, Castle Hill is where the Stars and Stripes first flew over Alaska in 1867.

START Sitka, 100 miles south of Juneau and 600 miles southeast of Anchorage.

1 ★ Old Sitka State Historic Site & Starrigavan Recreation Area. Alexander Baranof, agent for Russian businessmen, was the de facto ruler and conqueror of Russian America. After enslaving the people of the Aleutian Islands and Kodiak, and depleting the sea otters there for furs, he pushed eastward for fresh hunting grounds. His forces built a fort called Redoubt St. Michael on this site in 1799 and claimed the entire Pacific Northwest region. Perceiving this as an invasion, which of course it was, powerful and well-armed Tlingit chiefs in 1802 attacked the fort and killed almost everyone inside. Baranof, in Kodiak, began planning for a massive counterattack. The Tlingit got ready as well, digging in at the national historical park you will visit next (see **2**).

The Old Sitka site is merely a grassy lawn with interpretive signs. While you're here, enjoy the Starrigavan Recreation Area, joining

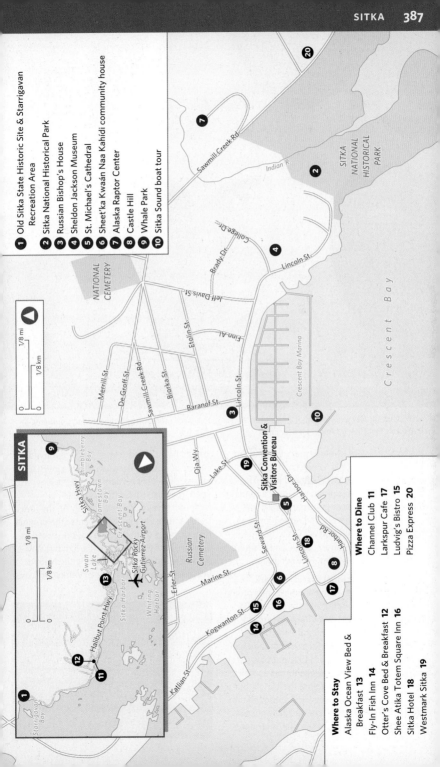

1. Old Sitka State Historic Site & Starrigavan Recreation Area
2. Sitka National Historical Park
3. Russian Bishop's House
4. Sheldon Jackson Museum
5. St. Michael's Cathedral
6. Sheet'ka Kwáan Naa Kahídi community house
7. Alaska Raptor Center
8. Castle Hill
9. Whale Park
10. Sitka Sound boat tour

Where to Stay

Alaska Ocean View Bed & Breakfast **13**
Fly-In Fish Inn **14**
Otter's Cove Bed & Breakfast **12**
Shee Atika Totem Square Inn **16**
Sitka Hotel **18**
Westmark Sitka **19**

Where to Dine

Channel Club **11**
Larkspur Cafe **17**
Ludvig's Bistro **15**
Pizza Express **20**

> *The Sheldon Jackson Museum is a repository for the 5,000-piece collection of Native artifacts gathered by Alaska's first General Agent for Education.*

the easy and very lovely Estuary Life and Forest and Muskeg trails, which connect just across the road and total about 1 mile. The bird-watching is excellent, including abundant ducks, geese, and songbirds and the occasional great blue heron. The recreation area has other easy trails and access to tide-pooling areas along the shore, as well as a superb campground. ⏱ **Half-day. Free admission.**

② ★★★ **Sitka National Historical Park.** Alaska's most interesting and best-interpreted historic site commemorates the great 1804 battle for Alaska between Russian forces under Alexander Baranof and Tlingit warriors under Katlian. The Russians already had conquered and enslaved Native peoples to the west, and now brought those forces as well as their own cannons against the Tlingit, but the Tlingit fought the siege and, although ultimately forced to retreat, never really gave up; they remained a threat when the Americans

arrived half a century later. Baranof moved the capital of Russian America to Sitka in 1808 and extended his settlements all the way south to Northern California.

Totem poles look down dourly on the forest trails, and inside the visitor center the original, historic poles from the area are preserved in a gallery with 30-foot ceilings. Exhibits and a film explain the history, taking the Native perspective, and in a series of workshops you

Getting Around Town

Sitka is compact and easy to get around, but just large enough that walking everywhere may be a bit much. I recommend renting bicycles. **Yellow Jersey Cycle Shop,** 329 Harbor Dr., is across from the Centennial Hall downtown (☎ 907-747-6317; www.yellowjerseycycles.com) and rents cycles for $25 a day.

can meet Tlingit craftspeople who are carrying on their people's traditions. ⏱ 2½ hr. 106 Metlakatla St. ☎ 907-747-0110. www.nps.gov/sitk. Admission $4. Visitor center summer daily 8am–5pm; winter Mon–Sat 8am–5pm. Park summer daily 6am–10pm; winter daily 7am–8pm.

❸ ★★★ Russian Bishop's House. After the brutality of Baranof and the other early Russian invaders, a cleric—now a saint in the Russian Orthodox faith—campaigned for and achieved more humane treatment of the Natives. Bishop Innocent Veniaminov translated the gospels into Alaska Native languages and wrote about the abuses of the military and fur traders. Thanks to him, the faith has had a lasting impact on Alaska, and there are currently 89 Russian Orthodox parishes in the state, mostly in tiny Native villages.

This house was built for him in 1843 of interlocking logs before being covered by siding; this construction held it together through decades of neglect until the National Park Service rescued the structure in 1972. It is by far the best building still standing from the time of Russian America. Do not miss the ranger tour of the second floor, a vivid window on that time, when Sitka was the largest city on the West Coast. ⏱ 1½ hr. Lincoln and Monastery sts. No phone. Admission $4 per person, $15 per family (family admission covers historical park, too). Summer daily 9am–5pm; by appointment in winter.

❹ ★★ Sheldon Jackson Museum. This museum, run by the Alaska State Museum, preserves an extraordinary collection of 5,000 Alaska Native artifacts gathered from 1888 to 1898, including the battle helmet worn by Katlian at the Battle of Sitka. It's amazing to see how much is here and how fresh it looks. The collector, Jackson, was a Presbyterian missionary who was given paternalistic care of Alaska Natives by the federal government. The museum shop is a good place to find authentic Native art. ⏱ 1 hr. 104 College Dr. ☎ 907-747-8981. www.museums.state.ak.us. $4 adults, free for children 18 and under. Summer daily 9am–5pm; winter Tues–Sat 10am–4pm.

❺ ★★ St. Michael's Cathedral. Besides being ornately beautiful, this church is full of interesting stories. For example, the icon of St. Michael, the farthest right of the six on the front screen, went down with a ship 30 miles offshore in 1813, only to wash ashore undamaged in its crate weeks later. When the church

Sitka Sound Tour Options

Depending on your interests and how much you want to spend, you have several choices for a wildlife cruise on the protected waters of the Sound or to the remarkable bird colony of St. Lazaria Island, which is accessible only in good weather.

• **Sitka Wildlife Quest** This tour by Allen Marine has a long-established reputation for excellence. The 3-hour tour operates Tuesday, Wednesday, Thursday, and Saturday afternoons. At Crescent Harbor. ☎ 888-747-8101 or 907-747-8100. www.allenmarinetours.com. $119 adults, $79 children.

• **Sitka's Secrets** A married couple, both former marine biologists, offer 3-hour charters on a small boat to St. Lazaria, seeking out whales along the way. ☎ 907-747-5089. www.sitkasecret.com. $120 per person, $300 minimum.

• **Esther G Sea Taxi** A friendly and enthusiastic guide takes passengers to St. Lazaria on 3-hour tours. ☎ 907-747-6481 or 907-738-6481 cell. www.puffinsandwhales.com. $150 per person.

• **Sea Life Discovery Tours** A specially built craft has large underwater viewing windows and a tide-pool touch tank. Although the 2-hour tours are geared to cruise-ship passengers and operate without regular times, independent travelers are welcome (with reservations). ☎ 877-966-2301 or 907-966-2301. www.sealifediscoverytours.com. $86 per person.

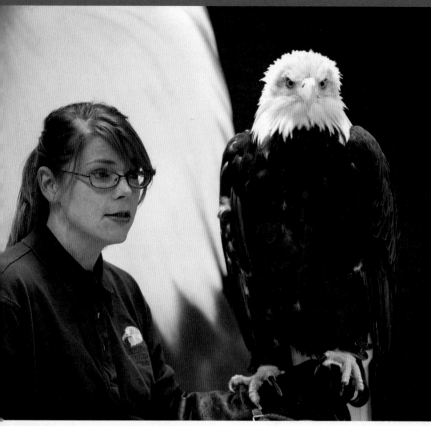

> *The Alaska Raptor Center trains injured eagles, like this one, to fly again in its $3-million flight training center.*

burned in 1966, a heroic human chain of rescuers saved the contents, and a replica building was completed in 1976 using Veniaminov's original plans. The door is usually unlocked and a guide or choirmaster on hand to tell you about it. ⏱ 1 hr. Lincoln and Cathedral sts. ☎ 907-747-8120. $2 donation requested.

⑥ ★ Sheet'ka Kwaán Naa Kahídi community house. The Sitka tribe built this modernized Tlingit clan house and furnished it with the largest house screen in the Pacific Northwest, a carved front wall inside the hall. Half-hour dance and storytelling sessions daily put visitors in touch with the Native traditions predating modern Sitka. ⏱ 1 hr. 200 Katlian St. ☎ 888-270-8687 or 907-747-7290. www.Sitkatours.com. $8 adults, $5 children. Call for performance times.

⑦ ★★ Alaska Raptor Center. This nonprofit center cares for injured birds of prey, primarily bald eagles; it nurses them back to health and, if possible, teaches them to fly again, in an enormous indoor flight-training center. The buildings are in the woods on a ridge, next to a stream where healthy eagles hunt. Outdoor cages contain birds in the process of recovery. Inside, the staff offers presentations that include a lot of information and a chance to see a huge, ferocious bird up close. ⏱ 1½ hr. 1000 Raptor Way (off Sawmill Creek Blvd.). ☎ 800-643-9425 or 907-747-8662. www.alaskaraptor.org. $12 adults, $6 children 12 and under. Daily 8am–4pm summer. No tours Oct–Apr.

⑧ Castle Hill. This fortified high point near Sitka's waterfront was used by each of the area's owners: Tlingit, Russian, and American.

Here the American flag first flew over Alaska. It's an open-air park now, known as Baranof Castle Hill State Historical Site, with cannons and markers on top. The grassy area on the north side of Lincoln Street was the military parade ground of this garrison town. The U.S. forces installed here after the Alaska purchase in 1867 were ill-disciplined and drunken and abused Tlingit villagers. When they departed after 10 years, tiny Sitka would have been destroyed by an angry clan leader if not for the intercession of another Tlingit clan. Cannons and historical markers are on top, along with a good view of the town and Sitka Sound. ⏱ 30 min. See p. 358, ❶.

❾ ★ **Whale Park.** Humpback whales are seen from boats all summer, but during migrations they are so common you can watch them from shore at the park, on a cliff overlooking the water just south of town. The whales pass southward from October to December, and return north in March. You can drive to the park, where staircases and boardwalks descend the cliff to viewing platforms. ⏱ 1 hr. Sawmill Creek Dr., 4 miles south of downtown.

❿ ★★ kids **Boat tour of Sitka Sound.** Voyage on the inviting waters surrounding Sitka on two sides and you're likely to encounter seabirds, sea otters, seals, sea lions, and whales. The wildlife is so abundant that it isn't necessary to go far from town, which means you can combine wildlife viewing with historic sightseeing in one day. Read up on the choices and reserve in advance to get the trip that appeals to you. ⏱ 3 hr. See "Sitka Sound Tour Options," on p. 389.

Getting Outdoors in Sitka

The Sitka area's choices for experienced outdoors people are truly extraordinary, including sea kayaking, hiking, fishing, camping, and visits to **Forest Service public use cabins** that you can rent (see "Cabin Preparations," on p. 372). The best local source of information is the **Sitka Ranger District,** 204 Siginaka Way (☎ 907-747-6671; www.fs.fed.us/r10/tongass/districts/Sitka). To get out beyond the road system, you will need a water taxi or air taxi. I recommend Davey Lubin's **Esther G Sea Taxi** (☎ 907-747-6481 or 907-738-6481 cell; www.puffinsandwhales.com) and Ken Bellows's **Air Sitka** flying service (☎ 907-747-7920). Both also offer sightseeing outings for those who don't want to be left in the wilderness.

Fishing Excellent fishing is found relatively near Sitka. I've covered the details earlier in this chapter (p. 369, ❹).

Hiking. I've mentioned the trails at the **Starrigavan Recreation Area** (p. 386, ❶), but the region has some 30 additional ones, varying in difficulty and accessibility. You can start from just east of downtown Sitka (take Indian River Road off Sawmill Creek Road) to hike the **Indian River Trail,** a 4-mile one-way rainforest walk rising gradually up the river valley to a small waterfall. **Gavan Hill–Harbor Mountain Trail** is a steeper climb, starting near the end of Baranof Street. The trail gains 2,500 feet over 3 miles to the peak of Gavan Hill, continuing another 3 miles along a ridge to meet Harbor Mountain Road.

Sea Kayaking. Sitka Sound and the myriad passages through the islands north and south are rich waters for paddling; you can see wildlife as well as remote and scenic little spots where only kayaks can explore. The town has a homegrown sea kayaking outfit, **Sitka Sound Ocean Adventures,** 112 Toivo Circle (☎ 907-752-0660. www.kayakSitka.com), that offers rentals and leads beginners on short paddles, as well as taking more ambitious trips and expeditions. A 2½-hour tour costs $69 for adults and $49 for children 6 to 12 years old (not appropriate for children under 6), while a half-day boat cruise and paddle will run $149 for adults and $109 for children 6 to 12.

Whale and Wildlife Viewing It's a crime to visit Sitka without getting out on these exquisite waters to see the otters, seabirds, and whales that frequent them. Choices are on p. 389.

Where to Stay

> *Shee Atika Totem Square Inn.*

★★★ Alaska Ocean View Bed & Breakfast

NORTH OF DOWNTOWN This is one of those wonderful B&Bs that reflects the personality of an enthusiastic owner who pours everything into it, like an over-the-top hobby. That's Carole Denkinger, who, with her husband, Bill, has thought of everything, even loaner laptops and HEPA air cleaners in every room. 1101 Edgecumbe Dr. ☎ 907-747-8310. www.Sitka-alaska-lodging.com. 3 units. Doubles $139–$229 high season; $85–$139 low season; w/breakfast. AE, DC, DISC, MC, V.

★★ Fly-In Fish Inn DOWNTOWN

On the water, just north of downtown, this stylish boutique hotel has an air-taxi service on-site that can take you out for a flight to fish in the wilderness. When you return, settle in to talk about it at the sumptuous bar, overlooking the harbor and with a big stone fireplace. Rooms are spacious, elegant, and well equipped. 485 Katlian St. ☎ 907-747-7910. www.flyinfishinn.com. 10 units. Doubles $159–$179 high season; $99 low season; w/breakfast. MC, V.

★ Otter's Cove Bed & Breakfast NORTH OF TOWN This B&B commands stunning ocean views with three downstairs units entered

separately from the family's living quarters, creating privacy for guests. The newly built house is full of fine details, stonework, and landscaping. 3211 Halibut Point Rd. ☎ 907-747-4529. www.ottercovebandb.com. 3 units. Doubles $130–$150 high season; $89–$109 low season. MC, V.

★★ Shee Atika Totem Square Inn DOWNTOWN Choose this hotel if you like a larger place with standard rooms. It stands across the street from the Tlingit community house and is owned by a Native corporation, which carries its people's red, black, and white artistic motifs through the hotel. Service is top-notch, and the building, with water views on two sides, has been continuously updated and is like new. 201 Katlian St. ☎ 866-300-1353 or 907-747-3693. www.totemsquareinn.com. 67 units. Doubles $139–$169 high season; $49–$119 low season. AE, DC, DISC, MC, V.

Sitka Hotel DOWNTOWN

The hotel has a prime location, facing the parade ground right downtown, though the building is old and has some rough edges. It's a clean place, however, and budget lodgings help save money. The rooms vary widely; the best are in the new wing in the back. 118 Lincoln St. ☎ 907-747-3288. www.Sitkahotel.net. 60 units. Double $105 high season; $70 low season. AE, DISC, MC, V.

★ Westmark Sitka DOWNTOWN

This hotel in the heart of the historic district was remodeled in 2009 with granite countertops and new furniture. Rooms have water views and all the amenities expected in a corporate hotel. But service was lacking on my last visit, a problem that extended to the Raven Dining Room restaurant. The dining room and the hotel's public spaces share an outdoorsy, decorative theme, including numerous mounted game trophies. 330 Seward St. ☎ 800-544-0970 for reservations, or 907-747-6241. www.westmarkhotels.com. 101 units. Doubles $159 high season; $99 low season. AE, DC, DISC, MC, V.

Where to Dine

> *An appetizer at the famous Channel Club.*

★★ **Channel Club** NORTH OF TOWN *STEAK*
This famous steakhouse overlooks the water from a simple, elegant dining room. Service is attentive, the steaks are expertly grilled, and the salad bar is unbelievable—it's really the highlight and most memorable aspect of the restaurant. The location is several miles out of town, but the restaurant offers a free shuttle. 2906 Halibut Point Rd. ☎ 907-747-7440. www.Sitkachannelclub.com. Entrees $16–$48. MC, V. Dinner daily.

★ **Larkspur Cafe** DOWNTOWN *CAFÉ* In the historic cable house building near the bridge, this happening coffee shop also serves terrific food, with items like cold smoked lox on rye toast with cream cheese and capers, and marinated black cod with brown rice and baby bok choy. The dining room is small, funky, and noisy; outside it's quieter, with water views. Check the blog for current live music listings. 2 Lincoln St. ☎ 907-966-2326. http://larkspur cafe.blogspot.com. All items $5–$15. MC, V. Lunch daily; dinner Wed–Sun.

★★ **Ludvig's Bistro** DOWNTOWN *MEDITER-RANEAN* Chef-owner Colette Nelson offers Sitka's most sophisticated meals in a tiny dining room. The dishes served to the few guests are memorably handcrafted, coming from a changing menu that has in the past included grilled marinated lamb chops and wild mushroom ragoût. 256 Katlian St. ☎ 907-966-3663. www.ludvigbistro.com. Entrees $17–$27. MC, V. Dinner daily.

kids **Pizza Express** SOUTH SIDE OF TOWN *MEXICAN* Near the Alaska Raptor Center and the historical park, this restaurant is really a Mexican place that also bakes good pizzas, which are delivered without fee. Sitka families love the place for the hearty, inexpensive food. 1321 Sawmill Creek Rd. ☎ 907-966-2428. Entrees $9–$19. MC, V. Lunch and dinner daily.

Travel Tip

Tent camping is available 7½ miles north of town, at Starrigavan Recreation Area (p. 386, ❶). RV camping is at the city-run **Sealing Cove RV Park** (☎ 907-747-3439), near the airport, for $22 per night.

Ketchikan

Alaska's most southern city, its fourth largest, grew up as a gritty waterfront logging and pulp mill town, but has transformed in the last 20 years into a major cruise port with little heavy industry. The visitor attractions tend to concentrate on the cruise trade, which floods the town with visitors during the day but leaves it quiet in the late afternoon and evening. The highlights for independent travelers are the totem pole parks, some nice walks, and access to wilderness areas such as Misty Fjords National Monument. For a complete visit, plan to spend at least 2 days.

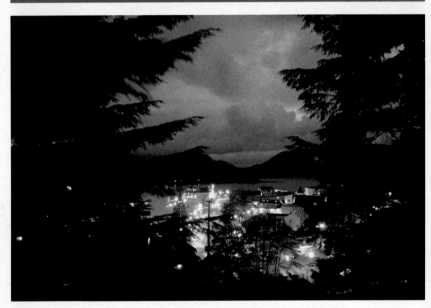

> *Like a tasteful cedar treehouse, Cape Fox Lodge overlooks Ketchikan from its high perch.*

START Ketchikan, 740 miles southeast from Anchorage.

① ★ Southeast Alaska Discovery Center. The Forest Service runs this big visitor center, but it provides information on outdoor activities on all public land in the state, regardless of which agency owns them. It's an invaluable information source for those planning an adventure, and interesting as well as a stop on a town tour to see the exhibits and films. Admission fees are summer only,

and they don't apply to those headed to the trip-planning room for advice and information. ⊕ 1 hr. 50 Main St. ☎ 907-228-6220. www. fs.fed.us/r10/tongass. Admission $5 adults, free for children 15 and under; $15 family maximum. May–Sept daily 8am–5pm; Oct–Apr Tues–Fri noon–4pm, Sat 10:30am–4:30pm.

② ★ Creek Street. This is a boardwalk running over salmon-laden Ketchikan Creek. It was the town's red-light district in the days when prostitution was permitted, until 1952,

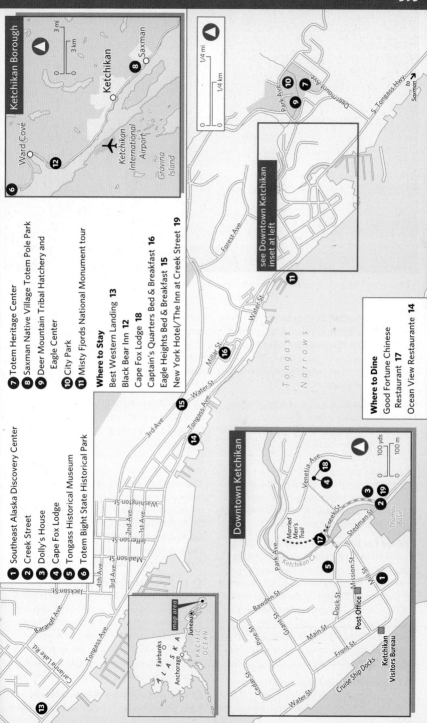

1 Southeast Alaska Discovery Center
2 Creek Street
3 Dolly's House
4 Cape Fox Lodge
5 Tongass Historical Museum
6 Totem Bight State Historical Park
7 Totem Heritage Center
8 Saxman Native Village Totem Pole Park
9 Deer Mountain Tribal Hatchery and Eagle Center
10 City Park
11 Misty Fjords National Monument tour

Where to Stay
Best Western Landing **13**
Black Bear Inn **12**
Cape Fox Lodge **18**
Captain's Quarters Bed & Breakfast **16**
Eagle Heights Bed & Breakfast **15**
New York Hotel/The Inn at Creek Street **19**

Where to Dine
Good Fortune Chinese Restaurant **17**
Ocean View Restaurante **14**

Ketchikan Borough

Downtown Ketchikan

see Downtown Ketchikan inset at left

> *Alaskan salmon at all stages of development at the Deer Mountain Tribal Hatchery and Eagle Center.*

and the neighborhood celebrates those wilder days. It is now home to shops and fun little attractions. The **Married Man's Trail**—the inconspicuous way to get to Creek Street — passes by a small waterfall that salmon try to leap over during runs.

3 Dolly's House. If you're interested in the town's racier days, stop in at what was once the home and workplace of Dolly Arthur, who set up shop, so to speak, in 1919. Dolly, who died in 1975, lived through Creek Street's wilder years and the not-so-wild years after prostitution was made illegal in 1952. It is a mildly amusing, slightly sad little museum. ⏱ 30 min. 24 Creek St. ☎ 907-225-6329. Admission $5. Summer daily 8am–4pm.

4 Cape Fox Lodge. The lodge is an Alaskan architectural masterpiece, situated among trees atop a cliff over Ketchikan. Take a look at the lobby by taking the fun-to-ride funicular car that climbs 211 feet up the cliff at the side of Creek Street. The summertime fare is $2, but if no one is around, just press the "up" button and go. The hotel's cafe has good food and an elegant dining room with wonderful views. See p. 399.

5 Tongass Historical Museum. This one-room museum is upstairs in the public library and features changing exhibits focused on the community. A small permanent area shows Native artifacts. ⏱ 30 min. 629 Dock St. ☎ 907-225-5600. Admission $2 summer; free winter. Summer daily 8am–5pm; winter Wed–Fri 1–5pm, Sat 10am–4pm, Sun 1–4pm. Library year-round Mon–Wed 10am–8pm, Thurs–Sat 10am–6pm.

6 ★★★ Totem Bight State Historical Park. In 1938, federal New Deal money hired Native carvers to copy rotting poles using traditional tools, and to build a clan house, which visitors can enter. These treasures stand above the shore, a fitting and even moving spot for them. This is the area's most aesthetic and educational place to see totem poles as they were meant to be presented, outdoors by the sea. ⏱ 1 hr. 10 miles out of town on N. Tongass Hwy. Alaska State Parks. ☎ 907-247-8574. www.alaskastateparks.org (click on "Individual Parks"). Free admission. Park always open.

7 ★★ Totem Heritage Center. This museum of historic totem poles up to 160 years old shows and interprets them in a spiritual and educational setting absent elsewhere in this city of totem poles. It's worth slowing down to enjoy. ⏱ 1 hr. 601 Deermount St. ☎ 907-225-5900. Admission $5 in summer; free in winter. Summer daily 8am–5pm; winter Mon–Fri 1–5pm.

8 ★★ Saxman Native Village Totem Pole Park. Set on a grassy slope overlooking the

> *Misty Fjords National Monument earns its name on a foggy day. The best way to see the wilderness is by boat and plane.*

ocean and the streets of the small village of Saxman, this park should not be missed. A 2-hour tour (including a dance performance in the clan house) is offered by the tribal group that owns the park, but the schedule is irregular, depending on the cruise ships. You can see the park's greatest highlight, the workshop, without taking the tour. There, some of the world's greatest totem pole carvers talk casually to visitors while they work. ⊕ At least 1 hr. Saxman, off S. Tongass Hwy. 2 1/2 miles south of downtown Ketchikan. ☎ 907-225-4846 for tour times and tickets. www.capefoxtours.com. Tour $35 adults, $18 children 12 and under; unguided visits $3 per person. Park always open. No tours Oct–Apr.

❾ ★★ Deer Mountain Tribal Hatchery and Eagle Center. This is a remarkably intimate setting to see the process of salmon being hatched, reared and harvested, and to get up close to live eagles. A pair of flightless bald eagles nest in an enclosure visitors walk through. Depending on the season, you can watch various parts of the salmon life cycle, including feeding thousands of tiny fish. ⊕ 1 hr.

1158 Salmon Rd. ☎ 800-252-5158 or 907-228-5530. Admission $9 adult, free for children 12 and under. May–Sept daily 8am–4:30pm; winter by arrangement.

❿ kids City Park. Kids love this park, where a creek divides into many channels, with small bridges. Adults can enjoy a pleasant stroll

Airport Water Taxi

Having the airport on a separate island from the town isn't particularly convenient, but it can be kind of fun. The usual way to get to ground transportation is on a ferry that runs every half-hour. But you can also catch a water taxi, a small boat that runs up Tongass Narrows directly to the downtown waterfront, just steps away from some of the hotels. That saves a cab ride and gives you the best possible introduction to watery Ketchikan. Tongass Water Taxi (☎ 907-225-8294) charges $19 for the first passenger and $8 for each additional person. The operator meets flights in the baggage claim area with a sign.

here, too. ⏱ 1 hr. Just up the creek from the Deer Mountain Tribal Hatchery and Eagle Center.

⓫ ★★★ **Misty Fjords National Monument tour.** Ketchikan is the jumping-off point for visits to this enormous wilderness, which contains some really astounding scenery. Sheer cliffs rise thousands of feet straight up from calm waters. Taking a boat into the wild and flying back is the best way to appreciate the immensity of the place. The national monument is a zone of extreme topography and remoteness. The wildlife viewing isn't great, but the mountains and cliffs are truly extraordinary, on a scale with famous places like Yosemite Valley. The boat ride to the fjords is relaxing and fun, if the weather is decent, and the entry into Punchbowl Cove, the highlight of the trip, is truly awesome. Best of all, you can get off the boat in Rudyerd Bay and board a floatplane for an utterly spectacular view of the fjords from above on your way back to Ketchikan. To save time and money, sacrifice the boat ride and fly both ways with **Island Wings Air Service** (below); a 2-hour excursion with 45 minutes on the ground is $249 per person. ⏱ half-day. Alaska Cruises. ☎ 800-323-5757 or 907-247-5295. www.bestofalaskatravel.com. $329 adults, $289 children; round-trip boat $158 adults, $105 children. ⏱ 1 day.

Getting Outdoors near Ketchikan

Bear Viewing. Brown and black bears congregate at several spots near Ketchikan. Black bears often show up near the road at **Herring Cove** (p. 363, ❹), where you can see them on your own or by joining a guided experience. Air services fly out from Ketchikan to other more exciting bear-viewing sites (p. 398). **Promech Air** (☎ 800-860-3845 or 907-225-3845, www.promechair.com) is a large, long-established operator that flies to Neets Bay. **Island Wings Air Service** (☎ 888-854-2444 or 907-225-2444; www.islandwings.com) is a small, woman-owned firm with limited-access permits that allow visits to the renowned Anan Wildlife Observatory and the Margarite Creek platform, both opportunities controlled by the Forest Service. In any event, expect to pay $330–$500 per person. If the price is too high, consider visiting the **Alaska Rainforest Sanctuary** (p. 363, ❹) instead.

Fishing. Ketchikan is famous for salmon fishing, which is mostly done on charter boats. Numerous operators offer outings. Daylong charters for salmon or halibut run around $300 per person; a half-day costs about $160. **Ketchikan Charter Boats** (☎ 800-272-7291 or 907-225-7291; www.ketchikancharterboats.com) is a good place to start.

Hiking The steep **Deer Mountain Trail** (p. 397, ❾), right behind town, is my favorite hike in Ketchikan, for its fantastic views. The **Ward Lake Recreation Area** and **Settlers Cove State Recreation Site** (p. 347, ❸) have good, level paths in beautiful surroundings.

Sea Kayaking. The narrow passages and small islands around Ketchikan, which itself sits on an island, create protected and scenic waters for a sea kayak outing, suitable for first-timers. **Misty Fjords National Monument** (p. 398, ⓫) is a great destination for experienced paddlers out for a longer expedition, perhaps using the Forest Service cabins that are available for rent in some spectacular spots (p. 373, ⓫). I recommend **Southeast Sea Kayaks,** 1621 Tongass Ave. (☎ 800-287-1607, www.kayakketchikan.com), because they specialize in taking small groups of independent travelers, not mobs of cruise-ship passengers. The half-day trips start with a boat ride to real wilderness for a maximum of six guests; these cost $159 for adults and $139 for children ages 6 to 15 (not appropriate for children 5 and under), including food and drink. A 2½-hour paddle costs $94 for adults and $64 for children.

Zip-Lining. The cruise lines brought this sport to Alaska from tropical destinations, along with the jargon of riding a line in the forest "canopy," not a word commonly used for these coniferous forests. It's fun and active, and it gets you into the woods—so, all good. You have three choices in Ketchikan; I pick **Southeast Exposure**'s Rainforest Ropes and Zipline Park (☎ 907-225-8829; www.southeastexposure.com) because it's less expensive and more self-directed than the competition. The course takes half a day and costs $95 per person.

Where to Stay

> *A room at the architecturally spectacular Cape Fox Lodge.*

★★ Best Western Landing NEAR FERRY DOCK
The hotel has a clean, corporate feel, with well-kept rooms in bright colors and friendly, professional service. There's a courtesy van to get downtown, but a car would be handy if staying here. One of the town's most popular family restaurants is on-site, the Landing Restaurant, a fountain and grill with lots of chrome. 3434 Tongass Ave. ☎ 800-428-8304 or 907-225-5166. www.landinghotel.com. 107 units. Doubles $200–$215 high season; $125–$142 low season. AE, DC, DISC, MC, V.

★★★ Black Bear Inn NORTH OF TOWN
This luxury inn stands on the waterfront with extensive gardens and a trail to a private beach. Everything is done in exquisite taste, and every amenity has been thought of. The hosts will even lend guests a crab pot or teach them how to smoke fish. Guests serve their own breakfasts from a shared kitchen while a suite and the cabin have their own cooking facilities. 5528 N. Tongass Hwy. ☎ 907-225-4343. www.stayinalaska.com. 6 units. Doubles $169–$189 w/breakfast. AE, MC, V. Children by arrangement only.

★★ Cape Fox Lodge DOWNTOWN
Alaska's most architecturally distinctive hotel, on a cliff top overlooking downtown, is

Camping

Three U.S. Forest Service campgrounds with a total of 47 sites are located at **Ward Lake Recreation Area** (p. 347, ❸). Sites at its **Signal Creek** and **Last Chance** campgrounds can be reserved through the national system at www.recreation.gov. The camping fee is $10 per night. At the end of North Tongass Highway, the **Settlers Cove State Park** (no phone) includes a sandy beach and 14 campsites. Camping costs $10 a night.

> *The New York Hotel's historic rooms are like a trip back in time.*

like a treehouse. Built with lots of cedar and consummate taste, it is reached from Creek Street by a funicular. It falls short only because the hotel and furniture are showing some age. The Heen Kahidi restaurant has a dining room of great elegance. The food is generally quite good, but prices are higher than other choices in town. 800 Venetia Way. ☎ 800-325-4000 or 907-225-8001. www.westcoasthotels.com. 72 units. Doubles $209–$229 high season; $99–$109 low season. AE, DC, DISC, MC, V.

★ **Captain's Quarters Bed & Breakfast** NORTH OF TUNNEL Big, light rooms attached to a family's house overlook Tongass Narrows from the steep mountainside just north of the downtown area. Guests enjoy the privacy and amenities of a hotel for a bargain price. 325 Lund St. ☎ 907-225-4912. www.captains quartersbb.com. 3 units. Doubles $105–$115 high season; $75 low season; w/breakfast. MC, V.

★ **Eagle Heights Bed & Breakfast** NORTH OF TUNNEL Immaculate, airy rooms built with remarkable skill, each with a private entry, overlook the water from the mountainside, a 20-minute walk from downtown. The hostess outdoes herself in terms of hospitality, even washing guests' laundry. 1626 Water St. ☎ 800-928-3308 or 907-225-1760. www.eagle heightsbb.com. 3 units. Doubles $105–$135, w/breakfast. MC, V.

★★ **New York Hotel/The Inn at Creek Street** DOWNTOWN There historic lodgings are right in the center of things, on Creek Street. The luxurious converted apartments are upstairs from some of the shops, and the small rooms are nicely done with antiques in a 1924 building by the harbor. The place is full of character but also comfortable and convenient. The on-site restaurant is a hip and friendly breakfast or lunch spot with many vegetarian choices, in a dining room with a strong historic feel. 207 Stedman St. ☎ 866-225-0246 or 907-225-0246. www.thenewyorkhotel.com. 14 units. Doubles $129–$229; $89–$119 low season. AE, DISC, MC, V.

Where to Dine

> *Good Fortune Chinese Restaurant on Creek Street.*

★ **Good Fortune Chinese Restaurant** DOWN-TOWN *CHINESE* This is an old standby serving consistently good meals for many years in a Creek Street building on pilings. The menu allows diners to choose by style of Chinese cuisine. Pick the broccoli beef. **4 Creek St.** ☎ 907-225-1818. Lunch $7; dinner entrees $12–$19. DISC, MC, V. Lunch and dinner daily.

★ **Ocean View Restaurante** NORTH OF THE TUNNEL *MEXICAN* This is a noisy family res-taurant doing what it takes to stay popular in a small town: offering a long menu with some-thing for everyone—Mexican, Italian, Greek, pizza—and food that's reasonably priced and reasonably well done. **1831 Tongass Ave.** ☎ 907-225-7566. Lunch $7–$9; dinner entrees $6–$20. MC, V. Lunch and dinner daily.

Petersburg

A reader once complained that I'd sent her to a small coastal town in Alaska where she found hardly any tourist activities. Funny, that's what I liked about it! In Petersburg, you'll meet few other visitors and find nothing touristy to do at all. But there are plenty of opportunities to enjoy the outdoors, the beauty of coastal Alaska, and exceptional whale-watching, sea kayaking, fishing, hiking, and other active pursuits. Petersburg lives by the sea, not the tourist trade, and its position far off the beaten track has kept it immune from the sad changes that have affected so many small towns in America. Thriving family businesses line the main street, crime is rare, and cruise ships are unknown. For a full visit, spend at least 2 days here.

> Clapboard houses line the waterfront of Petersburg, where the sea is their livelihood, not tourism.

START **Petersburg, 115 miles southeast of Juneau, 675 miles southeast of Anchorage.**

❶ ★★ **Hammer Slough and Sing Lee Alley.** Take a walk on the docks and dock-like streets of Petersburg's waterfront, where fishermen mend their nets and load their gear, totes of salmon move back and forth, and a park is built on a pier to honor lost mariners. I've described a walk here on p. 340, ❺ ⏱1 hr.

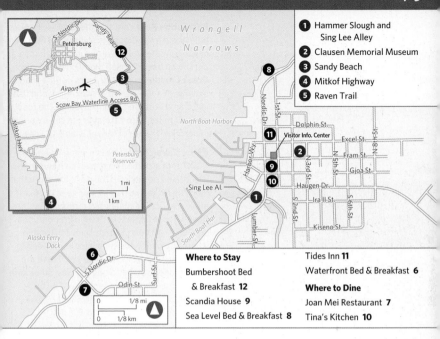

Where to Stay / Where to Dine legend:

Where to Stay

Bumbershoot Bed & Breakfast **12**

Scandia House **9**

Sea Level Bed & Breakfast **8**

Tides Inn **11**

Waterfront Bed & Breakfast **6**

Where to Dine

Joan Mei Restaurant **7**

Tina's Kitchen **10**

Map legend:

1. Hammer Slough and Sing Lee Alley
2. Clausen Memorial Museum
3. Sandy Beach
4. Mitkof Highway
5. Raven Trail

---

② ★ **Clausen Memorial Museum.** You might try to classify the town museum as its one tourist attraction, but you would be wrong. The museum's charm comes from its relevance for people who live here, as a storehouse for their collective memory. Consequently, there's a lot about fish and commercial fishing, including the display of the largest king salmon ever harvested, at 126.5 pounds, which a Petersburg commercial fisherman landed. ⏱ 1 hr. 203 Fram St. ☎ 907-772-3598. www.clausenmuseum.org. Summer Mon–Sat 10am–5pm; winter Tues–Sat 10am–2pm. Admission $3 adults, free for children 12 and under.

③ ★ **Sandy Beach.** Explore the coastal route north of town and a couple of miles around the north end of Mitkof Island to the beach, for bird watching, scenery, and walks. You can do it on a bike, on foot or by car. ⏱ 2 hr. See p. 370, **⑥**.

④ ★★ **Mitkof Highway.** The road that heads south from Petersburg leads to a series of inviting spots for exploration by car or bike. The Three Lakes Loop Road meets the highway at miles 10 and 20, and leads to the **Three Lakes Recreation Area** (p. 371, **⑧**), with a wonderful, easy trail; public rowboats; lots of berries

> The Clausen Museum houses 5,000 artifacts, 45,000 photographs and negatives, and 200 archival collections relevant to the town's history.

and wildflowers; and great bird-watching.

Back on the Mitkof Highway, a short trail at mile 14 leads to **Blind River Rapids,** a peaceful spot to fish for king salmon in June or for silvers in September. At mile 18, **Blind Slough**

> *Sandy Beach is a good spot for walking and exploring, especially for young ones.*

Recreation Area contains the local swimming hole; the narrow slough is so far from the open ocean that the water warms up enough for a dip (if you have Alaskan blood). The **Ohmer Creek Campground** is 22 miles out the road, again with a nice trail, a beaver pond, and fishing. Campsites are $6 for the night. The road ends 32 miles from Petersburg at the inspiring ocean views south of Mitkof Island. ⏱ 1 day.

5 ★★ **Raven Trail.** This is a steep hike with a 1,000-foot elevation gain, but the views of the islands and ocean from the ridge top more than make up for the work. The trail goes on, but the most practical destination is 4 miles in, at the **Raven Roost Cabin** (see "Cabin Preparations," on p. 372), a Forest Service public use cabin where you can spend the night (you'll need to make reservations before you go). There are some muddy patches along the way, so be sure to wear the appropriate footwear. The trailhead is behind the airport off Haugen Drive, about a mile from downtown. ⏱ 1 day.

Getting Outdoors near Petersburg

Fishing. The salmon fishing is excellent in Petersburg. Otherwise, there'd be no town here. Plenty of charter skippers take visitors out on the ocean. Half-day salmon charters cost around $175 per person, while halibut charters or longer salmon charters are $225 to $280 per day. Book through **Viking Travel** (p. 480).

Hiking. I've barely scratched the surface with my recommendations for hiking in Petersburg, including the steep **Raven Trail** (above), and the flat **Three Lakes Trail** (p. 371, **8**). For other ideas, get in touch with the Petersburg Ranger District, 12 N. Nordic Dr. (☎ 907-772-3871; www.fs.fed.us/r10/tongass/districts/petersburg).

Sea Kayaking. The waters around Petersburg hold infinite possibilities for sea kayaking expeditions. Beginners can do no better than to join **Tongass Kayak Adventures** (p. 370, **7**) for a half-day trip across Wrangell Narrows and up Petersburg Creek. The same firm leads overnight expeditions and can outfit you for a self-guided trip if you're up to it. Consider using a **Forest Service public use cabin** (see "Cabin Preparations," on p. 372) as a base, or paddle from cabin to cabin. A guided 3-night base-camp tour costs $950 per person.

Whale-Watching. Frederick Sound, Petersburg's home waters, is among the most productive humpback whale habitats in Alaska. Chances are excellent of seeing lots of whales performing their impressive behaviors, such as lunge feeding and spy hopping. Small boats make the trip, with a day lasting 6 to 10 hours and costing $150 to $210 per person. Barry Bracken of **Kaleidoscope Cruises** (☎ 800-868-4373 or 907-772-3736; www.petersburg lodgingandtours.com) is a marine biologist who carries a hydrophone to listen to the whales' intriguing underwater vocalizations. But other captains are good as well, and by booking through **Viking Travel,** 101 N. Nordic Dr. (☎ 800-327-2571 or 907-772-3818; www.alaskaferry.com), you can get matched up with a trip of the length you want.

Where to Stay & Dine

> The immaculately clean Scandia House.

★ **Bumbershoot Bed & Breakfast** NORTH OF TOWN A waterfront home overlooking Frederick Sound is offered by one of the warmest and most enthusiastic hosts you'll ever meet, Gloria Ohmer. You can get a simple, economical room, or take out the whole lower half (including a kitchen), where a family can spread out in great comfort. 901 Sandy Beach Rd. ☎ 907-772-4683. 4 units. Doubles $80–$90, w/breakfast. No credit cards.

★ **Joan Mei Restaurant** FERRY DOCK AREA *CHINESE* For many years this family has offered Americanized Chinese cuisine and an appealing salad bar. The dining room is bright, the service friendly, and the food satisfying. The menu also includes burgers and good fried fish and a few Mexican selections. 1103 S. Nordic Dr. ☎ 907-772-4222. Entrees $10–$25. MC, V. Lunch and dinner Tues–Sun. Closed mid-Jan to mid-Feb.

★★ **Scandia House** DOWNTOWN
The hotel reflects the solid simplicity of the town's Norwegian roots. Its elegant white rooms, trimmed in blond wood, are full of natural light. They're also some of the cleanest accommodations I've ever seen. The owners offer car rentals as well. 110 Nordic Dr. ☎ 800-722-5006 or 907-772-4281. www.scandiahousehotel.com. 33 units. Doubles $100–$130, w/breakfast. AE, DC, DISC, MC, V.

★ **Sea Level Bed & Breakfast** NORTH SIDE OF TOWN The building was constructed recently on pilings over the water, with a design intended to make it fit in with Petersburg's old marine warehouses and canneries. You can watch whales go by and even fish from the front deck at high tide. The hostess is a lifelong resident and political activist. N. Nordic Dr. ☎ 907-772-3240. www.sealevelbnb.com. 2 units. Doubles $110–$140 high season; $90–$120 low season. No credit cards.

★ **Tides Inn** DOWNTOWN
This is a friendly, well-run place offering good standard rooms for bargain prices. The pick of them have terrific views of Wrangell Narrows and the town below, but there are also money-saving kitchenettes without views. The hotel has an Avis car-rental franchise and an airport courtesy shuttle. 307 N. 1st St. ☎ 800-665-8433 or 907-772-4288. www.tidesinnalaska.net. Doubles $90–$120 high season; $65–$85 low season; w/light breakfast. AE, DC, DISC, MC, V.

★ **Tina's Kitchen** DOWNTOWN *FAST FOOD*
This is a booth with tables outdoors or in a tent, situated in a lot next door to the Scandia House. Food is quick and delicious, including Korean, Japanese, Mexican, and American items, all for reasonable prices. 104 N. Nordic Dr. ☎ 907-772-2090. All items $4.50–$11. No credit cards. Lunch and dinner daily. Closed Oct to mid-Apr.

Waterfront Bed & Breakfast FERRY DOCK AREA The location is prime, on a dock over Wrangell Narrows near the ferry terminal and Emily's Bakery. Rooms are basic but comfortable; Mission-style oak beds have excellent mattresses and down comforters. 1004 S. Nordic Dr. ☎ 866-772-9301 or 907-772-9300. www.waterfrontbedandbreakfast.com. 5 units. Doubles $100–$120, w/breakfast. MC, V.

Travel Tip

If you want to camp near Petersburg, your best choice is **Ohmer Creek Campground** (p. 371, ⑧).

Gustavus & Glacier Bay

Glacier Bay National Park is the definition of pristine—the land has only been out from under ice for a century or so, and for most of that time it has been under protection of the National Park Service. When you travel up the fjord by boat, you see a brand-new land, full of wildlife and devoid of human impact, *ever*—other than the passage of boats. The charming country town of Gustavus, threshold to the park, is its appealing mirror image. The presence of people here has been all for the good, creating in a remote, pastoral setting the opportunity to relax, eat, bike, fish, and feel as though you're in paradise. You'll want to spend at least 2 days to slow down and enjoy the outdoors.

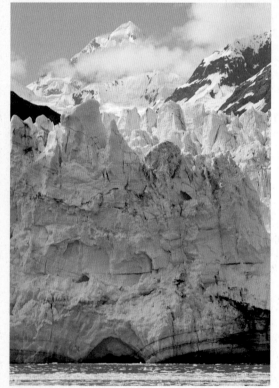

> *Marqerie Glacier in Glacier Bay National Park. Glaciers appear blue because ice absorbs shorter red and green wavelengths.*

START Gustavus, 90 miles west of Juneau. Alaska Airlines (p. 507) flies direct once daily, summer only.

❶ ★★ **Glacier Bay National Park boat tour.** The bay is in fact a fjord—a glacier-carved bay—that as late as 1879 was still full of ice. Now the water leads 65 miles back into the mountains through ice-carved rock, to a series of great glaciers still lurking there. The scenery is grand and unique, especially in the areas where the recent retreat of the ice has left the shore sterile of life. Marine mammal and bird life are abundant, however.

The main way into the park (other than by cruise ship) is on a tour boat from the park headquarters in Bartlett Cove, with a ranger onboard offering commentary. This 8-hour journey, with lunch provided, is too long for many kids, but there is no other tour option for most independent travelers. On the other hand, you can choose to fly over the bay (see the next item).

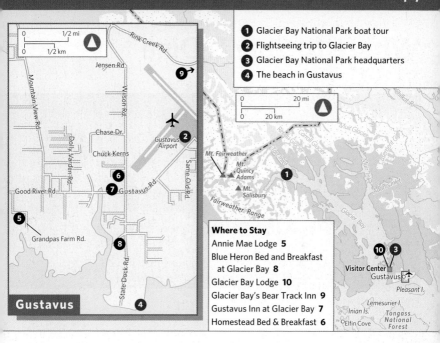

1 Glacier Bay National Park boat tour
2 Flightseeing trip to Glacier Bay
3 Glacier Bay National Park headquarters
4 The beach in Gustavus

Where to Stay

Annie Mae Lodge **5**

Blue Heron Bed and Breakfast at Glacier Bay **8**

Glacier Bay Lodge **10**

Glacier Bay's Bear Track Inn **9**

Gustavus Inn at Glacier Bay **7**

Homestead Bed & Breakfast **6**

Gustavus

⏱ 1 day. Glacier Bay Lodge & Tours. ☎ 888-229-8687 or 907-264-4600. www.visitglacierbay.com. The all-day tour departs at 7:30am. $200 adults, $100 children 2–12, free for children under 2.

2 ★★★ Flightseeing trip to Glacier Bay. A small plane can take you to unsurpassed

Planning Ahead: Spending the Night in Gustavus

There are no hotels in Gustavus; that doesn't mean you can't stay here, but it does mean advanced planning is required. It's not wise to simply show up for a spontaneous visit, as places book up early. The national park has a lodge, and Gustavus has country inns, wilderness lodges, and B&Bs. Most visitors stay at the park lodge or at a country inn in Gustavus, setting up the whole visit, including activities and meals, through their hosts. Also, note that the community lacks a bank or consistently available ATM, and some businesses don't take credit cards; stock up on cash before leaving Juneau.

views of the glaciers up the fjords, and for not much more than you would pay for the boat tour. While you give up the wildlife viewing of the boat tour's on-the-water perspective, instead you can see whales and other animals on a whale-watching ride from Gustavus with **Cross Sound Express** (p. 367, **13**). ⏱ At least 1 hr. p. 366, **12**.

3 ★ Glacier Bay National Park headquarters. The lodge and headquarters are at Bartlett Cove, far from the glaciers. There are several trails through the woods, such as the **Forest Loop Trail** (p. 367, **14**), and an opportunity to go paddling with **Glacier Bay Sea Kayaks** in the cove (p. 408), which is often frequented by whales.

4 ★ The beach in Gustavus. The town is on flat ground with meadows and forests, ending at the shore and the dock. From that dock, at the end of Dock Road, a sandy beach extends far in each direction. It's a peaceful place for a walk, where hardly anyone goes. ⏱ 2 hr. At the end of Dock Rd.

Where to Stay & Dine

> *Wildflowers surround Glacier Bay's Bear Track Inn.*

★ **Annie Mae Lodge** GUSTAVUS
This full-service lodge—in a cozy, old-fashioned post-and-beam building in the woods, near the Good River—offers rooms, food, and bikes, and arranges activities for guests. They charge lower prices than most. You don't have to eat at the lodge and can pay for meals separately, which gives you more flexibility than at other lodges. 2 Grandma's Farm Rd. ☎ 800-478-2346

or 907-697-2346. www.anniemae.com. 11 units. Doubles $185–$200 high season; $125 low season. AE, DISC, MC, V.

★ **Blue Heron Bed and Breakfast at Glacier Bay** GUSTAVUS Stay near the waterfront, among the wildflowers and marshland, in bright, well-equipped rooms with enthusiastic hosts. In the cottages, you can cook your own evening meal, while the rooms have access to

Getting Outdoors in Gustavus

Fishing Gustavus is a prime area for charter-boat fishing. The waters near the town are protected from large waves, so you're less likely to get seasick while fishing halibut than in some ports. The easiest way to plan a trip to Gustavus is to choose your inn and then have your host set up your activities, especially for fishing. Typically, you will pay $300 to $350 per person for a full-day charter.

Sea Kayaking The allure of sea kayaking here is that wilderness is so close at hand—from the first stroke of your paddle, you're into unspoiled waters rich with marine mammals. Groups often see whales in Bartlett Cove, the threshold to the national park, on half- or full-day trips run by **Glacier Bay Sea Kayaks**

(☎ 907-697-2257; www.glacierbayseakayaks. com). Trips cost $100 to $150 per person. From Gustavus, whale sightings are even more common, although the cost is higher. **Spirit Walker Expeditions** (☎ 800-KAYAKER (529-2537) or 907-697-2266; www.sea kayakalaska.com) takes kayakers by boat from Gustavus for surefire whale-watching in Icy Strait for $435 per person.

Whale-Watching For a boat to see the whales in Icy Strait, which may be Alaska's best whale-watching grounds for humpback and orca whales, contact **Cross Sound Express** (p 367, ⓭); they've never run a trip without seeing whales.

microwaves and refrigerators in the sunroom dining area. Off Dock Rd. ☎ 907-697-2337. www.blueheronbnb.net. 4 units. Doubles $145, w/breakfast. No credit cards.

★ **Glacier Bay Lodge** BARTLETT COVE
This is the national park lodge and headquarters, the only place to stay within the park. Common areas are comfortably old-fashioned, but the bedrooms, in buildings set among large rainforest trees, are aged and drab. The restaurant is wonderfully situated to look out on the cove, but it changes too much each year for me to offer an opinion on the food. It operates long hours in the summer season. Bartlett Cove. ☎ 888-229-8687 or 907-697-4000. www.visit glacierbay.com. 48 units. Doubles $171–$196. AE, DC, DISC, MC, V. Closed mid-Sept to late May.

★★★ **Glacier Bay's Bear Track Inn** EAST OF GUSTAVUS Even more remote than Gustavus, 6 miles down an unpaved road, the inn faces a field of wildflowers and the ocean. For such a spot, it's a remarkably grand place built of logs, with towering vaulted ceilings and rooms with a crisp finish. The dining room serves generous meals cooked to order. 255 Rink Rd. ☎ 888-697-2284 or 907-697-3017. www. beartrackinn.com. 14 units. $604 per person per night, double occupancy; discounts for additional nights. Rates include round-trip air from Juneau, transfers, and all meals. DISC, MC, V. Closed Oct–Apr.

★★★ **Gustavus Inn at Glacier Bay** GUSTAVUS
This is the area's original country inn, and the one that invented the Gustavus style more than 40 years ago: a comfortable, homey place with warm hosts, great food, free bike loans, and no need to deal with anyone else to set up your trip. The Lesh family is still at it and still winning awards for their incredible food and hospitality. The inn stands near the center of the community, surrounded by meadows and a big vegetable garden. 1 Gustavus Rd. ☎ 800-649-5220 or 907-697-2254. www.gustavusinn.com. 13 units. $205 per person per night, including all meals; half-price for children 11 and under. AE, MC, V. Closed Sept 16–May 15.

Homestead Bed & Breakfast GUSTAVUS
Relatively inexpensive but clean and attractive rooms are offered with breakfast at this family home at the center of Gustavus, near the Homeshore Cafe and Gustavus Inn, where you can buy other meals. 17 Faraway Rd. ☎ 907-697-2777. www.homesteadbedbreakfast.com Doubles $135, w/breakfast. No credit cards.

Why Go to Glacier Bay?

Some visitors seem to feel that visiting Glacier Bay National Park is a requirement. It is not. You can see fantastic fjords and glaciers at **Tracy Arm** (p. 381, ⑭), reachable on a day trip from Juneau . You can see plenty of whales from **Juneau**, too (p. 381, ⑭), or from **Petersburg** (p. 404), or in **Icy Strait** (p. 367, ⑬), near Gustavus, without going into the park at all. I think the best reason to go to Glacier Bay and the neighboring community of Gustavus is if you want to settle in and experience the place and its wilderness. The rural setting is unique, unlike the other communities I've described, because there's no real town here—the area is more of a collection of wilderness lodges. Yet as quiet and isolated as the place is, you can get there on a jet and stay in perfect comfort. Combined with the park's scenery, wildlife, and first-rate outdoor activities, it's an appealing package. But if you're not planning to take advantage of the rural setting by settling in to stay and relax—if your goal primarily is to see glaciers and whales—you can save money and time by going elsewhere.

Where to Dine?

Most accommodations in Gustavus have dining on-site, often included in the price of a stay. Most of the inns also take outside guests for dinner, with reservations. There's only one freestanding restaurant, the **Homeshore Cafe,** at Gustavus's central intersection on Wilson Road (☎ 907-697-2822). It's an all-purpose eatery, serving pizza, calzones, sandwiches, salads, and other casual food, and beer and wine; a large pizza is $20 to $25, while sandwiches are $10. In summer, lunch and dinner are served Tuesday through Saturday. The cafe accepts Visa and MasterCard. Internet access on a terminal is $5 for a half-hour, and they have Wi-Fi.

Haines

Haines is a bit different than Southeast Alaska's other towns: not as rainy, not as steep, not as busy with cruise ships. Also, it is connected by road through Canada to the rest of Alaska and the outside world. There are few compelling reasons to focus an entire trip on Haines, but still I find it among the must enjoyable of communities to visit, if only for a day or two. Its friendly, quirky character is charming, and you can have great fun while visiting the collection of odd museums and exploring the beaches and trails.

> The American Bald Eagle Foundation Natural History Museum is the brainchild of former Haines mayor Dave Olerud.

START Haines, 67 miles northwest of Juneau, 500 miles east of Anchorage.

❶ ★★ **Fort William Seward.** The dominant feature of Haines is a collection of white clap-board buildings around a big green lawn with a Tlingit clan house standing in the middle. This is Fort William Seward, an installation built for the gold rush that never served much of a purpose before being sold off after World War II. The veterans who bought it used it, in part, to help the rebirth of Tlingit culture, building the clan house and starting the **Alaska Indian Arts cultural center,** where visitors can see Native artists at work. ⏱1 hr. ☎ 907-766-2160. Free admission. Mon–Fri 9am–5pm.

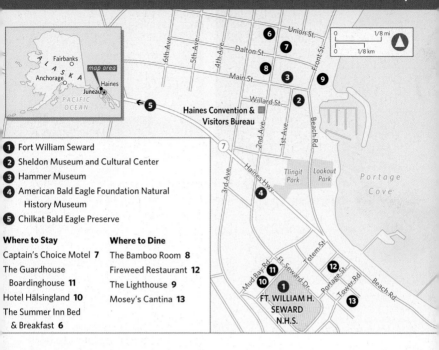

1 Fort William Seward

2 Sheldon Museum and Cultural Center

3 Hammer Museum

4 American Bald Eagle Foundation Natural History Museum

5 Chilkat Bald Eagle Preserve

Where to Stay

Captain's Choice Motel **7**

The Guardhouse Boardinghouse **11**

Hotel Hälsingland **10**

The Summer Inn Bed & Breakfast **6**

Where to Dine

The Bamboo Room **8**

Fireweed Restaurant **12**

The Lighthouse **9**

Mosey's Cantina **13**

2 ★ Sheldon Museum and Cultural Center. This is a serious town museum reflecting Haines's past and its current artistic output, and showing an extensive collection of Tlingit art and artifacts. It has a nice, personal feel and offers good interpretation. ⏱ 1 hr. 11 Main St. ☎ 907-766-2366. www.sheldonmuseum.org. $3 adults, free for children 11 and under. Summer Mon–Fri 10am–5pm, Sat–Sun 1–4pm; winter Mon–Sat 1–4pm.

3 ★ kids Hammer Museum. Perhaps your dreams of an Alaskan trip didn't include a visit to a museum devoted to hammers. But here you can learn something about the Alaska spirit. Possessed to live large, the owner followed his enthusiasm for hammers in a big way—there are more than 1,800 of them on display here. There are a lot of funny stories related to the museum, too, including a trademark dispute with a famous museum in L.A. named for philanthropist Armand Hammer. ⏱ 30 min. 108 Main St. ☎ 907-766-2374. www.hammermuseum.org. $3 adults, free for children 12 and under. In season Mon–Fri 10am–5pm; closed off-season.

4 ★ kids American Bald Eagle Foundation Natural History Museum. Another museum that came about due to the enthusiasm of one man, the center includes both a room full of mounted eagles and other animals and a facility where you can see live birds of prey. ⏱ 1 hr. 2nd Ave. and Haines Hwy. ☎ 907-766-3094. www.baldeagles.org. Admission $5 adults, $2.50 children 9 to 12, free for children 8 and under. Summer Mon–Fri 10am–6pm, Sat–Sun noon–4pm; closed winter.

Getting into Town

The state ferry dock is 5 miles out of town, and taxis are not consistently available; ask about transfers when you reserve your rooms. Or take another boat that arrives at a more convenient spot: The Port Chilkoot Dock right below Fort Seward, in town. It is used by the Haines-Skagway Fast Ferry (☎ 888-766-2103 or 907-766-2100; www.hainesskagwayfastferry.com), which carries passengers (but not cars) between the two communities daily. It charges $35 one way, $68 round trip.

> Rafting through the eagle preserve on the Chilkat
River.

5 ★★ **Chilkat Bald Eagle Preserve.** This state park along the Chilkat River protects an area that is home to the world's largest gathering of bald eagles, numbering up to 3,000, which comes together in the early winter for the food provided by a unique late-season salmon run. In the summer, just a few hundred eagles are present, but it's a good place to see them, perched in the cottonwood trees along the river and the Haines Highway, between 18 and 21 miles out of town. Guides bring groups to see the river; my favorite such trip is a river float through the preserve with **Chilkat Guides.** ⏱ Half-day. See p. 353, **14**.

Biking in Haines

A bike is a perfect mode of transportation for Haines. The town isn't large, but it's large enough that you might not want to walk everywhere, and you can explore by bicycle the little-used roads leading from the community. Rent bikes at **Sockeye Cycle Co.,** just up from the Port Chilkoot Dock on Portage Street in the Fort William Seward area (☎ 907-766-2869; www.cycle alaska.com); the cost is $14 for 2 hours or $35 for 8 hours.

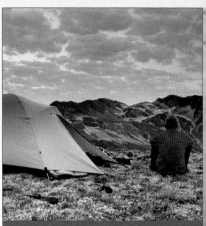

Getting Outdoors in Haines

Flightseeing. You're near enough to Glacier Bay National Park that you can fly over the mountains to see the glaciers and maybe even land on one. Paul Swanstrom of **Alaska Mountain Flying and Travel** (p. 367, **12**) specializes in putting people down in remote places in the park, including sightseers. Prices range from $149 to $499 per person.

Hiking. There are lots of trails to choose from in Haines; you can get advice and a free guide from the **Haines Convention and Visitors Bureau Visitor Information Center,** on 2nd Avenue near Willard Street (☎ 800-458-3579 or 907-766-2234; www.haines.ak.us). For an easy coastal hike, take the **Battery Point Trail,** which leads 2 miles along the shore from the end of Beach Road, southwest from the dock below the fort. The **Mount Ripinsky Trail** is a challenging all-day climb, 10 miles total, to a 3,650-foot peak north of town. The trailhead is at the top of Young Street.

Sea Kayaking. As in other Southeast towns, Haines offers the opportunity to sea kayak in the ocean waters nearby, but here the guides are from a well-known outdoors company that teaches mountain climbing and leads expeditions around the world: **Alaska Mountain Guides** (☎ 800-766-3396 or 907-766-3366; www.alaska mountainguides.com). Their half-day guided paddle is $85, including a snack; a full day, including lunch, is $125.

Where to Stay & Dine

★ **The Bamboo Room** DOWNTOWN *DINER* Everyone likes the halibut and chips here, and you can get most anything else from a menu that includes burgers, pasta, wraps, salads, and much seafood. The building was a gold-rush brothel and has been run by the same family for more than 50 years. 2nd Ave. near Main St. ☎ 907-766-2474. www.bambooopioneer.net. Entrees $10–$35. AE, DC, DISC, MC, V. Summer breakfast, lunch, and dinner daily; no dinner in winter.

★ **Captain's Choice Motel** DOWNTOWN This is Haines's only hotel with standard rooms similar to most American hotels—in this funny town, the normal place is the odd man out. Although on the dark side and some-what out-of-date, all rooms are clean and many have good views from a large sun deck. 108 2nd St. ☎ 800-478-2345 or 907-766-3111. www.capchoice.com. 39 units. Doubles $129 high season; $116 low season; w/breakfast. AE, DC, DISC, MC, V.

★ **Fireweed Restaurant** FORT SEWARD *PIZZA* This tiny restaurant in a nicely remodeled historic fort building packs in people for casual food, especially the good pizza and calzones. Historic building #37, Blacksmith Rd. ☎ 907-766-3838. Entrees $11–$20. MC, V. Summer lunch and dinner Tues–Sat; spring and fall dinner only. Closed Oct–Mar.

The Guardhouse Boardinghouse FORT SEWARD This is not a boardinghouse, but a comfortable, inexpensive B&B with central lodgings, where guests are treated as friends by the hostesses, Phyllis Sage and Joanne Water-man, and their spaniel. 15 Seward Dr. ☎ 866-290-7445 or 907-766-2566. www.alaskaguardhouse.com. 3 units. Doubles $85–$115, w/breakfast.

★ **Hotel Hälsingland** FORT SEWARD This big old wooden hotel with high ceilings is a National Historic Landmark, having served as the Com-manding Officer's Quarters for Fort William Seward during both world wars. It's by far the most interesting place to stay in town. Fort Wil-liam Seward parade grounds. ☎ 800-542-6363 or 907-766-2000. www.hotelhalsingland.com.

> *Get some 'za at Fireweed Restaurant.*

50 units. Doubles $89–$119. AE, DC, DISC, MC, V. Closed mid-Nov to mid-Mar.

★ **The Lighthouse** DOWNTOWN *SEAFOOD* The dining room is light and stylish and has a fine water view. In the evening it's a steak and seafood place, and the fish is done well—sim-ply, and not all fried. Breakfast is American traditional, and lunch mainly burgers and sandwiches. Main and Front sts. ☎ 907-766-2442. Entrees $15–$30. AE, DC, DISC, MC, V. Summer breakfast, lunch, and dinner daily; no breakfast in winter.

★ **Mosey's Cantina** FORT SEWARD *MEXICAN/SOUTHWEST* Authentic food made with hand-selected chiles warms up guests in the small dining room of this house with a big porch, south of the fort. The atmosphere is loud and festive. 1 Soap Suds Alley. ☎ 907-766-2320. En-trees $9–$18. MC, V. Lunch and dinner Mon–Sat. Closed Oct–Feb.

The Summer Inn Bed & Breakfast DOWN-TOWN Here is an old-fashioned B&B in a his-toric house with lacy fabrics and a claw-foot tub said to be Haines's first. The rooms are small but immaculate, and share three bath-rooms among them. No smoking or drinking is allowed. 117 2nd Ave. ☎ 907-766-2970. www.summerinnbnb.com. 5 units. Doubles $110 high season, w/breakfast. MC, V.

Skagway

The gold rush that rolled through Skagway in 1898
established the town's role in the world ever since. There's no industry here
other than tourism, and the buildings and stories left behind from that era are
the reason tourists come here. I've always enjoyed Skagway because the stories
are good and easy to imagine among the restored structures, but the place
can be overrun by cruise-ship passengers, and if the Wild West historic period
doesn't interest you, it's probably not worth a visit. If it does, you'll want a day
or two to explore.

> *In 1897, news of gold brought thousands of speculators to Alaska; the Klondike Gold Rush National Historic Park preserves that history.*

START Skagway, 86 miles north of Juneau, 500 miles east of Anchorage.

❶ ★★ Klondike Gold Rush National Historical Park. The National Park Service preserves and interprets many of Skagway's gold rush buildings and operates an interesting visitor center that is the best starting point for a visit. Besides viewing exhibits that explain the town's place in history, you can get free tickets for the walking tour of the main sites, many

of which have been restored. The 45-minute tours start at 9am, 10am, 11am, 2pm, and 3pm. Arriving 45 minutes early will help ensure that you receive a ticket and will give you time to look at the museum. If you choose to tour on your own, pick up the informative self-guided walking tour map. ⏱ 1½ hr. 2nd Ave. and Broadway. ☎ 907-983-9223; www.nps.gov/klgo. Free admission. May–late Sept daily 8am–6pm; late Sept–April no tours, museum open Mon–Fri 8am–5pm.

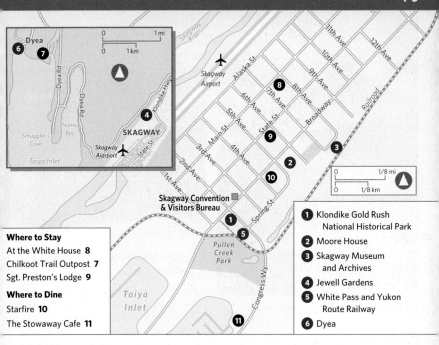

Where to Stay

At the White House **8**

Chilkoot Trail Outpost **7**

Sgt. Preston's Lodge **9**

Where to Dine

Starfire **10**

The Stowaway Cafe **11**

Skagway Convention & Visitors Bureau

1 Klondike Gold Rush National Historical Park

2 Moore House

3 Skagway Museum and Archives

4 Jewell Gardens

5 White Pass and Yukon Route Railway

6 Dyea

---

2 ★ **Moore House.** This spot has a story that neatly encapsulates gold-rush ethics: Captain William Moore brilliantly predicted that gold would be found in Yukon and that people would need to come through this area, and he obtained the title to the future town's land 10 years beforehand. But when the rush came, the gold seekers simply ignored his ownership and took his land. In a town without law or government, he was unable to get justice until long after the rush was over. ⏱ 30 min. 5th Ave. and Spring St. Free admission. Daily 10am–5pm; closed winter.

Getting Around Skagway

The central historic part of Skagway is easily walkable, but to reach some of the outlying attractions, you need to rent a bike from **Sockeye Cycle Co.** (p. 412) or take a shuttle or bus. **Dyea Dave Shuttle** (☎ 907-612-0290) operates like a taxi. Skagway's bus, called **SMART** (☎ 907-983-2743), runs a circuit around town for $2 a ride, leaving on the hour from City Hall at 7th Avenue and Spring Street.

---

3 ★ **Skagway Museum and Archives.** Occupying the town's most impressive building—a granite structure that began as a college and later was a courthouse and jail—this collection includes the best of the town's gold-rush memorabilia. ⏱ 30 min. 7th and Spring sts. ☎ 907-983-2420. Admission $2 adults, $1 students, free for children 12 and under. Summer Mon–Fri 9am–5pm, Sat 10am–5pm, Sun 10am–4pm; call for winter hours.

4 ★ **Jewell Gardens.** Original plantings from a garden dating to the gold rush have been augmented with an organic show garden and a glass-blowing studio where guests can watch artists at work. The proprietors teach about growing conditions and techniques in Alaska, including how to compost in cold weather. There's also a good restaurant on-site called Poppies at Jewell Gardens, which serves local seafood and the garden's own produce. ⏱ 1 hr. Mile 1.5, Klondike Hwy. ☎ 907-983-2111. www.jewellgardens.com. Admission $12 adults, $6 children 12 and under. Daily 9am–5pm. Closed mid-Sept to mid-May.

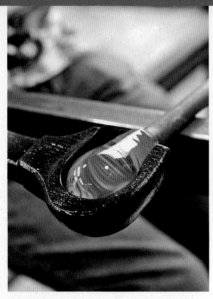

> *A glass artist works onsite at Jewell Gardens.*

> *The White Pass and Yukon Route narrow-gauge railway.*

5 ★★ **White Pass and Yukon Route Railway.** Two routes led over the mountains in gold-rush days: the famous Chilkoot Pass foot trail that led incredibly steeply from the now-disappeared town of Dyea, and the White Pass starting from Skagway, which was theoretically passable by horses although untold numbers of animals died on it. Either way, reaching the top meant you were in Canada, ready to build a boat to sail, row, and shoot rapids down to Dawson City. In 1900, in a miracle of engineering and rapid construction, the White Pass and Yukon Route narrow-gauge railway was completed from Skagway to Carcross, Yukon, spelling doom for Dyea, as few would walk anymore. The line still operates as an excursion train, and the ride is spectacular—incredibly steep and precipitous and historic. Some special trips use original cars and steam engines part of the way. The train is quite slow, however, and you see little in cloudy weather; reserve ahead, but consider canceling with a $10 penalty rather than going in a whiteout. ☉ Half-day. 2nd Ave. depot. ☎ 800-343-7373 or 907-983-2217. www.wpyr. com. Summit excursion $103 adults, half-price for children 3–12, free for children 2 and under.

6 ★★ **Dyea.** This ghost town lies at the start of the famed **Chilkoot Pass Trail** (at right). It's a challenging backpacking trip, but a lovely outing can be had by riding a bike to the area where Dyea once stood. The quiet road winds along the seaside. Dyea itself only suggests signs of its former existence, including historic debris and one false front. But it's a scenic and calming site, grassy and blanketed with wildflowers, and ranger-led tours daily at 10am and 2pm tell the story of the place. Best of all, away from the throngs and slick attractions in Skagway, the history starts to feel authentic.

The most powerful spot in town is the **Slide Cemetery**. On April 3, 1898, an avalanche swept almost 100 people to their deaths on the Chilkoot Pass. Most were buried here, although the number and their names are largely lost. It's a spooky place—a testament to the horrors of the gold rush, which are generally papered over in Skagway. ☉ Half-day. 8 miles out Dyea Road (turn left onto the road 2 miles out of Skagway, on Klondike Hwy. 2). Free admission. Always open.

Glacier Flights

The air services mentioned in Gustavus and Haines, **Air Excursions** (p. 367, **12**) and **Alaska Mountain Flying and Travel** (p. 367, **12**), also carry clients from Skagway over the spectacular glaciers of Glacier Bay National Park, which is just to the west.

Where to Stay & Dine

> *Locally brewed beers are popular—and generally excellent.*

★ **At the White House** DOWNTOWN
This gable-roofed inn with a gold-rush pedigree, fine woodwork, and wood floors contains modern, comfortable rooms, varying in size, that are in keeping with the style of the period. Besides the ceiling fans and quilts, they're equipped with refrigerators and Wi-Fi. Corner of 8th and Main sts. ☎ 907-983-9000. www.atthewhitehouse.com. 10 units. Doubles $125 high season; $85 low season; w/breakfast. AE, DISC, MC, V.

★ **Chilkoot Trail Outpost** DYEA
Staying in the nicely crafted log cabins here gets you away from the crowds in Skagway to a natural setting near the Chilkoot Pass Trail and Taiya River. Lodgings are up-to-date and have many amenities, but lack phones. In good weather, the hosts have a nightly campfire and provide supplies for s'mores. They lend bikes, too. Mile 7, Dyea Rd. ☎ 907-983-3799. www.chilkoottrailoutpost.com. 11 units. Doubles $145–$175, w/breakfast. Closed off-season.

★ **Sgt. Preston's Lodge** DOWNTOWN
Three buildings on a lawn contain typical, modern motel rooms with good amenities. It's the right choice if you simply want a comfortable place to sleep for a reasonable rate. 370 6th Ave. ☎ 866-983-2521 or 907-983-2521. www.sgtprestonslodge.com. 38 units. Doubles $85–$120, $80 low season. AE, DISC, MC, V.

★ **Starfire** DOWNTOWN *THAI* Besides the spicy Thai cuisine that is the specialty here—stir-fries, curries, soups, and salads—you can also get simply prepared local seafood or French cuisine. The service is quick and the dining room aesthetic, despite cramped quarters. 4th Ave. btw. Spring St. and Broadway. ☎ 907-983-3663. Entrees $14–$19. MC, V. Lunch Mon–Fri, dinner daily. Closed off-season.

★★ **The Stowaway Cafe** HARBOR *SEAFOOD*
This little restaurant has produced consistently excellent food for years, a feat no one else has managed in this highly seasonal community. Alaskan fish is prepared in many international styles—you can even get grilled halibut with Jamaican jerk spice and a cranberry chutney garnish. End of Congress Way, near the small boat harbor. ☎ 907-983-3463. Entrees $16–$29. V only. Lunch and dinner daily. Closed off-season.

> Juneau's Franklin Street.

Southeast Alaska Fast Facts

Accommodations Booking Services
Alaska Travelers Accommodations, LLC, for lodgings in Ketchikan and Juneau. ☎ 800-928-3308 or 907-247-7117. www.alaska travelers.com

Ketchikan Reservation Service. ☎ 800-987-5337 or 907-247-5337. www.ketchikan-lodging.com.

Getting There & Getting Around
BY PLANE The only jet carrier in the region is Alaska Airlines (☎ 800-252-7522; www. alaskaair.com). Commuter airlines connect many towns more frequently. Among the largest is Wings of Alaska (☎ 907-789-0790; www.ichoosewings.com). BY CAR No road connects most of the towns in the region. The only exceptions within Alaska are Haines and Skagway, at the north end of the Inside Passage waterway. Highways from there lead into Canada's Yukon. BY FERRY The main transportation link between communities is the Alaska Marine Highway System (☎ 800-642-0066, or 907-766-2111 locally; www.ferryalaska. com).

Emergencies
Dial ☎ 911.

Dentists & Doctors
If you need emergency dental care, go to the nearest hospital or medical center. KETCHIKAN Ketchikan General Hospital, 3100 Tongass Ave. (☎ 907-225-5171). WRANGELL Wrangell Medical Center , 310 Bennett St. (☎ 907-874-7000). PETERSBURG Petersburg Medical Center, 2nd and Fram streets (☎ 907-772-4291). SITKA Community Hospital (☎ 907-747-3241), 209 Moller Dr. JUNEAU Bartlett Regional, 3260 Hospital Dr. (☎ 907-796-8900), 3 miles out the Glacier Highway from downtown. HAINES Haines Medical Clinic (☎ 907-766-6300), on 1st Avenue, near the visitor center. SKAGWAY Dahl Medical Clinic (staffed by a physician's assistant), ☎ 907-983-2255 during business hours.

Internet Access
KETCHIKAN SeaPort Cyberstations (☎ 907-247-4615; www.seaportel.com), second floor at 5 Salmon Landing. WRANGELL Nolan Center, 296 Campbell Dr. (☎ 907-874-3770); access is $5 for the first 20 minutes, $10 an hour. PETERSBURG Free at the public library, at Nordic and Haugen drives (☎ 907-772-3349). SITKA Highliner Coffee, on Lake Street near Seward Street (☎ 907-747-4924). JUNEAU Copy Express, 230 Seward St. (☎ 907-586-2174). HAINES Haines Borough Library, 111 3rd Ave. S. (☎ 907-766-2545; www.ketchikan-lodging.com.). SKAGWAY Alaska Cruiseship Services, charging $6 an hour, at 2nd Avenue and State Street (☎ 907-983-3398).

Police
KETCHIKAN ☎ 907-225-6631. WRANGELL ☎ 907-874-3304. PETERSBURG ☎ 907-772-3838. SITKA ☎ 907-747-3245. JUNEAU ☎ 907-586-0600. HAINES Within city limits ☎ 907-766-2121; outside ☎ 907-766-2552. SKAGWAY ☎ 907-983-2232.

Visitor Information
KETCHIKAN Ketchikan Visitors Bureau, 131 Front St. (☎ 800-770-3300 or 907-225-6166; fax 907-225-4250; www.visit-ketchikan.com). WRANGELL Wrangell Visitor Center, in the Nolan Center, 296 Campbell Dr. (☎ 800-367-9745; www.wrangell.com). PETERSBURG Petersburg Chamber of Commerce, Visitor Information Center, corner of 1st and Fram streets (☎ 866-484-4700 or 907-772-4636; www. petersburg.org). SITKA Sitka Convention and Visitors Bureau (☎ 907-747-5940; www.sitka.org). JUNEAU Juneau Convention and Visitors Bureau, Visitor Information Center, in Centennial Hall, 101 Egan Dr. (☎ 888-581-2201 or 907-586-2201; www.traveljuneau.com).

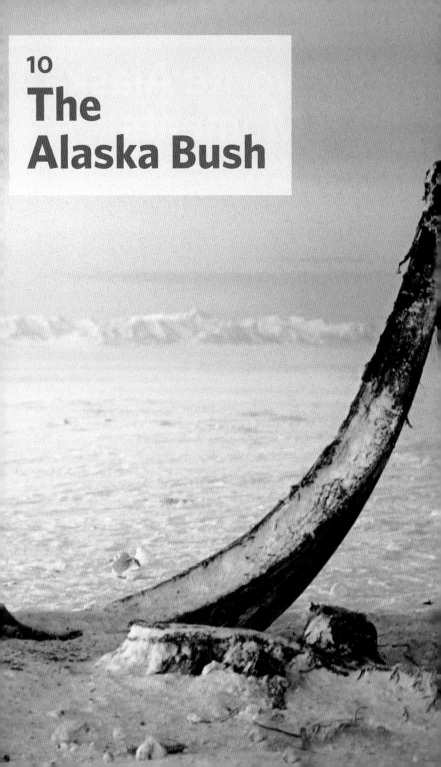

The Alaska Bush

My Favorite Alaska Bush Moments

Most of Alaska—all of the *real* Alaska, some would say— lies far beyond the end of the road system, in the vast area where towns and villages are specks dwarfed by the North's wild immensity. This is the land of adventure from childhood fantasies of Alaska, yet most visitors never make it there. The reasons are simple: Getting to the Bush is expensive, and there's not much to do once you arrive, unless you're bound for a rugged outdoor expedition (covered in chapter 12). But if you're determined, and you're prepared to appreciate these exotic places as they are—without attractions for visiting tourists—there's good reason to add a side trip of a day or two to one of these communities. You will see places, meet people, and perhaps have experiences that few can accurately imagine.

> PREVIOUS PAGE *A polar bear investigates a whale bone.* THIS PAGE *Midnight sun casts an eerie light over pack ice on the Chukchi Sea.*

❶ Midnight sun on the Arctic Ocean. Standing on the shore in **Barrow,** the farthest-north town in the United States, a new and unfamiliar ocean lies before you: an ocean that can freeze. In the early summer—when, for more than 60 days in a row, the sun never sets—ice often remains from the winter, glowing blue and white in the bright yellow light that beams from due north at midnight. See p. 429, ❸.

1 Midnight sun on the Arctic Ocean, Point Barrow
2 Iñupiat Heritage Center, Barrow
3 Musk oxen outside Nome
4 Flying above the Bering Strait
5 World War II ruins, Unalaska
6 Halibut fishing, Unalaska
7 Bear viewing Kodiak National Wildlife Refuge
8 Dinner cruise, Kodiak

> *Traditional music and dance performances help keep Inupiat culture alive in Barrow.*

❷ Meeting an elder at the Iñupiat Heritage Center. Barrow's living museum is for the indigenous residents of this Arctic community, and that's what makes the heritage center such an interesting place for visitors. Besides the exhibits that explain Iñupiaq culture, there are rooms where elders share their knowledge and a workshop where whaling crews build their seal skin boats. Try to attend for the afternoon dance performance. See p. 426, ❶.

❸ Seeing musk ox on the tundra outside Nome. This gold-rush town stands at a seemingly random spot where the tundra ends and the sea begins. You can see wildlife from a long way off on that tundra, and some very unusual animals are there to see. My most memorable Nome moment was driving up a gravel road and coming upon a herd of musk ox—shaggy monsters that look as though they've stepped out of a science-fiction movie. See p. 432.

❹ Flying above the Bering Strait and glimpsing Siberia. Nome-based **Bering Air** helped reopen the Bering Strait after the Cold War, reuniting Native families that had been separated by the Ice Curtain for half a century. The

> *The musk ox is so named for the strong odor emitted by males.*

> *The Kodiak* (Ursus arctos middendorffi) *is a distinct subspecies of brown bear that has been separated from other bears for 12,000 years.*

same firm still carries visitors for flightseeing or to view this strange landscape on scheduled village flights. You really can see Russia from up there! See p. 432.

❺ Climbing to the ruins of a forgotten war. The volcanic **Aleutian Islands,** swathed in tundra and swept by endless, foggy winds, are a world apart from anyplace else you've been. You may be equally unfamiliar with the fighting that occurred here during World War II, when thousands died in a struggle for two of the outer islands. On Unalaska you can climb to the remains of the American defenses. See p. 436, ❸.

❻ Hooking into a giant halibut. Unalaska and its port of **Dutch Harbor** see a greater volume of fish landed than any other port in the nation. This is the place to come if you're focused on catching a huge halibut. The location way out in the middle of the North Pacific puts it in an area of prodigious biological productivity (which means the bird-watching is great, too). The world's largest halibut, at 459 pounds, was caught here. See p. 437.

❼ Watching the world's largest bears. The Kodiak brown bear grows to enormous size—the largest of them can be 1,500 pounds and 10 feet tall when standing on its hind legs—thanks to the abundance of salmon returning here. These bears can be found only on **Kodiak Island,** which is America's second largest (only the big island of Hawaii is larger). By taking a floatplane to a salmon stream, you can get close to these giant bears in a remote, pristine setting. See p. 445, ❹.

❽ Dining on a yacht in a private cove. The waters around **Kodiak** are full of islands and narrow passages. Marty and Marion Owen take just six guests on their 42-foot *Sea Breeze,* anchoring up in a calm lagoon for a seafood dinner after a cruise to see puffins, sea lions, or whales. See p. 447.

Barrow

Visiting an Alaska Native community in the Arctic can feel like going to a foreign country. People speak English with an Iñupiaq accent and live and relate to each other according to the ways of their unique culture. The land is flat and treeless, melding into the sea, and the buildings, constructed on legs to avoid thawing the permanently frozen ground, don't collectively look like a town down south; there is no business district, no one has a grassy lawn, and snow machines and all-terrain vehicles are as common as cars. Barrow has all that, plus an added attraction: It's easy (if expensive) to get there, and the visitor infrastructure is adequately developed to make your stay comfortable and productive. You'll need to spend at least 1 full day here.

> A massive arch on the Arctic coast made of two whale bones pays homage to the Iñupiaq whale hunting heritage.

START Barrow is 760 miles north of Anchorage.

❶ ★★ Iñupiat Heritage Center. The Iñupiat used much of the money gained from the oil fields under their ancestral lands for education and protection of their cultural heritage. The center is a prime example. Rather than a tourist attraction designed to entertain visitors, it was built to keep Iñupiaq traditions alive by preserving artifacts, recording exchanges of traditional wisdom, and providing a place to build boats and drums and to create dance, theater, and art. You never know exactly what will be going on when you visit, but even if the place is quiet, there are fascinating museum exhibits; dance performances and craft fairs

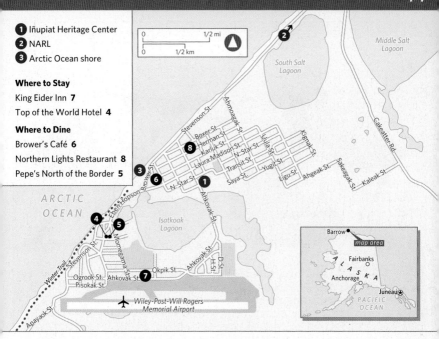

1 Iñupiat Heritage Center
2 NARL
3 Arctic Ocean shore

Where to Stay

King Eider Inn **7**

Top of the World Hotel **4**

Where to Dine

Brower's Café **6**

Northern Lights Restaurant **8**

Pepe's North of the Border **5**

are held daily for the Alaska Airlines Vacations tour, which independent travelers can see, too. ⏱ 2 hr. Ahkovak St. and North Star St. ☎ 907-852-0422. www.nps.gov/inup. Admission $10 adults, $5 students, free for seniors and children 6 and under. Mon–Fri 8:30am–5pm. Dance and craft fair (additional fee) 1:30–3:30pm most summer days (call ahead to confirm).

2 ★ **Naval Arctic Research Lab (NARL).** Barrow is among the furthest-north inhabited places in North America, which made it a natural site for the most important Arctic research field station on U.S. soil. For decades of the Cold War, the U.S. Navy conducted research here, building a complex of dozens of buildings on Point Barrow, the spit of land that reaches into the ocean north of town. Later the local community took over, supporting research and remodeling old labs into a community college. Cutting-edge climate change research continues here. The new Barrow Arctic Research Center stands behind the old buildings and is still managed by locals. You can go inside during normal business hours, and the center offers frequent public lectures

Getting to Barrow

The only way to get to Barrow is by air. The easiest and most popular way to visit is on an escorted tour offered by **Alaska Airlines Vacations** (☎ 866-500-5511; www.alaska airalaska.com). The tours can be done in a day or an overnight from Anchorage or Fairbanks. You'll be taken on a narrated bus tour to all of Barrow's attractions, including a stop at the Arctic Ocean and attendance at the dance program at the Iñupiat Heritage Center (see 1). If you go for a day, you'll have virtually no unstructured time to explore; if you want to wander on your own, take the overnight trip. The cost from Fairbanks is $499 for the day tour, $599 if you stay overnight at the **Top of the World Hotel** (p. 429). Going without the tour doesn't cost much less, and you'll still need to fly Alaska Airlines (p. 507). Most flights originate in Anchorage and stop in Fairbanks on the way to Barrow.

The Iñupiaq Whaling Tradition

For as long as the Iñupiat culture has existed, roughly 1,000 years, its heart has been the bowhead whale: the hunt, the harvest, and the sharing of the food. If your timing is good (and lucky), you'll have an opportunity to witness a part of this ancient tradition.

Bowhead commonly grow to more than 60 feet and reach an age of 150 years. Scientists established their longevity when Iñupiat hunters in 1992 found a stone spear tip in the flank of a landed whale—a tip that could not have been used since 1880. Bowhead numbers were driven down by commercial whaling, but are increasing well now despite Iñupiat hunting, which is limited by international agreement and closely regulated by the Iñupiat themselves.

Hunting occurs during the spring and fall migrations in Barrow. In the primary hunt, in the spring, crews cut trails through the rough sea ice to the edge of the lead, or open water area, and wait there in camp for a whale to approach. With luck, they can quietly launch a skin boat (pictured) near the whale and maneuver close enough to throw a harpoon. Traditionally, a number of strikes would have been used to tire the whale until a hunter could climb on its back, still in the water, and kill it with a spear. Today explosive weapons are used to kill the whale more humanely and safely.

Hundreds of villagers converge to pull a killed whale onto the ice and butcher it.

They eat nearly every part but no longer make much use of the bone, which once provided supports for houses. Everyone who participates receives an even share of meat and *muktuk*, or blubber with skin, as do the elderly or infirm. Then it is up to the successful crew to cook up whale delicacies and feed them to the entire community. The entire process can take days of continuous work to complete.

The spring hunt happens in early May. But the fall hunt, in early October, may be easier for visitors to witness, because then the whales are carried up on shore for butchering rather than onto the sea ice. The work typically takes place on the steel runway at **NARL** (p. 427, **②**). Ask if you can help, if you want; in any event, be friendly and open with people, and treat them respectfully.

If you come in late June, you might be on hand for Nalukataq, the festival when the successful captains are again obliged to feed the community; it takes place in the middle of town and is open to all. A highlight is the spectacular but dangerous Eskimo blanket toss: A group holding the edge of a walrus skin blanket uses it to hurl a person high into the air. Nalukataq is always on Saturday, but the exact day depends on the wishes of the captain.

You can learn much more about Iñupiat whaling and culture, and climate change in the Arctic, in my book The Whale and the Supercomputer *(www.charleswohlforth.com).*

by leading scientists (check the website). The entire complex is interesting in an odd way—it's easy to imagine Cold War scientists working here in the extreme cold. ☉ 1 hr. www.arcticscience.org.

❸ ★★★ Arctic Ocean shore. In Barrow, the sea is never far away. Classic photos are taken at the whalebone arch in the Browerville area, near Brower's Café, but it's common to find whale bones all along the beach. The community has used the bowhead whale as a key food for 1,000 years and still does so. If you come in May or June, join Arctic Tours for a ride in a Humvee, miles out along the beach beyond town, to look for polar bears. They are rare later in the summer, but are often seen in spring before the ice goes out. Call ahead to nail down a tour, as this is a casual home business. ☉ 2 hr. ☎ 907-852-4512 or 907-852-1462 cell. $70 per person, two-person minimum.

Where to Stay & Dine

Brower's Café BROWERVILLE *CHINESE*
The restaurant serves American and Chinese food in a historic whaling station built by Charles Brower, who a century ago established a family and cultural bridge between Barrow's Eskimo whalers and Yankee whalers from New England. 3220 Brower's Hill. ☎ 907-852-3456. Entrees $10–$47. MC,V. Lunch and dinner daily.

★★ King Eider Inn BARROW
This clapboard building near the airport is a place to escape the gritty, improvised atmosphere of most businesses in Barrow. One reason is the regulations: Smoking isn't allowed, and guests have to remove their shoes at the door. But it's also due to the solid, well-thought-out construction of the place, with quality materials and an airy design. 1752 Ahkovak St. ☎ 888-303-4337 reservations or 907-852-4700. www.kingeider.net. 19 units. Doubles $189 summer; $169 winter. AE, MC, V.

Northern Lights Restaurant BROWERVILLE *PIZZA* This is one of Barrow's more popular choices, with a clean dining room and a long menu that includes Chinese food, deli selections, burgers, and the best pizza in town. 5122 Herman St. ☎ 907-852-3300. Entrees $13–$30. MC,V. Lunch and dinner daily.

Pepe's North of the Border BARROW *MEXICAN*
Tour groups are dropped here for lunch and to receive souvenirs, such as a certificate showing you've crossed the Arctic Circle, from the

> *A well-used but comfortable room at the Top of the World.*

owner, Fran Tate. The place is in a time warp: Tate's claim to fame is a TV appearance with Johnny Carson, and the restaurant looks (and tastes) just like Americanized Mexican restaurants did in the 1970s. 1204 Agvik St. ☎ 907-852-8200. Entrees $20–$35. MC, V. Breakfast, lunch, and dinner daily.

★ Top of the World Hotel BARROW
This is the town's main hotel, where those on tours spend the night. You'll find standard rooms that are worn in spots but generally comfortable. Those on the water side look out on the Arctic Ocean. People gather to hang out in the lobby, a cluttered space with a TV and a stuffed polar bear. Agvik St. ☎ 907-852-3900. www.tundratoursinc.com. 44 units. Doubles $150–$220 summer; $125–$155 winter. AE, DC, DISC, MC, V.

Nome

Nome is unique as an Arctic gold-rush community and as a town that manages to keep intact the hard-charging, wacky spirit of that time. (In fact, Nome is a little south of the Arctic Circle, but it deserves to be called Arctic in every other respect.) It has a special quality for visitors. Unlike most rural Alaska communities, where outdoor activities require you to go with a guide or to be an expert yourself, this is a place where you can experience the Arctic on your own. There's plenty of stuff to do: Drive the long gravel roads looking for reindeer and musk ox. Go bird-watching for a remarkable variety of exotic species. Walk along a sandy beach that once was full of gold. Fly to tiny villages to get an aerial view of a strange landscape and unfamiliar way of life. The only way to get to Nome is by air—Alaska Airlines (p. 507) flies daily from Anchorage.

> An abandoned gold mining dredge once crept across the Seward Peninsula's tundra on ponds of its own making.

START Nome is 540 miles from Anchorage.
TRIP LENGTH At least 1 day.

❶ ★ Carrie M. McLain Memorial Museum. Nome is loaded with the best gold-rush stories in Alaska, but there's not much history in the streets. That's because until a sea wall was constructed in 1951, the town kept getting washed away. People rebuilt each time because gold was so plentiful; mining continued

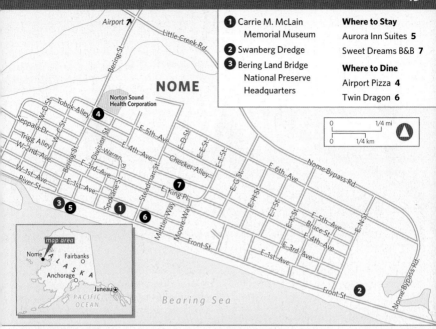

1 Carrie M. McLain Memorial Museum
2 Swanberg Dredge
3 Bering Land Bridge National Preserve Headquarters

Where to Stay
Aurora Inn Suites 5
Sweet Dreams B&B 7

Where to Dine
Airport Pizza 4
Twin Dragon 6

End of the Road: Nome & the Iditarod

When the **Iditarod Trail Sled Dog Race** ends under the burled arch in Nome (a log with a pair of lumps called *burls*), the town explodes into a giant party. Visitors come from all over the world along with the media, mushers, and helpers. Rooms book far in advance, but townspeople endeavor to find a spot for everyone in this festive atmosphere. Many community events take place, including a golf tournament out on the sea ice. Animal rights advocates may complain about the race on the Internet, but you won't hear anything but enthusiasm here.

The 1,000-mile Iditarod starts near Anchorage on the first Saturday in March.

Winners take about 9 days to get to Nome, during which time Alaskans and their media outlets can talk of little else, tracking mushers as they pass through remote checkpoints along the way. Air taxis such as **Rust's Flying Service** (p. 75, 4) carry visitors from point to point to follow along with the race. Another way to participate is by volunteering to help put on the race. Or just plan to be in Anchorage or Nome for the start or finish, and spend the rest of your trip seeing the various other winter festivals held around that period (see chapter 12). For more information, contact the Iditarod Trail Committee (☎ 907-376-5155; www.iditarod.com).

Getting Outdoors near Nome

The best reason to visit Nome is the surrounding wilderness. Here are three great ways to catch a glimpse.

Bird-Watching. The roads around Nome allow access to Arctic habitat of a type you've likely never explored, and you may even encounter some truly rare birds. The area is so close to eastern Siberia, it's possible to see Asian species. Chances are good you'll see bluethroats, yellow wagtails, wheatears, Arctic warblers, and Aleutian and Arctic terns. The best birding time is Memorial Day through June, when Bering Land Bridge rangers run Saturday bird outings, and in early August. Call the rangers for details (☎ 907-443-2522), or visit www.visitnome alaska.com/nome-bird-watching.html. Statewide bird tours, which often include Nome, are covered in chapter 12.

Flightseeing. Seeing the area from above is especially rewarding: The terrain is fascinating, there's plenty of wildlife, and the geography itself is an attraction, with the Bering Strait nearby and Russia just beyond. Bering Air pioneered flights across the strait and still flies charters there. A better plan is to organize a flightseeing charter on the American side or, if your group is small, to buy seats on one of the scheduled routes out to the tiny Native villages around Nome, which has the added bonus of allowing you a couple of hours to meet the locals before your return. Contact Bering Air (☎ 800-478-5422 in Alaska only, or 907-443-5464; www.beringair.com) and ask their advice, as making a good plan will depend on weather and schedules. Expect to pay $175 to $250 per person; on a loop flight, you can stay on board but pay only as far as the nearest village. Don't plan to stay overnight in a village without advance arrangements, and don't go in bad weather.

Wildlife Watching. The roads that radiate over the tundra and along the seashore from Nome are the town's most valuable feature for visitors. Your chances of seeing musk ox and reindeer right near town are often good. Rent a car from **Stampede Car Rental,** 302 E. Front St. (☎ 800-354-4606 or 907-443-3838; www.aurorainnome.com), and expect to pay more than $100 a day for an SUV you can take on the gravel roads. There are three main routes; the visitor center and **Bering Land Bridge National Preserve Head-quarters** (p. 433, ❸) are good sources of details. The Nome-Council Road is 72 miles long, half of it along the shore, and passes scenic bird-watching and fishing areas on the Solomon River. The Nome-Taylor road, also known as the Kougarok Road, runs 85 miles north of town over the tundra and through the beautiful Kigluaik Mountains. The Nome-Teller road leads 73 miles to the village of Teller, an authentic Alaska Native village with 260 residents and a store.

until fairly recently. You can learn about the history and see some fascinating artifacts, such as original *Nome Nugget* newspapers from the day, at this little museum, which is downstairs from the library. ⊙ 1 hr. Front St. and Lanes Way. ☎ 907-443-6630. www.nomealaska.org Free admission. Summer daily 9:30am–5:30pm; winter Tues–Fri noon–5:30pm.

② ★ **Swanberg Dredge.** The story of Nome's birth is an odd one. Gold seekers came to the area in 1898, and prospectors camped on the beach just south of what is now the town. In 1899 a man with an injured leg, whose name has since slipped away, was left behind in his tent while his companions looked for gold in the hills. Stuck, he decided to pan the sand around him. He hit pay dirt, sparking a much bigger gold rush in pursuit of the gold sand.

The beach is still a great place for a walk, although you're unlikely to find gold after a century of sifting. The Swanberg Dredge you see abandoned here operated until the 1950s.

It looks like a vehicle the size of a substantial building. Like the 38 huge gold dredges that once crept across the tundra of the Seward Peninsula, this behemoth dug its way across the land while floating on ponds of its own creation. If you get tired on the walk, get a cab back to town; the road is near the beach. ⊙ At least 2 hr.

③ **Bering Land Bridge National Preserve Headquarters.** The headquarters itself isn't particularly exciting, but it's a valuable source of information on the outdoors, which is the only good reason to go to Nome. The rangers here care for a rarely visited 2.7-million-acre national park unit, which covers much of the Seward Peninsula north of the Nome road system. They help visitors by offering advice and suggesting programs in and around Nome, including bird tours and ranger hikes. ⊙ 30 min. 214 Front St. ☎ 907-443-2522. www.nps.gov/bela. Daily 8am–4:30pm.

Where to Stay & Dine

★ **Airport Pizza** NOME *PIZZA*
This is a popular spot with a good reputation in town. It's also been covered by national media for packaging up pizzas and sending them on bush planes out to tiny villages. (Despite the name, it isn't at the airport.) Besides pizza, the restaurant serves sandwiches, Tex-Mex selections, steaks, and seafood; it brews fancy coffee, has 15 microbrews on tap, and offers free Wi-Fi. 406 Bering St. ☎ 907-443-7992. www.airportpizza.com. Entrees $11–$38. MC,V. Breakfast, lunch, and dinner daily.

★ **Aurora Inn Suites** NOME
This mock country inn on Nome's Front Street contains the best traditional hotel rooms in town. Nome has some awful, smoky dives, but here you'll be staying in accommodations as good as standard rooms anywhere. Owned by the Bering Straits Native Corporation, the inn also has an on-site car-rental operation. 302

E. Front St. ☎ 800-354-4606 or 907-443-3838. www.aurorainnnome.com. 56 units. Doubles $150–$250. AE, MC, V.

Sweet Dreams B&B NOME
Erna and Leo Rasmussen run the B&B. They're real pioneer treasures whom you'll love meeting, which happens when they pick you up from the airport. Their house has lots of Alaskan memorabilia. The B&B is near the Iditarod finish line and across from the good food at Airport Pizza. 406 W. 4th St. ☎ 907-443-2919. 3 units. Doubles $150, w/breakfast. MC, V.

Twin Dragon NOME *CHINESE*
This restaurant has survived for many years by serving food that keeps the locals coming back. That food includes Vietnamese noodles and pizza as well as Chinese cuisine. Front St. near Steadman St. ☎ 907-443-5552. MC, V. Entrees $11–$20. Lunch and dinner daily.

Unalaska & Dutch Harbor

A map of the Aleutian Archipelago, arching across the North Pacific almost to Asia, can stir the imagination, with thoughts of the extreme remoteness and distances, and of the weather that must batter these small, volcanic islands, exposed to the breadth of the world's largest sea. Indeed, the experience matches that image. Just getting to the largest community in the island chain, the industrial fishing town of Unalaska and its port, Dutch Harbor, takes a 3-hour flight from Anchorage or 4 days by ferry from Homer. Once there, the weather is extreme, but so are the views and the fishing, hiking, and bird-watching opportunities. There's perhaps a day's sightseeing to be had, focused mostly on World War II history; the last time war came to U.S. soil, it was here.

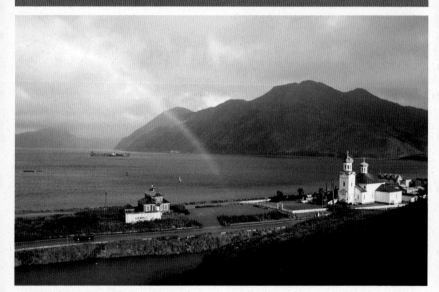

> Late-18th-century Holy Ascension Cathedral sits atop a wildflower-bedecked hill on Iliuliuk Bay.

START Unalaska is 800 miles from Anchorage. **TRIP LENGTH** At least 2 days.

❶ ★ Holy Ascension Cathedral. The 18th-century Russian invasion of Alaska started from the west, beginning with fur traders coming to the Aleutians from Siberia, and the influence of the Russian Orthodox church remains strong here among the indigenous people. A church first stood on this site in 1808, and the existing structure was completed in 1896. Besides being an important historic building, it's also a particularly lovely

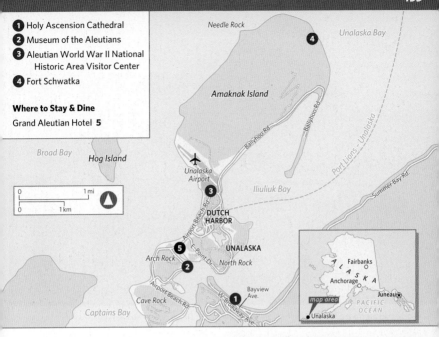

1 Holy Ascension Cathedral
2 Museum of the Aleutians
3 Aleutian World War II National
  Historic Area Visitor Center
4 Fort Schwatka

Where to Stay & Dine
Grand Aleutian Hotel 5

one, standing tall and white on the edge of Iliuliuk Bay. Take a walk there even if you can't go inside. The church often is not open, but if you're lucky enough to get in, it contains 697 icons and pieces of artwork dating back to its founding. Services are Saturday at 6:30pm; Sunday services are at 8:30am in the summer, 9:30am in the winter. On the waterfront of Iliuliuk Bay, Unalaska. Rector's home: ☎ 907-581-5883. ⏱ 30 min.

2 ★★ **Museum of the Aleutians.** The region has a history spanning 9,000 years, with some of North America's oldest coastal archeological sites here and on Umnak Island. Unlike most small town museums, which are set up by local enthusiasts, this museum was designed by professionals with academic training and with a mission of bringing ancient artifacts back to the culture that created them. In addition, you can see material on World War II in the Aleutians and exhibits focusing on relatively contemporary Alaskan art. ⏱ 1 hr. Next door to the Ounalashka Corporation on Margaret Bay, Dutch Harbor. ☎ 907-581-5150. www.aleutians.org. Admission $5. Summer Tues-Sat 9am-5pm, Sun noon-5pm; winter Tues-Sat 11am-5pm.

Getting to Unalaska & Dutch Harbor

This is a very expensive destination to reach, and getting there (and back) often involves delays or cancellations. The weather is frequently stormy, preventing landings on airport runways that were chipped from volcanic mountains, so it's not unusual for planes to be diverted to another landing strip to wait for a squall to pass. Only turbo-prop planes fly to the airport at Dutch Harbor, partly for this reason; they offer more flexibility in terms of where else they can land. The main carrier is PenAir (☎ 800-448-4226; www.penair.com). To reduce airfares of around $1,000 round trip from Anchorage, book your flight through **Alaska Airlines** (p. 507) and add it as a leg on your flight from home; that may save a lot. The flight from Anchorage takes 3 hours.

It's also possible to take the **Alaska Marine Highway** (p. 449) ferry to Dutch Harbor, but only for the adventure. The trip from Homer takes 4 days in open ocean, and unless you're really planning to linger, you'll have to fly back anyway, as the ferry stays only hours before returning and makes the trip only a few times a year.

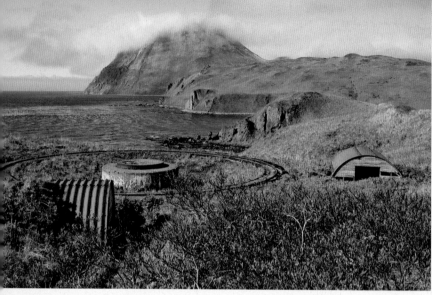

> *Fortifications from a World War II-era military build-up on Dutch Harbor still remain.*

❸ ★★ Aleutian World War II National Historic Area Visitor Center. Much of Dutch Harbor was built during World War II, when the Japanese captured two of the outer Aleutian Islands and bombed this community, killing 43 Americans. Some structures from the massive military buildup and counterattack are ruins while others remain in use—including the visitor center, in the Aerology Building (for the study of meteorology), which has exhibits and a restored radio room. Here the National Park Service interprets the historic assets in cooperation with the Ounalashka Native Corporation that owns most of them. The entry fee for the center does not cover the hiking fee to Fort Schwatka—that's another $6 per person (see ❹, next)—but make sure to pick up the booklet guide here for the hike. ⏱ 1 hr. At the airport. ☎ 907-581-9944, www.nps.gov/aleu. Admission $4. Thurs-Sun 1-6pm.

The Forgotten War

Not many Americans know about the terrible fighting that happened in the Aleutian Islands during World War II. The Japanese invaded early in the war, trying to create a diversion from the battle of Midway. The Americans had broken the enemy's codes and didn't fall for the trick, so the plan probably helped tip that key naval engagement in the direction of the U.S. But once the Japanese took the islands of Kiska and Attu, they made the Americans work to get them back.

The ensuing 15-month campaign, through fog and storms, involved battles that were among the Pacific war's costliest in terms of lives lost. About 900 U.S. service members died, and more than 2,300 Japanese (all but 28 fought to the death). Another tragedy paralleled that of the fighting: American troops forcibly removed the Native people of the islands and interned them in squalid camps in Southeast Alaska, supposedly to keep them from harm, but without real justification. Of the 800 imprisoned, more than 10 percent died before returning to ruined communities after the war. Many villages never recovered. In 1988, President Reagan apologized to the Aleut people for this injustice.

Getting Outdoors near Unalaska

Bird-Watching. Much of the land in the Aleutian Islands, if not owned by Alaska Natives, is within the **Alaska Maritime National Wildlife Refuge,** which protects the great abundance and diversity of avian life here. Refuge biologists have labored for many years, with some success, to rid rats and foxes from the islands to help bring back the area's many rare endemic species. For most bird-watchers, going to such a remote and exotic place provides an opportunity to see many unfamiliar birds. Among those you may not have seen before are the whiskered auklet and red-legged kittiwake, as well as occasional Asian species as accidentals. Go for a hike on your own, or charter a boat, perhaps combining bird-watching with fishing (see below).

Fishing. For anglers bent on catching the biggest halibut possible, Unalaska is the place to go. This Bering Sea region is among the most productive fisheries in the world, as the huge processing plants at the port attest. The largest halibut ever caught, at 459 pounds, was landed here; a replica hangs in the **visitor center** (p. 436, ❸). But with the difficulty of getting to the island, there's little sportfishing pressure, and big fish can be hooked relatively close to town. Weather can be an issue, but however bad it may look

on Discovery Channel's *Deadliest Catch,* it isn't always stormy here. Just plan for more than a day to make sure you get out on your charter. Contact a charter captain before coming through the visitor center, and plan everything carefully before flying out from Anchorage.

Hiking. In nice weather, the islands present a very inviting vista. In the absence of trees, the steep, rounded hills look like a park that one could casually cross in any direction. It's not quite that easy—the weather can change suddenly, and the heather hides foxholes that can turn an ankle—but Unalaska is fine for hiking. I've mentioned the hike to **Fort Schwatka** (p. 439, ❹). There are many other small peaks and beaches to explore, spontaneously or with advice from the visitor center. Always leave word where you're going and when you'll be back.

If you hike beyond the national historic area, you must pay an additional fee to the landowner, the Ounalashka Corporation. A 1-day hiking permit is $6 per person or $10 per family; you can buy one at the historic area visitor center (p. 436, ❸) or the corporation's office, 400 Salmon Way (☎ 907-581-1276; www.ounalashka.com), which is open Monday through Friday 8am to 5pm.

The Sea Ice Ecosystem

Ocean water creates extraordinary patterns when it freezes. You can see this by putting a glass of salt water in the freezer at home. Salt prevents freezing; the water solidifies by separating fresh from salt. The salt then resides in shrinking pockets of increasingly salty brine. During the cold months, liquid brine pockets stabilize within the ice's crystal structure, providing a tiny universe for organisms adapted to these very cold, very salty, very dark places. When conditions warm to a magic temperature in the spring, the brine suddenly melts into channels through the ice—it creates a beautiful, tree-branch pattern—and drains out from the bottom of the ice floes, building underwater icicles. The organisms that lived in the ice become food for an under-ice ecosystem as they are released. The solid ice left behind after the brine flushes out is fresh enough to provide drinking water when melted.

The sea ice harbors an extraordinary variety of specially adapted species, from peculiar salt-loving bacteria to unique, "antifreeze" species of fish and, of course, walruses, seals, polar bears, and whales. It's a much richer ecosystem than is found on land at these latitudes. Near the top of the food web, marine mammals feeding on plankton and on grazers like clams are able to store energy in thick layers of fat. The enormous polar bear thrives in this climate only because it has energy sources, primarily seal, that provide so many calories in so concentrated a form. Indeed, polar bears don't eat the whole seal, only the outer fat layer.

The ecosystem peaks in productivity in the spring, when the ice melts back and the organic material that had grown on and within it drops into the water, feeding many organisms up the food chain. The warming Arctic climate in recent decades has severely affected this system. Sea ice cover has rapidly reduced, pulling the ice edge farther from the shore. Where the ice edge retreats beyond the relatively shallow water of the continental shelf, the fertilizer falling from the melting ice edge is lost to the deep ocean abyss, out of reach of the ecosystem that could use it. Walrus, which normally live on the ice and feed on the bottom, can no longer feed when the ice is over very deep water. Polar bears, seals, and other marine mammals likewise suffer from the loss of ice. And, at the very bottom of the food chain, the loss of ice means a loss of habitat for many exquisitely adapted species on and within its crystal structure, most of which are not yet even known to science.

> *Bald eagles roost on a pile of crab pots in Dutch Harbor.*

4 ★★ **Fort Schwatka.** The fort, on Mount Ballyhoo at Ulakta Head, is reached after a hike of about an hour from the **Aleutian World War II National Historic Area Visitor Center** (see **3**, above). Starting from the airport, the hike is about 2 miles one way, with a climb of 800 feet; you can shorten it by half by getting a ride partway. The views are stunning.

The fort once had more than 100 buildings; many have collapsed, but some remain, including the best-preserved gun mounts and lookouts of all the nation's coastal defenses from the war. The fort itself is an abandoned ruin, but permits to go there cost $6; you can buy them at the historic area visitor center or, with more convenient hours, from the **Ounalashka Corporation,** 400 Salmon Way (see p. 436, **3**), which owns the land. ⏲ **Half-day.**

Staying & Dining in Unalaska

It's easy: The ★★ **Grand Aleutian Hotel** is the one place you'll want to stay and dine, and the folks here are an essential part of setting up a successful visit. Fortunately, the hotel is good. Built by one of the huge Japanese fishing companies operating here, it is the best in rural Alaska. While the rooms will be familiar to anyone used to a good midscale chain, the location on this rock in the Pacific, near the best fishing and bird-watching, makes them remarkable—as do the many ocean views. Common areas are grand, including the lobby with a big stone fireplace. The hotel also has a couple of bars, much more civilized than the rowdy fishermen's places the town is famous for.

At the **Chart Room** restaurant, on the second floor, you can dine on steak, seafood, or pasta while watching waterfowl paddle in the bay outside. The menu is brief, with entrees ranging from $18 to $65. The **Margaret Bay Café** is the place for breakfast or casual fare, and also has a good view. 498 Salmon Way. ☎ 866-581-3844 or 907-581-3844. www.grandaleutian.com. 112 units. Doubles $184. AE, DISC, MC, V.

RUSSIAN AMERICA

Before it became part of the United States,
Alaska belonged to another world power

BY MIKE DUNHAM

BITS OF RUSSIA REMAIN IN ALASKA—the Yup'ik Eskimo word for a non-Native person is "kass'aq," from "Cossack." But the clearest remaining signs of Russia's influence in Alaska are the onion-domed Russian Orthodox churches that can be seen in towns from Unalaska to Kenai to Sitka, as well as in many smaller villages. Christianity reached Alaska in 1794, when Russian Orthodox monks arrived in Kodiak led by Brother Herman—St. Herman of Alaska. He and other church-men worked to alleviate abuses against the Native people, building schools and orphanages, recording the language of the indigenous population, and recruiting Native church workers. Their devotion led many Native Alaskans to convert.

Indeed, Orthodoxy is still the dominant faith in places where it was established during Russian rule, albeit with some uniquely Native Alaska touches. The dead are sometimes buried above ground in colorful "spirit houses," such as those in the churchyard in Eklutna, near Anchorage. At Russian Christmas— celebrated on Jan-uary 7, according to the old Julian calendar—villagers go "starring," which involves following a decorated, spinning star from house to house and singing carols.

A Colonial Past

Trade and travelers had passed between Asia and North America by way of Alaska for centuries, but in 1741, Vitus Bering arrived from Russia and claimed his "discovery" for the Czar. For the next half century, lawless fur hunters spread along the Aleutian Islands to the mainland, seeking sea otter, seal and fox furs, setting up trading posts, and enslaving the Native population. Order wasn't imposed until 1799, when Alexander Baranof became colonial governor. He quickly extended Russian forts all the way to California, and after bloody fighting with Tlingit Indians (see p. 386, ❶), captured Sitka and made it the capital. Called "The Paris of the Pacific," Sitka prospered as the largest European settlement on the west coast of North America until the California gold rush in 1849. But by 1867, with sea otters hunted to near extinction, and a real threat that Britain might take the colony by force, Russia sold its claims in Alaska to the United States for $7.2 million.

Columbus of the Pacific

Vitus Bering, a Dane in the service of Czar Peter the Great, crossed Siberia to the Pacific Ocean, where he built ships, set sail, and mapped the eastern edge of Asia in 1728. His explorations were such a success that the czar then ordered him to find out just how close North America was to Asia. In 1741, he sailed into the unknown on a horrendous voyage beset by bad weather and illness. The expedition made contact with Alaska Natives and came within sight of Mt. Saint Elias, on the border of present day Canada. Shipwrecked on the way home, Bering and many of his crew perished before the expedition's survivors could build a new boat and return to Russia with news and maps of the land they called "Alyeska." Still, his efforts have not been forgotten, and the Bering Strait is named in his honor.

Kodiak

In some ways, Kodiak Island and its namesake town have more in common with fishing towns in Southeast Alaska or Prince William Sound than with the other Bush communities in this chapter. The town is a vibrant fishing port, reachable only by ferry or air, amid a forest of big trees on the north end of the island, which lies in the Gulf of Alaska. But in terms of your plans, Kodiak has this important fact in common with the Bush: The community is apart from any regular travel route you might choose, and you need a special reason to go there. Reasons do exist. This is the only place to see the world's largest bears (called Kodiak brown bears); the salmon fishing is exceptional; and the town is charming and historic, with good opportunities for outdoor exploration. Plan for 2 days here, including a day spent on an outdoor activity.

> A 1964 tsunami triggered by an earthquake sent fishing boats from Kodiak's harbor careening through downtown.

START Kodiak is 250 miles south of Anchorage.

❶ ★ Downtown Kodiak. Most of the downtown area in this town of 6,600 people is modern, thanks to the 1964 earthquake (see "Whole Lotta Shaking," on p. 208), which caused a tsunami that sent fishing boats from the harbor hurtling through town, knocking

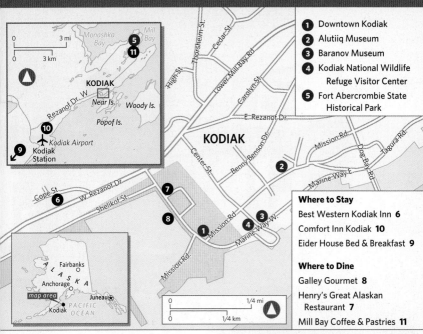

1 Downtown Kodiak
2 Alutiiq Museum
3 Baranov Museum
4 Kodiak National Wildlife Refuge Visitor Center
5 Fort Abercrombie State Historical Park

KODIAK

Where to Stay

Best Western Kodiak Inn 6

Comfort Inn Kodiak 10

Eider House Bed & Breakfast 9

Where to Dine

Galley Gourmet 8

Henry's Great Alaskan Restaurant 7

Mill Bay Coffee & Pastries 11

down buildings. At Mission Road and Marine Way, a warship is set in concrete: It's a **World War II Liberty ship,** the last one built. It was brought here to serve as a fish processing plant after facilities were destroyed by the earthquake, and is still in use. Toward the mountain along Marine Way, next to St. Paul Harbor, you reach the **fishermen's memorial,** with the many names of those lost at sea. Rounding the harbor's edge onto Shelikof Street, the **Kodiak Maritime Museum** has mounted excellent explanatory signs about the island's maritime industry. Stop in at **Kodiak Island Brewing Co.,** 338 Shelikof St. (☎ 907-486-2537; www.kodiakbrewery.com), where Ben Millstein brews the local beer and offers tours. ⏱ 1 hr.

❷ ★ **Alutiiq Museum.** The Natives of Kodiak Island created this museum to help bring back the Alutiiq culture that Russian and American invaders nearly destroyed. The owners' primary mission is to teach Alutiiq art and language to their own people, but for visitors the exhibits are well worth seeing. They come from a large and growing collection of artifacts and other materials, some unearthed in the museum's own digs. ⏱ 1 hr. 215 Mission

> A traditional canoe is one of more than 250,000 archaeological items in the Alutiiq Museum's repository.

> *Russian and Native artifacts mingle in the Baranov Museum, Alaska's oldest building, dating to 1808.*

Rd. ☎ 907-486-7004. www.alutiiqmuseum. org. Admission $5 adults, free for children 15 and under. Summer Mon–Fri 9am–5pm, Sat 10am–5pm; winter Tues–Fri 9am–5pm, Sat 10:30am–4:30pm.

Getting to Kodiak

From Anchorage you can fly to Kodiak on a jet with **Alaska Airlines** (p. 507) or a turbo prop with **Era Alaska** (☎ 800-866-8394 or 907-266-8394; www.flyera.com). Airfare is around $400 for a round-trip ticket. The ferries of the **Alaska Marine Highway System** (p. 449) connect Kodiak to Homer, a 10-hour voyage that's extremely scenic but can be quite rough. The one-way passenger fare is $74, half-price for children 6 to 11, and free for children 5 and under.

❸ ★ **Baranov Museum.** Kodiak was the original capital of Russian America, captured from the Natives in 1784 by Russian colonists in a bloody, unprovoked battle to win access to sea otter furs. Alexander Baranof (sometimes spelled "Baranov") built this log structure as a magazine and strong house to defend the pelts. Dating from 1808, it is the oldest building in Alaska. The tsunami in 1964 came to its doorstep but thankfully no higher. Inside, the museum holds Russian and early Native artifacts, and knowledgeable guides are eager to show off additional materials you can't see without their help. The gift store carries antique Russian items and authentic Native crafts. ⏲ 1 hr. 101 Marine Way. ☎ 907-486-5920. www.baranovmuseum.org. Admission $3 adults, free for children 12 and under. Summer Mon–Sat 10am–4pm, Sun noon–4pm; winter Tues–Sat 10am–3pm. Closed Feb.

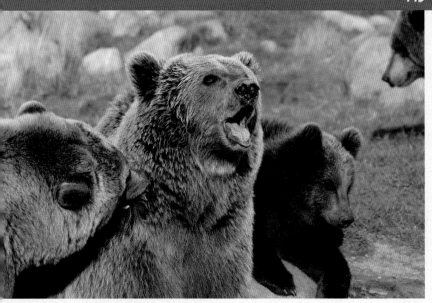

> *Young Kodiak brown bears pal around at the Kodiak National Wildlife Refuge.*

④ ★ Kodiak National Wildlife Refuge Visitor Center. The refuge takes in 1.9 million acres, two-thirds of the island on its southwest side. This is the domain of the huge **Kodiak brown bear,** and the center is the best place to learn about the bears and get advice for a good flight out to see them (p. 446). It's also worth a stop to see a complete gray whale skeleton, three full-size replicas of Kodiak brown bears, and other exhibits. ⏱ 30 min. Mission Rd. and Center St. ☎ 888-592-6942 or 907-487-2626. www.kodiakwildliferefuge.org. Free admission. Summer daily 9am–5pm; winter Tues–Sat 9am–5pm.

⑤ ★ Fort Abercrombie State Historical Park. The park is historical for its World War II ruins, but you may enjoy it more for the opportunity to walk in a glorious seaside forest among cliffs and huge trees, with paths to the beaches, good tide pooling, and a swimming lake. The ruins include gun emplacements, bunkers, and other concrete buildings built to keep the Japanese at bay after they took the islands of Kiska and Attu, in the western Aleutians (see "The Forgotten War," on p. 436). Local history buffs have made a museum in the ammunition bunker at Miller Point. Museum hours are changeable; check its website, www.kadiak.

org, or call ☎ 907-486-7015. ⏱ Half-day. 1400 Abercrombie Dr., off Rezanof Dr., 3K miles from downtown. ☎ 907-486-6339. Free admission. Park always open.

Living with the World's Biggest Bears

Rather than checking in on Kodiak's famous brown bears on a day trip, you can go into the wilderness for a few days of hiking, fishing, and extended bear viewing. The Kodiak archipelago is famous for its wilderness and fishing lodges. Check the **visitor center** (see ④, left) for a referral. An environmentally sensitive approach is taken by Harry and Brigid Dodge at their rustic, solar-powered **Aleut Island Lodge** (☎ 907-487-2122; www.kodiaktreks.com) in Uyak Bay. They take the time to know the bears and their habitat and to introduce visitors to the area rather than just quickly showing it off. Rates, which are $350 per person per night (3-night minimum), include food, bear-viewing excursions, and activities such as kayaking and fishing, but not the cost of getting there (about $350 per person, round trip from Kodiak).

Getting Outdoors on Kodiak

Bear Viewing. Most of the island lies within the **Kodiak National Wildlife Refuge** (p. 445, ❶), far from roads. The dominant inhabitants are giant brown bears that can grow to 10 feet when standing on hind legs and weigh up to 1,500 pounds. There are easier and less expensive places to see bears, but nowhere else can you see larger bears or encounter them in a more beautiful setting. Bears congregate during salmon runs, so viewing is best from early July to mid-August; at other times, you can probably do as well without making a trip all the way to Kodiak. Options include flights from **Anchorage** (p. 75, ❹), **Sterling** (p. 243, ❻), or **Katmai National Park** (p. 485). From Kodiak, the main way to get to bear-viewing sites is by floatplane; expect to pay around $475 per person, with a two- or three-person minimum, for a guided half-day trip—I suggest you go with **Sea Hawk Air** (☎ 800-770-4295 or 907-486-8282; www.seahawkair.com). After the plane lands, you may need to walk as far as a mile to reach the bears.

Fishing. In few places can you drive to fishing as good as at Kodiak. The roads from town reach eight good-sized rivers with runs of salmon and Dolly Varden char; sometimes you'll find spots as good as you would fly to from other towns. Taking a floatplane from town gets you to some of Alaska's very best fishing. About 50 charter boats are available for ocean fishing. You don't have to go far for big halibut, and boats troll for salmon during much of the summer. The **visitor center** (p. 445, ❹) has names of guides. Or seek advice and regulations from the helpful staff at the **Alaska Department of Fish and Game,** 211 Mission Rd. (☎ 907-486-1880; www.alaska.gov/adfg).

Sea Kayaking. Good sea kayaking waters start right from the Kodiak waterfront and continue through the Kodiak Archipelago, including some of the most beautiful and coveted places to paddle anywhere in Alaska. Andy Schroeder, a former Coast Guard officer, guides day trips as well as expeditions of several days through **Orcas Unlimited Charters** (☎ 907-539-1979; www.orcasunlimited.com). Expect to pay $200 per person for the day, with discounted rates for larger groups.

Where to Stay & Dine

> *Mill Bay Coffee & Pastries offers tasty treats along with excellent seafood lunches.*

★ **Best Western Kodiak Inn** KODIAK
Traditionally Kodiak's central hotel, this
wooden building perches on the mountainside
overlooking the boat harbor, with good views
from many units. Rooms are nicely furnished
with quality beds and lots of amenities. The
restaurant, the Chart Room, is good for a nice
meal out, with seafood on the menu and a
great ocean view. 236 W. Rezanof Dr. ☎ 888-
563-4254 or 907-486-5712. www.kodiakinn.
com. 81 units. Doubles $179 summer; $109 winter. AE, DC, DISC, MC, V.

★ **Comfort Inn Kodiak** AIRPORT
The hotel is directly across the parking lot
from the airport terminal; the back looks
out on woods. It offers good chain-standard
rooms with plenty of amenities. You will need
a car, as the town is 5 miles away. 1395 Airport
Way. ☎ 800-544-2202 or 907-487-2700. www.
choicehotels.com/hotel/ak025. Doubles $170
summer; $110 winter. AE, DC, DISC, MC, V.

★ **Eider House Bed & Breakfast** SOUTH OF
KODIAK The B&B is reachable by road 9 miles
from town but has the feel of a wilderness
lodge, near the seashore and Sargent Creek,
with excellent fishing. Rooms are attractive
and exceptionally clean, all with their own
bathrooms. Check-in isn't until 5pm except by
special arrangement. 782 Sargent Creek Rd.
☎ 907-487-4315. www.eiderhouse.com.
Doubles $145 summer; $90 winter. AE, MC, V.

★★ **Galley Gourmet** HARBOR *SEAFOOD*
Marty and Marion Owen take guests on an
hour-long cruise to see puffins, sea lions, and
whales before dropping anchor to serve dinner—seafood, of course—aboard their 42-foot
yacht, the *Sea Breeze.* They're personable folks
who take only six guests each evening. Marion
is an experienced professional photographer
and helps with getting good pictures; she also
teaches photography programs for visitors.
The entire evening lasts from 6pm to 9:30pm.
☎ 907-486-5079. www.galleygourmet.biz.
Reservations required. $125 per person. Dinner
daily. Summer only.

★ **Henry's Great Alaskan Restaurant** KODIAK
GRILL You'll meet commercial fishermen and
other locals in this energetic bar and grill. The
menu is lengthy, including steaks and seafood
as well as basic burgers and such. The smoked
salmon chowder is excellent. 512 Marine Way.
☎ 907-486-8844. www.henrysalaska.com.
Entrees $9–$39. MC, V. Lunch and dinner daily.

★★ **Mill Bay Coffee & Pastries** KODIAK
FRENCH This coffee shop seems to be the best
restaurant in town. It is run by an award-winning, Paris-trained chef and his wife, Joël and
Martine Chenet, who offer lunches of local seafood. The Kodiak sea burger, for $13, is salmon,
crab, shrimp, and cream cheese, among other
ingredients. The place is also a local social hub.
3833 Rezanof Dr. East, about 2 miles outside of
town. ☎ 907-486-4411. www.millbaycoffee.com.
Entrees $13–$15. MC, V. Breakfast and lunch daily.

Alaska Bush Fast Facts

Getting There & Getting Around
BY PLANE Alaska Airlines (☎ 800-252-7522; www.alaskaair.com) is the key travel link for these communities. BY FERRY Alaska Marine Highway System (☎ 800-642-0066; www.ferryalaska.com).

Emergencies
Dial ☎ 911.

Dentists & Doctors
If you're in need of emergency dental care, go to the local hospital or health center. BARROW Samuel Simmonds Memorial Hospital, 1296 Agvik St. (☎ 907-852-4611). NOME Norton Sound Regional Hospital, 5th Avenue and Bering Street (☎ 907-443-3311). UNALASKA/DUTCH HARBOR Iliuliuk Family and Health Services, 34 Lavalle Ct. (☎ 907-581-1202) is a clinic. KODIAK Providence Kodiak Island Medical Center, 1915 E. Rezanof Dr. (☎ 907-486-3281).

Internet Access
BARROW Free at the Tuzzy Library, at the Iñupiat Heritage Center in Browerville (☎ 907-852-1720). NOME Nome Public Library, 200 Front St. (☎ 907-443-6626). UNALASKA Unalaska Public Library, 64 Eleanor Dr. (☎ 907-581-5060). KODIAK A. Holmes Johnson Public Library, 319 Lower Mill Bay Rd. (☎ 907-486-8686).

Police
BARROW North Slope Borough Police Department, 1068 Kiogak St. (☎ 907-852-6111). NOME Nome Police Department, at Bering Street and 4th Avenue (☎ 907-443-5262). UNALASKA/DUTCH HARBOR Unalaska Department of Public Safety (☎ 907-581-1233) is just above the bridge on the Unalaska side. KODIAK Kodiak Police Department, 217 Lower Mill Bay Rd. (☎ 907-486-8000).

Visitor Information
BARROW City of Barrow, Office of the Mayor. Visitor center at Momegana and Ahkovak streets (☎ 907-852-5211, ext. 231; www.cityofbarrow.org). NOME Nome Convention and Visitors Bureau, Front and Division streets (☎ 907-443-6555; www.visitnomealaska.com). UNALASKA/DUTCH HARBOR Unalaska/Port of Dutch Harbor Convention and Visitors Bureau, 5th Street and Broadway (☎ 877-581-2612 or 907-581-2612; www.unalaska.info). KODIAK Kodiak Island Convention and Visitors Bureau, 100 E. Marine Way, Suite 200 (☎ 800-789-4782 or 907-486-4782; www.kodiak.org).

> The Star of Kodiak ship-turned-fish cannery is a landmark on St. Paul Harbor.

11
Alaska's Natural History & Culture

A Timeline of Alaskan History

PRE-HISTORY

10,000 B.C. Increasing glacial ice causes lower sea levels, allowing Alaska to connect with Siberia. Humans arrive in North America from Asia (pictured left).

LAST 10,000 YEARS People from Asia spread across North and South America. In Alaska, three racial groups and many cultural groups find homes.

800-1800

800–1200 Warm weather across the Arctic allows whaling culture from Alaska to spread across Canada and Greenland.

1200–1800 Colder climate increases ice, forcing the people of Arctic Alaska to concentrate in larger villages and establish the cultural practices they still have today.

1741 Vitus Bering (pictured left), on a mission originally chartered by Peter the Great, finds Alaska.

1743 Russian fur traders enter the Aleutian Islands before spreading eastward to Kodiak, becoming cruel slave masters to the indigenous people.

1778 British captain James Cook visits Alaska on his last voyage before his death in Hawaii, drawing the first accurate charts of the coast.

1800s

1799–1804 Russians and Tlingits fight a war for control of Sitka. Russians make it their capital, but never subdue the Natives.

1865 A Confederate navy ship attacks the whaling fleet in the Arctic, destroying 20 ships and capturing 4 more.

1848 New England whalers begin to exploit rich Arctic stocks; over the next 60 years, they decimate marine mammal numbers.

1867 Czar Alexander II sells Alaska to the United States for $7.2 million, roughly 2¢ an acre; the American flag is raised in Sitka under military rule.

1880 Joe Juneau and Richard Harris find gold on Gastineau Channel and found the city of Juneau; gold strikes are reported every few years across Alaska.

1898 Prospectors arriving in Seattle with a ton of gold spark the Klondike gold rush, populating Alaska with tens of thousands of Americans (pictured left).

1900s

1906 Alaska's first (nonvoting) delegate in Congress takes office; the capital moves from Sitka to Juneau.

1908 The Iditarod Trail, a dog-sled mail route, is completed, linking trails continuously from Seward to Nome.

1914 Federal construction of the Alaska Railroad begins; the first tents go up in the river bottom that will become Anchorage, a construction camp on the rail line.

1920 The first flights connect Alaska to the rest of the United States.

1942 Japan invades the Aleutians, taking Attu and Kiska islands and bombing Unalaska/Dutch Harbor; the military creates an overland link for the first time with the Alaska Highway.

1959 After a decades-long battle, Alaska overcomes objections of President Dwight Eisenhower and Republicans in Congress to become the 49th state.

1964 The largest earthquake ever measured in North America wipes out towns in Southcentral Alaska, but recovery brings economic development and modernization.

1968 The largest oil field in American history is found at Prudhoe Bay, on Alaska's North Slope.

1971 Congress acknowledges indigenous peoples' ownership of Alaska with transfers of 44 million acres of land and almost $1 billion to new Native-owned corporations.

1980 Congress sets aside almost one-third of Alaska in new parks and other land-conservation units.

1982 Alaskans receive their first Alaska Permanent Fund dividends, interest paid on an oil-wealth savings account.

1989 The tanker *Exxon Valdez* hits Bligh Reef in Prince William Sound, spilling 11 million gallons of North Slope crude in what was up to that date the worst oil spill in North America (pictured left).

2000s

2004 The FBI begins a broad-ranging political corruption investigation in Alaska.

2006 With nine political figures already convicted in the FBI probe, Sarah Palin (pictured left) is elected governor, advocating change and reform.

2008 Palin is nominated for vice president by the Republican Party.

2009 Palin resigns as governor and publishes her memoirs.

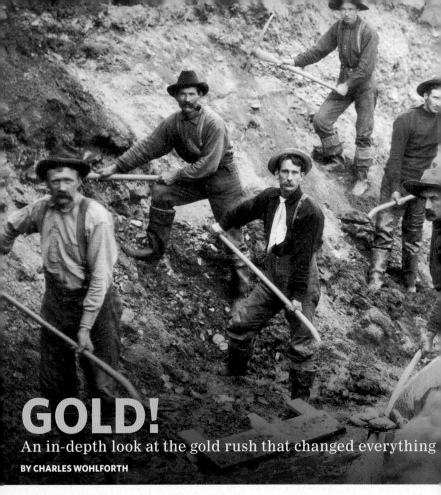

GOLD!

An in-depth look at the gold rush that changed everything

BY CHARLES WOHLFORTH

ALASKA'S GOLD FEVER BEGAN IN THE 1880S and has never really stopped—believe it or not, prospectors are still looking for gold, and finding it. But the one that started it all, and the one that so fundamentally shaped Alaska's development, was the Klondike Gold Rush of 1898, which lured an estimated 40,000 people from as far away as Australia to the wilderness of the Yukon Territory's Klondike River. To get there, stampeders, as they came to be called, had to cross Alaska—not an easy task today, let alone back then. But the routes they carved out helped draw the modern map, creating many of the towns that survive today.

Remnants of the Rush

LAST CHANCE MINING MUSEUM AND HISTORIC SITE, JUNEAU. Before the Klondike Gold Rush some of the largest gold mines in the world operated near Juneau, after a find by Joe Juneau and Richard Harris in 1880. The museum preserves the artifacts and feeling of the time. *See p. 378,* ❼.

KLONDIKE GOLD RUSH NATIONAL HISTORIC DISTRICT, SKAGWAY. The Wild West boom town that sprouted on the route to the gold fields was well-preserved from shortly after the ruckus had quieted, and the false-front buildings still stand along Broadway. *See p. 414,* ❶.

EL DORADO GOLD MINE, FAIRBANKS. Gold fever is still alive in Alaska, with billions to be made by huge mines operating or planned. This fun and corny attraction puts visitors in contact with real small-time miners and offers a chance to pan and find your own gold. *See p. 307,* ❿.

The Gold Rush: A Timeline

1896
On August 16, Skookum Jim Mason, his sister Kate, and her husband George Carmack, hit gold along Bonanza Creek in the Yukon.

1897
In July, Klondike prospectors arrive in San Francisco and Seattle bearing gold. The U.S. is in the midst of a series of financial crises, which helps fuel the stampede northward.

1898
Thousands flock north via two main routes: landing at Skagway or Dyea and going over the coastal mountains on the Chilkoot Trail, or by hiking to White Pass and taking a boat up the Yukon River.

1899
The Klondike gold rush dies down. Disappointed prospectors fan out across Alaska, spawning new gold rushes and founding new towns.

1900
Alaska's gold rush era reaches a peak as isolated Nome, in northwest Alaska, swells in size to over 12,000 residents.

1901
Swindler E.T. Barnette founds Fairbanks and attracts prospectors with exaggerated claims of gold.

1914
World War I brings the Gold Rush era to an end.

Going for the Gold

The Klondike gold strike began when George Carmack and Skookum Jim Mason located big lumps of gold, called nuggets, along the Klondike River. But that was unusual, and even the richest gold mines usually yield rocks or gravel containing only tiny grains of the metal. That's what makes finding gold so difficult—you're looking for minute flakes of yellow dust. Prospectors tend to search the beds of ancient or existing rivers that might have concentrated the stuff. Once they find a spot they think might yield results, they use a gold pan to agitate samples of sand and gravel in moving water. The weight of the gold makes it sink out of the mix. Here's how to find a bit of gold on your own:

1. Put your gravel or sand in the pan with water.

2. Holding the pan slightly tilted, swirl the water around the pan so the water and the lightest sand and rock spill over the rim.

3. Refill with water and repeat.

4. Eventually you're left with just a few grains of sand in the bottom of the pan, and, with luck, a few gold-colored specks.

A Brief History of Alaska

> PAGE 450-451 Watching for bowhead whales. THIS PAGE President Eisenhower admitted Alaska as the 49th state on January 3, 1959.

Former governor Sarah Palin has become perhaps the most famous Alaskan of all time, yet most Alaskans probably didn't know who she was until 2006, and she moved off the Alaska stage in less than 3 years. Even more than other Americans, many Alaskans had the sense that she appeared from nowhere, like a genie.

But although Palin may have become world-famous overnight, the conditions that set the stage for her political success had been developing for a century. She was elected and proved to be a popular governor because of her attitude toward Alaska's wealth, the natural resources that make the economy and government run, and the companies that exploit it.

Alaska's story, even before the arrival of non-Natives, has always been about the gifts of nature: the fish, furs, timber, minerals, and oil that come from the land and water. Agriculture has never amounted to much here, and no one has figured out how to manufacture products cost-effectively. Other than natural resources, money enters the state economy only through federal spending for defense and other activities, air cargo operations between the U.S. and Asia, and tourism.

Furs for Russians, Gold for Americans

When Russian invaders arrived, beginning in the 18th century, they were after valuable furs, not land. Beyond a few tiny coastal towns, including Sitka, Kodiak, and Kenai, they left Alaska unsettled and largely unexplored. After their hunters nearly wiped out their primary prey, the sea otter—and they did drive to extinction the manatee-like Steller's sea cow—Russian America declined, becoming a money-losing imperial backwater.

The United States bought Alaska from the czar in 1867—in fact buying what the Russians didn't even own, in the view of Alaska Natives—but the territory gained scant non-Native population for decades more. Only with the discovery of gold on the Klondike River, in Canada's Yukon, and the great, wild gold rush that followed in 1898 did pioneers spread across Alaska and begin to outnumber Natives.

Most of the newcomers, like the Russians before them, had a single thing on their mind: making money. Few came north with any idea of staying, although many ultimately did. Early travelers

> *The White Pass and Yukon Railroad was blasted through coastal mountains during the Klondike Gold Rush.*

described a population that really didn't care about the future of the place, stampeding from location to location in hopes of finding riches, building and rapidly abandoning new towns, and laying waste to salmon streams and the countryside when expedient.

Alaska and the Feds

President Theodore Roosevelt, the great conservation exponent, came to office in 1901 as the gold rush remained hot in Alaska. Among Roosevelt's concerns were outdated laws that allowed scammers across the American West to gain control of coal and oil reserves of enormous value for the cost of a few papers filed in the land office. He preferred a leasing system, wherein a company extracting resources would pay a portion of the value to the government. When Congress balked, the president froze disposal of coal and oil land. The stalemate lasted many years.

Roosevelt's freeze drove Alaskans crazy. Greed was partly to blame—those who went to Alaska to get rich on its resources were frustrated when encountering any barrier. But conservation also seemed absurd to many people. Alaska was so unimaginably vast, so packed with resources, so little touched—and now folks had to import coal from British Columbia.

The belief remains today that the federal government is a heavy-handed overlord, interfering with Alaskans' use of their own resources. Politicians regularly roll out the old rhetoric in speeches, attacking federal environmental controls or limits on oil drilling, and they still get cheers after a century of playing the same tune—even though the federal government spends far more per citizen in Alaska than in other states and is, in fact, the state's largest employer.

The Other Bad Guys

The Alaskans who arrived for the gold rush idealized the solitary prospector who could make it rich—like George Carmack, discoverer of the Klondike gold strike—but even in those days, big companies enjoyed most of the money to be made on natural resources, because developing remote industrial operations required a big investment. The Wall Street financiers behind these companies became popular villains as hated as the government.

The first and greatest of these perceived villains was the Alaska Syndicate, which

> *The Trans-Alaska Pipeline traverses 800 miles and three mountain ranges from the North Slope to Valdez and cost $8 billion to construct.*

developed the fabulously rich Kennecott Copper Mine, near Chitina, and built a railroad from the new town of Cordova, on Prince William Sound, to reach it. The syndicate's fight with the government for coal ultimately led to a national political scandal that helped cost the Republicans the White House in 1912 (see "Teddy Roosevelt & the Battle for Alaska," on p. 199).

In 1938, with copper prices low, the corporation abruptly shut down the mine, abandoned the towns it had built, and pulled up the railroad tracks to sell them for scrap in Japan. Alaskans cursed the fact that the iron from their rails was shot back at them in the form of bullets when the Japanese invaded the Aleutian Islands four years later.

A more lasting big-business influence held sway in the fishing industry through the territorial era, from the late 19th century onward. Outside corporate interests based mostly in Seattle bought up control of Alaska's salmon canneries and stream fish traps, the largest industry at the time. Using the time-honored methods of political influence in Washington, D.C., the corporations controlled the federal regulators who were supposed to protect the fish, and salmon numbers steadily declined.

The Cry for Statehood

By the 1950s, the federal government and large outside business interests controlled every aspect of Alaska's economy. Federal regulation even created a shipping monopoly that gouged Alaskan consumers with high prices for goods. Alaskans couldn't vote for president, nor could their one delegate to Congress vote on bills. But a growing, newly energetic population had arrived that wouldn't stand for it much longer.

Ironically, the federal government had itself brought the new migrants. World War II had caused a major economic boom, and the Cold War an even bigger one. This new non-Native population was young and optimistic, and many planned to stay and raise families. But as Alaskans, they still subscribed to the doctrine of opposition to big government and big business.

Military needs provided one of the objections to statehood. President Dwight Eisenhower stated that Alaska might be needed as a huge military reserve to defend against the Soviet Union. But that was a pretext—military officials admitted they didn't need the entire territory. Instead, Congressional politics were the real barrier. Alaska at that time was a Democratic state expected to support civil rights legislation. Republicans and southern Democrats opposed statehood to prevent election of two new Senators who would add to their adversaries in Washington.

When statehood came, in 1959, power over fisheries regulation was removed from the hated canned salmon bosses, and their fish traps were removed from Alaskan rivers. It would be Alaska for Alaskans. But statehood didn't prove to be that simple.

Statehood Challenges

Alaska was conceived as a new kind of state. The population was so small and the area so large and undeveloped that running a state government on taxes paid by Alaskans would be impossible. Instead, the Congress planned to transfer land, ocean, and underground resources that the state could use to make money to pay for services. The grant would include 103 million acres of land, an area the size of California and almost one-third of Alaska's total landmass.

The problem with the idea lay in some unfinished business. Alaska Natives had never been conquered by the Russians who sold Alaska, and from their perspective, they had never given up their ownership of the land. As long as the federal government held it all as public domain—under no one's control—the issue could stand

unresolved. But when the State of Alaska prepared to take ownership, the Natives had to act to protect their interests.

Faced with Native claims, federal authorities again froze Alaska lands, halting all transfer of federal land until the issue could be resolved. Non-Native Alaskans screamed in protest, but the conflict dragged on for years. Then, in 1968, a major oil company discovered the largest oil field in North America, on the North Slope, on land the state owned.

To get the oil out of Alaska would require a pipeline, one of the largest construction projects in history, and that would require settling the ownership of the land the pipeline would cross.

The Grand Compromise

A four-way struggle for ownership of Alaska had lingered since the gold rush. The four adversaries were the Alaska Natives, the non-Native Alaskans, national conservationists, and big-business interests. The need for legislation to authorize the Trans-Alaska Pipeline brought all four to the table, and their grand compromise was hammered out during the 1970s.

In 1971, Congress passed the Alaska Native Claims Settlement Act, at the time the best agreement any indigenous people in the world had received from those who had taken their lands. The bill created corporations to be owned by all Alaska Natives then living, paid them $1 billion, and gave the corporations first dibs on 44 million acres of Alaska's lands.

Subsequent legislation permitted the pipeline and set aside another 100 million acres of Alaska for preservation in national parks, refuges, and such. In 1977 the pipeline was completed, carrying one-fourth of the nation's domestic oil, and soon afterward oil prices shot sky-high. Alaska's state government became fabulously rich. It seemed everyone would be happy—but sometimes getting what you want doesn't work out the way you planned.

The Curse of Wealth

With oil wealth on the scale of an Arab nation, Alaska's state government went on a mad spending spree in the early 1980s. Individual taxes were cancelled, extraordinary benefits were created for people of every income level, and construction boomed. When oil prices crashed in 1985, all that came to a grinding halt and Alaska's overheated economy collapsed. A crushing 4-year depression depopulated neighborhoods and wiped out banks.

A new kind of economic stability came in 1990 and lasted 20 years. With Alaska dependent on the oil industry, its state government became responsive to industry wishes. The Republican Party, traditionally friendlier to the industry than Democrats—although Alaska Democrats were highly pro-oil, too—took ever-greater control until they held all major offices.

But that old-fashioned spirit of Alaska for Alaskans, of the lone pioneer having a chance—that spirit still remained, ready to rise again.

> *Sarah Palin campaigning for the gubernatorial nomination, 2006.*

The Old Guard Falls

The Republican old guard reached the apex of its power in 2002, when U.S. senator Frank Murkowski won election for governor and appointed his own daughter, Lisa, to his just-vacated Senate seat. He also found an appointment for a promising young woman who had run a strong but unsuccessful campaign in the Republican primary for lieutenant governor, installing her on an oil and gas regulatory commission. It was a well-paid but obscure post, perfect for setting aside a potential adversary.

But Sarah Palin didn't sit quietly at her new job. Her co-worker, the chair of the commission, also happened to be the chair of the Alaska Republican Party and Murkowski's strong supporter. Palin accused him of misusing his position with the oil industry and the party. Murkowski defended his friend and Palin resigned, coming to the attention of many Alaskans for the first time.

Murkowski also was working on a rewrite of oil tax laws. In exchange for industry support of a new gas line, he asked the legislature to lock in for decades the advantageous oil tax rates they wanted.

We now know that the oil industry's top lobbyist in Juneau, Bill Allen, head of the Veco Corporation, was paying cash bribes to legislators to get Murkowski's bill passed. We know this because the FBI had a camera hidden in Allen's hotel room.

Right Place, Right Time

Sarah Palin already looked like an ethical hero when the bribery scandal hit. She also looked like one of those independent pioneers of yore who weren't controlled by the federal government or big industry. She crushed Murkowski in the Republican primary in 2006 and handily beat the Democrat, also a pro-oil member of the older generation, in the general election.

As governor, Palin aligned with Democrats in the legislature to pass a strong ethics law and to fix the corrupted oil tax legislation. Her version increased the state's take of the oil resources, and in the bill she signed, Democrats increased it even more. Combined with the historic high oil prices of 2008, Alaska was awash in money once again. Palin sent out a lot of the money in "rebates" to individual Alaskans. Every man, woman, and child received $3,300 that summer.

No wonder Palin was hugely popular in Alaska when John McCain picked her as the Republican vice presidential nominee. She had tapped into Alaskans' strongest myth about themselves, about their independence and resistance to outside forces, and had sent them large checks of free money in the bargain.

It was a remarkable moment, but it didn't last. Palin's Alaska poll numbers slumped as she became a polarizing figure nationally and as her family became fodder for the tabloids. Other than the ethics law and the oil tax increase, she had no concrete accomplishments to her name when she abruptly resigned halfway through her first term as governor.

Alaska Today

Alaska remains reliant on big resource projects, which inevitably involve large corporations and the federal government, but resistant and antagonistic toward those same institutions. Politicians inveigh against Washington, D.C., in terms that would have sounded familiar to Teddy Roosevelt.

But some major aspects of Alaska's political and economic landscape have changed. The Native corporations are Alaska's largest homegrown businesses, with major economic and political power. Huge swaths of the state are permanently set aside as parks and wilderness. The oil companies don't call all the shots anymore. And the population has aged and settled down. Unlike the youthful transients of the gold rush, the Cold War buildup, or the oil boom, plenty of people plan to stay and do care about Alaska's future.

Alaska's Natural History

> *Glaciers are not static natural phenomena—they expand and retreat, melt and freeze, and even change course.*

In some ways, Alaska is easy enough to define. The boundaries are clear on a map. The people have some characteristics in common: as U.S. citizens, generally outdoorsy folk, participants in a shared history and cultural story. Certain adjectives cover the entirety of the land, too: vast, scenic, wild, extreme.

But such definitions are like a computer image with too little resolution: Zoom in a little bit, and the picture disappears. Alaska's boundaries, set by treaty in 1824, are essentially arbitrary. When the diplomats drew their lines, the shape of the place wasn't even clearly known. What those boundaries actually contain has as many differences as similarities.

The people are as various as members of the United Nations. The term "Alaska Native" takes in eleven peoples, and among them scores of tribes, called *villages,* with 20 unique languages and many dialects. The non-Native population is at least as diverse. No race holds a majority in the Anchorage schools, with students who speak 94 languages at home, the top five after English being Spanish, Hmong, Tagalog, Samoan, and Korean.

The land may be the hardest of all to pin down. Vast and wild, yes, but what else? In one region, a frozen desert that in summer is nonetheless swampy and nearly impassable, and in winter is a white sheet without landmarks except the wind patterns in the hardened snow. In another region, land that is among the rainiest and snowiest on Earth, a vertical landscape with waterfalls tumbling down and huge, ancient trees reaching up.

Simply put, Alaska is not one place. It is many, maybe an infinite number. Seeing it clearly requires taking it apart

> *Mount McKinley was formed 56 million years ago, when molten magma solidified deep beneath central Alaska; it still grows at about 1 mm per year.*

and looking at one piece at a time.

Understanding some of the natural history behind Alaska's landscapes and wildlife will give context and meaning to your visit. If you're not from a northern region, you may not have encountered glaciers, permafrost, or tundra before. Alaska, because of its size and location, is like an unfinished work of art, still being shaped by the fire of volcanoes and the ice of glaciers. And, like artwork, it is uniquely vulnerable, as the warming climate alters the processes that shape the land.

Glaciers

Bering Glacier, the largest in North America (about 30 by 145 miles in area), can't decide which way to go. Surging and retreating on a 20-year cycle, it reversed course in 1995 after bulldozing a wetland migratory bird stopover, and speedily contracted back up toward the mountains. Yanert Glacier surged 100 yards a day in 2000—after moving 100 yards a year since 1942. The next year, Tokositna Glacier started galloping after 50 years of quiet. In 1937, surging Black Rapids Glacier almost ate the Richardson Highway. In Prince William Sound, Meares Glacier plowed through old-growth forest. On a larger scale, all the land of Glacier Bay—mountains, forests, sea floor—is rising 1.5 inches a year as it rebounds from the weight of melted glaciers that 100 years ago were a mile thick and 65 miles longer.

In the last ice age, 15,000 years ago, much of what is Alaska today was a huge glacier. Looking up at the granite mountains of Southeast Alaska, especially in the Lynn Canal, you can see a sort of high-water mark near their towering peaks—the highest point to which the glaciers came in the ice age.

Today Alaska's 100,000 glaciers cover about 5% of its landmass, mostly on the southern coast. There are no glaciers in the Arctic—the climate is too dry to produce enough snow. The northernmost large glaciers are in the Alaska Range, such as those carving great chasms in the side of Mount McKinley. At that height, the mountain creates its own weather, wringing moisture out of the atmosphere and feeding its glaciers. The Kahiltna Glacier flows 45 miles from the mountain, descending 15,000 feet over its course. The Ruth Glacier has dug a canyon twice as deep as the Grand Canyon, half filled with mile-deep ice. Similarly, fjords and valleys all over Alaska were formed by the glaciers of 50 ice ages that covered North America in the last 2.5 million years.

Earthquakes & Mountains

Alaska has an average of 13 earthquakes a day, or 11% of all the seismic activity in the world, including 3 of the 10 largest ever recorded. On November 3, 2002, Alaska felt the world's largest earthquake of the year and one of the largest ever in the United States. Waves slopped across the bayous of Louisiana, and geysers at Yellowstone changed their size and period of eruptions. No one died, and few people were injured, because the quake occurred in such a sparsely populated area: the region between Anchorage and Fairbanks in the Alaska Range east of Mount McKinley. A 140-mile-long crack appeared right across that region, running over mountains and through glaciers. The land on each side moved laterally as much as 22 feet and vertically up to 6 feet. The Glenn Highway section known as the Tok Cut-Off, between Glennallen and Tok, broke into many deep cracks; a tractor-trailer fell

into one of them. Where the Interior highways crossed the big fault-line crack, lanes no longer lined up, and the road got a new jog where it used to be straight.

Any part of Alaska could have an earthquake at any time, but the Pacific Rim from Southcentral Alaska to the Aleutians is the shakiest. This is where Alaska is still under construction; the very rocks that make up the state are something of an ad hoc conglomeration, still in the process of being assembled. The floor of the Pacific Ocean is moving north, and as it moves, it carries islands and mountains with it. When they hit the Alaska plate, these pieces of land, called *terranes,* dock like ships arriving, but slowly—an island moving an inch a year takes a long time to travel thousands of miles. Geologists studying rocks near Mount McKinley found a terrane that used to be part of island geography in the tropics. In Kenai Fjords National Park, fossils have turned up that are otherwise found only in Afghanistan and China. The slowly moving crust of the Earth brought them here on a terrane that makes up a large part of the southern coast of Alaska.

The Earth's crust is paper thin compared to the globe's forces, and, like paper, it folds where two edges meet. Alaska's coast oscillates, bending up and down. At Kenai Fjords National Park, you can see steep little rock islands flocked with birds: They are old mountaintops, shrinking down into the earth. At Denali National Park, the earth is

bowing upward; the monolith of McKinley is a brand-new dent growing higher.

Here's how it works: Near the center of the Pacific, underwater volcanoes and cracks that constantly ooze molten new rock are adding to the tectonic plate that forms the ocean floor. As it grows from the middle, the existing sea floor spreads at a rate of perhaps an inch a year. At the other side of the Pacific plate, where it bumps up against Alaska, there's not enough room for more crust, so it's forced, bending and cracking, downward into the planet's great, hot, liquid, recycling mill of magma. Landmasses that are along for the ride smash into the continent that's already there. When one hits—the so-called Yakutat block is still in the process of "docking"—a mountain range gets shoved up. Earthquakes and volcanoes are byproducts.

Earthquakes that measure between 7 and 8 on the Richter scale occur once a year on average, and huge quakes greater than 8 occurred every 13 years on average over the last century. The worst of these, on March 27, 1964, was the strongest ever to hit North America. It ranked 9.2 on the Richter scale, twisting an entire region of the state so that land to the west sank 12 feet while in the east it rose more than 30 feet. More land moved laterally than in any other recorded earthquake as well. The earthquake destroyed much of Anchorage and several smaller towns, and killed about 131 people, mostly in sea waves created

> *In Alaska, people think of the Arctic as beginning at the Brooks Range, which is a bit north of the Arctic circle.*

by underwater landslides. In Valdez, the waterfront was swept clean of people.

But even that huge earthquake wasn't an unusual occurrence, at least in the Earth's terms. Geologists believe the same Alaska coast sank 6 feet in an earthquake in the year 1090.

Permafrost & Sea Ice

The northern Interior and Arctic parts of the state are less susceptible to earthquakes, and since they receive little precipitation, they don't have glaciers, either. But most of northern Alaska is solid only by virtue of being frozen. When it thaws, it turns to mush. The phenomenon is caused by permafrost, a layer of earth a little below the surface that never thaws—or at least, you'd better hope

it doesn't. With the climate warming, however, melting permafrost is affecting buildings and roads.

The Arctic and much of the Interior is actually a swampy desert. Annual precipitation measured in Barrow is the same as in Las Vegas. Most of the time, the tundra is frozen in white; snow blows around, but not much falls. It melts in the summer, but the water can't sink into the ground, which remains frozen. Water on top of the permafrost layer creates huge, shallow ponds. Alaska is a land of 10 million lakes, with 3 million larger than 20 acres. Birds arrive to feed and paddle around those circles and polygons of deep green and sky blue.

Permafrost makes the land do other strange things. On a

steep slope, the thawed earth on top of the ice can begin to slowly slide downhill like a blanket sliding off the side of a bed, setting the trees at crazy angles. You can see that at Denali National Park and elsewhere in the Interior. Permafrost also can create weird tundra, with shaky tussocks the size of basketballs that sit a foot or two apart on a wet, muddy flat. From a distance it looks smooth, but walking on real basketballs might be easier. In other places, freezing and thawing processes create ponds with straight sides and sharp corners, polygons that appear manmade. (For more, see "The Challenges of Frozen Ground," on p. 467.)

The permafrost also preserves many things. Although few and far between,

> *Adventurous visitors experience southern Alaska's temperate climate and primeval forests via zipline.*

tractor tracks remain clearly delineated for decades after they're made, appearing as narrow, parallel ponds reaching from one horizon to the other. The meat of prehistoric mastodons, still intact, has been unearthed from the frozen ground. On the Arctic Coast, the sea eroded ground near Barrow that contained ancient ancestors of the Eskimos who still inhabit the same neighborhood. In 1982, a family was found that apparently had been crushed by sea ice up to 500 years ago. Two of the bodies were well preserved, sitting in the home they had occupied and wearing the clothes they had worn the day of the disaster, perhaps around the time Columbus was sailing to America.

Sea ice is the frozen ocean that extends from the northern coast of Alaska to the other side of the world. For a few months of summer, it pulls away from the shore. Then, in October, icebergs floating toward land are cemented together by new ice forming along the beach. But even when the ice covers the whole ocean, it still moves under the immense pressure of wind and current. The clash creates towering pressure ridges—piles of broken ice that look like small mountain ranges and are about as difficult to cross.

Rainforest

Compared to the Arctic, southern coastal Alaska is warm and biologically rich. Temperate rainforest ranges up the coast from Southeast Alaska north into Prince William Sound and westward to Kodiak Island, with bears, deer, moose, wolves, and even big cats living among the massive western hemlock, Sitka spruce, and cedar. This old-growth forest, too wet to burn in forest fires, is the last vestige of the virgin, primeval woods that seemed so limitless to the first white settlers who arrived on the eastern coast of the continent in the 17th century. The trees grow on and on, sometimes rising more than 200 feet high with diameters up to 10 feet, and falling only after hundreds or even thousands of years. When they fall, the trees rot on the damp moss of the forest floor and return to the soil to feed more trees, which grow in rows upon their nursery trunks.

The rivers of the great coastal forests bring home runs of big salmon, clogging in spawning season like a busy sidewalk at rush hour. The fish spawn only once, returning by a precisely tuned sense of smell to the streams where they were hatched between 2 and 5 years before. When the fertilized eggs have been left in the stream gravel, the fish conveniently die on the beach, becoming a smorgasbord for bears and other forest animals.

The huge Kodiak brown bear, sometimes topping 1,000 pounds (the largest on record was 1,500 pounds), owes everything to the millions of salmon that return to the island each summer. By comparison, the grizzly bears of the Interior—the same species as browns, but living on grass, berries, and an occasional ground squirrel—are mere midgets, their weight counted in the hundreds of pounds. Forest-dwelling black bears grow to only a few hundred pounds.

Boreal Forest

Rainforest covers only a small fraction of Alaska, however. In fact, only one-third of Alaska is forested at all, and most of this is the boreal forest that covers the central part of the state, behind the rain shadow of coastal mountains that intercept moist clouds off the oceans. Ranging from the Kenai Peninsula, south of Anchorage, to the Brooks Range, where the Arctic begins, this is an area of taiga—a moist, subarctic forest of smaller, slower-growing, hardier trees that leave plenty of open sky between their branches. In well-drained areas, on hillsides and southern land less susceptible to permafrost, the boreal forest is a lovely, broadly spaced combination of straight, proud white spruce and pale, spectral paper birch. Along the rivers,

cottonwoods grow, with deep-grained bark.

Forest fires tear through Alaska's boreal forest each summer. In the newly warmed climate, million-acre burn seasons have become common; in 2004, a record 6.5 million acres burned—an area the size of Massachusetts—and in 2009 that number was almost 3 million acres. It's impossible to fight that much fire. In Alaska, the fire is always allowed to take its course unless structures or certain resources are at risk. In most cases, forest managers do no more than note the occurrence on a map. Unlike in the rainforest, there's little commercially valuable timber in these thin stands, and anyway, trying to halt the process of nature's self-immolation would be like trying to hold back a river with your hands. The boreal forest regenerates through fire—it was made to burn. The wildlife that lives in and eats it needs new growth from the burns as well as the shelter of older trees. When the forest is healthiest and most productive, the dark green of the spruce is broken by streaks and patches of light-green brush in an ever-changing succession.

The Warming Climate

In the past 2 decades, winters have warmed and shortened and summers have gotten hotter. Individual years are sometimes closer to the long-term norm, but the trend is toward warming. Years of bizarrely warm weather have become common, and records have been broken so often, they are hardly noted. In

Anchorage, where I live, that has meant ski seasons ruined by rainy weather, massive insect kills of trees, and extraordinary forest-fire danger, among many other changes.

In Arctic Alaska, the changes are much more pronounced: Sea ice is thinning and withdrawing from shore in ever-increasing record amounts. In 2007, the Northwest Passage over Canada and America was ice-free from one end to the other, completely navigable for the first time. The loss of ice has led to catastrophic erosion, washing away bluffs and villages. Permafrost has softened and given way. With winters warming and shortening, ecosystems are disrupted, with plant and animal life stressed by the new conditions. U.S. government scientists conclude that polar bears could go extinct, and the administration of President George W. Bush listed them as threatened. Without sea ice, it is difficult to imagine how they could survive.

Carbon dioxide warms the Earth by trapping the heat of the sun in the atmosphere, a phenomenon understood since the late 1800s. Climate records reconstructed from ancient ice show that the amount of carbon dioxide in the atmosphere has closely matched average temperature and climate conditions for half a million years. Due to human burning of fossil fuels, the carbon dioxide level in the atmosphere currently is higher than at any time in that period. And now Arctic temperatures are rising at a rate that appears unprecedented.

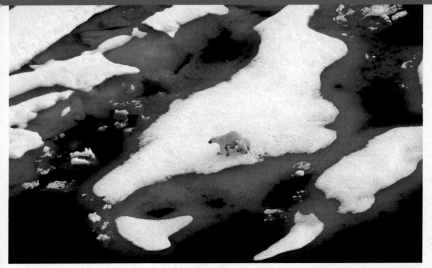

> *A decline in Arctic sea ice, which allows polar bears to hunt for seals, threatens the survival of the species.*

Does this mean adjusting your plans as a visitor? Yes and no. Tourists in recent years have enjoyed sunny weather but have also suffered through forest-fire smoke and rainy skiing. But how the changes will play out in any particular year cannot be predicted, just as you cannot set your vacation dates based on a TV weather forecast.

On the other hand, we may all need to adjust our plans.

The amount of carbon dioxide each of us is responsible for emitting relates directly to the nonrenewable energy we use. You can help save Alaska by carpooling or turning off an extra light.

The Challenges of Frozen Ground

The cold of northern Alaska chills the ground in winter, and the summer sun is warm enough to thaw only the top layer of soil. This permanently frozen ground is called permafrost, and the surface soil that freezes and thaws each year is called the active layer. In southern Alaska, the ground's surface also freezes, but that freeze goes down only so many feet and thaws completely in the summer. In between the Arctic and the south, in the Interior region, permafrost is patchy.

The presence of permafrost is a challenge for plants and for people. Permafrost stops soil from draining, so the active layer is often swampy. Not many species grow well in such cold, undrained soils; the black spruce is the only conifer that can make it. It's a thin, gnarled tree that grows a trunk a few inches thick in 100 years. Full of pitch, it burns readily, powering huge fires across the Interior that regenerate the land and open the cones of the next generation of black spruce, which otherwise remain permanently sealed.

For people, permafrost is tough to build on. When permafrost melts, it turns to mush, the land collapses, and structures placed on top sink into the earth. The warming climate of recent decades has melted a lot of patchy permafrost, causing roads to fall apart across the middle part of Alaska. State transportation officials have allocated millions of dollars to rebuild highways that slump when the permafrost melts underneath. The Trans-Alaska Pipeline has faced the same problem, although not to the same extent, since its supports are designed to get rid of heat. In the Arctic, many buildings stand on pilings to keep their warmth out of the ground.

Alaska's Native Peoples

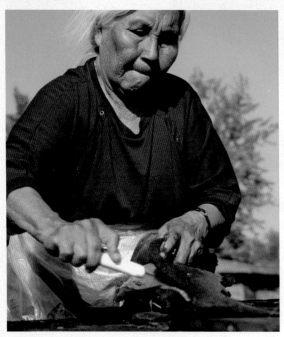

> *A Native woman cleans a fish at an Athabascan fish camp.*

Theories differ about how North America was originally populated. The textbook lesson says the first people walked across a land bridge from Asia (over the dry Bering Sea) around 15,000 years ago, when glacial ice had sequestered enough of the Earth's water to lower the sea level. The bridge, up to 1,000 miles wide, included the entire west coast of Alaska at its largest size and lasted longest in the area between Nome and Kotzebue.

But new archaeology and geology throw doubt on that theory, suggesting a migration story that's much more complex. People who know the Arctic know the land bridge simply wasn't necessary for migration: In the winter, you can sometimes walk on ice between Siberia and Alaska even today, and the seafaring skills of Alaska's Aleuts and Eskimos would have enabled them to travel back and forth to Asia at any time. Siberian and Alaskan Natives share language, stories, and kin.

Perhaps the connection across the north was continuous and followed many routes after northern people learned to sew skin boats and clothing about 15,000 years ago. Certainly, the idea that they walked across land seems increasingly questionable. Geologists now believe the route south was largely impassable during the last glacial period; if migrants did follow it, they must have used boats to connect coastal pockets that remained free of glacial ice.

However and whenever the first people arrived, they quickly spread through the Americas, creating cultures of incredible complexity and diversity. Most scientists believe migrants through Alaska were the ancestors of indigenous peoples all over the hemisphere, from the Inca to the Algonquin. In Alaska, those who stayed fit into two racial groups, the Indians and Eskimos (within Alaska, at least, these terms are accepted and used by the people themselves). The division between these two groups is typically marked by certain aspects of physical appearance, and by qualities of traditional culture. For example, the creation stories and spiritual world views of Arctic people around the world show interesting similarities among themselves, but are different from those of Indian groups. In Alaska the Eskimos include the Iñupiat of the Arctic, the Yup'ik of the Southwest, and the Alutiiq of the Gulf of Alaska coastline. The Indians include the Athabascan of the Interior and the Tlingits, Haida, and Tsimshians of Southeast Alaska and British Columbia.

The Native groups of Alaska have a lot in common culturally, but before the white invasion, they had well-defined boundaries and didn't mix much. They didn't farm, and the only animal they domesticated was the dog; dog teams and boats were the primary means of transportation and commerce. But they generally were not nomadic, and no one in Alaska lived in ice igloos. (Farther east, in Canada, igloos were used as winter dwellings on the ice pack.) On the treeless Arctic coast, houses were built of sod atop supports of whalebone and driftwood; where wood was plentiful, in the rainforests, large and intricately carved houses sheltered entire villages.

Typically, a family-connected tribal group would have both a winter village and a summer fish camp for gathering and laying up food. Elders guided the community in important decisions. A gifted shaman led the people in religious matters, relating to the spirits of ancestors, animals, trees, and even the ice that populated their world. Stories passed on through generations explained the universe.

Those oral traditions kept Native cultures alive. Twenty distinct Native languages were spoken. A few elders still speak only their Native language today, and only one language, Eyak, is essentially extinct. The languages break into four major families: Eskimo-Aleut, Athabascan-Eyak-Tlingit, Haida, and Tsimshian (the last two are primarily Canadian). The Eskimo-Aleut language group includes languages spoken by coastal people from the Arctic Ocean to the Gulf of Alaska, including Iñupiaq in the Arctic; Yup'ik in the Yukon–Kuskokwim and Bristol Bay regions; Aleut in the Aleutian Islands; and Alutiiq on the

> *Iñupiaq whalers with a seal skin boat at the edge of the pack ice on the Chukchi Sea.*

Alaska Peninsula, Kodiak, and Prince William Sound. There are 12 Athabascan and Eyak languages in Alaska, and more outside, including Apache and Navajo. In Southeast Alaska, Tlingit was spoken across most of the Panhandle. Haida was spoken on southern Prince of Wales Island and southward into what's now British Columbia, where Tsimshian also was spoken.

The first arrival of whites was often violent and destructive, spanning a 100-year period that started in the 1740s with the coming of the Russian fur traders, who enslaved the Aleuts, and continued into the 1840s, when New England whalers first met the Iñupiat of the Arctic. There were pitched battles, but disease, resource depletion, and nonviolent destruction of oral traditions were more influential forces. Protestant missionaries, backed by government assimilation policy, drove the old stories and even Native languages underground. Lela Kiana Oman, who published traditional Iñupiaq stories to preserve them, told me about

her memories of her father secretly telling the ancient tales at night to his children. She was forbidden to speak Iñupiaq in school and did not see her first traditional Native dance until age 18.

For the Aleuts, whose cultural traditions were almost completely wiped out, the process of renewal involves archaeology, repatriation of stolen objects, and a certain amount of invention. On the other hand, some villages remain with unbroken traditions, especially deep in the country of the Yukon–Kuskokwim Delta, where Yup'ik is still the dominant language and most of the food comes from traditional subsistence hunting and gathering, altered only by the use of modern materials and guns.

Today's young adults have grown up in a Native cultural renaissance, and it's come not a moment too soon. Television, the Internet, and the lure of teen rebellion—common all over the world—compete with healthier traditional activities. Schools in many areas now require Native language classes, or even teach using language-immersion techniques.

Alaska Natives also are fighting destruction of their communities fueled by alcohol and other substance-abuse problems. Rates of suicide, accidents, and domestic violence are high in the Bush. Statistics show that nearly every Alaska Native in prison is there because of alcohol. Current efforts include a sobriety movement that attacks the problem one person at a time; one of its goals is to use traditional Native culture to fill the void of rural despair where alcohol flows in. From a political angle, a "local option" law provides communities the choice of partial or even total alcohol prohibition; it has been successfully used in many towns but remains controversial in others.

There are social and political tensions between Natives and whites on many levels and over many issues. The Alaskan city and Alaskan village have less in common than do most different nations. Although village Natives come to the city to shop, get health care, or attend meetings, urban Alaskans have no reason to go to the villages, and most never have made the trip.

The most contentious rural–urban issue concerns allocation of fish and game. Some urban outdoorsmen feel they should have the same rights to hunt and fish that the Natives do, and the state's Supreme Court has interpreted Alaska's constitution as saying that they're correct. But rural Natives have federal law on their side, which overrules the state. A decade of political stalemate over the issue divided Alaskans until, in 2000, the feds finally stepped in and took over fish and game management in the majority of Alaska to protect Native subsistence. Many Natives were glad to see that happen, as humiliating as the move was for independent-minded Alaskans. Natives feel that subsistence hunting and fishing are an integral part of their cultural heritage, far more important than sport, and should take priority. Darker conflicts exist, too, and it's impossible to discount the charges of racism that Native Alaskans raise when faced with issues as diverse as school funding and public safety.

Alaska Natives have essentially become a minority in their own land. In 1880, Alaska contained 33,000 Natives and 430 whites. By 1900, with the gold rush, the numbers were roughly equal. Since then, non-Natives have generally outnumbered Natives in ever greater numbers. Today there are about 98,000 Alaska Natives—27,000 of whom live in the cities of Anchorage and Fairbanks—out of a total state population of 627,000 people of all races.

Consequently, Alaska Natives must learn to walk in two worlds. The North Slope's Iñupiat, who hunt the bowhead whale from open boats as their forefathers did, must also know how to negotiate for their take in international diplomatic meetings. And they have to use the levers of government to protect the whale's environment from potential damage by the oil industry.

Non-Natives traveling to the Bush also walk in two worlds, but they may not even know it. In a Native village, a newly met friend will ask you in for a cup of coffee; it can be rude not to accept. Too much eye contact in conversation also can be rude—that's how Native elders look at younger people who owe them respect. If a Native person looks down, speaks slowly, and seems to mumble, that's not disrespect but the reverse. Fast-talking non-Natives have to make a conscious effort to slow down and leave pauses in conversation because Natives usually don't jump in or interrupt—they listen, consider, and then respond. Of course, most Native people won't take offense at your bad manners. They're used to spanning cultures. When I was in a village a few years ago, I looked in confusion at a clock that didn't seem right. "That's Indian time," my Athabascan companion said. Then, pointing to a clock that was working, he said, "White man time is over there."

Urban visitors who miss cultural nuances rarely overlook the apparent poverty of many villages. Out on a remote landscape of windswept tundra, swampy in summer and frozen in winter, they may secretly wonder why Natives endure the hardships of rural Alaskan life when even the most remote villager can see on television how easy it is in, say, Southern California. Save your pity. As Yup'ik social observer Harold Napoleon once said, "We're poor, all right, but we've got more than most people. Our most important asset is our land and our culture, and we want to protect it, come hell or high water."

Alaska in High & Popular Culture

Awareness of Alaska has reached a new level in the popular imagination, with an abundance of new books and movies about the state. As has always been the case, most of the material merely uses Alaska as a blank page for fantasies from the minds of their creators. One cannot learn much about Alaska from fictional movies or books, although there are always other reasons for watching or reading them.

Literature

The Alaska Native experience is covered by *50 Miles from Tomorrow,* by Willie Hensley (Farrar, Straus and Giroux, 2009), the memoir of a key leader in the Alaska Native land claims movement who became a towering figure in politics and government. He tells his life story, especially focusing on his Iñupiaq childhood in a traditional sod hut in the Arctic.

Seth Kantner also grew up in a sod hut, although he and his parents were white. In his novel *Ordinary Wolves* (Milkweed Editions, 2004), Kantner describes his youth in the Arctic wilderness, where his family's way of life was little different from that of pre-contact Eskimos. This autobiographical tale conveys the hardships of that life and of his introduction to the city, with devastating emotional clarity.

The pioneer rather than the Native perspective comes from the work of Klondike gold prospector Jack London, whose most famous book was

> *Jack London, author of the classic* Call of the Wild *(1903), was once an unsuccessful gold prospector.*

The Call of the Wild, (Aladdin, 1903). Literature was London's payoff for a short and unsuccessful sojourn in the gold rush. He never got much chance to look for gold after wintering in a Yukon cabin and getting scurvy, but he found great inspiration. This classic, published just 5 years later, tells its story from the point of view of a dog.

A latter-day classic about pioneers, *Coming into the Country,* (Farrar, Straus and Giroux, 1976), was written

by John McPhee. Although it describes a world that is now in the past, McPhee's closely observed and vividly told profile of Alaska remains valuable as a snapshot of a key time of transition. The Alaskan spirit he conveys through profiles of strange characters in the Bush remains with us.

Here are two books for learning about contemporary Alaska, from decidedly different points of view: My own book *The Fate of Nature* (Thomas Dunne/St. Martin's

> *Director Werner Herzog's* Grizzly Man *(2005) is a study of Alaskan brown bear enthusiast—and prey—Timothy Treadwell.*

Press, 2010) uses the history, science, and people of Prince William Sound as a lens to examine one of the largest questions facing humankind: Is it within our nature to share the Earth with wilderness and wild creatures? Sarah Palin, on the other hand, sees nothing but economic development opportunity in Alaska's future. *Going Rogue* (HarperCollins, 2009) is her memoir of her youth in Wasilla and run for the vice presidency. It was a cultural phenomenon when it came out, with even the purchase of the book interpreted as a political statement. Critics were unimpressed, but believers loved it.

Film & Television

Since most people don't know much about Alaska, filmmakers often use it as a setting for exploring their own ideas and stereotypes about the wild (although hardly any filming actually happens here). Sometimes the results are good. The Hollywood movie *Insomnia* (2002) includes Al Pacino's powerful performance as a detective whose ethical lapses won't let him sleep when he visits a small Alaska town where the sun never sets in the summer. Take-home message: Bring eye shades if light bothers you at night. Many newcomers do find the midnight sun unsettling.

Similarly, the film *Into the Wild* (2007), which dramatizes Jon Krakauer's book of the same name, investigates ideas about a character rather than the reality of a misguided young seeker who hiked into the wilderness near Denali National Park, only to starve to death in an abandoned school bus. Director Sean Penn made the unusual decision to film on location in Alaska, filling the movie with spectacular scenery.

A rather more cynical (but in some ways, more accurate) portrayal of Alaska comes from *The Simpsons Movie* (2007). Alaskans seemed to have fully arrived in the forefront of national consciousness when subjected to the ridicule of the creators of this animated family, and many found it uncomfortable. Homer, having caused environmental devastation at home, finds he fits right in when he gets to Alaska, where "you can never be too fat or too drunk."

> *Homer thinks he's found his own personal heaven in Alaska in the* The Simpsons Movie *(2007).*

The most perceptive and accurate film about Alaska comes from German director Werner Herzog, who made the documentary *Grizzly Man* in 2005. Herzog used real video made by Timothy Treadwell, who treated dangerous brown bears as pets on his camping trips on the Alaska Peninsula—and then was eaten by them. Rather than exploiting the situation, Herzog uses it for a profound exploration of society's misunderstanding of the nature of the wild.

On the small screen, *Northern Exposure* (1990–95) captured something true about Alaska, too, although the factual details were strange and off-base. The fictional TV series followed a spoiled New York doctor forced to relocate his practice to a small town in Alaska. The feeling the show created of life in a

> *The television show* Northern Exposure *(1990–1995) won two Emmy Awards and two Golden Globes.*

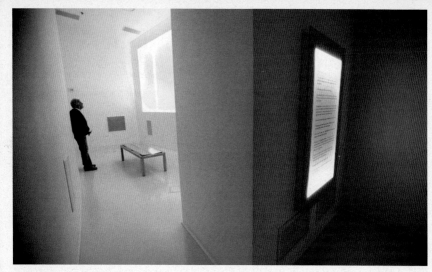

> *A visitor enjoys composer John Luther Adams's sound installation at the UA Museum of the North.*

Southeast Alaska community was remarkably accurate, with its odd characters and events and the sense of casual familiarity with the surrounding wilderness. The early seasons are strongest.

More recently, reality TV has focused on Alaska. The hit show *Deadliest Catch: Crab Fishing in Alaska* premiered in 2005 on the Discovery Channel. The unlikely stars—rugged, hard-driving crab fishermen working in the dangerous waters of the Bering Sea—now appear in the tabloids and on television. Another Alaska-based show, from the same producers, is *Ice Road Truckers,* about truck drivers hauling equipment on the Dalton Highway, made Alaskans start to wonder what part of life in the state *wouldn't* become grist for the national media mills.

Popular Music

Alaska doesn't produce a lot of famous musicians; Alaskan artists have to leave to make it in the big time. The most famous to have done so is Jewel, whose 1995 album *Pieces of You* put her on the cover of *Time* magazine. She began life as Jewel Kilcher, a pioneering family in Homer known for their folk singers and yodelers. After Jewel, the list of national acts that started in Alaska is not long. Recently a homegrown bluegrass band called Bearfoot made a splash with a terrific pop/bluegrass

album called *Doors and Windows,* and Kate Earl, who started as an Anchorage folk singer, has made her way as a pop musician on the national scene.

Big-name acts do occasionally pass through Alaska, usually in the winter, but that's certainly nothing to plan a visit around. A better bet is the local music scene in several communities, which blossoms for festivals in Anchorage and Juneau during the winter and spring (see chapter 14). Anchorage promoters and venues are listed in chapter 4.

Classical Music

Anchorage (p. 119) and **Fairbanks** (p. 321) have symphonies. Alaska's best-known composer is John Luther Adams, who works in a cabin outside Fairbanks; his work has been performed all over the country and lavishly praised by the *New Yorker* and the *Village Voice.* You can encounter his music at a much-admired sound installation at the **UA Museum of the North** (p. 317, **7**), called "The Place Where We Go to Listen."

The **Sitka Summer Music Festival** (☎ 907-747-6774; www.sitkamusicfestival.org) is a chamber music series nearing its 40th birthday. Performances and other events take place over 3 weeks in June. **Juneau Jazz and Classics** (☎ 907-463-3378; www.jazzandclassics.org) is a 9-day festival in late May.

Eating & Drinking

> *A fresh growler at Skagway Brewing Company.*

> *King crab legs are one of Alaska's delicacies.*

Beer drinkers will find that many small towns in Alaska have their own brews. Usually there is no bottling plant, so you have to enjoy the beer in a bar or restaurant, or get a growler—a returnable jug that is filled at the brewery and should be drunk fresh. In Anchorage there are several breweries and brewpubs; you really would have to put your mind to it to try everything. The state's most popular beer is Alaskan Amber, brewed in Juneau by Alaskan Brewing Co, based on a gold-rush recipe—in any bar in Alaska, you get one just by saying, "Amber." (I don't know how barmaids named Amber handle this.)

Alaska cuisine is mostly about salmon and halibut—other fish and shellfish, too, and game, if you feel like something exotic. But salmon or halibut will be on virtually any restaurant menu in the summer and is likely offered as the highlight of the offerings. The key to cooking Pacific salmon—or to ordering it in a restaurant—is to avoid any preparation that spoils the rich flavor. With halibut, it's important to choose the right cut and preparation for enjoying this flaky, delicate fish. I love eating halibut and chips or salmon tacos from a stand, but even then the fish needs to be treated and prepared right to do it justice.

12

The Best Special Interest Trips

> PREVIOUS PAGE *Kayaking near Johns Hopkins Glacier.* THIS PAGE *Camping at Glacier Bay National Park.*

Escorted General Interest Tours

A large fraction of visitors to Alaska see the state from buses and rail cars on escorted tours, usually before or after a cruise. Passengers who fly to Alaska also join escorted tours, although almost exclusively with companies owned by the cruise lines. The positive reasons for choosing this approach are simplicity and the opportunity to travel with other people, perhaps making friends. For older singles, that can be a big plus; many folks on these escorted tours are members of the "gray hair and tennis shoe" set. Costs are controlled and known in advance. Typically, a weeklong escorted tour is around $1,400 per person.

You do give up major advantages when you have someone else run your vacation for you. Groups are large, and visitors sometimes feel as though they are being herded around. Stops at sights of interest tend to be brief, hitting the highlights only, which can risk missing the whole point of an experiential wilderness destination. Accommodations and facilities are the largest and most standardized. You won't meet many Alaskans, as staff is imported. Outdoor activities are few and are geared to the least fit member of your group.

The two largest tour companies are **Holland America Line** (☎ 800-544-2206; www.graylineofalaska.com or www.hollandamerica.com) and **Princess Tours** (☎ 800-426-0500; www.princesslodges.com). Both are owned by Carnival Cruise Lines, and the differences between the two are narrowing. In general, Holland America has more choices around the state, with unique itineraries and activities, while Princess offers higher quality, with better hotels and first-rate food and service.

Organized Tours: Finding Your Guide to the Great Outdoors

If the point of your Alaska trip, as for most visitors, is to experience wilderness and to see wildlife and scenery, it makes sense to orient your tour to outdoor activities. I've focused on the outdoors throughout the book, and you'll find advice for self-guided and locally guided activities in each chapter. That independent approach allows you to save money by getting help only when you need it and by calibrating your activities to your interests and ability level.

But if you don't want to take on all the details yourself, it's also perfectly reasonable to sign up for a tour with a company that specializes in the outdoors. This approach costs more, but offers the benefits of saving time on planning and during your trip. You'll be certain of a quality experience without doing research or legwork.

The next step up from an outdoors-oriented vacation is a multiday expedition into the wilderness. For such a trip, you probably need a guide with the equipment, know-how, and organization to make it happen safely and smoothly. Only those experienced in providing such trips in more forgiving environments should consider leading their own expedition in Alaska. The hassle of lining up the equipment and transportation may persuade even some experts to join a guided group.

Alaska Discovery (☎ 800-586-1911; www.akdiscovery.com) pioneered eco-tourism in Alaska with the mission of saving wild places, and even after being bought by the international Mountain Travel Sobek expedition company, it is still known for a local and environmentally positive ethic. Trips concentrate on sea kayaking in Southeast Alaska, where the company started, but also include rafting expeditions and complete vacations. Among the unique offerings are the kayak tours to the rationed Pack Creek brown bear viewing site and the cushy inn-to-inn kayaking trips. The Glacier Bay paddles are famous, and the company also leads floats in the Arctic National Wildlife Refuge. A 3-day kayak expedition near Juneau is $995, while 10 days in the Arctic is around $4,695.

Alaska Wildland Adventures (☎ 800-334-8730 or 907-783-2928; www.alaska wildland.com) is a well-run company based in Southcentral Alaska that has created a set of first-class wilderness lodges and outdoors-based escorted tours for travelers who want to experience the wild but aren't interested in being uncomfortable or doing anything difficult. The mood is positive and outdoorsy, the facilities are in great places and of excellent quality, meals are plentiful, and beds are soft. Days are spent on outings—rafting, kayaking, hiking, glacier cruises, or wildlife watching. An 11-day group safari is around $5,696; shorter trips, trips for families with kids, fishing trips, and other choices are available, too.

Equinox Wilderness Expeditions (☎ 206-462-5246; www.equinoxexpeditions.com) reflects the expertise of its owner, Karen Jettmar, whose two decades of work have made her famous as a guide and an author about Alaska's wilderness. Offerings include challenging rafting, sea kayaking, and hiking trips and less strenuous base-camp wildlife viewing. The expeditions go to the state's most remote and exotic areas. Groups are limited to five to eight members. You can set up a custom trip with your own group. A 10-day Arctic float trip costs around $4,200.

The specialty at **St. Elias Alpine Guides** (☎ 888-933-5427 or 907-345-9048; www.steliasguides.com) is mountain climbing and backpacking, and the focus is Wrangell–St. Elias National Park. Not a bad combination, since that's some of Alaska's most extraordinary and least used wilderness, with such an abundance of mountains that the company can offer first ascents as part of its product line. For those who aren't up to a mountain-climbing expedition (most of us), the company also offers more manageable treks and extraordinary multiday rafting trips.

Self-Guided Tours

For a fraction of the cost of an all-inclusive tour, you can travel by car or ferry and do self-guided hikes or sea kayaking and wildlife-viewing day trips. The following are agencies with expertise setting up that kind of tour. As always when using a travel agent, you'll get the best results if you do your research first and have a fair idea of your interests and goals before getting started. Also, take care of your money when using any trip-planning agency; use a credit card that will cover you if the agency goes broke, and buy travel insurance separately (see p. 511).

Bob Kaufman, an accomplished outdoors athlete, designed **www.alaska.org**, a website that contains lots of advice and details and an incredible number of videos showing what places are really like. The site is not focused specifically on the outdoors, but Bob's philosophy (and smiling face) shine through, and the site is a good tool for putting together an outdoors-oriented trip, especially in the Southcentral-to-Denali zone. Using the site commits you to nothing; when you've seen enough, book online or call the toll-free number (☎ 888-ALASKA-8 [252-7528] for questions and booking, or do the booking yourself.

> *A program at the Alaska Raptor Center shows off a bald eagle.*

Alaska Tour & Travel (☎ 800-208-0200; www.alaskatravel.com) specializes in the territory between Denali and Kenai Fjords national parks—Alaska's most popular travel area—which they also link with a shuttle service, critical for those who don't rent a car, called the Park Connection. The website is very handy, allowing you to buy packages or build your own itinerary.

Energetic Matthew Lowe's specialty is setting up outdoors-oriented trips, especially in the Southcentral region. His company, **AskMatt Alaskan Adventures & Tours** (☎ 907-868-1786; www.askmatt.com) is a great source for anyone interested in fishing charters, remote lodges, and winter trips.

If your primary goal is to catch fish, a $95 upfront fee is well worth the cost to get specialist Sheary Suiter, owner of **Sport Fishing Alaska** (☎ 888-552-8674 or 907-344-8674; www.alaskatripplanners.com) on your side. A former lodge owner, she knows where fish are running each week—and the best lodge to stay at or air taxi to get you there. That's critical information not easy to find on your own.

Lodges hate to tell visitors not to come; Sheary could save you thousands if she helps you avoid a fishing lodge with poor fishing.

If you want to plan a Southeast Alaska ferry odyssey, **Viking Travel** (☎ 800-327-2571 or 907-772-3818; www.alaskaferry.com) can be a big help. Besides handling ferry bookings—and getting clients to the front of the line for hard-to-get vehicle or cabin reservations—this Petersburg-based travel agency can arrange rooms and outdoor activities for you, too.

Volunteering

The sorts of organizations that can always use volunteers are happy to get the help in Alaska, too, including museums and such, but here are a couple of ideas for a more uniquely Alaskan volunteer vacation. The **Iditarod Trail Sled Dog Race** (p. 121) uses many volunteers to put on the race; contact them through the website, and act early, because they typically get more help than they can use. The **Alaska SeaLife Center** (p. 268, **1**) also uses volunteers; it is a research aquarium and animal rescue center in Seward. In Sitka, the **Alaska Raptor Center** (p. 390, **7**) rehabilitates eagles and other birds of prey, with volunteers helping each summer.

Outdoor Activities A to Z

Backpacking

The best places for backpacking on trails are in Chugach National Forest and Chugach State Park, near Anchorage, and Chena River State Recreation Area, near Fairbanks. In the national forest, the **Resurrection Trail** leads from **Hope** (p. 234, **3**) to **Cooper Landing** (p. 238, **5**), a trip of 39 miles that makes a good three-day trip, although you have to station a car at the far end to get back. Also in the Chugach forest, the **Primrose Creek** (p. 252, **3**) and **Lost Lake trails** connect for a glorious 16-mile (one way) overnight.

More practical for most visitors are trips that start and end at the same trailhead. Of course, any trail can be done that way. Among the best are in Chugach State Park, from Anchorage, starting at **Glen Alps** (p. 74, **1**), **Eklutna Lake** (p. 73, **5**), or the **Eagle River Nature Center** (p. 72, **2**).

Near Fairbanks, the 15-mile **Granite Tors**

Trail (p. 288, **7**), in Chena River State Recreation Area, is among my favorites. You can camp among the tors; be sure to bring food and plenty of water with you.

For off-trail backpacking, the destinations are infinite. If you haven't done it before, consider going with an outfitter like **St. Elias Alpine Guides** (p. 218). You need to know how to find your route and avoid the hazards of cold rivers and bad weather, among other things. **Denali National Park** is a good place for a first off-trail backpacking experience, because rangers offer advice (and potentially rescue) and the **shuttle bus** (p. 149) gets you to your starting point. Wherever you go, leave a trip plan with someone who will alert authorities if you don't come back.

Biking

Bicycles are a good way to get around most Alaskan towns, and Anchorage has an extraordinary network of paved bike trails that provide the best way to enjoy the city. I've mentioned bike rental agencies throughout the book.

For a bike-oriented vacation, consider **Alaskabike** (☎ 907-245-2175; www.alaska bike.com), which leads trips on the rural highways, with activities along the way. An 8-day tour over the spectacular Richardson Highway costs $2,995, all-inclusive.

Mountain biking opportunities in Alaska are many. Again, the local rental agency is the best source for where to go depending on when and where you arrive. I've also given specific ideas at **Denali National Park** (p. 146), **Anchorage** (p. 63), and **Homer** (p. 260).

Bird-Watching

Many birders come to Alaska in search of species and habitat types they haven't encountered before. Make birding an aspect of your trip using the advice in each chapter to find good spots near Alaska towns; they're too numerous to call out individually here, but among the best are **Kenai Fjords National Park** (p. 30, **3**), **Sitka Sound and St. Lazaria Island** (p. 33, **1**), the **Copper River Delta** near Cordova (p. 208, **10**), and the roads near **Nome** (p. 432).

One other destination is only for birders: the **Pribilof Islands.** Considered among the world's best birding destinations, the islands

> *Hiking in Wrangell-St. Elias National Park.*

are remote rocks far out in the Bering Sea. Accommodations are rough, and meals are served only in a fish cannery cafeteria, but the abundance of avian and marine mammal life is unequalled. Trips are offered by **TDX Corporation** (☎ 877-424-5637; www.alaskabirding.com).

If birding is a primary purpose of your trip, consider joining a group with a guide who will take you to the best spots along with others who share your interest. Among well-reputed operators coming to Alaska are Arizona-based **High Lonesome Bird Tours** (☎ 800-743-2668 or 520-458-9446; www.hilonesometours. com) and Texas-based **Victor Emanuel Nature Tours** (☎ 800-328-8368; www.ventbird.com).

Camping with a Car or an RV

Camping along Alaska's roads is a fun and authentically Alaskan alternative to staying in hotels and eating meals in restaurants. The advantages for families are decisive with this spontaneous, outdoor style of travel. Campgrounds are everywhere outside the cities, and RV parks are easy to find as well.

My preference is to go with a tent and cooler packed in the trunk of the car,

> *Casting on the Kenai River.*

maximizing freedom and closeness to nature and minimizing cost. On the other hand, you'll find no flush toilets or showers in most public campgrounds, and it can get quite cold at night, even in the summer. For advice on how to arrange a camping trip in the face of airline baggage fees and TSA regulations, see p. 157.

I've also toured with a rented RV, which provides more protection from the elements, a soft bed at night, cooking facilities, and a built-in toilet. On the downside, touring by RV doesn't save money over staying in hotels; driving and parking the big rig reduces the spontaneity; and someone has to deal with draining that convenient toilet, which is not fun.

RVs are for rent in Anchorage, Fairbanks, or Skagway, or in Seattle if you want to tackle the Alaska Highway odyssey. Operating in each of those locations, **Alaska Motorhome Rentals** (☎ 800-323-5757; www.bestofalaskatravel. com) is the best choice for one-way rentals. Here is an example that should allow you to evaluate your costs: Skagway to Anchorage carries a drop-off fee of $795 to $995; plus the cost of the rental, $209 to $249 a day in the high season; plus mileage (or pay $35 a day for unlimited mileage), gas (allow 50¢ a mile), and any taxes.

I've mentioned campgrounds at towns and parks throughout the book, but there are many others. A widely distributed free map put out by the Alaska Public Lands Information Centers lists all public campgrounds. One book with detailed reviews of every campground and RV park in Alaska is *Traveler's Guide to Alaskan Camping,* by Mike and Terri Church (Rolling Homes Press).

Canoeing

A canoe can be the easiest way to experience the wilderness. You don't have to carry your stuff on your back, and if you match the place you paddle to your skills, you don't need a guide. I've highlighted some of the best and most accessible canoeing at the **Kenai National Wildlife Refuge** (p. 274, **❶**), along the **Chena River** in Fairbanks (p. 299, **❽**), and on the **Copper River Delta** near Cordova (p. 408, **❿**). In each case, canoe rental and shuttle services make it easy.

Dog Mushing

If you come in the winter, I hope you can catch a dog-sled race. It's a singular experience to see these powerful, intelligent animals speeding by. You can also drive a team yourself, although to really learn how is beyond the means and interest of most visitors. Fairbanks is the center of mushing. **Sun Dog Express Dog Sled Tours** (☎ 907-479-6983; www. mosquitonet.com/~sleddog) charges just $15 for a short ride, $250 to learn to drive a team in a half-day, or $475 for a three-day expedition.

More visitors encounter mushing in the summer. Demonstrations without snow are common, with the classic being at **Denali National Park** (p. 161). But you really need a sled to mush, and that's accomplished in warmer months by flying to a glacier, such as **Norris Glacier** near Juneau (p. 381, **⓯**) or **Godwin Glacier** near Seward (p. 271).

Fishing

The fishing industry remains Alaska's largest employer, and angling is among the most popular reasons to make the trip here. Besides the world's largest salmon and halibut, anglers also pursue thriving wild stocks of steelhead,

> *White water rafting on the Nenana River.*

cutthroat, and rainbow trout; Dolly Varden and Arctic char; and Arctic grayling.

You can catch fish when they're running almost anywhere in Alaska except at high elevations in the Arctic or Interior. You'll need information, equipment, and skills, and for that it makes sense to fish with a guide or charter skipper the first time out. Fly-in fishing with a guide is the best of all. I've listed those providers throughout the book.

If fishing is an overriding goal, I recommend contacting **Sport Fishing Alaska** (p. 259) or **AskMatt Alaskan Adventures & Tours** (p. 480) to make sure you end up where the fish are. A trip to a fishing lodge or a fly-in to Bristol Bay can give you the kind of fishing that will assure you are called a liar when you share your tales at home. At best, you can pull in big, beefy trout and salmon one after another. Expect to pay $1,000 a day for such a trip.

To learn more about Alaskan salmon, see "Salmon," on p. 254.

Flightseeing

Seeing the scenery from the air is an essential element of an Alaska vacation. Small planes are the primary means of transportation for much of the state and the best way to get to many remote places. Getting on one for aerial views is easy and worth the money if you plan well and wait for good weather. The very best flights go from **Talkeetna** to see Mount McKinley (p. 130, ❶), but there are good choices all over the state, which you will find described in each of the chapters.

Hiking

Hiking is the least expensive and most natural way into Alaska's wilderness, possible from many communities without even a drive to the trailhead, and virtually always within easy reach. You don't need a guide, just good shoes and clothing and your common sense (leave word of where you're going for solo hikes). Trails are listed throughout the book.

Rafting

A raft can be the best way to see a big swath of remote Alaska or enjoy a speedy thrill ride for an afternoon. River floats range in duration from an afternoon of crazy rapids at **Sixmile Creek** near Hope (p. 232, ❷) to a couple of weeks in the Arctic with **Alaska Discovery** (p. 479) or **Equinox Wilderness Expeditions** (p. 479). I've covered white-water guides in many towns. One of the best operators, with options in several parts of the state, is **Nova** (☎ 800-746-5753 or 907-745-5753; www. novalaska.com), which has been in business since 1975. Their daily floats are on Sixmile Creek at **Matanuska Glacier** (p. 194, ❷) and in Copper Center under the name **Alaska's River Wrangellers** (p. 191, ❾); they also offer longer wilderness trips. I mark them highly for being serious about the hazards of floating on these cold, fast waters; you shouldn't discount the risks, either.

Winter Festivals & Sled Dog Races

Visitors who come to Alaska in the wintertime experience even more beautiful scenery—under snow, it's more dramatic—and can enjoy many more authentic community events and sports, including skiing and dog mushing. Hotel rates drop drastically, often to half of their summer highs (or less). On the other hand, wildlife viewing and fishing are essentially nil, most tourist-oriented attractions are closed, the days are short, and travel options are limited by weather—unless you're skilled and equipped to drive long, lonely distances on icy highways. Some coastal and island communities can be grim in winter, with nothing to do.

The best area for a winter visit is the central part of the state, from Anchorage to Fairbanks, and the best time is February and March, with the peak in the middle of that period. Now the sun is in the sky past midafternoon and temperatures have moderated, but there's still plenty of snow on the ground. This is the time when Alaska comes alive with its biggest events, races, and festivals.

The **Anchorage Fur Rendezvous Festival** (☎ 907-274-1177; www.furrondy.net), during the last weekend of February and first weekend of March, is packed with fun and interesting activities, including the running

of the reindeer and the World Championship Sled Dog Races, both of which occur the first weekend. The second weekend of the festival, the **Iditarod Trail Sled Dog Race** (☎ 907-376-5155; www.iditarod.com) leaves from downtown Anchorage, running all the way to Nome.

Fairbanks begins the big mushing races of the year in early February with the **Yukon Quest International Sled Dog Race** (☎ 907-452-7954; www.yukonquest.com), which links across the border with Canada to Whitehorse, Yukon, 1,000 miles away. The **World Ice Art Championships** (☎ 907-451-8250; www.icealaska.com) happen later in the month and last into early March, attracting international carvers who create massive sculptures. The ice park usually also has fun slides and mazes for kids. The **Open North American Championship Sled Dog Race** (☎ 907-457-6874; www.sleddog.org) comes later in March.

While you won't be participating in those events, there's plenty to do in the region: cross-country or downhill skiing (p. 299, ⑩), watching the aurora or soaking in a hot pool at **Chena Hot Springs Resort** (p. 289, ⑧), and maybe even checking out other extreme winter events. The list here is only the start; see "Going to Extremes," on p. 96.

Sea Kayaking

In coastal Alaska, sea kayaking is like hiking in most other places: It's the best chance to get up close to marine life and the rocky shoreline. Every coastal community from Kodiak to Ketchikan has a small-town sea kayaking company with local guides leading day trips. I recommend a paddle for anyone who is reasonably fit and doesn't have back or knee problems. Renting and paddling on your own is advisable only after you've had some experience and lessons; while you don't need lessons for a guided multiday trip, it's wise to do a day trip first and make sure you enjoy it. **Alaska Discovery** (p. 479) offers some of the best expeditions.

Skiing, Cross-Country

Alaska's long, snowy winters, well-developed trail systems, and active skiing community have developed a steady stream of national champions and Olympians, in numbers vastly out of proportion to the state's population. The best trails are in Anchorage, at **Kincaid Park** (p. 70, **6**), and at **Birch Hill** in Fairbanks (p. 299, **10**), but other communities in Southcentral and Interior Alaska also have great Nordic skiing. Races mostly happen in February and March, at the same time as other **winter festivals** (at left), with many of the long-distance events welcoming novices who just want to participate for fun (see "Going to Extremes," on p. 96). You can tap into information for the whole state at the website for the **Nordic Ski Association of Anchorage** (www.anchoragenordicski.com; click on "Links" for clubs around the state).

Skiing, Downhill

There are community alpine skiing areas in several towns, but the only mountain worthy of focusing a trip on is **Alyeska Resort** in Girdwood (p. 87, **7**), south of Anchorage. Skiing is best in the late winter, when the sun returns, and during the week, when Anchorage families are at school and work.

Snowmobiling

We call them snow machines, and they're basic transportation for many Alaskans. Give it a try from Girdwood with **Glacier City Snowmobile Tours** (p. 93).

> *Shredding powder at Alyeska Resort.*

Wildlife Viewing

Seeing wildlife is a major focus of every chapter in the book. The best inexpensive wildlife safari is on the shuttle buses of **Denali National Park** (p. 132, **3**). There are also places to go where the entire objective is seeing animals, the most important of which is **Brooks Camp** in Katmai National Park, in southwest Alaska. During salmon runs, peaking in early July and to a lesser extent again in September, large numbers of huge brown bears congregate at a waterfall on the Brooks River where salmon have to leap to get upstream. If you've seen film or pictures of bears catching jumping salmon, they probably came from here. Lodgings are available at Brooks Camp, but they're so difficult to reserve that there's hardly reason to mention them. Instead, go on a day trip from Anchorage. You will fly an Alaska Airlines jet to King Salmon, and then take a small plane to the camp. Book it as a package through the concessionaire, **Katmailand** (☎ 800-544-0551 or 907-243-5448; www.katmaiair.com), for about $620. That may seem a lot, but it isn't out of line for fly-in bear viewing, and here you see one of the most impressive bear gatherings. However, do not go outside of salmon peak times, as then you may see no bears at all.

13
Guide to Alaska's Flora & Fauna

> *OPPOSITE PAGE The white Arctic wolf.* THIS PAGE *A pod of humpback whales summers in polar waters.*

The flora and fauna of Alaska are not particularly diverse. One of the pleasures of learning the names of plants is that you soon can be an expert. Instead, what's special about Alaska's living world is its abundance. Much of America used to be as rich, according to the journals of Lewis and Clark. In Alaska, though, the great herds of land mammals were never extirpated; caribou still migrate in herds of 100,000. Fences never were built, and roads are too scarce to have eviscerated ecosystems as they have done in the Lower 48. Human impact is certainly a factor here, but much of Alaska looks as it probably did when the ice retreated at the end of the Pleistocene.

Get a Good Guide

To dig deeper into animal and plant identification, get a hold of the proper field guides. For plants, trees, and fish, you will need an Alaska-specific book, which is easiest to find after you arrive in the state.

Birds. Any comprehensive field guide will do. I use the *National Audubon Society Field Guide to North American Birds,* Western Edition (Alfred A. Knopf, $20).

Fish. Anglers should pick up a colored identification guide printed on either side of a plastic laminated card. Various versions are available in Alaskan book, sporting goods, and gift stores.

Flowers. A general North American guide isn't much help. The classic is a locally published book widely available here: *Field Guide to Alaska Wildflowers,* by Verna E. Pratt (Alaskakrafts, $16).

Mammals, Birds & Fish. Although its illustrations are not in color, the best single source of information is the *Alaska Department of Fish and Game Notebook Series* (Alaska Department of Fish & Game, $13). It is for sale in bound form or available for free as a download. Go to www.adfg.state.ak.us/pubs/notebook/notehome.php.

Trees. The best book, though it offers more detail than most visitors will want, is *Alaska Trees and Shrubs,* by Leslie A. Viereck and Elbert L. Little (University of Alaska Press, $25).

Land Mammals

Arctic Fox

SCIENTIFIC NAME *Alopex lagopus*

WORTH NOTING Closely related to the red fox, the Arctic fox has a luxurious white pelt, perfect camouflage for its snowy habitat of treeless coastal areas from the Aleutian Archipelago to the sea ice of the Arctic Ocean. The Arctic fox will eat anything—from eggs to berries to lemmings—and often will follow a polar bear, eating the seal remains left behind.

PRIME VIEWING You can encounter Arctic foxes on the tundra near Barrow or Nome.

Beaver

SCIENTIFIC NAME *Cebus capucinus*

WORTH NOTING Beavers occupy most of Alaska's forests. They grow up to 4 feet long including the tail and can weigh 100 pounds. The decline of trapping in recent decades has led to an increase in beavers, with dams flooding new areas and blocking fish streams. A rounded beaver lodge is not surprising to find in slow-moving water, but it takes patience to spy a beaver.

PRIME VIEWING Along Interior and Southcentral highways and trails.

Black Bear

SCIENTIFIC NAME *Ursus americanus*

WORTH NOTING Smaller than the brown bear, growing to 200 pounds, the black bear has a straighter nose and lacks the distinctive hump on the back. Black bears are commonly jet-black but can also be brown or even bluish. They're found throughout forested Alaska. They're mostly vegetarian, subsisting on berries and insects, but they gorge on salmon when it is available.

PRIME VIEWING Concentrated near salmon streams and, in some communities, near garbage sources. The top viewing site is the Anan Wildlife Observatory in Southeast Alaska (see "Seeing Bears in Southeast Alaska," on p. 366).

Brown Bear

SCIENTIFIC NAME *Ursus arctos*

WORTH NOTING Brown bears are identical to grizzly bears, but larger because they live on the coast and eat salmon. Coastal bears can grow to 1,000 pounds or more, while inland bears, dining on plants, rodents, and young moose and caribou, reach only a few hundred pounds. Brown bears are far more dangerous than black bears, as they do kill large mammals.

PRIME VIEWING **Katmai National Park** (p. 485); Pack Creek, on Admiralty Island (p. 365,); and Denali National Park (p. 132). Or fly out on bear-viewing excursions from Anchorage (p. 75, ❹) or Ketchikan (p. 365, ❿).

Kodiak Brown Bear

SCIENTIFIC NAME *Ursus arctos middendorffi*

WORTH NOTING While coastal brown bears and inland grizzly bears are genetically identical and differ only because of diet, the huge brown bear living on Kodiak island are a distinct subspecies that has evolved in isolation. Those special genes and the prodigious salmon runs on the island contribute to enormous size: the record is 1,500 pounds, with giant 1,000-pound male bears not uncommon.

PRIME VIEWING Kodiak National Wildlife Refuge (p 445, ❹).

Caribou

SCIENTIFIC NAME *Rangifer tarandus*

WORTH NOTING Genetically identical to reindeer, Alaska's barren-ground caribou are gentle, skittish deer that migrate over the Arctic tundra and, farther south, over alpine tundra, sometimes in vast herds. They graze on grasses, leaves, and flowers in summer, lichen in winter.

PRIME VIEWING **Denali National Park** (p. 132), Glenn Highway east of **Matanuska Glacier** (p. 191, ❿), **Dalton Highway** north of the tree line (p. 310).

Dall Sheep

SCIENTIFIC NAME *Ovis dalli dalli*

WORTH NOTING Resembling bighorn sheep with their curling horns, but smaller, Dall sheep occupy the rocky high country, where their agility allows them to escape predators. Powerful lenses are required to get a good look at one, since you're unlikely ever to get near a band of them. Look for white spots on high gray peaks, and then focus in.

PRIME VIEWING **Denali National Park** (p. 132), Seward Highway on **Turnagain Arm** (p. 84), and other mountain areas.

Moose

SCIENTIFIC NAME *Alces alces gigas*

WORTH NOTING Moose are the world's largest deer, and Alaska's moose is the largest of them, growing bigger than a horse and weighing up to 1,600 pounds. They are found all over Alaska, but most commonly in brushy or swampy areas in the Interior and Southcentral regions. Stressed moose can suddenly and fatally attack; keep your distance. Highway collisions can be deadly, too.

PRIME VIEWING Keep your eyes open while on any highway or trail in central Alaska. Moose are common in Anchorage's wooded parks, too.

Mountain Goat

SCIENTIFIC NAME *Oreamnos americanus*

WORTH NOTING Shaggy mountain goats look as if they are wearing thick white parkas. Their horns are short and black. They favor the same rocky alpine habitat as the Dall sheep, but farther south, along the Gulf of Alaska coast and into the Talkeetna Mountains in the Southcentral region.

PRIME VIEWING Seward Highway on **Turnagain Arm** (p. 84) and along rocky coastal mountains accessed by boat.

Musk Ox

SCIENTIFIC NAME *Ovibos moschatus*

WORTH NOTING An Arctic animal with a coat of extraordinary warmth that hangs to the ground, the musk ox is an ice-age survivor with few relatives. Eliminated from Alaska and nearly driven globally extinct by hunting, the species was reintroduced from Greenland in the 1930s and is still increasing steadily in Alaska.

PRIME VIEWING See musk oxen in the wild on the roads near Nome (p. 432).

Sitka Black -Tailed Deer

SCIENTIFIC NAME *Odocoileus hemionus sitkensis*

WORTH NOTING This small deer lives in the temperate rainforests of Southeast Alaska, Prince William Sound, and Kodiak Island. The big trees and patchy clearings of the old-growth forest provide critical habitat, because thick branches reduce deep snow, which deer cannot navigate, but allow enough light for forage to grow.

PRIME VIEWING By chance on hikes or boat rides in the rainforest.

Snowshoe Hare

SCIENTIFIC NAME *Lepus americanus*

WORTH NOTING This hare has interesting characteristics that allow it to adapt to the snowy boreal forest. Its coat is camouflaged brown in the summer and snowy white in the winter. Its hind feet are large and thick with fur, functioning as natural snowshoes. The species ranges across Alaska, south of the Brooks Range and east of the Yukon–Kuskokwim Delta

PRIME VIEWING With sharp eyes, you can catch sight of hares along roadways or trails in the early morning or at dusk

Wolf

SCIENTIFIC NAME *Canis lupus*

WORTH NOTING Adaptable wolves live all over Alaska but are most common in the Interior. They are also Alaska's most controversial animal, as the state government has pursued a policy of killing wolves to increase moose numbers. Wolves have never been endangered in Alaska.

PRIME VIEWING Wolves are rarely seen except in areas without cover, such as on the tundra of **Denali National Park** (p. 132) or along the **Dalton Highway** (p. 310).

Marine Mammals

Beluga Whale

SCIENTIFIC NAME *Delphinapterus leucas*

WORTH NOTING The adults are white, while juvenile belugas are gray. They're toothed whales, like killer whales or dolphins, and they grow to 10 to 15 feet long. Huge herds of belugas feed in summer in coastal waters, on spawning fish such as herring or salmon. In the water, their arched white backs are easy to see in groups.

PRIME VIEWING The endangered Cook Inlet population of belugas can be seen on **Turnagain Arm** along the Seward Highway (p. 84) and at the mouth of the Kenai River near **Kenai's Old Town** (p. 239, **6**).

Gray Whale

SCIENTIFIC NAME *Eschrichtius robustus*

WORTH NOTING Measuring about 45 feet when fully grown, these baleen whales are notable for the abundance of barnacles and scars on their mottled gray heads and back, and the presence of a low hump and series of knobs rather than a dorsal fin. Their 10,000-mile migration along the shore from Baja California to Arctic Alaska takes them through the Gulf of Alaska in early spring.

PRIME VIEWING Viewing in Alaska is not easily accessible except in April, by boat from **Seward** (p. 270).

Harbor Seal

SCIENTIFIC NAME *Phoca vitulina*

WORTH NOTING These are the seals you are most likely to see on Alaska's southern coast, although their numbers are in serious decline for reasons that are unknown. Harbor seals are half the length and one-tenth the weight of Steller sea lions. When distinguishing a harbor seal from a sea otter, pay attention to how the animal floats; the seal stays belly down and lower in the water.

PRIME VIEWING Rocky coastal areas in the Gulf of Alaska. Seals congregate around special haul-out rocks that are locally known, so just ask.

Humpback Whale

SCIENTIFIC NAME *Megaptera novaeangliae*

WORTH NOTING This baleen whale species is the most frequently seen in Alaska, with a population that winters in Hawaii and feeds during summer in certain areas along the state's southern coast. Adults are over 40 feet long and easily identified by the humped back, the small dorsal fin, and the habit of raising the flukes, or tail, vertically above the surface when diving.

PRIME VIEWING In Southeast Alaska, in **Icy Strait** (p. 367, **13**) near Juneau and in **Frederick Sound** near Petersburg (p. 404). Also in north Gulf of Alaska waters, near **Kenai Fjords National Park** (p. 30, **3**) and in Prince William Sound from **Whittier** (p. 201, **3**).

Killer Whale

SCIENTIFIC NAME *Orcinus orca*

WORTH NOTING The most distinctive and exciting whale to watch, the killer whale, or orca, has sharp black-and-white markings and a tall, erect dorsal fin. In Alaskan waters, killer whales form two distinct groups that never mix: resident whales, which feed only on fish and live in large matrilineal pods, and transient whales, which feed on marine mammals, roaming widely and hunting in smaller groups.

PRIME VIEWING The best areas are similar to those for humpback whales, though with less predictability.

Polar Bear

SCIENTIFIC NAME *Ursus maritimus*

WORTH NOTING The polar bear is classified as a marine mammal because it normally spends its entire life on the ocean, on the sea ice north and west of Alaska. Polar bears in this region primarily eat ringed seals, rarely seen by visitors, stripping the rich fat layer. Their threatened status is owing to the rapid loss of sea ice in recent years due to climate change, which affects habitat and food.

PRIME VIEWING In spring and early summer, polar bears can sometimes be seen from **Barrow** (p. 429, **3**).

Sea Otter

SCIENTIFIC NAME *Enhydra lutris*

WORTH NOTING Driven to the brink of extinction a century ago, sea otters are now quite common in southern coastal Alaska, and they can be seen in boat harbors and along town beaches. They float on their backs, using their tummies for a table and a nursery. With care, viewers can get a close look from boats and kayaks.

PRIME VIEWING Prince William Sound from **Cordova** (p. 212, ❹), Kachemak Bay from **Homer** (p. 239, ❽), **Sitka Sound** (p. 391, ❿), other coastal waters.

Steller Sea Lion

SCIENTIFIC NAME *Eumetopias jubatus*

WORTH NOTING Despite their enormous size—males normally grow to 11 feet long and 1,250 pounds—Steller sea lions are astoundingly swift and graceful in the water, allowing them to feed on a wide range of fish. Their numbers in western Alaska have declined drastically in recent decades, leading to intensive conservation efforts.

PRIME VIEWING Encounters are usually incidental to marine wildlife cruises in Southeast Alaska and Prince William Sound.

Fish

King (or Chinook) Salmon

SCIENTIFIC NAME *Oncorhynchus tshawytscha*

WORTH NOTING The largest and most prized of all Pacific salmon, the king commonly grows to more than 30 pounds in its 5 years at sea before spawning in rivers. Landlocked and immature kings can be much smaller, however. Identify kings by the black spots on the back, dorsal fin, and tail. They also have black pigment in the mouth, along the gums.

PRIME FISHING In May and June. Most famous is the **Kenai River** (p. 256, ❷), but kings run in many other streams and can be caught at sea outside of runs.

Silver (or Coho) Salmon

SCIENTIFIC NAME *Oncorhynchus kisutch (Walbaum)*

WORTH NOTING A hard-fighting and delicious fish that grows to around 10 pounds and 2 feet long, returning from the sea to spawn typically in less than 2 years. Distinguish silvers from kings by their lack of black spots on the lower half of the tail, and by the gray rather than black gums.

PRIME FISHING Run timing differs but generally takes place in August and September. Resurrection Bay near **Seward** (p. 270) is famous for silvers.

Pink (or Humpy) Salmon

SCIENTIFIC NAME *Oncorhynchus gorbuscha*

WORTH NOTING This abundant salmon lacks the rich flavor of other species and is sometimes regarded by anglers as a nuisance, but it can be fun to catch on light tackle. They spawn on a biannual cycle and grow to 4 pounds. Recognize pinks by the blue back, small scales, spots over the entire tail, and lack of vertical marks; when nearing spawning, males grow a hooked jaw and humped back, and females get green splotches.

PRIME FISHING All over coastal Alaska from midsummer into the fall.

Arctic Grayling

SCIENTIFIC NAME *Thymallus arcticus (Pallus)*

WORTH NOTING The grayling is a rare and beautiful relative of the trout, found in clear northern streams. Its unmistakable feature is a sail-like dorsal fin that runs most of the length of its back, with iridescent spots of red or purple. The back is otherwise dark, and the sides are gray. Grayling bite anything and are popular sport for fly fishermen. They're typically about 12 inches long.

PRIME FISHING Roadside and trailside streams in Interior and Arctic Alaska.

Dolly Varden Char

SCIENTIFIC NAME *Salvelinus malma*

WORTH NOTING Closely related to eastern brook trout, the Dolly Varden takes its name from a beautiful character in Charles Dickens's *Barnaby Rudge* for its bright coloring: red on the lower body, with red and orange spots on the silvery sides. It lives in lakes, streams, and coastal waters, with both sea-run and nonmigratory populations. Dollies are popular sportfish, usually less than 18 inches long.

PRIME FISHING In streams or coastal waters through spring and summer; local knowledge is important.

Lingcod

SCIENTIFIC NAME *Ophiodon elongatus*

WORTH NOTING When fishing for halibut, chances are good of instead hooking these eager-biting and hard-fighting greenlings, which are typically over 2 feet and can grow much larger. The flesh is delicious. Their color is blotchy brown, and they have a dorsal fin that runs almost the entire length of the body.

PRIME FISHING Common near reefs up to 300 feet deep near the Kenai Peninsula, Kodiak, Prince William Sound, and Southeast Alaska.

Pacific Halibut

SCIENTIFIC NAME *Hippoglossus stenolepis*

WORTH NOTING After salmon, halibut are Alaska's most coveted sportfish, thanks to their great size and delicate white flesh. They're flat, bottom-dwelling fish, with a gray top and white bottom, and with both eyes on the gray side. Over decades, halibut can grow to several hundred pounds. Fishing is from boats over deep water; the challenge is to pull in such a large fish from such a great depth.

PRIME FISHING Homer (p. 259, ❶), **Unalaska/Dutch Harbor** (p. 237), **Gustavus** (p. 408), and various other ports in southern Alaska.

Rainbow Trout

SCIENTIFIC NAME *Oncorhynchus mykiss*

WORTH NOTING Among the most sought of freshwater fish in Alaska, the rainbow looks like a salmon, to which it is closely related. Identify a rainbow by the reddish or pinkish band along its side and by a mouth that does not extend past the back of the eye. They normally grow to 8 pounds, but much larger trophies have been caught.

PRIME FISHING Rainbows are widely distributed in lakes and clear streams from Southeast Alaska to western Alaska, and are stocked in some popular spots.

Rockfish

SCIENTIFIC NAME *Sebastes*

WORTH NOTING This is a group of some 30 species found in deep coastal waters. All have large eyes and long, spiny fins, and some are brightly colored. The flesh is delicious, but you need to hook a large fish to get much of it from among the bones. Rockfish reproduce slowly and live decades—some species up to a century—and are killed simply by being brought to the surface, so anglers need to avoid hooking many of them.

PRIME FISHING Caught incidentally on halibut charters.

Steelhead Trout

SCIENTIFIC NAME *Oncorhynchus mykiss*

WORTH NOTING Although genetically the same species as the rainbow trout, the steelhead's ocean life cycle gives it a different appearance, more silvery and streamlined. Like salmon, the steelhead returns to spawn in a particular stream, but unlike salmon, it lives to repeat the process. It's a rare, coveted, and difficult to catch fish; conservation law often requires catch-and-release only.

PRIME FISHING Run timing depends on the stream. Certain deep, clear streams in Southeast Alaska and the Kenai Peninsula have runs.

Birds

American Golden Plover

SCIENTIFIC NAME *Pluvialis dominica*

WORTH NOTING In the spring, clouds of migrating shorebirds, including plovers, land on the beaches and mud flats of southern coastal Alaska, running ahead of waves to poke their narrow bills into the sand. The American golden plover and similar Pacific golden plover fly incredible distances: The former come from Tierra del Fuego and Patagonia, and the latter from Polynesia.

PRIME VIEWING Shorebird festivals celebrate the early May arrival of migrations in **Homer** (p. 260) and in **Cordova** (p. 210).

Bald Eagle

SCIENTIFIC NAME *Haliaeetus leucocephalus*

WORTH NOTING The national symbol of America, almost eliminated from the other states, has always been common in Alaska, especially in southern coastal areas where fish are abundant, but also along Interior rivers. The bald eagle takes 5 years to mature into the distinctive white plumage on its head, before which it can look like a golden eagle. Adults have a wingspan of up to 7 feet.

PRIME VIEWING **Chilkat Bald Eagle Preserve,** near Haines (p. 353, **14**); however, eagles are as common as pigeons in many coastal towns.

Boreal Owl

SCIENTIFIC NAME *Aegolius funereus*

WORTH NOTING These small owls are spread throughout Interior forests and into the Southcentral region, wherever the boreal forest contains some deciduous trees, but are not easily seen because of their nocturnal habits. They hunt small rodents, using a powerful sense of hearing. They are around 9 inches long with a two-foot wing span.

PRIME VIEWING During late winter and spring breeding season, skilled birdwatchers track boreal owls by their mating calls.

Common Murre

SCIENTIFIC NAME *Uria aalge*

WORTH NOTING Like other alcids, a family of web-footed diving birds, this murre spends its entire life on the water except when nesting on rocky sea cliffs. Roughly the size and shape of a football, the common murre resembles a penguin when standing, with a white chest and a black head and back. Their colonies can be numerous, but murres lay only one egg a year.

PRIME VIEWING Rocky shores in **Kenai Fjords National Park** (p. 30, **3**), **Kachemak Bay** (p. 239, **8**), and Southeast Alaska.

Common Raven
SCIENTIFIC NAME *Corvus corax*

WORTH NOTING The intelligent raven has found ways to adapt to various habitats, from the coastal rainforest to the oil fields of the Arctic (not to mention the deserts of the American Southwest). The species holds an important place in Alaska Native mythology; the Tlingit creation story tells of how Raven stole the sun, moon, and stars and put them in the sky.

PRIME VIEWING Urban ravens congregate around food sources. In natural areas like the coastal forest, they're easy to locate by their distinctive and varied deep-throated calls.

Glaucous-Winged Gull
SCIENTIFIC NAME *Larus glaucescens*

WORTH NOTING These are the most common sea gulls of the southern Alaska coast, with white heads and bodies and gray backs and wings. They naturally scavenge along coasts and at river mouths, and their populations can explode when they gain access to human food sources. Don't feed the gulls!

PRIME VIEWING Boat harbors, fish processing plants, near-shore areas of schooling fish.

Harlequin Duck
SCIENTIFIC NAME *Histrionicus histrionicus*

WORTH NOTING This is the most striking of several beautiful sea ducks found on Alaska's coasts. The name comes from the bright plumage of the adult male, reminiscent of a jester's costume. Harlequins nest inland on streams but spend the fall through spring seasons on the ocean, preferring rugged shores; nonbreeding ducks can be seagoing all summer.

PRIME VIEWING Prince William Sound and other coastal areas; however, getting to their shallow haunts can require a sea kayak outing.

Horned Puffin & Tufted Puffin
SCIENTIFIC NAME *Fratercula corniculata & Fratercula cirrhata*

WORTH NOTING Horned puffins have the more familiar, T-shirt profile, while tufted puffins have feathers that curl back from their heads and have black instead of white chests. Both are alcids, like the common murre, and spend most of their time floating on ocean waves. They're comical when taking off and landing, but much more graceful underwater. Adults are about a foot long.

PRIME VIEWING **Kachemak Bay** near Homer (p. 239, **8**), **Kenai Fjords National Park** (p. 30, **3**), **Sitka Sound** (p. 391, **10**), and other rocky waters.

Sandhill Crane
SCIENTIFIC NAME *Grus canadensis*

WORTH NOTING Among the most dramatic of Alaskan birds, these cranes stand 3 feet tall and have a wingspan of 6 feet. Their throaty call is loud and haunting, and aloft their long necks and legs float gracefully. Cranes nesting around Cook Inlet and westward migrate to California's Central Valley; those in the Interior and the Yukon–Kuskoskim Delta winter in Texas and Mexico.

PRIME VIEWING Local knowledge helps, but you can find sandhill cranes in **Anchorage** (p. 63), **Homer** (p. 260), and **Fairbanks** (p. 316).

Trumpeter Swan
SCIENTIFIC NAME *Cygnus buccinator*

WORTH NOTING The world's largest waterfowl, trumpeter swans average 28 pounds for males and 22 pounds for females; their eggs are 5 inches long. The vast majority nest in Alaska, where they never were endangered. They're found in forested areas of the Interior and Southcentral regions. You may also see tundra swans, which are nearly identical, but distinguished by their smaller size and a yellow spot near the eye.

PRIME VIEWING **Copper River Delta** near Cordova (p. 408, **10**), **Creamer's Field Refuge** in Fairbanks (p. 320, **13**).

Willow Ptarmigan
SCIENTIFIC NAME *Lagopus lagopus*

WORTH NOTING Found all over Alaska in high, treeless areas, ptarmigan live on the ground and can surprise a hiker by appearing underfoot and running along a trail without effectively getting away. They look like grouse, with winter plumage of pure white and, in summer, mottled brown or red feathers with white wings.

PRIME VIEWING Along mountain or tundra trails anywhere in the north. Ptarmigan often let viewers walk right up to them.

Trees & Plants

Alpine Forget-Me-Not
SCIENTIFIC NAME *Myosotis alpestris*

WORTH NOTING Alaska's state flower shows the colors of its flag, blue and yellow, in many small blossoms no larger than ⅜ inch. The plant is perennial and grows about a foot high in alpine meadows and open coastal areas. It blooms in late May and June on warmer slopes, and into early August where the snow sticks later in the spring.

PRIME VIEWING Roadsides and trails on the Kenai Peninsula, and mountain hikes in Interior and Southcentral Alaska.

Black Spruce
SCIENTIFIC NAME *Picea mariana*

WORTH NOTING This rather pathetic tree of the boreal forest makes use of habitat where no other can grow—boggy, cold Interior Alaska lands on top of permafrost—and thus covers a vast area in the center of the state. It is easy to recognize by its stunted appearance, with sparse, short, drooping branches and dark bark. The species can be hard to distinguish from the other important boreal forest conifer: the white spruce, which is tall and conical, growing on drier ground, often mixed with birch.

PRIME VIEWING All along Interior highways.

Bog Blueberry
SCIENTIFIC NAME *Vaccinium uliginosum*

WORTH NOTING There are a number of varieties of blueberries in Alaska, generally blooming in early summer and yielding fruit from July to early September, depending on the latitude, elevation, and year. In the mountains, this is a short tundra plant, while on the shore it grows up to 2 feet. Berries are small and more flavorful than commercial blueberries, with a slight tartness.

PRIME VIEWING Found over most of Alaska in bogs, woodlands, and tundra and on alpine slopes.

Common Fireweed
SCIENTIFIC NAME *Epilobium angustifolium*

WORTH NOTING Along Alaska highways in July or August, the hills are painted pinkish purple with this plant, which can grow 5 feet high, its single, straight stalk surrounded by blossoms. The name comes from fireweed's quick regrowth after fires or other disturbances. The pace at which the flowers go to seed is used to predict the onset of winter.

PRIME VIEWING Any disturbed land over most of Alaska.

Cow Parsnip
SCIENTIFIC NAME *Heracleum lanatum*

WORTH NOTING This plant with juicy stems, large leaves, and white flowers grows head-high in meadows and forest clearings. It helps make up for Alaska's lack of poison ivy: The sap is highly allergenic for some people and has the quality of intensifying the skin's sensitivity to the sun, causing sunburns. In a fire, it creates toxic smoke.

PRIME VIEWING Common in Southcentral and Southeast Alaska.

Devil's Club
SCIENTIFIC NAME *Echinopanax horridum*

WORTH NOTING This tall, woody plant with large leaves gets its name from sharp spines that are painful and difficult to remove, and it can cause infections. The bright red berries that appear in August are toxic. Devil's club grows in thickets on steep ground in the moist coastal forest of Southcentral and Southeast Alaska and is impenetrable without a machete.

PRIME VIEWING Best avoided, devil's club is found in woods around Anchorage and many other coastal communities.

Labrador Tea
SCIENTIFIC NAME *Ledum palustris*

WORTH NOTING This evergreen shrub with narrow leaves and tiny white flowers is common on the forest floor and in bogs. Rub the leaves between your fingers for the fragrant aroma. They can easily be made into tasty tea, but start slowly, as it can be a diuretic.

PRIME VIEWING Forests, bogs, and mountains in Southeastern, Southcentral, and Interior Alaska.

Nootka Lupine
SCIENTIFIC NAME *Lupinus nootkatensis*

WORTH NOTING This showy blue perennial has large flowers around a thick, woolly stalk. Near the coast, the Nootka lupine grows to 2 or 3 feet; the Arctic lupine is similar but smaller, about a foot tall, and grows in the rest of the state. After blooming in early summer, lupines produce pealike pods of poisonous seeds.

PRIME VIEWING Beach tops and slopes near roadsides throughout much of Alaska.

Nootka Rose & Prickly Rose
SCIENTIFIC NAME *Rosa nootkatensis & rosa acicularis*

WORTH NOTING These fragrant and lovely wild pink roses bloom in early summer over most of Alaska. The thorny bushes grow from a couple of feet tall to head-height in forest openings and meadows with direct sun. The petals can be made into tea or jelly, and the red rose hips have various culinary or medicinal uses, but don't eat the seeds.

PRIME VIEWING Often found in gardens, Alaska's wild roses are easily recognized on open slopes, such as the trails along **Turnagain Arm** on the Seward Highway (p. 84).

Paper Birch
SCIENTIFIC NAME *Betula papyrifera*

WORTH NOTING A common species among various birches, this is the main constituent (along with the white spruce) of the birch-spruce boreal forest on uplands across the center of Alaska from Southcentral to the Brooks Range. It is a beautiful tree, with white bark and wide-reaching black branches. Other common deciduous trees are aspen, willow, and cottonwood or poplar.

PRIME VIEWING Common in dry, open boreal forest, such as in Anchorage's **Kincaid Park** (p. 70, **6**).

Salmonberry
SCIENTIFIC NAME *Rubus spectabilis*

WORTH NOTING One of many edible berries that may be new to those who reside in the Lower 48, the salmonberry is juicy with delicate flavor and looks like an extra-large, pinkish raspberry (it's the color of salmon flesh), ripening in late summer. The thornless bushes grow 3 to 5 feet tall near streams, especially on the southern coast. Similar berries include nagoonberry, trailing raspberry, and cloudberry.

PRIME VIEWING Streamside in the temperate rainforest of coastal Alaska.

Sitka Spruce
SCIENTIFIC NAME *Picea sitchensis*

WORTH NOTING Alaska's state tree is the giant of the southern coast's temperate rainforest, often growing to more than 200 feet tall, 8 feet in diameter, and 750 years old. Distinguish it from the huge western hemlock growing in the same habitat by the hemlock's softer needles and floppy top. Where the moist temperate climate of the coast transitions to the drier Interior, the Sitka spruce hybridizes with the white spruce.

PRIME VIEWING The Alaska coast, from Southeast Alaska to Kodiak.

14
The Savvy Traveler

> Scenic, if chilly, cruising on Tracy Arm fjord near Juneau.

Before You Go

Government Tourist Offices

Alaska Travel Industry Association; 2600 Cordova Street, Ste. 201 Anchorage, AK 99503; www.travelalaska.com. No telephone inquiries.

Alaska Public Lands Information Center; 605 W. 4th Ave, Suite 105, Anchorage, AK 99501; ☎ 866-869-6887 or 907-644-3661; www.alaskacenters.gov.

Best Times to Go

The peak season for Alaska tourism is June 15 to August 15, when the weather is at its best; salmon fishing is in full swing; and activities, tours, and parks are open. But crowding and prices peak, too. May 15 to June 14 and August 16 to September 15 are the "shoulder seasons," months that may still have excellent weather, although it's a dicier proposition. Salmon fishing is scarce in May but excellent in the fall. Prices are lower and crowds few—this can be an excellent time to visit.

The worst times to visit are from September 16 to November 30 and from April 1 to May 14. Weatherwise, you might have good luck with early May and late September into early October, but for the most part there's not much to do, and weather conditions lend themselves to neither summer nor winter activities.

Winter, on the other hand, is a wonderful time to visit for skiing, skating, dog mushing, snowmobiling, aurora viewing, and community festivals. Typical tourist activities, such as guided tours or wildlife viewing excursions, aerial trams, zip-lines and many historic sites, don't operate in winter, but on the plus side, hotel rates can be very low. March is best, when the sky is light and the calendar full.

Festivals & Special Events

FEBRUARY

The Yukon Quest International Sled Dog Race (☎ 867-668-4711; www.yukonquest.com) is a 1,000-mile race between Fairbanks and Whitehorse, Yukon Territory—the direction alternates each year. The race begins the first weekend in February. For around 2 weeks at the end of February and the beginning of March, the **Anchorage Fur Rendezvous Festival** (☎ 907-274-1177; www.furrondy.net) brings a citywide winter celebration including many community events and the 3-day World Champion Sled Dog Race.

MARCH

The famed **Iditarod Trail Sled Dog Race** (☎ 907-376-5155; www.iditarod.com) starts on the first Saturday in March, ceremonially in Anchorage and the next day for real in Willow, before running 1,000 miles to Nome. The winning run usually takes 9 days. The **Nenana Ice Classic** (☎ 907-832-5446; www.nenanaakiceclassic.com) is a century-old betting pool that tracks the exact time the ice will give out on the Tanana River in Nenana. **Tripod Days,** the first weekend in March, is a community celebration of the erection of the marker on the river. The jackpot typically exceeds $300,000. In Fairbanks, the **World Ice Art Championships** (☎ 907-451-8250; www.icealaska.com) get underway in late February and early March. Ice carvers sculpt spectacular works from crystal-clear chunks, some as large as small buildings—the best viewing is before the middle of the month.

APRIL

In Juneau, the **Alaska Folk Festival** (☎ 907-463-3316; www.alaskafolkfestival.org) involves folk music performances in many venues and casual jam sessions for a week in early April.

MAY

In early May, Homer's **Kachemak Shorebird Festival** (☎ 907-235-7740; www.homeralaska.org) includes hikes, cruises, workshops, and performances to mark the arrival of massive flocks of migrating birds on beaches. The **Little Norway Festival** (☎ 907-772-3646; www.petersburg.org), in Petersburg, celebrates the May 17, 1814, declaration of the independence of Norway from Sweden; events are held on the third full weekend in May. Memorial Day weekend brings the **Kodiak Crab Festival** (☎ 907-486-5557; www.kodiak.org) to Kodiak, and events include a carnival, a blessing of the fleet, and a service for lost mariners.

JUNE

Celebration is the name of a Juneau event, sponsored by the **Sealaska Heritage Institute** (☎ 907-463-4844; www.sealaskaheritage.org), that brings together Alaska Natives from

WEATHER

	JAN	FEB	MAR	APR	MAY	JUNE	JULY	AUG	SEPT	OCT	NOV	DEC
ANCHORAGE: SOUTHCENTRAL ALASKA												
Average high	21	26	33	44	55	62	65	63	55	40	28	22
Average low	8	11	17	29	39	47	51	49	41	28	16	10
BARROW: ARCTIC ALASKA												
Average high	−8	−12	−8	6	25	39	46	43	34	20	5	−6
Average low	−20	−24	−21	−8	15	30	34	34	27	10	−6	−17
FAIRBANKS: INTERIOR ALASKA												
Average high	−2	−8	24	42	60	71	73	66	55	32	11	1
Average low	−19	−15	−2	20	38	52	52	47	36	17	−5	−16
JUNEAU: SOUTHEAST ALASKA												
Average high	29	34	39	48	55	62	64	63	56	47	37	32
Average low	18	23	27	32	39	45	48	48	43	37	28	23

every part of the state to share dance and art. The event takes place in even-numbered years, in early June. The **Sitka Summer Music Festival** (☎ 907-747-6774; www.sitkamusic festival.org) offers chamber music with international performers over 3 weeks in June.

In Fairbanks, the **Midnight Sun Baseball Game,** hosted by the **Alaska Goldpanners** (☎ 907-451-0095; www.goldpanners.com), brings together semipro baseball players for a game on the longest day of the year, typically June 21. The game is played without lights, with the first pitch at 10:30pm. Nome's **Midnight Sun Festival** (☎ 907-443-5535) marks the solstice and includes a parade, softball tournament, raft race, and polar bear swim on the weekend closest to June 21.

In Valdez, the **Last Frontier Theatre Conference** (☎ 907-834-1614; www.pwscc.edu) is a weeklong national gathering of playwrights and directors for seminars and performances. It is usually held in mid-June, but dates change annually.

JULY

On July 4, Independence Day is celebrated with events in many towns, including Seward, Seldovia, Ketchikan, Skagway, and Juneau. Seward's celebration includes the legendary **Mount Marathon Race** (☎ 907-224-8051; www.seward.com), from city streets to the 3,022-foot peak and back in less than 40

Making Advance Reservations

If you plan on coming to Alaska in peak season, you may find some reservations difficult—even if you start booking them 6 months early. The very best bear-viewing opportunities are rationed, including **Pack Creek** (p. 365, ⑩) near Juneau and the campground and lodge rooms at **Brooks Camp** (p. 485) in Katmai National Park; you should seek those reservations the moment you know you want to go. Reservations for cabins and vehicle slots on the most popular ferry routes of the **Alaska Marine Highway System** (p. 507) sell out soon after they become available, typically the winter before the trip. The most coveted Forest Service public use cabins in Southeast Alaska and Prince William Sound can book up the instant they appear on the reservations system, 6 months before the stay (www.recreation.gov). It's also a good idea to reserve campsites and shuttle bus tickets at **Denali National Park** (p. 132) as soon as you can, although booking isn't as urgent as with some of the other opportunities I've mentioned here. Reservations for rooms and activities are also required in peak season, but you have more time and flexibility with these.

minutes. Late July sees the 4-day-long **Southeast Alaska State Fair** (☎ 907-766-2476, www.seakfair.org) in Haines.

AUGUST
Palmer hosts the **Alaska State Fair** (☎ 907-745-4827; www.alaskastatefair.org) for the 12 days before Labor Day. It's a quintessential state fair with the addition of the giant vegetable competition, where world records are regularly broken.

OCTOBER
The **Alaska Day Festival** (☎ 907-747-8806) is a celebration of the Alaska purchase on October 18, 1867, in the former Russian America capital of Sitka.

NOVEMBER
Over a weekend in early November, the fall congregation of humpback whales in Sitka Sound is marked by a symposium, tours, concerts, and other community events as part of **Sitka WhaleFest** (☎ 907-747-7964; www.sitkawhalefest.org). The mid-November **Alaska Bald Eagle Festival** (☎ 907-766-3094; www.baldeaglefestival.org), in Haines, follows Sitka's WhaleFest and features seminars and town events meant to mark the world's largest gathering of bald eagles, which happens annually on the Chilkat River. Over Thanksgiving weekend, the University of Alaska Anchorage hosts top-ranked college teams at the Sullivan Arena as part of the **Carrs/Safeway Great Alaska Shootout** basketball tournament (☎ 907-786-1250; www.goseawolves.com).

DECEMBER
As part of the **Anchorage International Film Festival** (www.anchoragefilmfestival.org), a dizzying variety of films is shown all over the city during 2 weeks in mid-December.

Weather
Climatic conditions can change drastically from region to region, and from season to season. For more information on each of Alaska's unique regions, see "Alaska's Natural History," on p. 461.

The National Weather Service, Alaska Region Headquarters (www.arh.noaa.gov) is a good resource for understanding the weather experienced throughout the state.

The Geophysical Institute at the University of Alaska Fairbanks offers aurora predictions: www.gedds.alaska.edu/AuroraForecast. For more extreme events, learn about volcano predictions and updates at www.avo.alaska.edu, and find earthquake information at www.aeic.alaska.edu. Discover more about Alaska's climate and geography at the Alaska Public Lands Information Center website: www.alaskacenters.gov.

Road conditions can be found at http://511.alaska.gov.

Contact the Alaska Department of Fish and Game for fishing information (www.sf.adfg.state.ak.us) or wildlife viewing information (www.wildlife.alaska.gov).

Getting There

By Plane
The Ted Stevens Anchorage International Airport is by far the main air gateway to Alaska, with numerous carriers flying direct from cities all over the United States, but mostly from Seattle. The flight from Seattle to Anchorage takes 3½ hours. A few flights also enter Alaska at Fairbanks, Juneau, or Ketchikan.

The dominant airline to Alaska, and the only airline offering jet service beyond Anchorage and Fairbanks, is Alaska Airlines (☎ 800-252-7522; www.alaskaair.com). Check with other carriers to see if they have flights or partnerships with Alaska Airlines.

International travelers usually have to fly through Seattle or another major U.S. city before changing to a domestic flight to Anchorage, with just a few weekly exceptions. From North America: All major U.S. carriers and Air Canada fly to Seattle. From Seattle, fly onward to Alaska. From the United Kingdom: More than a dozen airlines connect Seattle from London. British Airways (☎ 800-AIRWAYS (247-9297); www.britishairways.com) offers some nonstop flights. In Seattle, change to a domestic carrier for the flight to Alaska.

From Australia: Many airlines connect Sydney and Seattle. The busiest on the route include Qantas (☎ 131313 in Australia; www.qantas.com) and United (☎ 131777; www.unitedairlines.com.au). From Seattle, United flies to Anchorage, but Qantas passengers have to transfer to a domestic U.S. carrier.

From New Zealand: Air New Zealand (☎ (0)9 357 3000 in New Zealand; www.airnewzealand.co.nz) offers direct flights from

Auckland to Seattle. In Seattle, change to a domestic carrier to reach Alaska.

By Train

It isn't possible to ride a train from the Lower 48 or Canada to Alaska. Taking the train to Bellingham, Washington, or Prince Rupert, BC (Canada), and then continuing to Alaska by ferry is covered below.

By Car

Driving a car to Alaska from the rest of the U.S. is a journey of 2,500 miles or more that is most suitable for those with unlimited time and a high tolerance for cheap motels and greasy hamburgers. Bringing an RV or tent along the way, however, makes it an adventure. Taking the ferry part of the way is covered below. The route within Alaska is covered within tours when relevant. The Canadian part of the drive, which is the majority of it, is beyond our scope. *The Milepost* (Morris Communications, $30) is the classic guide to that route.

By Ferry or Cruise

Coming to Alaska by ferry is covered below. For complete coverage of the many cruise lines that sail to Alaska, see *Frommer's Alaska Cruises and Ports of Call*, by Fran Wenograd Golden and Gene Sloan.

Getting Around

By Plane

Alaska Airlines (☎ 800-252-7522; www.alaskaair.com) connects Alaska's larger towns and Bush hub communities. Commuter airlines offer many of the same links, often saving time, since passengers don't go through security checks. The largest commuter line, covering most of the state, is Era Alaska (☎ 800-866-8394; www.flyera.com). In Southeast Alaska, use Wings of Alaska (☎ 907-789-0790; www.ichoosewings.com).

By Ferry

The Alaska Marine Highway System (☎ 800-642-0066; www.ferryalaska.com) connects coastal towns along the route from Ketchikan to Unalaska, with the bulk of the system concentrated on the Inside Passage of the Southeast region.

By Train

The Alaska Railroad (☎ 800-544-0552 or 907-265-2494; www.alaskarailroad.com) operates in the center of the state, connecting Anchorage with Seward and Whittier to the south and with Fairbanks, Denali National Park, and Talkeetna to the north. It's a nice way to travel, but expensive and slow. Treat it as a tour feature rather than an efficient means of travel when evaluating whether the trade-offs make sense for you.

By Bus

Generally, intercity bus service is poor in Alaska and used only by the backpacker and hostel set. One exception is the Park Connection Motorcoach Service (☎ 800-266-8625; www.alaskatravel.com/bus-lines), which offers the only way other than a private car to get from Seward (and Kenai Fjords National Park) to Denali National Park in a single day. It uses large, comfortable highway coaches.

By Car

For the central part of the state, including the corridor connecting Kenai Fjords National Park to Denali National Park, which is the most popular, driving is the least expensive and most flexible way to get around. For Southeast Alaska and the Bush, on the other hand, most communities are not connected by roads, and air and ferry are more important.

For those not coming by cruise ship, the most popular approach to visiting Alaska is to fly to Anchorage and rent a car there, touring according to your plans and then returning the car to Anchorage. All major rental agencies are represented. In the summer, base rental rates are around $50 a day; taxes and fees imposed by the city, state, and airport add more than 40% more. You can avoid almost half those extra charges by renting outside of the city.

A key consideration if you plan to drive any of Alaska's unpaved highways is to rent from an agency that allows the vehicle's use on those roads. See "Renting the Right Car for Going Off-Pavement" on p. 509.

Except near the largest cities, all of Alaska's highways are two-lane roads, and they generally pass through wilderness without much in the way of human settlement. Speed limits are up to 65 miles per hour, and you can be tempted to go fast because of the lack of traffic, but there are special hazards here: dips and humps in the road, called *frost heaves,* and large animals that can run into the road, including moose and caribou. Driving slowly is safer. Passing is dangerous on these roads; the law requires slower vehicles to pull over and let others pass.

Before traveling on a rural highway, especially one of the long, unpaved routes (such as the Dalton and Steese highways), prepare for many hours of travel without gas or services available. In winter, be prepared for survival in extremely cold weather without help for hours. In general, I recommend that visitors fly rather than drive between communities in the winter.

Check current road conditions and hazards by calling ☎ 511 or going to http://511.alaska.gov.

Tips on Accommodations

In the high season, you should book your rooms in advance to have any selection. The best accommodations are booked months out for the peak summer period. In the fall and winter, rooms are usually easy to obtain, except in particular winter destinations at peak times, including Alyeska Resort in Girdwood and Chena Hot Springs Resort near Fairbanks.

You'll find rooms similar to those in national and international chains in Alaska's cities, with the same features—televisions, phones, private bathrooms, boring art—found in business hotels in every developed nation. Good standard rooms are available even in the small towns. For something more uniquely Alaskan, choose small inns or B&Bs, which sometimes use extra bedrooms in family homes; this may save you money and will put you in closer contact with the places you aim to visit. There are hostels in almost every town as well, though outside the cities they are seasonal. Those with generous budgets may want to consider a visit to a fly-in or boat-in wilderness lodge, although that is beyond our scope here. The ferries of the Alaska Marine Highway System also have cabins, which rent for reasonable rates (p. 373).

Backpacking, tent camping, or RV camping are wonderful ways to visit Alaska. I've covered some of the details in chapter 12.

Fast Facts

ATMs/Cashpoints

Cash machines are ubiquitous, even in convenience stores and Native villages, although I've noted some exceptions. You generally can use plastic to pay for everything, except some small B&Bs and some very expensive purchases such as wilderness trips or fly-in lodges.

Banking Hours

Banks are typically open Monday through Friday 9am to 5pm and Saturday at least until noon.

Bike Rentals

I have mentioned bike rental agencies in each town where bicycles are practical to use. Bicycles are of greatest use in small towns where distances are not as great and traffic not as fast, including smaller communities in Southeast Alaska and little coastal towns on the Kenai Peninsula and Prince William Sound. Anchorage has a network of wooded bicycle paths that make cycling one of the best activities there.

Business Hours

Grocery stores in the cities—which typically also carry a wide range of merchandise, from clothing to fishing rods—are open until late at night, every day of the year. Smaller shops typically operate at least from 10am to 7pm. In small towns, where businesses may be family run, expect shorter hours.

Customs and Wildlife Products

Passing back and forth between Alaska and Canada is more complicated than it used to be, and international travelers have additional issues to consider. Since Alaska's border crossings are remote, it's wise to plan before starting your trip. Here are contact phone numbers for questions: Canadian Customs in Whitehorse (☎ 867-667-3943); U.S. Customs and Border Protection on the highways (☎ 907-774-2252), in Skagway (☎ 907-983-2325), or in Anchorage (☎ 907-271-6855).

There are no duties on products made in the United States or Canada going back and forth between those two countries. International travelers are exempt from duties on personal effects, which are items you use yourself, such as clothing, cameras, and fishing rods. In addition, every visitor over 21 years of age may bring in limited quantities of various items without duties, which you can learn about from U.S. Customs and Border Protection at its website (www.cbp.gov).

International visitors should not consider bringing firearms except for a hunting trip. You will need your hunting license first, and the Alaska Department of Fish and Game issues licenses to nonresident aliens only for hunts with registered guides. Consequently, you must begin the process by retaining a guide; ask him or her to do the extensive paperwork that will follow, and allow several months for the bureaucracy.

U.S. residents traveling through Canada should do some research before taking firearms. Guns other than hunting rifles or shotguns generally are not allowed, and you need to fill out a form and pay a $25 fee for those guns that are allowed; contact the Canadian Firearms Center (☎ 800-731-4000; www.cfc-cafc.gc.ca) before you go in order to avoid problems. You should also register your firearms with U.S. Customs and Border Patrol (no fee) before entering Canada, to ease your return to the United States.

Laws and treaties designed to protect endangered species can make it difficult to bring home authentic Alaska Native art and crafts that are perfectly legal to buy and own under U.S. and Alaska law. Alaska Natives have used these materials for thousands of years, and their subsistence harvest is not a danger to the species. Some individual U.S. states have more restrictive laws, however, and generally marine mammal products made of any threatened or endangered species cannot be taken out of the country unless at least 100 years old. In addition, even if you can legally take home the item, and even if you're only carrying it through Canada, a permit is required in order to comply with the Convention on International Trade in Endangered Species, known as CITES; permit applications take up to 90 days for processing.

For international visitors, the most practical advice is simply to avoid buying anything that requires a CITES permit—that is, anything made from a marine mammal or any other species on the CITES list, which includes brown or black bear, wolf, lynx, bobcat, or river otter (although none of those are endangered in Alaska). If it is legal to take the item home, have the shop mail it to you insured, and have them take care of the paperwork. Otherwise, contact the U.S. Fish and Wildlife Service for help, in Anchorage (☎ 907-271-6198; http://alaska.fws.gov/law). Foreign visitors exporting wildlife products may also need to contact the agency's Division of Management Authority in Washington, D.C. (☎ 800-358-2104; http://international.fws.gov) regarding permit requirements.

Drinking Laws
The minimum drinking age in Alaska is 21, and ID is frequently checked. Most restaurants sell beer and wine, while some have full bars that

---

Renting the Right Car for Going Off-Pavement

When you sign a car rental contract with a name-brand firm, you usually agree not to drive the car off pavement. If you violate the agreement and damage the car, especially out in the wilderness, you could be liable for extraordinary costs to tow and repair it, and for the rental firm's lost business while it is out of service. Here are much better rental alternatives in Fairbanks (one, in Anchorage, is on p. 194, and another, in Nome, is on p. 432).

GoNorth Car and Camper Rental (☎ 866-236-7272 or 907-479-7272; www.gonorth-alaska.com), rents SUVs, vans and trucks, and also campers on four-wheel-drive pickups and motorhomes. With unlimited mileage, a pickup camper is $137 to $252 a day (7-day minimum rental); insurance of $21 to $27 a day is required unless you present proof of your own coverage, so be sure to ask about what paperwork you will need when you reserve. GoNorth also rents camping gear. If you prefer a car, **Arctic Outfitters** (☎ 907-474-3530; www.arctic-outfitters.com), rents the Ford Escape with CB radios, maintenance kits, and two full-sized spare tires. Drivers must be at least 30 years old and have their own insurance. One-day rental rates exceed $200, with discounts for additional days, and mileage charges start after 250 miles.

serve hard liquor as well. Packaged alcohol, beer, and wine are sold only in licensed stores, not in grocery stores, but these are common and are open long hours every day. Under state law, bars don't have to close until 5am, but many communities have an earlier closing, generally around 2am. Open containers of alcohol are not allowed in your car or, with few exceptions, in any public place outside a bar or restaurant. Don't even think about driving while intoxicated, which in Alaska carries mandatory jail time for the first offense.

More than 100 rural communities have laws prohibiting the importation and possession of alcohol (this is known as being "dry") or prohibiting the sale but not the possession of alcohol (known as being "damp"). With a few exceptions, these are tiny Bush communities off the road network; urban areas are all "wet." Of the communities featured in this book, Barrow is damp and the rest are wet. Before flying into a Native village with alcohol, ask about the law, or check a list online (go to www.dps.state.ak.us/abc and click on "Dry/Damp Communities"). Bootlegging is a serious crime.

Electricity

As in Canada, the United States uses 110–120 volts AC (60 cycles), compared to 220–240 volts AC (50 cycles) in most of Europe, Australia, and New Zealand. Downward converters that change 220–240 volts to 110–120 volts are difficult to find in the United States, so bring one with you.

Embassies & Consulates

The following nations have consulate offices in Anchorage: Canada, 310 K Street, Suite 220 (907-264-6734; www.anchorage.gc.ca); Japan, 3601 C Street, Suite 1300 (☎ 907-562-8424; www.anchorage.us.emb-japan.go.jp); Korea, 800 E. Dimond Boulevard., Suite 3-695 (☎ 907-339-7955; http://usa-anchorage.mofat.go.kr/eng/am/usa-anchorage/main/index.jsp); and Mexico, 610 C Street, Suite A 7 (☎ 907-334-9573). You can contact the following embassies in Washington, D.C.: Australia, 1601 Massachusetts Ave. NW, Washington, DC 20036 (☎ 202-797-3000; www.usa.embassy.gov.au); Canada, 501 Pennsylvania Ave. NW, Washington, DC 20001 (☎ 202-682-1740; www.canadainternational.

gc.ca/washington); Ireland, 2234 Massachusetts Ave. NW, Washington, DC 20008 (☎ 202-462-3939; www.embassyofireland.org); New Zealand, 37 Observatory Circle NW, Washington, DC 20008 (☎ 202-328-4800; www.nzembassy.com); United Kingdom, 3100 Massachusetts Ave. NW, Washington, DC 20008 (☎ 202-588-6500; http://ukinusa.fco.gov.uk).

Emergencies

Dialing ☎ 911 will reach an emergency dispatcher almost anywhere there is phone service.

Family Travel

Activities and businesses appropriate for families are noted throughout the book with a 🄺🄸🄳🅂 icon. In addition, each chapter has a tour designed with children in mind. The drawbacks of bringing a family on an Alaska trip are worth noting as well: The travel and activities are expensive, and children's discounts tend to be small. Many popular activities aren't suitable for young children, such as rafting or sea kayaking outings; long fishing charters; and most wildlife viewing, which usually involves a lot of time to find animals that, in the end, may be far away and difficult for young children to see. When planning your trip with children, focus on a smaller area of the state and include plenty of energetic outdoor activities such as hiking.

Gay & Lesbian Travelers

Anchorage, Juneau, and Fairbanks have active gay and lesbian communities. In Anchorage, Identity Inc. (www.identityinc.org) offers referrals, publishes a newsletter called *Northview*, sponsors activities throughout the year, and operates a gay and lesbian helpline (☎ 888-901-9876 or 907-258-4777). The June Pridefest includes a parade and picnic, among other events. Identity Inc.'s Gay and Lesbian Community Center of Anchorage is at 336 E. Fifth Ave. (☎ 907-929-GLBT (929-4528).

Gays and lesbians can find some Alaska B&Bs and tours specifically marketing to them. For example, Olivia Cruises and Resorts (☎ 800-631-6277; www.olivia.com) typically brings a lesbian cruise to Alaska each year, with well-known entertainers on board. In Fairbanks, a small but growing company specializes in outdoor tours and backcountry trips statewide for gays and lesbians. It's called Out in Alaska (☎ 877-374-9958; www.outinalaska.com).

Holidays
Banks and state and local government offices close on two state holidays: Seward's Day (the last Monday in March) and Alaska Day (October 18, or the nearest Friday or Monday if it falls on a weekend).

Banks, all government offices, post offices, and many stores, restaurants, and museums are closed on these national holidays: January 1 (New Year's Day), the third Monday in January (Martin Luther King, Jr., Day), the third Monday in February (Presidents' Day), the last Monday in May (Memorial Day), July 4 (Independence Day), the first Monday in September (Labor Day), the second Monday in October (Columbus Day), November 11 (Veterans' Day/Armistice Day), the fourth Thursday in November (Thanksgiving Day), and December 25 (Christmas). The Tuesday after the first Monday in November is Election Day, a federal government holiday in presidential-election years (held every 4 years, and next in 2012).

Insurance
Travel insurance is available for trip cancellation or interruption, for medical costs, and for lost or delayed luggage. Typically all those types of coverage are sold together in a per-trip or an annual comprehensive plan. Look for the best deal on travel insurance by going to www.insuremytrip.com. Also consider purchasing insurance on rental cars and health care before leaving home. Details follow.

Trip Cancellation: Insurance for trip cancellation or interruption is a must if you have paid the large cash deposits demanded by many Alaska outfitters, fishing guides, wilderness lodges, package tour operators, and cruise companies. A premium of 5% to 7% of the cost of the trip is well worth the protection against the uncertainty of Alaska weather (most deposits are lost in case of weather delays or cancellations) or unexpected crises that might prevent you from being able to depart as planned. Interruption insurance will get you home under covered circumstances. Major insurers offer policyholders access to 24-hour phone assistance to help handle crises. Read the policy carefully to find out when you

are covered. Do not buy insurance through the operator holding your deposit, even though the insurer itself is a different entity. Instead, buy your insurance directly from the insurance company without the involvement of anyone selling you travel products.

Baggage: Insurance on your baggage is included in most travel insurance plans. If an airline loses or damages your bags, it is usually responsible for up to $2,500 per passenger on domestic flights (on international flights, up to approximately $635 per checked bag), excluding expensive items such as jewelry and cameras. Good luck getting an airline to actually pay in a reasonable period of time, however, as this is notoriously difficult. The simplest course is to leave valuables at home or carry them with you, insuring your baggage only if justified by the worth that you can prove. You would need to establish the value of your lost clothing and such with bills of sale or similar documentation for each item.

Internet Access
Alaska is wired, and Wi-Fi hotspots are common and often free—for example, in the entire Anchorage airport. Finding a connected terminal is easy, too, generally in libraries, coffee shops, and hotel lobbies. BlackBerrys and iPhones work in most populated areas, too.

Legal Aid
If you are pulled over for a minor infraction while driving (such as speeding), never attempt to pay the fine directly to a police officer; this could be construed as attempted bribery, a much more serious crime. Pay fines by mail or directly into the hands of the clerk of the court. If accused of a more serious offense, say and do nothing before consulting a lawyer. In the U.S., the burden is on the state to prove a person's guilt beyond a reasonable doubt, and everyone has the right to remain silent, whether he or she is suspected of a crime or actually arrested. Once arrested, a person can make one telephone call to a party of his or her choice. International visitors should call your embassy or consulate.

Mail & Postage
At press time, domestic postage rates are 28¢ for a postcard and 44¢ for a letter. For international mail, a first-class letter of up to 1 ounce costs 98¢ (75¢ to Canada and 79¢ to Mexico);

a first-class postcard costs the same as a letter. For more information, go to www.usps.com and click on "Calculate Postage."

Money

Visitors can handle their money in Alaska as they would in the rest of the United States or any developed country. Credit and debit cards are accepted widely, and ATMs are found almost everywhere except in remote wilderness areas without communications. Foreign visitors should exchange any foreign cash into U.S. dollars before leaving home or in a major American city outside of Alaska; currency exchange is virtually nonexistent within the state. Foreign travelers to the U.S. should beware of hidden credit-card fees while traveling. Check with your credit or debit card issuer to see what fees, if any, will be charged for transactions while you are in the U.S.

Outdoor Health & Safety

Here are some basic safety issues to be aware of when you're outdoors in Alaska. If unsure of how to handle them, get informed before heading out into the wilderness—or go with a guide.

Avalanche Sliding snow hardens to a consistency that only metal tools can dig through. If you're buried, self-rescue is usually impossible, and you don't have long to live; most people don't survive. Don't go into snowy backcountry without training in avalanche avoidance and recovery equipment, including locator beacons, probes, and shovels.

Bears & Other Wildlife Deaths from wild animal attack are rare, but why take chances? Don't attract bears. Be tidy with your food and trash when you're camping; don't spread food odors; clean fish away from your campsite; and never keep food, pungent items, or clothing that smells like fish in your tent. Make noise when walking through brush or thick trees to avoid surprising a bear or moose. Bear and moose are strongly defensive of their young, so stay away. If you encounter a bear, stop, wave your arms, make noise, and, if you're with others, group together so you look larger to the bear. Depart by slowly backing away, not running. The bear will usually lose interest. If you encounter a moose, keep your distance and find a way around without going close.

Boating Safety Cool temperatures, unpredictable weather, and cold water add to the hazards of boating or floating in Alaska. Go only with an experienced, licensed operator unless you know what you're doing. Wear a life jacket so you don't sink if shocked by a fall into frigid water. After coming to your senses, you have 15 minutes to half an hour before cold immobilizes you. Always be prepared to quickly warm a wet person with warm, dry clothes and hot drinks (see "Hypothermia," below).

Drinking Water Avoid the chronic diarrhea caused by *Giardia lamblia* by purifying river or lake water before you drink it. Hand-held filters are the best solution. They're available from sporting-goods stores for around $75. Giardiasis may not show up until weeks after you get home; tell your doctor that you may have been exposed so you can get tested and be treated and cured.

Hypothermia Dying of cold can happen even in the summer when you aren't properly dressed and get wet, especially if hungry or exhausted. Dress in material (whether wool or synthetic) that keeps its warmth when wet, choosing layers so you can avoid chilling perspiration. Symptoms of hypothermia include cold extremities, being uncommunicative, displaying poor judgment or coordination, and sleepiness. A shivering victim still has the ability to warm up if better dressed; a lack of shivering means the body has gone beyond that point and warmth must be added from the outside or from warm drinks. Get indoors, force hot liquids into the victim (except if he or she is not fully conscious, as this could cause choking), and, if shelter is unavailable, apply body heat from another person, skin on skin, in a sleeping bag.

River Crossings Hiking off trail sometimes requires that you ford a river. It's easy to get in trouble in glacial meltwater—barely above freezing, heavy with silt that makes it opaque. If in doubt, don't do it. If you do decide to cross, unbuckle your pack, keep your shoes on, face upstream, use a heavy walking stick if possible, and rig a safety line. Children should go in the eddy behind a larger person, or be carried.

Seasickness Your trip will probably include a

boat ride, perhaps to fish or see wildlife. Avoid seasickness by abstaining from alcohol the night before, eating a light breakfast, limiting coffee, and sitting low and near the middle of the boat, away from odors and with your eyes on the horizon. The very best seasickness remedy is the scopolamine skin patch, available only by prescription, which lasts up to 3 days. Over-the-counter choices are meclizine (brand names Bonine, Antivert, or Dramamine II) and dimenhydrinate (original Dramamine). Both are drowsiness-inducing antihistamines, but there's less of that side effect with the newer meclizine. For the drugs to be effective, take them at least 2 hours before you get on board.

Wilderness Communications If you are unsure of your navigational skills, maps, or equipment, don't go into the wilderness on your own. In case you get lost or in trouble, make sure someone knows where you went and when to expect you back. Even on a short dayhike, leave a note in your car indicating where you are bound. You can't count on cell phones. For serious outdoors people, a personal locator beacon with a built-in GPS is a safety backup that will bring help in a real emergency wherever you are.

Satellite phones work everywhere, too; you can rent one from **RoadPost** (☎ 888-290-1616 or 905-272-5665; www.roadpost.com).

Passports

Many visitors travel between Alaska and Canada. An adult U.S. citizen needs a passport, passport card, or enhanced driver's license to reenter the country over the road or water; an American child under age 18 needs a passport or a birth certificate combined with photo identification. A website explaining the requirements is at www.getyouhome.gov. Canadians and nationals of most other countries need passports but not visas.

See "Embassies & Consulates," above, for whom to contact if you lose your passport while traveling in the U.S. For other information, contact the following agencies:

For Residents of Australia: Contact the Australian Passport Information Service at ☎ 131 232, or visit www.passports.gov.au.

For Residents of Canada: Contact the Passport Office, Department of Foreign Affairs and International Trade, Ottawa, ON K1A 0G3 (☎ 800-567-6868; www.ppt.gc.ca).

For Residents of Ireland: Contact the Passport Office, Setanta Centre, Molesworth Street, Dublin 2 (☎ 01/671 1633; www.foreign affairs.gov.ie).

For Residents of New Zealand: Contact the Passport Office, Department of Internal Affairs, 47 Boulcott Street, Wellington, 6011 (☎ 0800/225 050 in New Zealand or 04/474 8100; www.passports.govt.nz).

For Residents of the United Kingdom: Visit your nearest passport office, major post office, or travel agency, or contact the Identity and Passport Service (IPS), 89 Eccleston Square, London, SW1V 1PN (☎ 0300/222 0000; www.ips.gov.uk).

For Residents of the United States: To find your regional passport office, check the U.S. State Department website (http://travel.state.gov/passport) or call the National Passport Information Center (☎ 877-487-2778) for automated information.

Safety

Muggings are rare, but crime rates in general are high in Alaska's cities, especially for sexual assault and other violent crime. Avoid conflict or vulnerable situations in bars or late at night. Women do travel alone but should avoid walking by themselves at night, especially in wooded or out-of-the-way areas, even when the midnight sun is out. Women should never hitchhike alone.

Alaska's cities all have full-service hospitals. Even tiny towns have clinics, although often without a physician. Medical facilities are listed in the "Fast Facts" section of each chapter; they can provide referrals for dentists or other health professionals. In an emergency, call ☎ 911.

For tips on staying safe in the wilderness, see "Outdoors Health & Safety" on p. 512.

Senior Travelers

The National Park Service offers a free admission and discount program to seniors age 62 or older, under the ungainly name America the Beautiful—National Park and Federal Recreational Lands Pass—Senior Pass (formerly called the Golden Age Passport). The pass is good for lifetime free entrance to national parks, monuments, historic sites, recreation areas, and national wildlife refuges, for a one-time processing fee of $10. Buy the pass in person at any park that charges an entrance fee. For more information, go to www.nps.gov/fees_passes.htm or call the United States Geological Survey, which issues the passes, at ☎ 888-275-8747.

People over age 65 get reduced admission prices to many Alaska attractions, and some accommodations have special senior rates. Be sure to bring identification to prove your age.

Most towns have a senior center where you'll find activities and help with any special needs. The Anchorage Senior Center (☎ 907-258-7823; www.anchorageseniorcenter.org) offers guidance for visitors; use of the restaurant, gift shop, and fitness room; and a chance to meet locals. Dances are held most Friday nights.

Exploritas, formerly called Elderhostel, (☎ 800-454-5768; www.exploritas.org), operates many weeklong Alaska learning vacations for groups of people 55 and older. The catalog of choices is on the website.

Smoking

In Alaska's cities, smoking is prohibited in most indoor public places. In Anchorage and Juneau, smoking is prohibited even in bars. Smoking is more common in small towns, where rules are usually less strict. Smoking is generally prohibited in hotels and B&Bs; if you must smoke in your room, make that your first question when you book.

Taxes

Alaska imposes no state sales tax, but most local governments have a sales tax and a bed tax on accommodations. All prices and rates are listed without tax unless otherwise noted. The United States has no value-added tax (VAT) or other indirect tax at the national level.

Telephones

The least expensive ways to call home are by purchasing a by-the-minute calling card, for sale in grocery stores, or by using your computer with www.skype.com or a similar voice over Internet service. Connection speeds are spotty in little Alaskan hotels, so don't count on Skype working for video calls. The largest phone company in Alaska eliminated pay phones in 2010, and now they are almost impossible to find.

Most long-distance and international calls can be dialed directly from any phone. For calls within the United States and to Canada, dial 1 followed by the area code and the seven-digit number. For other international calls, dial 011 followed by the country code, the city code, and the number you are calling. Calls to area codes 800, 888, 877, and 866 are toll-free but won't work from outside the U.S. or Canada, and occasionally won't work from outside Alaska. For local directory assistance ("information"), dial 411; for long-distance information, dial 1, then the appropriate area code and 555-1212.

Time Zone

Alaska naturally spans five time zones, but Alaska Standard Time (AST) was stretched to include almost the entire state. It's 1 hour earlier than the U.S. West Coast's Pacific Time and 4 hours earlier than Eastern Standard Time. Crossing over the border from Alaska to Canada adds an hour and puts you at the same time as the West Coast. The balance of the continental United States is divided into four time zones: Eastern Standard Time (EST), Central Standard Time (CST), Mountain Standard Time (MST), and Pacific Standard Time (PST). When it's 8am in Anchorage, it is 9am in Los Angeles (PST), 10am in Denver (MST), 11am in Chicago (CST), noon in New York City (EST), 5pm in London (GMT), and 2am the next day in Sydney. Daylight saving time is in effect from 1am on the second Sunday in March (turn your clocks ahead 1 hour) until 1am on the first Sunday in November (turn clocks back again).

Tipping

Tips make up a major part of the compensation for many service workers. To leave no tip in a restaurant is socially unacceptable and leaves your server unpaid. In restaurants, bars, and nightclubs, tip your server 15% to 20% of the check, depending on the quality of service. Tipping is not expected in cafeterias or fast-food restaurants where you order at a counter. Tip fishing guides and outfitters $10 to $20 per person per day. For outings of less than a day, adjust the tip accordingly. At wilderness lodges, which normally have all-inclusive rates, ask the proprietor to distribute a tip for the entire visit rather than trying to do it at each meal; a blanket tip of $15 per person per day is acceptable. In hotels, tip bellhops $1 per bag and tip the housekeeper at least $1 to $2 per day. Tip checkroom attendants $1 per garment, and tip valet-parking attendants $1 each time you get your car. Tip cab drivers 15% of the fare, and tip hairdressers and barbers 15% to 20%. Do not tip gas-station attendants and ushers at movies and theaters.

Toilets

You won't find public toilets, or "restrooms," on the streets in most U.S. cities, but they can be found in hotel lobbies, bars, restaurants, museums, department stores, railway and bus stations, and service stations. Large hotels and fast-food restaurants are often the best bet for clean facilities. It can be a long way between toilets on rural Alaskan highways; see "Keeping the Wilderness Clean" (at right).

Travelers with Disabilities

Hotels have rooms accessible for people with disabilities, and many B&Bs have made the necessary adjustments as well. Make sure to ask for the special rooms when making reservations. People with permanent disabilities can get a free lifetime pass to National Parks and many other federal public lands, as well

Keeping the Wilderness Clean

Backpackers and sea kayakers are used to leaving the wilderness as they found it, but anyone driving a remote highway in Alaska needs to take the same care. It doesn't take much thoughtless use to diminish the wilderness, and finding toilet paper or human waste by a trail or a highway is disgusting and discouraging. Whether driving or camping, follow the simple rule to leave no trace. It's easy if you plan ahead. Bring some kind of digging tool with which to bury organic waste (but nothing more!) and sealable plastic bags with which you can pack out toilet paper and any other trash. To learn more, see the website of the Leave No Trace Center for Outdoor Ethics, at www.LNT.org.

as a 50% discount on some camping fees and the like. Apply in person at any facility (such as a park) that charges an entrance fee. You will need to show proof of a medically determined disability. Other details (including the program's absurdly long name) are the same as those listed for the seniors' pass on p. 513.

Index

A

Accommodations. *See also specific hotels/areas*
best, 11-13
catering to cruises, 165, 322
tips on, 508
Advance reservations, for tours/ activities, 157, 233, 407, 505
Arctic Ocean trip, 311, 313, 315
bear-viewing, 362, 382, 479, 485, 505
Denali backcountry hikes, 161
Denali shuttle bus, 143
Adventure Bound Alaska (Juneau), 45, 381
Air Excursions (Gustavus and Juneau), 367, 416
Airport Dike Trail (Juneau), 367
Air Sitka, 391
Air travel, 21, 22, 376, 506-7. *See also* Alaska Airlines
Alaganik Slough (Copper River Delta), 185, 209
Alaska Aces Hockey (Anchorage), 116, 120
Alaska Airlines, 485, 506, 507
Alaska Bush, 427, 430, 444, 435
Anchorage, 45, 203
Cordova, 210
Gustavus, 34, 406
Juneau, 333, 335, 351
Alaska Airlines Vacations, 41, 427
Alaska Aviation Heritage Museum (Anchorage), 56-57, 75
Alaska Backpackers Inn (Anchorage), 110, 111
Alaska Bird Observatory (Fairbanks), 288, 306, 320-21, 324
Alaska Bush, 422-49. *See also* Barrow; Kodiak; Nome; Unalaska and Dutch Harbor
favorite moments, 422-25
Fast Facts, 449
Alaska Canoe & Campground (Sterling), 60, 231, 249, 251, 253, 277
Alaska capitol building (Juneau), 337, 376, 377
Alaska Car Rental (Ketchikan), 348
Alaska Center for the Performing Arts (Anchorage), 82, 116, 119
Alaska Discovery tours, 52-4, 382, 479, 483, 485
Alaska Eagle Arts (Ketchikan), 339
Alaska Fly 'N' Fish Charters (Juneau), 365, 382
Alaska Goldpanners baseball club, 307, 505
Alaska Governor's Mansion (Juneau), 337, 377
Alaska Highway, 283, 293, 294, 296, 297, 453, 482

Alaska Indian Arts cultural center (Haines), 352, 410
Alaska Islands & Ocean Visitor Center (Homer), 39, 239-40, 248, 253, 260, 263
Alaska League Baseball (Anchorage), 67, 116, 120
Alaska Marine Highway System. *See* Ferry travel
Alaska Maritime National Wildlife Refuge (Unalaska), 260, 437
Alaska Motorhome Rentals (Anchorage), 58, 373, 482
Alaska Mountain Flying and Travel (Haines), 367
Alaska Mountaineering & Hiking (Anchorage), 96, 101
Alaska Mountaineering School (Talkeetna), 163
Alaska Mountain Guides (Haines), 412
Alaska Museum of Natural History (Anchorage), 78
Alaskan Amber beer, 475
Alaska Native Arts Foundation Gallery (Anchorage), 96, 97
Alaska Native Heritage Center (Anchorage), 8, 29, 66, 72, 123
Alaska Native Medical Center gift shop (Anchorage), 97
Alaskan Yurt Rentals (Kachemak Bay State Park), 253
Alaska Outdoor Rentals & Guides (Fairbanks), 299, 300, 309, 317
Alaska Public Lands Information Center, 482, 504, 506
Anchorage, 83, 123
Fairbanks, 312, 316, 327
Interior Alaska, 293, 327
Alaska Railroad, 21, 56, 151, 165, 507
Anchorage, 122
Denali Nat'l Park, 129, 133, 135, 151
Fairbanks, 326
history of, 174, 299, 309, 453
Kenai Peninsula, 279
Spencer Glacier, 56, 86, 92, 230, 236-37
Turnagain Arm, 6, 185
Whittier, 185, 200
Alaska Rainforest Sanctuary (Herring Cove), 363-64, 398
Alaska Raptor Center (Sitka), 33, 331, 335, 390, 480
Alaska River Expeditions (Cordova), 212, 213
Alaska Rivers Company (Cooper Landing), 39, 238
Alaska Salmon Bake (Pioneer Park, Fairbanks), 309
Alaska's Capital Inn (Juneau), 13, 359, 383
Alaska Sea Kayakers (Whittier), 202
Alaska SeaLife Center (Seward), 30, 60, 235, 237, 247, 268-69, 480
Alaska's River Wrangellers (Copper Center), 191, 483

Alaska State Fair (Palmer), 138, 506
Alaska State Museum (Juneau), 35, 337, 343, 351, 358-59, 374
Alaska State Trooper Museum (Anchorage), 69
Alaska Syndicate, 195, 199, 216, 457-58
Alaska Travel Adventures (Juneau), 381, 382
Alaska Vistas (Wrangell), 366
Alaska Wilderness Outfitting and Camping Rentals (Ketchikan), 372
Alaska Wildland Adventures (Cooper Landing), 238, 241, 479
Alaska Wildlife Conservation Center (Seward Hwy), 86
Alaska Zoo (Anchorage), 46, 66,74, 79
Aleut, 436, 468, 469
Aleutian Islands, 187, 425, 437
Native peoples of, 386, 452, 469
under Russian rule, 386, 441, 452
in World War II, 425, 436, 439, 453, 458
Aleutian World War II National Historic Area Visitor Center (Unalaska), 436, 439
Aleut Island Lodge (Kodiak), 445
All-terrain vehicles (ATVs), use of (Denali Nat'l Park), 158
Alpine skiing, 485. *See also* Alyeska, Mount; Alyeska Ski Resort
Anchorage, 92
Fairbanks, 287
Alutiiq, 443, 468, 469
Alutiiq Museum (Kodiak), 443-44
Alyeska, Mount (Girdwood), 66, 86, 87, 92, 113
Alyeska Ski Resort (Girdwood), 66, 86, 87, 92, 485, 508
aerial tram, 38, 87, 113
hotel, 38, 87, 110, 113
American Bald Eagle Foundation Natural History Museum (Haines), 352, 411
Anan Wildlife Observatory (near Wrangell), 366, 398, 488
Anchorage, 28-29, 36, 45-46, 56, 57, 58, 64-123, 152 157, 206
with children, 58, 76-79
Fast Facts, 122-23
favorite moments, 64-67
hotels, 12, 110-15
nightlife/entertainment, 116-21
outdoor activities, 64-67, 88-95
restaurants, 14, 66, 102-9
shopping, 96-101
suggested itineraries, 68-71, 72-73, 74-75, 76-79, 80-83
Anchorage Downtown Marriott, 110-11
Anchorage Fur Rendezvous Festival, 67, 116, 121, 484, 504
Anchorage Grand Hotel, 110, 111
Anchorage Market & Festival, 83, 99
Anchorage Museum at Rasmuson Center, 29, 67, 68-69, 78, 97

Anchorage Senior Center, 514

Anchorage Symphony Orchestra, 116, 119, 474

Angel Rocks Trail (Chena River State Recreation Area), 289, 307

Aquariums/Sea life attractions
Homer, 10, 39, 239–40, 242, 248, 253, 260, 263
Seward, 30, 60, 235, 237, 247, 268–69, 480

Arctic Caribou Inn, 311, 315

Arctic Circle, 302, 312, 429, 430

Arctic Getaway Bed and Breakfast (Wiseman), 314

Arctic National Wildlife Refuge, river floating in, 10, 479

Arctic Ocean, 311, 313, 315, 422, 427. See also Barrow; Dalton Highway
shore of, 4, 429

Arctic Road Runner (Anchorage), 102, 103

Art, ice, world championships of (Fairbanks), 283, 285, 287, 320, 484, 504

Art, Native. See Native arts; Athabascans; Tlingit, cultural attractions of; Totem poles

Art, public
Anchorage, 80, 81, 82, 83
Denali visitor center, 133
Seward, 234, 246

Art galleries/museums/shopping
Anchorage, 81, 96, 97, 99, 121
Anchorage Museum at Rasmuson Center, 29, 56, 67, 68–69, 78, 97, 123
Fairbanks, 317, 474
Homer, 39, 242, 248, 253, 260, 262
Juneau, 379

Artique, Ltd. (Anchorage), 96, 99

Artists' communities
Halibut Cove, 14, 39, 230, 240
Homer, 39, 242, 260, 262
Juneau, 379
Ketchikan, 339

AskMatt Alaskan Adventures & Tours (Anchorage), 480, 483

A Taste of Alaska Lodge (near Fairbanks), 13, 287, 300, 322

Athabascans, 135, 468, 469
cultural sights/attractions of
Anchorage, 73, 82, 440
Copper Center, 40, 49, 191, 194–95, 206
Denali National Park Visitor Center, 133

Atigun Pass (Dalton Hwy), 312, 314

ATMs/Cashpoints, 313, 407, 508

Auke Village Recreation Area (Auke Bay), 344, 384

Aurora borealis. See Northern Lights

Aurora Express B&B (Fairbanks), 13, 322

Avalanche safety, 512

B

Backcountry Connection van (Copper Center to Kennicott/McCarthy), 195

Backcountry Information Center (Denali Nat'l Park), 161

Backcountry trips, 10, 24
health/safety in, 512–13
preparing for, 147, 160

Backdoor Cafe (Sitka), 358

Backpacking, 480–81
Granite Tors Trail, 282, 289, 480–81
Primrose Creek/Lost Lake Trails, 251, 252, 480
Resurrection Pass Trail, 238, 480

Baja Taco (Cordova), 197, 213

Bald eagles, 196, 496
Anchorage, 64, 72, 89, 480
Haines, 333, 352, 353, 411, 496, 506
Juneau, 337, 351, 374
Ketchikan, 44, 339, 347, 397
Sitka, 33, 331, 335, 390, 480
Petersburg, 340, 342

Ballinger, Richard, 199

B&J Sporting Goods (Anchorage), 96, 99

Banking hours, 508

Baranof, Alexander, 357, 386, 388–89, 441, 444

Baranov Museum (Kodiak), 444

Barnette, E.T., 298, 317, 455

Barrow, 4, 41, 426–29, 464, 465
Alaska Airlines tours of, 41, 427
Iñupiaq culture/whaling tradition, 424, 426–27, 428, 470
staying/dining in, 429

Barrow Arctic Research Center, 427

Bars and nightclubs, 117, 119, 321, 381

Baseball
Anchorage, 67, 116, 120
Fairbanks, 283, 307, 505

Battery Point Trail (Haines), 412

Beaches
Anchorage, 71, 89
Arctic Ocean, 4, 429
Chena Lake, 306
Copper River Delta, 209
Fox Island (near Seward), 235
Gustavus/Glacier Bay, 35, 345, 367, 407
Homer area, 12, 39, 240, 242, 267
Juneau and area, 35, 381
Kenai, 239
Ketchikan, 348, 399
Mendenhall Glacier area, 34, 344, 365–66
Nome, 430, 433
Petersburg/Mitkof Island, 370, 371, 403
Peterson/China Poot Bays, 248–49, 253, 263, 264
Prince William Sound, 224
Sitka area, 369
Unalaska/Kodiak, 437, 445
Valdez, 190, 223
Wrangell, 351

Bears, 157, 488–89, 492, 512. See also specific bear species
advance bookings, 339, 485, 505
costs, 242, 382
flightseeing trips, 57, 75, 230–31
safety tips, 25, 157, 161, 512

Bear Tooth Grill (Anchorage), 102, 103

Bear Tooth TheatrePub (Anchorage), 116, 120

Beaver Sports (Fairbanks), 317

Bed and breakfasts, 12–13 , 20, 122

Beer, 70, 82, 116–20, 361, 443, 475

Begich, Boggs Visitor Center (Seward Hwy), 36–38, 54, 86

Begich Towers (Whittier), 51, 189, 201, 203

Bellingham, Washington, ferries from, 373, 507

Beluga Point (Seward Hwy), 85

Beluga whales, 187, 491
Seward Highway, 85
Turnagain Arm, 6, 29, 187, 491

Bering, Vitus, 441, 452

Bering Air (Nome), 424–25, 432

Bering Land Bridge National Preserve Headquarters (Nome), 432, 433

Bering Strait, 441, 468

Bering Strait and Siberia, flights over, 424–25

Bernie's Bungalow Lounge (Anchorage), 116, 117

Best Western Lake Lucille Inn (Wasilla), 138, 139

Big Delta State Historical Park (near Delta Junction), 294

Bike rentals, 481, 508
Anchorage, 70, 88, 89
Denali Nat'l Park, 162
Southeast, 35, 335, 349, 353, 361, 369, 388

Biking/mountain biking, 21–22, 481
Anchorage, 66, 88–89, 481
Denali Nat'l Park, 162, 481
Homer area, 263, 481
Southeast, 35, 412

Birch Hill Recreation Area (Fairbanks), 287, 299–300, 321, 485

Bird Creek (Seward Hwy), 85

Bird Creek Alaska State Parks Campground (Seward Hwy), 58, 85, 110, 115

Bird Point (Seward Hwy), 85

Bird Ridge Trail (Seward Hwy), 85, 89

Birds, 496–98. See also Bald eagles

Bird-watching, 5, 481
Anchorage, 64, 67, 71, 84, 89, 498
Copper River Delta, 50, 198, 209, 212, 481, 498
Fairbanks, 288, 292–93, 306, 320–21, 324, 498
Glacier Bay, 406
Homer, 39, 498
Juneau area, 344, 365–66, 367, 382
Kenai Fjords Nat'l Park, 9, 30, 60, 234, 463, 481

Nome area, 5, 430, 432, 433, 481
Petersburg, 370, 403
Pribilof Islands, 9, 481
Sitka area, 33, 368, 386–88, 389
Seward area, 29, 234, 248, 250
Unalaska/Dutch Harbor area,
425, 434, 437, 439
BJ Boat Rentals (Sitka), 370
Black Bear Inn (Ketchikan), 13, 399
Black bears, 466, 488
Juneau area, 9, 34, 332, 336,
344, 380, 382
Ketchikan area, 339, 363, 366, 398
Wrangell area, 366, 398, 488
Black Rapids Glacier (Richardson
Hwy), 462
Blind River Rapids (Petersburg), 403
Blind Slough Recreation Area (near
Petersburg), 403–4
Blueberry Lake State Recreation Site
(Valdez), 61, 207, 208, 224
Blues Central/Chef's Inn (Anchorage),
116, 117
Boat tours/cruises
Chena River (Fairbanks), 286, 320
College Fjord (Chugach
Mountains), 38, 185, 201
Kenai Fjords Nat'l Park, 9, 60,
234–35, 243, 246–47
Kodiak, 425, 447
Petersburg, 45, 404
Prince William Sound, 15, 38,
202, 203, 222
Sitka Sound, 335, 389, 391
Boating safety, 512
Bob's IGA (Wrangell), 350
Bonanza Mine Hike (near Kennicott),
218
Boreal forest, 466
Bowhead whales, 41, 428, 429, 470
Bowman's Bear Creek Lodge (Hope),
12, 246
Bristol Bay, fly-in fishing, 10, 259, 483
Brooks Camp (Katmai Nat'l Park),
485, 505
Brown bears, 489
viewing of, 57, 230–31
Katmai Nat'l Park, 485, 505
Ketchikan area, 366, 398
Lake Clark Bear Camp, 231, 243
Pack Creek, 365, 366, 382, 479
Wrangell area, 366
Bunnell Street Arts Center (Homer),
39, 242, 260–62
Bun on the Run (Fairbanks), 305
Bureau of Land Management, 61, 312
Business hours, 508
Bus travel, 507
Byers Lake (Denali State Park), 129,
141, 154, 161

C
Cabin Fever (Anchorage), 96, 100
Cabin Nite Dinner Theater (Nenana
Canyon), 142, 170

Caines Head State Recreation Area
(near Seward), 247, 270
Campbell Creek (Anchorage), 89
Camp Denali/North Face Lodge
(Kantishna), 11, 166
Campfire programs (Denali Nat'l
Park), 129, 154, 163
Campgrounds in/near Denali Nat'l
Park, 129, 154–55, 157, 160, 169
Camping, 20, 23, 157, 481–82
Chugach Nat'l Forest, 246, 251
Cordova, 213
Deadhorse, 315
Denali Nat'l Park, 129, 152–57, 169
Fairbanks, 323
Homer Spit, 267
Juneau, 384
Kenai/Soldotna, 277
Ketchikan, 372–73, 399
Petersburg, 371, 404, 405
Sitka, 368–70, 393
Southeast Alaska, 368–73
Valdez, 224
Campobello Bistro (Anchorage),
102, 103
Camp stoves, 157
Canada
customs duties/regulations, 508–9
Dawson City tour, 296
firearms regulations, 509
and Klondike Gold Rush, 296,
452, 454–55, 456
passport requirements, 296
travel from/to, 296, 326, 347,
373, 419, 506–7, 513
Canoeing, 482
Byers Lake (Denali State Park),
129, 141, 154, 161
Chena River (Fairbanks), 282–83,
299, 309, 320, 482
Copper River Delta, 184–85, 209
Kenai Nat'l Wildlife Refuge, 4,
60, 231, 249, 482
Tangle Lakes (Denali Hwy), 145,
161
Canopy tours. See Zip-lining
Cape Fox Lodge (Ketchikan), 339, 396,
399–400
Captain Cook monument
(Anchorage), 83
Carl E. Wynn Nature Center (Homer),
243, 248, 263
Car rental, 122, 238, 251
Anchorage, 122, 133, 238, 251
and camping, 157
Fairbanks, 326, 509
Nome, 432, 433
off-pavement, 194, 432, 509
Seward, 238
Southeast, 348, 351, 371, 405
Carrie M. McLain Memorial Museum
(Nome), 430–32
Carrs/Safeway Great Alaska Shootout
(Anchorage), 120, 506
Car travel, 20–21, 22, 23, 507–8

Castle Hill (Sitka), 32, 358, 390–91
Cathedral Mountain (Denali Park
Road), 148, 160
Cemeteries
Dyea, 361, 416
Eklutna Historical Park, 73, 82, 440
Juneau, 376, 377
Talkeetna, 132, 163, 175
Center for Alaskan Coastal Studies
(Homer), 10, 39, 242, 248
Central (Steese Hwy), 303
Chair 5 (Anchorage), 102, 103
Champions Choice skate rentals
(Anchorage), 93
Channel Club (Sitka), 14, 393
Chatanika River (Steese Hwy), 303
Chena Hot Springs Resort (near
Fairbanks), 7, 61, 287, 289, 300,
302, 307, 484, 508
Northern Lights viewing at, 7,
282, 287, 291
Chena Lake Recreation Area (North
Pole), 306, 323
Chena River (Fairbanks). See also
Pioneer Park
canoeing on, 282–83, 299, 309,
320, 482
Discovery riverboat cruises on,
286, 320
Chena River State Recreation Area
(near Fairbanks), 288–89, 302,
307, 323
trails, 282, 289, 307, 480–81
campgrounds, 288, 307, 323
Chief Shakes Island (Wrangell),
350–51
Children, traveling with, 58–61, 510.
See also specific towns and cities
Anchorage, 58, 76–79
Denali Nat'l Park, 61, 155
Fairbanks/Interior, 304–9
Juneau, 351–52
Kenai Peninsula, 244–49
Southeast, 346–53
Childs Glacier (near Cordova), 7, 50,
184, 198, 208, 209, 212, 213
Chilkat Bald Eagle Preserve (near
Haines), 412, 496
rafting through, 333, 353, 412
Chilkat Guides rafting tours (Haines),
353, 412
Chilkoot Charlie's (Anchorage), 116, 117
Chilkoot Pass Trail (from Dyea), 416,
455
China Poot Bay (near Homer), 248–
49, 253, 264
tide pooling at, 10, 249, 263
Chitina, 195, 206, 458
Chugach Mountains (Seward Hwy), 66
Chugach National Forest, 38, 64, 86,
189, 199, 201, 212, 246 , 480
camping, 246, 251
Cordova Ranger District, 208, 210
Chugach Outdoor Center (near
Girdwood), 39, 232–33, 245

Chugach State Park (Anchorage area), 46, 55, 58, 64, 480. *See also* Glen Alps trailhead

Chum (dog) salmon, 255

Circle (Steese Hwy), 303

Circle District Historical Society Museum (Steese Hwy), 303

City Hall murals (Anchorage), 82

City Park (Ketchikan), 339, 347, 397–98

City Park (near Wrangell), 351

Clarence Strait ferry ride (near Ketchikan), 348–49

Clausen Memorial Museum (Petersburg), 342, 403

Cleary Summit (Steese Hwy), 303

Climate change, 42–43
loss of sea ice, 43, 438, 466, 492
NARL research on, 427

Club Paris (Anchorage), 102, 104, 116, 117

Coldfoot (Dalton Hwy), 311, 312–13

Coldfoot Camp (Dalton Hwy), 312–13

College Fjord (Chugach Mtns), 208
boat tours of, 38, 185, 201

Communications, wilderness, 513

Conservation, 453, 457–58
Roosevelt and, 199, 359, 457, 458
Southeast Alaska, 356

Consulates and embassies, 510

Cook, James, 83, 86, 223, 452
monument to (Anchorage), 83

Cook Inlet (Anchorage), 12, 28, 71, 83, 239, 259, 262
beluga whales in, 187, 491

Cooper Landing, 39, 231, 238, 258, 480

Cope Park (Juneau), 337, 377

Copper Center, 40, 49, 145, 191, 194–95

Copper River, 206, 209
and Childs Glacier, 7, 50, 184, 212

Copper River and Northwestern Railroad line, 216

Copper River Country. *See* Prince William Sound and Copper River Country

Copper River Delta, 50, 184–85, 198, 203, 208–9. *See also* Prince William Sound and Copper River Country
bird-watching at, 198, 209, 212, 481, 498
canoeing on, 184–85, 209, 482

Copper River Highway, 50, 198, 208, 212, 213

Copper River Princess Wilderness Lodge (near Copper Center), 191

Copper Whale Inn (Anchorage), 12, 110, 111

Cordova, 5, 50, 197, 199, 203, 208, 210–13, 458, 481
camping in, 213
ferry rides to, 203
outdoor activities in, 212
staying/dining in, 213

Cordova Coastal Outfitters, 50, 184, 197, 208, 209, 212

Cordova Historical Museum, 203, 211

Cosmic Kitchen (Homer), 243, 266

Courthouse Totem Poles (Anchorage), 83

Coyote Air (Coldfoot), 313

Crackerjack Sportfishing Charters (Seward), 270

Creamer's Field Refuge (Fairbanks), 288, 306, 320, 324, 498

Creek Street (Ketchikan), 44, 339, 346, 394–96

Crime, 513

Crooked Creek and Whiskey Island Railroad (Pioneer Park, Fairbanks), 309

Cross-country skiing, 485
Anchorage, 4, 92–93, 485
Fairbanks, 287, 299–300, 321, 485
Hatcher Pass, 134, 140
The Homer Bench, 243
Matanuska Glacier area, 191, 207, 221

Cross Sound Express (Gustavus), 367, 407, 408

Crow Creek Mine (Girdwood), 87

Cruise lines, 165, 322, 324, 336, 338, 478
and crowding, 336, 338
ferries as alternative to, 339
hotels catering to, 165, 322
stores catering to, 336, 337, 360, 379

Culture, 471–74. *See also* Art; Films; Literature; Music; Performing arts; Television series; Theater

Currency/currency exchange, 512

Customs regulations, 508–9

Cyrano's Off-Center Playhouse (Anchorage), 116, 120–21

D

Dall sheep, 489
best viewing of, 6, 29, 85, 148

Dalton Highway, 20, 282, 302, 310–15, 508

Danny J ferry (Homer to Halibut Cove), 39, 240

Darwin's Theory (Anchorage), 116, 117

David Green Master Furrier (Anchorage), 96, 99

Davidson Ditch (Steese Hwy), 303

Dawson City (Yukon Territory, Canada), 296, 359, 416

Deadhorse (Dalton Hwy), 312, 314, 315

Deer Mountain Trail (Ketchikan), 363, 364, 398

Deer Mountain Tribal Hatchery and Eagle Center (Ketchikan), 44, 339, 347, 397

Delta Junction, 283, 294, 326, 327

Dena'ina Civic and Convention Center (Anchorage), 82

Denali Air, 161

Denali and Kenai Fjords National Parks, 28–31, 56–57

Denali and Mat-Su, 126–79. *See also* Denali National Park; Talkeetna
with children, 61, 155
camping, 129, 152–57, 169
dining near, 170–71
Fast Facts, 178–79
favorite moments, 126–29
outdoor activities, 158–63
staying near, 11, 164–69
suggested itineraries, 130–35, 136–45, 146–51

Denali ATV Adventures, 158

Denali Backcountry Adventure, 149

Denali Fly Fishing Guides, 161

Denali Highway, 20, 129, 142, 144–45

Denali Junior Ranger Program, 61, 155

Denali National Park, 4, 6, 9, 10, 11, 31, 61, 126–79. *See also* Denali and Mat-Su; McKinley, Mount; Mount Healy Overlook trail
advance bookings for, 143, 505
bus tours of, 31, 142, 147, 143, 149, 156–57, 160, 172, 481
Discovery Hikes, 142, 160
entrance to, 132–33, 142, 155
hiking in, 4, 10, 24, 31, 61, 126, 128, 135, 142, 156, 158, 160, 162
Natural History Tour, 147, 149
ranger-led programs at, 61, 129, 142, 149, 150, 154, 155, 160, 163
train travel to, 133, 151
Tundra Wildlife Tour, 142, 149
Visitor Center, 31, 61, 133, 141–42, 155, 160, 161, 162, 163
Wilderness Access Center, 141–42, 143, 161, 162, 169
wildlife viewing, 9, 31, 128, 142, 146–49, 157

Denali Outdoor Center, 31, 61, 135, 162

Denali Park Road, 134–35
suggested itinerary, 146–51
wildlife viewing along, 142, 146–49

Denali Park Salmon Bake, 133, 170

Denali Princess Lodge (Nenana Canyon), 165, 170

Denali Southside River Guides, 141

Denali State Park, 129, 141, 154, 161

Dentists and doctors. *See* Fast Facts *for specific areas*

Dianne's Restaurant (Anchorage), 72, 102, 104

Disabilities, travelers with, 243, 515

Discount passes/free travel
for disabled travelers, 515
for seniors, 513–14

Discovery Hikes (Denali Nat'l Park), 142, 160

Discovery riverboat cruises (Chena River, Fairbanks), 286, 320

Discovery yacht cruises (Prince William Sound), 203

Dock Point/Dock Point Trail (Valdez), 190, 223

Dog-sled demonstrations (Denali Nat'l Park), 142, 149, 156, 161, 482

Dog-sled races/festivals, 8. *See also*
Iditarod Trail Sled Dog Race
Anchorage, 484, 504
Fairbanks, 287, 484
Yukon Quest, 285, 317, 484, 504
Dog-sled rides/mushing, 482
Anchorage area, 168
Juneau, 35, 343, 381, 382
Norris Glacier/Juneau Ice Field, 35,
342–43, 381, 382, 482
Seward, 271, 482
Dolly's House (Ketchikan), 339, 396
Double Musky Inn (Anchorage),
102, 104
Doyon, Limited, lobby of (Fairbanks),
284, 317
Doyon/ARAMARK booking firm,
143, 149
Driftwood Inn (Homer), 12, 266, 267
Driftwood Lodge (Juneau), 378, 383
Drinking laws, 509–10
Drinking water, 512
Dyea, 361, 416, 455

E

Eagle (near Yukon Territory border),
296, 298
Eagle Beach State Recreation Area
(near Juneau), 344
Eagle Historical Society and
Museums, 296
Eagle River Campground (near
Anchorage), 115, 152
Eagle River Nature Center (near
Anchorage), 64, 72, 89, 480
Eagle Roost Park (Petersburg), 340–42
Eagle Summit (Steese Hwy), 283, 303
Earthquake Park (Anchorage), 71
Earthquakes, 208, 506. *See also* Great
Alaska Earthquake (1964)
2002 earthquake, 463
East Glacier Loop (Mendenhall
Glacier), 336, 380
Eielson Visitor Center (Denali Park
Road), 134, 142, 149–50, 160
Eisenhower, Dwight D., 453, 458
Eklutna Historical Park, and "spirit
houses" of, 73, 82, 440
Eklutna Lake, 73, 88, 89, 480
Elderberry Bed & Breakfast
(Anchorage), 110, 112
Elderberry Park (Anchorage), 76, 82
El Dorado Gold Mine (near Fairbanks),
307, 321, 454
Electricity, 510
Embassies and consulates, 510
Emergencies, 510
Environmental issues
climate change, 42–43, 466–67
conservation, 199, 356, 359, 453,
457–58
Exxon Valdez oil spill, 189, 196,
201, 211, 222, 224, 268, 453
loss of sea ice, 43, 428, 438,
465, 466, 492

Equinox Wilderness Expeditions,
479, 483
Era Alaska (Anchorage), 444
Era Helicopters (Juneau), 35, 162, 343,
381, 382
Esther G Sea Taxi (Sitka), 389, 391
Estuary Life Trail (Starrigavan
Recreation Area), 368, 388
Evergreen Cemetery (Juneau), 376, 377
Exit Glacier (near Seward), 30, 235,
238, 247, 271
Exploritas (formerly Elderhostel), 514
Extreme sports, 94–95
Exxon Valdez oil spill, 189, 196, 201, 211,
222, 224, 268, 453

F

Fairbanks, 40–41, 61, 282–327. *See also*
Dalton Highway
camping in/near, 323
with children, 304–9
Fast Facts, 326–27
favorite moments, 282–83
nightlife/entertainment, 321
shopping, 317, 320
staying/dining in, 322–24, 325
suggested itineraries, 284–89,
292–303, 310–315
Fairbanks Community Museum,
285, 316
Fairbanks Ice Museum, 285, 297, 320
Fairbanks Symphony, 321, 474
Family travel, 510
Fast Facts, Alaska, 508–515
Fauna, 9, 487, 488–98. *See also specific
mammals, birds, and fish*
Ferry travel, 21, 22, 507, 508
advance bookings for, 373, 505
as alternative to cruise, 339
Clarence Strait, 348–49
from Homer, 435, 444
Lynn Canal, 353, 359
Peril Strait, 33–34, 331, 358, 370
Prince William Sound, 182, 189,
201, 203
Wrangell Narrows, 7, 340,
371–72, 404
Festivals and special events, 504–6
5th Avenue Mall (Anchorage), 81, 122
Films, 472–73
Finger Mountain (Dalton Hwy), 312
Firearms, 509
Fireweed 400 bike race (Matanuska
Glacier), 207
Fish, 493–95. *See also specific fish*
Fish and Game, Alaska Department
of, 263, 509
fishing information, 89, 258, 446,
506
wildlife guide, 487
Fish Central (Valdez), 190, 202–3
Fisherman's Memorial Park
(Petersburg), 340
Fishermen's memorial (Kodiak), 443
The Fish House (Seward), 270

Fishing, 482–83. *See also specific
species of fish;* Fly-in fishing
Alaska Bush, 425, 432, 437, 445,
446, 495
Anchorage, 67, 70, 83, 89, 259,
480, 483
Bristol Bay, 10, 259, 483
Cooper Landing, 39, 231, 238
Denali Nat'l Park, 161
government information, 89, 258,
506
Gustavus, 35, 345, 408, 495
Homer area, 8, 15, 39, 240–41,
259, 263, 495
Juneau, 382
Kenai Peninsula, 4, 39, 231,
256–59
Ketchikan, 44, 398
Petersburg, 403–4, 480
Prince William Sound, 38, 190,
202–3
Resurrection Creek (Hope), 246
Seward, 270, 493
shipping fish home, 259
Sitka, 333, 369, 391
Talkeetna, 175
Valdez, 190, 191, 202–3
Whittier, 202
"The Fishing Hole" (Homer), 263
Flightseeing, 21, 483
Anchorage, 11, 45, 57, 67, 75, 89,
168, 431
Bering Strait/Siberia, 424–25, 432
Cordova, 203, 212
Denali Nat'l Park, 161–62
Fairbanks & Interior, 313, 315
Glacier Bay, 366–67, 407, 412
Gustavus, 367, 407, 408, 416
Haines, 367, 412, 416
Juneau, 13, 35, 162, 343, 367, 381,
382, 416
Ketchikan, 44, 330, 372, 398
McCarthy, 195, 218
Mount McKinley, 31, 47, 130, 132,
141, 151, 161, 172, 174, 483
Nome, 424–25, 432
Norris Glacier/Juneau Ice Field,
35, 343, 381, 382
Seward area, 271, 482
Talkeetna, 31, 47, 130, 132, 141,
161, 172, 174
Floatplane, travel by, 21, 45, 57, 66–67,
75, 89
Flora, 499–501
Flume (Juneau), 377
Fly and camp trips, 157
Fly-in fishing, 10, 21, 259, 483
Anchorage, 45, 57, 67, 75, 89,
259, 431, 480, 483
Sitka, 13, 392
Cordova, 203, 212
Fly-In Fish Inn (Sitka), 13, 392
Food and drink, 475
Forest and Muskeg Trail (Starrigavan
Recreation Area), 368, 388

Forest Loop Trail (Glacier Bay Nat'l Park), 367, 407

Forest Service public use cabins (Southeast Alaska), 372, 373, 391, 404, 505

Fort Abercrombie State Historical Park (Kodiak), 445

Fort McGilvray (near Caines Head), 247, 270

Fort Schwatka (Unalaska), 436, 439

Fort William Seward (Haines), 352, 410, 413

40 Below Fairbanks (Pioneer Park, Fairbanks), 297, 309

4th Avenue Market Place (Anchorage), 70, 81, 97, 123

4th Avenue Theatre (Anchorage), 83

Fox Island (near Seward), 235

Frederick Sound (Petersburg), whale-watching on, 45, 187, 331, 342, 367, 404, 409, 492

G

Galbraith Lake (Dalton Hwy), 282, 315

Gavan Hill-Harbor Mountain Trail (Sitka), 391

Gay and lesbian travelers, 510–11

Gayle Ranney's Fishing & Flying (Cordova), 203, 212

Geography, 42–43, 177, 428, 438, 461–67, 492, 506

Geophysical Institute (UA Fairbanks), 287, 291, 506

Georgeson Botanical Garden (UA Fairbanks), 41, 286, 304, 317

Getting to/around Alaska, 506–08

Girdwood, 38, 86, 87. *See also* Alyeska, Mount; Alyeska Ski Resort

Glacier Bay, 52, 462
  flightseeing over, 366–67, 407, 412, 416
  sea kayaking in, 332–33, 479

Glacier Bay Lodge & Tours, 35, 345, 367, 406–7, 409

Glacier Bay National Park, 35, 52, 54, 55, 367, 406–9
  flightseeing over, 366–67, 407, 412, 416
  sea kayaking in, 10, 35, 332–33, 407, 408, 479
  whale-watching in, 35, 407

Glacier Bay Sea Kayaks, 35, 407, 408

Glacier Brewhouse (Anchorage), 104–5, 117

Glacier City Snowmobile Tours (Girdwood), 93, 485

Glacier cruises, on Prince William Sound, 15, 38, 202

Glacier Gardens (Juneau), 380

Glacier Highway (near Juneau). *See* Out Juneau's Glacier Highway

Glacier hiking (Mount McKinley), 128, 151, 161, 172, 174

Glacier Park (Matanuska Glacier), 191, 194, 220

Glaciers, 42, 177, 462–63
  Bering, 462
  Childs, 7, 50, 184, 198, 208, 209, 212, 213
  Columbia, 222
  Exit, 30, 235, 238, 247, 271
  Kahiltna, 130, 132, 151, 163, 463
  Matanuska, 49, 55, 191, 194, 204, 206, 220–21
  Meares, 222, 462
  Mendenhall, 9, 34, 332, 335–36, 344, 380, 382
  Muldrow, 150–51
  Norris, 35, 342–43, 381, 482
  Portage, 42, 51, 86
  Root, 49, 55, 195, 206, 217
  Shoup, 40, 190, 223
  Spencer, 56, 86, 92, 93, 230, 236–37
  Worthington, 190–91, 195–96, 207

Glacier View Campground (near Kennicott), 207, 219

Glen Alps trailhead (Chugach State Park), 46, 55, 64, 74, 78–79, 88–89, 480

Glenn Highway, 122, 463
  in Matanuska Glacier area, 49, 55, 191, 192, 194, 204, 206, 220

Godwin Glacier Sled Dog Tours (Seward), 271, 482

Gold Creek (Juneau), 337, 359, 376, 377

Gold Creek Salmon Bake (Juneau), 337, 381

Gold Dredge No. 8 (Fairbanks), 300–1, 303, 321

Golden Heart Park (Fairbanks), 285, 317

Gold in Alaska. *See also* Klondike Gold Rush
  founding of Fairbanks, 298, 455
  Juneau–Harris find, 337, 359, 376, 452, 454

Gold panning, 455
  Fairbanks, 300–1, 303, 321
  Girdwood, 87
  Juneau, 337, 381
  Kantishna, 149, 151, 166

Gold rush, attractions/exhibits on. *See also* Gold panning (*above*)
  Fairbanks area, 307, 309, 321, 454
  Juneau, 337, 359, 376, 377, 378, 379, 454
  Skagway, 360, 414, 415, 454
  Steese Highway, 302–3

Gold rush, towns of
  Dawson City, Yukon Territory, 296, 359, 416
  Dyea, 361, 416, 455
  Skagway, 360, 414–16, 454–55

Gold Rush Town (Pioneer Park, Fairbanks), 309

GoNorth Alaska Adventure Travel Center (Fairbanks), 317, 509

Goose Lake (Anchorage), 78, 88, 92

Governor's Mansion (Juneau), 337, 377

Granite Tors (Chena River State Recreation Area), 282, 289, 480–81

Gray whales, 187, 491

Great Alaska Adventure Lodge (Sterling), 258

Great Alaskan Earthquake (1964), 453, 463–64
  Anchorage, 70, 71, 80, 81, 208
  Kodiak, 442–43
  Portage, 86
  Seldovia, 265
  Seward, 269
  Valdez, 190, 196, 201–2, 208, 222, 224

The Greek Corner (Anchorage), 102, 105

Grizzly bears, 366, 466
  viewing of, 126, 128, 148, 315

Gull Rock Trail (Hope), 246

Gustavus, 35, 52, 336, 343, 345, 367
  beach in, 407
  getting to, 34
  outdoor activities in, 35, 345, 408
  wilderness travel in, 363

Gustavus & Glacier Bay, 406–9
  staying/dining in, 407, 408–9

Gustavus Inn at Glacier Bay, 13, 332, 409

H

H_2Oasis (Anchorage), 79, 92

Haida, 8, 468, 469

Haines, 366, 410–13
  with children, 352
  outdoor activities in, 412
  staying/dining in, 413

Haines Convention and Visitors Bureau, 412

Haines-Skagway Fast Ferry, 411

Halibut, 475, 482, 495
  fishing for, 259
  Gustavus, 35, 345, 408, 495
  Homer/Kachemak Bay, 15, 39, 240–41, 259, 263, 495
  Juneau, 382
  Ketchikan, 44, 398
  Kodiak, 446
  Petersburg, 404
  Sitka Sound, 369
  Unalaska, 425, 437, 495
  Valdez/Prince William Sound, 202

Halibut Cove, 14, 39, 230, 240

Halibut Cove Lagoon, 253

Hammer Museum (Haines), 352, 411

Hammer Slough (Petersburg), 330, 402

The Hangar (Juneau), 381, 385

Harbor Cafe (Valdez), 190, 225

Harding, Warren G., 302, 309

Harv & Marv's Outback Alaska (Juneau), 382

Hatcher Pass (near Willow), 129, 134, 139, 140

Hatcher Pass Lodge, 140

Healy, Mount. *See* Mount Healy Overlook trail

Herman, Saint (Kodiak), 440

Herring Cove (near Ketchikan), 363–64, 398

High Country Car and Truck Rental (Anchorage), 194
Highway Pass (Denali Nat'l Park), 126, 149
Hiking/Walking, 24, 483
  Anchorage area, 89
  Cordova, 208, 212
  Denali Nat'l Park, 4, 10, 24, 31, 61, 126, 128, 135, 142, 156, 158, 160, 162
  Girdwood, 38
  Glacier Bay Nat'l Park, 407
  Haines, 412
  Homer, 248, 263
  Hope, 246
  Juneau, 35, 343, 359, 376–80, 382
  Kachemak Bay, 263
  Ketchikan, 363, 364, 398
  Matanuska Glacier, 194, 220, 221
  Mendenhall Glacier, 335–36, 380, 382
  Petersburg, 370, 403–4
  Root Glacier, 49, 55, 195, 206, 217
  Seward, 270
  Sitka, 368, 369, 386, 388, 391, 393
  Unalaska/Dutch Harbor area, 437
  Wrangell–St. Elias Nat'l Park, 10
History, 452–60
Holidays, 511
Holland America Line cruises, 165, 322, 324, 478
Homer, 5, 39, 239–40, 253, 259, 260–67. See also Homer Spit
  with children, 248
  fishing in, 8, 15, 39, 240–41, 259, 263, 495
  museum/art galleries in, 39, 242, 248, 253, 260, 262
  outdoor activities in, 263
  staying/dining in, 262, 266–67
  trips to Seldovia from, 262, 263, 265
The Homer Bench, 243
Homer Saw and Cycle, 263
Homer Spit, 262
  art galleries on, 39, 242
  camping on, 267
  fishing on, 263
The Homestead Restaurant (Homer), 14, 231, 267
Homestead Trail (Homer), 248, 263
Hood, Lake. See Lake Hood entries
Hope, 12, 234, 245–46
Hope and Sunrise Historical Mining Museum, 234, 245–46
Horseshoe Lake Trail (Denali Nat'l Park), 156, 162
Hotel accommodations, 23. See Accommodations; see also specific hotels/areas
Hotel Alyeska (Girdwood), 38, 87, 110, 113
Hotel Captain Cook (Anchorage), 110, 113
Hotspot Cafe (near Yukon River Bridge), 312

Howling Dog Saloon (Fairbanks), 321
Humpback whales, 187, 492
  Frederick Sound, 45, 187, 331, 342, 404, 492
  Glacier Bay Nat'l Park, 10, 332–33
  Icy Strait/Gustavus, 4, 187, 367, 408, 492
  Juneau area, 351, 382
  Kenai Fjords Nat'l Park, 9, 187, 234, 492
  Orca Inlet (Cordova), 187, 212
  Prince William Sound, 187, 222, 492
  Sitka Sound, 33, 370
  Whale Park (Sitka), 391
Humpy's Great Alaskan Alehouse (Anchorage), 70, 82, 117
Hypothermia, 161, 512

I

Ice art, world championships of (Fairbanks), 283, 285, 287, 320, 484, 504
Icy Strait, whale-watching in, 4, 187, 345, 367, 408, 409, 492
Ididaride Sled Dog Tours (Seward), 271
Iditabike race, 95
Iditarod Trail (original mail route), 453
Iditarod Trailhead (Seward), 269
Iditarod Trail Invitational, 95
Iditarod Trail Sled Dog Race, 8, 67, 80, 95, 121, 134, 431, 484, 504
Igloo Mountain (Denali Park Road), 142, 148, 160
Ilanka Cultural Center (Cordova), 203, 211
Imaginarium Discovery Center (Anchorage Museum), 68–69, 78
Independence Mine State Historical Park (Hatcher Pass), 139–40
Indian River Trail (Sitka), 391
Inlet Charters Across Alaska Adventures (Homer), 39, 241, 259
Inns, best, 12–13
Insurance, travel, 25, 376, 479, 511
Interior Alaska, 282–327
  with children, 304–9
  Fast Facts, 326–27
  favorite moments, 282–83
  suggested itineraries, 284–89, 292–303, 304–9, 310–315
  winter travel in, 287
International Gallery of Contemporary Art (Anchorage), 81, 99
Internet access, 511
Iñupiat, 468–70
  culture of, 424, 426–27
  whaling tradition of, 424, 428, 470
Iñupiat Heritage Center (Barrow), 8, 41, 424, 426–27
Iron Dog Snowmobile Race, 95
Island Wings Air Service (Ketchikan), 44, 372, 398
Izaak Walton State Recreation Area (Sterling Hwy), 252, 277

J

Jakolof Bay (near Homer), 263, 265
Jakolof Road (Seldovia), 265
Japan, and invasion of Aleutian Islands, 247, 436, 445, 453, 458
Jens' Restaurant (Anchorage), 14, 102, 105
Jewel (singer), 474
Jewell Gardens (Skagway), 415
Juneau, 34–35, 45, 337, 343, 351–52, 358–59, 365, 374–85
  back streets of, 352, 377
  camping near, 384
  with children, 351–52
  nightlife/entertainment, 381
  outdoors activities in, 382
  shopping, 337, 379
  staying/dining in, 359, 383–85
Juneau, Joe, and Richard Harris, 337, 359, 376, 452, 454
Juneau Convention and Visitors Bureau, 382
Juneau–Douglas City Museum, 337, 359, 376–77, 380
Juneau Ice Field/Norris Glacier, 35, 343, 381, 382
Juneau International Airport, visibility problems at, 376
June's Whittier Condo Suites, 203

K

Kachemak Bay, 240–42, 265
  halibut fishing, 240–41
  hiking, 263
  sea kayaking, 230, 241–42, 263
  wilderness lodges, 11, 264
Kachemak Bay State Park, 253
Kachemak Bay Wilderness Lodge (near Homer), 11, 264
Kahiltna Glacier, 130, 132, 151, 163, 463
Kaleidoscope Cruises (Petersburg), 45, 404
Kantishna (Denali Nat'l Park), 135, 151, 166
Kantishna Experience (Denali bus tour), 149
Kantishna wilderness lodges, 11, 128, 129, 151, 166
Kantishna Wilderness Trails, 149
Katmai National Park, bear-viewing, 243, 446, 485, 489, 505
Kayaking. See Sea kayaking
Kenai, 239, 256, 274–75. See also Soldotna
  camping in/around, 277
  Old Town of, 239, 256, 274
  staying/dining in, 276–77
  visitors/cultural center, 239, 274
Kenai Canyon, 238
Kenai Fjords National Park, 9, 28–31, 56–57, 252, 271, 463
  boat tours of, 9, 60, 234–35, 243, 246–47
  with children, 60
  killer whales at, 187, 230, 234

Kenai Fjords Tours, 30, 60, 235
Kenai Fjords Wilderness Lodge (Fox Island), 235
Kenai Mountains, 38–39
Kenai National Wildlife Refuge, 4, 249, 252, 274
    with children, 60, 249
Kenai Old Town, 239, 256, 274
Kenai Peninsula, 29, 230–79. See also Homer; Kenai; Seward; Soldotna
    avalanche conditions in, 279
    with children, 244–49
    Fast Facts, 279
    favorite moments, 230–31
    outdoor adventures on, 250–53
    suggested itineraries, 36–41, 232–35, 236–43, 256–59
Kenai River, 4, 238, 239, 256–57, 275
Kenai River, Lower, 256–58
Kenai River Sportfishing Lodge (Cooper Landing), 258
Kenai Visitors and Cultural Center, 239, 274
Kennicott, 214–19
    general store/visitor center, 216
    original spelling, 195, 199, 214, 458
Kennicott & McCarthy, 5, 49, 195, 199, 206, 214–19
    getting to, 195, 217
    staying/dining in, 219
    wilderness activities near, 218
Kennicott copper mine, 5, 195, 199, 214, 216, 218, 457–58
Kennicott Glacier Lodge, 216, 219
Kennicott Mill Town, 184, 214–17
    concentration mill, 216
    power plant, 216
    train depot, 216
Kennicott River footbridge, 195, 217
Ketchikan, 338–39, 394–401
    camping near, 372–73, 399
    with children, 346–47
    Creek Street shopping, 44, 339, 346, 394, 396
    outdoor activities in, 398
    staying/dining in, 399–400, 401
    totem poles of, 8, 44, 339, 348, 355, 396
    wildlife/scenery of, 362–63
Ketchikan Charter Boats, 44, 398
Kids. See Children, traveling with
Kigluaik Mountains (near Nome), 432
Killer whales (orca), 187, 196, 492
    Aleutian Islands, 187
    Frederick Sound, 187, 331
    Icy Strait/Gustavus, 187, 345, 367
    Juneau area, 352
    Kenai Fjords Nat'l Park, 187, 230, 234
    Orca Inlet (Cordova), 187, 212
    skeleton of (Ilanka Cultural Center, Cordova), 203, 211
Kincaid Park (Anchorage), 28, 70, 71, 88, 89, 92–93, 501
    cross-country skiing, 92–93, 485

King (chinook) salmon, 255, 259, 493
    Homer, 259, 263
    Kenai River, 4, 256–57, 275
    Petersburg area, 402–4
    Resurrection Bay (Seward), 270
    Seldovia Slough, 265
    Ship Creek (Anchorage), 67, 70
Klondike Gold Rush, 296, 452, 454–55, 456
Klondike Gold Rush National Historical Park and Visitor Center (Skagway), 360, 414, 454
Klondike Highway, 296
Kobuk Coffee Company (Anchorage), 81, 100
Kodiak, 442–47
    as capital, 444
    outdoor activities in, 446
    staying/dining in, 425, 447
Kodiak brown bears, 445, 466, 489
    viewing of, 425, 445, 446, 489
Kodiak fishermen's memorial, 443
Kodiak Island Brewing Co., 443
Kodiak Maritime Museum, 443
Kodiak National Wildlife Refuge and Visitor Center, 445, 446
Kumagoro (Anchorage), 102, 105, 107

L
Lake Clark Bear Camp (Sterling), 231, 243
Lake Hood floatplane base (Anchorage), 45, 57, 66–67, 75, 89
Lake Hood Inn (Anchorage), 12, 110, 113
Lakeshore Motor Inn (Anchorage), 110, 113–14
Land's End Resort (Homer Spit), 262, 267
Lanie Fleischer Chester Creek Trail (Anchorage), 88, 92
Large Animal Research Station (UA Fairbanks), 286, 305, 317
Larkspur Cafe (Sitka), 369, 393
Last Chance Mining Museum (Juneau), 359, 377, 378, 379, 454
Lavelle's Bistro (Fairbanks), 14, 285, 325
Legal aid, 511
Liberty Falls (near Chitina), 206
Lifetime Adventures (Eklutna Lake), 73
Lightspeed Planet Walk (Anchorage), 70, 82
Lincoln, Abraham, 35, 350, 355
Literature, 471–72
Lodges, wilderness. See Wilderness lodges; see also specific hotels/areas
Lost Lake Trail (Seward), 252 , 480
Lower Kenai River, 256–58
Lunch Creek Trail (near Ketchikan), 348
Lunch Falls Loop Trail (near Ketchikan), 348
Lynn Canal, and ferry ride through (near Haines), 353, 359, 462

M
Macaulay Salmon Hatchery (near Juneau), 364–65, 380
Maclaren Pass (Denali Hwy), 145
Mahay's Riverboat Service (Talkeetna), 47, 141, 175
Mail and postage, 511–12
Majestic Valley Wilderness Lodge (Matanuska Glacier), 55, 207, 221
Mako's Water Taxi (Homer), 253, 263
Mammals, land, 488–91. See also specific animals
Mammals, marine, 491–93. See also Polar bears; Whales; Whale-watching
Marathon, Mount (Seward), 270, 505–6
Marion Creek Campground (near Coldfoot), 313
Married Man's Trail (off Creek Street, Ketchikan), 339, 396
Marx Bros. Cafe (Anchorage), 14, 102, 107
Matanuska and Susitna Valleys ("Mat-Su"). See Denali and Mat-Su
Matanuska Glacier area, 49, 55, 191, 194, 204, 206, 220–21
    staying/dining in, 221
Matanuska Glacier State Recreation Site, 191, 194, 220
Matanuska River, rafting/sea kayaking on, 49, 92, 185, 194, 204, 221, 483
Maxine & Jesse Whitney Museum (Valdez), 190, 196–97, 202, 224
McCarthy, 5, 49, 195, 206, 217, 218. See also Kennicott and McCarthy
McHugh Creek (Seward Hwy), 85
McKinley, Mount (Denali Nat'l Park), 6, 135, 163, 462–63
    air taxi tours over, 31, 47, 128, 130, 132, 141, 151, 161, 172, 174
    Climbers' Memorial (Talkeetna), 132, 163, 175
    glacier landings/hiking on, 128, 151, 161, 172, 174
    viewing, 128, 146, 149–51, 157
McKinley Lake, 209
Meares Glacier (PWS), 222, 462
Medical assistance, 513.
Mendenhall Glacier (near Juneau)
    black bear viewing at, 9, 34, 332, 336, 344, 380, 382
    campground of, 384
    hiking at, 335–36, 380, 382
    visitor center of, 380
Mendenhall Wetlands State Game Refuge, 365–66, 367, 382
Midnight sun, 422, 472, 513
Midnight Sun Baseball Game (Fairbanks), 283, 307, 505
Midnight Sun Run (Fairbanks), 307
Miller's Landing water taxis (Seward), 247, 270
Million-Dollar Bridge (Copper River Delta), 209

Mining museums/attractions. *See also* Gold panning; Gold rush, attractions/exhibits on
  Fairbanks area, 307, 321, 454
  Girdwood, 87
  Hatcher Pass, 139–40
  Hope, 234, 245–46
  Kennicott and McCarthy, 5, 49, 195, 199, 206, 214–19
  Kennicott area, 218
  Last Chance Mining Museum (Juneau), 359, 377, 378, 379, 454
  Treadwell Mine Historic Trail (Juneau), 359, 376, 379–80, 382
Misty Fjords National Monument (Ketchikan), 44, 330, 364, 398
Mitkof Highway, 403
Mitkof Island, 5, 371
MJ's Bread N Butter Charters (Whittier), 202
Money, 512
Moore House (Skagway), 360, 415
Moose, 490, 508, 512
  Anchorage, 66, 92
  Denali Nat'l Park, 128, 146, 157
The Moose's Tooth Pub and Pizzeria (Anchorage), 102, 107
Morris Thompson Cultural and Visitors Center (Fairbanks), 284, 316
Mosquito Cove Trail (Starrigavan Recreation Area), 369
Mountain biking. *See* Biking and mountain biking
Mountain climbing, 163
  off Seward Highway, 66
  Denali Nat'l Park, 142, 163
  Kachemak Bay State Park, 253
  Wrangell–St. Elias Nat'l Park, 10, 218
Mountains, and earthquakes, 463–64.
Mount Alyeska Tram (Girdwood), 38, 87, 113
Mount Healy Overlook trail (Denali Nat'l Park), 4, 31, 61, 128, 135, 156, 162
Mount Marathon Race (Seward), 270, 505–6
Mount McKinley Climbers' Memorial (Talkeetna), 163, 175
Mount Ripinsky Trail (Haines), 412
Mount Roberts Tramway (Juneau), 351, 377, 382
Movie theaters
  Anchorage, 83, 116, 120
  Fairbanks, 321
  Juneau, 381
Mulcahy Baseball Stadium (Anchorage), 67, 116, 120
Muldrow Glacier (Denali Park Road), 150–51
Murals
  Anchorage, 80, 81, 82
  Denali visitor center, 133
  Seward, 234, 246

Murie, Adolph, 148
Murie Science and Learning Center (Denali Nat'l Park), 155, 163
Murkowski, Frank, 460
Museum of Alaska Transportation and Industry (near Wasilla), 138–39
Museums. *See also* Art galleries/ museums/shopping; Mining museums/attractions; Native arts; Transportation museums/ attractions
  Alaska Bush, 430, 432, 435, 444
  Anchorage, 29, 56, 68–69, 78, 97, 123
  Cordova, 203, 211
  Eagle, 296
  Fairbanks, 40–41, 285, 286, 291, 297, 304, 316, 320
  Haines, 352, 411
  Homer, 39, 242, 248, 253, 260
  Juneau, 35, 337, 343, 351, 358–59, 374, 376–77, 380
  Ketchikan, 347, 396
  Petersburg, 342, 403
  Seward, 234, 269
  Sitka, 357, 389
  Skagway, 360, 415
  Steese Highway, 303
  Talkeetna, 46, 132, 141, 163, 174
  Valdez, 40, 61, 190, 196–97, 202, 207, 224
  Wrangell, 349–50
Music, 474
  Anchorage, 116, 119, 474
  Fairbanks, 321, 474
  Sitka, 474, 505
Musk oxen, 5, 138, 490
  viewing, in Nome, 424
Musk Ox Farm (near Palmer), 99, 138

N

Nalukataq (whale feeding festival, Barrow), 428
Native arts, 99, 509. *See also* Athabascans; Tlingit, cultural attractions of; Totem poles
  Anchorage, 8, 29, 66, 70, 72, 81, 96, 97, 99, 123, 138
  Barrow, 8, 41, 424, 426–27
  Cordova, 203, 211
  Eklutna Historical Park, 73, 82, 440
  Fairbanks, 284, 317, 320
  Haines, 352, 410
  Ketchikan, 339
  Kodiak, 443–44
  Sitka, 334–35, 357, 389, 390
  Wrangell, 349–50
Native peoples, 4, 8, 461, 468–70. *See also* Athabascans; Iñupiat; Tlingit
  enslavement/assimilation, 355, 386, 388, 441, 469
  land ownership settlement, 453, 459
  and Russian Orthodox Church, 73, 378, 389, 434, 440

Native Village of Eyak's Ilanka Cultural Center (Cordova), 203, 211
Natural history, 461–67
Natural History Tour (Denali bus tour), 147, 149
Nature walks/Dayhikes (Denali Nat'l Park), 162. *See also* Hiking/Walking
Naval Arctic Research Lab (NARL, Barrow), 427, 428, 429
Nenana, 302
Nenana Ice Classic/Tripod Days, 302, 504
Nenana River (Denali Nat'l Park), white-water rafting on, 129, 135, 156, 162
Nenana stern-wheeler (Pioneer Park, Fairbanks), 283, 309
Nick Dudiak Fishing Lagoon ("The Fishing Hole") (Homer), 263
Nightlife and entertainment
  Anchorage, 116–21
  Fairbanks, 321
  Juneau, 381
Nolan Center Museum (Wrangell), 349–50
Nome, 5, 430–33, 455
Nordic Ski Association of Anchorage, 93, 485
Nordic Ski Club of Fairbanks, 287
Norris Glacier/Juneau Ice Field, 35, 342–43, 381, 482
North American Sled Dog Championships (Fairbanks), 287
Northern Lights (*aurora borealis*), 70, 287, 290–91
  Fairbanks area, 7, 282, 287, 291, 322
  forecasts of, 287, 291, 506
  research on, 287, 303, 304
Northern Nights Inn (Cordova), 198, 213
North Pole (town), and Santa Claus House, 295, 297, 306
North Tongass Highway (north of Ketchikan), 347, 399
Northwestern Fjords sea kayaking trip (Kenai Fjords Nat'l Park), 252
Northwest Passage, 43, 466
  Cook's search for, 83, 86
Nova Raft and Adventure Tours (Matanuska Glacier), 220–21
  glacier hikes, 49, 194, 220
  rafting, 49, 185, 194, 204, 221, 483

O

Off-pavement travel, and car/vehicle rentals, 194, 432, 509
Off-road stopping, on Dalton Hwy, 313
Ohmer Creek Campground (near Petersburg), 371, 404, 405
Oil industry, 459–60
  native land ownership settlement, 453, 459
  Prudhoe Bay fields, 310, 311, 453
  Trans-Alaska Pipeline, 195, 207, 295, 303, 311, 459, 467
Old City Hall (Anchorage), 80

Old Portage and the Train Depot (Seward Hwy), 86

Old Sitka State Historic Site, 357, 368, 386

Oomingmak Musk Ox Producers' Cooperative (Anchorage), 99, 138

Orca Enterprises (Juneau), 351–52, 382

Orca Inlet (Cordova), 187, 212

The Oscar Gill House Historic Bed & Breakfast (Anchorage), 110, 114

Ounalashka Native Corporation (Unalaska), 436, 437, 439

Outdoor activities, 15, 52–55, 88–93, 204–09, 250–53, 480–85. *See also entries for specific areas/activities*
guides for, 55, 478–79
self-guided tours, 479

Outdoor Adventures Program (UA Fairbanks), 317

Outdoor health/safety, 25, 512–13

Out Juneau's Glacier Highway, 34, 342, 344, 353, 364, 381

The Overlook Bar & Grill (Nenana Canyon), 171

P

Pablo's Bicycle Rentals (Anchorage), 70, 88

Pack Creek (Admiralty Island, near Juneau), bear-viewing at, 365, 366, 382, 479

Palace Theatre (Pioneer Park, Fairbanks), 309, 321

Palin, Sarah, 138, 139, 453, 456, 460

Palmer, 48, 136, 138

Pangaea Adventures (Valdez), 40, 190, 223

Park Connection Motorcoach Service (Seward to Denali), 480, 507

Parks Canada, 296

Passports, 296, 513

Pearson's Pond Luxury Inn & Adventure Spa (Juneau), 13, 384

Pedro, Felix, 298, 303

Performing arts, 121. *See also* Nightlife and entertainment
Anchorage, 119–20
Fairbanks, 321
Juneau, 381

Peril Strait, ferry trip through, 33–34, 331, 358, 370

Permafrost, 43, 464–65, 466, 467

Perseverance Trail (Juneau), 35, 343, 359, 378, 382

Petersburg, 5, 45, 336, 340, 342, 370, 371, 402–5, 419
camping near, 371, 404, 405
and Hammer Slough, 330, 402
Norwegian roots of, 5, 340, 504
outdoor activities in, 5, 45, 370, 403–4
staying/dining in, 370, 405

Petersburg Creek and Wrangell Narrows sea kayaking with Tongass Kayak Adventures, 370

Peterson Bay (near Homer), nature tours of, 39, 248

Petroglyph Beach State Historic Site (Wrangell), 351

Phillips Cruises and Tours (Whittier), 38, 202

Pike's Waterfront Lodge (Fairbanks), 322, 323–24

Pink (humpy) salmon, 85, 207, 246, 255, 494

Pioneer Air Museum (Pioneer Park, Fairbanks), 309

Pioneer Avenue art galleries (Homer), 39, 242, 262

Pioneer Park (Fairbanks), 283, 299, 306, 307, 308–9, 317, 320
40 Below Fairbanks, 297, 309
Palace Theatre, 309, 321

Point Bridget State Park (near Juneau), 344, 382

Point Woronzof (Anchorage), 71

Poker Flat Research Range (University of Alaska Fairbanks) (Steese Hwy), 303

Polar bears, 41, 74, 429, 438, 492
loss of sea ice, 43, 438, 466, 492

Polychrome Pass (Denali Park Road), 148, 157, 162

Portage Glacier, 42, 51
boat tour of, 86

Postage and mail, 511–12

Potter Marsh (Anchorage), 67, 84, 89

Potter Section House (Anchorage), 84–85

Pratt Museum (Homer), 39, 242, 248, 253, 260

President Harding's rail car (Pioneer Park, Fairbanks), 309

Primrose Creek Trail (Seward), 251, 252

Primrose Landing Campground (Seward), 60, 251

Primrose Ridge (Denali Park Road), 146, 160

Prince Rupert, British Columbia, ferries from, 347, 373, 507

Princess Tours cruise line, 165, 478
Copper Center area, 191
Nenana Canyon, 165, 170
Cooper Landing, 241
Denali State Park, 169

Prince William Sound, 38, 51, 92
boat tours/cruises of, 15, 38, 202, 203, 222
Exxon Valdez, 196
ferry crossings of, 182, 189, 201, 203

Prince William Sound and Copper River Country, 182–226. *See also* Chugach National Forest; Cordova; Kennicott and McCarthy; Matanuska Glacier area; Valdez
Fast Facts, 226
favorite moments, 182–85
outdoor adventures in, 204–9
suggested itineraries, 188–91, 192–98, 200–3

Prince William Sound glacier cruises, 15, 38, 202, 222

Prince William Sound Kayak Center (Whittier), 202

Prince William Sound Lodge (near Ellamar), 224

Promech Air (Ketchikan), 398

Prudhoe Bay oil fields, 310, 311, 453

Puffins, 9, 30, 33, 234, 425, 497

Pump House Restaurant & Saloon (Fairbanks), 282–83, 299, 325

R

Rafting, 24, 479, 483. *See also* White-water rafting
Anchorage area, 86, 92
Haines area, 333, 353, 412
Cooper Landing, 39, 238, 241, 479
Copper Center, 191, 483
Cordova, 212
Haines, 353, 412
Kenai Canyon, 238
Matanuska Glacier, 49, 92, 185, 194, 204, 221, 483
Sixmile Creek, 233
Talkeetna, 135, 175
Valdez, 190, 191

Rainbow Falls Trail (near Wrangell), 351

Rainbow Tours (Homer), 265

Rainforest, 465–66

Ranger, educational, and field programs (Denali Nat'l Park), 61, 129, 154, 155, 163
ranger-led hikes, 142, 149, 150, 160

Ranger-led activities/tours
Homer, 260
Bering Land Bridge Nat'l Preserve Headquarters, 433
Dyea (Chilkoot Pass Trail), 416
Glacier Bay Nat'l Park boat tour, 406
Hatcher Pass, 139
Skagway, 360
Prince William Sound ferry, 189, 201
Sitka, 389
Wrangell-St. Elias Nat'l Park, 191

Raven Roost Cabin (Petersburg), 404

Raven Trail (Petersburg), 404

Red (sockeye) salmon, 255
Chitina/Copper River, 206
Russian River, 258

Red Squirrel Campground (Chena River State Recreation Area), 288

REI (Anchorage), 96, 101, 157

Remembering Old Valdez Exhibit (Valdez Museum and Historical Archive annex), 190, 196, 202, 207, 224

Residence Inn by Marriott (Anchorage), 110, 115

Resolution Park (Anchorage), 83

Restaurants, 14, 23. *See also specific restaurants/areas*

Resurrection Bay (Seward), 30, 60, 234, 235
salmon fishing in, 270, 493

Resurrection Creek (Hope), 246

Resurrection mural (St. Peter's Episcopal Church, Seward), 234

Resurrection Pass Trail (Hope to Cooper Landing), 238, 480

Richardson Highway, 7, 40, 61, 462
biking tour of, 481
Trans-Alaska Pipeline, 195, 207

Rika's Roadhouse (near Delta Junction), 40, 294-95

Riley Creek Campground (Denali Nat'l Park), 129, 154-55, 169

River crossings, 512

River floating, Arctic, 10, 479

River's Edge Resort Cottages (Fairbanks), 322, 324

RoadPost satellite phone rentals, 513

Roosevelt, Theodore, 199, 298, 359, 378, 457, 458, 460

Root Glacier Trail (Kennicott), 49, 55, 195, 206, 217

Roseship Campground (Chena River Recreation Area), 288, 307, 323

Running of the Reindeer (Anchorage), 67, 121, 484

Russian America, 440-41. See also Baranof, Alexander
capital of, 334, 376, 379, 388, 441, 444, 452, 506

Russian America, Native peoples in, 440-41. See also Tlingit
enslavement of, 386, 388, 441, 469
Orthodox Church, 73, 378, 389, 434, 440

Russian Bishop's House (Sitka), 33, 357, 369, 389

Russian Orthodox Church, 440
Eklutna, 73
Juneau, 337, 378
Kenai, 239
local clergy/saints of, 33, 357, 389-90, 440
and Native peoples, 73, 378, 389, 434, 440
Sitka, 32-33, 357, 389-90
Unalaska, 434-35

Rust's Flying Service (Anchorage), 45, 57, 67, 75, 89, 431

RVs, 20, 23, 57, 157, 373, 481-82, 507, 508

RVs, rental/park facilities, 482
Anchorage, 59, 115, 373
Chena Lake, 306
Dalton Highway, 313
Denali Nat'l Park, 169
Fairbanks, 323
Homer, 267
Juneau, 384
Kenai/Soldotna, 277
Sitka, 393
Valdez, 224

S

Sable Mountain (Denali Park Road), 148, 160

Sable Pass (Denali Park Road), 128, 148

Sacks Cafe & Restaurant (Anchorage), 66, 102, 108

Safety, 512, 513

St. Elias Alpine Guides, 218, 479, 481
Kennicott tours, 49, 195, 206, 214, 216
Root Glacier hikes, 49, 55, 195, 206, 217

St. Lazaria Island bird colony (Sitka), 33, 389, 481

St. Michael's Cathedral (Sitka), 32-33, 357, 389-90

St. Nicholas Orthodox Church (Eklutna), 73

St. Nicholas Orthodox Church (Juneau), 337, 378

St. Thérèse, Shrine of (near Juneau), 34-35, 332, 344, 381

Salmon, 66, 196, 254-55, 398, 404, 475, 482, 493-94. See also Fishing; specific salmon species

Salmon bakes
Denali area, 133, 170
Fairbanks, 309
Juneau, 337, 381

Salmon hatcheries
Ketchikan, 44, 339, 347, 397
Juneau area, 364-65, 380
Valdez, 207

The Saltry Restaurant (Halibut Cove), 14, 39, 240

Sanctuary River Campground (Denali Nat'l Park), 169

Sandy Beach (Petersburg), 370, 403

Santa Claus House (North Pole), 295, 297, 306

Satellite phones, 326, 513

Savage River Bridge (Denali Park Road), 146, 160

Savage River Campground (Denali Nat'l Park), 129, 169

Savage River Loop hiking trail (Denali Nat'l Park), 156, 162

Saxman Native Village Totem Pole Park (Ketchikan), 355, 363, 396-97

Scandia House (Petersburg), 371, 405

Scenery and wildlife, best (Southeast Alaska), 362-67

Science and natural history museums/ attractions
Anchorage, 29, 56, 67, 68-69, 70, 78, 82, 123
Anchorage area, 64, 72, 89, 480
Fairbanks, 40-41, 286, 291, 297, 304, 320
Homer, 10, 39, 239-40, 242, 243, 248, 253, 260, 263
Juneau, 35, 337, 343, 351, 358-59, 374
Ketchikan, 339, 346, 362-63, 372, 394
Seward, 30, 60, 235, 237, 247, 268-69, 480

Sea Breeze, yacht cruises and dining on (Kodiak), 425, 447

Sea Hawk Air (Kodiak), 446

Sea ice, 465
ecosystem of, 438, 466
loss of, 43, 438, 466, 492
whaling on, 428

Sea kayaking, 23-24, 485
Anchorage area, 92
Cordova, 212
Glacier Bay, 10, 35, 332-33, 407, 408, 479
Gustavus, 345, 408
Haines, 412
Homer, 230, 241-42, 263
Juneau area, 382
Kenai Fjords Nat'l Park, 252
Ketchikan, 44, 330, 364, 398
Kodiak, 446
Matanuska River, 49, 92, 185, 194, 204, 221, 483
Petersburg, 15, 45, 370, 404
Prince William Sound, 184, 202
Seward, 30, 60, 252, 270
Sitka Sound, 391
Shoup Glacier, 40, 190, 223
Wrangell Narrows, 370

Sea Life Discovery Tours (Sitka), 33, 389

Sea Otter RV Park (near Valdez), 224

Sea otters, 196, 230, 234, 269, 270, 493
Cordova, 50, 184, 197, 208, 212, 493
historical hunting of, 223, 386, 441, 444, 456
Kachemak Bay, 230, 493
Sitka Sound, 33, 335, 391, 493

Seasickness, 512-13

Seldovia, 262, 263, 265
kayak tours of, 265

Seldovia Slough, 265

Senior travelers, 513-14

Settlers Cove State Recreation Site (near Ketchikan), 348, 398, 399

Seward, 30, 56, 235, 237, 243, 246-47, 268-73
with children, 60, 246-47
outdoor activities in, 270, 271
staying/dining in, 272-73

Seward Highway, 29, 36, 38, 54, 58, 66, 122, 188, 198, 244, 250
and Exit Glacier, 30, 235, 238, 247, 271
at Turnagain Pass, 39, 230, 232-33, 244, 250

Seward Museum, 234, 269

Seward Windsong Lodge, 273

Sheep Mountain Lodge (Matanuska Glacier), 49, 55, 206, 207, 221

Sheet'ka Kwáan Naa Kahídi (Tlingit clan house, Sitka), 334-35, 357, 390

Sheldon Jackson Museum (Sitka), 357, 389

Sheldon Museum and Cultural Center (Haines), 411

Ship Creek (Anchorage), 67, 70, 83, 89

Shoemaker Bay Recreation Area (near Wrangell), 351

Shoup Glacier sea kayaking with Pangaea Adventures (Valdez), 40, 190, 223

Shoup Glacier trail (Valdez), 190, 223

Shrine of St. Thérèse (near Juneau), 34–35, 332, 344, 381

Silverbow Bakery (Juneau), 358

Silverbow Basin (Juneau), 359, 376, 378

Silver salmon (coho), 255, 493
Anchorage area, 67, 70, 85, 89
Blind River Rapids, 403
Homer Spit, 263
Lower Kenai River, 257
Seward, 270, 493
Valdez, 202–3
Tongass Highway, 348

Simon & Seafort's Saloon and Grill (Anchorage), 70, 108–9

Sing Lee Alley (Petersburg), 340, 402

Sitka, 32–33, 334–35, 336, 369, 386–93
bike rentals in, 335, 369, 388
camping near, 368–70, 393
as capital, 334, 376, 379, 388, 441, 452, 506
history/culture of, 356–58, 441
outdoor activities in/near, 369, 391
staying/dining in, 392, 393

Sitka National Historical Park, 33, 335, 357, 388–89
totem poles in, 4, 33, 331, 335, 355, 369, 388–89

Sitka Ranger District, 391

Sitka Sound, 369–70
bird/wildlife viewing in, 33, 389, 481
boat tours of, 335, 389, 391
salmon/halibut fishing in, 333, 369, 391
sea kayaking in, 391

Sitka Sound Ocean Adventures, 391

Sitka's Secrets fishing/wildlife tours, 370, 389

Sitka Summer Music Festival, 474, 505

Sitka Wildlife Quest, 33, 389

Sixmile Creek, white-water rafting on, 39, 92, 232–33, 245, 250, 483

Skagway, 359, 414–17, 360–61
and Klondike Gold Rush, 360, 414–16, 454–55
staying/dining in, 417

Skagway Museum and Archives, 360, 415

Skiing. See Alpine skiing; Cross-country skiing

Slide Cemetery (Dyea), 361, 416

SMART (Skagway bus system), 415

Smoking, 514

Snow City Cafe (Anchorage), 102, 109

Snow Goose Restaurant & Brewery (Anchorage), 116, 119, 120

Snowmobiling, 56, 93, 95, 207, 485

Sockeye Cycle Co. (Haines and Skagway), 353, 361

Soho Coho (Ketchikan), 339

Soldotna, 249, 256, 257, 274–75. See also Kenai
camping in/around, 277
staying/dining in, 276–77

Soldotna Visitor Center, 257

Solomon Gulch Hatchery (Valdez), 207

Sons of Norway Hall (Petersburg), 340

Sophie Station Hotel (Fairbanks), 322, 324

Southcentral Alaska, 45–47
and climate change, 43

Southeast Alaska, 32–35, 44–45, 330–419. See also Gustavus and Glacier Bay; Haines; Juneau; Ketchikan; Petersburg; Sitka; Skagway
camping in, 368–73
with children, 346–53
Fast Facts, 419
favorite moments, 330–33
suggested itineraries, 334–37, 338–45

Southeast Alaska Discovery Center (Ketchikan), 339, 346, 362–63, 372, 394

Southeast Alaska State Fair (Haines), 506

Southeast Exposure (Ketchikan), 372, 398

Southeast Sea Kayaks (Ketchikan), 398

Special-interest trips, 478–85

Spectator sports. See also Dog-sled races/festivals
Anchorage, 67, 116, 120, 506
Fairbanks, 283, 307, 505

Spenard Roadhouse (Anchorage), 102, 109

Spencer Glacier, 56, 86, 92, 93, 230
backcountry trips through, 56, 236–37

"Spirit houses," of Eklutna Historical Park, 73, 82, 440

Spirit Walker Expeditions (Gustavus), 35, 345, 408

Sport Fishing Alaska (Anchorage), 259, 480, 483

Stan Stephens' glacier and wildlife cruise (PWS), 222

Starrigavan Recreation Area (near Sitka), 368, 369, 386, 388, 391, 393

State Court House (Juneau), 377

State Office Building (Juneau), 337, 377

Steese Highway, 21, 283, 302, 303, 311, 508

Sterling
bear camp flights from, 230, 243, 446
camping/outdoor rentals in, 60, 231, 249, 251, 253, 277

Stony Creek (Denali Park Road), 149, 160

Stony Hill Overlook (Denali Park Road), 149

Strategies for travelers, 18–25

Sukakpak Mountain (Dalton Hwy), 314

Sullivan Roadhouse (Delta Junction), 40, 294

Summer solstice, events/activities celebrating, 283, 307, 505

Summer vs. winter travel, 121, 134, 135, 167, 170. See also Winter travel

Sunny Cove Sea Kayaking (Seward), 30, 60, 252, 270

Susitna Place (Anchorage), 110, 115

Susitna Valley, viewing, 145. See also Denali and Mat-Su

Swanberg Dredge (Nome), 433

Swan Lake canoe route (Kenai Nat'l Wildlife Refuge), 60, 249, 252–53, 274

Sweet Mo's Simple Pleasures Ice Cream (Hope), 234, 246

Swimming. See also Beaches
Anchorage, 92
Chena Hot Springs Resort (near Fairbanks), 289, 302

Symphony orchestras, 321, 474

T

Taft, William Howard, 199

Talkeetna, 31, 41, 46–47, 61, 132, 141, 172–77
staying/dining in, 176–77
suggested itinerary, 130–35
travelling by rail, 133, 151

Talkeetna Aero Services Denali National Park tour, 172

Talkeetna Air Taxi, 31, 47, 130–32, 141, 161, 172, 174

Talkeetna Historical Society Museum, 46, 132, 141, 163, 174

Talkeetna Ranger Station, 132, 141, 155, 163, 174

Talkeetna River Guides rafting floats and fishing, 175

Tanana River (Fairbanks area), 286, 295, 298, 299, 302, 504
and Trans-Alaska Pipeline, 295

Tangle Lakes Archaeological District (Denali Hwy), 145

Tangle Lakes (Denali Hwy), 145, 161

Tangle River Inn (Denali Hwy), 145

Taxes, 514

Taxis. See Fast Facts for specific areas

Taylor Highway, 20, 296

Teklanika River (Denali Park Road), 147

Teklanika River Campground (Denali Park Road), 169

Telephones, 514

Television series, 472–74

Teller (Native village near Nome), 432

Ten-Mile bird-watching area (Copper River Delta), 209

10th and M Seafoods (Anchorage), 96, 100

Tern Lake (near Seward), 29, 234, 248, 250

Tetlin National Wildlife Refuge (Alaska Hwy), 292–93

Theater
Anchorage, 116, 119, 120–21
Fairbanks, 309, 321
Juneau, 381
Valdez, 505

Thompson Pass (Richardson Hwy), 50, 54, 190–91, 195–96, 207, 208

Thorofare Pass (Denali Park Road), 134, 149

Three Lakes Recreation Area (near Petersburg), 403

Three Lakes Trail (near Petersburg), 371, 403, 404

Thunderbird Falls (Glenn Hwy), 73, 89

Tide pooling
Homer area, 10, 242, 249, 260, 263
Wrangell area, 351
Kodiak, 443
Petersburg, 370
Juneau area, 344
Sitka area, 369, 388

Tide-pool touch tank (Sea Life Discovery Tours, Sitka), 389

Time zone, 514

Tipping, 514–15

Tlingit, 334–35, 358, 384, 468, 469
and battles with Russians, 440–41, 452
eagle and raven of, 83, 355, 497
gold finding by, 376
Old Sitka State Historic Site, 357, 368, 386
Sitka Nat'l Historical Park, 4, 33, 331, 335, 355, 357, 386, 388
and U.S. forces, 391

Tlingit, cultural attractions of. See also Totem poles
Castle Hill (Sitka), 32, 358, 390–91
Haines, 352, 410, 411
Juneau, 337, 351, 374, 377
Ketchikan, 396
Sitka, 334–35, 357, 368, 386, 390
Sitka National Historical Park, 4, 33, 331, 335, 355, 357, 369, 386, 388–89
Wrangell, 350–51

Toilets, 515

Tok, 283, 293, 296, 326, 327, 463

Toklat River (Denali Nat'l Park), 126, 134, 142, 148–49, 160

Tongass Historical Museum (Ketchikan), 347, 396

Tongass Kayak Adventures (Petersburg), 45, 370, 404

Tongass National Forest, 339, 340, 359, 371, 372, 373

Tongass Water Taxi (Ketchikan airport), 347, 397

Tony Knowles Coastal Trail (Anchorage), 12, 28, 56, 66, 70, 71, 76, 82, 88, 89

Top of the World Highway, 20, 296

Top of the World Hotel (Barrow), 427, 429

Totem Bight State Historical Park (Ketchikan), 44, 348, 355, 396

Totem Heritage Center (Ketchikan), 44, 339, 355, 396

Totem Ocean Trailer Express (Anchorage), 373

Totem poles, 354–55
Anchorage, 35, 83
Haines, 352, 355, 410
Ketchikan area, 8, 44, 339, 348, 355, 363, 396–97
Sitka National Historical Park, 4, 33, 331, 335, 355, 369, 388–89

Totem Heritage Center (Ketchikan), 8, 44, 339, 355, 396
Wrangell, 350, 355

Tour companies, 165, 478–85. See also Fishing; Flightseeing; Fly-in fishing; Rafting; Wildlife viewing tours/ attractions

Tourist/Visitor information, 504.

Town Square Park (Anchorage), 66, 80, 81, 93

Tracy Arm, 6, 381, 409

Tracy Arm–Fords Terror Wilderness, 6, 45, 331, 337, 381

Train travel, 21, 22, 327, 373, 507. See also Alaska Railroad
White Pass and Yukon Route (Skagway), 21, 331, 361, 416

Trans-Alaska Pipeline, 459, 467
at Richardson Highway, 195, 207
at Steese Highway, 303
at Tanana River crossing, 295
at Yukon River crossing, 311

Transportation information, 21, 507–8

Transportation museums/attractions, 56–57, 75, 138–39, 309, 443

Transportation Security Administration (TSA), 157, 482

Travel insurance, 25, 376, 479, 511

Treadwell, John, 359, 379

Treadwell Mine Historical Trail (Juneau), 359, 376, 379–80, 382

Trees and plants, 499–501

Tripod Days/Nenana Ice Classic, 302, 504

Tripod Mountain hiking trail (Cordova), 208, 212

Troll, Ray, 339

Trout, 483, 495
Bristol Bay, 259
Campbell Creek (Anchorage), 89
Chena Lake Recreation Area, 306
Kenai Nat'l Wildlife Refuge, 4, 60, 252
Ward Lake Recreation Area, 348

True North Kayak Adventures (Homer), 230, 242, 263

Tundra Wildlife Tour (Denali bus tour), 149

Turnagain Arm, 6, 29, 66, 84–87, 185, 244, 246, 250
wildlife viewing along, 67, 489, 490, 491, 501

Turnagain Arm Trail, 84–85, 89

Turnagain Pass (Seward Hwy), 39, 230, 232–33, 244, 250

Twelvemile Summit (Steese Hwy), 303

Twisted Fish Company Alaskan Grill (Juneau), 365, 385

U

Ulmer's Drug and Hardware (Homer), 263

Umnak Island (near Unalaska), 435

Unalaska & Dutch Harbor, 434–39
outdoor activities in, 425, 437, 495
Russian heritage of, 440–41
staying/dining in, 439
World War II, 425, 436, 439, 458

University of Alaska Fairbanks, 286
cross-country trails at, 287
Georgeson Botanical Garden, 41, 286, 304, 317
Large Animal Research Station, 286, 305, 317
Outdoor Adventures Program, 317
Poker Flat Research Range (Steese Hwy), 303

University of Alaska Geophysical Institute (Fairbanks), 287, 291, 506

University of Alaska Museum of the North (Fairbanks), 40–41, 286, 291, 297, 304, 317, 320, 474

University of Alaska Poker Flat Research Range (Steese Hwy), 303

V

Valdez, 40, 190, 196–97, 201–3, 207, 222–25, 311
camping in/around, 224
with children, 61
staying/dining in, 225

Valdez Museum and Historical Archive, 40, 61, 190, 196, 202, 207, 224
annex of, 190, 196, 202, 207

Van Gilder Hotel (Seward), 234, 273

Veniaminov, Bishop Innocent, and house of (Sitka), 33, 357, 389–90

Viking Travel (Petersburg), 404, 480

Vogel, Paula, 381

Volunteer vacations, 431, 480

W

Walking tours
Eagle Historical Society and Museums, 196
Juneau attractions, 359, 376, 377
Skagway attractions, 360, 414
University of Alaska Fairbanks, 286

Ward Lake Recreation Area (near Ketchikan), 347–48, 398, 399

Wasilla, 138–39
Water, drinking, 512
Weather, 20, 505, 506
Wedgewood Resort (Fairbanks), 306, 320–21, 322, 324
Westchester Lagoon (Anchorage), 28, 66, 71, 76, 78, 88, 93
Westmark Fairbanks Hotel & Conference Center, 322, 324
Whale Park (Juneau), 391
Whales, 9, 186–87, 491–92. *See also specific whale species*
   Petersburg, 45, 187, 331, 342, 367, 404, 409, 492
   Glacier Bay Nat'l Park, 35, 407
   Gustavus, 367
   Icy Strait, 4, 187, 345, 367, 408, 409, 492
   Juneau area, 351–52, 367, 382, 391, 409
   Sitka, 367, 391
Whistling Swan Productions (Anchorage), 116, 119
White Pass (Skagway), 455
White Pass and Yukon Route, 455
   railway trip along (Skagway), 21, 331, 361, 416
White-water rafting, 483
   Copper Center, 191, 483
   Denali Nat'l Park, 31, 61, 142
   Kenai Canyon, 238
   Matanuska Glacier, 185, 221
   Nenana River, 129, 135, 156, 162
   Sixmile Creek, 39, 92, 232–33, 245, 250, 483
Whittier, 51, 189, 200, 201, 202
   and Prince William Sound, 15, 38, 51, 92, 184, 185, 187, 201, 202
   staying in, 203
Wickersham, James, 298, 359, 378
Wickersham House State Historic Site (Juneau), 359, 378
Wilderness, keeping it clean, 515
Wilderness Access Center (Denali Nat'l Park), 141–42, 143, 161, 162, 169
Wilderness communications, 513
Wilderness lodges, 11, 479. *See also specific lodges*
   Denali Nat'l Park, 11, 164–69
   fishing at, 10, 259, 480, 483
   fly-in, 11, 168
   Gustavus, 407, 409
   Homer/Kachemak Bay, 264
   Kantishna, 11, 128, 129, 151, 166
   Kenai Peninsula, 235, 241
   Matanuska Glacier, 49, 55, 206, 207, 221
   Prince William Sound/Copper River, 191, 224
Wildlife. *See also* Fauna; *see specific animals*
   guides to, 487–98
   safety tips, 512
Wildlife products, buying/exporting, 508–9

Wildlife refuges
   Alaska Maritime Nat'l Wildlife Refuge (Unalaska), 260, 437
   Arctic Nat'l Wildlife Refuge, 10, 479
   Creamer's Field Refuge (Fairbanks), 288, 306, 320, 324, 498
   Kenai Nat'l Wildlife Refuge, 4, 60, 231, 249, 252, 274, 482
   Kodiak Nat'l Wildlife Refuge, 445, 446, 489
   Mendenhall Wetlands State Game Refuge, 365–66, 367, 382
   Tetlin Nat'l Wildlife Refuge (Alaska Hwy), 292–93
Wildlife viewing, 9, 485. *See also specific animals and species; "wildlife viewing" under specific areas*
   Alaska Zoo, 46, 66, 74, 79
   Denali Park Road, 142, 146–49
   Fairbanks, 286, 305, 317
   Katmai Nat'l Park, 485, 505
   Kenai Fjords Nat'l Park, 187, 230, 234–35
   Nome area, 432
   Sitka Sound, 33, 369–70, 389, 481
Wilson, Woodrow, 174, 199
Windy Point (Seward Hwy), 85
Winner Creek Trail (Girdwood), 38, 87, 89
Winterlake Lodge (near Anchorage), 11, 168
Winter travel, 24
   Denali Nat'l Park, 134, 135, 167
   Skagway, 361
Wiseman (Dalton Hwy), 311, 313–14
Women travelers, safety of, 513.
Wonder Lake (Denali Nat'l Park), 128, 151, 156–57
Wonder Lake Campground (Denali Nat'l Park), 151, 157, 160, 169
World Champion Sled Dog Race (Anchorage), 484, 504
World Ice Art Championships (Fairbanks), 283, 285, 287, 320, 484, 504
World War II-era sights/attractions
   Aleutian Islands, 425, 436, 439, 458
   Caines Head, 247, 270
   Kodiak, 443, 445
   Whittier, 51, 189, 201
Worthington Glacier, 50, 190–91, 195–96, 207
Worthington Glacier State Recreation Site, 191, 195–6, 207
Wrangell, 331, 336, 349–51, 355
   with children, 349–51
Wrangell Mountain Air, 195, 218
Wrangell Narrows, ferry trips through, 7, 340, 371–72, 404
Wrangell Narrows and Petersburg Creek sea kayaking, 45, 370, 404
Wrangell-St. Elias National Park, 5, 10, 55, 191, 195, 206, 218
   mountain climbing in, 10, 218
   visitor center, 40, 49, 191, 195, 206

Wynn Nature Center (Homer), 243, 248, 263

Y
Yachts, traveling/dining on, 203, 223, 425, 447
Yellow Jersey Cycle Shop (Sitka), 335, 369, 388
Yukon–Charley Rivers National Preserve (near Eagle), 296
Yukon Quest Sled Dog Race, 285, 317, 484, 504
Yukon River Bridge area, 302, 311–12
Yukon River Camp (near Yukon River Bridge), 312
Yukon Territory
   Dawson City, 296, 298, 359, 416
   Klondike Gold Rush, 296, 452, 454–55, 456
   Yukon Quest Sled Dog Race, 285, 504
Yurt rentals
   Peterson Bay field station, 249
   Fairbanks, 289
   Kachemak Bay State Park, 253

Z
Zimovia Highway (south from Wrangell), 351
Zip-lining
   Herring Cove, 364
   Ketchikan, 372, 398
Zyphyr (Juneau), 14, 385

Photo Credits

Note: l= left; r= right; t= top; b= bottom; c= center